Strategic Human Resources

Frameworks for General Managers

Strategic
Human Resources

Frameworks for General Managers

JAMES N. BARON
Stanford University

DAVID M. KREPS
Stanford University
and Tel Aviv University

JOHN WILEY & SONS, INC.
New York • Chichester • Weinheim • Brisbane • Singapore • Toronto

ACQUISITIONS EDITOR	Brent Gordon
MARKETING MANAGER	Carlise Paulson
SENIOR PRODUCTION EDITOR	Kelly Tavares
SENIOR DESIGNER	Laura Boucher

This book was set in Palatino by Matrix Publishing Services and printed and bound by Malloy Lithographers. The cover was printed by Lehigh Press.

This book is printed on acid free paper. ∞

Library of Congress Cataloging-in-Publication Data
Baron, James N.
    Strategic human resources : Frameworks for general managers /
James N. Baron, David M. Kreps.
        p.   cm.
    Includes index.
    ISBN 0-471-07253-2 (cloth : alk. paper)
    1. Personnel management.   I. Kreps, David M.   II. Title.
HF5549.B286   1999
658.3—dc21   98-55272
                                                                                  CIP

Printed in the United States of America

10 9 8 7 6 5

For Isaac and Nina, and Tamar, Oren and Avner.

PREFACE AND ACKNOWLEDGEMENTS

A few years back—actually, more than either of us cares to admit—we came up with the idea of jointly developing and teaching a required course on human resource management for the MBA students at Stanford University's Graduate School of Business (GSB). The goal was to impart a "general manager's perspective" to managing employees, enlisting the disciplines of economics, psychology, and sociology, and drawing on careful disciplinary scholarship that had been done on the topic. We couldn't find a textbook that was suitable for the sort of course we wanted to teach, so we began writing notes for the students to read, notes that have evolved into this book.

The broad themes and perspectives that we will emphasize throughout this book are described in Chapter 1, and we don't want to rehash all that here. But it is worth highlighting one point: We undertook this venture in large measure because we each wanted to learn from the other about how our respective disciplines approach employment relationships. (We also thought the exercise would be fun.) We initially expected that "the Economics way of thinking" and "the Organizational Behavior way of thinking" would be substitutes for one another, and consequently that we'd educate students by debating the differences in how our disciplines viewed the world. We've found instead that the disciplines are complementary; each helps to fill in holes left open by the other, thereby sharpening and clarifying what the other has to say. In fact, there is not a single chapter in this book that isn't truly collaborative; in every case, whoever penned the first draft of each chapter found that not only his prose but—more importantly—his thinking about the subject at hand was significantly altered and improved through the efforts of the other. (One telling indicator of this is that on various occasions while writing this book, each of us has provided scathing feedback to the other concerning a particular passage of text that was absolutely intolerable, only to discover that the person criticizing the passage at issue was the one who long ago had originally drafted it.)

As with any venture that has taken a long time, there are a lot of folks to thank. We've abused the patience of many editors at John Wiley & Sons, who nonetheless have remained committed to—and even excited about—this project. We are indebted to the administration of the Stanford GSB; they gave us time to teach this course and they supported us in developing it, even in the early days when we were still trying to figure out what we were doing. That we were given free rein (indeed, even *encouraged*) to pursue this venture illustrates the best elements of HRM in leading academic institutions, where intrinsically motivated faculty are given considerable autonomy in choosing what projects to pursue. This is an approach toward managing human resources that we suspect is well-suited to many other organizational settings. We are very grateful for the latitude and for the many forms of support, tangible and otherwise, we've received over the years from the Stanford GSB.

Generations of students who sat through our courses—in the MBA program and in various Executive Education offerings—read through our notes and made many valuable contributions. A complete list is too long to give, but Lisa Auerbach and George Snelling, who were part of the group that suffered through our first painful attempt, deserve a particularly heartfelt thank-you.

Our colleagues at Stanford have been very generous in furnishing comments, suggestions, references, and information. Bob Flanagan, Eddie Lazear, Charles O'Reilly, and Jeff Pfeffer have co-taught the HRM course with us at various times, and we appreciate their encouragement, willingness to share ideas and materials, and help in letting us try out our ideas on their students. Other colleagues at the GSB who helped us include: Connie Bagley, David Baron, David Brady, Alain Enthoven, Roberto Fernandez, Mike Hannan, Chuck Horngren, Chuck Holloway, Rod Kramer, Rick Lambert, Jim March, George Parker, Joel Podolny, John Roberts, Garth Saloner, Mike Spence, and Mark Wolfson.

We are grateful for assistance we received from colleagues at other institutions, who read draft chapters, used some of our materials in class and provided feedback on students' reactions, steered us to relevant literature and cases, and tactfully encouraged us to finish. At the risk of missing some names that ought to be on the list, we would like to acknowledge: George Baker, Avner Ben-Ner, Mike Beer, Bill Bielby, Jeff Bradach, Diane Burton, Tom DeLong, Richard Freeman, Jack Gabarro, Bob Gibbons, Michael Gibbs, Robert Graham, Dana Heller, Bengt Holmstrom, Rakesh Khurana, Mark Knez, Kazuo Koike, Brigitte Madrian, Nitin Nohria, Craig Olson, Jim Rebitzer, Alvin Roth, Carl Sloan, and Peter Zemsky, in addition to the very helpful anonymous reviewers who provided comments via our publisher.

As Ivory Tower shut-ins, we have been privileged to be able to pick the brains of a number of very talented people from the real world. They have shared information about their organizations, which aided us in writing this book; helped us in developing materials for our Stanford course; and in some cases visited our classes, sharing their wisdom with our students. Again, at the risk of overlooking someone, we would particularly like to thank: Mary Dumont, Esquire; Debra Engel, 3COM; James Hresko, General Motors; Robert Koski, Sun Hydraulics; Richard Kovacevich and Stephen Hansen, Norwest Corporation; Ayman Hindy, Long-Term Capital Management; Jean Mandeville and Philip Rawlings, British Telecom; Andreas Mattmueller, Mandarin Oriental Hotel Group; Susan Mendelsohn, Pillsbury Madison & Sutro LLP; John Morgridge and Barbara Beck, Cisco Systems; Lewis Platt, Hewlett-Packard; John Reed and Lawrence Phillips, Citigroup; Dr. Parichart Suksongkroh, The Oriental (Bangkok); Thomas J. Tierney, Bain & Co.; Paul Varacalli, Service Employees International Union; Michael Vartain (formerly of Stanford University's Office of General Counsel); and Andrew Wold, PACCAR.

Clerical and research assistance at Stanford were provided by Vanessa Chiniquy, Aishya Earls, Barbara Firpo Laing, Matthew Lonergan, Megan Miller, Linda Taoka, and the members of the GSB's FIRST team. Our thanks to all of them.

Much of the writing for this book occurred during the 1997–98 academic year, while Baron was a Marvin Bower Fellow at the Harvard Business School and Kreps was on sabbatical leave at the Berglas School of Economics at Tel Aviv University. Each of us is deeply grateful for the generosity and hospitality displayed by the institution that hosted him during the 1997–98 year. Mavis Carroll and Allison Ounanian at Harvard Business School assisted in the preparation of several chapters.

Finally, we have accumulated more than our fair share of debts on the home front. Our gratitude to our spouses, Mary Dumont and Anat Admati, cannot be conveyed with glib or succinct turns of phrase of the kind that suit a preface. Suffice it to say that as glad as we are that this book is done, Mary and Anat are probably even happier. Our children—Isaac and Nina, and Tamar, Oren, and Avner—too often had to put up with "Daddy's working" when truly important things came up. Though it is far from adequate compensation, we're delighted to dedicate this book to them. They are, after all, the most important human resources that we have a role in developing.

CONTENTS

Chapter 4   Employment and Economics   62

Chapter 5   Employment as a Social Relation   95

Chapter 6   Voice: Unions and Other Forms of Employee Representation   118

Chapter 7   Employment, Society, and the Law   153

Chapter 8   Internal Labor Markets   167

Chapter 9   High-Commitment HRM   189

Chapter 10 Performance Evaluation   **210**

Chapter 11 Pay for Performance   **243**

Chapter 19   HRM in Emerging Companies   471

Chapter 20   Organizing HR   503

Appendix A   Transaction Cost Economics   537

Appendix B   Reciprocity and Reputation in Repeated Interactions   548

Appendix C   Agency Theory   566

Appendix D   Adverse Selection and Market Signaling   577

Index   587

List of Tables, Figures, and Exhibits

1

INTRODUCTION

Imagine that you have the job of evaluating applications for new business loans at a major bank. One day, you find the following two loan applications in your in-basket.[1]

The first application consists largely of a thirty-four page, handwritten document entitled "Sun Hydraulics Corporation: Plans and Objectives," describing a manufacturing start-up that will produce hydraulic valves and other fluid power products. The document contains *pro forma* income statement and balance sheet projections for ten years, with supporting documentation that discusses the fluid power product industry in general. The document clearly states, however, that the company has (as yet) no prototype products. The proposal's centerpiece is a section detailing the company's corporate creed, which states:

> The creed (or philosophy) of a company when clearly expressed and enthusiastically used creates the foundation of a corporation's internal and external personality.
>
> For this new corporation to quickly establish itself and maintain a high product standard while growing rapidly it will be important to develop an ethical, aggressive, responsive and stable impression on customers, distributors, employees and vendors as soon as possible.
>
> Perhaps most importantly, the ultimate quality of a corporation is largely determined by the character of its employees who are attracted into employment and develop because of the corporation's environment.

Elsewhere, a description is given of the management procedures that will be employed. In brief, the plan describes an enterprise with no organization chart, no job titles, no hierarchy at all. Workers themselves will determine on a day-to-day basis what they will do (working in "natural groups" that will be allowed to form spontaneously). Except perhaps for information on compensation, all information held by members of the organization will be open and available to every other member. Suppliers and customers will deal directly with the workforce. There will be no quality control managers. Decisions will be made by the "soldiers." Elsewhere in the application is a short biography of the founder, Mr. Robert Koski, who most recently held the position of VP–Corporate Development in a traditionally run firm in the industry. Koski, an engineer by training, receives rave reviews from the CEO/Founder of his old firm, who states that he would hire Koski back in an instant, given the chance.

The second application concerns a large hotel project, to be built in San Francisco, California, by John Portman, a noted architect and developer of luxury hotels. Portman views this as the capstone of his career—it will be the first hotel that his firm will manage once built—and he plans to name it The Portman Hotel. The Portman will be relatively small, extremely luxurious, in an excellent location in San Francisco. The key element of the hotel's strategy is that it will bring Asian standards of hostelry to San Francisco. Specifically, each floor in the hotel will be staffed by a team of Personal Valets (PVs), whose job description comes down to "do whatever the guest asks, as long as it is neither illegal nor immoral." PVs will draw baths, iron clothing, mix drinks, and so on. They will also be responsible for keeping the rooms clean and in order.

Of course, the brief descriptions given above are inadequate for you to evaluate the prospects of the two firms. (Some readers may view Koski's vision of a structureless firm as sufficiently crazy, especially in a job-shop context, that his application can be rejected out of hand.) But we hope these brief descriptions are sufficient to make the point that a key element in each proposal concerns human resource management (HRM). Koski is banking on a radically nonstandard relationship between his firm and its employees; the Portman Hotel proposal makes the PVs the centerpiece of its marketing strategy, and it will succeed or not depending on how the PVs perform (and how customers react to the PV concept and execution).

As an outside analyst, to evaluate the two proposals you must judge whether the human resources (HR) policies that are contemplated will work. How would you structure your analyses? What considerations would be important? Suppose your financial institution made a substantial loan and, as an officer of your bank, you were put on the board of either of these ventures as an outside member. How important is it that you come to grips with the HR policies of the organization? If we assure you that it is *crucially* important (and we can give those assurances), are you equipped to come to grips with those policies?

We will return to these cases in the course of this book, but here is the bottom line. The Portman Hotel failed (the building is now the Pan Pacific Hotel), substantially because its HR strategies failed. Sun Hydraulics, conversely, has been a substantial success and underwent its first public offering in January of 1997. The company's 10-K for 1996 states:

> Management believes that the Company's success during its 27-year history is due in large part to its emphasis on innovative product designs and vertically integrated, state of the art manufacturing processes. Management attributes the Company's ability to continuously implement process improvements to its horizontal management structure that encourages employee contribution at all levels. The Company does not have a formal organizational chart and employee responsibilities do not devolve from titles or narrow job descriptions. This management philosophy is utilized throughout the Company's operations.[2]

TABLE 1-1 Relative Compensation of Top Executives Across Functional Areas: Large U.S. and Japanese Companies[3]

FUNCTION	JAPAN	U.S.
Manufacturing	1.00	1.00
Sales/Marketing	0.93	0.91
R&D	0.87	0.90
Finance	1.00	1.32
Human Resources	1.02	0.83

For now our point is simple: Until quite recently, the management of human resources was regarded (in the United States, at least) as a low-level technical specialty, involving people who specialize in filling out government-mandated forms, conducting wage and morale surveys, handling initial recruitment interviews, and the like. Few (if any) American managers, told that their next assignment was going to be in the Personnel department, would stop on the way home to pick up a celebratory bottle of champagne. Instead, the HR department has been one of the places to send good, solid managers who fell off the fast track at some stage or another. Accordingly, most general managers had few and limited tools with which to think intelligently and analytically about HRM in particular organizations. You will certainly not be unique if you found our two cases intriguing, but you didn't quite know where to begin your analysis.

In other countries, the picture has been somewhat different. The contrast is most vivid with traditional Japanese firms, where managing human resources is the single most important duty of middle-level general managers, and success in these tasks is a prerequisite for advancement into top management. As Table 1-1 shows, senior HR managers in large Japanese corporations are, if anything, treated as the elite.

And in the United States, the picture is changing. There is an increasing awareness of the importance of managing the workforce. The shelves of airport bookstores are filled with titles such as *Putting People First*. The VP for HR is getting invited more frequently to top management strategy formulation sessions and is even speaking up. As we discuss in Chapter 20, HR departments are outsourcing some of their lower value-added activities, such as payroll and benefits processing, to remake themselves into leaner, more "high-end" business partners. General managers are increasingly aware that their skills in thinking about HRM need polishing at least and, in many cases, a complete makeover.

THE PREMISES OF THIS BOOK

We applaud these changes, and we've written this book to help accelerate them. Our efforts are based on the following four premises:

First, *human resources are key to organizational success or failure*. It is perhaps going too far to say that excellent HR policies are sufficient for success. But success with poor HR policies is probably impossible, and the effects of improved HR policies on organizational success are potentially enormous. We contend that the central importance of HRM to the viability of Sun Hydraulics and the Portman Hotel is hardly atypical, especially given the abilities, knowledge, and skill possessed by employees today. Moreover, we will suggest how and why competitive advantage built and achieved through superior human resource management is more sustainable and harder for competitors to emulate than some other bases of achieving competitive advantage.

Second, HRM is too important to be left to HR specialists. *For HRM to be successful, general managers must be involved.* From the overall strategy of the organization to day-to-day logistical operations, management must understand and be sensitive to the role played by the organization's human resources.

Third, *for general managers to understand and be sensitive to HRM, the basic issues in the management of human resources must be laid out in nonspecialist terms,* without a lot of concern for the nitty-gritty of government mandates and technical concerns that permeate specialist books and courses in HRM. It is especially important that HRM be presented in a way that links it to the other concerns of general management, and in particular to the organization's (overall) strategy.

And finally, nostrums are just that, nostrums. HRM is too complex to be turned into slogans. *To understand the management of human resources, we must reach back to the basic economic, social, psychological, and legal forces that impinge on employment,* which means that we must reach back to Economics, Psychology, Sociology, and the Law. And we must reach back to *all* of these complementary ways of thought. Any approach that stresses one to the exclusion of others will be incomplete and potentially misleading.

Based on these four premises, our objectives for this book are to construct frameworks by which you—as a general manager or a student of general management—can better analyze and craft HR policies in your organization. We will also examine what light these frameworks can shed on some crucial HR issues confronting management today, such as the outsourcing of labor, management of a diverse workforce, downsizing a too-large organization, and total quality management (TQM).

Each of these premises is a matter of (almost religious) dogma. We can (and, in a moment, will) cite strong empirical evidence for the first, but the second, third, and fourth are to a large extent bald (and bold) assertions. Even so, we can say a few things about each.

Human Resources Are Key

Human resources are key to organizational success or failure. Until recently, something of a leap of faith was required to believe the management of human resources has big effects on the bottom line. But no longer: There is a fast-growing and high-quality body of empirical research demonstrating that HRM policies have an impact on organizational performance.[4]

Not surprisingly, much of this work has focused on the effects of pay systems—how much workers are paid and to what extent pay is performance based.

A number of recent studies suggest that firms paying above-market wages relative to their competitors experience lower rates of absenteeism, disciplinary discharge, and turnover, as well as greater job satisfaction and performance.[5] There are also various studies reporting that gain-sharing and profit-sharing plans are associated with superior group- or organizational-level productivity and financial performance; and that under certain circumstances performance-based pay plans can increase performance and facilitate attraction and retention of high performers.[6]

Other researchers are finding that the level and performance-sensitivity of pay may be less important for the bottom line than how workers are *treated* and the broader set of human resource policies within which pay regimes are embedded. For instance, after a thorough and careful review of existing studies relating pay systems and worker participation schemes to productivity, Alan Blinder—Princeton economist and former vice chairman of the Federal Reserve System's Board of Governors—concluded: "[Unexpectedly], it appears that changing the way workers are treated may boost productivity more than changing the way they are paid, although profit sharing or employee stock ownership combined with worker participation may be the best system of all."[7]

Very interesting evidence has also been collected concerning TQM. An MIT study of the automotive industry gathered detailed information on plant technology, human resource practices, productivity, and quality for automobile plants throughout the world. This study showed that organizations whose HR systems incorporate a cluster of "high-commitment" practices (teams, more participation, employment security, intense screening and socialization, etc.) obtain greater productivity and (especially) higher quality than other plants, even after controlling for differences in plant technology, age, model mix, and the like.[8] Moreover, the returns to high-commitment work systems were found to be especially great among organizations utilizing lean manufacturing processes (just-in-time, kanban methods, etc.). In another study of 102 business units in North America and Europe (primarily U. S. manufacturers), Douglas Cowherd and David Levine document that enterprises with narrower pay differentials (between top executives and line workers and between top executives and first-level managers) are perceived by customers as having significantly higher product quality (relative to competitors), even after controlling for differences in unionization, size, workforce composition, market share, and technology across the business units.[9]

And recent research on the evolution of human resource systems in technology start-ups suggests that founders' early decisions regarding HR philosophy and practice exert enduring effects on their companies. For instance, a recent large-scale study of Silicon Valley start-ups interviewed founders, CEOs, and key HR managers to gather information on the HR philosophies and practices espoused by the founder as well as information on subsequent developments within the companies. The researchers found that—even after controlling for differences in the companies' age, industry, occupational mix, public versus private status, growth rate, and other relevant factors—those start-ups whose founders had initially espoused a commitment-based employment model (strong attachment to the company, screening of workers based on cultural fit, security of employment, etc.) subsequently required fewer managerial and administrative specialists to oversee the activities of their nonadministrative employees.[10] In other words, firms that invested heavily in building a strong system of employee commitment and organizational attachment from the outset required significantly fewer administrative overseers some years later. We discuss this body of research in greater detail in Chapter 19.

When you add to these careful empirical studies the vast array of impressionistic or casually gathered data, it becomes clear how important HRM can be to organizational evolution and success.

General Manager Involvement

For HRM to be successful, general managers must be involved. Just because successful HRM is a key element to success of the organization, we can't necessarily conclude that the concern and involvement of general managers is *crucial*. To give an analogy, maintenance of the package trucks at United Parcel Service is crucial to that company—if those brown trucks were subject to frequent breakdown, the organization's performance would fall precipitously. But this doesn't mean that UPS top management necessarily needs to concern itself with maintenance procedures.

The argument for general (and top) management involvement in HRM instead turns on three ideas that we will develop in this book: First, human resources constrain the strategies that the organization can and should carry out, so that insofar as general managers are concerned with setting and implementing overall strategy, they would be foolish to ignore the organization's HR policies. Second, workers' expectations and attitudes are crucial to HRM, and general managers have a preeminent role to play in setting the "tone" of the employment relationship. Third, the implementation of the firm's HR policies is best done with *at least* the participation of line managers in the field, rather than being left to HR specialists.

Top managers are increasingly aware of the important role they play in their firm's HR administration. The general business press has featured HRM recently; survey data attesting to the importance of HRM are rampant. (Indeed, why else would you have picked up this book?) This sentiment is captured vividly by Richard Kovacevich, president and CEO of Norwest, a rapidly growing global financial services company headquartered in Minneapolis, with $88.5 billion in assets at the end of 1997. (In mid-1998, Norwest announced its merger with Wells Fargo Bank, based in San Francisco.) The firm has been enormously successful; a Norwest stockholder who reinvested dividends experienced an annualized return of roughly 33% for the decade ending at year-end 1997, compared to 18% for the S&P 500 over that same period. When Kovacevich describes his responsibilities to employees and external audiences, he typically states that his main job is to manage human resources at Norwest and asserts that: "The primary responsibility of business managers is to influence the hearts and minds of our people, consistent with the culture of Norwest, so they care more about our business than competitors care about theirs."[11]

Plain Language and Connections to General Management Concerns

For general managers to understand and be sensitive to HRM, the basic issues in the management of human resources must be laid out in nonspecialist terms, and the connections between HRM and other concerns of general managers must be made. Despite increasing recognition of the importance of HRM, interest in HRM courses within MBA programs has been dwindling. We think that this has been true because those courses, with a few welcome and important exceptions, tend to be courses for HR specialists, focused on the minutiae of running a personnel system, rather than on the strategic issues associated with human resources that are critical for the general manager or the entrepreneur or the consultant. Traditional HRM texts and courses focus on how to carry out job analyses and wage surveys, conduct employment interviews and set up performance appraisal systems, comply with employment laws and deal with unions, conduct training programs, and the like. Very few texts and courses focus on how to align the HR practices of the organization with its strategy or technology or culture. Even fewer address how, once an organization has invested in developing an effective reputation as an employer and developed a time-tested set of HR practices and policies, managers ought to think about molding their decisions regarding technology, structure, strategy, plant siting, and the like to the company's HR system. And none of the existing texts with which we are familiar provides managers or entrepreneurs with a systematic framework for thinking through these issues.

What has been missing in the HR domain is something analogous to Michael Porter's "five forces" framework for competitive strategy—an organizing scheme which, although an oversimplification, helps give general managers the lay of the land and focus their attention on the key issues they need to consider in managing human resources. We, somewhat immodestly, hope to provide one such framework.

The Basic Disciplines

To understand the management of human resources, we must reach back to the basic economic, social, psychological, and legal forces that impinge on employment. This leads us into the most distinctive element of this book. We are not the first to claim that an organization ought to align its HR policies and practices with its strategy, technology, and environment. This point is central to the literature dealing with what is called "strategic human resource management." Nor are we the first writers to suggest that the influence should go in the opposite direction as well—that is, an organization's HR system represents an important constraint on choices of strategy and technology. (However, this second point has seldom been stated explicitly or emphasized.) Finally, you can find a number of books, some good and some . . . not so good, which adopt the general manager's perspective on the issues.

We assert that the management of human resources is complex because the basic element is the behavior of people, whose perceptions and expectations are colored by their perceptual abilities and by their social experiences, and whose objectives mix (to varying degrees) pure self-interest, comparisons with others, and some sense of social obligation. Moreover, because the issues involved are so important to individuals, society has an enormous stake in the outcome, and societies will express their interests in the outcome through both social and legal constraints on organizations and their relationships with employees.

This complexity has two consequences. First, it is dangerous to rely on folk wisdom, best current practice, and a few war stories to get a sense of what works and what doesn't. To the extent that it is possible, we will try to enlist careful empirical study of organizations and their HR policies. And second, to understand the careful empirical work we cite and to try to make sense of folk wisdom and best current practice, we will enlist the basic social sciences of economics, sociology, and psychology. We will try to understand why people act as they do by going back to the economic, social, psychological, and legal forces that drive their actions and impinge on employment.

We explicitly eschew nostrums that are meant to apply universally; we don't believe that universal truths in this domain exist. This doesn't mean that there is no wisdom in popular nostrums—they wouldn't be popular if they didn't contain some wisdom—but we will try to understand *why* and *when* they are more applicable, and why and when they are dangerous. We also aim to enlist all three of economics, psychology, and sociology. Some excellent books on "strategic HRM" have been written that take the perspective of one of these disciplines. But we believe that all three are important to a full understanding of HRM, and that the three are complementary—each improves rather than competes with the others.

Consider, for example, performance evaluation. When economists think about performance evaluation, they tend to focus on its use as a monitoring and incentive device—that is, how to align the interests of the employee with the goals of top management so that the behaviors most valued by the organization are carried out, monitored, and rewarded. Economic reasoning will indicate some harmful effects that performance appraisal schemes can have, such as encouraging people to focus too much on the aspects of a job that are easiest to measure, but not necessarily the most valuable. Economic analyses focus on technological and informational concerns: the kind of job being done, how objectively and accurately outcomes can be measured, how much control the individual worker has over his or her outcomes, and so on. But economics does not concern itself with what basic objectives the worker seeks, nor how the process of evaluation itself affects the worker's expectations about the nature of the relationship and (thus) his or her behavior. Sociologists, in contrast, tend to focus on the institutional and cultural forces that impinge on performance evaluation—how social and organizational relationships between the people being appraised and those doing the appraising may affect the outcomes of performance appraisal; differences in norms governing performance appraisal across occupations, countries, and the like; and ways in which organizations design performance evaluation schemes to create favorable perceptions in the eyes of key external stakeholders (government, unions, etc.). Psychological work on the topic, in turn, has a lot to say about the factors that influence how valid, reliable, and fair a particular appraisal instrument or technology is judged to be.

It should be clear that each of these facets of performance appraisal is important and that a good deal is lost if we do not consider all of them. For instance, economic reasoning might recommend a particular appraisal technology in a specific organizational setting where relevant psychological or sociological work would suggest that very same technology is actually infeasible, illegitimate, unreliable, or counterproductive. Conversely, an approach to performance appraisal based solely on psychological principles might overlook unintended incentives or pathologies created by a particular appraisal regime that economic models would illuminate. Accordingly, throughout this book, we try to meld insights from the different disciplines (and to acknowledge where there are disagreements and differences of opinion), rather than adopt a single disciplinary orientation and examine every HRM issue through that one lens.

Although we will invoke the social sciences, we will try to minimize the jargon and maximize plain English, and we will appeal to concrete examples instead of abstract principles when we can. But we won't always succeed. Because we attempt to integrate three social sciences that have a tradition of mutual hostility (or, at least, indifference), readers who are disciples of one may find parts of this book off-putting. If you are not a (single-) disciplinarian and if your previous studies haven't permanently put you off one or more of the three social sciences, you probably won't have a problem here. But otherwise . . .

PAYBACK TIME

To make it through this book, you'll have to recall (or learn) some economics, some sociology, and some social psychology. And the economics, sociology, and psychology that are important to this book are generally not what is taught in undergraduate courses on the subjects. (Actually, we think this will turn out to be a bit of a plus, because we'll be "reviewing" what you need to know in a way that we hope won't seem too tedious.)

But if you persevere, we think the conceptual frameworks we create will illuminate some important issues of current concern. For example, one of the most fundamental decisions an organization must make concerns which activities to conduct internally and which ones to contract out to other organizations. Outsourcing is nothing new, of course, but quite a lot of evidence suggests that organizations are outsourcing more and more and relying on various "contingent" and flexible forms of employment such as employee leasing, use of independent contractors, and hiring individuals on a project basis. The old conventional wisdom about the virtues of vertical integration has been supplanted by a belief in the virtues of being "lean and mean," of maximizing flexibility, and of sticking to your knitting by contracting out non-core activities. We will suggest that decisions about what activities to conduct inside versus outside the organization are fundamentally human resource decisions—assessments about the distinctive competence of the organization's workforce and about which tasks complement the organization's existing

HR system. Thus, armed with our conceptual framework, you will be in a better position to think about key factors to consider when deciding what jobs to outsource and about HR practices that will reduce potential adverse effects of outsourcing.

Another hot issue nowadays is workforce diversity, including not only demographic diversity within one country, but also diversity across countries and cultures. Most of what has been written about diversity, especially for managers, consists of practical tips aimed at helping managers and individual employees to acclimate to an increasingly heterogeneous workforce. There has also been a fair amount of scholarly and practitioner writing, targeted principally toward the HR executive, concerning the HR practices and systems that are necessary to attract, develop, and retain a diverse workforce. We'll attack diversity along different lines, thinking about diversity in *strategic* terms: In what kinds of organizational and environmental settings is diversity a particular asset (or liability)? What implications does an increasingly heterogeneous workforce have for a firm's human resources strategy and for the "fit" among particular human resource practices? How is the manner in which diversity is sought and achieved in an organization likely to alter the organization's culture and reputation?

We've already mentioned TQM, but given that there can be few managers left on the planet who aren't at least somewhat preoccupied with total quality—whether or not those precise buzzwords are used—a few more words won't hurt. The main challenges that organizations are facing in pursuing total quality nowadays, as best we can tell, concern the management of human resources. It is not difficult for an organization to acquire the necessary knowledge of principles of statistical process control, inventory management, continuous improvement, activity-based accounting, and the like, which are advocated by quality gurus (and which may have very wide applicability across a diverse range of organizations). What seems much tougher, however, is designing and implementing the HR systems that will drive a quality program: restructuring selection, training, compensation, performance appraisal, and promotion systems to support team-based work systems, the delegation of power to those lower down in the organization, and an intense focus on customer satisfaction. We assert that such a restructuring of the HR system must necessarily be keenly sensitive to the organization's context; and we believe that we will give you some tools for thinking strategically about human resource concerns that will be extremely valuable if you seek to design and implement quality programs.

THREE AXES WE WILL GRIND

We don't believe in nostrums, and we will try to avoid them. But we have three general sermons that we will be preaching constantly:

First, *HR policies cannot be considered piecemeal*. Because of basic economic, social, and psychological considerations that we address in this book, HR practices either work together as a package or they fight each other. Quite different "packages" or systems can work well together in the same setting, while a mix of bits from each will fall flat. Treatments of personnel management targeted toward HR specialists often treat topics like compensation, job design, and recruitment separately. When it comes to meeting legal mandates or day-to-day administration, this is somewhat sensible. But from the standpoint of the general manager, it is almost certainly less valuable to have mastery over the details within each relevant topic area of HRM than it is to comprehend how the various elements of the HR system interrelate and under what circumstances they support or impede one another. We will get to evidence on this point (and a fuller explanation of what all this means) in Chapter 3, but for now, a metaphor will probably make the point: The general manager doesn't need a large cookbook listing recipes for every course of a meal, but rather some guidance about how to construct menus so that all the courses go well together.

Second, managers must think of human resources as something in which to invest. Human assets are hard to evaluate quantitatively, so they don't show up on the balance sheet. But whether or not the bean counters can assign dollar values to them, assets they are, and *general managers must think of human resources as a form of capital.*

Third, continuing this line of thought, *human resources are a particularly difficult form of capital to shift or modify.* It is possible, with a lot of time and effort, to shift the HR policies of an established enterprise, or to change dramatically the composition of the organization's human resources. But as a practical matter, general managers should consider their human resources as something of a constraint on their actions. And they should be careful, especially early on, in setting the right policies and tone when it comes to HRM.

THE STRUCTURE OF THE BOOK

We proceed along the following route. The book is divided into two main parts. The first part is devoted to basic frameworks and ideas. In Chapter 2 we develop the fundamental checklist for the study of the organization's HR practice in context. Called the "five factors" (the parallel with Michael Porter's "five forces" is painful but, as far as we can tell, unavoidable), it gives a categorization of factors in the larger context that bear on HR practices: the business strategy, work organization, culture, workforce demographics, and the external environment (economic, social, legal, and political). As with any checklist, this one is incomplete and, in some cases, has overlapping categories. But we (and you) will find it very useful for filing away the "facts" about a particular organizational context and for disciplining your thinking about the HR issues involved in specific settings. We will use this framework frequently, focusing especially on business strategy and work organization, to organize our thinking about particular HR issues. In Chapter 3 we develop a second fundamental thesis of this book—that HR systems must be thought of as just that: *systems.*[12] Chapters 4 and 5 flesh out our basic framework by bringing some basic insights from the social sciences to bear on HR and employment. Chapter 4 looks at employment through the lens of economics, and Chapter 5 complements this by looking at employment as a social and psychological relationship. Chapter 6 blends ideas from Chapters 4 and 5 by considering the general topic of giving workers a "voice" or a say in what they do and how they do it. Chapter 7 briefly discusses the role of law and society in HRM. Chapters 8 and 9 wrap up the first part of the book by applying the ideas of earlier chapters to important examples of HR systems: internal labor markets and high-commitment work environments.

In the second part of the book, we (mostly) study the various elements that constitute an HR system. Here you'll find separate chapters on performance evaluation (Chapter 10), pay for performance (Chapter 11), compensation systems and benefits (Chapter 12), job design (Chapter 13), staffing and recruitment (Chapter 14), training (Chapter 15), promotion and career concerns (Chapter 16), downsizing (Chapter 17), and outsourcing (Chapter 18). In view of our notion that HR systems cannot be understood very well decomposed into constituent pieces, these chapter divisions are somewhat artificial; the chapter on performance evaluation, for example, will spend a lot of time on issues of compensation and job design, and vice versa. So a fair amount of flipping back and forth, as you read these chapters, is a good idea.

We wrap up with two *sui generis* chapters. In Chapter 19, we survey some recent work done at Stanford on HR policies in emerging firms, using this as a springboard to revisit issues of alignment and complementarities among HR practices and to discuss change and the evolution of HRM in organizations. And in Chapter 20, we look at the HR function: Who should set strategy?; Who should implement strategy?; What role should HR specialists play? Our philosophy is that general managers should be intimately involved in setting HR strategy and then in the implementation of the strategy. But HR specialists do have a role to play—a role that we explore in concluding the book.

WHAT THIS BOOK LACKS

Although it is probably already clear from what we've had to say, we reiterate that our primary focus is *not* on the operational details of personnel administration that preoccupy HR specialists. If you are an HR specialist or aspire to be one, we hope you will find this book interesting and informative. But neither we nor you should expect it to give you the detailed information that your specialty requires.

Indeed, even if your aspirations fall short of specializing in HRM, you may well have questions about operational details that we don't answer. For example: What are the advantages and disadvantages of different types of gain-sharing plans? How large do performance bonuses have to be for bonus schemes to be motivating? How does one conduct a "comparable worth" study to examine whether there are inequities in the pay structure? What kinds of information should employees be allowed to see in their personnel record? Happily, academic researchers and HR practitioners alike have paid considerable attention to these kinds of nitty-gritty concerns. Wherever possible, we provide references to reviews of such literatures that we believe are helpful and accessible to the generalist.

Perhaps the most important nitty-gritty concerns for general managers are legal considerations. For reasons we will discuss in Chapter 7, employment is perhaps the most closely regulated and legislated type of economic transaction. Although we will discuss some of the legal issues involved and summarize some of the statutory and regulatory constraints on human resource management, it is impossible to provide a comprehensive (or even satisfactory) treatment in this book, and you would be well advised to do some independent reading to familiarize yourself with the legal dimensions of HRM in your legal environment.[13]

IN REVIEW

At the end of each chapter, we provide a brief outline to help readers review what they have read.

⇒ The main premises of this book are:
1. Human resources are the key to organizational success or failure. HR policies and practices must be tied to overall organizational strategy.
2. For HRM to be successful, general management must be involved
3. For general managers to understand and be sensitive to HR issues, those issues must be laid out in nonspecialist terms
4. To understand HRM, you must reach back to the basic economic, social, psychological, and legal forces that impinge on employment, which means you have to understand some basic economics, sociology, and social psychology. One-size-fits-all nostrums and prescriptions built from one and only one disciplinary lens may contain wisdom, but they may miss as much as they hit.

⇒ If this sounds like painful reading, there is a reward: If you persevere, you will get insights into issues of current topical interest such as outsourcing, workforce diversity, and TQM.

⇒ HR policies are part of a system—they shouldn't be considered piecemeal.

⇒ Human resources are capital—think *investment* and not *cost*.

⇒ Human resources are difficult to shift or modify—get HR strategy right at the start (if you can), or you'll probably pay the price later.

⇒ This book lacks the important, nitty-gritty detail of typical HRM courses, and it especially lacks material on the legal constraints on HR that apply in different jurisdictions around the world. You'll have to look elsewhere for such stuff, and we strongly urge you to do so.

ENDNOTES

1. Reprinted from Louis B. Barnes and Colleen Kaftan, Sun Hydraulics Corporation (A), case 485-169. Boston: Harvard Business School, 1985, p. 7.

2. Reprinted from Louis B. Barnes and Colleen Kaftan, Sun Hydraulics Corporation (A), case 485-169. Boston: Harvard Business School, 1985, p. 7.

3. Copyright © 1991, A. T. Kearney, Inc. All rights reserved. Reprinted with permission. These data are based on manufacturing companies with sales in excess of $2.0 billion. With the compensation for top manufacturing executives within the country used as an index, Table 1-1 shows relative average compensation (salary plus bonus) for top executives in different functions. For example, specialists in finance in Japan receive approximately the same average compensation as do Japanese specialists in manufacturing, whereas U.S. specialists in finance receive 32% more than U.S. specialists in manufacturing. Note that at the top of these companies, the HR function is (on average) the most highly paid specialty in Japan and the lowest-paid specialty in the United States.

4. Helpful reviews of some of this literature are provided in Alan S. Blinder (ed.), *Paying for Productivity: A Look at the Evidence* (Washington, DC: The Brookings Institution, 1990); George Milkovich and Alexandra Wigdor (eds.), *Pay for Performance: Evaluating Performance Appraisal and Merit Pay* (Washington, DC: National Research Council, 1991); Ronald G. Ehrenberg (ed.), *Do Compensation Policies Matter?* (Ithaca, NY: Cornell ILR Press, 1990); Morris M. Kleiner et al. (eds.), *Human Resources and the Performance of the Firm* (Madison, WI: Industrial Relations Research Association, 1987); U. S. Department of Labor, "High Performance Work Practices and Firm Performance" (Unpublished manuscript, August 1993); Brian Becker and Barry Gerhart, "The Impact of Human Resource Management on Organizational Performance: Progress and Prospects," *Academy of Management Journal* 39 (August 1996): 779–801; Keith Whitfield and Michael Poole, "Organizing Employment for High Performance: Theories, Evidence, and Policy," *Organization Studies* 18 (no. 5, 1997): 745–64; Brian E. Becker, Mark A. Huselid, Peter S. Pickus, and Michael F. Spratt, "HR as a Source of Shareholder Value: Research and Recommendations," *Human Resource Management* 36 (Spring 1997): 39–47; and Jeffrey Pfeffer, *The Human Equation: Building Profits by Putting People First,* Chapter 2 (Boston: Harvard Business School Press, 1998).

5. For reviews of the literature, see Lawrence Katz, "Efficiency Wage Theories: A Partial Evaluation," in Stanley Fischer (ed.), *NBER Macroeconomics Annual* (Cambridge, MA: MIT Press, 1987); James M. Rebitzer, "Efficiency Wages and Implicit Contracts: An Institutional Evaluation," in Robert Drago and Richard Perlman (eds.), *Microeconomic Issues in Labor Economics: New Approaches* (New York: Harvester Wheatsheaf, 1989).

6. See Milkovich and Wigdor (eds.), *op. cit.*; Pfeffer, *op. cit.*; Edward P. Lazear, "Performance Pay and Productivity," National Bureau of Economic Research Working Paper #5672 (Cambridge, MA: NBER, August 1996).

7. Blinder, *op. cit.,* p. 13.

8. John P. Macduffie and John F. Krafcik, "Integrating Technology and Human Resources for High-Performance Manufacturing: Evidence from the International Auto Industry," pp. 209–25 in Thomas A. Kochan and Michael Useem (eds.), *Transforming Organizations* (New York: Oxford University Press, 1992).

9. Douglas M. Cowherd and David I. Levine, "Product Quality and Pay Equity Between Lower-level Employees and Top Management: An Investigation of Distributive Justice Theory," *Administrative Science Quarterly* 37 (June 1992): 302–20.

10. James N. Baron, Michael T. Hannan, and M. Diane Burton, "Determinants of Managerial Intensity in the Early Years of Organizations," Research Paper 1550, Graduate School of Business, Stanford University.

11. Quoted in Bruce A. Pasternack, Shelley S. Keller and Albert J. Viscio, "The Triumph of People Power and the New Economy," *Strategy & Business* (Booz-Allen & Hamilton, Second Quarter, 1997), viewable online at: http://www.strategy-business.com/strategy/97203/pagc6.html.

12. Similar emphasis on the connections (or "complementarities") among human resource practices can be found in Paul Milgrom and D. John Roberts, *Economics, Organization, and Management* (Englewood Cliffs, NJ: Prentice-Hall, 1992); Edward P. Lazear, *Personnel Economics for Managers* (New York: Wiley, 1998); Jeffrey Pfeffer, *Competitive Advantage Through People* (Boston: Harvard Business School Press, 1994); Macduffie and Krafcik, *op. cit.*; and Casey Ichniowski, Kathryn Shaw, and Giovanna Prennushi, "The Effects of Human Resource Management Practices on Productivity: A Study of Steel Finishing Lines," *American Economic Review* 87 (June 1997): 291–313.

13. Good background sources for the U.S. context include William B. Gould, *A Primer on American Labor Law,* 3rd edition (Cambridge, MA: MIT Press, 1993); and Constance E. Bagley, *Managers and the Legal Environment: Strategies for the 21st Century,* 2nd edition (St. Paul, MN: West, 1995).

2

THE FIVE FACTORS

The most important question about the human resources policies of any firm is: *How well do those policies fit?* HR systems are precisely that—systems—whose components sometimes work together and sometimes clash. And they are embedded within larger systems of relationships: the firm and its diverse stakeholders; the society or societies the firm inhabits; and so on. Thus, the question *How well do the firm's HR policies fit?* can be divided into two parts. First, do the HR policies fit in the broader context of what the firm is trying to do, where it is located, and how it operates? Second, to what extent are the individual pieces of the HR system internally complementary or consistent?

The notion that an organization ought to craft HR policies that are internally consistent and that suit its strategy, technology, and context is hardly controversial. Yet it is much harder to pull off than it sounds. Conspicuous examples of misaligned and/or internally inconsistent HR practices are not hard to find, and we'll provide numerous illustrations throughout this book. Imitation may be the sincerest form of flattery, but it is also one of the ways in which organizations can develop human resource practices that are either misaligned with their strategy and context or internally inconsistent with other policies and practices already in place. One sometimes observes a frenzied and indiscriminate rush to emulate the human resource practices of highly successful companies—for instance, emulating a competitor's pay system without due regard for the delicate interplay *among* different elements of an HR system or for differences in strategy, technology, and context between your organization and your competitor's that (should) impinge on the choice of HR practices. It is not difficult to find examples of organizations that have embraced initiatives around total quality, empowerment, and teams—simultaneously producing mission and value statements that champion their commitment to these endeavors—but whose HR practices regarding recruitment and selection, compensation, performance management, and promotion are essentially unchanged from an earlier era in which individual contribution, narrow jobs, and risk aversion were the ways of the world. Another common source of HR misalignment (particularly among organizations that are growing, diversifying, or globalizing rapidly) is the wholesale transfer of HR practices that were well suited to a specific line of business, geographical locale, organizational scale, or segment of the workforce to another context to which they are distinctly mismatched.

In this chapter, we will describe the framework we use to assess the fit of an HR system within the organization's broader context. Issues of internal consistency among HR practices are taken up in Chapter 3.

When asking *Does the HR system fit?* in a specific situation, it helps to have a general framework for analysis, which directs your attention to important categories of issues and key concerns within each category. A well-known example of such an framework, used to analyze business strategy, is Michael Porter's *Five Forces*.[1] We follow Porter's lead and provide a list of five categories of factors that bear on the HR system of any organization. The five factors are: (1) the social, political, legal, and economic environment; (2) the workforce; (3) the organization's culture; (4) the organization's strategy; and (5) the technology of production and organization of work.

In this chapter, we will discuss each of these features of the organizational context. Our objectives for now are modest. Except for technology, we'll be quite brief about things we will be looking at within each category, making lists and giving a few simple illustrative examples. We won't come to many conclusions in this chapter about how these things interact with the firm's HR system; such conclusions will be reached throughout the course of the book.

THE EXTERNAL ENVIRONMENT: SOCIAL, POLITICAL, LEGAL, AND ECONOMIC

The boundaries among social, political, legal, and economic pressures on the organization are fuzzy, so we group them in a single general category. But, trying hard to separate them into subcategories, here are the sorts of things we have in mind:

Social forces impinging on HRM begin with the local society's norms about work and employment in general. What in the society lends status to individuals? What sorts of behavior are frowned upon and what sorts are condoned? What are viewed as the social responsibilities of the firm? What types of organizational control are (not) acceptable and legitimate?

Concerning the political environment, how do political pressures work on the organization in terms of HR policies and practices? What do local governments expect? What support can be obtained from the political system? What impediments are imposed by the political system? Are aspects of employment relations subject to centralized bargaining and negotiation? Are employees and employers politically organized and mobilized?

Moving a small step to the legal environment, what are the statutory responsibilities of the organization? What rights do workers have, both individually and collectively? What sorts of employment practices are sanctioned? What legally enforced distinctions must be made among workers (e.g., exempt versus nonexempt in the United States)? What distinctions are impermissible?

As for the economic environment, what conditions exist in the local labor market? How great is labor mobility? What economic pressures does the organization face in other product and factor markets?

As an example of how the external environment can affect HR practices and policies, consider how the employment systems and internal labor markets of top-tier Japanese corporations are supported by Japanese institutions and environmental conditions. A detailed discussion of these firms and their HR practices will be given in Chapter 9, but for now, suffice it to say that these practices involve a lot of investment by the firm in the employee's skills and training, early in the employee's career. These practices make sense for the firm *if* the firm can be relatively sure that employees will not depart for other jobs—that is, if labor mobility is low. And, in Japan, it is: Putting it a bit thickly, it is sometimes said (among Japanese) that it is better to be a substitute on the championship team than to be the star of a second-place team. Status accrues to workers at the elite firms, status that they (at least until recently) lose if they shift jobs, especially to move to a lower status firm, even in a higher-status position. This is complemented and enhanced by low economic rewards for mobility. Finally, Japanese labor unions are organized on a company basis. These external social and economic factors work together to lower labor mobility and thus complement the array of HR practices employed by the Japanese elite firms. Of course, to the extent that economic and social conditions are changing in Japan, elite Japanese companies are changing their HR policies. And when they go overseas, these firms both adapt to the different environments they face and consciously attempt to site their facilities in locales that foster low labor mobility and so fit relatively better their distinctive HR practices.

Environmental factors are particularly important for multinational firms, especially those that seek (sometimes under political or legal pressure) to have a workforce that is representative of the host country. Note, for example, the relative difficulties that Japanese firms have had in the United States in building paternalistic relationships with workers, faced with a culture of labor–management antagonism and legal limits on what can be discussed directly with workers.

Even the physical environment can have significant implications for HRM! When confronted (in an international executive education session) with the case of the United Parcel Service (UPS), with its "cradle-to-grave" employment system and strong conformist culture, an astute participant from the Arabian Gulf asserted that the UPS employment system would not work well in his country: Because of his country's "itinerant" culture and oppressive climate, few workers are willing to remain employed there more than a few years, making it impossible for UPS to recoup the large front-end investment it makes in individual workers.[2]

THE WORKFORCE

The key factors here are mostly demographic. How old is the workforce? How well educated? How homogeneous or heterogeneous socially? Social homogeneity refers to uniformity with respect to social characteristics—sex, race, age, income group, education—*and* to norms of behavior derived from the society that workers come from. Another important form of workforce homogeneity is partly social, partly technical—namely, the occupational mix required in the organization. For instance, a law partnership that specializes in business law will be much more homogeneous than a "full-service" law partnership, which in turn is much more homogeneous than, say, Unilever.

The demographic distribution of the workforce can powerfully constrain employment strategy. For example, firms with a bulge of middle-level managers hired in anticipation of growth that fizzled out may be unable to sustain lifetime employment policies. Organizations with workers who are, on average, less well educated, will find total quality initiatives more difficult to implement successfully (see Chapter 9). The amount of workforce heterogeneity (e.g., in age, gender, education, occupation) also has implications for the degree of diversity an organization should display in its personnel practices (recruitment, performance evaluation, compensation, benefits, etc.). And heterogeneity can fundamentally affect basic motivational techniques. For instance, peer pressure as a motivational tool or control device works best in general when the workforce exhibits a fairly high degree of social homogeneity.

Especially in the United States, firms are exhorted by political forces to diversify their workforces. As we will see in Chapter 14, there can be substantial potential benefits from doing so. But when we come to this discussion, we will be especially concerned with challenges that arise generally in dealing with demographic heterogeneity.

THE ORGANIZATION'S CULTURE

The organization's culture refers to norms of conduct, work attitudes, and the values and assumptions about relationships that govern behavior at the organization. Many variables enter here, including: Is the culture egalitarian or hierarchical? Is the culture one of cooperation or competition among co-workers? Is work itself regarded as a joy or as drudgery that provides a means to some other end? Is conformity important, or does the organization encourage diversity or even contention in thought and action? Are workers regarded as mere employees—that is, is the labor exchange largely "economic" in character?—or are workers regarded more as family members?

Research on organizational culture suggests several important caveats and reminders in thinking about the topic.[3] First, please be sure to distinguish the organization's culture from the norms of the society in which the organization is embedded. General social norms can either support or derogate a particular organization's culture, but organizations sometimes display significantly diverse organizational cultures within a single social environment.

This raises a second caveat: Many studies of organizations and their cultures suggest it is misleading to speak of "organizational culture," because in fact organizations often display quite distinct *subcultures,* even within a single locale or organizational unit. Obviously, variations in culture, within and between organizations, are likely to have a lot to do with the kinds of work being performed (i.e., the core technology). For instance, we would not be surprised to observe different value systems among those who heal the sick versus those who manufacture vacuum cleaners. However, technological determinism isn't likely to get us very far, because we also observe substantial variations in norms and value systems among organizations doing roughly the same things. Consider as examples: Ben and Jerry's ("hippie" ice cream manufacturers in the United States) versus most of their competitors; or the fun-loving culture of get-it-done cooperation among employees in various jobs at Southwest Airlines, versus the more strait-laced, bureaucratic, "I don't do it if it isn't part of my job description" approach at most U. S. airlines. (We summarize evidence in Chapter 19 regarding the very different values and assumptions reflected in the organizational blueprints espoused by the founders of Silicon Valley technology start-ups, even within the same industry.)

A final caveat concerns the manageability of organizational culture. There is considerable debate, among both scholars and practitioners, about whether managers can (or should) consciously manipulate the system of workplace norms and values, or whether instead culture must be informal and emergent, either because that is its nature or because that is when it is most beneficial for an organization. We will not make strong assumptions about the ability of managers or others to engineer cultures according to a particular blueprint they seek, but we will assume that the HR policies and practices in effect, as well as how they are implemented, can send powerful messages that are likely to influence organizational norms and values as experienced by employees.

For that reason, the implications of organizational culture for HR policies (and vice versa) can be enormous, because culture is either reinforced by or clashes with specific practices and policies, rendering the culture more or less effective as a means of coordinating and controlling activities. In Chapter 10, for instance, we will see that a culture that stresses cooperation generally won't mesh well with a system of performance evaluation (to determine raises, bonuses, or promotion) employing a strictly enforced curve to make large distinctions. Wide pay dispersion according to rank fits well with a hierarchical culture and poorly with an egalitarian culture. A firm that seeks to encourage individual creativity through explicit rewards and recognition will find that this is more difficult in a culture stressing conformity (in attire and behavior). An organization that wishes to foster a feeling of family might structure compensation along lines that has the symbolic nature of a gift.

THE ORGANIZATION'S STRATEGY

By the organization's strategy, we mean the answers to the following questions: What are the organization's distinctive competencies, things it can do better than the competition (or, at least, nearly as well as the best)? On what basis does the organization hope to achieve competitive advantage—for instance, technical innovation, premium customer service, superior quality, an integrated line of products or services, or low-cost production? On what basis will its competitive advantage be *sustained*—is the company relying on financial and knowledge-based barriers to entry, on legal protection, on a reputation for aggressive behavior in response to challenges? What are the long-term objectives—for instance, growth, market share, or niche penetration? What actions are being taken to get there? We also include here the firm's financial strategy, especially its financial structure; for instance, the use of debt versus equity financing and whether its equity is widely and publicly held versus privately and closely held.

It is not hard to think of connections between business and financial strategy, on the one hand, and HR policies on the other. Here are four examples.

1. *Nordstrom versus traditional retailers.* A retailer whose strategy is predicated on the quality of its customer service should structure its employment relationships differently than does a firm aiming to be a low-cost provider of some good. In the United States, for example, the Nordstrom chain of department stores has managed to differentiate itself from the competition—and generally to make handsome profits in a period of declining profitability within retailing—by giving unparalleled service to the customer. The centerpiece of their strategy is the personal relationship between the customer and the Nordstrom "associate." Nordstrom's particular retailing strategy drives their recruitment, training, compensation, promotion system, job design, and other personnel practices. They recruit highly educated and aggressive sales people, who resemble the upscale clientele to whom they will be selling, train them incessantly so they know all the merchandise and can therefore advise customers and engage in cross-selling, provide long-term advancement opportunities to cut down on turnover, and so on.

   Conversely, much of Nordstrom's volume-oriented competition has viewed the sales force as an unfortunate expense item required to ring up the merchandise. These companies tend to believe that economies of scale, skilled buyers, and shrewd financial management, rather than a highly motivated sales force, are the key strategic weapons. Accordingly, they rely more on harsh discipline, close supervision, and low wages for the sales force; offer few, if any, promotion opportunities for sales personnel; and typically provide little or no training.[4]

2. *RE/MAX versus traditional realty firms.* RE/MAX, a real estate network, tries to attract clients by having very active and aggressive agents, whom it attracts with a compensation system that is nonstandard in the industry. Most real estate sales agents working for a large agency will keep some fraction of their commissions, giving the rest to the agency to pay for clerical support, advertising, office and phone services, and the like. In some cases, agencies will pay their agents a base wage, as a buffer against a run of bad luck or a downturn in sales in general. Agents working for RE/MAX, however, keep 100% of their commissions, get no base wage, and in fact must pay the agency "rent" for office space and related overhead expenses. Accordingly, the agent who elects to work for RE/MAX must be confident about her abilities and willing to work hard for sales.[5]

3. *Financial structure in the United States and Japan.* An organization's financial strategy can have important implications for its HR system (and vice versa). It is not altogether surprising, for instance, that Japanese or-

ganizations, noted for their long-term employment relationships and treatment of workers as strategic assets, have traditionally secured external financing from institutions with whom they are tied through long-term collaborative relationships. Less subject to the vagaries of an anonymous and short-term-oriented stock market and financial community, Japanese firms have had more latitude to pursue a high-commitment approach to HRM, even during periods when it might be tempting to do what many U. S. firms have done: downsize, renege on past promises, impose tighter controls over workers, and the like.[6] Similarly, many companies in the United States that display high-commitment work systems and long-term employment relations exhibit little debt, fund their growth internally, and retain all or most of the stock among employees (or owners). Typically, these are companies whose competitive strategies are predicated on long-term relations with customers and/or suppliers, and therefore on long-term relations with employees, requiring that the workforce be perceived as an investment or asset to be nurtured and protected for the long haul, rather than an expense item to be pruned whenever this is expedient in the short term.

4. *Investment banking and market making.* Some investment banks pursue both traditional investment banking and trading and market-making activities because of perceived synergies in these activities. But this strategy can lead to difficulties in the HR domain. Because investment banking and trading are quite different tasks, appropriate incentive systems, means of control, and so on are also likely to be quite different, which can lead to tension between the two groups within the firm.[7] The broader point here is that decisions about whether or not an organization follows a strategy of product diversification and/or vertical integration will have enormous implications for HRM, including whether jobs and career paths are defined narrowly or broadly, how performance is evaluated and managed, and how desirable it will be for compensation schemes to be uniform versus differentiated among parts of the organization. Conversely, it should be clear that an organization's human resource practices can constrain choices of business and financial strategy in important ways.

THE TECHNOLOGY OF PRODUCTION AND ORGANIZATION OF WORK

We assume that you were not surprised by our definitions of the political, social, legal, and economic environment, the organization's culture, and its strategy. But by *technology of production,* we mean something a bit broader than you might think, so we will be more detailed in this section.

Under the general rubric of technology, we include factors and conditions that bear on how labor inputs are converted to outputs. We have in mind the broad picture of how tasks are organized and coordinated, not simply what kinds of machines (if any) are employed. A list of some of these factors and conditions follows, together with some examples of how each bears on important HR policy issues.

Physical Layout, and Worker Privacy and Proximity

Is the work conducted in a single location, with workers in close proximity to one another, or is the work conducted at isolated locations? This is potentially important in at least two ways: First, work conducted in isolation will be harder to monitor and harder to direct. Consider far-flung service-oriented companies, such as United Parcel Service or Federal Express. It is not surprising that such companies typically combine information technology (e.g., on-board devices that transmit data to central mainframes) with strong inculturation of their workforce in order to ensure compliance with company policies and quality standards. In contrast, when work is conducted in an environment with many (similar) workers present, peer pressure can more readily be employed (for good or, in the case of peer-induced output restrictions, for bad). Second, when workers are in close proximity and technically interdependent, it also becomes harder to treat differently workers who see themselves as similar (in social science jargon, forces of social comparison are stronger; see Chapter 5) and worker dissent is more easily mobilized. It is hardly a coincidence that unions are more prevalent in such settings.

Required Skills

What skills are required? Are those skills acquired externally or on the job? Are those skills firm-specific or are they transportable? When workers' skills are acquired on the job, new hires are usually less productive than workers with longer job tenures, because the new hires invest a fraction of their time learning what to do and how. Even when skills can be acquired off the job, the firm often pays for their acquisition (see Chapter 15). In either case, the costs of turnover can be high and the firm will take steps to retain its already-trained workers and attract workers it will want to keep. When skills are acquired on the job and skill requirements increase with rank, promotion-from-within systems acquire substantial advantages (see Chapters 8 and 16). When workers acquire skills on the job, they often do so from co-workers, which has implications for how rewards are distributed. In particular, seniority-based pay and promotion systems are often employed under these circumstances, so that senior workers are willing to share their knowledge with their junior colleagues.

Monitoring Employee Input

For a variety of reasons, it is often important to monitor what the employee does on the job. This can mean monitoring the employee's overall level of effort, the quality and care taken, or how the employee allocates time among tasks. Setting aside for now the question of why we might want to monitor the employee, the technological questions are, How and how well can we do it? How expensive is it to monitor? To be sure, this is connected to matters of physical proximity and privacy: How easy is it to observe the employee? How intrusive would direct monitoring be?

In many cases, direct monitoring of activity is either too costly or too intrusive to undertake. In such cases, indirect measures of employee contributions are sought. Often these measures are simply the level of output achieved by the worker: How many pieces of fabric does a fabric cutter cut? What are the unit costs achieved by a plant (measuring the performance of the plant manager)? What profits are achieved by the firm, and what happens to the market value of its equity (measuring the performance of a corporation's CEO)? The relevant technological questions here are:

1. *To what extent can the employee, by her levels of input, control these measures of output?* In almost every job, the tangible measures of output are not completely under the control of the individual employee. Raw materials may be bad. Uncontrollable factors may intervene, such as a crippling natural disaster in a salesperson's or plant manager's territory. If we measure a salesperson's output by the dollar volume of sales or the number of units sold, we will be looking at a very noisy measure of labor input because so many factors outside the salesperson's control can influence a good or bad result. In contrast, if we look at the output of a piece-rate cutter of fabric, there is a much more direct and noiseless connection between labor input and the level of output.

2. *When employee input is multifaceted, are there good (relatively noise-free) measures of the different facets? Can we find a good summary measure of the many facets, good in the sense that it captures what is important to the firm?* For instance, fabric cutters might sacrifice quality for speed. It is probably cheap and easy to monitor the speed with which a fabric cutter works, but it may be very difficult or expensive to get good contemporaneous information about the quality of his work.

As we will see in Chapter 11, these two factors play a critical role in designing extrinsic incentives. When workers have little control over tangible measures of output, it can become next-to-useless to base incentive compensation on those measures of output. Furthermore, when a job involves a number of tasks, only some of which are easy for the individual to control, performance-based rewards will often encourage a risk-averse employee to focus on those tasks over which he or she has the greatest control. But it is often the hardest-to-measure stuff that is most important from the organization's viewpoint. This dilemma was dramatically illustrated by the trouble that Sears encountered in the early 1990s with their automotive repair centers, in which mechanics and managers were rewarded based on the volume of certain kinds of repairs. Perceiving that they would be evaluated based on the quantity of repairs that they carried out, some Sears employees performed unnecessary repairs and did not focus much attention on the harder-to-measure dimension of the work *quality* (including the evaluation of what work was needed).

There are two further technological considerations connected to the ability to monitor worker inputs, but they are sufficiently important to warrant their own subsections:

Task Ambiguity and Creativity

When "what to do" is reduced to a standard operating procedure, task ambiguity is low. But some jobs score quite high on task ambiguity and requisite discretion, such as physicians, self-directed research scientists, and high-level general managers. In these jobs, it can be just as important (if not more so) to exercise good judgment in selecting *what* tasks to carry out as it is to execute those tasks well. A physician who selects the wrong procedure but performs it masterfully is of little use to the patient! In extreme cases, *creativity*—finding entirely new tasks to perform or, at least, new ways to perform old tasks—is the most important factor in good performance.

In general, the greater the level of task ambiguity, the harder it is to control performance by explicit incentives, because it is harder to measure performance. At the very least, explicit incentives should be based on long-term performance, usually defined in a broad, diffuse, and subjective manner. Reliance on intrinsic goals or rewards is often more effective still.

An interesting case in point concerns medicine and the impact of medical malpractice suits. It has been argued that in response to costly malpractice suits, medical practice (at least, in the United States) has been reduced more and more to going "by the book"—following a sequence of steps, performing batteries of tests, and otherwise limiting the use of the physician's subjective judgment. It is clear why defensive, by-the-book medicine is practiced—it makes it easier to refute malpractice after the fact—but it is far from clear that the benefits (discovering truly incompetent physicians) outweigh the costs of overtesting and other forms of defensive medicine.[8]

Patterns of Worker Interdependence and Cooperation

By worker interdependence, we mean the extent to which the product of one worker's efforts is affected by the efforts of other workers. In some cases, each worker's efforts stand or fall on their own; examples might include writers and traveling salespersons (except insofar as a writer's success depends on the editor or publisher, and a salesperson's success might depend on the quality of the product being sold or on after-sale service given by others). In other cases, interdependencies are *sequential*—each person depends on a sequence of "predecessors" but not on anyone further down the chain. Sequential manufacture along an assembly line or in a batch process often has this character. In still other cases, interdependencies are *complex and reciprocal*; the results of one person's efforts depend on the efforts of others, whose results depend in turn on the efforts of the first. Many sorts of team production (e.g., hospital care) have this character.

The greater the interdependence, the harder it is in general to untangle the level of one worker's performance from the overall performance of the group. For that reason, extrinsic, single-worker incentive schemes are harder to maintain, especially if they generate wide disparities in rewards. How would you like to fly on an airplane in which the pilot and copilot were fighting over the controls, competing to receive "credit" back at headquarters for landing the plane? When interdependence is high, group-based incentive systems are often employed, with some reliance on peer pressure (when feasible) to control free-riding.

When workers must cooperate extensively, there is the same kind of potential for distortion of incentives discussed above in the case of Sears' automotive repair centers. The extent of an employee's cooperation will often be harder to measure and take longer to reveal itself than other aspects of that same employee's job performance (such as the quantity of output, attendance, etc.). Performance evaluation and reward schemes that focus too much on shorter-term and easier-to-measure outcomes can provide inadequate incentives for workers to cooperate. For this reason, for example, the most experienced or lead workers in a piece-rate facility (such as fabric cutting), who are expected to devote some of their time to training new workers and solving problems that arise, sometimes receive time-based pay rather than piece-rate wages.

The impact of patterns of interdependence doesn't end with questions of monitoring and incentives. There are also social ramifications; for instance, high levels of interdependence generally involve high levels of personal interaction, which can trigger processes of social comparison (see Chapter 5).

The Distribution of the Outcomes: Stars, Guardians, and Foot-Soldiers[9]

In some jobs, such as basic researcher, one or two home runs in a lifetime make for a successful career, and the firm is willing to try out a lot of players to find the one home-run hitter in the crowd. In selling big-ticket items, it may take more than one or two home runs to make a career, but a single high-margin sale is worth a lot, and it may be worth losing a lot of potential sales to hold out for the big win. In other jobs, it is the failures that loom large. Aircraft pilots want to get their planes down nice and smooth, and they want to stick to the schedule when possible. But a failure (that is, a crash) is a lot worse for an airline than sticking to a schedule is good. In still other jobs, variations in individual performance don't matter too much; organizational success depends on the aggregated performance of large numbers of individuals, none of whose individual performance is decisive.

The observed distribution of outcomes reflects two sets of forces: (a) each worker faces (uncontrollable) environmental uncertainty that makes the outcome of his efforts somewhat random; and (b) different workers in the same job, acting in the same circumstances, may get different outcomes because of variations in skill level, ability, determination, and the like. The issue here is the *distribution* or *range* of possible outcomes of a worker's efforts on both these grounds, measured in terms that are meaningful for the firm.[10]

Consider the range of possible outcomes, centered around the "average":

1. When a bad performance isn't too bad, but a good performance is very good for the firm, we call this a *star* job. Jobs involving the production of knowledge or innovation, where only the (occasional) good idea is adopted after being thoroughly vetted, are usually star jobs.[11]

2. When a bad performance is a disaster, but a good performance is only slightly better for the firm than an average performance, we will call this a *guardian* job. Guardian jobs are often found when the work technology involves a complex, interdependent system of production, and overall performance is determined largely by the worst individual contribution. A special case of this involves workers who represent the organization to a key external constituency in settings where the organization's reputation is a valuable asset. In this case, insofar as word of a single screw-up will be spread among the external constituency, the organization suffers disproportionately from the single screw-up.[12]

3. A *foot-soldier* job is one in which the range is concentrated near the average.

We can give two pictorial depictions of these three cases. Drawing the range of possible outcomes gives us Figure 2-1.[13] Alternatively, we can draw the probability distribution (density) of possible outcomes: In the case of a star, because the average outcome is on the left-hand side of the range of outcomes, the odds of a good outcome are quite low, with most outcomes in the average-to-mediocre range. The reverse is true for a guardian; most of the time the outcome should be average to slightly above average, with small probability of a disaster. And for a foot-soldier, the distribution of outcomes will be roughly symmetric around the average, within a fairly narrow range. Taking artistic license with the shape of the probability distributions, we get the three distributions shown in Figure 2-2.

We have applied these descriptive terms to the *job,* by which we mean a position held by a single individual in the firm. In some cases it is more meaningful to think of star, guardian, and foot-soldier *teams,* especially when production is so interdependent that it makes little sense to try and disentangle the impact of different workers' contributions.

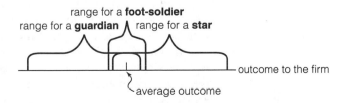

Figure 2-1 Ranges of outcomes for different types of jobs.

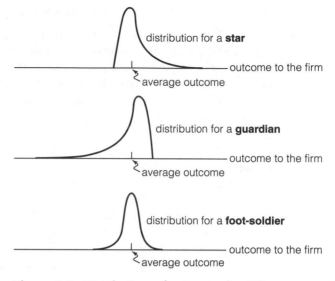

Figure 2-2 Distributions of outcomes for different types of jobs.

Obviously, if the firm can affect (through job design or other choices) the types of jobs it has, it will opt for star and against guardian jobs. Thus, for example, total quality management strives to design products and processes that are foolproof (eliminate the possibility of bad outcomes) and to take advantage of the insights and inspirations of individual workers (extend the range of possible good outcomes). To the extent that it can, the organization will put redundancies in place for guardian positions, such as an airline equipping a plane with both a pilot and copilot or a bank requiring two signatures on very large checks. But sometimes the firm can have only limited impact on the sorts of jobs it possesses, and then HR policies will change depending on the qualities of those jobs.

For example, when employees can choose between relatively risky versus risk-free outcomes, the organization will want to encourage "gambling" among stars and discourage it among guardians. This can be done through compensation practices: for stars, small penalties (or none at all) for failure, and large rewards for success; for guardians, severe penalties for any failure. This can also be achieved through more intrinsic methods of motivation, such as culture. For foot-soldier positions, HR practices should be directed at raising the average level of performance instead of focusing on the extremes of the distribution. Although the firm doesn't benefit much by raising a single worker's performance, it may do quite well by raising slightly the average performance of a large number of workers.[14]

If the variation in outcomes is due (in part) to variations in employee skills, then recruitment and training strategies will also vary among the different job types. For a star job, the costs of a hiring error are small relative to the upside potential from finding an exceptional individual. Therefore, the organization will wish to sample widely among many employees, looking for the one pearl among the pebbles. For guardian jobs, in contrast, the firm will be very careful to screen initial job applicants and may require long apprenticeship periods before giving the employee responsibility, both in order to screen further and to train the individual. And for foot-soldier positions, the firm will be relatively content to take in whatever applicants are willing to work at the going wage, or it may pursue some other recruitment objectives (e.g., social homogeneity).

Of course, the three patterns in Figures 2-1 and 2-2 do not exhaust all the possibilities. In some cases, for example, the range of possible outcomes extends both far above and far below the benchmark of average performance. For example, in a firm that thrives on innovations, the single researcher looking for an innovative idea is a star. But when a manager must decide which innovations to fund or to adopt companywide, that manager can have tremendous positive *and negative* impacts on the organization. When reputation is important and can be shaped by both outstandingly good and appallingly bad individual performances, the employee can have a widely varying impact on the fortunes of the firm.

What are the implications of this sort of combined star–guardian pattern? Typically, workers whose jobs have this pattern are difficult to control. To guard against disasters, failure must be severely punished and great care must be taken in selection and training. Yet to get star performances, risk taking needs to be encouraged, and the organization should be open to running a lot of candidates through the position to see who has what it takes to be a star. Obviously, the twin goals of minimizing disasters and promoting risk taking to obtain stellar performances are difficult to reconcile, and we typically find in this sort of job that more effort goes into disaster avoidance than into encouraging risk-taking. One reason for this is the well-documented tendency for losses to loom larger than gains—that is, employees and managers perceive a loss of K units (sales, dollars, company image, or whatever) as hurting more than a gain of K units helps.[15] Because of the basic inconsistency in motivating/selecting for the star and guardian aspects of a single job, the combined star–guardian pattern should be avoided if possible. Given the bias toward avoiding failures, when the combined pattern cannot be avoided, extra attention should paid to the "star" aspects in order to correct the balance. We will have more to say about these issues later in this book when we discuss job design, performance evaluation, and compensation issues.

APPLYING THE FIVE FACTORS: THE CASE OF IBM

The story of the rise and decline of International Business Machines (IBM) has been told many times, in many ways. We will not go into great detail here, and we will oversimplify, but to illustrate broadly the use of five-factor analysis, it helps to recount the story in our terms.[16]

From the perspective of 1978, IBM was one of the great success stories of American industry. Earnings had grown at a compounded rate of 17.7% from 1950 to 1960. Over the next decade, the annual percentage growth in earnings *improved* to 19.7%. From 1970 to 1978, growth in earnings was "only" 15% per annum. Although IBM had a substantial business in office products ($3 billion in revenues), in 1978 the bulk of its business was in data processing (computers, peripheral devices, and software), which contributed 81% of its revenues and 92.4% of its operating income.

A brief rendition of the five factors in the early 1970s might run as follows:

- *Strategy.* IBM was a centrally directed, product-focused company. It developed—and then sold and serviced—the products that it decided were needed, and it prospered because, by and large, its preeminence allowed it to control the product agenda of the information processing industry. Especially with the 360/370 series of computers, IBM defined how data processing was done—by specially trained computer staffs, working with so-called mainframe computers and complete (and complex) large-scale systems for information storage, manipulation, and communication. Time sharing had moved computer control and use out of the era of punch cards and batch processing, but computing was still largely the realm of staff specialists, whom IBM's sales and service staffs cultivated. IBM manufactured its own products and tried to control its product line through patents and patent-infringement lawsuits. It bundled hardware with dedicated software that appealed to the computer specialist because it reinforced the power of the specialists and appealed to their own tastes and skills; general managers couldn't hope to cope with the highly specialized and arcane systems. Because automated information processing was quite novel, IBM put great stress on delivering error-free products to the market; it didn't want potential customers to be scared off by stories of bugs encountered early in a product's life cycle. Much of IBM's growth in the 1970s came overseas, and IBM's strategy there was to be a true multinational: IBM Japan would look like a traditional Japanese firm; IBM France would have French top management; to the fullest extent possible, production would take place worldwide; and although R&D was somewhat concentrated in the United States, it was consciously being spread overseas.

- *Workforce.* IBM's workforce was occupationally fairly diverse, including R&D and product design engineers, computer assemblers, sales and service staff, support personnel (clerical, custodial, etc.), and even a (very) few pure scientists, who were largely kept hidden away in research facilities such as the Watson Labs in Yorktown Heights, New York. But the bulk of the core workforce (at least in the United States) consisted of career employees with an engineering background, largely white, male, and middle to upper-middle class.

- *Culture.* IBM's culture was starched white shirt. This is more literal than might be imagined; a somber blue suit with a discreet tie and an ever-so-slightly off-white shirt was regarded as one small step away from a clown suit. Conformity, teamwork, and dedication to Big Blue (i.e., IBM) were central norms.

- *Technology.* In a corporation as large and diverse as IBM, the technology of work varies enormously and, even looking at a single job, it has many distinct and important elements. However, we want to focus on three aspects of the core workers in the value chain running from product development to sales and service. First, the "big systems, mainframe, arcane technology" approach to information processing means that teams are vital. Individuals could and did have brilliant ideas, and disastrous screw-ups could and sometimes did take place. But by and large, IBM's army was an infantry of foot-soldiers, each contributing a small piece to a very large mosaic. Second, and relatedly, individual performance was hard to measure. Performance of the team or business unit could be better observed, but even measuring performance at these levels was difficult when outcomes took time to clarify and involved a number of factors outside of IBM's control. Third, to reduce the chances of an imperfect product reaching the market, IBM's development efforts involved redundancies and competitions: If, say, a subcomponent system to accomplish a particular task was required, different approaches to the system would be taken by different groups, and then a "jury" would decide which version would be adopted.

- *Environment.* We will not discuss IBM's multinational strategy, except to note that it responded in part to political pressures on the corporation (which in turn strongly colored some of IBM's multinational HR policies). Instead, under the category of "environment," we stress: (a) substantial status accrued, in the 1950s and 1960s, from working for a premium employer (such as IBM); (b) the more specific professional norms of engineers and scientists to some extent tied their identities more strongly to their profession than to their employer; and (c) the power that IBM had in the labor market for information technology specialists during this period. Insofar as IBM could and did set the product agenda for the industry (except for specialty players such as Cray), it was an attractive employer to those who wanted to work with the best colleagues and machines, to help set the agenda.

How did IBM's HR policies fit with these factors? Extremely well. IBM ran a paternalistic internal labor market. (See Chapter 8 for more discussion of internal labor markets.) Employees had a no-layoff guarantee, premium wages, and outstanding working conditions. Employees expected and were expected to have a career at IBM, moving from entry-level positions through various technical and managerial hierarchies. This promoted identification with IBM, gave workers a better sense of the big picture, helped develop wide competencies, promoted team play and team spirit, and gave the company longer lead times for evaluating employees. Specific compensation and bonus systems for higher-level managers reinforced IBM's top-down control of its product mix. The strong internal culture helped to homogenize the different national and international units of IBM.

Recall the annual growth figures for net earnings cited earlier: 17.7% from 1950 to 1960; 19.7% during the 1960s; and 15% from 1970 to 1978. But then, from 1978 to 1986, earnings grew at only 5.5% per annum. As for 1986 until today, the recent hard times experienced by IBM make it difficult to make economic sense out of earnings figures, but earnings for 1996 imply a growth rate of less than 5% per annum for that decade. Share prices fell from a high of around $75 in the late 1980s (adjusting for splits) to around $20 in late 1993. The stunning market rally since 1996 has vaulted IBM's share price above $185 (as of December 1998), but this still leaves IBM's equity holders with much smaller gains in the last decade or so than were experienced by the technology sector or the market as a whole over that period. What happened, and how did this affect HRM?

We focus on several related changes in the five factors:

- *Strategy*. IBM is no longer able to adopt the attitude of, "Make it (the product), and they (the customer) will buy." It has had to shift from a centrally directed product focus to a much more market-driven focus. Although the goal of error-free product introductions remains admirable, speed to market in an increasingly competitive environment has become critical.

- *Workforce*. Its workforce, especially at upper, decision-making echelons, was wedded philosophically and emotionally to the big-systems, technical-language vision of computing. (Compare the operating systems of the PCs to the early Macintoshes, or OS/2 to Windows.) This turned out, with hindsight, to be the wrong strategy in software. Also, the workforce was attuned to a world in which hardware manufacture and sale was a large part of the value chain. But, increasingly (in the micro, workstation, and minicomputer end of the market), profits come from software. In hardware, IBM manufactures excellent products, but so do Compaq and Dell. IBM has no true relative advantage as a manufacturer, and some of its competitors (e.g., Sun Microsystems) do little or no manufacturing in-house.

- *Culture*. Its old top-down management style slowed its rate of response to its new environment. The white-shirt/Big Blue culture made it harder to bring in an increasingly iconoclastic workforce. To speed response to market, IBM began to abandon its previous system of multilevel competition in development, but this system (and the notion of error-free new products) had become an ingrained cultural icon, complicating implementation of the new development process.

- *Technology*. In product development, especially in software, there is relatively more emphasis nowadays on star performance and relatively less on foot-soldiery. It is too strong to say that a single individual can create on her own a commercially successful software application, but the number of individuals needed is relatively smaller, and the impact a single individual or small team can have is relatively greater.

- *External (economic and social) environment*. IBM's labor market environment has shifted adversely. It has lost its attractiveness as the font of new technology, and in an industry in which the technology has shifted relatively to more of a star pattern, venture-capital-fueled start-ups have raised the stakes for what a star can expect to command. This has also affected the internal culture of IBM vis-à-vis the external professional culture of engineers: It is harder to achieve worker identification with Big Blue, when good outside employment opportunities exist and mobility is high. Finally, the status conferred generally for working for a Fortune 50 firm is relatively less than it once was.

If no layoffs and a strong internal labor market were the hallmarks of IBM's HR policies, the changing factors given above have significantly affected how those policies fit. IBM nowadays risks losing its best personnel to established competitors and to start-ups; if it retains all that want to remain, it winds up with a disproportionate number of folks from the bottom of barrel. This is especially costly in a world that is more star-driven. In addition, it can no longer be sure that it can supply its labor needs internally; it may have to reach outside for key employees. Of course, IBM has officially abandoned its no-layoff policy, and it has reached outside for talent, even to the level of its CEO. Compensation policies have had to be adjusted. Incentives have been reformed, to decentralize decision making, and so on.

Did IBM blow it? With hindsight, we can say that many of its strengths in the 1960s became relative weaknesses in the 1980s. But when climatic conditions on the savanna change in a way that favors gazelles and is problematic for elephants, we can't blame an elephant for not being a gazelle. IBM has adjusted to its new world with some measure of success; not surprisingly, given the deeply ingrained culture that had developed over the years, an important aspect of IBM's resurgence and realignment has come about through acquisitions which have brought new technology, people, and values to the company. It can't be held accountable for the fact that the new world is not as hospitable to it (especially given the legacies of its workforce and culture) as was the world of the 1960s and 1970s.

ONE SIZE DOES NOT FIT ALL

Another general lesson about fit can be drawn from the IBM story. If a firm's HR system fits well with one specification of strategy, technology, workforce, culture, and environment, then it is bound to fit some other set of factors poorly. In HRM, there is no one size that fits every situation. IBM had a superlative HR system for the world it inhabited in the 1960s. It comes as no surprise, therefore, that IBM's system was not ideally suited to the changed world of the 1980s. As you examine an HR system and its fit with the five factors, it can often be useful to answer the question: *What does the firm's HR system preclude it from doing well?* To learn what a firm *can* do well, it often helps to specify what it cannot.

THREE CAVEATS ABOUT THE "FIVE FACTORS"

We hope you will find the five factors helpful when organizing your observations about the context of a firm's human resources system. But as with all frameworks for organizing the data, the five factors, if taken too seriously, can lead you into nonproductive or counterproductive intellectual straitjackets. For one thing, you may become more concerned with getting everything to fit neatly into one of the five slots than with understanding the important factors and (especially) their interrelationships.

A second intellectual straitjacket that is particularly dangerous with the five-factor approach is that it can cause you to think in one direction, *from* the environment, technology, culture, workforce, and strategy, *to* the HR system of the organization. You might regard the five as fixed, with HR practices adjusting to fit. Yet an organization has some control over each of the five factors. This is clearest when it comes to its strategy, but is also somewhat true about culture, workforce, and technology. (Indeed, management decisions that influence workforce and culture are a vital part of its HR strategy.) It is even true to some extent about the environment, insofar as the organization can choose where to locate its facilities. For instance, think of the Japanese auto manufacturers and where they chose to locate their American assembly plants: not in Detroit, but in rural Ohio, Kentucky, and Tennessee. No doubt some significant tax advantages were at work here but, as we'll see when we return to this example later in the book, a lot of strategic HRM was involved, as well.

This is not to say that management has complete control over the five factors it faces. Once a plant is sited in one location, it can be very expensive to move. A technology, once fixed, is hard to change. Once a cohort of managers of a certain age is hired, it can be hard to dispose of. A strategy or culture, once put in place, can be very difficult to shift (for reasons we will develop over the next few chapters). And the choice of location, technology, strategy, workforce, and environment, even at the outset, is not unencumbered by circumstances; for instance, when Toyota decided to assemble automobiles in the United States, siting the facility in, say, Honduras, was not a viable option.

So as you examine the five factors in specific cases, keep in mind that they aren't fixed and unalterable, but neither are they infinitely adaptable. The key is to fit them to HR practices and HR practices to them to the greatest extent feasible, where the fitting goes in both directions.

A third problem with a five-factor list is that it can lead you to draw connections between each of the five factors and the specific components of the organization's HR system, without paying enough attention to the key linkages *among* those HR components. For instance, you might be tempted to think separately about how the five factors impinge on compensation, promotion, job design, recruiting, employee development, and so on. But thinking of compensation as separable from promotion or how jobs are designed is fatuous. The interrelationships among these things are at least as important as their individual attributes. Thus, we turn next to the second aspect of fit concerning strategic HRM, namely how the constituent pieces of an HR system *fit* together (or don't).

IN REVIEW

⇒ An organization's HR policies and practices must fit, both together (internal consistency) and with the broader context of the organization (alignment). This chapter concerns fitting the broader context.

⇒ To help you understand the broader context in specific cases, we suggest organizing your observations into five boxes, the five factors: the external environment; the workforce; the organization's culture; the organization's strategy; and its technology of production.

⇒ The first four of the five factors have fairly straightforward definitions, but by technology, we mean more than the types of machines used. We define technology broadly to include
  • Physical layout, worker privacy and proximity
  • Required skills
  • Ability to monitor worker inputs
  • Levels of task ambiguity and creativity required
  • Patterns of worker interdependence and cooperation
  • The distribution of workers' outcomes: stars, guardians, and foot-soldiers

⇒ The case of IBM illustrates how an organization's HR practices can be beautifully crafted to fit the broader context of one time and place, but fit less well as conditions shift.

⇒ One size does not fit all when it comes to HR systems. To understand what a specific HR system is good for, it often helps to ask what it fits poorly.

⇒ When applying the five factors, avoid:
  • Spending too much time trying to stuff each important factor into one and only one box.
  • Taking the five factors as fixed and immutable, and thinking that HR practices must adapt to fit. (The fitting goes both ways.)
  • Paying too little attention to how the pieces of the HR system fit with *each other.*

ENDNOTES

1. See Michael Porter, *Competitive Strategy* (New York: Free Press, 1980).

2. The case of UPS will be discussed in some detail in Chapter 3.

3. For a good overview, see Joanne Martin, *Cultures in Organizations: Three Perspectives* (New York: Oxford University Press, 1992).

4. This tendency for strategies centered on long-term, high-quality relations with customers to favor longer-term, high-commitment employment relations is also evidenced in research on the HR systems of emerging technology companies (see Chapter 19).

5. See Chapter 14 for a more detailed discussion of how the RE/MAX strategy works.

6. Front-line Japanese firms also tend to be less vertically integrated than their American and European counterparts and depend instead on a tight network of suppliers. When times are tough, the front-line firms will maintain lifetime employment by disproportionately passing on the bad times to their suppliers, including the "loan" of workers to the suppliers, who must lay off their own workers to make room. Of course, these time-honored features of Japanese organizations are being strained by the economic, social, and demographic changes occurring in present-day Japan.

7. See, for example, Ken Auletta, "Power, Greed, and Glory on Wall Street: The Fall of Lehman Brothers," *New York Times Magazine* 134, Section 6 (Sunday, February 17, 1985): 29.

8. See Daniel Kessler and Mark McClellan, "Do Doctors Practice Defensive Medicine?," *Quarterly Journal of Economics* 111 (May 1996): 353–90.

9. The material in this subsection is adapted from David Jacobs, "Toward a Theory of Mobility and Behavior in Organizations: An Inquiry into the Consequences of Some Relationships Between Individual Performance and Organizational Success," *American Journal of Sociology* 87 (November 1981): 684–707.

10. We will not be precise concerning the units in which outcomes for the firm are measured. But to operationalize this, we would use something like long-run impact on the firm's profits, or impact on its growth rate, or something similar. Because this is meant to be used to help a firm analyze and improve its own HR system, the appropriate measure will be determined by the objectives of the firm.

11. The potential for being a star in a creative position can be attenuated, however, by the way the organization is structured—for instance, when the creative worker faces powerful forces within the organization that insist on conformity, or where creative efforts can be defeated by others pursing a different agenda (e.g., when the legal office squelches new product lines to reduce product-liability exposure).

12. However, in some cases a single exceptionally good performance will also attract disproportionate notice among constituents, in which case the job is neither a star nor a guardian position, but a mixed star–guardian. See below for further discussion of this mixed case.

13. The "size" of the range is measured in units that are meaningful to the firm. For example, piece-rate workers can vary widely in terms of the number of pieces completed over the period of a day; differences in output measured in hundreds of percent are not atypical. But if (as is usually the case) these differences have only modest financial implications for the firm, we still have a foot-soldier. Also, any employee could, potentially, cause a disaster for the firm—the employee could, for example, suddenly go berserk—and any employee could, potentially, discover and reveal some astonishing breakthrough that revolutionizes what the firm does. The ranges in Figure 2-1 are meant to accommodate those outcomes that are reasonably contemplated as part of the job.

14. Because the firm's impact through compensation and other policies on foot-soldier performance is small, there is a tendency for the impact that is there to go unrecognized or under-appreciated. Jacobs, *op. cit.,* suggests that for foot-soldiers, this may mean that meritocratic reward policies are more apt to go by the board: The firm may set its policies to accomplish broad political aims—for example, it may adopt seniority-based pay systems in societies where seniority-based pay is socially acceptable. Or re-

wards may be doled out on more personal or political grounds: Superiors may curry favor by rewarding and promoting their favorites, thereby creating dependencies that solidify their power base in the organization. But we suspect these regimes may not be stable. Individuals in foot-soldier positions may be able to exert profound negative effects on organizations in ways that don't relate directly to the performance of their jobs—for instance, by mobilizing opposition, creating negative publicity, instigating lawsuits and filing grievances, or gunning down a supervisor or co-worker. Furthermore, the performance of foot-soldiers *en masse* may have an appreciable impact on the firm, even if no single foot-soldier does so. Therefore, there is still an important role for performance-based rewards and sanctions in a foot-soldier setting. (See the discussion of Safelite Glass in Chapter 11.)

15. See Daniel Kahneman and Amos Tversky, "Prospect Theory: An Analysis of Decision Making Under Risk," *Econometrica* 47 (March 1979): 263–91; and Max Bazerman, *Judgment in Managerial Decision Making,* 3rd edition (New York: Wiley, 1994): Chapter 3.

16. For further detail, see Richard F. Vancil, Arvind Bhambri, and James Wilson, "IBM Corporation: Background Note," Harvard Business School note 9-180-034; David B. Yoffie and Andrall E. Pearson, "The Transformation of IBM," Harvard Business School case 9-391-073; and David B. Yoffie and Jeffrey M. Cohn, "The Transformation of IBM: Supplement," Harvard Business School supplement 9-792-105.

3

Consistent HR Practices: The Whole Can Be More than the Sum of the Parts

In this chapter, we examine the proposition that the HR systems of successful firms often display practices reinforcing consistent themes or messages. Organization A operates as "one happy family"—extrinsic rewards are deemphasized; explicit guarantees of lifetime employment are offered; pay differentials are minimized; few obvious status differentials exist among members (few organizational charts, no reserved parking spaces, etc.); more compensation is given in the form of personalized gifts and benefits that reinforce the psychological bond between the employee and the organization; performance is appraised on the basis of doing things "our way" and conforming with broader company goals, rather than based purely on measurable outputs; upper-level vacancies are filled exclusively from within; and so on. Organization B, on the other hand, has a consistent "dog-eat-dog" philosophy that appeals to self-interested behavior: It emphasizes extrinsic rewards; new employees must sign a document acknowledging that they understand their employment is "at will" and can be terminated at any time by the employer; compensation is based on comparative performance (e.g., salesperson or branch manager of the year); status differences are emphasized (keys to an executive washroom, reserved spots in the parking lot, a carpeted area in the cafeteria for managers and an executive dining room for upper managers); incumbent employees are given no advantage over outsiders when filling a vacancy; few benefits are offered, and those that are offered are distributed according to a "cafeteria" plan, in which workers can customize their own benefits package or even trade off some of their benefit entitlement for additional pay.

Our stereotypical Organizations A and B may have radically different HR systems simply because they face radically different external forces. But we believe that such radically different HR systems can flourish reasonably well in very similar situations. Indeed, the differences in HR policies may be attributable entirely to the histories of the two organizations. Very distinct arrays of HR policies can fit a given external environment quite well *if* the arrays are internally consistent; and for the same reason that internal consistency is valuable, it isn't easy to tinker successfully with such arrays at the margins, nor, once established, to reconfigure the array from scratch.

In this chapter, we will explore the issue of internal fit or consistency among HR practices, focusing on four questions: Why is consistency useful and/or desirable? Along what dimensions can consistency be measured? Over what span should consistency be pursued? What role do history and organizational inertia play in discussions of consistency?

But before getting to these questions, we should be clear about what sorts of consistency we have in mind. There are (at least) three aspects of consistency: (1) Different parts of the overall HR system that bear on individual employees—recruitment, compensation, performance appraisal, promotion, training, and so on—should be consistent or (perhaps a better word) complementary. For example, policies that emphasize extensive and expensive training should be complemented by compensation, promotion, and recruitment policies that reduce turnover. We will call this *single-employee* consistency, emphasizing that the different pieces of HR policy that bear on a single employee should be consistent with one another. (2) The treatment of different workers should, at least over some span, be consistent. If employee A is treated in a particular fashion, a similarly situated employee A' should be treated similarly. We will call this *among-employee* consistency. (3) The HRM philosophy and premises of the organization should demonstrate some degree of *temporal consistency* or continuity. The appropriate extent of temporal consistency will depend, of course, on a number of factors, not the least of which is the rate of change in the organization's environment. But in general how employee A is treated today should not differ radically from how she was treated yesterday.

These represent different aspects or meanings of consistency in HRM, and at different points in this chapter we will focus on one to the exclusion of others. But we deal with them together because they are interrelated through their rationales.

WHY IS CONSISTENCY OF HR PRACTICES DESIRABLE?

Consistent HR practices are desirable for (at least) five sets of reasons. First, there are some obvious technical benefits of consistency. For example, a firm choosing to invest heavily in training its employees will see increased value in careful screening of applicants and in practices that are intended to decrease turnover. When on-the-job training accumulates over a period of years, practices that reward seniority (and thus reduce turnover among employees with longer tenure) make sense. When the firm employs informal training, provided by more senior workers to their more junior colleagues, seniority-based rewards also help by putting senior workers at no disadvantage when they share their knowledge. To cite another example, a firm that wishes to broaden its workforce (hiring, say, more women and minorities) may find it relatively advantageous to move to a cafeteria-style benefits plan. These reasons all pertain to single-employee consistency. At the same time, temporal consistency and among-employee consistency have different (and fairly obvious) technical benefits, having to do with economizing on costs of administration.

A second set of reasons why consistency is desirable concerns the psychology of perception and cognition. From basic psychology, we know that messages are more salient and recalled better when the multiple stimuli being transmitted are simple and support the same theme, as in an effective advertising campaign. Consistency, which also entails simplicity (i.e., everything follows the same basic principles), is thus desirable because it aids in the learning process that individuals must undertake, to understand what is expected of them and what they can expect in turn.

For example, owing to their technologies, some firms find that they must give their personnel wide discretion in some (but not all) matters. In these cases, the firms must choose whether to provide direct incentives for employees to perform as desired versus using indirect control based on the perception of mutual interests. When it comes to other activities that these individuals perform, the firm may be able to monitor its personnel quite closely and thus control them by rules. Should the firm use rules? The choice whether to do so depends on how the firm aims to control its employees in the first set of activities. If the firm chooses close supervision of those activities that can be closely supervised, its employees may infer that they are not trusted and adjust their behavior accordingly by acting in ways that are consistent with not being trusted.[1] Control of the first set of activities by trust will then be compromised: Employees will infer that they are not trusted (and thus not trust*worthy*), and react accordingly. A pharmaceutical company, for instance, will often need to give bench scientists wide discretion in project selection and choice of techniques. The same company presumably could monitor their scientists' attendance and punctuality easily by using time clocks. However, doing so would clash with—and thus undermine—the autonomy and trust involved in other, more important, facets of the employment relationship.

This category of reasons—largely about single-employee consistency as phrased above—can be extended to among-employee and temporal consistency. In most cases, an employee assumes that how she and others have been treated in the past, as well as how other similarly situated employees are being treated contemporaneously, provides good data for how she can expect to be treated now and in the future. Consequently, if HR practices changed frequently or varied considerably across similar employees, the process of learning what to expect and what is expected would be seriously impaired.

A third category of reasons for pursuing consistent HR practices involves social forces. Consistency—in the sense of congruence with external social norms and preconceptions—aids learning. It is easier to mold individuals' tastes and expectations when the organization's practices consistently (and symbolically) mimic previously internalized patterns of relationships in other contexts, whether these patterns are akin to an anonymous marketplace (dog-eat-dog) or a family relationship (mutual caring). This factor may help explain, for instance, why Japanese corporations setting up operations in the United States have often opted to site their plants in small towns and rural locations, where the strong "group ethic" and family atmosphere sought at work may mirror workers' roles outside the workplace more than would be the case in an urban environment. For the same reasons of inference and cognition cited in the previous paragraph, this rationale for consistency extends from how a single employee is treated to how groups are treated through time—for instance, only a dysfunctional family would extend mutual caring to some siblings and adopt a dog-eat-dog stance of (non)care toward other siblings, or oscillate back and forth between these two distinct modes of interaction.

A fourth advantage of consistent HR practices relates to recruitment and selection. Workers are not all alike, and they will do better or worse in a given organization according to how well they are matched to its attributes. Just to keep turnover costs in line, the firm should hope that prospective employees can understand the nature of employment on offer, so that mismatching and concomitant quits don't result. Indeed, even if a somewhat mismatched worker doesn't quit, he may be less happy and productive if the job doesn't fit his tastes in employment.

Consistency in HR practices allows for better initial matches in three ways. First, insofar as consistency promotes understanding, prospective employees are better able to comprehend at the outset what they are getting themselves into. Second, to the extent that there are correlations among the preferences of a given worker—for example, someone who feels comfortable with performance-based compensation also desires similar hard-edged practices when it comes to promotion criteria, benefits, decision-making authority, and the like—then clusters of HR practices that are consistent in matching those correlations will achieve better matches. Third, individuals may have a taste for co-workers who have the same preferences they do—warm and fuzzy types may not interact well with very competitive types—and consistent HR practices, insofar as they lead to a workforce that is homogeneous in terms of such preferences, may promote teamwork and worker cohesion. Of course, all three aspects of consistency are desirable for these job-match considerations.

Finally, among-employee consistency is desirable because it defuses invidious social comparisons and feelings of distributive injustice. These jargon-laden terms are treated in depth in Chapter 5, but for now the simple idea to keep in mind is that people tend to resent it when someone "just like them" receives significantly different (especially better) treatment, apparently for no good reason. Favored treatment may buy the good will of the person receiving it. But because people focus on the injustices they face, the cost of malcontents will usually exceed the benefits provided by those receiving favored treatment. Thus, defusing these comparisons is a good idea.

MEASURING CONSISTENCY

Having extolled the virtues of consistency, how do we measure it? When it comes to among-employee and temporal consistency, measures are fairly straightforward: the uniformity of practices and treatment among similarly situated individuals (defined in terms relevant to the specific organization—see below); and the continuity in HR philosophy and practice over time for the organizational unit under study. But how do we measure single-employee consistency? Alas, there is no precise formula or litmus test to use in assessing the consistency among the distinct pieces of an organization's employment practices. (If it were that easy, we would never observe companies making mistakes in aligning their HR practices!) But our four categories of reasons for seeking single-employee consistency provide several general suggestions for how to gauge this aspect of consistency in an organization's employment practices.

In view of technical complementarities among policies and practices, a good starting question is: How does a given policy or practice being contemplated affect the costs and benefits associated with other HR activities? If a new training program or compensation system is contemplated, for instance, will it increase or decrease the returns from the company's current practices concerning recruitment, employment security, job design, performance appraisal, diversity, collective bargaining, and the like? Is a policy of frequent rotation among specific tasks for production workers—aimed at increasing worker knowledge and stimulating suggestions among employees—consistent with piece-rate compensation? (Probably not; see Chapter 9.) Does a contemplated system of detailed peer review make current compensation and promotion practices more valuable or less?

Other reasons for seeking consistency are psychological or social in nature and lead us to ask whether the various messages communicated are congruent with one another, especially within the broader social context. HR policies or practices should be analyzed for (in)consistency not only in terms of their substance but also in terms of *process* and *symbolism*. Although we can't provide anything like a comprehensive checklist, here are some themes that represent important sources of potential (in)consistency among human resource practices:

- Does the organization presume trust or distrust in relations between the firm and its employees (and among employees themselves)?

- Does it assume an inherent desire to do good work or an inherent tendency for employees to shirk unless they are motivated and controlled by incentives or fear?

- Is the emphasis on egalitarianism or meritocracy? centralization versus local decision making and control? openness or secrecy? competition or cooperation? tradition and stability or flux and change?

- Is the focus on individuals or on groups as the key organizational units?

- Is the emphasis primarily on outcomes (getting the job done) or process (following rules)?

- Is the organization viewed primarily as an economic entity devoted to making money, a noneconomic entity devoted to the maintenance of its members (or its own perpetuation), or an organization serving some higher calling?

- Does the organization offer "jobs" or "careers"?

To the extent that an organization's HR practices provide unambiguous and consistent messages about these topics, employees will have a clearer and more powerful sense of what they can expect and what is expected of them, thereby aiding in the attraction, motivation, and retention of people best suited to the enterprise. This suggests that a test of consistency along these dimensions is: How consistent are the expectations of employees, both in terms of what (they believe) is expected of them, and what they expect of their fellow employees and the organization? How quickly and effectively do new recruits come to learn these things?

As for screening of prospective employees, tests of consistency include homogeneity of the workforce in terms of their tastes in personal (co-worker) relationships and the extent to which prospective employees are able to anticipate what a job with the organization entails, what will be expected of them, and what they can expect in return.

THE ORGANIZATIONAL MENAGERIE

Do not be misled by our juxtaposition of Organizations A and B at the start of this chapter. These are hardly the only two consistent patterns of HR practices. For one thing, consistency is culturally relative; a pattern or practice that is viewed as consistent in Japan might send very mixed signals to a German workforce. But even more, "visionary" organizations are often those that, in a particular time and social and economic context, find practices that fit together technologically and allow employees to anticipate what they can expect and what is expected of them. Because of heterogeneity in the workforce, in the legal, economic, and technological environment, and (even) in the population of other functioning organizations, it is witless to try to give a short list of consistent organizational types.

For instance, one of the authors of this book, together with Professor M. Diane Burton of Harvard University and Professor Michael T. Hannan of Stanford University, has conducted a study of the "HR blueprints" of over 150 emerging, high-tech companies located in the Silicon Valley. The nature of this study and specific data are reported in detail in Chapter 19 (where further references are given). Rather than repeat definitions and data here, we'll simply give you an important bottom line from the perspective of this chapter: The data collected indicate that when it comes to founders' HR blueprints for this collection of firms, there are five fairly distinct and prevalent types of organization in the "menagerie," together with a number of close cousins and hybrid mixes. These distinct types are: commitment-model firms, somewhat like our organization B; bureaucratic firms, which to some extent approximate the classic portrait of bureaucracy sketched by Max Weber; star-model firms that resemble academic departments in elite universities; the autocratic model, in which the founder is more or less (and for better or worse) a virtual dictator; and the engineering-model firm, a peer-driven, team-oriented model in which skills are valued and cool technology motivates the troops (sort of an engineering fraternity house). We want to stress two conclusions that emerge from this research:

- There is no consensus as to the best HR blueprint for a high-tech start-up in the Silicon Valley, even within particular industry niches, at least based on what the researchers observed. And there aren't two polar organizations. Instead, the data suggest a richer menu of consistent possibilities.

- Each of these five models "resonates" with—is consistent with—organizational forms that exist in the larger social environment from which employers and employees are drawn. Consistency, at least in part, derives from the preexisting conceptions of the people involved, about how organizations can and should be structured and managed.

CONSISTENCY AND INCONSISTENCY: TWO ILLUSTRATIVE CASES

We'll mull over these data in detail in Chapter 19, so here we just want to summarize two cases—examples of particularly strong and weak consistency in HR practices that bear on individual employees—to illustrate what consistency and inconsistency among HR practices mean in reality.

Hewlett-Packard: A Model of Consistency

Hewlett-Packard (H-P), a U.S. multinational producer of electronic equipment, provides an excellent illustration of strong consistency and alignment among a firm's HR practices. H-P is widely regarded as a pioneer in high-commitment work systems. (For more detail on this general type of organization, see Chapter 9.) Their progressive employment policies are designed to cultivate and convey trust in the workforce, provide a superior quality of work life, and "create an environment in which employees can fulfill their natural desires to do good, creative work."[2] To return for a moment to Chapter 2, this approach fits their business strategy of designing, manufacturing, and then servicing top-quality, leading-edge, and somewhat premium-priced products. Among the policies H-P has employed toward these ends are: long-term employment and efforts to minimize layoffs; above-market compensation; extensive discretion for employees; extremely liberal benefits; intensive (and continual) training; and programs aimed at providing flexibility to workers in balancing work and family responsibilities.[3] Not surprisingly, these "investments" are supported by careful screening of initial hires, promotion from within, reliance on peer pressure and peer review, and programs aimed at minimizing turnover, which all interact to ensure that H-P reaps a good return from these investments in its workforce. (For instance, the firm's CEO, Lewis Platt, related to one of us how potential abuses of flex-time are effectively sanctioned by peer pressure, due to a general fear that conspicuous abuses will cause H-P to abandon the flex-time policy.)

The benefits to H-P from such a consistent and tightly aligned set of HR policies seem clear. In an industry characterized by intense competition for technical and marketing talent, H-P is able to attract and retain highly gifted and motivated personnel. H-P's system of promotion from within, the expectations of long-term employment, and the intensive training and professional development provided have historically reinforced the basic message that workers at H-P can have a gratifying career there. Those practices also help the firm ensure that employees internalize and embody the company's values, which is particularly important insofar as H-P cannot closely supervise some work activities (especially the creative work) and has chosen instead to cultivate a relationship of trust and rely on peer pressure. Its compensation and evaluation procedures reinforce the message of trust and of being part of a family; for instance, there are no individualized bonus systems anywhere within H-P, even for the CEO, only generally awarded rewards based on H-P stock. Of course, these practices leave H-P open to opportunistic behavior by some of its employees; for example, because it would muddy the message of trust to rely on methods such as surveillance of the workplace or lie detector tests, H-P does not employ these intrusive methods.[4] Instead, H-P is famous for its use of "Management By Wandering Around" (MBWA), which represents a more informal and less intrusive form of monitoring that ostensibly enables managers to communicate trust and concern, rather than distrust and suspicion. (The company's Web site proclaims: "Trust and respect for individuals are apparent when MBWA is used to recognize employees' concerns and ideas.")

Compare H-P to IBM, as we described it in Chapter 2. IBM also offered lifetime employment and careers instead of jobs. But IBM was much more of a bureaucracy, and (especially) a bureaucracy directed from above. H-P's product line spans many industries—computers and peripherals, of course, but also medical instrumentation, telecommunications equipment, test and measurement equipment—because H-P bench engineers are given a lot of freedom to use their engineering skills as they choose.[5] IBM, in contrast, kept a tighter and more centrally determined rein on their product line. It isn't hard to imagine that H-P's system makes for relatively happier creative workers, or that IBM's makes for a more focused product-line strategy. Both are internally consistent; and both are well tuned to certain environmental conditions. The difference is that IBM's system became externally less fit, as the information processing industry matured and evolved.[6]

We noted above that an organization's culture may limit the sorts of monitoring and control strategies it wishes to deploy. Yet it is worth noting that H-P *does* use metal detectors to screen production workers at some facilities outside the United States (e.g., in Singapore). Such tactics, if employed in the United States, would presumably be inconsistent with the basic message of trust that H-P aims to cultivate. But in some East Asian countries, such as Korea and Singapore, where citizens confront more extensive governmental control over their lives, there is probably little contradiction between H-P's reputation as a progressive, caring, trusting employer on the one hand, and, on the other hand, using metal detector technology on the shop floor to deter theft. In other words, when we measure consistency of HR practices in terms of *consistency with a standard pattern of social relationships,* the society within which the enterprise is embedded can greatly affect internal consistency.

To summarize: H-P's human resource policies and value statements communicate a remarkably consistent set of messages about what the firm and employees have a right to expect of one another, to the point that employees can (and do) characterize reliably whether or not a given action or decision was undertaken in accordance with "the H-P way."

The Portman Hotel: An Example of Inconsistency

The importance of internally consistent HR policies is illustrated perhaps even more dramatically when consistency is not realized. One of the most dramatic examples we know of internally inconsistent and poorly aligned HR policies concerns the Portman Hotel, which opened in San Francisco in 1987.[7] The hotel, designed by noted hotel architect John Portman, was the first hotel to bear his name and be run by his management company. Portman sought to replicate in the United States the service and ambiance provided by premier Asian hotels, such as the Oriental Hotel in Bangkok and the Regent in Hong Kong. To differentiate itself among high-end hotels in San Francisco, of which there were many, Portman sought to create a "no rules" environment for guests.

At the center of the hotel's marketing strategy were the hotel's personal valets (PVs), who would be available to perform any (legal and moral) task requested by the guest, and who would also be responsible for the normal custodial and maintenance activities associated with hotel rooms. Thus, the PVs were to have extremely broad jobs, bearing somewhat autonomous responsibility for duties normally carried out under close supervision by numerous specialists in traditional hotels. Delivering the exceptional service the Portman sought would obviously require tremendous interdependence and coordination, not only among PVs, but also between PVs and other areas of the hotel. Territoriality needed to be avoided at all costs. Flexibility was critical, along a number of dimensions: within individuals (multitasking); across individuals (cross-training and teamwork); across parts of the hotel; and over time (the ability to upsize and downsize in response to seasonal, day-of-the-week, and even time-of-day fluctuations in guest requests). By empowering PVs and reducing costly management layers, Portman also hoped to minimize overhead costs. Given the importance of the PVs to the hotel's strategy, as well as the desire of hotel management to avoid unions, the hotel offered new hires a contract, providing certain guaranteed rights and entitlements, and it sought to create a culture of mutual trust, membership (versus employment), pride, openness, voice, and fairness.

It didn't work. Portman's management created a set of HR policies and procedures that were internally inconsistent and poorly aligned with the firm's strategy and technology. And as time passed and events unfolded, Portman's management reacted to events in ways that sent glaringly inconsistent messages to the PVs.

To begin with, when recruiting PVs, Portman (working through a recruitment consulting firm) sought out individuals who, among other things, scored high on assertiveness and need-for-structure. The high need for structure was touted as important for workers who would be tending to the custodial needs of the guest rooms, but it was incongruent with Portman's "do anything" policies and the hotel's own amorphous organizational structure. Moreover, stressing assertiveness resulted in hiring some PVs who saw this job as a means to an end outside of work and others who were seeking a career in the hotel industry. Because of the lean hierarchy at Portman, a career at Portman itself was impossible for many PVs, and thus both of these groups of PV recruits were susceptible to turnover.

Compensation practices also displayed substantial inconsistency. Base pay was very low, at a level commensurate with maids at more traditional hotels. Yet the PVs were expected to do lots more and harder work. Moreover, 20% of the PVs had college degrees and 15% were trade-school graduates, so their pay was hardly commensurate with their social status. The benefits were liberal, but the workforce was very young (80% were under 35 years of age), so the generous long-term disability, retirement, and medical benefits were less salient to them, and the high rate of turnover built into the recruiting practices made these benefits less salient still.

Customer satisfaction depended on the performance of several PVs who (at various times of the day, and over a period of several days) served the guest, as well as the performance of other service personnel in the hotel (e.g., the concierge and the switchboard). Cooperation among PVs and between the PVs and other service personnel was thus very important. Management talked about the importance of cooperation, but they also acted in ways inconsistent with promoting cooperation. Most notably, they initially forecast that the very low base wages would be supplemented by very high tip income. Management spoke of how PVs could become "independent capitalists," working on their own to please guests and thus achieve higher tips, hardly an image conducive to teamwork and cooperation. Moreover, staffing decisions resulted in PVs being shunted from one floor to another as needs arose, making it harder to achieve the sort of personalized relationship with a guest that would lead to a large tip at time of departure. There were also "competitions" for associate of the month and associate of the year, which we would not expect to promote cooperation. Happily (perhaps), taking into account the relatively small prizes and the very small chances of winning, these competitions could not have had much of an impression on the PVs. But the symbolism, recognizing outstanding individual performance, was not ideal.

Despite the obvious importance of training in an organization devoted to such a novel and challenging service concept, there was essentially no follow-on training or development beyond an initial two week orientation. Perhaps management hoped that a lot of training would occur on the job, with PVs sharing their accumulated knowledge with one another. But the incentive system didn't reward this (if anything, it promoted competition among co-workers for tips); the PVs were kept very busy, due to chronic understaffing; and the constant shuffling of job assignments disrupted stable relationships among PVs.

Perhaps most significantly, management sent two sets of conflicting messages to the PVs. The first concerned the nature of the PV job itself, which entailed a range of tasks—from cleaning toilets to serving drinks to ironing clothes to fulfilling extraordinary requests (such as procuring theater tickets or locating jogging routes). The stress on tip income, the novelty of the job, and initial training on how to judge a guest's personality emphasized the extraordinary-service part of the job. Yet at the same time, rooms were being inspected by supervisors for cleanliness and readiness. Moreover, PVs were left to themselves to balance their workload, to decide when to delay cleaning a bathroom in order to serve drinks to a different guest. In the jargon of Chapter 2, the job design mixed both star and guardian elements, fostering ambiguity among individual PVs about whether they were to take risks for big successes or be careful to avoid failures.

Second, the firm sent the message that employees are important ("Associate" titles, formal employment contract and bill of rights, etc.), but then management did not listen when the PVs complained and made suggestions during the early months in which the hotel was struggling to get off the ground. PVs complained that despite management's fine rhetoric, other service personnel treated them like glorified maids. When occupancy rates were lower than anticipated in the first few months, management tried to save on operating expenses by cutting back on staffing levels and by moving PVs from floor to floor as needed.

Problems arose from the start: occupancy rates stayed below expectations; tip income was (on average) one-fifth of what was expected; guests seemed unclear on how to use the PVs; turnover among PVs was high. Management earnestly attempted to solve these problems. Most notably, they reorganized the PVs into stable teams that would each staff a particular floor. This was successful at first, but as occupancy rates stayed low, management began to corrupt the team concept, decreasing (via attrition) the number of PVs to reduce the operating budget, assigning part-time "floating PVs" at peak-load times to understaffed teams. Problems arose anew; the hotel was eventually bought out, and today it is part of the Singapore-based Pan Pacific Hotel chain, which is part of Japan's huge Tokyu Corporation.

What could management have done? Despite the attractiveness of the notion of bringing East Asian standards of hostelry to the United States, it is debatable whether there is any way to manage human resources to make this marketing concept fly. Returning to the five factors and, in particular, the external (economic and social) environment: labor costs in San Francisco are at least three times what they are in East Asia, so that East Asian hotels can staff at a level that isn't feasible in San Francisco; hotels are premium employers in East Asia and hence have far less trouble retaining their staff than the Portman did; and the ethic of "service" on which Asian hotels draw is buttressed by a set of cultural norms and institutions that are much less prevalent in American society, making the PV job much more of an outlier in the United States than in Asia.

However, if the attempt was to be made, Portman should have recognized by deed as well as by word the central importance of PV performance for the success of its marketing strategy. Training should have been much more extensive. PVs should have been listened to when they made suggestions. When tip income fell well below expectations (and promises), the hotel should have increased base pay. Cooperation should have been stressed; the idea of setting up teams that work a single floor together was a good starting point, especially if a way could have been found to share tips equitably. But those teams should have been maintained even in the face of low occupancy rates. Portman needed to think of their human capital as *capital*—as something to invest in, with returns accruing only after a while.

Instead, Portman's management treated their labor resources—the key to their strategy—as an expense item. Management invested heavily in the physical plant, with stunning public areas, expanses of elegant marble in each bathroom, green Rolls Royce limousines to ferry guests around San Francisco, and an extensive array of business tools and technologies made available to guests. There can be little doubt that Portman's management would have shelled out big bucks without a moment's hesitation to repair malfunctioning air conditioning had the hotel confronted an unexpected heat wave during its first summer of operation. Yet management was reducing the PV workforce—a key element of their marketing strategy—to save $16,000 per month (1.5% of their operating budget), an outlay that the hotel could have recaptured by increasing occupancy a mere two-thirds of one percent! Somehow, Portman's management believed that they could deliver unparalleled service and attract, motivate, and retain superior people without hiring more people or paying higher wages than their competitors. It isn't enough to talk a good and consistent game about the importance of human resources; indeed, talking one way and acting another is as detrimental as anything to getting a consistent story out to your workforce.

THE SPAN OF CONSISTENCY

Returning to the H-P example for a moment, you might object that (as we've told the story) they take consistency too seriously. H-P's business strategy fits well with a stable, trusting, risk-encouraging environment for their creative employees. But does this imply that they can't or shouldn't closely monitor, say, assembly-line workers or clerical personnel? To be sure, devotees of TQM tell us that assembly-line workers are an important creative force, and in fact H-P practices TQM, so it may make sense to extend an atmosphere of trust and stability to assembly-line workers (see Chapter 9). But suppose H-P didn't practice TQM and didn't otherwise see a direct benefit in promoting an atmosphere of trust and stability among assembly-line workers. In this case, what should H-P do? Should it strive to create the same type of atmosphere among assembly-line workers as elsewhere in the firm so as not to confuse or dilute the message sent to its engineers? Alternatively, could (and should) H-P maintain two (or more) HR systems, one for engineers and the other for assembly-line workers, each internally consistent but not necessarily consistent with the other?

Framing this issue more generally, much of our discussion so far indicates that each employee should face a consistent set of HR practices as they bear on him or her. We've argued earlier in this chapter that it is advantageous to have HR systems be consistent across employees, but *to what extent?* What is the appropriate span for consistency? Where can the firm safely "break" its HR policies, without endangering an overall sense of consistency?

A general principle that provides some insight into this question is that people tend to compare their plight with the situations of those whom they perceive as being similar to themselves, and confusion or resentment arises most when treatment is different among people who perceive themselves as similar. (See the discussions of social comparisons and distributive justice in Chapter 5.) Thus, complete consistency across all employees is often unnecessary; social, economic, demographic, and even symbolic differences between groups of workers can serve as workable points of discontinuity or change in employment practices. For example, confusion might appear in the minds of the H-P design engineers if engineers who work on mainframes were treated very differently from those who worked on microcomputers. But H-P can sustain some differences in how it treats its engineers on one hand and its clerical staff on the other, because the demographic and socioeconomic distinctions between the two groups are fairly clear.

Economic forces play a powerful role in shaping how different segments of the workforce are treated within an organization, at least within the context of a market-based economy. If British Petroleum treated its R&D staff the way it treats its sales staff, it might well lose its R&D staff to competitors. Ben and Jerry's, the ice cream manufacturer, had a company rule that no-one could be paid more than five (later, seven) times the pay of the lowest-paid full-time employee.[8] But when, in 1995, they sought an outsider for CEO (to satisfy a perceived need for professional managerial skills that the founders lacked), they were prepared to abandon that policy. And within our own business school, a long-standing practice of seeking to minimize wage dispersion, particularly among incoming rookie professors, has begun eroding to some extent, in response to intense competitive pressures to hire young finance and accounting talent, including from Wall Street firms.[9]

Indeed, in a market-focused society, distinctions that are based or justified on market forces—by occupational group, region, and the like—can become socially valid (and even self-reinforcing) to some extent. For example, to put the best face possible on their change in policy, Ben and Jerry's asserted that a highly paid CEO was needed because the ability to command a high salary implies possession of needed managerial skills. To cite another example, the historian Margo Conk has described how, in the late nineteenth and early twentieth centuries, the U.S. Census Bureau defined detailed occupational categories so as to capture cultural and demographic distinctions then thought to exist among people who typically did different types of jobs.[10] In that time period, for instance, it was presumed that the work women and nonwhites did was less skilled and afforded a lower standard of living than work done by white males. Accordingly, lacking any clear *technical* criteria for differentiating among occupations, the government created distinctions among skilled, semiskilled, and unskilled roles to reflect and preserve these beliefs. Ironically, as Conk observes, differences in the occupational distributions of men versus women and whites versus blacks eventually were used to "explain" or justify differences in labor market attainment by race and sex, even though those presumed differences helped determine the occupational categorization in the first place.

Of course, the legitimacy of certain distinctions can also depend on the host society. For example, Japanese firms, at least until recently, had less difficulty than their U. S. counterparts sustaining a "dualist" regime that favors certain segments of the workforce (males, older employees) over other segments (particularly women), because these social and demographic distinctions have been viewed as more legitimate within the Japanese context. When these social distinctions erode, so can the legitimacy of differentiation based on them. For example, as the traditional rigid divisions between physicians and nurses have started to erode (in the United States, at least) in terms of their gender composition, level of education, and professionalization, so too have differences in how they are managed (such as freedom from bureaucratic intrusion) begun to erode.

Creating Distinctions

At the time this book was being written, it was alleged that some prominent Silicon Valley firms were engaged in rather stark two-tier employment practices. Specifically, some systems programmers for these firms worked in modern, plush corporate facilities—they could lunch in well-tended garden courtyards, or work out in corporate gymnasiums—while others could be found in locations that resembled warehouses. The work done by the two groups was quite similar; indeed, to some extent the groups were interdependent. But Group A seldom or never saw Group B workers, and visa versa. In other firms, the two groups were found in the same building, but still in very different physical surroundings, and again fraternization between the two groups was discouraged. Personnel records of the two groups showed that Group A employees were paid far more than Group B; in fact, members of Group B were not employees of the firm whose name was on the facility at all; they were employees of a labor contractor from countries such as India, who had been retained by the host firm to provide the contract labor.

These alleged practices have been hotly disputed and the subject of media investigations and lawsuits recently. But suppose that these allegations were true. It is not hard to figure out a purpose of such stark stratification. Judgments of similarity are often outside the control of the firm, reflecting such factors as socioeconomic status, level of education, gender, ethnicity, and alternative wage opportunities in the labor markets. But organizations can sometimes create—or at least encourage—distinctions and give distinctive treatment where they would not otherwise arise. In the particular instance, the host firm and the labor contractor are using an arsenal of symbolic acts to distinguish the well-paid, well-treated employees of the host firm from the contract laborers.

Job titles are sometimes used to create these distinctions (see Chapter 5). There may be little difference in the skills required or tasks undertaken by administrators versus clericals, but in many organizations the administrators command much higher wages and respect than clericals (holding constant years of service) and, perhaps not coincidentally, the latter category is more likely than the former to be female-dominated. In some societies, the difference in gender might suffice to legitimate differences in compensation; in the United States, the difference in job title helps confer the perception of legitimacy. On Singapore Airlines flights, service attendants wear different garments denoting their rank; the in-flight magazine provides a key, so that passengers will know the rank corresponding to each outfit. Visit a Japanese assembly line and you may see workers employed side by side, doing nearly identical tasks, but wearing different colored caps. One color denotes a permanent employee of the firm, while another denotes a seasonal or limited-contract worker, with enormous differences in job security and benefits between the groups. Of course, distinctions are formed simply by the fact that some line workers are permanent employees and others are seasonal or limited-contract workers. More generally, outsourcing labor (discussed in depth in Chapter 18) is a powerful tool for creating initial distinctions between permanent employees—the insiders—and the outside "temps."

Efforts to create and reinforce distinctions in order to legitimate differential treatment among employees don't always work. IBM had a hard time in personal computers because the HR practices that seemed necessary in this field conflicted with employment practices that were the hallmark of IBM. In the early days of personal computers, IBM tried to solve this problem by removing its PC Division geographically from the rest of the firm; more recently, IBM spun off its PC operations as a separate entity. To cite another case, numerous airlines have tried to implement two-tiered employment systems; there are workers-hired-before-such-and-such-a-date, who get substantially better pay and benefits than those hired after that date. Such systems have been acceptable to some unions, who have seen this as a way of protecting the salary, benefits, and jobs of existing members. But basing differences in treatment on such distinctions has rarely been successful; the second-tier workers naturally resent their second-tier treatment and can respond with second-tier efforts.[11]

Such distinctions can be especially hard to maintain when the organization has a strong internal labor market or a lot of lateral transferring occurs. The basic characteristic of an internal labor market is that the firm hires workers at low-level entry ports and then (pretty much) promotes from within (see Chapter 8). Internal labor markets are used, in part, to increase workers' identification with the firm rather than with their profession. If you take a worker who is employed in this kind of lifetime employment situation (e.g., as was the norm until very recently at IBM), and you wake that worker up in the middle of the night and ask "What do you do for a living?," the answer is supposed to be: "I work for IBM" and not "I sell typewriters" or "I am a company comptroller." If the aim is to have the employee's primary identification be to the firm and not to the specific job or department, then trying to sustain distinct employment practices based on rank or function will be more difficult.

Treating employee subgroups differentially can also be troublesome when the nature of the work throws together workers from different subgroups who receive different treatment. Consider, for instance, pilots working in an airline cockpit under a two-tiered personnel system. In these systems, the flight captain, who is an older, more senior pilot, typically receives job security, traditional benefits, higher pay, and the like; the co-pilot or first officer, who was hired more recently and belongs to the second tier, may not enjoy all (or any) of these advantages. Such conspicuous distinctions in the treatment of crew members do little to promote the harmony required of an effective flight crew. As noted above, the broader social, political, and cultural environment can serve to deter (or legitimate) such distinctions. For instance, we would expect less difficulty implementing two-tiered personnel systems that favor senior pilots—who are likely to be older and, given historical hiring practices, more likely to be white and male—in countries that are less egalitarian and that associate age with status more than the United States does.

Differentiating among employee subgroups is also particularly divisive when a strong, cohesive organizational culture is sought. It is difficult to persuade people to identify with a single overarching goal or identity while simultaneously promoting rampant distinctions among segments of the workforce. In teaching the Portman Hotel case to MBA students and executives, for instance, a solution often proposed for the hotel's problems is to split off the maid duties from the PV duties, reducing the number of PVs, paying them higher wages, and hiring a number of maids at market wages. This suggestion is typically offered with an analysis that—due to differences in the job task, as well as educational, gender, and (perhaps) even racial/ethnic differences in the respective labor pools—such distinctions between maids and PVs can be sustained. Yet going back to the context of the organization shows that this solution poses some difficulties. Given the necessity of delivering consistently outstanding service and the high degree of interdependence required of everyone on the hotel staff, the PVs and maids would presumably have to work in close collaboration. Certainly there would be a significant guardian element to the maid job in the Portman Hotel context. Suppose a crew of low-wage (perhaps non-English-speaking) maids were brought on board, isolated from the contractual guarantees and liberal benefits made available to the rest of Portman's "associates." Although the social distinctions between this group of maids and the PVs might facilitate differential treatment of the two groups, trying to segment the workforce in this way would work at cross-purposes with some aspects of the organization's strategy and culture: How effectively would you expect the maids to perform and to work with the rest of the hotel's staff to provide unparalleled service? How successful do you think the hotel would be in its efforts to avoid unionization?

Faced with this argument, students who propose the two-tier system at Portman will often rejoin that East Asian hotels successfully rely to some extent on this sort of split-job design. That is correct. But compare the economic, social, and cultural environments of San Francisco and East Asia: Labor is cheaper in East Asia; personal service is more acceptable as a profession; gender and ethnicity are sometimes viewed as more legitimate bases of job assignment; and the legal environment is less hospitable to aggressive unionization. Don't misunderstand us: The two-tier strategy for Portman is certainly worth pondering. And if the hotel should choose to pursue it, it would do well to create social distinctions between the two tiers—for instance, require some college education for PVs (to the extent that this doesn't run afoul of discrimination laws), provide separate canteen facilities for the two groups, and so on. But our guess is that, on balance, the environmental factors in San Francisco, combined with the hotel's overall strategy and general culture, would have worked against successful implementation of a two-tier design.

Because it is often highly contentious to treat distinct segments of the workforce differently, it is not uncommon for strong-culture firms to spin off completely separate subunits for freestanding activities that require a distinct pay regime or set of HR practices, such as an entrepreneurial research team (e.g., IBM and its personal computer staff). This is done to reduce the dissent that might ensue if the same differentiation was more conspicuous. This shows how an organization's HRM system can shape its strategy and structure, and not just vice versa: Here, the desire of certain firms to foster high-commitment employment systems can shape organizational boundaries, suggesting that certain activities be spun off into distinct entities rather than grouped together with other (interconnected) activities.

An Illustration: Information Services at United Parcel Service

A real-world example of a firm that has struggled with these issues concerns United Parcel Service (UPS).[12] Known throughout the world for their distinctive chocolate-brown package cars, UPS has for decades been the largest private package delivery firm in the world. UPS has developed a very strong culture of trust and independent action among its regular workforce; managers and package-car drivers have a clear mandate to do whatever it takes to get packages delivered on time and in good shape. One means by which the firm has inculcated this strong sense of dedication is by rotating people throughout the organization, including stints as package sorters and package-car drivers, the company's key line positions. (Even corporate attorneys have served stints driving a package car.) The UPS culture is also no-nonsense; for example, managers may not drink coffee at their desks.

In the 1970s and 1980s, UPS faced a new form of competition: overnight air package delivery, led by Federal Express. While UPS's volume, which was concentrated in ground freight, was not appreciably diminished, UPS management: (a) worried that the air package segment would grow; (b) worried that the U.S. Postal Service would challenge their ground freight business; and (c) wished in any case to capitalize on their extensive fleet of package cars to move into the overnight business. As part of their response, they felt the need to upgrade significantly their information systems (IS) technology, so they could be competitive on tracking packages, billing, and so on.

Traditionally, UPS would have upgraded its IS technology by having some of its home-grown managers train in IS and then bring their training back to UPS. Given the time lags this would have involved, and also the limited available pool of IT expertise among its personnel, UPS considered the radical idea of bringing in IS professionals from outside. This second route presented UPS with a number of dilemmas: How should the outsiders be compensated? Should IS professionals be given ownership shares in UPS? Should they be eligible for higher managerial ranks at UPS? Should they be allowed a cup of coffee at their desks (given that coffee is essential fuel for computer types)? Should they go through the normal orientation and rotation schedule? Compounding the difficulty of these questions was an understanding that information technology for tracking packages would have to be deployed by package-car drivers, who (therefore) would have to buy into the ideas and designs created by the IS professionals. In a culture in which being a package-car driver is the equivalent of attending boot camp, management was rightfully concerned that the drivers would regard IS professionals as aliens—treated differently—and thus would resist implementation of the IS systems. (Indeed, unless the IS folks could get a good understanding of what a package-car driver did, they might come up with unworkable or at least poorly designed technologies.)

In the end, UPS opted to bring in some outsiders but to give them an abbreviated form of boot camp—all the IS people hired spent time in package cars and sorting centers and, especially during the Christmas season, helped out in the field. For the most part, the IS professionals were injected with a fairly strong dose of the same "brown blood" that flows in the veins of the rest of the UPS workforce. (We are unsure whether the IS people were allowed coffee at their desks.) In the final analysis, UPS determined that given its strategy, technology, and culture, it could not tolerate rampant segmentation or differential treatment among its ranks without potentially undermining the integrity of the HR system that had historically made the company's workforce so productive and loyal.[13]

TEMPORAL CONSISTENCY AND ORGANIZATIONAL INERTIA

Organizational arrangements are path dependent, meaning that whatever initial approach the organization takes in dealing with a particular concern (e.g., compensation or job design) will tend to persist over time and shape subsequent decision making, even when changing environmental circumstances warrant modifications. This, of course, can have extremely detrimental effects on an organization. But we outlined earlier why temporal consistency—which breeds this sort of organizational inertia—can also be desirable.

We will elaborate on these points in Chapters 4 and 5, but essentially the desirability of maintaining continuity in HR policies comes down to two things. First, it is important that employees understand well the HR policies under which they labor, and, just as consistency of different pieces of those policies and consistency of those policies applied to different employees promote understanding, so too does constancy or continuity of policies promote the ability to learn and remember. (The same argument pertains as well to *prospective* employees, insofar as cultivating and sustaining a distinctive reputation in the labor market is a valuable asset for the organization.) Second, the HR practices of an organization provide a framework for relationships between employees and management (and among employees), but they do not fully specify those relationships. Instead, within the framework, workers and managers negotiate by word and deed a set of expectations and modes of behavior. When the firm changes this framework, it can upset the basis of these informal and highly complex understandings, and workers and managers must then spend time and energy renegotiating the relationship each bears to the other. Insofar as this is time and energy diverted from more directly productive activities, it is bad for the firm.

Notice that achieving temporal consistency and continuity need not require that an organization refrain completely from changing its HR practices. Our arguments about the virtues of temporal consistency basically revolve around stability in the expectations that employees (and prospective employees) have about their roles, the norms and values that govern conduct in the organization, and the treatment an individual can expect from co-workers, one's supervisor, and others in the firm. It may be possible in some cases to preserve stability along those lines while implementing fairly considerable changes in specific HR policies. For instance, numerous organizations that traditionally offered lifelong careers have, like H-P, recently retreated from an iron-clad pledge of employment security, viewing such commitments as overly constraining given rapid changes in technologies and business environments. Yet quite a few of these firms also (like H-P) retain a strong emphasis on the personal and professional development of their employees, manifested in extensive training, broad job designs, generous benefits, a holistic view of employees, and the like. They explain the changes in their HR systems (toward more career self-management and less assurance of secure employment) as a continuation and evolution of—not a retreat from—their time-honored HR philosophy. They argue that these modifications in particular HR practices do not reflect a change in the firm's basic norms and values, but rather a recognition that in today's economy, sometimes the best contribution a firm can make to employees' professional and personal development is to help some individuals recognize they are no longer well-suited to working there, and then provide them with the tools necessary to compete effectively for jobs elsewhere (including retraining, outplacement assistance, and generous severance benefits).

Of course, in trying to preserve temporal continuity while adapting its specific HR practices to environmental changes, the firm faces a dilemma: It can take the "gradualist" route, evolving a mishmash of poorly articulated, badly matched practices as it responds to each source of environmental pressure in a piecemeal way, or it can pay the costs of making wholesale changes in its HR practices and philosophies to meet the new situation. An example of a firm confronting this dilemma of late is Lincoln Electric Company.

An Illustration: Change at the Lincoln Electric Company

Lincoln Electric manufactures arc welding equipment. The company has long been held up as a paragon of manufacturing excellence; the Harvard Business School case on Lincoln Electric is the historic best seller of all Harvard cases,[14] and Lincoln has been the subject of television documentaries and numerous glowing reviews in the business press. Lincoln's production technology has been a worker-paced assembly line, with work-in-process buffers between each stage in the assembly process. The worker-pacing of assembly is an important part of Lincoln's distinctive HR system; compensation is based in substantial measure on a system of piece-rates, which allows each worker to choose a pace that matches his or her desire for compensation with his or her desire to bust a gut working. (Lincoln supplements the piece-rate system with a complex and generous bonus system that rewards productivity and other activities, and workers are held accountable for the quality of their output. Also, the company is renowned for a very strong, no-nonsense, no-frills culture.)

In recent years, Lincoln has sought to modernize its manufacturing operations by adopting so-called lean production, including just-in-time techniques. These techniques reduce buffer inventories and thus seem at odds with the piece-rate practices that are integral to the Lincoln Electric HRM system. Lincoln could abandon or modify its piece-rate compensation system, but then the company would confront: (1) possible inconsistencies this might create with other long-standing HR policies (e.g., performance evaluation, recruitment, job design); and (2) potential adverse effects on its valued reputation in the labor market, a reputation gained by never wavering from the philosophies and practices advocated by Lincoln's founder nearly eight decades ago. (The power of this reputation is attested to by a story, perhaps apocryphal, that in Cleveland, Ohio, the home of Lincoln, grade-school children sometimes bring home year-end report cards that read "Joanie is a real Lincoln Electric kind of person," meaning someone industrious and independent.) Little surprise, then, that in trying to adapt Lincoln to its changing environment, which includes more intense global competition and increased scrutiny from outside shareholders, top management has proceeded with extreme caution, convening internal committees and retaining an outside consulting firm to examine productivity and compensation issues at the firm.[15]

INCONSISTENT CONSISTENCIES

Pulling together ideas from the last chapter and this one, organizations simultaneously seek various forms of consistency: consistency between HR practices and current initiatives in business strategy and technology; consistency of HR practices with one another; consistency in practices across (at least similar) employees; and consistency or continuity between HR practices in the past, present, and future. Unhappily, it isn't always possible to achieve consistency on all these fronts simultaneously. In other words, sometimes the various forms of consistency aren't mutually consistent!

For instance, when two firms merge or one acquires a second, conflicts between temporal consistency and among-employee consistency can arise. In some cases, the two merging organizations have quite different HR philosophies and practices. To achieve consistency among all employees, one or both organizations must change. But this means that temporal consistency must be compromised. To take two specific examples, as we wrote this book, the mergers of Citicorp and Travelers Group and of Germany's Daimler-Benz AG with U.S.-based Chrysler Corporation were announced and consummated. A great deal of speculation in the business press concerned how and how well each company in these proposed pairings, reputedly with very different organizational cultures and HR systems, would be intertwined. When an acquisition involves, say, a large pharmaceutical firm purchasing a small biotech start-up—to "merge" the pharmaceutical's capabilities in manufacturing, marketing, and regulatory affairs with the basic science the start-up has created—careful management may be able to preserve distinctive treatment for the old employees of the biotech firm. But the mergers of Daimler with Chrysler and (especially) of Citicorp with Travelers are touted as paying off because of synergies that will involve close interdependencies between the employees of the partnering firms. Maintaining distinctions in this case will be hard, perhaps too hard. These will be interesting cases to watch.

SUMMARY AND ROAD MAP

In this chapter and in Chapter 2, we have sketched the basic concepts and frameworks we will use to evaluate an organization's HR practices, to gauge whether they are consistent with one another and with the broader context. We will use these frameworks to study specific issues and analyze particular organizational forms throughout this book.

You are entitled at this point to raise (at least) two concerns. First, our frameworks have been skeletal—we have provided vague generalities buttressed by quick examples. We haven't yet put meat on these bones by looking at such substantive questions as: What activities should be carried out by regular employees versus outsiders or contingent employees? When should employment be long-term and promotion be from within? What principles should guide job design and the allocation of rewards to positions? How should performance be evaluated and by whom? When should a firm pay above-market wages? How extensive should the benefits package be and what kinds of benefits should be emphasized? What advantages accrue from a diverse workforce, and how can these advantages be maximized (and the costs minimized)? The bulk of this book will concern such questions.

But before getting to the meat, we deal with a second legitimate concern. In this chapter and, to a lesser extent, in Chapter 2, we have made vague reference to notions such as reputation (and its importance in employment relationships), processes of social comparison, psychological theories of learning, perception, and cognition, and the like. We hope our vague references have not unduly confused you, but to support those hopes with action, in the next two chapters we will discuss the basic economic, social, and psychological factors that impinge upon HRM and the relationships between employer and employee(s). In other words, we have a bit more place-setting to do at the table before getting down to the main course, but (we assert) a properly set table will make consumption more enjoyable and more fruitful.

IN REVIEW

⇒ In addition to being consistent with the broader context facing the firm (the subject of Chapter 2), HR policies and practices should be internally consistent. We focus on three aspects of internal consistency:
- *Single-employee consistency:* consistency among the different elements of the firm's HR system, such as compensation, recruitment, and performance evaluation
- *Among-employee consistency:* consistency of HR policies applied to different (but similarly-situated) employees within an organization

- *Temporal consistency:* continuity and consistency of an organization's HR philosophy (though not necessarily all of its specific HR practices) through time

⇒ Consistency among the elements of an organization's HR system and consistency in HR philosophy over time and across employees are desirable for various reasons, which include:
  - Technological complementarities
  - Helping employees learn about and internalize the "nature" of their employment relationship, by being internally consistent and consistent with common patterns of social relationships
  - Improving the match of individuals to work settings

⇒ In addition, consistency in HR practice among similarly situated individuals is desirable to defuse invidious social comparisons and to foster feelings of distributive justice.

⇒ Measuring single-employee consistency is difficult, but each of the reasons why it is desirable (listed above) suggests some possible metrics and tests. Measuring among-employee and over-time consistency in HRM is more straightforward.

⇒ In specific cases, a variety of substantially different systems can pass the test of consistency.

⇒ The desired span of consistency (e.g., should shop floor workers be treated similarly to research scientists?) depends on numerous factors, including:
  - Technological interdependencies
  - Degree of fraternization, demographic similarities, and other factors that govern processes of social comparison (see Chapter 5)
  - Economic forces (which, in turn, can legitimate distinctions, at least in some societies and some organizations)
  - General societal and cultural norms

⇒ Distinctions, which can be the basis for "breaks" in how different groups of employees are treated, can be artificially created or reinforced by a variety of means. (Outsourcing—dealt with at length in Chapter 18—is a currently fashionable way to try to make distinctions.) However, there are limits to how effective this can be, particularly in interdependent settings and in organizations whose cultures emphasize "membership" (one-big-family) or deemphasize differentiation.

⇒ Though temporal consistency in HR philosophy has desirable features, it can also give rise to organizational inertia.

⇒ The three different aspects of consistency may themselves be mutually inconsistent. There are also often real conflicts to be resolved in seeking alignment of HRM with the business context while simultaneously preserving single-employee, across-employee, and temporal consistency.

ENDNOTES

1. See Jeffrey Pfeffer, *Competitive Advantage Through People: Problems and Prospects for Change* (Boston: Harvard Business School Press, 1994): Chapter 4.

2. Jennifer J. Laabs, "Hewlett-Packard's Core Values Drive HR Strategy," *Personnel Journal* 72 (December 1993): 38–48.

3. Though H-P continues to emphasize employee development and "employment security based on performance," its leadership has sought to spearhead an evolution of the "H-P way" that places more emphasis on results, accountability, and employees' responsibility for managing their own careers (versus employer paternalism). See the discussion of "Why Work at H-P?" on the company's Web site (http://www.jobs.hp.com/USA/why/).

4. See http://www.jobs.hp.com/USA/why/hpway/#href2.

5. A matter of ongoing debate at H-P as this book was written is whether the firm should be more directive in promoting "interdisciplinary" projects, or should leave these up to the bench engineers to initiate.

6. Differences in the companies' respective HR systems may also help illuminate why H-P appears to have suffered less from the "brain drain" that, as we noted in Chapter 2, has plagued IBM. First, recall that no employees at H-P are on bonus plans; rather, more emphasis is placed on companywide stock ownership, perhaps reinforcing a stronger sense of economic and psychological ownership at H-P than at IBM, where elaborate bonus plans have tended to focus primarily on the top management ranks. Second, if scientists and engineers are tempted to join a start-up for greater breadth, variety, and autonomy on the job, then the broader job designs and more flexible career paths for which H-P is well known are likely to be assets in attracting and retaining entrepreneurially minded scientists and engineers. Finally, anticipating our discussion of trust and reputation in Chapter 4 and Appendix B, bear in mind that IBM conspicuously reneged on its long-standing policy of lifetime employment, whereas H-P has gone to much greater and more visible lengths in trying not to violate implicit contracts with its workforce.

7. See Charles C. Heckscher and Philip Holland, *The Portman Hotel Company,* Harvard Business School case 9-489-104 (revised 9/89).

8. Jay Mathews, "Ben and Jerry's Melting Social Charter: Ice Cream Maker Abandons Progressive Pay Policy to Find New CEO," *Washington Post* 117 (June 14, 1994): D3; Jennifer J. Laabs, "Ben & Jerry's Caring Capitalism," *Personnel Journal* 71 (November 1992): 50–7.

9. Returning to considerations of strategy and technology emphasized in Chapter 2, this pay differentiation may be more contentious in the context of a business school like ours—which has long emphasized the interrelation of research and teaching and which seeks to promote interdependence and cooperation among faculty both within and between academic units within the school—than in schools with a tradition of greater Balkanization along disciplinary lines, such as Wharton.

10. Margo A. Conk, "Occupational Classification in the United States Census: 1870–1940," *Journal of Interdisciplinary History* 9 (Summer, 1978): 111–30; also see James G. Scoville, *Concepts and Measurements for Manpower and Occupational Analysis* (Washington, DC: U. S. Department of Labor, Report to Office of Manpower Research, 1969).

11. For a discussion of one recent failed attempt at creating a two-tiered system (at Lincoln Electric Company, a manufacturing firm we discuss below), see Zachary Schiller,

"A Model Incentive Plan Gets Caught in a Vise," *Business Week,* no. 3459 (January 22, 1996): 89–92.

12. See Jeffrey A. Sonnenfeld and Meredith Lazo, *United Parcel Service* (A), Harvard Business School case 9-488-016.

13. Recent years, however, have witnessed increasing antagonism (including a crippling strike in 1997) between UPS and its unionized workforce over a variety of issues, including efforts by the company to differentiate among segments of its workforce—particularly full- versus part-timers—in terms of pay, benefits, and other job conditions. See Paul Magnusson et al., "A Wake-up Call for Business," *Business Week,* no. 3542 (September 1, 1997): 28–9; and "The Teamsters and UPS," *Economist* 344 (August 16, 1997): 14–5.

14. See Norman A. Berg and Norman D. Fast, *The Lincoln Electric Company,* Harvard Business School case 9-376-028.

15. Schiller, *op cit.*

4

EMPLOYMENT AND ECONOMICS

Employment is clearly an economic affair. Except for the occasional professional athlete who claims she would pay to play the game, or the starving artist driven by his muse to create without tangible reward, people work in substantial measure for the economic rewards they earn. Even more so, most employers hire their employees primarily for economic reasons. This is not to say that wages (or other economic benefits) are the be-all-and-end-all of employment from either the employee's or employer's perspective; personal and social fulfillment play important parts, which we will emphasize throughout this book. But it would be hard to deny that economic factors play a huge part.

In this chapter, we will build an economic framework for studying employment. The framework we build is not the sort of economics that most people know—supply equals demand—because the exchange of labor for money often doesn't fit that economic model. Instead, our framework will employ concepts such as balance of power, reciprocity, reputation, and reserved rights. If you are like most readers, this sort of economics may be a bit new to you. The underlying economic foundations are *Transaction Cost Economics,* especially as developed and exposited by Oliver Williamson, and the theory of reciprocity and reputation in repeated games.[1] We'll try in this chapter to give you all the tools you will need for the applications we will meet later in the book. But in case you want some background in these two foundations, Appendices A and B of this book give a nontechnical introduction to each.

THE BASIC FRAMEWORK

The economic view of employment that we will adopt involves a sequence of ideas and observations. We will provide an outline of the basic framework in this section. When this is done—when the "big picture" is all laid out—we will elaborate and analyze the individual steps in the sequence.

(1) *Employment is often an open-ended transaction, with the details of the transaction specified only as time passes and relevant contingencies arise.* This assertion probably doesn't come as a surprise to you. The idea is simply that when the employee takes a job, the duties entailed a month or six months or three years ahead are not precisely specified. Moreover, details about salary a year or two or five

years hence, future promotion prospects, and the like are left vague. This isn't to say that these so-called "terms of trade" aren't vaguely anticipated. Each side has at least a rough idea about what will be involved. But the details—some of which are quite important to the value of the transaction to two sides—are left to be determined later.

Why? The simple answer is that many employment relations are enduring, or at least hold the possibility that they will be enduring, and the parties involved either can't anticipate all the possible future contingencies or don't want to waste time and energy at the outset detailing how each contingency, however unlikely, will be met. The aphorism *We'll cross that bridge when we come to it* captures what is going on, where some of the bridges to be crossed aren't even foreseen at the outset.

In recent years, firms have increasingly opted for temporary workers, workers hired on a single-project basis, and the like. To the extent that this is true, employment relations are increasingly less open-ended. (We'll examine these trends later in the book, especially in Chapters 17 and 18.) But note well: If someone hired by a firm to work on a project has reasonable prospects of being hired on future projects, then the overall "employment relationship" between the two is open-ended, in the sense that the terms under which reemployment is possible are left open at the start. Similarly, a company may hire temps or contract employees repeatedly from the same personnel agency, in which case one could think of the company as having developed an open-ended enduring relationship with the labor contractor in lieu of an enduring relationship with the workers *per se*. Moreover, notwithstanding these recent trends toward more flexible forms of labor contracting, we think that the most prevalent and interesting employment relations remain open-ended in just the sense we've described.

(2) *The way in which this open-ended transaction is filled in—the determination of the precise terms of trade, as time passes and contingencies arise—depends on decision-making rights and privileges that are specified by law, by explicit contractual agreement, and (often most importantly) by tradition and common practice.* For instance, in most societies today, employees always retain the right to quit—slavery is illegal—although employees can sometimes voluntarily surrender rights to what they can do after they quit, in so-called noncompete agreements. On the other side, employers' rights to terminate an employment relationship are often circumscribed under law—in legal jargon, employment is not at will—and employees in certain cases can be fired only for just cause, following due-process procedures.[2]

Although the law and explicit contractual agreements are important, so too is common practice, which can vary from one organization to the next. In one organization, bosses generally tell employees what to do. Other organizations cultivate bottom-up decision making. A third possibility is typified by Sun Hydraulics— the firm we met in Chapter 1 and to which we will return near the end of this chapter—where tradition and custom dictate that each employee decides each day for himself or herself what to do that day.

Traditions and customs that determine who fills in the employment contract day-to-day are almost always informal, based on history and implicit understandings between employees and employer. The questions then arise, Why do these traditions or customs have any force? Why does anyone believe in them? For instance, at Sun Hydraulics, custom dictates that employees do what they want. What guarantees are there that, one morning, an employee of Sun Hydraulics doesn't arrive at work and find that a time-clock has been installed, shop supervisors have been appointed, and he (the employee) has an assignment handed to him with the admonition that if he doesn't complete the assignment by quitting time, he will be fired?

To understand the guarantees, we take a momentary detour. Consider an individual—call him A—who for years has shopped for salads, breads, cheeses, cold cuts, and prepared foods at a local delicatessen, and who expects to continue shopping there for years to come. This individual has an open-ended economic relationship with his deli, in the sense that the items that will be available six months hence, their prices, and A's purchases are all left open today. (For instance, A is going to have a fancy dinner party in a year's time that he can't possibly anticipate today. But that's okay, because a few days before the party A will know about it and will be able to order then what he wants for his fancy dinner party, based on availability, prices, and A's budget then.) The details of this open-ended transaction are "filled in" according to law and custom. Under law, A can go to another deli if he wants to, and the deli can refuse to serve A (with some limitations). And by custom, the deli quotes prices to A, and A selects what he wants according to his tastes and budget constraint. If A wants a special item, he can order it, but special orders must be made in advance (say, a week ahead of time, or whatever is customary in this setting). Note well, the custom (at least in the United States) is that A and his deli don't haggle over food prices. In contrast, A and his rug merchant *do* haggle. The customs are different, so the ways in which the transactions are "completed" are different.

Thus, A's relationship with his deli fits the structure for employment relations that we've created so far. And A and the deli benefit from this enduring relationship; for instance, A comes to know how the deli's roast chickens taste, what cheeses it stocks, and so on. Yet there is a substantial difference between A's relationship with his deli and the relationship between A and his employer, which is the crux of the matter in our model of employment. Suppose that A's fancy dinner party comes around, and A asks for a price on stilton cheese, which he is eager to serve with a rare bottle of port. If the deli owner knows how desperately A wants the stilton for dessert, he could conceivably try to "hold up" A by asking for three times the normal price. But this hold-up, if attempted, would not work, for the obvious reason that A has recourse to other delis. In effect, the deli owner is substantially constrained or disciplined by competitors who would be happy for A's business. To be sure, A can't quite replicate (immediately) all the aspects of his relationship with his old deli; if he goes to someone new, he'll need to check that the cheese is well-kept, the salads well prepared, and so on. But as long as A has friends who shop at other delis, who can provide recommendations, advice, and other information, then the "costs" incurred in a switch are not large.

But suppose A's *employer* tried to take advantage of A, by insisting that A undertake certain arduous tasks. Could A switch employers so easily?

(3) *As time passes and a particular employment relationship matures, the immediate terms of trade between employee and employer are less and less disciplined by market competition, because the fortunes of the two parties involved become more and more intertwined through the development of relation-specific assets.* For both employer and employee (to differing degrees in different cases), finding a new match is usually *much* less economical—and often increasingly so—than keeping on with the current relationship. (Indeed, both parties have an interest in taking steps to increase the ties that bind the other party, simply to improve their bargaining positions.)

What sorts of "costs" are involved? For the employee: A new job must be found. A spell of unemployment may have to be endured. A move may be required, which means uprooting spouse and family. Treasured social relations with co-workers may be lost. Note well, the employer may also suffer if she has to replace this employee with a new recruit: The employee may have accumulated specialized knowledge that a replacement will acquire only at a cost in time and out-of-pocket expense. The employee may have cultivated a network of connections within the firm that permits efficient communication. The social relations between the employee and other employees may be valuable to the employer, as may (more directly) the social relations between the employee and employer. The employee may have a network of connections with the firm's suppliers or customers, and thus the employer can lose twice if the employee walks: first, by losing those connections; and second by the possibility that the employee will walk away with some of the employer's clientele.

Economists call these things *relation-specific assets*. The *relation-specific* part means that they are things that bind each side of the transaction to the other specific trading partner. If you take a job as an accountant with Price Waterhouse (which was merging with Coopers & Lybrand as this book came to press), and you acquire general knowledge about accounting, this isn't relation-specific: You can move to KPMG Peat Marwick and use this knowledge just as well. But if, in the course of your employment, you make connections with other folks at Price Waterhouse, those connections are less likely to be useful elsewhere, and so they are relation-specific assets. As for *assets,* the idea is that these things have a relatively long useful life, and you (and your employer) invest time and energy in them.

It is stretching the terminology a bit, but we mean to include in the category of relation-specific assets the match itself, insofar as being matched with an employer or employee is valuable for the other side. In particular, employees, except in a very tight labor market, usually attach significant value to being matched with an employer—that is, having a job—because finding another match consumes time and energy and involves worry.

You can probably add to our list of relation-specific assets. The point is that these assets often have substantial value, and to the extent that they are valuable, they weaken considerably the "discipline of the market" that keeps each side from trying to take advantage of the other. Of course, the costs of a severed relation are not symmetrical. One side may be more at risk than the other; indeed, it is generally felt that employees are more at risk in this sense than are employers.[3] If it would "cost" you $75,000 in terms of loss of value in these assets to have to leave your current employer, then your employer has a $75,000 bargaining chip to hold over you. Your value to your employer, measured relative to her next-best alternative (of finding and training a replacement), may be only $25,000. Then you have to worry that she will use this leverage to your detriment.

(4) *In place of the discipline of the market, employer and employee are restrained—not always perfectly—by a host of factors: goodwill and warm feelings for the trading partner; an ethical aversion to taking undue advantage of one's trading partner; the legal rights of the other side; the ability of the other side to threaten in return (a balance of power); and the desire to maintain a general reputation as a good employer or employee.*

We probably don't need to explain goodwill and warm feelings or ethics, but their powerful effects (particularly of goodwill) should not be underestimated. Throughout this book, we'll be looking at ways that employers and managers (because we are writing for those audiences) can enhance these feelings in their employees.

Legal rights—for instance, the right of employees to quit; to be free of intrusive surveillance; not to be fired without good cause and due process; and to organize collectively so as to present management with a united front—are very important in employment relationships. We'll spend a lot of time on these as well, especially in Chapter 7.

But it is the ideas of reputation and balance-of-power (or, if you prefer, terror) that most directly concern us here. To give an example: the reason it would be unwise for management at Sun Hydraulics to suddenly insist on time clocks and to hand out daily assignments—even for a single employee—is that this could seriously compromise relations with all employees for a long time to come. Both the management and owners of Sun (who are, in this case, a substantially overlapping group) benefit from the excellent relations they have with the line employees, and so members of management find it in their own interest to protect the valuable and valued relationships they have with employees by not suddenly reverting to time cards, daily assignments, and similar practices.

How exactly do balance of power and reputation work? In what circumstances will they work well, or at all? To the extent that they do work, who benefits by them, and by how much? These are the central questions of this chapter, which we will address at length as we proceed.

(5) *Efficiency in employment relationships depends both on adapting flexibly and well to contingencies that arise and on sustaining and promoting long-term investments by both parties in the relationship, including a willingness to sacrifice immediate self-interest if doing so will substantially improve the common good.* In the next section we'll give examples of these things. The critical idea for now is that *both* flexibility *and* long-term cooperation and investment should be achieved, to the greatest extent possible.

But these twin goals are somewhat in conflict. Flexible adaptation to possible contingencies entails a particular distribution of decision rights and privileges, giving authority to the party (or parties) with the relevant information and decision-making capabilities. If this distribution puts one side or the other in danger of being exploited, it may result in withdrawal of cooperation, unwillingness to invest in productive relation-specific assets, and/or insistence on rigidifying contractual guarantees. Guarantees of the sort enumerated in point (4) may help resolve the conflict. Thus:

(6) *To achieve efficiency in employment relations, decision-making rights and privileges must be assigned—by law, contract, and custom—in a way that takes advantage of the information and capabilities of the parties involved and at the same time provides adequate safeguards to each side.* In this respect, the relative efficiency of employment relationships becomes a matter of "institutional design," where the institutions are primarily the patterns of decision-making authority regarding how the open-ended contract between employer and employee gets fleshed out from day to day. In one setting, it may be best to grant the employer most of the decision-making authority. In another, the employee may be best suited to call the shots. Most often, decision-making authority should be shared in one way or another. And sometimes outside and objective third parties should be involved.

To understand the relative efficiencies of these different institutional arrangements in specific cases, we need to understand the ways in which balance-of-power and reputation safeguards work, a topic we examine later in this chapter. In doing so, we will see that getting these institutional arrangements right is only part of the battle:

(7) *Whether efficient outcomes are reached, and the precise nature of those outcomes, will depend crucially on the psychology and sociology of the relationship, which in turn is powerfully influenced by: (a) the history of relations between the two parties themselves; (b) the history of each of the parties in other employment situations; and (c) local norms and customs concerning "appropriate" relations between employers and employees.* Institutional arrangements that are "efficient" according to point (6) above may or may not work well in practice, depending on the two parties' expectations and objectives. To sustain cooperation, for instance, each side must either expect that their trading party will reciprocate good for good (and bad for bad), or they must internalize the welfare and interests of the other party. (And really robust cooperation often entails both of these.) After all, the mere fact that a marriage persists over time doesn't mean that it is necessarily harmonious or healthy, and so too with employment relations. We will have a bit to say on this score in this chapter, and much more to say about it throughout this book, especially in Chapter 5.

The key, especially for the last two steps in the argument, is understanding how and when balance of power and reputation "work," in the sense of providing guarantees for the employee and/or employer that permit and promote cooperation. But before we discuss those key ideas, we begin our detailed discussion with point (5) and properties of employment relations that make them more or less efficient.

ACHIEVING EFFICIENT EMPLOYMENT RELATIONS

In the best of all possible worlds, what would lead to economically efficient employment relations? We focus on three basic categories:

1. *Efficient adaptation and coordination.* The circumstances facing a firm change. Old opportunities whither and new opportunities appear. Employees discover both talents and shortcomings. Clearly, it benefits the firm (in the sense of producing value) if employees can be deployed and redeployed in ways that take advantage of these changing circumstances and new information. Moreover, because production is often interdependent, the actions of employees have to be coordinated. (When we write "have to be coordinated," it sounds as if we implicitly mean by the bosses. But we don't mean that; employees can, in some cases, do a very good job of coordinating themselves.)

2. *Investing in productive human capital.* Employer and employee can and sometimes do take actions that improve their ability to work productively together. For instance, the employee may take time and effort to build up a network of useful contacts in the organization, or he may try to acquire skills that are particularly useful in his current job. The employer can subsidize the employee's training, and she can provide opportunities for network building.

3. *Sacrificing immediate self-interest for the common good.* Both employer and employee are often faced with a temporary dilemma of sacrificing self-interest to improve the general welfare. A clerical worker might stay late—in a situation where the accrued overtime wages don't compensate for the inconvenience—because a crucial report must be finished. A line supervisor may permit an employee to depart early or arrive a bit late, even if the employee isn't strictly speaking entitled to this "favor," because it is important to the employee. An experienced employee may spend time assisting a new recruit, even if this help is unlikely to be recognized in any official way.

We've only given examples for each category, but the general ideas should be clear. Moreover, it should be clear that a willingness to cooperate is basic to all three: A willingness to respond flexibly to circumstances, to invest today in anticipation of returns tomorrow, and to sacrifice self for the common good, all involve the spirit of cooperation. What does it take to achieve this sort of cooperation? Employees and employers must believe that proffers of flexibility will not be used to harm their interests, that they will recoup investments they make in the relationship, and that a sacrifice of self-interest today will yield greater dividends in the future. In a nutshell, the parties involved must believe that the benefits accruing jointly will be *shared,* if not today, then in the future.

For instance, when it comes to designing and managing employment relationships, most employers have mixed objectives, but at or near the top of the list is getting the most value or contribution to long-term profit out of those employees. Many employers mix in with this a genuine concern for the welfare of their employees, but efficiency *per se*—increasing the joint welfare of the two sides to the exchange—isn't quite the same as improving the welfare of each party. It is conceivable that concrete steps needed to improve the efficiency of the firm's employment relations would *decrease* profits, because those steps would cause wages and benefits to employees to rise by more than the joint increase in surplus.[4] In a case like this, we don't expect the employer to go along. And, even more so, we don't expect employees to offer themselves up voluntarily for the "common good" if the common good means big profits for the employer and worse conditions (including employment insecurity) for themselves.

Thus, trust by each side that they will get their share is a necessary adjunct to efficiency. What gives rise to that trust? As we noted earlier, goodwill and ethical restraints are both sources. The law provides a measure of guarantee. Explicit contractual provisions are often enlisted.

We believe that goodwill and ethics, to the extent they work, almost always work well. But legal guarantees and explicit contractual provisions are often less than ideal, because they engender further costs for the parties involved. Obvious costs include administrative costs of monitoring compliance (for legal guarantees), negotiation costs (for contractual guarantees), attorney compensation and (when necessary) court fees, and so on. Less obvious costs arise because such means of achieving "trust" can harm flexibility: The law is generally a fairly blunt instrument, because it must be crafted to suit a huge diversity of cases. And contractual guarantees, because they must be written in advance, often fail to fit well the specific contingencies that arise as time passes. Finally, relying on courts and contracts (or even threatening to do so) may provoke an atmosphere of confrontation that harms goodwill.[5]

To engender trust (and thereby cooperation) without harming flexibility or cooperation itself, we look for other mechanisms.

BALANCE OF POWER AND REPUTATION

Now we turn to the heart of our economic framework, the twin notions of balance of power and reputation. The idea is that a balance of power between the contracting parties or the concern of one party for her reputation generally can provide safeguards and guarantees that sustain long-term cooperation. How do these things work? When do they work? When might they fail? How can they be strengthened? When they work, what determines precise terms of trade?

Simple Hierarchy

To begin to answer all these questions, it is easiest to focus on a specific (and stylized) form of employment relation, *simple hierarchy*.[6] Imagine a firm with a single boss and a number of employees. Employees of this firm retain the right to quit and, we will assume, this employer retains the right to discharge workers (i.e., employment continues only if both parties wish it to). Employees cannot be compelled to work more than eight hours a day, five days a week. However, except for that and for some other basic rights (such as, employees cannot be compelled to do anything illegal or immoral), the custom in this firm is that employees work at whatever assignments they are given by the boss. If she tells them to dig ditches, they dig ditches. If she tells them to file papers, they file papers. If she insists that they work a night shift, from 10 P.M. to 6 A.M., they must do that. Or, rather, they must do these things or else be fired or quit—they always retain that right—or convince the boss to give them a different assignment.

Why do the employees agree to such a terrible scheme of employment? That's a loaded question, and we should be clear in the ways it is loaded. First, whether terrible or not, it is certainly a contractual arrangement that *a priori* is open-ended in precisely the sense we described in our outline of the framework: What employees will be doing a day or a month or a year hence is initially unspecified, to be determined only as necessary. Second, there is nothing terrible about the scheme if the employees can quit and find other employment without cost. If, say, the work involved is carpentry, if the employees are all skilled carpenters, and if skilled carpenters can find work easily in the local economy, then the boss is disciplined by the market; she can't ask for labor more onerous than the market-determined conditions without paying better-than-market wages, or her employees will exercise their right to quit.

But suppose the employees are in thrall to the employer, and increasingly so. That is, it becomes increasingly costly for them to quit, because this would mean a spell of unemployment, possible relocation, loss of friendships with co-workers (which might even deter quitting by the skilled carpenter mentioned in the previous paragraph), and so on. They have to worry that the boss will insist on night shifts or onerous work, up to the limits imposed by employees' willingness to quit and suffer the associated costs if the boss's demands become too harsh. And then our question *Why do the employees agree to such a terrible scheme of employment?* is loaded only insofar as it prejudices us to think that the boss will use her power to the detriment of her employees. But for three categories of reasons, she may not do so.[7]

We cited employer goodwill as one guarantee for the employees in this situation, and we reiterate here that this should not be dismissed lightly. The employer may turn out to be a nice person who is concerned for the welfare of her employees. Extending this explanation a bit, she might feel strongly that exploitation of employees in this fashion is unethical and so refuse to do so.

A second source of security for the individual employee is, potentially, a balance of power or threatened damage: He can threaten to quit, *which may levy subsequent costs on the employer* if she attempts to exploit him. If this individual employee walks off with a lot of skills that will be hard or costly to replace, or with a big chunk of the employer's clientele, or even if his departure means a period (until the vacancy is filled) during which the firm is short-staffed, the employee's threat may be credible and may restrain the employer from trying to take advantage. Note well, it may be the custom that the employer (she) decides what the employee (he) does, day after day. But if she is clear that treating him unfairly will induce him to quit, causing the firm to incur the costs associated with his departure, she is restrained in what she proposes.

Because carrying out the threat to leave is costly for the employee, it is sometimes asserted that such a threat is just a bluff from which he will retreat if the employer steadfastly insists on onerous tasks. Whether the threat is a bluff depends on a host of factors, such as how stubborn the parties are, how much each will be hurt by severing their relationship, their experiences as bargainers, and the expectations they have developed about each other. But the notion that the employee is inevitably bluffing and will back down flies in the face of both real-life experience and more carefully controlled evidence from the laboratory, both of which demonstrate that people will refuse to be exploited and instead will punish the would-be exploiter, even if this is personally costly.[8]

This sort of balance-of-power argument depends, however, on the individual employee having a credible and *significant* threat to hold over the employer. Very often it is the case that individual employees can't do much *on their own* to materially affect their employer. The employer may not be too worried about the departure of any single employee, because she (the employer) has plenty of alternative employees. Hence, the single employee cannot credibly threaten the employer that he will quit if she attempts to exploit him; the employer can simply shrug her shoulders and say, "Adios."

But suppose you observed your employer exploiting the relative bargaining weakness of some fellow employee. Fearing that you might be the next victim, an entirely reasonable response on your part might be to polish your resume quietly, or start looking for another job, or insist on greater contractual guarantees against exploitation in your case, or at least insist on more pay, before you consent to invest yourself further in this employment relationship. Perhaps most significantly, you may be less inclined to take actions that are costly to you but that would promote the common good, because you are less convinced that your cooperation will be reciprocated later. And if you are a prospective employee, you are likely to be less inclined to take a job with this sort of employer—at least, you will want a higher initial salary and more guarantees in writing before doing so.

This illustrates the third type of restraint against exploitative treatment of employees: The employer's treatment of *each* employee can affect her general *reputation* as employer with *all* her employees, current and prospective. (As we will note below, this is particularly true to the extent that social and/or technical connections among the employees facilitate greater communication and affinity among them.) Exploitative treatment of one employee may generate some short-run benefits, but if the cost is a damaged reputation and concomitant reactions by other employees, the cost may be too high.

Note that we aren't speaking here of formal collective action by the employees. Rather, we have in mind independent, individual action by a number of employees, each observing the actions of the employer, and each taking independent steps to protect himself, given the employer's now-soiled reputation. Formal collective action—by a union, for instance—fits into this general picture in a category between balance of power and reputation. But the fit is sufficiently interesting and nuanced to deserve separate treatment, which we provide in Chapter 6.

Thus, employer goodwill (or ethics), a balance of power with individual employees (or with an employee collective, if they have formed one), and/or reputation with the workforce as a whole, can answer the question *Why would the employee consent to be employed in a relationship that, by custom, leaves so much decision-making authority to the employer?*

Other Forms of Governance

In the hierarchical caricature of employment sketched above, we have supposed that the employer retains the bulk of authority to determine the terms of trade in the employment relationship as events unfold; the employee can trust the employer not to abuse that authority despite the lack of market-based discipline because of goodwill, a balance of power, or the employer's desire to protect her reputation.

This—the boss demands and the worker accedes—is the standard caricature image of employment; why else use the term *boss?* Yet although it is the standard caricature, in other employment relationships, custom and law dictate other decision-making procedures or what, in the jargon of economics, is called *governance.* There are cases, for example, in which the employee has most of the discretion. One example of this is the relationship between the CEO and the board of directors; the CEO is the employee of the Board, but (in large part) it is the CEO who determines what to do on a day-to-day basis. A second example is the relationship between client (employer) and lawyer or physician (employee); the latter will in many, if not most, instances decide what tasks to perform and even what fees to charge.

Even more often, the division of discretion does not exclusively favor one party. In some cases, employee and employer retain discretion over different decisions. Teachers might be assigned courses to teach by their Dean or Department Chair, but be free to determine what to put into those courses, how to deal with specific issues that arise in class, and so on. Research scientists determine what they will do on a day-to-day basis, subject to broad directions from their superiors. Assembly line operators at Toyota are given the discretion to stop the assembly line when a problem appears before them, but others in the company determine what mix of cars will be assembled and (in large measure) what position on the line the worker will fill on a day-to-day basis. Self-managing teams (see Chapter 13) are given general tasks to accomplish but are left to work out among themselves how to accomplish those tasks. This sort of division of authority/discretion must be accompanied by a level of trust on both (or all) sides.

In some cases, consensus between the parties is required for some decisions; neither party has individual discretion. Consider, for example, factories in which employees elect a Workers' Council, and management, either by statute (as in Germany) or voluntarily, must obtain the Council's agreement to make changes in plant staffing levels, work practices, and so on. In these cases, the trust that is required on both sides is that neither will be recalcitrant in day-to-day negotiations;

recalcitrance on one side would be met with recalcitrance on the other, to the detriment of both.

In still other cases, third-party adjudication of disputes takes place. Whenever the courts intervene in employment relations, interpreting the rights and privileges that the two parties have under law, we have an example of third-party adjudication. But beyond this, there are cases in which the parties agree privately and contractually that disputes that arise will be settled by appeal to a neutral arbitrator. In these cases, each must trust in the neutrality of the arbitrator, and professional arbitrators protect the substantial income they gain from arbitration by preserving their reputations for neutrality and fairness.

Choosing Among the Forms of Governance

Why do we observe one of these forms of governance in a particular setting and not another? What leads to having discretion distributed in one way versus another in specific cases? Why is the standard caricature what it is? In most cases, the answers to these questions mix three factors. First, there is tradition. Things tend to be done in ways similar to how they were done previously. This isn't blind obedience to the past—there are solid reasons for it, which we discuss below. Second, there is law. Society intervenes heavily in employment, giving by statute particular powers and reserved rights to one party or the other. There are good reasons for society to do this—we discuss them at length in Chapter 7—but, as we shall observe later in this chapter, management can sometimes benefit from such restrictions on its own prerogatives. And finally, there is efficiency: The forms of governance used in particular circumstances will tend to be those that enhance efficiency, because it is generally in the interests of the parties involved, and also because more efficient arrangements will tend to survive and be imitated.

But what leads to a governance form that enhances efficiency? Returning to our discussion of what makes for efficient employment relations, we find that two factors dominate.

Superior Information

The authority to call the shots should, on efficiency grounds, rest with the party who best understands what the immediate circumstances call for. In many cases it is the employer and not the employee who possesses the required information and the ability to use it. This happens because the employer specializes in information acquisition and processing, both as a natural consequence of her job as manager, and because she, as (probable) supervisor of a number of employees, can best exploit economies of scale and scope in gathering and processing information. Indeed, because employers coordinate the actions of a number of subordinates, they are in a better position to know what each is doing and what must be done to coordinate their efforts.

This is true in some cases, but not all. When employees form a collective—a labor union or a workers' council—the union or council can have officers (or its own employees) who specialize in gathering and analyzing information about the firm, so that on information grounds, a sharing of decision authority becomes feasible. Indeed, for particularly effective use of workers' councils, firms have found it useful to share information freely both with the officers of the council and with individual employees. Line workers at Toyota are given the discretion to shut down the production line because, management believes, they possess valuable information about how to improve the manufacturing process, information that management lacks. Even so, for them to use their discretion and knowledge effectively, it is important for line workers to have a broader picture of the production process, leading to policies of frequent job rotations, increased levels of managerial communication with line workers concerning strategy and even financial matters, and so on.[9] Or, to go to the extreme cases where it is the employee who dictates to the employer: Both the CEO of a corporation and the family lawyer or doctor are usually in a much better position to know what ought to be done (at least, on a day-to-day basis) than are their respective employers, the board of directors and the client.

Adequate Reputation Stake

Although it makes sense to assign decision-making authority to the better-informed party, to encourage cooperation it is also necessary to offer guarantees to the other side that this authority won't be abused. Insofar as we rely on the decision-maker's reputation as an assurance or guarantee for the other party, we should look for reasons why the party with authority will have a reputation stake adequate to offer the needed guarantees. Going back to the caricature of a simple hierarchy that we sketched above, the employer presumably deals more frequently with more employees, finds it harder to relocate if she sullies her reputation in one locale, and undergoes greater scrutiny by external forces. These factors all increase the relative reputation stake of the employer and therefore push toward giving her discretion, banking on her desire to protect her reputation.

But when employees form a collective, the collective is enduring, lacks mobility, and deals frequently with management in ways that single employees do not. Hence, worker collectives can have a reputation stake that single workers do not have, and we can contemplate power sharing with a collective in cases where power sharing with individual workers is much harder to imagine. To be sure, one can point to cases where individual employees have substantial reputations at stake—such as CEOs, lawyers, movie directors, and physicians—and consequently they are granted very wide discretion by the employer concerning what tasks will be done, when, and how. When it becomes desirable to give discretion to individuals who do not have such strong reputational stakes, employers will want to promote the accountability of those employees; lifetime employment guarantees or dealing with a workforce that is naturally less mobile are means to this end.

Please do not confuse *reputation stake* with what the respective parties have at stake more generally. In drafting a will, an estate lawyer certainly has less in total at stake (by any reasonable metric) than does her client. Yet the attorney has the greater reputational stake in the transaction. The lawyer must be concerned that she is not perceived by potential clients as someone whose wills frequently are successfully challenged or lead to enormous and unnecessary tax liabilities. The client, in comparison, probably doesn't carry much of a reputation among estate lawyers. Similarly, the individual patient undergoing heart surgery clearly has much more at stake in this task than does the surgeon performing the service. But his concern for his reputation as a patient is probably insufficient to guarantee his good behavior toward his surgeon, while the surgeon doesn't want to become known as someone who buries her mistakes.[10]

In some cases, one party has both access to superior information and an adequate reputation stake, and so it is clear that this party should be granted the preponderance of authority. But in other cases, the two factors work in opposite directions, and efficient governance may not be clear. This is almost always the case, for instance, where trilateral governance is found—that is, where the two parties agree *a priori* that disputes are to be resolved by an independent arbitrator. Because the arbitrator's income depends on having other parties perceive that she is fair and neutral, it is clear that she has a very large reputation stake in specific decisions she is asked to render. But it is typically the case that she will be less well informed about the particulars of the situation than are either of the two parties principally involved. Thus, in most trilateral governance, a relatively ill-informed party who has a very strong reputation stake calls the shots![11]

QUALIFICATIONS AND AMENDMENTS

The previous section paints a pretty picture about the role of balance-of-power and reputation in employment relationships. But it is too pretty a picture, on several grounds.

Inefficient Expectations

In all the cases we've discussed, we assumed that if an opportunity for cooperation is there, it will be grabbed by both sides. In a balance-of-power situation, the two parties will cooperate. When employer reputation is the driving force, it will be a reputation that promotes efficiency. But things aren't so simple. Employers who maintain a simple hierarchy sometimes have terrible reputations, which leaves their employees defensive and aggressive in turn. When workers form a collective—a union—and decision-making authority is shared, union-management relations can and sometimes do lead to constant, grinding confrontation.

The problem is one of reciprocity and expectations. Each side to the transaction is willing to trust the other, to give a little today, to refrain from taking maximum immediate advantage of the other side, *if* each side anticipates that the other side will reciprocate good for good and bad for bad. But when one side expects that any attempt at trust, any proffer of cooperation, or any restraint in exploiting the other side will be met with a sneer and subsequent attempts by the other side to take maximum immediate advantage, then the first party will behave accordingly. Those expectations, in turn, are driven by the history of relations between the two parties themselves; their (possibly diverse, and partially vicarious) experiences in other, similar situations; and general local norms and customs concerning "appropriate" relations between employers and employees.

The story of New United Motors (NUMMI) illustrates this point powerfully. NUMMI, a joint venture of General Motors (GM) and Toyota, is based at an old GM plant in Fremont, California, a plant that was known within GM for its hostile labor–management relations, high levels of absenteeism, and other undesirable characteristics. Under the NUMMI agreement, GM provided the plant and Toyota supplied the management. Because of political pressures, the workforce was largely drawn from the former GM employees at the plant, represented by the same United Auto Workers local with which GM had had such adversarial relations in the past. The change in management from GM to Toyota supervisors and managers had an enormous impact. Worker expectations shifted, and the plant has been a (relative) model of cooperative labor–management relations, to the benefit of each side. We are not saying that the only changes that resulted from the change in management were changes in worker expectations. Management actions had to change to justify those expectations. But it seems fairly clear that GM management would have had a significantly harder time bringing about on their own such a sudden change in employees' expectations; GM management were trapped by the past. It is interesting to speculate on what will happen over the next few years, as the agreement winds down and Toyota withdraws, leaving the plant back in the hands of GM management. We've heard optimistic reports that the changed expectations (toward a cooperative environment) are persisting. And we've heard more ominous reports that these cooperative expectations are winding down as well. Only time will tell.

Changing HR Practices: Inertia and Expectations Traps

This bears strongly on a lot of the content of this book. We hope that some of the HR practices we describe in this book will seem appealing to you, in the context of a particular organization you know about and in contrast to that organization's existing HR practices. But identifying a better way of doing things is generally a lot easier than implementing it, especially when the better way depends, as it so often does in HRM, on joint and cooperative efforts between labor and management or even simply on changing the expectations of employees. So as we talk about change, we'll spend a lot of time worrying about how to unfreeze expectations and beliefs that impede efficient employment relationships and how to refreeze (or create) helpful expectations and beliefs.

To develop this idea, a short digression is helpful. It is sometimes alleged that some firms "overpay" their workers. Average wages paid by these firms are considerably in excess of the pay earned in the local community, and this higher pay is accompanied by higher levels of benefits, better working conditions, and so on. In the jargon, such premium compensation is called *efficiency wages,* because it is meant to lead to a more efficient workforce: Premium-wage payers are more attractive firms to work for and hence receive job applications from more workers in a local area, so (to the extent that they are able to screen) they can cream-skim, choosing the most able. Further, because workers will wish to remain with a premium-wage-paying firm, the firm will be able to screen for the best workers based on their track records on the job. Workers faced with the threat of being discharged for sub-par performance will have a greater incentive to supply consummate performance, to avoid being discharged from a plum job. Premium-wage payers will therefore have lower levels of voluntary turnover, and, as a consequence, have lower training costs and suffer fewer disruptions. And as we will see in the next chapter, workers who view the premium wages and working conditions as a gift from the firm may reciprocate with the gift of consummate performance, independent of any calculations concerning the chance of discharge, through a psychological process of gift exchange.[12]

To the extent that these things are true—and the available evidence documents, at a minimum, lower turnover rates at premium-wage paying firms—then the assertion that premium-wage payers overpay their workers is erroneous or, at least, not clearly proven. These firms pay more, but they purchase a better quality of labor services and/or experience lower recruiting, severance, and training costs. We would expect to find premium-wage payers concentrated among firms for whom a better quality of labor is more important—for instance, firms that require a high level of job-specific knowledge (so that turnover would be particularly expensive), or firms for whom difficult-to-monitor quality efforts are particularly important (so that consummate effort by workers is crucial). And, looking at the data, this is indeed what we generally see.[13]

Imagine, therefore, that an executive reading these paragraphs has become persuaded of the merits of paying efficiency wages in her firm, which until now has not paid premium wages because the costs outweighed the benefits. Suppose the firm has changed its production technology or strategy so that the tradeoffs now run the other way; now the firm would like to become a premium-wage payer. Can she simply announce that, henceforth, the firm will pay premium wages and expect to procure higher-quality labor? Of course she cannot. For one thing, her firm's in-place workforce was built up in a period of nonpremium wages, and to the extent that premium wages attract employees of inherently better quality, it will take a while to turn over the workforce and enhance its quality. Moreover, to the extent that premium wages elicit consummate performance from employees, squelch voluntary turnover, and attract talented job applicants, it is not today's offer of premium wages that matters as much as the expectations in the minds of current and prospective employees that premium wages will be paid in the future. The firm needs to change employees' expectations, which can take time. The first step in doing so is to offer premium wages today. But this alone may be insufficient, and the firm may find it too costly to change those expectations. It may be trapped with a less-than-premium workforce, without a good way out, or at least without a good-and-quick way out.

We earlier asserted that the governance structure used in a particular employment situation is often influenced by tradition. It should now be clear why tradition plays a role here; tradition strongly colors expectations, and employee and employer expectations about how things "ought" to be done are often crucial to whether a particular form of governance gives efficient or inefficient outcomes.

Short-Run Temptations and Voluntary Restraints

A second qualification to the pretty picture of the last section concerns short-run temptations. Take the case of simple hierarchy, where the employer retains almost all the decision-making authority, and employees depend on guarantees wrought from balance of power or the employer's desire to maintain her reputation. (Extending this idea to other forms of governance is straightforward.)

The calculus that keeps the employer from exploiting her hold over her employees is simple: The short-run benefits are outweighed by the long-term costs of (possibly) losing the specific employee or, even worse, of sullying her reputation with her entire workforce. But in some cases, the employer's immediate temptation to exploit workers is overwhelming and dwarfs future considerations. To take an extreme case, consider an employer who (without giving notice) is planning to shut down a factory in a particular locale, moving operations off-shore. She doesn't fear the future actions of her current employees, because she plans that they will soon be ex-employees. Thus, balance-of-power and reputation considerations don't restrain her from moving off-shore, or even from exploiting her current employees in anticipation of the move. When short-run gains from exploitation are high, or the long-run pain associated with exploitation is low, balance-of-power and reputation are inadequate restraints on employer behavior.

If one party has a powerful short-run incentive to exploit the other, then the cooperative arrangement may break down or even fail to take effect. Both sides, anticipating the relatively imminent disruption of the cooperative scheme, see little future in cooperating relative to extracting the most they can immediately. Because of this, the party facing the short-run temptation may actually benefit from voluntarily restricting her options *ex ante* or submitting to statutory restrictions. For example, when the employees have a formal collective such as a union, the employer can offer contractual guarantees about maintaining work at a facility. When employees bargain individually, contractual guarantees concerning severance payments, triggered if (say) more than half the workforce is discharged, may do the trick.

Reputation and the Problem of Free-Riding

Another qualification concerns the reputation construction. This guarantee for the employees works because employees react independently (but *en masse*) when the employer exploits fellow employees. But will employees pay attention to how their colleagues are treated? And will they independently sanction the employer, if they themselves have not been directly abused?

There is something of a free-rider problem here. It is costly for employees to keep track of how other employees are treated. And it is presumably even more costly to sanction one's own employer. If an individual is himself mistreated by the employer, pride or a desire for revenge may make his counter-threat credible. But in the reputation story, it is not the single employee who harms the employer, but the mass of them acting independently but similarly. So, consider the decision by a single employee about whether to sanction the employer for mistreating a colleague. If other employees are keeping track and will sanction the employer, what do his efforts along these lines add? And if others aren't getting involved, why should he step out of line (presumably only to be squashed)?

To be sure, there is some self-interested force for doing so; recall Benjamin Franklin preaching the merits of cohesion among signers of the Declaration of Independence by asserting that "We must all hang together, or assuredly we shall all hang separately." But Franklin's admonition followed the signing of the Declaration of Independence, which marked out the signatories as rebels together, distinct from the crowd. In the workplace, what takes the place of this symbolic act of defiance? What binds the employees together?

One obvious factor is the extent of interdependence and proximity among workers. If Fred and Ethel work closely together and the employer tries to exploit Fred (e.g., assign him work not in his job description or demand overtime work without pay), Ethel is likely to have a strong interest in rising to Fred's defense for at least three reasons: (1) the employer's actions toward Fred are likely to have an adverse effect on Ethel's capacity to do her own job; (2) Ethel will worry about being punished by Fred for not having risen to his defense (e.g., perhaps Fred will try to sabotage Ethel's contributions to their joint work); and (3) if Ethel sits on her hands at Fred's expense and Fred observes this, she certainly won't be able to count on help from Fred should the employer try to exploit *her* sometime in the future.

Social homogeneity of the workforce is another factor likely to help overcome the free-rider problem that employees face in sanctioning an employer who behaves exploitatively. Employees are more apt to pay attention and then, as needed, to react, when one of "their own" is being abused. Correspondingly, this sort of individual-but-collective response is less dependable the more socially diverse is the workforce. Peer pressure, which is enhanced by social homogeneity, is another helpful force. An employer who understands the benefits that accrue when trust arises from reputation might even seek to promote bonding among the workforce—for instance, through company jargon, shared titles, and common socialization experiences that level preexisting differences and encourage affinity among segments of the workforce. But social homogeneity, peer pressure, and organizationally induced bonds aren't always sure-fire solutions. As we will see in Chapter 6, that is why employee collectives (such as unions) can sometimes benefit not only employees but the employer as well: By institutionalizing employee collective response to abuse, which otherwise might not be forthcoming, an employee collective gives employees needed safeguards that *may* enhance trust and thus redound to the benefit of the employer. (But see Chapter 6 before accepting this argument!)

Knowing What to Expect: Consistency Once Again

Another qualification concerns the notion that an employee—or any party that must trust another—knows when that trust has been violated. We've used the term *exploitation* as a colorful way of saying that the employer breaks faith with employees to their detriment, requiring more of them than they expected or changing implicit agreements that she had with them. But the demands of a job vary over time and with the circumstances of the moment. When the employer insists that an "eager beaver" employee move to the night shift, is this an attempt at exploitation of the employee's relative eagerness, or is it a legitimate response by the employer to some changed circumstance? When an employee is sent out on the road for the fourth time in a month (when the implicit understanding has been two trips on average per month), is this exploitation or a temporary increase reflecting scheduling irregularities?

If employees can't tell the difference, they don't know whether to carry out threats against the employer or how to reassess her reputation. Doing nothing invites exploitation; perhaps the employer is pushing the envelope, to see if the employees will respond. But overreacting is bad for both: Threatening to quit, or actually quitting, costs both sides. Withdrawing cooperation only shrinks the pie the two sides have to split. Insisting on written guarantees in place of implicit agreements reduces flexibility and pads the pockets of the lawyers. Employers and employees both benefit when balance-of-power and reputation-based guarantees can be monitored easily and without too many mistakes being made.

This takes us back to Chapter 3 and the benefits of consistency in HR practices. How do the employer and employees reach a state where each understands what is permissible and what is not? How do the parties ensure their ability to monitor compliance? The keys are often explicit, formal rules or simple (somewhat implicit) principles, based on observable actions. When the rules can be made explicit and formal—no more than five hours overtime per week; no assignment to tasks not in the current written job description; promotions based on objective measures—it is relatively easy to understand what they are and whether they are being applied. But this can unduly restrict managerial discretion in situations where discretion is valuable. When managerial discretion is particularly valuable, then simple general principles—no one works more than his boss, everyone shares in the dirty work—are often more useful. Of course, this is a powerful rationale for consistency (and simplicity) in HR practices; consistency promotes understanding and clarity, and understanding and clarity are prime virtues whenever reputation and implicit agreements are the focus of attention.[14]

DETERMINING THE TERMS OF TRADE

Return for a moment to the case of Mr. A and his delicatessen. What determines the terms of trade between the two parties, where the terms of trade are things like the price of stilton cheese, and the amounts of cheese, roast chicken, prepared salads, and so forth that change hands? To a large extent, the price of goods bought and sold are determined in the larger marketplace of delis (as suppliers) and consumers (as demanders). To be sure, roast chicken or ratatouille from one deli is not identical to the same products at a different deli, nor is the shopping experience at one store identical to the experience elsewhere; there is a measure of so-called product differentiation here. Thus, the price of roast chicken can vary from one deli to another. Nonetheless, the variations can't become too large, at least in locales with several delis. As for the amounts bought and sold, buyers determine how much to buy and sellers how much to sell. In sum, the market in prepared roast chicken fits well the classic economic model of supply and demand; the fit isn't perfect, but it is adequate for many purposes.

As we've already noted, if we assume that relation-specific assets have developed, the discipline of the market is dulled. The ongoing bargain between employer and employee isn't determined by market prices and alternatives, but instead by historical precedent within the organization, bargaining strength, and each side's concern for its future relations with this and other trading partners. The market exerts a bit of discipline: The exact terms of trade that result cannot be so bad for one side or the other that it leaves a party worse off than that party would be by exercising all its legal options (to quit, say, for an employee). But typically this leaves a lot of room for bargaining. And although economics (and common sense) can help us to understand qualitatively what makes for a stronger or weaker bargaining position, it won't pin down the precise terms of trade that result.

This affects what we get out of our economic framework for studying employment. If the government imposes a chicken tax of $0.50 per pound of prepared chicken, or if the price of raw chicken increases by 20%, the economics of supply-equals-demand allows us to make pretty good predictions about what will happen to the price of roast chicken. But if the government increases payroll taxes by 3%, or if a firm decides to institute pay for performance, it is harder to get exact predictions from the economic model about what this will mean for the terms of trade in a particular ongoing employment relationship. We will be making qualitative predictions about such things throughout the book, but because of the fuzziness inherent in bargaining processes, quantitative predictions are difficult, and often our predictions will be hedged with all sorts of caveats about the psychology of the workplace and the like.

Indeed, we saw an important example of this when we discussed inefficiency and expectations. The exact same "tangibles" concerning employment practices, labor supply and demand, job requirements, and so on can lead to vastly different terms of trade between employer and employee, depending on intangibles such as the level of trust and reciprocity between them. Although that discussion focused on whether efficient employment relations would always happen (conclusion: no), the same sort of "fuzziness" pertains to how the parties split the gains from trade they produce, even assuming they reach an efficient relationship.

When Is Market Discipline Strong?

We should be clear: This indeterminacy stems from the conditions that: (a) the employment transaction will be incomplete *a priori,* to be "filled in" as contingencies arise; and (b) when the filling in takes place subsequently, the discipline of the market will be dulled. In some exchanges, especially short-term ones, employer and employee don't get their fortunes so entangled as this; in such cases, we would abandon the economic framework we've set up in this chapter for more standard economic approaches. Our motivation for laying out the framework of this chapter is that we believe that conditions (a) and (b) hold in most (and certainly in most *interesting*) employment situations. But (a) and (b) are conditions that are met or missed in specific examples, and the appropriate economic framework for studying employment is determined in consequence.

There is one further caveat to note about trusting market discipline to determine the terms of trade in employment. Market discipline—the notion that with many buyers and sellers of a particular good, the good's price will be determined by market forces and market forces alone—depends on the further condition that the good in question isn't very differentiated. Because roast chicken from the corner deli isn't quite the same as roast chicken from the local supermarket, the price per chicken or per pound isn't exactly the same. And what is somewhat true for roast chicken is all the more true in many cases for jobs: A job with Firm A is often very different from a similarly titled job with Firm B. For instance, associate positions at Boston Consulting Group (BCG) are viewed as fairly differentiated from associate positions at McKinsey, even though BCG and McKinsey are both high-profile, U.S.-based management consulting firms.

In part, this differentiation reflects the business strategies of the firms, which informs what associates do for their living. But the differentiation reflects two other facts of life concerning employment. First, in contrast to the deli example, employment tends to be a "bundled good" transaction. This is economics fancy talk for the fact that Mr. A can buy roast chicken and salads at his regular deli, cheese at a local supermarket, wine at a local discount wine store—in short, his "deli-needs" can be split among several trading partners. Hence, we can (to some extent) consider the terms of trade in roast chicken distinctly from those in cheese. But Mr. A's labor transaction, which often involves a number of different tasks, is usually with one employer. This isn't invariably the case, but it is the case often enough. Thus, jobs are bundles, and this raises enormously the scope for differentiation.

And at the same time, because employment is open-ended and market discipline tends to be (at least somewhat) weakened over time, there is scope six months or two years hence for differences to arise between two otherwise "similar" jobs. To the extent that those differences down the line are anticipated *ex ante*—for instance, owing to differences in tradition or HR practices or reputation—the jobs are differentiated at the outset. Thus, even when an employee is choosing among jobs to take, before relation-specific assets have been formed, market discipline is somewhat muted: Because conditions (a) and (b) will hold later, jobs at different firms are already substantially differentiated from the outset.

Having said all this, we reiterate that there are certainly cases where the traditional economics of supply-equals-demand is quite appropriate. A part of the economics of employment, called *Human Capital Theory,* uses this more traditional economic framework to study personnel issues. We'll discuss ideas from Human Capital Theory occasionally (particularly in Chapter 15, when we discuss training), but we don't do much of it. This alternative approach to the economics of employment can yield some valuable and important insights, however, and we recommend that anyone interested in HRM should study the subject through this alternative economic lens.[15]

LONG-TERM EMPLOYMENT RELATIONSHIPS

Our basic framework in this chapter began with the assertion that most interesting employment relationships endure (at least potentially) for months or even years. The prevalence of long-term employment is probably fairly obvious to you—notwithstanding recent trends toward shorter job tenures—but of course not all employment relations are long-term. As we just said, when employment relationships last only a little while, the economics of the situation shift. (In particular, market discipline becomes much more important.) It is interesting, therefore, to ask why and when employment relations are or are not long-term.

The rationales for long-term employment relationships can be partitioned into two sets: direct benefits of long-term employment to the parties involved; and the desire of each party to increase bargaining leverage with the other, by tying down the other in a fashion that promotes long-term relationships.

Direct Benefits of Long-Term Employment

To begin, there are a number of reasons why long-term employment benefits either the employer or employee (or both) directly. Included on a list of benefits to the employer are:

Amortizing Recruitment Costs

There are often fixed costs associated with recruiting and selecting a new employee. A longer spell of employment lowers the number of times this fixed cost must be incurred, or (what is the same thing) amortizes these expenses over longer periods of time.

Amortizing the Cost of Training

Many jobs require the employee to have firm- and job-specific knowledge and/or skills. When the employer pays for this training up front, she benefits if the cost of training is amortized over a longer spell of employment.[16]

Evaluation of Employee Abilities for Purposes of Job Assignment

Long-term employment relationships provide relatively cheap and (often) more accurate access to information about employees' abilities, so that employers are better able to match employees over time to specific tasks that need to be done.

Performance Evaluation and Incentives

For reasons we discuss at length in Chapters 10 and 11, a longer-term relationship will often (but not always) allow the firm to measure performance more accurately and along more dimensions, which is useful for a variety of purposes, including the design of effective incentives.

Loyalty to One's Co-workers and to One's Employer

When workers are loyal to one another, employers can motivate them as a group and then depend on peer pressure and mutual monitoring to enhance individual performance. Group-level incentives can be particularly important in cases where it is difficult after the fact to disentangle from the joint production of a work group who did how much. Of course, social bonds are more likely to form the longer the group has been together.

And just as social bonds are more likely to form the longer that employees are together, employees are more likely to develop loyalty to the organization itself the longer they are associated with it. At least, a longer-term association creates the *possibility* of strong loyalty ties. There are at least three explanations for this. First, employers can encourage loyalty in long-term employment relationships by promising large rewards for long-term employees, such as wages that rise dramatically with seniority. To safeguard the promised benefits, a self-interested employee will contribute to the long-term success of the firm. Second, the promise of attractive long-term employment will often incline employees to feel better about the employer and thus incline them to reciprocate (see the discussion of gift exchange in Chapter 5). Third, the longer an employee stays with an organization, the greater his loyalty is likely to be, because of psychological processes of escalating commitment and effort justification (see Chapter 5).

Long-term employment also directly benefits employees. One set of reasons concerns the costs of finding work and the chances of enduring long spells of unemployment. Included in the costs of finding work are search costs and, if necessary, relocation costs: Employees will form attachments in their community—children will be in school, spouses may have jobs that are not easily changed, friendships with others will form—and shorter-term employment relationships may result in employees having to uproot themselves and their families to find work. An extensive literature also documents considerable adverse psychological and medical effects of involuntary job loss (see the citations in Chapter 17). And employees form social bonds with their co-workers, which they clearly value. Longer-term employment relationships will promote these social bonds, which (holding other things constant) will be beneficial to the employees.

Costs of Long-Term Employment

Of course, there are direct costs as well as benefits to long-term employment relationships. Several disadvantages are worth mentioning:

Variable Labor Demands

Labor demand by an employer usually varies through time. Ideally, the employer will want to retain some flexibility in the amount of labor that is purchased. There are many techniques for retaining some flexibility while offering long-term employment to (at least) a core of employees—we will discuss these at length in subsequent chapters—but even given these techniques, long-term employment relationships can reduce the ability of the employer to match levels of employment with demand.

The Dark Side of Loyalty

Loyalty can be beneficial, but it can have deleterious effects as well. To provide appropriate incentives to employees, employers must sometimes take actions that hurt employees. If the employer and employee have a long-term social relationship, it can be hard (to say the least) for the employer to be as hard-edged as is sometimes warranted. And employee loyalty to co-workers can be detrimental to the employer, if employees protect each other or, especially when comparative evaluation systems are used, adopt a group norm against providing consummate effort.

Dysfunctional Behavior

Long job tenures by employees may give them greater opportunities for harming the employer, intentionally or otherwise.[17] For example, subordinates in a long-term employment situation may try to influence or lobby superiors; we will later see that such so-called influence activities can have substantial adverse consequences for promotion systems, monitoring, and job design.

Familiarity (Sometimes) Breeds Contempt

We asserted previously that long-term employment facilitates cooperation among employees. This benefit is not automatic, however. It takes careful management to be realized. For example, long-term employment relationships can intensify fractious personal relationships among competitors for the same job, or between younger workers and more senior employees who view the neophytes as potential rivals.

Strengthening the Employer's (and Employee's) Bargaining Position

If the employer can increase her hold on the employee, by increasing the desirability of the job she offers relative to the employee's outside opportunities, then she strengthens her bargaining leverage. Thus, employers—both to pursue the direct benefits of long-term employment enumerated previously and to increase their bargaining leverage—will take steps to tie the employee to the current job. Of course, to the extent that such steps are effective, they result in longer-term employment.

And, on the other side, the employee will take steps to increase his relative desirability as an employee to his employer, both to realize the direct benefits listed earlier and to strengthen his bargaining position. This also promotes longer-term employment.

Actions that Lengthen Employment Duration

Although long-term employment has both advantages and disadvantages, the advantages tend to prevail; both sides tend to benefit from long-term employment. But this general tendency doesn't mean that the desires of employee and employer will coincide in each and every case. Employees will sometimes leave a job of their own volition. They may find a better job. They may be impelled to quit for personal reasons. They may simply lose interest in the current job. Employers, to realize the benefits of long-term employment and to improve their bargaining position, will want to discourage voluntary turnover among employees. We will discuss turnover-reduction strategies at length later in the book, especially in Chapter 16. But it is worth mentioning three examples, just to give a flavor:

We've already discussed the first: efficiency wages. Employers pay above-market wages along with above-market benefits and working conditions, so that employees will be less inclined to leave the firm for another employer. (As we observed, efficiency wages come with other benefits for the employer.)

Second, employers can also promote a strong and distinctive culture; workers who self-select into this organization because of the culture or who are socialized into it will be less likely to leave for another firm.

And third, employers may operate an internal labor market (ILM): New employees of the firm enter from the outside into a few, generally low-level, port-of-entry jobs and then rise through the firm; promotions are internal, and competition for a plum job is restricted to those already employed by the firm. Put baldly, the firm offers not jobs but careers. ILMs decrease voluntary turnover by giving incumbent workers promotion prospects, by building worker loyalty to and identification with the organization, and by increasing social connections among workers. Overall, ILMs confer substantial advantages and entail substantial costs. We will explore this sort of arrangement in Chapter 8.

SUN HYDRAULICS: TRUST AND LOVE

We discussed Sun Hydraulics briefly in Chapter 1, and we mentioned it in a couple of places in this chapter. Both because it is an extraordinary company and because, in part, it illustrates some of the ideas of this chapter, we close by taking a more detailed look at it.[18]

Sun Hydraulics was founded in 1970 by Robert Koski, to manufacture fluid power products used in large nonavionic applications. He founded the company along very nontraditional lines. Koski believed that such standard management tools as organization charts and quality control departments were tremendously destructive of outstanding performance, and he proposed (in his initial business plan) an organization that would eschew all forms of hierarchy. His firm would have no organization chart. Workers would themselves determine what they would do day-by-day, self-organized into informal work teams as needed. Decisions would be delegated to the "soldiers" in the organization. All information (except for information about compensation) would be shared within the organization.

In the year ending in June 1997 (six months after its initial public offering), Sun's sales were $56.8 million. Its products had lower prices and (apparently) higher margins than the products of competitors, and Sun enjoyed a reputation among its clientele for outstanding quality. The operations in Sarasota had expanded to about 340 employees, of whom over 80% are engaged in manufacturing functions, over 10% are in engineering and marketing functions (Koski asserts that of the ten most creative hydraulic engineers in the United States, Sun employs a majority), and the remainder are "office" people performing other support functions. Two successful foreign subsidiaries exist—one in England (70 employees), and the other in Germany (10 employees). A second, largely independent plant opened in the Sarasota area, in March 1997.

The organizational "structure" (in quotes because there isn't a formal structure) is as Koski initially envisioned. There are no organization charts, reporting relationships, job descriptions, or titles. (To deal with State of Florida incorporation laws, there are a President and Controller. And according to the Harvard case on Sun, one worker who had decided on her own to tend the hundreds of house plants in the Sarasota facility has styled herself as the company's Plant Manager.) Work is self-organized. Natural teams have formed (and reformed as necessary) spontaneously to organize work, but individual workers retain the right and responsibility to choose how they spend their own time. Teams self-select "leads." Production is "job shop" in character (meaning that scheduling is all-important), but line workers, possessed of all necessary information, turn out product efficiently, both in terms of time required and costs incurred. Computer software to aid in scheduling was developed internally and was so successful that Sun has developed an ancillary business to sell the software. Koski, worried for awhile that the organization would not survive his retirement, has already arranged his succession; Clyde Nixon is now the president, and Koski has gone back (largely) to engineering.

Students encountering a much more detailed version of this story (in the Harvard cases) are sometimes skeptical. But Sun and Koski have been nice enough to allow some of our MBA students to go on a plant tour—actually, they mostly just wander around—and those that have made the trip have come back zealots, the more so the more skeptical they were going in.

How does this work? How does this extraordinary organization hold itself together? From the perspective of this chapter (and the next), two basic forces seem to be at work. From the perspective of this chapter, there is a very strong implicit contract among all the workers at Sun—in return for work at good wages, in very good conditions, in an extremely nice locale, and with unparalleled opportunities for autonomy and creativity, workers are responsible for getting product done in a timely and efficient manner. Peer pressure is strong—in such a (relatively) small facility, a lot of workers' social life is bound up with their workmates, strengthening the forces of peer pressure. The nature of the implicit contract is relatively clear and straightforward (but see below for some caveats). And, at the same time, the nature of work at Sun and the relatively small numbers of employees have led workers to internalize the welfare of their workmates and the firm—the preferences of workers increasingly reflect a desire to see Sun and the people at Sun do well.

To add three further points to these basic themes: (1) Sun has a strong reputation as an employer in the Sarasota region and, among fluid power engineers, in the engineering community, a reputation that screens for individuals whose tastes for work and working conditions fit well with Sun. Turnover at Sun is low in general; it is (relatively) higher for new employees who learn quickly whether they fit in or not, but even new employees come with a lot of knowledge about what working at Sun means. (2) After almost thirty years, and given the extraordinary nature of Sun's employment system, it is perhaps not surprising that Sun has a strong reputation in Sarasota. But how did this begin? How was Koski able to attract his initial employees to what many people, accustomed to more traditional forms of management, initially think is a hare-brained, can't-work scheme?

Koski asserts that among his earliest hires was an operator with a strong reputation in the community—having convinced this individual that he (Koski) was serious and worth a gamble, this individual could "lend" Koski reputational capital, just as Koski borrowed financial capital from other sources. (3) Sun Hydraulics enjoys a very strong reputation for quality and ethical behavior among customers as well. And Koski points here as well to the early days of the business. After filling his first major order, he became concerned that there was a small chance that the product was defective. Koski immediately called back the product to check and rework, which was extremely expensive for him, especially for a new business with negative cash flows. It turned out that the defect wasn't there. But the reputation Koski "bought" in this fashion was (he asserts) crucial in winning the loyalty of Sun's clientele.

The story seems—and is—quite inspirational. Yet there are certainly potential problems and limitations with Sun's HRM system. (1) Sun is a very successful company, but it is not and never will be an industrial giant. It is not clear that Sun Microsystems could function with a system so radical as this. (But this is not to say that large organizations can't learn from Sun Hydraulics. See Chapter 9, which discusses high-commitment HR in general.) Indeed, management at Sun Hydraulics recognizes this; a second facility in Sarasota was opened because Sun decided that the first facility was close to the largest size at which their HR system could be sustained. (2) Sun has had difficulty getting some less "sexy" tasks done. For instance, for a long time Sun operated without an up-to-date product catalog—a real marketing disadvantage—because no one would step forward to take charge of first creating and then maintaining a catalog. (3) People at Sun sometimes worry that as the company matures, "new ventures" such as the scheduling-software business will mushroom and dull the company's focus on its core business. (4) Going back to the five factors from Chapter 2, it is not difficult to imagine settings in which the costs and pitfalls of the Sun Hydraulics approach would loom larger and the potential benefits of their model would be much smaller.[19]

TAKEAWAYS

The economic framework we've outlined here will be an important touchstone for our study of HR policies and practices throughout this book. Notions of employee and employer trust, decision-rights and privileges, enhancement of reputation, and the like will prove quite important when we get to the nuts and bolts of HRM. But even before we get to those nuts and bolts, the framework suggests some points that merit emphasis.

Perhaps the most important point concerns the practical application of these ideas in a specific setting. We suggest that, confronted with a specific organization, you begin by answering the following questions:

- How efficient are the employment relationships? Are they appropriately flexible? Are employees and employers willing to contribute to the common good? Are the parties involved making appropriate (efficiency-enhancing) investments in human capital?

- In what ways are employment relations open-ended? In what ways are they tied down by contract or law?

- Who makes important decisions about how the open clauses are filled in? Is this party the appropriate decision-maker, in terms of possessing relevant information and the capability of using it?

- What relation-specific assets bind employees to employer, and vice versa?

- To the extent that parties are at risk (because they hold relation-specific assets but lack decision-making authority over matters that are important to them), what protections do they have? To what extent are the employment terms-of-trade driven solely by the market?

- If there is a lack of cooperation, or flexibility, or investment, what stands in the way? Is it a lack of credible guarantees? If so, what can make those guarantees more credible? Is it simply an adverse set of expectations regarding how cooperation will be met? If so, how can you turn those expectations around?

These are pretty general questions, and we don't pretend that they are easy to answer in a specific case. The first question is particularly difficult; we suggest organizing your analysis of this question in terms of the five factors from Chapter 2. But even an imperfect attempt to answer these questions, especially if done by a team of managers (or employees generally) who bring different perspectives to the table, can help you to diagnose the basic economics of employment in the organization.

As you do so, the following list of general "morals" from this chapter should be kept in mind:

- Just as "goodwill" with customers and a strong brand are acknowledged to be economically valuable—if intangible—assets, so too does employee goodwill and a strong reputation in the labor market represent an enormously valuable asset, which deserves comparable attention.

- To have a clear reputation for what employment means in a given setting, consistency in the organization's HR policies and practices and some measure of continuity in its HR philosophy over time is valuable.

- Reputation depends in large measure on how it is transmitted. You can't (and probably shouldn't) control this transmission. But you should consider whether it might suit your purposes to improve channels of communication among employees.

- Management should weigh very carefully the short-term impact of any actions vis-à-vis employees against the longer-term impact of those actions on the firm's reputation. In particular, it should anticipate the impact of its treatment of a particular employee or subgroup on the expectations of other employees within the organization, especially when employees are interdependent, in close proximity, socially homogeneous, subject to strong peer pressure, or otherwise bonded to one another.

• Reputations, once established, are often difficult to change. It is best to get these right from the start. Organizations seeking to re-craft the expectations that exist between the firm and employees (or to build a set of expectations different from what is standard within the industry or local labor market) will frequently have to take bold, dramatic, and symbolic actions to "unfreeze" the past, perhaps even bringing in new management and/or employees.

• Employee empowerment—an enormously popular idea nowadays—is typically predicated on direct benefits that ensue from granting power and autonomy to employees (see Chapter 9). But the framework of this chapter suggests that an indirect benefit arises through the enhancement of trust in the employee-employer relationship; by giving employees a hammer with which to hit management if management gets out of line, employees can be relatively more assured that management won't get out of line.

BEYOND ECONOMICS

Throughout this book, we'll be exploring the implications of the economic framework in this chapter for particular facets of HRM. Yet the economic framework is clearly lacking in two important respects. The first concerns expectations about what is appropriate, how much reciprocity can be anticipated, and the like. The economic framework makes it quite clear that these expectations are critical drivers of the employment relationship, determining in part whether the relationship achieves efficiency or not. But the framework only points out the importance of those expectations; it doesn't do much at all to identify what they might be in specific cases. We said that these expectations are formed out of experience and from social norms and conventions. If so, then we must be concerned with the cognitive skills and processes of employees and employers: What cues do they attend to? What sort of data will be salient? And to the extent that these expectations are bound up in social conventions and norms held more generally, we must be concerned with those norms and conventions.

The second shortcoming of the economic framework is how it conceives of the interests of the parties in an employment relationship. For the most part, we followed the economist's tradition of assuming that individuals are ultimately self-interested and selfish; the employer and employee could trust each other because the party being trusted was given a self-interested, selfish reason to justify that trust. (That is, the employer doesn't exploit the employee because she fears retaliation, either by the exploited employee himself or by all the employees, responding to her now-sullied reputation.) We paid generous lip service to the notion that employer (and employee) goodwill are important factors in our economic framework.

But we didn't do anything analytical with this idea. The case of Sun Hydraulics makes clear that forces like goodwill are somewhat endogenous, determined, at least in part, by the experiences and social environment of the individual. So to understand employment more fully, we should explain what leads to things like goodwill (or bad will).

These two matters—studying how expectations are formed, and how things like goodwill are created and evolve—take us outside the realm of economics, to psychology and sociology. So we next examine employment through lenses that those disciplines provide.

IN REVIEW

⇒ Employment relations are often—though not always—enduring and open-ended, with details that are left unspecified at the outset being "filled in" on a day-to-day basis.
  • Long-term employment is usually beneficial to both employer and employee.
  • Because employment is open-ended, governance—the rules and procedures by which the "filling in" is done—becomes important.
  • Governance combines legal rights and contractually granted authority with custom and tradition.

⇒ In many employment situations, employees and employer are increasingly "bound" to one another as they develop relation-specific assets, which dulls the discipline of market forces.
  • This can subject either side to the threat of exploitation or a hold-up, leading to inefficient employment relationships if the parties demand inflexible contractual guarantees, refuse to invest in the relation, or simply refuse to contribute to the common good, fearing that any such contributions will go unreciprocated.

⇒ But the threat of hold-up—say, of the employee by the employer—can be defeated by at least three means other than by law or contractual provision:
  • Goodwill on the part of the employer, or an ethical aversion to exploiting employees
  • A balance of power, arising from the credible threat by the employee to retaliate (to the extent possible) if he is exploited
  • The desire of the employer to maintain a reputation generally among employees (and prospective employees) for not being exploitative

⇒ Governance in employment is efficient if decision-making authority vests in a party (called "shc") that: (a) has access to and ability to use information to make efficient decisions; and (b) can be trusted by the other side because, say, she has an adequate reputation stake.

⇛ Several qualifications to the balance-of-power and reputation stories must be given.
- Efficiency is a product of well-designed governance *and* "cooperative" expectations. Neither alone is sufficient.
- Expectations are formed only through time, based on experience, which can make it difficult to change HR practices and policies.
- Trust is destroyed when a party with decision-making authority can take enormous immediate advantage of the other side.
- Reputation faces a free-rider problem that is not always easily solved. Employees are most likely to solve the free-rider problem and sanction an exploitative employer when they are interdependent and/or proximate, socially homogeneous, subject to peer pressure, or organizationally bonded (e.g., through common language, titles, or socialization experiences).
- In both the balance-of-power and reputation stories, the "contract" between parties must be clear, giving a rationale for the sort of consistency discussed in Chapter 3.

⇛ In the balance-of-power and reputation stories, the exact "terms of trade" are not fixed by economic factors alone, but depend on bargaining ability, expectations, social custom, and the like.

⇛ This economic framework is silent in two important ways (taking us to Chapter 5):
- It highlights the crucial importance of the parties' expectations but offers little insight into where those expectations come from.
- It is silent on the formation of things like employer and employee goodwill.

ENDNOTES

1. For textbook treatments, see (respectively): Oliver E. Williamson, *The Economic Institutions of Capitalism* (New York: Free Press, 1985); and David M. Kreps, *A Course in Microeconomic Theory* (Princeton, NJ: Princeton University Press, 1990), Chapter 14.

2. The (in)ability to fire employees at will depends, at least in the United States, on a variety of factors, including (importantly) the organizational level of the employee. For example, boards of directors can generally discharge CEOs at will and without risk of a wrongful discharge lawsuit.

3. But one can certainly think of examples in which an organization would stand to lose more by severing employment relations with star individuals or teams than would the employees involved, particularly if the enterprise has built its strategy around those key personnel (who can ply their trade elsewhere).

4. This is not simply a hypothetical possibility, as we'll discover in Chapter 6.

5. This doesn't necessarily happen, but it is a real possibility. See the discussion concerning extrinsic incentives and intrinsic motivation in Chapter 5.

6. Our discussion in this section is drawn from the classic article by Herbert Simon, "A Formal Theory of the Employment Relationship," *Econometrica* 19 (July 1951): 293–305.

7. Simon, *ibid.*, adds a fourth reason: The task assignments that lead to the greatest immediate profit for the boss may not in fact be onerous for the employees. But to the extent that the employer controls wage levels, she could exploit the employees by paying them wages that are lower than "market wages" but not so far below the market that employees are induced to quit (and suffer the costs of finding a new job, etc.).

8. See, for example, Alvin Roth, Vesna Prasnikar, Masahiro Okuno-Fujiwara, and Shmuel Zamir, "Bargaining and Market Behavior in Jerusalem, Ljubljana, Pittsburgh, and Tokyo: An Experimental Study," *American Economic Review* 81 (December 1991): 1068–95.

9. See Chapter 9.

10. Of course, it bears noting that in each of these cases, the reputational concerns of the service provider are buttressed by the threat of a malpractice suit and by sanctions imposed on the provider by her professional association and colleagues, who seek to preserve a positive collective reputation for themselves.

11. For readers who understand a bit of the subtleties of game-theoretic reputation, a word more about this may be helpful: A virtue of trilateral governance is that the *ex post* response to it is clear cut. If the arbitrator says to do X, then both parties must do X to keep faith with the deal. Hence, trilateral governance rates high in terms of *ex post* observability on both sides, which is a crucial factor in the efficiency of reputation and/or balance of power equilibria. We could achieve similarly high levels of *ex post* observability through the procedure of having each party choose one way to proceed and then flipping a coin to determine which will be adopted, but this can promote extreme demands. Indeed, one form of third-party arbitration (used, for example in some professional sports) has the two parties concerned making specific final offers, and then the arbitrator is constrained to choose between them, according to her (the arbitrator's) sense of which is the more equitable. This scheme promotes reasonable demands by each side, and at the same time gives each side the ability to use the information they possess (in such cases, about their tastes and preferences, and about the range of possible deals) to structure a deal that is more efficient than what we might expect to emerge from a relatively ill-informed arbitrator who had to craft the deal himself.

12. For some of the empirical evidence, see Carl M. Campbell III, "Do Firms Pay Efficiency Wages? Evidence with Data at the Firm Level," *Journal of Labor Economics* 11 (July 1993): 442–70; Alan Krueger and Lawrence H. Summers, "Efficiency Wages and the Inter-industry Wage Structure," *Econometrica* 56 (March 1988): 259–93.

13. It is worth noting, however, that empirical studies tend to show that firms paying premium wages for employees in their core occupations tend also to pay above-average wages for the rest of their workforce (e.g., clerical workers), suggesting perhaps that considerations of internal equity are at work.

14. This line of argument also suggests why organizations seeking to establish and maintain trust with employees might rely more on general norms and codes of conduct and less on specific rules and procedures, even if this exposes the firm to the risk of intentional or unintentional abuses by employees. The cost of excessively detailed rules and procedures is not only that they can hamper managerial and/or employee discretion in some important cases, but also that they send the message that employees are not trustworthy or trusted, which prompts employees to behave accordingly. Afraid to

start down the slippery slope of promulgating rules and procedures, which naturally tend to promote more of the same, a trust-seeking organization may elect instead to adhere to the opposite extreme, preferring to err in the direction of having too few formal controls rather than having too many.

15. We particularly recommend Edward Lazear, *Personnel Economics for Managers* (New York: Wiley, 1998).

16. In Chapter 15 we will study why and when the employer bears the costs of training.

17. Some crimes (e.g., embezzlement, industrial espionage) almost by their very nature presuppose a long-term relationship between the victim and the perpetrator.

18. You can read more about Sun Hydraulics in the Harvard Business School case studies: Louis B. Barnes and Colleen Kaftan, "Sun Hydraulics (A), (B), and (C)" (HBS 9-485-169, 9-485-170, and 9-491-125, respectively).

19. At the same time, one can identify striking examples of other organizations, located in very different business contexts than Sun Hydraulics, which nonetheless seem to have been successful applying an approach similar to Koski's. One well-publicized example is the Brazilian company Semco, which is similar to Sun Hydraulics in many ways, despite facing a very different workforce and economic, social, and cultural environment (including unions). Details on HRM at Semco are provided by CEO Ricardo Semler in his book *Maverick: The Success Story Behind the World's Most Unusual Workplace* (New York: Warner Books, 1993).

5

EMPLOYMENT AS A
SOCIAL RELATION

In the early 1980s, the employees of Delta Airlines presented top management with a gift: a promise to purchase a brand new Boeing 767 airplane for the company.

Motivated by rising evidence of workplace stress and *karoushi* (death from overwork), Japan's Ministry of Labour has been trying since 1986, with little success, to institutionalize a five-day work week and to get workers to increase their use of vacation time.[1]

The Dean of the Stanford Business School appointed a task force of faculty and staff to examine ways of improving the delivery of support services to faculty. The task force found widespread and intense resentment among faculty support staff over being called "secretaries," a title that was perceived to be demeaning and not reflective of their talents and contributions.

A 1991 article in *Sports Illustrated* reported: "On November 22, 1989, . . . the Minnesota Twins made outfielder Kirby Puckett [baseball's] first $3 million-a-year player. Just six days later, the Oakland Athletics agreed to pay outfielder Rickey Henderson roughly the same amount. Their milestone signings opened the floodgates, and today, 16 months later, those two stars are among 40 players making at least $3 million a year. . . . Henderson, last season's American League MVP, now says he was having second thoughts about his four-year, $12 million contract almost from the minute he signed it, and last summer, after teammate Jose Canseco received a five-year, $23.5 million package, Henderson openly complained that he was underpaid. . . . He stayed away from the A's training camp in Phoenix until March 7, eight days past the date he was asked by Oakland to show up and one day after the mandatory major league reporting date. And when he did arrive, he immediately informed the A's that they had until the end of spring training to renegotiate his contract. 'It's pride, period,' Henderson said. 'I don't think my contract is fair. I don't think I'm 40th or 50th on the list. . . .'

'How can a guy making $3 million be underpaid?' Chicago White Sox catcher Carlton Fisk says, referring to Henderson. 'They [complaining players] can go kiss my ass. Whose fault is it? Rickey just signed last year, didn't he?'"[2]

These vignettes underscore an obvious, yet powerful, fact: The employment relationship is about much more than the exchange of labor services for a paycheck. It is an economic relation in part, but it is a potent social and psychological one as well. Effective human resource management depends on process and symbolism no less than on the content and financial value of company personnel policies and practices. Taking a purely economic perspective on employment can blind you to important forces at work in HRM.

For instance, consider the design and administration of compensation and performance evaluation systems. A number of prominent theories in economics and psychology imply that it is invaluable (even essential) to differentiate rewards based on effort and performance, and that informing employees about those reward differences is a prerequisite for an organization to have an effective motivational system. Yet when we look at the data, we often see both substantial pay compression[3] and strenuous attempts by firms to conceal whatever *differentiation* exists in compensation levels. Why? The answer lies in the ways in which people perceive their situation, how they evaluate specific types of treatment and rewards, and what arrangements they view as (il)legitimate.

This chapter concerns some of the cognitive, social psychological, and social forces that impinge on HRM by influencing what employees expect at work and how they perceive, evaluate, and respond to employment policies.[4] Our survey of relevant concepts from cognitive psychology, social psychology, and sociology is not intended to be anything like comprehensive or exhaustive (though it may prove exhausting!). Rather, we focus selectively on a few key cognitive and social-psychological processes and benchmarks that influence how people form expectations and make evaluations, which must be understood to craft effective HR policies and to which we will return in subsequent chapters.

ANCHORING AND EXPECTATIONS

Cognitive psychologists have demonstrated that individuals attend to many cues and sources of information in forming judgments and making sense of social life (including the employment relationship). Recognizing the benchmarks that employees use in making assessments and forming work-related attitudes is critical to understanding employee (dis)satisfaction.

Psychologists have shown that individuals make judgments with reference to various cognitive "anchors" that are available and salient. For instance, in one study a wheel with random numbers on it was spun before asking experimental subjects to guess the ambient room temperature in the room in which they were seated. Subjects' temperature estimates actually gravitated toward the number that came up on the wheel during their particular trial of the experiment! In other words, people anchored their temperature estimates in terms of a reference value (the wheel number), which they knew to be completely meaningless, failing to adjust their estimates adequately away from the initial anchor point.[5] Similar studies have been conducted concerning the pay rates that subjects think various jobs deserve, in which judgments are unduly influenced by arbitrary reference points, such as an estimate provided by someone known to have no relevant knowledge or experience on the subject.[6]

The expectations communicated by others around us can also serve as powerful attitudinal and behavioral anchors. Numerous studies in work settings, schools, and other contexts have documented the powerful effects of expectations on performance. Just communicating the expectation, even ever-so-subtly, that someone will perform well (poorly) makes the person more likely to do so, which suggests that the expected level of performance that is communicated (by co-workers, superiors, etc.) can serve as an anchor in terms of which people adjust their actual behavior.

Such behavioral tendencies have a number of important implications for human resource management. For instance, some surveys have shown that organizations having more generous employment policies and well-defined internal promotion ladders often exhibit higher levels of employee *dis*satisfaction.[7] Anchoring may provide one explanation for this seemingly puzzling finding. In an organization with generous reward possibilities and well-defined career ladders, employees will often develop a clear notion about how far it is possible to advance within a specific period of time. Indeed, recruiters sometimes come to business schools to recruit MBAs, armed with slick charts describing precisely how far and how fast an entry-level manager can expect to progress from position to position within their firms. But an unanticipated effect of such charts and the promotion systems they describe is to encourage employees to assess their career accomplishments by anchoring on the *maximum* attainable rank for a person of a given age or tenure. (Presumably, the same process may take place with respect to salary when there are clearly defined and well-understood salary ranges.) Employees who have accomplished an enormous amount and experienced quite rapid promotion may nonetheless be frustrated or dissatisfied because they aren't focusing on how far they have advanced from the base of the mountain, as it were, but instead on how far away they still are from the summit. By encouraging employees to anchor on how fall short they have fallen relative to the best-case scenario, rather than how much better they have done than the worst case, organizations may inadvertently foster aversive comparisons.[8]

THE PSYCHOLOGY OF ATTRIBUTION AND MOTIVATION

Psychologists argue that individuals come to make attributions about their own attitudes, motivations, and behaviors from observing their conduct and trying to infer what caused the behavior. Moreover, these attributions can have powerful effects on our future conduct.

Commitment

One manifestation of these processes of attribution and self-perception concerns the formation of commitment. The balance between effort and reward has powerful effects on the attributions people make about why they engage in certain behaviors. For instance, it possible to induce commitment by persuading individuals to expend considerable effort on an activity in the absence of a clear external reward for doing so. Psychologists call this *insufficient justification*; unable to identify a clear external rationale for exerting effort on a task, the person can either believe that the effort was wasted or, alternatively, that there was some higher purpose served by the effort. Because we generally dislike perceiving ourselves as having done things that are foolish or that lack efficacy, there is a tendency to take the other cognitive route and divine a higher purpose in our behavior, thereby psychologically inducing commitment to that course of conduct.

The process of commitment has a strong self-reinforcing quality. The more we invest in a specific course of conduct, the more difficult it is psychologically to abandon that path, and therefore the stronger the inclination is to reaffirm our commitment to the activity. This process of *escalating commitment* is strongest when the person got involved in the activity voluntarily (rather than through coercion), has exerted considerable effort, has done so visibly and publicly, and when the course of conduct is difficult or impossible to undo.

Intrinsic versus Extrinsic Motivation

These processes of attribution and self-perception have implications for how individuals come to perceive their motivations for engaging in certain behaviors. Numerous psychological studies of adults and children have shown that calling attention to external (especially monetary) rationales for behavior can diminish performance and intrinsic motivation (i.e., the desire to perform an activity because of inherent enjoyment of the activity and the desire to improve). This is especially likely when the tasks involved are either inherently interesting or involve substantial cognition and initiative. As in the case of commitment, the underlying argument is that people come to make attributions about themselves and their motivations from observing their own behavior. Perceiving that they needed to be externally and financially induced to carry out a task, people come to the point of view that they must not have had any other motivation for performing that task. Thus, it may be possible to stifle a person's underlying intrinsic motivation by calling attention to strong external rationales for his or her behavior, especially if the person was already inclined to engage in that behavior without the external inducements.

Consider, for instance, the issue of how frequently to evaluate performance and dispense rewards. Edward Lazear shows that, according to economic principles, employees prefer more frequently timed evaluations and rewards (rather than, say, equivalent career-end balloon payments): More frequent assessments and payouts help the individual learn more about the quality of his or her match with the employer. This positive value of information for employees is then to be traded off against the cost of acquiring and providing that information.[9]

But this economic analysis ignores a second impact of frequent performance evaluation and reward on employees: As Edward Deci has shown experimentally, frequent evaluation and reward can have a *controlling* element, whereby the person cognitively is "controlled" by the reward and comes to perceives the locus of causality as external.[10] Individuals may wish to avoid perceiving their own actions as extrinsically motivated and to avoid having their actions perceived in that light by relevant others. Systems of workplace control, performance evaluation, and reward allocation that frequently and conspicuously call attention to the formal calculation of rewards and sanctions associated with an employee's conduct are therefore likely to encourage employees to attribute their behavior purely to the desire to garner those rewards (or avoid those sanctions).[11] Where intrinsic motivation can be effective, economic considerations alone may lead to too-frequent evaluation and reward.

This argument is consistent with evidence about the disdain with which employees often view piece-rate compensation schemes. Amitai Etzioni has argued that workers find the control of their behavior via blatant pecuniary incentives such as piece rates "alienating" and "dehumanizing." Similarly, Ronald Dore writes that "there is a further, intangible cost [of piece rates] in disaffection and suspicion. Because the whole system is geared to keep their earnings level constantly salient in the workers' consciousness, they carefully calculate what their earnings *ought* to be."[12] We do not mean to condemn piece-rate systems or pay-for-performance categorically; in some contexts, these incentive devices can be quite beneficial. (See Chapter 11 for more on when and where.) But there is no doubt that the benefits of such systems can be considerably compromised when the systems undermine workers' intrinsic motivation.

The same basic idea has broader ramifications. For instance, recall a point we made in Chapter 4: Implicit motivations for cooperation in an employment relationship—such as viewing cooperation as ethical or perceiving the other party's welfare as important to you—may be dulled when the parties involved negotiate and formalize in advance the extent of their cooperation. In such cases, the parties are more likely to attribute their cooperative behavior purely to external influences—for instance, a desire to avoid contractual penalties or a lawsuit—and hence to infer that this is in fact what motivates their cooperation. Along the same lines, when employees are subjected to close external monitoring or surveillance, they may draw the psychological inference that they are not trusted and thus not trustworthy, acting in ways that reinforce that perception.[13] Recall an observation we made about Hewlett-Packard in Chapter 3: An organization (like H-P) that offers employees wide discretion in choosing and executing tasks and that encourages participatory decision-making should be very wary of intrusive monitoring and surveillance, because the combination could be deadly—workers infer that they are not trusted (and thus not trust*worthy*) and yet have wide latitude in performing their jobs.

An anecdote to illustrate the practical relevance of this theory concerns an executive who managed to dampen intrinsic motivation markedly by encouraging employees to make materialistic attributions for their own behavior. During the mid-1980s, corporate law firms dramatically increased the salaries paid to associate (non-partner) attorneys. The increases were prompted initially by large raises given by the firm of Cravath, Swaine, and Moore in New York to its attorneys, prompting their direct competitors in the labor market to match Cravath's lucrative salary schedule.[14] Corporate associates throughout the country waited in eager anticipation to see how much of these increases would trickle down. Responding to these pressures, the partners of a large corporate law firm headquartered in San Francisco decided to adjust associate salaries upward to restore the previous relationship between its starting salaries and those offered by the large New York law firms. This decision was announced at a general meeting of the associates.

Imagine that the associates were randomly assigned to hear one of two different versions of a presentation being given by the same managing partner, explaining the rationale for the raises. In the first speech, the managing partner explains that the raise was "forced" by the large raises being doled out by law partnerships in New York. He notes that "when the cost of lemons goes up, lemonade manufacturers have to pay more or they will be unable to buy lemons of the same quality as in the past." The managing partner underscores that this raise is not being paid because the associates had earned it, but simply because the partners were afraid that the associates might jump ship if their compensation wasn't increased a similar percentage.

In version two of the speech, the managing partner makes an announcement along the following lines: "We all know that law firms are facing salary pressures. Obviously, our firm needs to remain competitive, and so we shall. [Here, the managing partner succinctly spells out the details of the raises.] Let me hasten to point out that we understand that what will keep you here and stimulated in the long run is our firm's sterling reputation, the caliber of our clients, the extraordinary legal minds who work here, the interesting work we provide, and the training and mentorship we offer. We appreciate all the important contributions each of you makes every day. We're delighted to be able to match the competition on salary, and we'll keep working to make it hard for them to match us on all the other, truly important dimensions that make for a great law firm."

Given that the associates' wealth would be completely unaffected by the content of the speech, would the content have any effect on the reactions of associates? It is impossible to know, because, not surprisingly, the law firm did not carry out this intriguing experiment. Had they done so, we would have expected the raise to produce a positive motivational boost among the associates who heard the second version of the speech. At worst, there is no reason to expect that speech to do any harm (unless it is perceived as hypocritical). What we *do* know, however, is what happened when version one was communicated, because this is the essence of the speech that the managing partner actually delivered, including the lemons analogy. Needless to say, this announcement did *not* have desirable effects on the lawyers. The associates left the meeting much wealthier—about a 33% pay increase for starting associates, who had been at the firm only a month or two—and significantly angrier and demotivated.

There are some powerful psychological reasons for expecting this episode to have demotivated the attorneys in this firm. To be sure, corporate lawyers care about their compensation; the fact that the law firm felt obliged to match the competition suggests that they perceived this to be the case, and indeed one of the factors precipitating the initial pay hikes in New York was the fact that lawyers doing deals with investment bankers were becoming tempted by the prospect of the higher compensation received by those bankers. But the point here is not whether the lawyers care about money. The key points are: There are strong reasons (including the professional socialization of lawyers) for the associates to want to *perceive* themselves as being motivated by things other than money; and, more importantly, it is advantageous for the firm to have lawyers who perceive themselves to be motivated less by money and more by intrinsic rewards such as the reputation and quality of the firm and its clients, the variety and challenge associated with the legal work, the co-workers, and the amount of training and mentorship provided.[15] Although associates at this firm might have departed over money, they certainly wouldn't have *stayed* simply for money. But what the managing partner's speech communicated, in stark and explicit terms, was: "We know you're here for the money. Here it is. Now get back to work."

Should the law firm have matched its competitors' salary offers? Absolutely. We are not suggesting that people shouldn't be paid (even handsomely) for their efforts. What is critical here are the kinds of attributions and self-perceptions that a given reward system encourages people to make. In the law firm case, it is quite clear that the way the raises were explained encouraged the attorneys to perceive themselves as money-grubbing mercenaries. This undercuts the significance of various other motivations that not only are potentially cheaper to the law firm, but that also distinguish it more from its competitors, who all pay the same wages. Moreover, the speech sent the psychological message to the lawyers: *You are in this simply for the money.* Lawyers who perceive themselves in that light are unlikely to exert the same quality or quantity of effort on behalf of the firm and its clients.

How Prevalent Is Intrinsic Motivation?

Admittedly, some jobs provide few opportunities for intrinsic motivation. Someone cleaning toilets in a hospital may be able to derive some pride from making a contribution (however indirect) to health care, but it's harder to imagine such lofty motivations operating for the person who cleans toilets in a bowling alley. Yet intrinsic motivation is perhaps more generic, more important, and more valuable to organizations than we often recognize.

For instance, consider some survey results from the 1977 "Quality of Employment Survey."[16] According to this survey, a large percentage of employees seem motivated at work by something other than the compensation received. For instance, 76.3% disagreed with the statement that "I'd be happier if I didn't have to work at all." In the same vein, 72% responded that they'd continue to work even if they were already financially comfortable for the rest of their lives. Half the survey respondents agreed with an item stating that "what I do at work is more important to me than the money I earn," and an even higher percentage expressed disagreement with the statement that their main interest in working was to get money in order to do other things. Finally, more than 58% reported that they put "a lot" of extra physical or mental effort into their jobs beyond that which is required, and another 35% said they expend at least "some" effort above what is required.[17] More recent workplace surveys corroborate these findings.

The Value of Intrinsic Motivation

As we noted in the law firm example, having employees who are motivated by intrinsic elements of the job itself offers a variety of advantages. Obviously, it may not be necessary for the organization to expend as much on incentives and elaborate control technologies if employees are intrinsically motivated to do a good job. Moreover, in many jobs, workers can survive by doing a merely satisfactory job, but the organization seeks outcomes that are better than satisfactory. Intrinsic motivation is often the most powerful way of getting a worker to take the extra steps to move from "satisfactory" to "more than satisfactory." This is particularly true if trying to move to "more than satisfactory" is risky—for instance, in jobs involving innovation, risk taking, and the like. It is often extremely difficult to induce the optimal mix of risk taking and risk avoidance through explicit incentives, whereas an employee who is motivated by innate curiosity, a drive to excel, or personal growth may naturally be more willing to take more risks of the type the firm would like.

Summary

The psychological literature on attribution and social perception suggests that we form attachments to courses of action through a cognitive process of reconciling our behaviors with our beliefs and making attributions about the causes of our behavior. The key point of this discussion is to emphasize how an organization's HR practices (and the processes by which those practices are implemented) can affect commitment and motivation, sometimes in ways that those who design and implement those practices did not anticipate. Accordingly, as we analyze specific elements of HRM throughout this book, we will want to consider carefully how specific policies and their implementation are likely to influence the kinds of attributions and inferences that employees make about their motivations and their ties to the organization.

SOCIAL COMPARISON

People often make inferences and form judgments using others as points of reference. Rickey Henderson, the baseball player (mentioned at the outset of this chapter) who was originally thrilled to sign a contract for $3,000,000 per year, became indignant once other players began to make as much or more money. People care deeply about relative, not just absolute, standing, a fact that is painfully obvious when you observe the ferocity with which academics maneuver, plot, and fret concerning differences in resources that would be clinically imperceptible to many readers of this book. (Henry Kissinger, himself a former professor, is reported to have once quipped that academic politics are so vicious because the stakes are so low.) In this section, we summarize some of psychologists' main findings about social comparison processes, which will have important implications in subsequent chapters concerning particular domains of HRM.[18]

First, there are many motives for social comparison, which influence the referents that individuals are likely to use in gauging their behavior or outcomes. In some cases, particularly when self-esteem may be threatened, individuals seek self-enhancement through social comparison, searching for individuals whose situation or performance is worse than their own to promote a sense of superiority. Interviews of breast cancer victims, for instance, reveal that they frequently cope by comparing themselves to others who are even less fortunate (downward comparisons).[19] Similar patterns have been discovered for individuals facing job disruptions and other employment-related events.[20] On other occasions, individuals seeking to improve or motivate themselves may make upward comparisons.

In general, however, many (if not most) of the social comparisons people make are motivated by a desire for self-evaluation or self-definition, to assess how one stacks up against some relevant individual or group of individuals. For such purposes, individuals exhibit a strong tendency to make social comparisons vis-à-vis individuals who are similar to themselves. Similarity here is a function of both personal characteristics—such as age, gender, education—and being in a similar situation (for instance, within a work organization, in the same occupation, job title, department, or entry cohort).

There are several reasons for similarity-based comparisons. First of all, for diagnostic purposes, comparisons vis-à-vis similarly-situated individuals are obviously the most informative. If an engineer at Renault wishes to gauge how well she is performing or how well she is being treated, there is likely to be little information gained by comparing herself to the CEO of Deutsche Telekom. A second reason for similarity-based comparisons is that we typically have the most information about people similar to ourselves. On a personal level, it is well known that people are attracted to others like themselves, which means that the available referents for most people will tend to have similar characteristics. Furthermore, it is often easiest for us to make comparisons against those who are in the same organizational situation (e.g., the same department, rank, entry cohort) and in our social network, because these are the people with whom we generally tend to interact the most. In most organizations, interaction patterns will be circumscribed to a large degree by job title, department, rank, date of entry, and the like, which again will reinforce the tendency for individuals to make social comparisons against people who are like themselves and in similar organizational situations.

This suggests that formal organizational categories are likely to shape the kinds of social comparisons employees can and do make, and that organizations can more readily differentiate among employees in allocating pay or other valued rewards when more extensive formal distinctions prevail among individuals. Differentiating among employees in terms of treatment and rewards will generally be most problematic when the employees are: socially homogeneous; personally close; working in close proximity with one another; working interdependently; and knowledgeable about the differentials. But the causal arrows operate in the opposite direction as well: The existence of wide reward differentials has been shown to act as an impediment to developing close, interdependent working relations.

The tendency for reward differentials based on category membership to be viewed as more legitimate no doubt helps explain why pay is so often attached to job titles, rather than to individuals, within organizations. Psychological studies have shown that even when individuals are assigned to categories that they know to be clearly random or arbitrary, they will tend to internalize an identification with the category and come to perceive members of the category as more alike and members of other (random) categories as more different.[21] This process presumably provides some psychological basis for justifying differences in treatment across categories.

This is not to suggest, of course, that organizations should always tie pay rates to job titles or some other categorical designation. Contemporary organizations are experimenting with many innovations in pay systems that move in the opposite direction, toward greater individuation in pay. We will have much more to say on these topics in subsequent chapters. Here we are simply making the point that to the extent that individuals in an organization are similarly situated or perceive themselves as similar, efforts to differentiate them in terms of rewards and treatment are likely to be more contentious and harder to justify. For instance, we noted in Chapter 3 how organizations seeking to implement two-tiered employment systems or to utilize contingent workers often rely on subtle devices to reinforce differentiation between the two groups, including differences in: formal job titles and/or informal labels; shift assignments or geographical locations; employee uniforms and badge colors; demographic attributes of the two workforces (e.g., gender, ethnicity, age); reward and benefit entitlements; and access to company social events.

CATEGORIZATION PROCESSES IN ORGANIZATIONS

Because monetary and nonmonetary rewards in many organizations are so often attached primarily to jobs or other categorical distinctions, rather than to individuals, the topic of where the categories come from is very significant. Organizational categories are important because they shape social comparison processes (and, in turn, reward allocations).

Many treatments of the division of labor in organizations presume that "jobs" represent neutral, logical, and efficient bundles of interrelated activity that somehow emerge naturally. However, a variety of studies suggest some powerful social and psychological forces that shape how activities actually get bundled, differentiated, and ultimately categorized into jobs.

In-Group Biases

First, the identity of the person or persons doing the categorization—the membership of the "in-group"—can have important effects on the categorization itself. One such in-group bias is a tendency for members of the in-group to distinguish its members from nonmembers. This tendency is well documented when it comes to gender and job classification, where men are the in-group. A study of the California state (government) civil service system found that, all else being equal, job title distinctions were greatest within those lines of work (occupations) that were most balanced in their race and gender composition, and these distinctions reintroduced segregation by race and gender.[22] In a large sample of California (private and public sector) work enterprises, more than 75% of the individuals classified as "personnel managers" were male, while five-sixths of the "personnel clerks" were female. This tendency was evident *even in organizations in which there was no more than one full-time equivalent position devoted to personnel duties.*[23] Focusing exclusively on establishments with one full-time (or part-time) personnel specialist makes it reasonable to assume that the personnel-related tasks involved were fairly similar across organizations. Moreover, if there is no more than one full-time equivalent personnel specialist, it is hard to believe that a "personnel manager" is really doing much managing, as there are no subordinates specializing in personnel to manage.

Why would in-group members seek to foster and preserve separations from outsiders? For one thing, members of the in-group report higher job-related psychological well-being in segregated settings. And this sort of separation can be used to rationalize pay inequality along social and demographic lines within organizations. Researchers have demonstrated that jobs done primarily by women and nonwhites tend to be devalued socially and economically (e.g., to have prescribed pay rates lower than otherwise comparable jobs staffed primarily by white males).[24]

A second in-group bias concerns the fineness of distinctions. People generally are able to make finer distinctions among people like themselves. For example, an economist can make many more distinctions among a representative set of one hundred economists than she can among one hundred representative sociologists, and she may be hard pressed indeed to see many distinctions among one hundred representative scholars of French literature. Experimental studies have shown that even perceptions of facial distinctions and behavioral and personality characteristics are more fine-grained among member's of one's own group. Out-group members, in contrast, are typically perceived as being more similar to one another, with actual differences among them minimized.[25] The tendency toward in-group bias suggests, for instance, that engineers would recognize more distinctions among engineering employees than are likely to be recognized by marketers; therefore, if people in a position to determine the formal job structure of the organization are engineers (or identify with engineers), we would expect to see finer vertical and horizontal distinctions made among those engaged in engineering activities within the company.[26]

One way of illustrating this sort of in-group bias within the work setting is to look at when organizations are most likely to proliferate job titles. The most extreme case of differentiation involves crafting a distinct category (job title) for a single individual. We expect one-person job categories in organizations to be populated primarily by people from powerful or favored in-groups, because finer distinctions are recognized among their duties and abilities. In the world of work, in-group and out-group membership is largely (although not exclusively) defined by gender and race, so we would expect to see one-person job titles filled disproportionately by white males. This is exactly what we find, even when we look *within* high-status and highly paid categories.[27]

Where finer job category distinctions are made, we expect to see (and do in fact find) greater pay dispersion. But this fineness bias has also been used to rationalize pay inequality. A study of the Washington state civil service system showed that external market surveys were used more often in setting the wages of female-dominated job classifications. This was justified on the grounds that female-dominated job classifications were bigger and less internally differentiated, whereas activities done by males were more finely subdivided into specialized jobs, having fewer incumbents and less likelihood of a clear counterpart on the external labor market. Explaining the lower pay of women in Washington's state government with reference to "market forces" thus overlooks the systematic manner in which jobs were differentiated along gender lines, in ways that, in turn, insulated men more from external market comparisons.[28]

Divide and Conquer

Besides being used to elevate the in-group, it is sometimes argued that employers exploit the power of formal distinctions to subdivide the remaining workforce in particular ways, to set one group or category off against another, rather than encouraging them to identify with one another in terms of an overarching common identity. In the early 1980s, for instance, the Diamond Shamrock Corporation faced an intense effort to unionize chemical workers in one of its U.S. plants. One of the company's strategies for responding to its disgruntled workforce was to subdivide the chemical operatives into horizontally and vertically differentiated job categories (i.e., a set of specialties and a set of rank distinctions).[29] Some students of organizations, especially those with a Marxist orientation, have argued that employers deliberately create such formal divisions and foster rivalries along gender, ethnic, and related lines, to weaken the collective power of labor. By creating job titles corresponding to specialized tasks and a set of graded ranks, these authors would argue, Diamond Shamrock was able to differentiate among various groups of employees and foster a preoccupation with rank among the chemical workers, thereby undercutting an overarching collective identity among the workforce that might have fostered unionization.

DISTRIBUTIVE AND PROCEDURAL JUSTICE

People care deeply about being treated fairly. Research in experimental and real-world settings—for instance, in the workplace, the criminal justice system, and schools—has demonstrated that perceptions of justice exercise powerful effects on how individuals and groups respond to their treatment within an organization or institutional domain. Not surprisingly, those people receiving the most favorable treatment on an absolute basis tend to perceive things as most just. Nonetheless, the evidence suggests that people can and do distinguish their own absolute outcomes from two key dimensions of justice: *distributive,* or how they did relative to others; and *procedural,* the process by which the outcome was achieved.

These two dimensions have somewhat different impacts on the employee. Distributive justice perceptions seem to be consistently related to workers' satisfaction with their jobs and pay, whereas perceptions of procedural justice seem to be more strongly related to perceptions of the supervisor, attachment to the organization, and willingness to engage in various kinds of "organizational citizenship behavior."[30]

Distributive Justice

Distributive justice concerns whether people believe that outcomes or rewards are allocated among people in a way that is fair and equitable. *Equality* is one allocation norm that is sometimes espoused, especially in settings where group members are close to one another and/or it is difficult, costly, or contentious to try and pinpoint precisely who did what and with what effect. Another entitlement norm sometimes employed emphasizes *needs,* though this is much less prevalent in work settings than in other social settings, such as families, voluntary organizations, and educational institutions. A third justice principle that has been shown to prevail in many settings, especially where performance varies significantly across individuals, is *simple equity.* According to the equity principle, individuals ought to be rewarded commensurate with the outcomes they generate, factoring in the inputs—effort, ability, and so on—they brought to bear in performing the task.

Of course, it's often much trickier in practice than in theory to define what outputs and inputs ought to be considered in creating an equitable reward formula.[31] Consequently, we often observe reward systems that pursue distributive justice through other means. Seniority, for instance, is a popular allocation principle that does not directly reward performance, except insofar as retention decisions are based on performance and acceptable performance is therefore a prerequisite for attaining high seniority. But seniority is a reward principle that tends to be seen as fair in a variety of circumstances, because it is a basis for allocating rewards from which every employee can expect to benefit eventually and because it can be measured objectively and precisely. Seniority is especially likely to be employed in allocating rewards when production is interdependent or when the consequences of employees' actions cannot be discerned for a long while.

What employees will perceive to be distributively just obviously depends on a variety of factors, many of which we will discuss in subsequent chapters. There are important cultural variations here; for instance, in some Asian societies, age and gender were seen as just bases for allocating rewards, in contrast to the state of affairs in the United States. Criteria for gauging justice may also vary across occupational groups, demographic groups, and types of organizations and industries.

What matters, of course, is not whether a reward system or other employment practice is just in some absolute sense, but rather what employees *perceive.* Consequently, efforts to demonstrate internal and external equity are crucial in establishing perceptions of distributive justice. Seemingly objective data can be remarkably persuasive in creating such perceptions, even when the consumers of such data recognize the subjectivity involved. For instance, each year the Stanford University faculty–staff newspaper publishes charts showing salary distributions by rank and department for Stanford faculty. (The charts typically show the 25th, 50th, and 75th percentile for salary plotted against years of experience for faculty at a particular rank in a specific part of the University.) Everyone seems to know that these data are cooked in a variety of conspicuous ways. For example, economics professors, who make more than other social science professors, are grouped in with natural science professors so as not to make the other social scientists feel too bad.[32] Many private side deals involving hidden compensation are presumably not represented in these plots, and so on. And yet our faculty colleagues nonetheless seem to focus quite a bit of attention on gauging where they show up in such plots relative to others. Consistent with the literature on anchoring we discussed previously, it is as if people cannot avoid utilizing information they are given for comparison purposes, even if they recognize that the information has been deliberately concocted in order to influence how they will construe it.

The key points to keep in mind for now are: Perceptions of distributive justice matter a lot; they are not simply a function of how people are treated objectively; and perceptions of distributive justice appear to be susceptible to influence.

Procedural Justice

Whether we are talking about bonus awards, performance reviews, decisions about who should participate in a special training program, or who receives a plum assignment, employees will have strong perceptions not only about whether the outcome itself was fair, but also about whether the processes and procedures used to make the decision were fair. Not surprisingly, perceptions of procedural justice tend to be correlated with perceptions of distributive justice (if you think the outcome was fair, you are more likely to believe the process was fair, and vice versa), and to be correlated with how well the person fared in absolute terms (if you fail to be promoted, you are less likely to think the selection process was fair than is your colleague who *was* promoted). Nonetheless, evidence suggests that perceptions of procedural justice are distinct and have important implications for organizations.

The key findings in the literature on procedural justice are that people generally judge procedures to be more fair when: decisions or allocations are based on criteria that are valid (job-related), consistently applied, and clearly explained; the procedures used reinforce and are consistent with the organizational culture (e.g., if the culture espouses the virtues of open communication, then the process is conducted openly); the principles or procedures used do not denigrate the individual (e.g., performance reviews are conducted in a way that does not humiliate or belittle employees) or encroach on personal privacy; the people involved in determining the decision outcome are perceived to be competent and not to have a vested interest in the decision outcome; individuals are given ample opportunity to participate in the decision process and to respond to negative allegations or evaluations; and there are established mechanisms for individuals to appeal or grieve unfavorable outcomes.

RECIPROCITY AND GIFT EXCHANGE

Closely related to the idea of equity is sociologists' notion of a ubiquitous *norm of reciprocity,* whereby individuals feel strongly that:

> (1) people should help those who have helped them, and (2) people should not injure those who have helped them. . . . Such obligations of repayment are contingent upon the imputed value of the benefit received. The value of the benefit and hence the debt is in proportion to and varies with—among other things—the intensity of the recipient's need at the time the benefit was bestowed ("a friend in need . . ."), the resources of the donor ("he gave although he could ill afford it"), the motives imputed to the donor ("without thought of gain"), and the nature of the constraints which are perceived to exist or to be absent ("he gave of his own free will"). Thus, the obligations imposed by the norm of reciprocity may vary with the status of the participants within a society.[33]

Sociologists' ideas about reciprocity thus provide another rationale for long-term employment relations, internal labor markets, and efficiency wages, which previous chapters have rationalized primarily in economic terms (e.g., as encouraging firm-specific human capital investment, reducing opportunism, etc.). The logic of reciprocity suggests that employers benefit from offering employees stable, long-term employment, above-market pay, and opportunities for internal advancement and career growth in part because these represent gifts that employees feel obliged to reciprocate through increased loyalty and effort.

Note well that the extent of obligation that a gift creates depends on perceptions of the recipient's need, how affluent the donor is, and how pure are the donor's motives. It is hard to imagine that a colleague creates much obligation on your part by giving you a fruit cake that you know she received as a gift long ago and has been waiting to pawn off on someone else, or if you know full well that your boss gave you a holiday gift instead of a bonus purely as an income-tax-avoidance device. The psychological impact of providing tangible or intangible gifts to employees is likely to depend not only on the magnitude of the gifts, but also on the gifts being seen as: sincere and benevolent, rather than selfishly motivated; having a symbolic or nonmonetary significance, rather than purely equivalent to or a substitute for cash compensation; tailored to the needs of the recipient; and costly to the donor in terms of time or effort. Thus to reap the same motivational benefits, an organization's "gift exchange" regime would have to become more magnanimous: as employees become better off (less needy); as the organization comes to be perceived as more affluent; and as a given gift exchange practice becomes more commonplace among competing organizations.

Organizations obviously can—and do—manipulate employees' perceptions of these things, which can have huge effects on the motivational benefits received through gift exchange. For instance, within academia (and, we presume, most industries), there is usually a strong "home court advantage" in recruiting wars when a faculty member receives an attractive outside offer from another institution. In large part, the advantage stems from the obvious costs of moving. But there are other components: The individual's current employer has better information about the individual's tastes, and the individual knows more about what can or cannot be done for her. Information isn't an unalloyed good; it is harder for the home team to turn down a request with the excuse that "we can't do that administratively," when it is apparent to everyone that they just did. But the home team usually has somewhat more ability to match the tastes and desires of the individual both materially and symbolically. And, to the current point, the home team is often better able to dress up the offer as a gift. The home institution is often agonizingly slow and recalcitrant in responding, but at the very last minute, fever-pitch negotiations and Herculean efforts, often involving management at the highest levels, produce a package that induces the person to stay. This often conveys how enormously difficult, time consuming, and costly it has been to amass a satisfactory response, creating a much stronger sense of obligation and gratitude on the part of the recipient.

Conversely, there are also things that organizations can do to undercut the gift exchange properties of things they do for employees. For example, Cisco Systems is a rapidly growing high-tech firm that is the world leader in networking technology. In its early days, Cisco provided free nonalcoholic beverages to employees, who often worked eighty-hour weeks. After having grown to more than 1,500 employees in the early 1990s, the company found it was supplying more than 80 different selections (including four varieties of mineral water), at an annual cost of roughly $1,200,000. Cisco's purchasing department undertook not to eliminate the benefit but simply to reduce by 50% the number of available selections, hoping to reduce costs through greater purchase volumes on a smaller number of beverage brands.

According to John Morgridge, who was CEO at the time, the outpouring of complaints and protests via the company's e-mail system was so intense that it literally shut down their central computer system, suspending normal business operations. The efforts of Cisco's purchasing department jeopardized the gift exchange properties of the free beverage policy in at least two ways: By casting the issue in terms of cost savings, they suggested that these beverages were a "normal" business expense rather than a gift; and for those employees whose favorite beverages were to be eliminated, they undercut the personal element of the gift and the sense that Cisco was providing something especially for them.

STATUS (IN)CONSISTENCY

When individuals attend to their relative standing or status within a particular group or organization, the relevant dimension of status might be pay in one organization, authority level in a second, and technical expertise in a third. The factors that produce status obviously vary among groups of employees and across occupations, organizational contexts, and countries. Yet although money (or authority, or expertise) may be the dominant dimension in a given situation, other dimensions cannot be completely ignored, particularly because studies have shown that people are also attentive to the degree of *consistency* in their statuses across multiple dimensions and across multiple social contexts.

Sometimes an individual occupies high status along one dimension and low status along another. Examples include: the highly compensated salesperson with only a seventh-grade education; the senior executive who is much younger than her subordinates; the task-force leader from Marketing in an Engineering-dominated organization; or the non-physician hospital administrator. This sort of *status inconsistency* can create an incongruity that has been shown to promote various undesirable outcomes. People who occupy wildly different status positions on different social hierarchies face confusion over how they should act and how they should expect to be treated by others. This confusion creates ambiguity and strain, sometimes producing nontrivial psychological (and even medical) maladies.[34]

Accordingly, organizations must be sensitive to what can happen when an individual changes status on one dimension but stays at the same status or loses status on another dimension—for instance, the rapidly promoted superstar whose organizational rank is soon incommensurate with her age or tenure. Moreover, because we occupy many different statuses, including ones derived from activities outside of work, there are abundant opportunities for inconsistency between *organizational status* and *social status*. The literature on the adverse effects of status inconsistency implies that organizations should try to alleviate or mitigate such inconsistencies as well.

An intriguing example of how one company dealt with this challenge involves the early days of Apple Computer. A number of descriptions of the early Apple corporate culture have emphasized the powerful symbolism associated with company badges. Each badge had a prominent number, with the numbers assigned increasing consecutively as additional employees entered the company. Having a very low badge number thus identified someone as a pioneer from the early days, which was highly respected within the company culture.

The badge numbers nicely alleviated a potentially troublesome status inconsistency: In our society, younger and less-educated individuals typically receive lower status than their older, more-educated counterparts. In the early days of Apple, there was a strong imbalance between the high organizational status of Steve Jobs, Steve Wozniak, and other high-ranking pioneers within the company and their relatively low social status along lines of age and education. (Neither Jobs nor Wozniak had graduated from college when they co-founded the company). The badge numbers conveniently made organizational age (tenure) prominent and conspicuous, thereby making chronological age less salient.

The bottom line here is that we cannot understand how someone is treated and rewarded within the work setting in isolation from that person's other social roles, statuses, and characteristics.

LEGITIMACY AND ORGANIZATIONAL INERTIA

As we noted in the last chapter, the employment relationship is fundamentally based on expectations and trust, which typically must be built up gradually over time. Consequently, continuity in employment practices (or at least in broad HRM philosophy) will often be highly advantageous to an organization. Of course, there are "switching costs" associated with making changes in any kind of transaction, such as sourcing components with a new supplier, taking your business to a new law firm, or relocating your physical plant. These costs arise because you (and members of your firm) must learn new routines and reconstruct networks of connections. In trying to alter its HRM practices or premises—either by replacing workers or transforming personnel policies—the employer faces these generic switching costs. In addition, however, changing HRM philosophies, policies, and procedures entails another switching cost that is perhaps less tangible yet no less important: what we might call "legitimation costs."

Much of what makes HRM function smoothly involves employment practices that are traditional, customary, and unquestioned or taken for granted by employees. Dramatic changes in HR practices require that the old order be renegotiated and legitimated anew. For example, early students of labor relations argued that much of the benefit of long-term employment, promotion from within, and the other characteristic features of internal labor markets, such as pegging pay to jobs rather than to individuals, had to do with the *legitimacy* associated with these practices.[35] Analogies were made between modern-day internal labor markets—which tied employees to an organization essentially for life—and feudalism, where the sense of mutual obligation among lords, vassals, and serfs and well-entrenched customs ensured that relationships persisted smoothly and harmoniously across generations. Over time within an internal labor market, it has been argued, a similar set of customs and rules develops that provides an invaluable form of social glue within the workplace. If the organization's job structure or reward system or performance appraisal system were to change on a daily basis, it is hard to believe that employees would ever view them as legitimate, much less take them for granted. The rub, of course, is that the very properties that tend to foster trust and legitimacy in an organization's HR system tend to make that same system resistant to change, a reality with which many prominent companies have grappled in recent years.

SUMMARY AND PROSPECTUS

This chapter has surveyed some important ideas from psychology, social psychology, and sociology that bear on employment relationships. Each of these ideas helps illuminate how people perceive and respond to how they are treated and rewarded at work. Economic models of employment contracts typically pay little attention to issues of *process,* assuming that *what* the firm gives to its employees (and vice versa) is what matters, rather than *how* rewards are determined and framed. The ideas reviewed here reveal why and how the same objective bundle of policies or rewards might engender quite different reactions among different groups of employees or in disparate organizational contexts.

Consider, for example, the question: *What is the effect of giving employees a voice in what they do and how they do it?* Of course, when employees have a voice, they may use that voice to make choices that management would not itself choose.

But ignore this for the moment and consider: Holding fixed the choice that is made, what would be the impact of employee participation in important decisions by the firm? The considerations raised in this chapter lead us to conclude that employees would be more likely to judge the choice as having been correct and thus they would be more committed to making it work out, through processes of effort justification and the closely related cooptive effects of participation. Furthermore, insofar as the choice has consequences for the distribution of rewards, those consequences would be more likely to be regarded as procedurally just (at least, if the participation process is itself equitable).

This question deserves more than these cursory answers, however. A complete discussion blends together ideas from this chapter and the economic framework sketched in Chapter 4. The question raises a host of issues that are crucial to the management of human resources. Hence, we move next to a chapter-length examination of the issue of employee voice.

IN REVIEW

⇒ Employment relations are shaped by economics *and* by social and psychological forces. Process and symbolism are at least as important to effective HRM as are the content and economic values of HR practices.

⇒ A number of cognitive and social-psychological processes are key to employment relationships:
- Anchoring on available and salient cognitive anchors—for example, the level of performance expected by superiors often anchors the level of performance that is provided.
- Attributions about attitudes, motivations, and behaviors, based on inferences from observing our own conduct:
  ○ Intrinsic motivation to do a task can be muted by calling conspicuous attention to extrinsic rationales for doing the task. When extrinsic rationales are absent, individuals tend to attribute effort they expend to their liking of the task or some other higher purpose, thereby enhancing commitment.
  ○ Commitment so derived escalates the longer the individual performs the task without attributing motivation to external influences.
  ○ Intrinsic motivation is probably more prevalent than you think and represents a powerful motivational device in situations where extrinsic incentives are hard to get right.
- Individuals evaluate their position relative to others, in a process of *social comparison*:
  ○ Social comparisons sometimes occur upward and downward, but in work settings the most common comparisons are horizontal, vis-à-vis others who are similar demographically, in terms of status, or with whom much contact takes place.

- ○ Formal organizational categories shape the social comparisons individuals make. For this reason and others (in-group biases, attempts to divide and conquer), organizations use categorization processes strategically to affect outcomes and behavior.
- Individuals attend not only to the absolute rewards they receive, but how they fare relative to others (distributive justice) and the processes by which outcomes are determined (procedural justice):
  - ○ Distributive justice can be assessed based on ideas of equality, meeting needs, or (more prevalent in work settings) the equity principle that rewards should go to those who contribute the most.
  - ○ Perceptions of procedural justice tend to rise when procedures: are based on valid criteria; are applied consistently and explained clearly by competent individuals; reinforce organizational values and culture; do not denigrate the individual; and involve participation and a right of appeal.
- Gift exchange—the desire to reciprocate "gifts" in kind—can be a powerful force for eliciting consummate effort from employees. The nature of the "gift" and the situations of the gift giver and receiver all affect the extent to which a gift is perceived as such.
- Status inconsistency—occupying discrepant positions on multiple organizational and/or social hierarchies—can have negative effects. Unnecessary status conflicts should be avoided; where they are necessary or unavoidable, artificial means for reinforcing the desired status hierarchy can help.
- An important source of organizational inertia is a need for legitimacy in organizational practices. Constant change de-legitimizes practices.

ENDNOTES

1. Charles Smith, "Working on a Change: Japan Steps Gingerly Towards a Five-day Week," *Far Eastern Economic Review* 140 (April 14, 1988): 62–3; Walter Tubbs, "Karoushi: Stress-death and the Meaning of Work," *Journal of Business Ethics* 12 (November 1993): 869–77.

2. Reprinted courtesy of SPORTS ILLUSTRATED (March 18, 1991). Copyright © 1999, Time Inc. "Bawl Players: As Big Bucks Proliferate, More and More Stars are Suffering from Salary Envy" by P. King. All rights reserved.

3. Economist Robert Frank, for instance, reports evidence of drastic compression in compensation paid to auto and real estate salespersons and to grant-writing research faculty in universities, relative to observed variations in the incremental revenues these people bring into their respective organizations. See Robert Frank, *Choosing the Right Pond: Human Behavior and the Quest for Status* (New York: Oxford University Press, 1985).

4. Sections of this chapter borrow heavily from James N. Baron, "The Employment Relation as a Social Relation," *Journal of the Japanese and International Economies* 2 (December 1988): 492–525.

5. For some examples of this type of research, see Amos Tversky and Daniel Kahneman, "Availability: A Heuristic for Judging Frequency and Probability," *Cognitive Psychology* 5 (September 1973): 207–32; and "Judgment Under Uncertainty: Heuristics and Biases," *Science* 185 (September 1974): 1124–31.

6. Interestingly, paying people based on the accuracy of their judgments does not seem to reduce the magnitude of this type of anchoring effect.

7. For examples, see Randy Hodson and Teresa Sullivan, "Totem or Tyrant?: Monopoly, Regional, and Local Sector Effects on Worker Commitment," *Social Forces* 63 (March 1985): 716–31; James Lincoln and Arne Kalleberg, "Work Organization and Workforce Commitment: A Study of Plants and Employees in the U.S. and Japan," *American Sociological Review* 50 (December 1985): 738–60.

8. We may be divulging valuable trade secrets here, but another example of anchoring comes to mind, which no doubt has broader application in the management of human resources. As professors, we have found that students are much less troubled by a three-hour final exam if course materials originally advertised a four-hour final rather than a three-hour final, and much *more* troubled by a three-hour exam if a two-hour final was originally advertised. Of course, it is inconceivable that faculty members might use such knowledge strategically!

9. E. Lazear, "The Timing of Raises and Other Payments," *Carnegie–Rochester Conference Series on Public Policy* 33 (Autumn 1990): 13–48.

10. Edward Deci, *Intrinsic Motivation* (New York: Plenum Press, 1975).

11. See Alfie Kohn, *Punished by Rewards* (New York: Houghton-Mifflin, 1993).

12. Amitai Etzioni, *Modern Organizations* (Englewood Cliffs, NJ: Prentice-Hall, 1971); Ronald Dore, *British Factory–Japanese Factory* (Berkeley, CA: University of California Press, 1973).

13. See Jeffrey Pfeffer, *Competitive Advantage Through People: Problems and Prospects for Change* (Boston: Harvard Business School Press, 1994), Chapter 4.

14. Law firms like Cravath, in turn, were responding in part to the exodus of corporate lawyers in the mid-1980s to Wall Street. Working closely with young investment bankers, who garnered a share of the lucrative financial deals on which they were working, young corporate attorneys found it hard not to use the I-Bankers as an anchor or reference point for evaluating their own compensation. Having done so, corporate lawyers were increasingly tempted to follow in the footsteps of their banker acquaintances.

15. Intrinsic motivation is advantageous in this setting because it is especially difficult to provide extrinsic incentives for lawyering, with its emphasis on quality of work and teamwork. (See Chapter 11.)

16. This survey involved a nationally-representative sample of the U.S. labor force aged 16 and above. The figures reported here are taken from Robert P. Quinn and Graham L. Staines, *The 1977 Quality of Employment Survey: Descriptive Statistics with Comparison Data from the 1969–70 and 1972–73 Surveys* (Ann Arbor, MI: Institute for Social Research, University of Michigan, 1979).

17. Of course, the mere fact that people report such behavior in surveys does not guarantee that their reports are accurate. But a number of different literatures suggest the prevalence and importance of intrinsic motivation. Even laboratory studies of animals have demonstrated that holding constant the amount of reward available, subjects have

a preference for activity over doing nothing. There also seems to be ample anecdotal evidence to support the argument, such as the lottery winners who stay in their jobs, or the superwealthy tycoons who remain obsessed with doing the next deal.

18. Good overviews of this literature are provided by Morton Deutsch, "Experimental Studies of the Effects of Different Systems of Distributive Justice," pp. 151–64 in John C. Masters and William P. Smith (eds.), *Social Comparison, Social Justice, and Relative Deprivation* (Hillsdale, NJ: Lawrence Erlbaum, 1987); Joanne V. Wood, "Theory and Research Concerning Social Comparisons of Personal Attributes, *Psychological Bulletin* 106 (September 1989): 231–48; Shelley E. Taylor, Bram P. Buunk, and Lisa G. Aspinwall, "Social Comparison, Stress, and Coping," *Personality and Social Psychology Bulletin* 16 (March 1990): 74–89.

19. Joanne V. Wood, Shelley E. Taylor, and Rosemary R. Lichtman, "Social Comparison in Adjustment to Breast Cancer," *Journal of Personality and Social Psychology* 49 (November 1985): 1169–83.

20. Leonard I. Pearlin, Morton A. Lieberman, Elizabeth G. Menaghan, and Joseph T. Mullan, "The Stress Process," *Journal of Health and Social Behavior* 22 (December 1981): 337–56; Joel M. Brockner, "The Effects of Work Layoffs on Survivors: Research, Theory, and Practice," pp. 213–55 in Barry M. Staw and L. L. Cummings (eds.), *Research in Organizational Behavior,* Volume 10 (Greenwich, CN: Jai Press, 1988).

21. For instance, see Roderick M. Kramer, "Intergroup Relations and Organizational Dilemmas: The Role of Categorization Processes," pp. 191–228 in Barry M. Staw and L. L. Cummings (eds.), *Research in Organizational Behavior,* Volume 13 (Greenwich, CN: Jai Press, 1991).

22. David M. Strang and James N. Baron, "Categorical Imperatives: The Structure of Job Titles in California State Agencies," *American Sociological Review* 55 (August 1990): 479–95.

23. James N. Baron, *Economic Segmentation and the Organization of Work,* unpublished doctoral dissertation, Department of Sociology, University of California–Santa Barbara (1982). Nineteen of the 49 organizations meeting this criterion used a professional or managerial job title (e.g., director of industrial relations, personnel manager) to refer to their one personnel specialist; the remaining thirty used a clerical title (e.g., payroll clerk, timekeeper). Men represented 11 of the 19 people with professional or managerial titles, but only two of the 30 clerks. The odds of observing a difference of that magnitude purely by chance are less than one in a thousand.

24. See Amy Wharton and James N. Baron, "So Happy Together?: The Impact of Gender Segregation on Men at Work," *American Sociological Review* 52 (October 1987): 574–87; and James N. Baron and Andrew E. Newman, "Pay the Man: Effects of Demographic Composition on Prescribed Wage Rates in the California Civil Service," pp. 107–130 in Robert Michael, Heidi Hartmann, and Brigid O'Farrell (eds.), *Pay Equity: Empirical Inquiries* (Washington: National Academy Press, 1989).

25. Marilynn B. Brewer and Roderick M. Kramer, "The Psychology of Intergroup Attitudes and Behavior," *Annual Review of Psychology* 36 (1985): 219–43.

26. We aren't aware of any empirical studies that speak directly to this kind of prediction, but we can cite a compelling illustration of this kind of effect. A group of industrial psychologists who created the occupational classification scheme used in the U.S. Department of Labor's *Dictionary of Occupational Titles* managed to concoct 37 separate job titles within Psychology, whereas they created only 30 titles to capture all jobs within the fields of Economics, Political Science, Sociology, and Anthropology com-

bined! For a discussion of this example, see James N. Baron and Jeffrey Pfeffer, "The Social Psychology of Organizations and Inequality," *Social Psychology Quarterly* 57 (September 1994): 190–209.

27. See Baron and Pfeffer, *op cit.*

28. William P. Bridges and Robert L. Nelson. "Markets in Hierarchies: Organizational and Market Influences on Gender Inequality in a State Pay System," *American Journal of Sociology* 95 (November 1989): 616–58. These authors also found that in deciding which "benchmark" or market-related job classification a given job title was linked to in setting pay, the State of Washington assigned female-dominated titles to female-dominated benchmarks more than was warranted given the similarity in skills between the focal job title and its benchmark or market counterpart. In other words, the gender composition of job titles affected which external labor market occupations were defined as relevant for the process of wage determination.

29. See Stuart M. Klein and Kenneth W. Rose, "Formal Policies and Procedures Can Forestall Unionization," *Personnel Journal* 61 (April 1982): 275–81.

30. For instance, see Dean B. McFarlin and Paul D. Sweeney, "Distributive and Procedural Justice as Predictors of Satisfaction with Personal and Organizational Outcomes," *Academy of Management Journal* 35 (August 1992): 626–37; Stephen W. Gilliland, "The Perceived Fairness of Selection Systems: An Organizational Justice Perspective," *Academy of Management Review* 18 (October 1993): 694–734.

31. Although individuals sometimes disagree about precisely which inputs ought to be considered, the principle of equity generally entails the view that individuals should not be rewarded or penalized for outputs or inputs that were outside of their control. For instance, if one production worker receives a batch of defective raw materials that adversely affects her output or quality, it is not equitable to penalize her for that, nor to reward someone who produces more than his co-workers because they experienced an uncontrollable power outage whereas he did not.

32. An individual economist can compare her salary with salaries in the other social sciences generally, but an individual sociologist cannot disentangle the salaries of economists from the salaries of all those (presumably) well-paid physicists.

33. Alvin Gouldner, "The Norm of Reciprocity: A Preliminary Statement," *American Sociological Review* 25 (April 1960): 161–78.

34. For instance, see Samuel B. Bacharach, Peter Bamberger, and Bryan Mundell, "Status Inconsistency in Organizations: From Social Hierarchy to Stress," *Journal of Organizational Behavior* 14 (January 1993): 21–36.

35. Internal labor markets are discussed in detail in Chapter 8.

6

VOICE: UNIONS AND OTHER FORMS OF EMPLOYEE REPRESENTATION

In the late 1980s, Magma Copper, then the fourth largest U.S. copper mining company, found itself in the unenviable position of being the industry's highest-cost producer, in an industry plagued by violent incidents of labor unrest, and facing a dwindling supply of accessible ore deposits.[1] Just spun off from Newmont Mining, Magma was also heavily saddled with debt, largely as a result of an earlier agreement with its labor unions. (In exchange for major wage givebacks, the company implemented a bonus plan linked to the copper price, which skyrocketed shortly thereafter. This forced Magma to pay out some $56 million in bonuses in 1987–88, which in turn required the company to borrow at high interest rates.)

In 1988 a new CEO, Burgess Winter, arrived and turned the situation around. Between 1988 and 1991, operating costs per pound of copper declined by 24%, production from Magma's mines increased 30%, and productivity increased by 50%. Winter achieved this turnaround in large measure by forging a cooperative partnership with labor. He began with the contract negotiations of 1989, taking a series of steps designed to build trust and credibility with the union leadership and rank-and-file. This included (importantly) extensive leadership training for supervisors, to help them be effective in a new cooperative work environment. Winter also took some steps that were fraught with symbolism; for instance, he appeared at the plant gate shoulder to shoulder with union leaders, to pass out copies of a new proposed accord outlining union–management cooperation.

But perhaps most importantly, Magma management and its unions put into place structures within which labor and management could work together to improve Magma's plight. A Joint Union–Management Cooperation Committee (JUMCC) was created to oversee the new cooperative relationship, and the JUMCC in turn created a structure for joint labor–management problem-solving teams. Each division in Magma was challenged by the JUMCC to identify a team project capable of making a "quantum breakthrough" contribution to Magma. In response, over forty projects were initiated, tackling a vast array of work-related issues. One group elected to tackle the vexing challenge of developing reserve ore deposits (the so-called Kalamazoo or "K" ore body) located adjacent to Magma's largest currently operating mine, the San Manuel mine. The San Manuel was scheduled to close down by 1997 (with 1,300 jobs slated to be lost), due to dwindling reserves that could be mined economically. This "K" ore body could keep the mines open but seemed inaccessible; management was convinced that it was prohibitively expensive to mine the "K" using traditional techniques. But after studying the issue, the labor–management team that took on this issue asserted that by exploiting job flexibility, improving scheduling, and developing new work methods, the "K" could be mined effectively. The JUMCC authorized a pilot project on a small portion of the ore body, and results were encouraging enough to authorize a second, larger study, financed by savings realized when the unions agreed to use the new work methods on the San Manuel. The second study was equally successful, and the "K" was fully developed at a cost of nearly $100 million.

Before giving the green light to develop the whole "K," however, labor and management took further steps to guarantee that development could not be interrupted by strikes or a change in management. Eight months before the 1989 contracts were due to expire, labor and management ratified a new contract. The contract was unusual not simply because both parties volunteered to work out an agreement before the existing contract expired, but also for the way it was negotiated: not in the traditional one-bargaining-table format whereby labor and management confront one another, but instead by a number of joint labor–management teams, each given responsibility for pieces of the contract, which were then knitted together by the JUMCC. And the new contract was unusual for some of its key features. It was to last fifteen years (instead of the normal three); this tied management's hands considerably, but it also avoided the enormous loss of productivity characteristically experienced in the industry during the last year of each three-year contracting cycle, as well as the frequently ensuing strikes as the parties prepared to face off against each other. Through a system of binding arbitration, the contract essentially guaranteed that there would be no work stoppages for a minimum of eight years, enough time to put the broad changes in labor–management relations implemented at Magma to the test. The contract was equally innovative in formalizing the idea that contract disputes should be resolved by joint problem-solving teams, and that labor and management would work together continually over the life of the contract to refine work practices and methods.[2]

We draw four morals from this story:

1. The basic relationship between employer and employee can be friendly and cooperative or antagonistic and conflictual. Friendly and cooperative—based on trust and reciprocity—is the more efficient, but this requires a partnership between labor and management.

2. Despite all we have said in previous chapters about inertia in the relationship between employer and employee, change—even rapid change—is possible. We meant what we said about how hard it can be to change the character of the employment relationship, but stories such

as Magma Copper and NUMMI show that "hard" doesn't mean "impossible." Indeed, for reasons we discuss later, employee collectives such as unions may aid in making a change. And the importance of symbolic acts in effecting such changes should not be minimized.

3. The workforce at Magma contributed ideas—very impressive ideas—as well as muscle in turning the situation around.

4. The turnaround at Magma involved important concessions on both sides. Management gave workers a chance to contribute ideas—a voice—but just as importantly, this was a voice with real authority behind it. To build trust, both labor and management gave up some of their traditional autonomy and flexibility.

This chapter is devoted to several general issues raised by the Magma case: How much say should workers be given concerning their work lives? Should workers be consulted about work practices? Should they be allowed to *determine* work practices? Should they be given a veto over large-scale layoffs or decisions to send work outside the firm or overseas? Should they have a say in major strategic decisions made by management?

These questions all concern what is called *worker voice,* although the term *voice* needs some clarification:

- We aren't talking solely about consultations with workers, where management asks workers what they would like yet essentially reserves all decision-making authority to determine what workers will get. This sort of consultation is only *part* of giving workers a voice. We are also concerned with giving workers genuine decision-making power.

- Individual workers can be given a voice, or workers can be given a formal *collective* voice, through a union or some other "representative" body. In this chapter, we will deal almost exclusively with formal, collective voice. In Chapter 9, which discusses high-commitment HRM, we explore possibilities for less formal, more individualized voice.

- The imperative *should* must be clarified: In this chapter, we take the narrow perspective of management and the owners of the firm and ask, Is it in their interests for workers to have a say?

EMPLOYEE VOICE AS A MATTER OF LAW

Of course, workers may have a (collective) say regardless of the interests of management and owners. We will leave until next chapter the topic of why society intervenes in the private relationship between an employer and employee(s). But it ought to be noted at the outset that worker voice is not simply a matter of employer volition.

Laws concerning collective and individual employee rights vary markedly from country to country (and, within the United States, from state to state), so we cannot hope to give a blanket statement of what kinds of say workers are legally entitled to. But, to take two important and illustrative examples:

In the United States, nonsupervisory employees are entitled to organize themselves into a union. A single union may represent all or most nonsupervisory employees in a single firm—this is typical in so-called *industrial union* settings like automobile assembly (the United Auto Workers). Or workers may be organized into several unions on the basis of the types of work they do. In newspaper publishing, for example, the typesetters, printers, paper handlers, mailers, and journalists each have their own *craft* union. But whichever form it takes, employees are entitled to organize. If enough employees request it (through a very precise procedure), the National Labor Relations Board (NLRB) will hold a certification election in which all eligible workers can vote for or against union representation. Management can campaign against the union, but its election-related activities are circumscribed by law. And if a majority of the eligible workers vote for union representation, management is required by law to bargain in good faith with the union over a host of issues. The covered workers—the technical term is the *bargaining unit*—can subsequently decertify the union as their bargaining agent, in an NLRB-supervised decertification election.[3]

In Germany, an employer with more than five employees must allow those employees to elect a representative Works Council, which has formal decision-making (or, at least, decision-blocking) power in matters of hiring, firing, work practices, and scheduling. The Works Council also plays a role in the event of plant closures and work relocation—roughly, the Works Council cannot prevent a plant closure, but it can delay one. In larger organizations, moreover, workers are entitled by law to elect representatives to the firm's Supervisory Board, which (akin to the Board of Directors in the United States) chooses management and must approve the overall strategy of the firm. The owners of the firm—the equity holders—have their own representatives on the Supervisory Board, and equity's representatives can outvote the representatives of the employees. But not by much; the employees, acting through their representatives on the Supervisory Board, have a lot of power over the firm's basic strategic direction. Indeed, just being at meetings of the Board and having access to the media gives workers' representatives a lot of power. Day-to-day and month-to-month strategic decisions taken by the firm are set by the firm's Economic Committee (the American parallel would be the Executive Committee of Management), which includes representatives of the Works Council along with management. Workers are also entitled to union representation; unions (and not the Works Council) negotiate with management over economic conditions such as wages and benefits. This negotiation is generally done on a national basis—for example, the national unions representing workers at auto assembly plants will bargain with an association of auto manufacturers.

These are but two examples. Things are different still in Great Britain, in France, in Japan, in Mexico, and in Singapore. And things can change quite rapidly: Mrs. Thatcher had enormous impact on labor law in Great Britain and, as this book was written, President Clinton was sponsoring legislation that would profoundly affect U.S. labor law (see endnote 15). Though we have given a few details of the

U.S. and German systems, our descriptions are quite cursory; as a manager, you should carefully and thoroughly inform yourself of the rights your employees currently have to organize themselves in the locales in which you operate.

WHY SHOULD YOU CARE ABOUT UNIONS?

Our experience teaching to an audience drawn largely from the United States is that, at this point, the objections begin to fly. Why bother discussing unions? In the United States, the extent of unionization is small (around 16% of the nonagricultural workforce, 12% if one looks at the nongovernmental sector only) and falling. But the United States is hardly typical. To provide a better sense of how unionization rates and trends look elsewhere, we provide some descriptive data. Table 6-1 reproduces statistics from the *OECD Employment Outlook*[4] on unionization rates between 1970 and 1988 for various countries. Table 6-2 reports more recent data from the International Labour Organization's *World Labour Report 1997–98* on trade union density for a sampling of countries worldwide.

TABLE 6-1 Unionization Rates in the OECD

Country Grouping	Unionization Rates			
	1970	1980	1985	1988
Europe[a]	38%	44%	40%	38%
North America[b]	30%	26%	19%	18%
Other OECD[c]	37%	35%	33%	30%
Seven large countries[d]	33%	32%	27%	25%
Eleven small countries[e]	50%	57%	55%	52%
Seven adversarial systems[f]	33%	32%	26%	25%
Eleven cooperative systems[g]	39%	40%	38%	36%

[a]Austria, Belgium, Denmark, Finland, France, Germany, Ireland, Italy, the Netherlands, Norway, Sweden, Switzerland, and the United Kingdom.

[b]Canada and the United States.

[c]Australia, Japan, and New Zealand.

[d]Canada, France, Germany, Italy, Japan, the United Kingdom, and the United States.

[e]Austria, Australia, Belgium, Denmark, Finland, Ireland, the Netherlands, New Zealand, Norway, Sweden, and Switzerland.

[f]Australia, Canada, France, Italy, New Zealand, the United Kingdom, and the United States.

[g]Austria, Belgium, Denmark, Finland, Germany, Ireland, Japan, the Netherlands, Norway, Sweden, and Switzerland.

Source: Adapted from *OECD* data taken from *OECD Employment Outlook, 1991:* Table 4.2, p. 102. Copyright © OECD, 1991.

In reflecting on these data, you should bear in mind the following:

- Unionization rates in major manufacturing industries tend to be substantially higher.

- If your firm is not unionized, you may someday face the "threat" of unionization. If this happens, knowing something about unions, worker rights, and limitations on what management can do to fight union representation may keep you out of jail. (It may even cause you to welcome the union!)

- There have been swings in unionization rates over time. In the United States, for instance, the Teamsters' recent gains and show of strength in their confrontation against United Parcel Service have emboldened many in the labor movement. There is no ironclad guarantee that the recent trend toward lower unionization rates in the United States will continue.

- As Table 6-1 shows, the low rate of unionization in the United States is way out of step with the rest of the OECD. If your business takes you to Northern European countries, such as Germany, you are more likely to find unions, and (by law) you are very likely to find a works council and worker representatives on your Supervisory Board.

- In many industries and countries, collective bargaining agreements extend to a much larger group of workers than just those employees who belong to trade unions. In some cases, this occurs formally, because collective bargaining agreements pertain to union members and nonunion employees alike within the bargaining unit. In France, for example, only 10% of the workforce are trade union members, but 92% are covered by collective bargaining agreements; in Spain, the corresponding percentages are 11% and 68%, respectively, and for Germany they are 32% and 90%.[6] (In contrast, within the United States, collective bargaining agreements usually bind only on union members; 16% of the workforce is unionized and only 18% are covered by collective bargaining agreements.[7] And in Japan, the percentage of workers covered by collective bargaining is actually slightly *less* than the percentage of the workforce that is unionized, because unionism is strongly enterprise-based in Japan and not all enterprise unions in Japan conclude a collective bargaining agreement.[8]) In other cases, terms negotiated between unions and leading firms dictate informally the contours of labor–management relations more broadly within an industry or region, not only within smaller union enterprises but within nonunion firms as well. This occurs, for instance, in the U.S. automobile industry and in the Japanese *Shunto* (or so-called "Spring wage offensive") negotiated annually between the leading national employer federations and trade union confederations.

- Finally, and most importantly, organized labor presents us with the best data we have about giving workers a voice. If we want to understand employment relationships in general, studying a wider collection of forms and variations will presumably give us more to chew on as we try to derive general

TABLE 6-2   Trade Union Density for Selected Countries in the 1990s

Country	Year	Union membership as a percentage of:		
		Nonagricultural Labor Force	Wage and Salary Earners	Formal Sector Wage Earners[a]
Africa				
Egypt	1995	29.6	38.8	
South Africa	1995	21.8	40.9	51.9
Americas				
Argentina	1995	25.4	38.7	65.6
Brazil	1991	32.1	43.5	66.0
Canada	1993	31.0	37.4	
Mexico	1991	31.0	42.8	72.9
United States	1995	12.7	14.2	
Venezuela	1995	14.9	17.1	32.6
Asia				
Australia	1995	28.6	35.2	
China	1995	54.7		70.0
India	1991	5.4		22.8
Japan	1995	18.6	24.0	
Korea	1995	9.0	12.7	
Malaysia	1995	11.7	13.4	
New Zealand	1995	23.2	24.3	
Philippines	1995	22.8	38.2	
Singapore	1995	13.5	15.9	
Taiwan	1995	27.9	33.1	
Europe				
Austria	1995	36.6	41.2	
Belgium	1995	38.1	51.9	
Bulgaria	1993	51.4	58.2	
Czech Republic	1995	36.3	42.8	
Denmark	1994	68.2	80.1	
Finland	1995	59.7	79.3	
France	1995	6.1	9.1	
Germany	1995	29.6	28.9	
Ireland	1993	36.0	48.9	
Israel	1995	23.1	23.0	
Italy	1994	30.6	44.1	
Netherlands	1995	21.8	25.6	
Norway	1995	51.7	57.7	
Poland	1995	27.0	33.8	
Portugal	1995	18.8	25.6	
Russian Federation	1996	74.8		
Spain	1994	11.4	18.6	
Sweden	1994	77.2	91.1	
Switzerland	1994	20.0	22.5	
United Kingdom	1995	26.2	32.9	

[a]"Formal sector wage earners" adjusts for prevalence of individuals working in the informal economy, such as employers, the self-employed, unpaid family workers, farm workers and domestic workers; people earning less than the minimum wage; or employed on irregular contracts or working only a few hours a week.

Source: Copyright © International Labour Organization 1997, *World Labour Report, 1997–98*: Table 1-2.[5]

principles. Specifically, although there are some instructive examples where managers have freely granted workers a voice, much of what we know about the impact of worker voice comes from instances where workers have *taken* the voice the law gives them.

For this reason, most of this chapter will concern unions and HRM in unionized settings. And what the data show may come as something of a surprise, at least to many U.S.-based managers.

WHAT IS THE IMPACT OF WORKER REPRESENTATION?

Among practicing managers, there is a wide variety of opinion about the impact of unions and worker representation. The typical American manager, based more on press reports and anecdote than on direct experience, may view unions as corrupt, featherbedding institutions that promote inefficiency and industrial strife and that waste the dues collected from members on perks for the union bureaucracy and on promoting political causes. The typical German manager (or, more precisely, the typical German manager circa 1987—the stresses of German reunification have clouded this rosy picture) is more likely to view her Works Council as a productive and cooperative partner that contributes substantially to productive efficiency; and to see her union as, if not benign, then certainly not a malignant or malevolent force.

These are stereotypes, of course, but as with all stereotypes, they contain some truth. In some cases, bodies that represent workers cause substantial inefficiencies; in others, they promote efficiency. They can impact worker behavior, attitudes, and discipline for good and bad. Even if they promote efficiency, they may cost the firm more in increased wages and benefits than they provide through increased efficiency. So rather than relying on stereotypical anecdotes, we might begin by asking, What is the *average* impact of worker representation?

A lot of empirical work has been conducted to try and answer this question. We will rely primarily on the work of Richard Freeman and James Medoff concerning the average impact of unionization in the United States.[9] Before summarizing the results of this work, however, two cautions are in order.

Problems in Empirical Design

First, much of the empirical work on unionization is far from ideal in its research design. Two different sorts of empirical designs have been used: *Cross-sectional analysis,* in which union and nonunion firms are compared at a given time; and *longitudinal analysis,* which examines what changes occur over time once a firm's workforce either becomes unionized or loses its union status.

The hardest task for empirical researchers in this domain (as in most) is to control for other relevant factors. If we looked cross-sectionally at all the firms in the United States, comparing (say) average return on equity (ROE) in union firms versus nonunion firms, we would see statistically significant differences. But unionization rates vary considerably across different industries—higher in manufacturing and lower in services, for example. Do observed differences in ROE reflect an effect of unionization, or do they simply pick up differences in the industry mixes in the two populations? To control for this, investigators use either multiple regression techniques (putting in controls for things like industry type, degree of competition in the industry, and so on), or a "paired-sample" technique, in which each unionized firm in the sample is matched or paired with a nonunion firm that (except for the unionization) has similar objective characteristics.

The specific controls that are used and the particular paired samples that are created matter to the results. Arguments ensue over what is the "pure" effect of unionization; one researcher's analysis shows one thing, and another's shows something else. Moreover, there is a final "uncontrollable" variable to worry about, namely, the fact of unionization itself. For example, suppose we found cross-sectionally that unionized firms are more profitable on average.[10] We might conclude that somehow unions promote profitability. But a skeptic might argue that we have the causation backwards: Firms that are profitable attract unions, because there is more opportunity in such firms for unions to obtain benefits for their members. Or it might be that there is some third, omitted factor, which both improves profitability and attracts unionization; if we controlled for this omitted variable, we might see that unions *decrease* profitability.

Similar problems arise in longitudinal studies. Suppose that, over a period of time, a firm both gets rid of its union and becomes relatively less profitable. Did the loss of the union cause profits to decrease? Or did the (possibly) apparent signs that profits were going to decrease cause the firm to get tough with its workers, breaking the union in order to survive economically?

Ideally, we should learn about the effects of unions by taking a sample of comparable new firms and randomly causing half to have unions and half not, following them forward through time. We aren't able to do this—the subjects in the population will not cooperate with this experimental design—and consequently the problems noted above intrude. If you are trained in empirical methods, this is nothing new conceptually, and indeed you should be keeping these same methodological cautions in mind throughout this book in weighing the evidence bearing on the issue at hand. These cautions warrant particular attention as we review empirical results on unions in this chapter (specifically, those of Freeman and Medoff); because of these methodological complexities, the findings we report are not settled facts. If you read in the literature, you will have no problem finding other empirical researchers who dispute the conclusions we are about to list.

Averages Are Only Averages

The second caution is that we report *average* effects of unionization. There is a good deal of dispersion around these averages, however. Given the emphasis we put in Chapters 2 and 3 on alignment of HR practices with one another and with the business context, and given our discussion in Chapter 4 about how expectations are important to whether labor and management manage to cooperate, it is not surprising to find that the effects of unionization vary, even among firms that are quite similar in many ways.

If we find, for example, that union firms on average have a lower return on equity than nonunion firms do, this is not the same as saying that every union firm will have a lower ROE than every nonunion firm, nor that a given firm, if it is suddenly unionized, can expect its ROE to decrease. Averages mean something, and if we can offer a good explanation for a particular average effect, we may learn something. But averages don't mean everything. Indeed, when we get around to rationalizing the research findings we will report, we will see that this is a case in which there may be even less to "average effects" than usual.

What Do Unions Do?

So what, according to Freeman and Medoff (and other empirical studies), is the average impact of unions?

- Wages and benefits are higher on average in union firms than in nonunion firms, although the union wage differential varies across different circumstances: It is larger in highly regulated industries, in industries with high rates of unionization, and among less-educated workers; and it is smaller among white, middle-aged males.

- The threat of unionization by itself will on average cause an increase in the level of wages and other forms of compensation.

- Unionization generally causes a shift in the *mix* of compensation: Union workers usually receive a greater proportion of their compensation in the form of fringe benefits, contributions to pensions, and so on.

- In unionized firms, seniority is typically much more important (for promotions, transfers, layoffs, wages) than in nonunion firms. Unionized firms are more likely to deal with business cycle fluctuations by using temporary layoffs (for the less senior workers, especially) than by slowing or stopping wage growth. (Incidents of wage "givebacks" in the 1980s by unions muddied this picture, by putting into the data some cases of unionized firms with substantially reduced wages in response to economic slowdowns.)

- Work rules in unionized firms are more likely to be written down and the subject of negotiation. (But see the discussion below concerning distinctions between industrial and craft unions.) However, employers in the United States remain more or less free to set employment *levels* unilaterally.[11]

- On average, turnover is lower in union settings.

- Workers in unionized firms are much more likely to have access to formal grievance procedures, and thus unionized firms have a higher average incidence of registered grievances. But (on weaker evidence) if we look only at firms with grievance procedures, the impact of unions is *not* to raise, and possibly to lower, the rate of grievances.

- Unionized workers express lower job satisfaction and greater discontent with working conditions than do nonunion workers.[12]

- In the average strike, workers lose more in wages and benefits from their employer than they gain back in increased subsequent wages and benefits *in the current contract cycle.*[13]

- According to Freeman and Medoff, unions have had relatively little success politically in extending their legal rights, although they have been fairly successful in protecting the rights they do have and in lobbying for bills that benefit workers in general.

- Freeman and Medoff also report that, notwithstanding some notable exceptions that tend to be widely reported by the press, labor unions tend to be fairly democratic institutions, affording their members good access to decision-making processes.

- *Finally, getting to the bottom line (for management and owners of the firm):* Unionization is on average associated with lower profits, when profits are measured by return to capital or return on equity. But the decline in profits is more than exceeded (on average) by the increase in wages and benefits, so that the overall effect is to improve productivity. This is the key finding for our purposes, so let us restate it in somewhat more colorful language. *On average, unions create a bigger pie to be split between the workers and the owners of a firm. But, on average, the slice of the pie taken by unionized workers is so much bigger than the slice taken by nonunionized workers, that the owners of unionized firms are left on average with a smaller slice (in absolute terms) than the slice taken by owners of nonunionized firms.* Using nonfinancial measures of productivity tends to confirm that unionized firms are more productive on average. The most negative finding along these lines concerns dynamic efficiency: There is some indication that unions take away so much profit that unionized firms are unable to finance the R&D needed to keep on the technological frontier.[14]

It is worth juxtaposing this evidence concerning how unions affect productivity and profits against the American manager's stereotype of unions as corrupt, "featherbedding" institutions. The stereotype tends to focus on the outdated and inefficient work rules that union agreements sometimes foster and on the wage premia associated with unions. But the productivity evidence suggests that this is only looking at the cost side of the coin. Based on existing empirical evidence, the components of increased efficiency from unionization come principally from lower turnover, lower administrative costs, and more efficient and rationalized management practices in the face of unionization. If unionized settings are split according to measures of the quality of labor–management relations, the increased efficiencies are typically found in settings with good labor–management relations. In settings with bad labor–management relations, unions do indeed conform to the stereotype and degrade efficiency.

THE TWO FACES OF UNIONS

Let us say again that the facts just recorded are not established to everyone's satisfaction. Although Freeman and Medoff (and other labor economists who agree with them) base these assertions on careful empirical investigation, the empirical work is fraught with complications, and other labor economists dispute many of the assertions listed above.

We will not be able to resolve these disputes here. But it is actually somewhat unimportant that we do so. What is important, and what seems beyond serious dispute, is the empirical finding that unions *may* increase productivity, and at the same time they tend to increase their share of the total pie. The question then becomes: How do we explain this collection of observations? Freeman and Medoff begin their explanation by citing what they refer to as the *two faces of unions*. This refers to two basic economic functions played by unions.

First, unions *enhance the power of workers* in their relations with employers, because under U.S. labor law workers gain something of a monopoly right to provide the employer with labor services; the employer cannot credibly play one employee off against another, nor can the employer threaten employees (except at great cost) with competition from prospective employees outside the firm.[15] In this *market-power* role, unions can gain for their members higher wages and benefits, better and more explicit working rules/conditions, and arrangements such as seniority provisions that tend to protect incumbent members of the union from competition by new hires.

If there is a union wage differential that arises from the union's market power, and if workers' alternative job prospects lie largely or even partly in the nonunionized sector, then unions should be associated statistically with lower quit rates, because workers in union settings will be earning relatively premium compensation.

The second function of a labor union is to *give workers a means to express and enforce their opinions,* a *voice* in how the firm is managed. The mere expression of those opinions can improve efficiency. Of course, workers will evince greater satisfaction—or at least voluntarily quit less frequently—the more they like their compensation package and the rules under which they work. Thus, to the extent that management isn't sure what workers would like, giving employees a chance to express their collective opinion can improve the match between what they get and what they want. Moreover, as discussed at the end of Chapter 5, the ability to express one's opinion may increase feelings of procedural justice and buy-in, which presumably has a positive impact on worker's attitudes and efforts. (However, see the discussion of *Voice Without Authority* below.)

But giving workers a voice via a union has broader consequences. Most importantly, perhaps, it shifts management's attention from the desires of younger workers to the desires of older workers. In designing HR policies and practices, management will naturally be concerned with whether those policies and practices appeal to workers. Yet workers are not unanimous in what they want. Which workers will be the focus of management's concerns? Some workers are *infra-*

marginal, which is a fancy way of saying that they are unlikely to leave in the short-run even if they perceive conditions at the firm as worsening. The infra-marginal workers tend to be those with longer tenures at the firm, who have established greater ties to co-workers, to the firm, and to the community, and who are more likely to have family responsibilities, all of which dampen mobility. Other workers are *marginal,* meaning that they are more likely to leave if the policies and practices of the firm have less appeal to them. The marginal worker in most cases will be a younger worker with less-entrenched roots, fewer family responsibilities, and so on.

Absent a union, management will be inclined to give greater weight to the tastes of the marginal worker, because the marginal worker is going to be the first to act if working conditions, compensation, and the like become unappealing. Management can be relatively more sanguine about infra-marginal workers, because the costs to them of leaving are much higher. Unions, however, are political organizations, and the politics of unions frequently tend to favor those with longer tenure in the organization and those with more at stake, who are therefore willing to devote themselves more to union activities. Therefore, the balance of power in the union shifts toward the more experienced, older workers. The voice of the worker that emerges from a union will be the voice of an infra-marginal worker rather than the voice of the worker that, in a nonunion setting, management is most likely to hear (imperfectly) and heed.

Some consequences of this shift are fairly obvious. For example, union contracts tend to emphasize seniority rights. Insofar as the infra-marginal worker is more likely than the marginal worker to value benefits such as family health care and pensions, relatively more of the compensation in a union setting will lie in these areas than would be the case in nonunion settings. Consequently, infra-marginal workers will be more satisfied and turnover among them will decrease. On the other hand, turnover among the marginal workers ought to increase, relatively.[16]

Do these shifts in managerial priorities and attention that are associated with unionization mean greater efficiency overall? They may do so, but an argument to that effect is unconvincing.[17] So we look elsewhere—beyond the general effects of voice noted above—for why union representation may promote efficiency.

WHY UNIONS MAY ENHANCE EFFICIENCY: TRANSACTION COST RATIONALES

Our search begins with ideas developed in Chapter 4. Recall the basic hierarchical model of employment, in which the employer calls the shots and the employee must therefore trust the employer not to abuse her (the employer's) authority. This trust can be important in all sorts of ways for gaining efficiency; employees are more willing to accept management direction or to volunteer information if they believe that doing so will not lead to grief. When we look more closely at the argument, we see several rationales for how unions can enhance this trust–reputation construction.

Collective Action, Collective Punishment, and Free-Riding

Our first rationale picks up on a story already started in Chapter 4, which applies when the basis of worker trust is the employer's concern to preserve her reputation, given the impact of that reputation on independent but collective actions by workers. The employer refrains from taking advantage of Employee A because she fears the independent responses of Employees B, C, D, and so on. But this presupposes two conditions that do not automatically hold: (1) Employees B, C, and D are paying attention to the employer's dealings with A; and (2) they are prepared to act against the employer if she abuses A. Suppose that monitoring the relationship between A and the employer is costly for other workers. Or suppose that sanctioning the employer, if she abuses A, is costly for B, C, and D, in terms of lost wages, having to seek a new employer, and the like. Given these costs, can we trust that B, C, and D will do the necessary monitoring and sanctioning (if needed) of the employer? If not, the reputation construction falls apart and workers are not protected by the employer's concern for her reputation.

Perhaps B, C, and D will, individually and independently, undertake the necessary monitoring and sanctioning. Each may see it as in his own interest to hold the employer accountable. There may be job interdependencies or affiliative ties among the employees that give added personal value to each for taking actions that protect others. But as we saw in Chapter 4, in settings with a large number of employees, a free-rider problem arises. Employee B understands that his *own* monitoring (and, when necessary, his sanctioning) of the employer doesn't have much impact on the employer's actions. The employer is concerned with responses by large numbers of workers. If C and D are going to do the necessary work of keeping the employer in line, B's efforts don't add much, so why should he suffer the costs? On the other hand, if C and D are not going to monitor and sanction the employer as needed, what's the point of B trying to do so on his own? Even worse, if B suspects that C and D may not sanction the employer, B may worry that, were he to do so, things would be correspondingly worse for himself. Either way, B sees little personal gain to counterbalance the personal costs he would incur, and he chooses not to monitor or sanction. Of course, if everyone thinks this way, the basis for trust is lost.

Now add to this scenario a union or some other collective organization of workers. The lines of communication and coordination among workers are thereby clearly established. Employees B, C, and D can meet and decide collectively that they will act to sanction the employer, if sanctions are in order. The cost of monitoring the employer's actions can be handled by a specific worker–designee, the shop steward. Moreover, free-riding may become costly for the free-rider; if the shop steward calls for an industrial action, those workers who refuse to participate can be subjected to formal union discipline or informal sanctions (the latter whether or not they are union members).

To rely on anecdotal evidence, how often have you heard of wildcat strikes taking place in a unionized plant simply because a single worker was mistreated by a single supervisor? In contrast, how often have you heard of similar actions by workers in a nonunion setting? The point is that organized workers, by virtue of their organization, are better able to exercise their collective economic might, which can make them feel more secure, thereby *increasing* the level of efficient cooperation.[18]

Interpreting Management Actions: The Routinization of Dispute Resolution

When we discussed reputation constructions in Chapter 4 and Appendix B, we said that one limiting factor is noise in observables. Suppose the employer takes some action against Employee A, who cries foul. Employees B, C, and D must ponder whether they should respond. Did the employer act abusively, violating the informal understanding between management and employees? Or were the employer's actions against A justified in this instance? The testimony of neither the employer nor A can be trusted entirely in such a case; each has an obvious bias. But if B, C, and D can't be sure whether sanctions are called for, then they may either let the employer off when she should be sanctioned or engage in sanctions that are costly to all when sanctions aren't called for. This sort of "noisy observation" can be killing to reputation, both because it gives the employer some incentive to push the envelope in gray cases, which means less protection for workers, and because it sometimes punishes her unfairly, meaning less incentive for her to keep to the arrangement.

The presence of a union may not, on its own, reduce the noise in any single case. However, by centralizing the monitoring function—creating among the workers someone who specializes in interpreting management actions generally—unionization may lead to more accurate interpretations of specific cases. It gives workers collectively the ability to talk back to management; if management is pushing the envelope in some area, a union representative may be able to warn management that this is being viewed unfavorably before it goes too far. And, when management acts within the legitimate parameters of the employer–employee implicit contract, the union can legitimate management's position. If a boss says, "Employee A had it coming," this is less likely to be accepted by B, C, and D than if the shop steward, however reluctantly, agrees that A was mostly at fault.

In effect, in a three-party relationship (management, union leadership, union rank-and-file), union leadership is acting as a somewhat objective third party. If a union official is viewed by workers as being "one of us"—which is more likely when the union official is drawn from the rank-and-file of workers, resembles them socially and demographically, and is subject to recall by workers collectively—then rank-and-file workers (and even the aggrieved Employee A) are more apt to accept the union official's determination that management was not abusive than if some management designee looks into the matter and decides against the worker. At the same time, management and union officials can (possibly) build a more objective and positive relationship concerning dispute resolution than can management and individual workers, because the greater number and frequency of ongoing negotiations in the first case gives the parties greater opportunity and incentive to find common ground. In addition, the frequency of interactions between union officials and management can permit a greater degree of trust; management is more apt to accept a union official's statement that Supervisor X really screwed up this time, if the union official's track record in negotiations with management is one of reasonableness, truthfulness, and (to some extent) willingness to compromise. Conversely, if a manager maintains that Supervisor X may have seemed capricious in this case but—appearances notwithstanding—actually acted in good faith, this is more likely to be accepted by a union official who has had a long-term relationship with the manager in which the manager has been reasonable, truthful, and (to some extent) accommodating. In general, then, union officials may be more selective in pursuing disputes with management than individuals would be because of the union's concern with preserving long-term union-management harmony and its greater experience in adjudicating past disputes.

When these conditions pertain, disputes between management and individual workers can be settled by management and the union officials in a prompt, businesslike manner. Formal grievance procedures may be avoided, if informal negotiations between management and the union officials can result in a compromise agreeable to management and to the specific worker, where the acquiescence of the specific worker is based on his trust of the union official. Efficiency will in some cases be increased, as the routinization of disputes and avoidance of formal grievance procedures lessens *ex post* bargaining and enforcement costs.

Note that the union official walks a fine line here, having to maintain the confidence of both rank-and-file workers and management. If the union official is too accommodating to management, rank-and-file workers may conclude that the official has sold out and they may be unwilling to accept the official's judgment about specific matters. Disputes that might have been settled informally may then be pressed to the formal grievance stage by the aggrieved employee. Management that tries to build a positive relationship with the union must be careful in doing so not to cause union officials to lose credibility and legitimacy with the rank-and-file. Of course, management must also be ready to admit fault, when it is at fault in particular instances. To be stubborn forces the union leadership either: (a) to be stubborn in return, which will effect no efficiencies at all; or (b) to sell out in fact to management, which (one assumes) the rank-and-file will perceive.

On the other hand, the union officials must be somewhat accommodating, ready to see management's side in disputes and to compromise when appropriate. If, to maintain its credibility with the rank-and-file, union leadership must be implacably stubborn, then management will have no choice but to be stubborn in return. This is likely to cause any efficiencies to evaporate and, insofar as the union official galvanizes the entire rank-and-file, can even lead to increased inefficiency.

Keep in mind that the union rank-and-file is itself a diverse group—some more interested in positive labor–management relations, and some more interested in confrontation. Moreover, unions are political organizations; union representatives (especially, professional labor representatives supplied by the national union) may be attending to agendas other than constructive labor–management relations at this locale. All of these factors can interfere with a positive labor–management relationship, because the union officials have a different agenda (e.g., increasing tension to secure a larger base of members), or because the shop steward must protect her political flank by appeasing the militants, or because she may be drawn from the militants. It is no slam dunk that union representatives will improve matters in the manner sketched above—it is perhaps only a bare possibility—but the possibility is there.

Voice and Responsibility: Balanced Bilateral Relationships

Thus far our explanations for efficiency enhancement by unions have involved enhanced communication and coordination. These stories don't depend very much on actual authority granted to the union. But unions and other worker collectives often have real decision-making authority. Setting aside the issue of whether management should be willing to grant this authority, we can ask: How might such a grant of authority to worker organizations enhance productive efficiency?

In general, workers have access to information that management lacks. Workers may be unwilling to give up that information without some guarantees that the information won't be used against them, and the best guarantee they can receive is to become decision-making partners with management.

Then why not grant decision-making authority to *individual* workers? The problem is one of worker abuse of decision-making authority. Will an individual worker use this authority constructively, for the good of the entire enterprise? Or will he use this power solely to further his own ends, enhancing his bargaining power with management to the greatest possible extent? When we grant management decision-making authority, the protection afforded workers comes from management's concern with its reputation among workers. Some individual employees—such as top-level managers in their relationships with the Board of Directors—have similar reputation concerns and can be granted substantial decision-making authority. However, the requisite reputation stake isn't always there, especially with employees nearer to the bottom of the organization's hierarchy. A shop floor employee can relocate too easily to be effectively restrained by his personal reputation as an employee.[19]

A union, on the other hand, is ostensibly an enduring partner with management. Think of the union as an ongoing enterprise that represents the interests of workers, just as the firm is an ongoing enterprise that represents the interests of its current owners and managers. Unions can and do have reputation stakes in their dealings with management. To the extent that union officials want to protect their union's reputation with a particular employer, their concern for its reputation can be the guarantee that management needs of good, constructive behavior, just as the strongest guarantee to employees of good, constructive behavior by management is management's reputational stake. Moreover, just as management speaks with a collective voice (more or less), having a union allows the employees it represents to speak to management with a single voice (again, more or less). The union is a party that can be held accountable for the actions of its members; if one of its members misbehaves, management can hold the union responsible, just as unions hold management in general accountable for the misdeeds of any single manager.

Needless to say, this rosy picture must be qualified. Cooperation between labor and management is just one possibility; intense antagonism between them is another. Simply having a union is no guarantee of good relations, and when labor-management relations are sour, unions are more apt to use their legal entitlements to get what they can in the short-run from management, expecting management to reciprocate by trying to take maximal advantage of labor. In such cases, the antagonistic relationship that is created, with constant sparring between the two sides, can lower efficiency relative to what would obtain if management could somehow make the union disappear. This is the main reason why average effects in this instance are less meaningful than might appear: There is a lot of dispersion around the average, depending on the sort of relationship that exists between the two parties (amicable and cooperative versus hostile and antagonistic). The dispersion is less a product of uncontrollable noise than it is the product of history and management practice.

A second qualification concerns the relationship between the union rank-and-file and its officials. As we have intimated, there need not be perfect alignment between the interests of these two groups. In effect, the union acts as the agent of its rank-and-file members, and we have to ask how and why rank-and-file members go along with the deals negotiated on their behalf by their agent.

Take the case of an individual rank-and-file union member, who has no particular reputation stake in his dealings with his employer. How does the existence of a union permit management to grant discretion to this worker, trusting that the discretion won't be abused? Why, in other words, should the mere presence of a union cause the individual worker to internalize the interests of his colleagues, both those employed today and those who will be employed in the future, enough so that he acts with concern for the general reputation of workers with management? An important factor here is that unions form a large part of the social environment of the individual worker. Unions can, by consensus of their members, enforce social sanctions on miscreants, sanctions that are less readily available to management. Especially when the union is organized along craft lines (see below), the union is better able to control workers because it presumably has greater control over the worker's access to jobs in general than does the individual employer.[20] One would therefore expect more extensive grants of discretion to workers in settings where the union plays a greater social role in the lives of its rank-and-file and where the union controls access to the individual worker's trade. As we will see further on, that prediction is borne out, if we compare craft unions with industrial unions. Workers may be more likely to internalize the interests of the union than those of the firm because of general societal norms of worker solidarity, greater social similarities with members of the union, and because unions are often based more on principles of "kinship" than are firms.[21] For these reasons or others, individual workers may become more likely to act for the good of the union, as defined by the union hierarchy, even at a cost to the individual worker's narrow self-interest. And the issue may be somewhat moot, insofar as discretion is granted not to single workers but to the workers collectively—that is, to the union that represents them. In other words, it may not be prudent for management to allow single workers to determine their own work rules, but it may be safe to delegate this authority to the union, giving the union the task of enforcing those rules among its members.

In thinking about the relationship between the union rank-and-file and its officials, again you should keep in mind that unions are political entities and not purely economic bodies. Managers work for the owners of the firm. The owners of the firm are presumably concerned with the market value of their equity. So to the extent that owners of the firm can provide suitable incentives for the managers who work for them, and to the extent that the value of equity depends in some measure on the firm's reputation as an employer, we can see a link between that reputation and the actions of management.[22] The authority of the current union leadership, in contrast, is subject to repeal by election of *current* members of the union. Thus, union leadership will be more concerned with the economic well-being of current members, as perceived by those members. This by itself leads union officials to be more concerned with the here-and-now than is (enlightened) management. And worse still, suppose management concludes an agreement with union officials, an agreement that entails long-term commitments on both sides and that depends on the union leadership seeking to preserve its reputation with management. Management must then worry that this particular set of union leaders will be thrown out of office. Will the next group of elected union officials that comes along be willing to honor commitments given by their predecessors? Especially in settings where newly elected union officials are likely to have been elected by running against the old officials, this is somewhat doubtful.[23] Moreover, as union elections approach, incumbent union officials may feel a need to bash management in order to protect their political flanks. The periodic occurrence of union-leadership elections can wreak havoc with even the best intentions regarding reputable, consistent behavior.

Giving Protection Against Big-Stakes (Single) Actions by Management

To promote efficiency, one wants to give workers discretion in matters where they have the information needed to make more efficient decisions. For example, it can promote efficiency to allow workers to control their work rules, if employees can be trusted not to abuse this authority. But should they be given any authority to block or delay management action in matters where, presumably, management has most or all of the relevant information? For example, should workers collectively have a say in whether the firm outsources some of its work or relocates work overseas?

A simple argument leads to the (incorrect!) conclusion that it is never in management's interest to allow workers this sort of discretion, because workers' and management's interests in such matters are naturally opposed. No union will be in favor of losing work for its members. Hence, when such actions are important for increased efficiency and profits of the firm, worker authority in these matters must necessarily be obstructionist.

The problem with this simple argument is that it ignores several things. First, workers have a wide variety of interests, and trade-offs are possible. If it enhances productive efficiency to ship some work overseas, this presumably means more profits. To gain worker acquiescence, it may be necessary to give employees more in return than they give up, but enhanced efficiency means that they can be given that something more, while still leaving increased profits for management and owners. Thus, workers will not necessarily be obstructionist.

In rebuttal one might ask, Why should management have to give workers this sort of "bribe"? Why share the increased efficiencies with workers, when, if workers had no power in these matters, management could keep all the goodies for itself and for the owners of the firm? This brings us back to the basic trust–reputation story of Chapter 4. When one party—the employees, say—trusts the employer, this is often motivated by the belief that the employer will be restrained by its concern for continued good relationships. But, to reiterate from Chapter 4, when it comes to decisions such as moving work overseas, management's concern for its reputation with its current workers may evaporate, because those workers will shortly be ex-workers.[24] In terms of basic reputation constructions, when the party with a reputation stake will sometimes take a single action for such large stakes that its reputation stake is dwarfed by immediate considerations, the basis for trust is lost. And then workers, knowing that such decisions may be in the offing (with predictable consequences) may be disinclined to trust management at all. If the relationship is going to be sundered when the next big-stakes decision comes along, management is less restrained in today's low-stakes actions by its concern for the future.

To put it succinctly, to preserve its reputation stake, management may have to offer guarantees to workers that big-stakes unilateral decisions will not be coming down the pike. To get the trust of workers—for purposes of amicable and efficient transactions *today*—management may need to tie its hands or limit its options concerning *tomorrow*. It isn't clear that tying tomorrow's hands is worth it, compared to the benefits accrued today. But the simple argument, which focuses entirely on preserving management's prerogatives over tomorrow's decisions, misses the bigger picture.

At this point, the story of Magma Copper should be recalled. All sorts of things were at work in that episode—a basic change in the attitudes and expectations of workers and management, a movement to a more balanced bilateral relationship, increased perceptions of procedural justice and employee buy-in (see the following section)—but a key factor was that management was willing to tie its own hands with a fifteen-year contract that called for binding arbitration and with guarantees that the "K" ore-body would be developed if extraction costs were sufficiently low. This represents a real loss of flexibility for management, but it simultaneously gives workers the sort of guarantees they need to cooperate with management.[25]

Moreover, management should remember that the working population is not entirely powerless. It does have political power that it can exercise, even at a local level. If management does not offer workers guarantees voluntarily, it may find that much cruder and more onerous "guarantees" are forced upon it under law. To take a simple example, suppose management wishes to relocate some, but not all, work at a plant to some out-of-state or overseas location. If the current workforce has no say in the matter, it may see this as the opening wedge of a process that will swallow all that it has, and it may act collectively to stop the process before it starts, whether through legislation, informal political pressure, or a general work action. If, on the other hand, workers have authority in the matter in general, they may feel secure enough to seek a compromise in the current matter. Sure, management has to give up something—a "bribe" must be given—but it may prove better to share the increased efficiencies with workers than to be compelled to forgo them altogether.

WHY UNIONS MAY ENHANCE EFFICIENCY: PSYCHOLOGICAL AND SOCIAL RATIONALES

Up to this point, our rationales for an efficiency-enhancement effect of unions and other forms of worker collectives have relied largely on economic explanations, drawing on ideas from Chapter 4. These rationales are strengthened by considerations from sociology and social psychology, the stuff of Chapter 5.

In some of what has preceded, we enlisted ideas from Chapter 5. Specifically, when we considered the trilateral relationship between workers, management, and union representatives, an important reason why union representatives might have credibility with the rank-and-file was the attraction associated with social similarity. Beyond this, we turn back to some of the closing ideas of Chapter 5. When workers have a say in the conditions and nature of their work, worker buy-in and a sense of procedural justice are more likely to flourish. Take the case of giving workers a say in the outsourcing of work or in large layoffs. The workers who remain are much more likely to accept the actions taken and to proceed in businesslike fashion—perhaps even assisting in the implementation—if they had a say and a hand in framing the actions taken.

Moreover, to be granted real authority—to be trusted—can engender trustworthiness. To the extent that management wants to grant some discretion to unions in, say, matters of work rules, in order to take advantage of line workers' knowledge, it would send a very mixed signal indeed to simultaneously deny the union a say in matters such as outsourcing, which have such a potentially tremendous impact on the welfare of union members. It sends the signal that management is willing to give employees (through the union) discretion when the employees can be helpful, but it really doesn't trust them or view them as partners. This is not an ideal message to send to employees who are handling work rules on the shop floor!

The shift in management attention, from marginal to infra-marginal workers, can also have positive sociological and social-psychological impact. If management listens to and heeds the concerns of infra-marginal workers, and infra-marginal workers are elected to represent workers generally (which, for reasons given earlier, they will tend to be), they gain authority and respect among their co-workers. To the extent that the infra-marginal workers—older and more stable, with greater concerns for their families and the future—are good role models (from management's point of view) for workers generally, management can benefit from this gain in authority, respect, and status.

VOICE WITHOUT AUTHORITY

Managers should be wary of what may seem like having one's cake here and eating it too. Namely, management may decide to give workers a voice but no authority—workers are given a forum to make suggestions and express their concerns, likes, dislikes, and suggestions, but they are given no power to enforce their desires.

If we think solely in economic terms, such a general policy of voice without authority can't hurt, relative to no voice and no authority, and it may help. It can't hurt, because management presumably has no interest in harming workers gratuitously, and if it did, workers would simply withhold information. To the extent that management is genuinely uncertain what workers want, it can use what it learns from workers' remarks to better attune compensation, work-rules, and the like to employee preferences, at least insofar as the changes don't compromise profits.

This, however, ignores the dark side of things like buy-in, procedural justice, and trustworthiness engendered by trust. Suppose management continually seeks the opinions, advice, and information of workers, but then management is perceived by those workers as using what it learns solely for its own benefit (with any benefits to workers occurring purely by coincidence). Imagine, for example, that management learns that workers have a greater-than-anticipated taste for benefits in the form of subsidized child care, which can be efficiently provided in the sense that the cost of the child care to management is less than the pecuniary benefits to workers of the child care. In response to this information, suppose that management provides child care *and* cuts salaries so that total compensation is held fixed and profits go up. Or imagine that management continually seeks employee "suggestions," but fails to act on repeated suggestions of a particular sort. It is easy to imagine the resentment that would ensue, resentment that might well be manifested in the form of collective action, higher turnover, or reduced worker effort.

Finally, although voice without authority may not hurt (at least, on economic grounds), it misses many of the advantages of voice with authority—namely, all the advantages that accrue from giving workers guarantees and getting in return their trust and cooperation.

FURTHER REMARKS ON UNIONS

Although this chapter is not about unions *per se,* a few final observations about unions and union practices are worthwhile.

Unionization in the United States versus Europe: The Legacy of Gompers

In most parts of Europe, few people question the legitimacy of workers taking an interest and active role in the management and strategic directions of the firm for which they work. Workers are an important constituency of the firm, perhaps the constituency with the largest fraction of their net wealth at stake if things go bad; their interests in such matters as strategic decisions the firm is taking, where it is siting its facilities, and what markets it plans to develop are clear and accepted. This reaches its zenith in the German system of co-determination, in which workers are legally guaranteed representation on the Supervisory Board nearly equal to that of shareholders, and moreover, the Works Council and management together form the firm's Economic Committee, which determines day-to-day and month-to-month strategic directions for the firm.

In comparison, organized labor in the United States has traditionally taken a hands-off attitude about managing the firm. Labor unions have been interested in so-called bread-and-butter issues of wages, benefits, and working conditions. They have traditionally abjured any interest in the strategic directions of the firm, except insofar as this affects bread-and-butter issues.[26] (For example, a decision to move production facilities to the Far East may be considered a matter for union concern, but a decision to shift product lines or to develop a new product probably would not.)

The reason for this difference in philosophy traces back to Samuel Gompers, the father of the modern American labor movement. Gompers was a strong believer in bread-and-butter unionism, restricted to highly skilled workers, and he opposed the general collectivization of industrial workers. While Gompers was leading the craft unions in the American Federation of Labor or AFL (see below), industrial labor unions were formed and led by members of the Industrial Workers of the World (IWW) and other socialist organizations. To say the least, socialism in the United States in the early part of the twentieth century was not well received by the general public, and the failure of the IWW (and industrial unions early in the century) can be attributed in some measure to a lack of public support for "socialists." Gompers' natural predilections against socialist philosophies and their advocacy of workers' role in the management of capital was reinforced by his shrewd political sense that it was essential to distance himself from those philosophies. Under his direction, the AFL made it clear that they had no desire to supplant or subvert the prerogatives of owners to employ their capital as they wished. In Europe, in comparison, organized labor has always had strong connections with socialist movements, especially with socialist political parties, so a philosophy of worker control over capital comes much more naturally there.

There are also significant differences in the bargaining structures observed in Germany and other countries compared to the United States. To simplify, collective bargaining agreements tend to be more centralized in Europe than in the United States, sometimes negotiated between a national employers' association and a national labor organization, with provisions for local adaptations. Moreover, in some countries (unlike the United States), nonunion workers are automatically extended the rights and benefits guaranteed to union members in collective bargaining agreements. Not surprisingly, given these differences, union-nonunion differentials tend to be more pronounced in the United States.

These differences in philosophies and bargaining structures have had enduring consequences. The bread-and-butter unionism of Gompers accentuates the "market power" side of unions—not trying to make the firm more efficient, which is management's role, but trying to extract from management the best possible wages, benefits, and working conditions through the exercise of market power. The more proactive unionism of European unions leads to greater interest in the efficient management of the firm. It is reducing the issue to somewhat of a caricature, but in Europe labor and management view their respective roles as economic partners, while in the United States the dominant culture has positioned labor and management as natural antagonists, so that cooperative union–management relations are somewhat less natural.[27] In particular instances, then, union leadership in the United States has a hard time accepting management overtures for cooperative relationships; union membership is socialized to regard such behavior as something of a sellout, delegitimizing the leadership's role (and power base) as representatives of the rank and file. Note that this doesn't mean that the average effect in the United States of having unions is necessarily to reduce efficiency. Rationalization of management practices, routinization of dispute resolution, giving workers a voice in the composition of their compensation, and (thereby) reducing turnover still count for a lot. But this tradition can impede efforts by organized labor and management to work together to promote efficient work practices.

Indeed, some provisions of labor law in the United States (specifically, the National Labor Relations Act) have been construed as barriers to labor–management cooperation and worker empowerment. For instance, some experiments with work teams and quality circles (e.g., at Electromation and DuPont) have been alleged before the NLRB to represent unfair labor practices, because: (1) they circumvent collective bargaining agreements that require employers not to alter work methods or job structures without union consent; and (2) more generally, they subvert the union's role as the sole bargaining agent for workers in the bargaining unit. In the last few years, the NLRB and U.S. courts have upheld this interpretation. An effort to amend the National Labor Relations Act—so that joint labor–management committees discussing items of mutual interest that are not the subject of collective bargaining are exempted from coverage—passed the House and Senate during the 104th Congress, but was vetoed by President Clinton in 1996. As of this writing, another effort along these lines, which is likely to share the same fate, is pending before the 105th Congress.

Industrial versus Craft Unions in the United States

One legacy of Gompers' early rejection of militant industrial unionism is two distinct categories or strands of unions. There are the *craft* unions, whose members all practice a particular skilled craft, and the *industrial* unions, which try to organize all eligible workers in a particular industry. In industries organized along craft union lines, such as newspaper publishing, management must deal with a host of different craft unions, such as the Typesetters, the Pressmen, the Paper Handlers, and so on. In industries organized by industrial unions, management deals primarily with a single union, such as the United Auto Workers in automobile manufacture. (Some unions have changed their basic orientation over time. For example, the Teamsters began life as something of a craft union, but they have tended more recently to behave like an industrial union.) Indeed, the distinctions are sufficiently marked so that until 1955 there were two large labor federations in the United States, the American Federation of Labor (AFL), composed of craft unions, and the Congress of Industrial Organizations (CIO), composed of industrial unions. In 1955 the two merged, forming the AFL-CIO.

Craft unions tend to represent skilled workers, whose skill, typically acquired through a union-directed progression from apprentice to journey to master status, gives them monopoly power with the employer. Craft unions tend to wish to control their own work practices, without specifying those practices in writing in the contract. (What is specified is the list of tasks that "belong" to the particular *craft*. The typical anecdote in this regard concerns the case of a power cord of a machine that was pulled out by accident: Work must stop until a member of the electrician's union can be found, because only an electrician is allowed to plug in power cords.) In the caricature of a craft-union shop, the shop steward will be the key figure in determining who does what job, who gets overtime, and so on. The membership of craft unions tends to be socially homogeneous; in the caricature, all the members (middle-aged white men and their sons and nephews) belong to the same lodge and bowl in the same league. Because of this, a craft union is often much more able to keep workers "in line," if the union chooses to cooperate with management (or to enforce a collective action *against* management).

Industrial unions tend to represent unskilled or semiskilled workers (though the recent growth of industrial unionization among two groups of workers—clericals and government employees—has muddied things somewhat). Hence, industrial unions tend to depend much more on their legally chartered power to be effective. This is why industrial unions find it attractive to organize the entire workforce of the plant; if they represented only some fraction of the workers and they withdrew their labor services, management might be able to get other workers to cover for those on strike. This has several consequences:

- Agreements with industrial unions tend to be much more explicit about work practices. Detailed job descriptions are often included; tasks are assigned to specific worker grades. Thus, were there a spill on the shop floor, it would not be just any member of the maintenance workers' union who must be found, but rather a Maintenance Technician Grade IV. The union, in representing many diverse workers, establishes formally and explicitly the rights of each.

- Politics in industrial unions tend to be more fractious and exciting, especially when the demographics of the company's workforce is changing (because of a change in production methods, say, or product mix).
- Workforce heterogeneity, in terms of social characteristics and skill levels, tends to be greater in industrial unions than in craft unions.[28] This can hurt the ability of shop stewards in an industrial union to bargain informally over grievances with management; shop stewards in industrial unions do not, on average, carry the confidence and trust of workers in their shops as strongly as do the stewards in a craft union.

THE BOTTOM LINE FOR MANAGEMENT

We are now ready to tackle the questions with which this chapter began: Taking the perspective of management, how should management view worker collectivization, whether through unions or other forms?

Should Management Welcome Unionization?

Although they needn't do so and sometimes don't, unions *can* increase productive efficiency. To reiterate, they do this by giving workers a voice with which to express opinions; by helping routinize day-to-day disputes and negotiations between labor and management; by increasing the extent to which management can delegate to and trust in labor; by increasing commitment through enhanced opportunities for participating in workplace governance; by enhancing perceptions of distributive and procedural justice; and, in some cases, by offering workers protection against adverse large-stakes decisions by management.[29]

Given these positives, should management welcome or even invite a union to organize its workforce? *Going by the averages* (in the United States), the answer appears to be *no*. On average, unions take more using their monopoly power than they add in increased efficiencies. As noted earlier, however, looking at the averages in this instance can be quite misleading. If, for example, your workforce is being courted by a union with a track record for positive union–management relations, then you may be better off (in terms of profits) having them in; they may enhance productivity by more than they take out in profits. (To the best of our knowledge, the data neither support nor refute the hypothesis that more constructive unions take back more in increased compensation than they give in enhanced overall productivity.) Indeed, a first step in developing positive relations with the union can be to recognize them forthrightly. Jim Casey, the founder of United Parcel Service, *invited* the Teamsters to organize his company very early in the firm's history, believing that unionization was inevitable and that his overture would produce a more cooperative relationship.[30] Bear in mind, of course, that workers are free to vote for a union, whether or not the employer has welcomed or invited them to do so. The result at UPS was a very positive and constructive relationship over many decades. (Recent dealings between the Teamsters and UPS, however, suggest that this historically constructive relationship may have gone somewhat sour. You might ponder how much of this is attributable to decisions on the part of UPS management that appeared to violate long-standing implicit understandings with its workforce.)

However, Casey's perspective definitely seems to be the minority point of view in the United States, given the enormous resources employers continue to devote to strategies designed to avoid unions. Some examples of these strategies include: retaining labor lawyers and consultants who specialize in union avoidance;[31] relocating plants in states (or foreign countries) where unions are not powerful; isolating workers from one another, to make it more difficult for them to solve the collective action problem;[32] and installing grievance systems, work teams, and other alternatives to collective bargaining.

Kiss 'em, Kill 'em, or Co-Exist? What If You Have a Union?

Suppose you are managing in a setting with an established union. Suppose further that the relationship is not particularly constructive. The question arises, Should you try to turn the relationship around, make the union disappear, or live with what you've got?

Because both sides may win if you pursue the first option, we begin there. It has been done, as we saw with Magma Copper. But understand that the constructive relationship you are seeking is based on mutual respect and trust, and the union officials that you have to deal with are elected representatives of the rank-and-file. Insofar as your firm has a long history of enmity with a union, turning things around can be difficult. You should consider this activity as a risky investment. It will probably be costly in the short-run—you'll need to give more than you get—and the returns aren't guaranteed.

If you do decide to make the attempt, experience offers a few pointers.

- It helps if this is a response to a real crisis, perceived as such by labor and management. If everyone understands that what is at stake is the equity of equity holders and the jobs of management and workers, they are more likely to respond positively.

- Symbolism counts for a lot. Bringing in labor relations people with a history of constructive labor relations and giving them authority has been effective, as has having the CEO and other top managers directly involved, treating their counterparts in labor as equals and partners.

- Resistance to cooperative labor–management relationships is often most acute among particular segments of management, such as first-line supervisors acclimated to a more adversarial regime and among lawyers and HR specialists whose jobs revolve around handling labor–management conflicts. Recall that one of the first (and most important steps) that Burgess Winter took at Magma was to work with this segment of management.

- Remember the political reality that union officials face: Even if they believe in your good will and understand intellectually that a positive relationship is good for them and the employees they represent, they cannot be seen to get too far out in front of beliefs of the rank-and-file. If the membership is sufficiently embittered, support for management initiatives stressing a new cooperative relationship with the union may not be a politically viable course of action.

And if you are going to make the attempt, you can probably be glad that your workers are organized. Turning around bad labor–management relations with unorganized workers is tremendously difficult; essentially, you have no single partner to deal with. The union gives you the opportunity to talk with a representative of the workforce—if that representative is at all inclined to cooperate, you have a shot. And to the extent that the workers' representative is drawn from and represents the infra-marginal employee who is older, with greater family responsibilities, he or she is more likely to be so inclined.

On the other end of the spectrum is the option of trying to weaken or even oust the union. A number of techniques have been tried with some success to achieve this objective, including using bankruptcy protections to abrogate union contracts; subcontracting work to nonunion concerns; and increasing reliance on "contingent" personnel (part-timers, etc.) as a device to restrain union demands. If you are considering this option, think hard. Unions can be very powerful foes, and trying strategies like these is something akin to betting on the lottery. If you win, you may win big. But if you don't win, and the odds may well be against you, you are likely to wind up with a thoroughly embittered partner whose protector (the NLRB) is apt to be keeping a close eye on you. Finally, if you are seriously considering a "kill 'em" strategy, take good legal advice.

Obviously, we can't offer general advice among kiss 'em, kill 'em, or co-exist. The specific history of relations, the players currently involved, the anticipated duration of the relationship, and the economic and social costs and benefits of various outcomes all need to be considered carefully. Inasmuch as most managers will probably come down in favor of co-existence, we offer some gratuitous general advice: The relationship you have with your union is potentially productive capital. It is more complex capital than, say, your plant and equipment; the machines on an assembly line don't vote every so often on how fast the assembly line will move next time you turn it on. But it is capital, and managers (in the United States, at least) are usually too pessimistic about the rates of return that can be achieved from investing in it.

NONUNION WORKER REPRESENTATION?

Given unionization rates in the United States, if you manage in the United States you are unlikely to face the choice of the previous subsection. But even if you decide against inviting a union to organize your firm's workforce, you might still learn from the productive efficiencies that the data suggest can be provided by unions.

Providing a forum for worker complaints and suggestions is an obvious first step, including quality circles that can make suggestions for management approval. Allowing workers to select advocates whom they bring to grievance hearings is another. The "voice without (real) authority" option is there, and it can be tried, but we firmly believe that efficiency enhancement will be greater insofar as genuine authority is granted along with voice. This leads to further steps you might take, such as: general policies of worker empowerment to control working conditions and to monitor and control production methods, including giving quality circles the authority (within limits) to decide whether to implement their own ideas; having worker representatives on the management committee of the organization, with a vote; allowing workers to select one or more of the firm's outside directors; having grievances adjudicated by objective third parties (e.g., a labor lawyer who provides mediation services) or providing for an elected representative of labor on whatever panel hears grievances.[33]

To make such arrangements work, management must understand that some setbacks will occur. Workers, if they are going to have authority, will have to be given information relevant to the exercise of that authority. A management style of holding all the cards close to the vest will not work. And if workers have access to important proprietary information, some may sometimes leak out. More importantly, worker interests are rarely aligned perfectly with those of management or the firm's owners. The alignment is unlikely to be one of perfect opposition, and granting workers authority may improve the alignment (through a sense that the relationship is longer term and through psychological processes of buy-in and escalating commitment). But workers may sometimes use authority they have been granted in ways that run against the immediate interests of management. At such times, management must keep in mind that these "suboptimal" (from management's perspective) decisions are part of the investment it is making in good labor–management relations, paid for by increased efficiencies at other times.

The hard question for management is *Will the investment give a sufficient return?* The answer depends on too many specifics. But in cases where labor–management relations have a healthy history, where worker efforts are not easily monitored (so that some degree of discretion is technologically necessary), and where workers have access to information that could be used to increase productive efficiency, the investment should be considered very seriously. We'll return to this topic and some of the details in Chapter 9, when we discuss high-commitment HRM.

WHAT NEXT?

We noted at the outset of this chapter that workers have statutorily established rights to some forms of voice, although those rights vary across locales. Workers enjoy a lot of other protections under law. Why should the government intercede in the private exchange of labor services for pay? Regardless of why it should or shouldn't, why *does* it? It is to these questions that we turn next.

IN REVIEW

⇒ To achieve efficient, cooperative relations in employment, it can be helpful to give employees real decision-making authority.

⇒ The most systematic data we have on this point concern the impact of unions in the United States.
- Employees' rights to be represented by a union (or another employee collective) are usually established by law; the relevant laws vary greatly from jurisdiction to jurisdiction.
- Although unionization rates in the United States are low and have been falling over recent decades, the study of unions remains of interest because of the concentration of unionization in key industries; because the prospect of unionization is ever-present; because you are much more likely to face unions or other worker collectives outside the United States; and because unions give us insight into worker voice in general.
- The average impact of unionization on a number of dimensions has been tabulated (see pages 127–9); the bottom line in terms of efficiency and profits is that, in the United States, unionization seems to raise efficiency but to reduce profits.

⇒ Explanations of these data have stressed the "two faces" of unions:
- They enhance the bargaining power of workers.
- They give workers a voice, and in particular, they give a voice to older, more stable (infra-marginal) workers.

⇒ Why does unionization seem to enhance efficiency?
- Unions help solve the free-rider problems of collective employee action, strengthening employee safeguards based on employer reputation.
- Unions help to routinize dispute resolution.
- Management can delegate to unions in ways it cannot delegate as safely to individual workers, because of the union's stake in an enduring relation. And for a variety of reasons, such delegation can improve efficiency.
- Unions can offer employees protection against single big-stakes actions by management.
- By promoting employee trustworthiness and thus trust in employees, unionization helps to enhance worker buy-in and commitment.
- Unions can raise perceptions of distributive and procedural justice.
- Unions provide status and clout to infra-marginal workers, who tend to be older and more stable—and therefore perhaps more desirable role models for the workforce from management's perspective.

⇒ Voice without authority can help improve efficiency, but it can also frustrate employees and lead to resentment.

⇒ The bottom line:
  • A case can be made for welcoming unionization of your workforce, but the case usually doesn't impress managers in the United States.
  • If you have a unionized workforce in the United States, promoting more positive, efficient relations is a long-term investment strategy well worth considering.
  • Trying (in the United States) to rid yourself of union representation for your workforce is a dangerous proposition.
  • If you don't have a union, it can still make a lot of sense to give your workers a voice (with authority), a topic to which we return in Chapter 9.

ENDNOTES

1. For informative discussions of the evolution in labor relations at Magma, see William H. Miller, "Metamorphosis in the Desert," *Industry Week* (March 16, 1992): 27–34; George W. Bohlander and Marshall H. Campbell, "Problem-solving and Work Redesign: Magma Copper's Labor-management Partnership," *National Productivity Review* 12 (Autumn 1993): 519–33; and Jeffrey Pfeffer, *The Human Equation: Building Profits by Putting People First* (Boston: Harvard Business School Press, 1998), Chapter 8.

2. We will not go into greater detail about this one specific story. But aficionados of governance provisions in contracts, and particularly those interested in trilateral governance through arbitration, will find specifics of the Magma contract to be quite interesting. See Bohlander and Campbell, *op. cit.*

3. More details about unions in the United States are scattered throughout this chapter.

4. Adapted from OECD data taken from OECD Employment Outlook, 1991, Table 4.2, p. 102. Copyright © OECD, 1991.

5. The complete table is viewable online at: http://www.ilo.org/public/english/80relpro/publ/wlr/97/annex/tab12.htm.

6. OECD, *Employment Outlook* (July 1994), Chart 5.1, p. 173.

7. *Ibid.*

8. *Ibid.*; also see Y. Suwa, "Enterprise-Based Labor Unions and Collective Agreements," *Japan Labor Bulletin* 31 (September 1, 1992), viewable on-line at http://www.jil.go.jp/bulletin/year/1992/vol31-09/03.htm.

9. Empirical studies for Great Britain have also been done, and work is being done on other European contexts. The only results we will report here are for the United States, however. The work of Richard Freeman and James Medoff that we will report may be found in their book, *What Do Unions Do?* (New York: Basic Books, 1984). Their empirical studies were conducted in the early 1980s; subsequently, follow-up studies have been conducted which by and large confirm what Freeman and Medoff found—for example, see Lawrence R. Mishel and Paula B. Voos (eds.), *Unions and Economic Competitiveness* (Armonk, NY : M.E. Sharpe, 1992). Despite being more than a decade old,

the Freeman and Medoff book remains a valuable source, which you would do well to read, especially if you will be working in an American context that is unionized.

10. We don't in fact find this, but suppose for the moment that we did.

11. Collective bargaining agreements will often specify *how* layoffs must be handled, with what notification, and what alternative solutions must be tried before layoffs ensue. Similarly, union agreements sometimes give priority to certain groups (e.g., recalling unemployed union members based on accumulated seniority) if the employer wants to hire additional personnel, and some unions have recently bargained for the right to bid on certain projects before they are contracted out. But unions in the United States seldom have control over the number of employees, nor, in most cases, whether work will be outsourced.

12. You may find this somewhat paradoxical: If unionized workers have lower job satisfaction, why do they also have lower turnover rates? Recall from last chapter that job satisfaction is a tricky thing, which has to do with anchoring and salience. In the context of unions, a common explanation for low job satisfaction is that organized workers are more likely to expect to be able to change their working conditions for the better, and therefore they spend more time examining those conditions to see what changes for the better could be made. This raises the contrast or vividness between what current conditions *are* and what they *might be,* lowering job satisfaction.

13. The italics are there for a reason: We can measure the value of increased wages and benefits in 1999 of a strike conducted in 1998. But if contract negotiations in 1998 concluded without a strike, how were current terms affected by the 1995 strike? Insofar as negotiations are focused on percentage raises—which is true to some extent—there is an enduring impact on wages and benefits of earlier strikes. And, more directly, the 1995 strike may have sufficiently chastened management so that they gave good terms in the 1998 negotiations.

14. Barry T. Hirsch, *Labor Unions and the Economic Performance of Firms* (Kalamazoo, MI: W.E. Upjohn Institute for Employment Research, 1991).

15. Some terminology and institutional facts are helpful here. A *closed-shop* setting is one in which the employer may hire only union members. In this case, the union is clearly the monopoly supplier of labor services to the employer. But closed shops are illegal in the United States A *union-shop* setting is one in which new employees who hold a union-eligible job are required to join the union upon taking up employment. In union shops, then, every union-eligible employee must pay union dues and is subject to union discipline. Most states in the United States permit union shops; some—primarily those in the South, Midwest, and Southwest (but not California)—have right-to-work laws that make union shops illegal. In an *agency shop,* new workers are not compelled to join unions but must pay the equivalent of union dues to hold a union-eligible job, on the theory that the union acts as the worker's agent and deserves compensation for this. So especially where the union has only agency-shop powers, it is not the sole supplier of labor to the employer. Still, the employer must negotiate bread-and-butter terms of employment (wages and benefits) exclusively with the union, and the employer may and often does negotiate work-rule issues. To the extent that the union can compel its members to go on strike—and informal union discipline often gives it this power *de facto* if not *de jure*—and to the extent that a large percentage of the workforce belongs to the union, the union retains a lot of bargaining power. Management can, under current law, break a union, but it must first negotiate seriously ("in good faith," as interpreted by the NLRB) with the union, make a final offer,

and, if the offer is rejected, declare impasse, after which it can hire permanent replacements. These permanent replacements can then vote to decertify the union as their bargaining agent. However, the costs of busting a union by going through this process are usually quite high. (Although this is an accurate description of current law as of this writing, the Clinton administration has had as a centerpiece of its legislative agenda the withdrawal of the right to hire permanent replacements, and only permanent replacements can vote to decertify the existing union as the bargaining agent. It seems unlikely that this will become law before the next [2000] Congressional elections, at the earliest. But by the time you read these lines, the law may have changed.)

16. This projected increase in turnover among marginal workers is confounded by the general decrease in turnover that results because: (1) management has better (more direct) information about the preferences of workers in general; (2) increased feelings of procedural justice, increased buy-in, and the like associated with unionism; and (3) wages and benefits in union firms are somewhat better than in the nonunion sector. Hence, although we would expect to see that unionization is associated with a pronounced decrease in turnover among more senior workers, the overall prediction for less senior workers is ambiguous.

17. If they did, and if managers understood this connection, then profit-maximizing management would cater to the interests of more senior workers. Thus, to assert that this union-induced shift in attention is efficiency-promoting is to assert that the promotion of efficiency occasioned by the shift is too subtle for management to divine without being forced to do so by unionization.

18. There is a subtlety to note here. When bosses act capriciously, the presence of a union ought to raise the odds of a wildcat strike. But bosses, aware of this, are no doubt less likely to act capriciously when a union is present than in a nonunionized setting. Thus, the fact that wildcat strikes are much less frequent in nonunionized settings makes our point with emphasis: In nonunionized settings, the probability of worker action *conditional on a supervisor's transgressions or caprice* apparently falls so much that—despite the higher marginal rate of supervisor caprice that is likely in such settings—we nonetheless see far fewer collective actions by workers.

19. We will have more to say about this in Chapter 9, in the context of high-commitment HR practices.

20. Control is also facilitated in craft unions by the social homogeneity of members and the inculcation of shared skills and values that occurs through union-controlled training apprenticeships.

21. Although sexist, a standard term for members of a union local, *the brethren,* is indicative.

22. Both "to the extents" can be and have been extensively questioned. And because many considerations motivate managers, there is a substantial political component to managerial decision-making. "Power and Politics" is a popular MBA course for good reason. So the link between the economic well-being of the firm and the decisions of its managers is not as tight as might be hoped. But the link is there, to a greater extent than the corresponding link in a union.

23. On the other side, the union leadership must be wary of agreements and arrangements made with management, which are subject to change or cancellation whenever there is a change in the relevant management. The unions at Eastern Airlines tried to foster good relations with Eastern's management during the tenure of Frank Borman as CEO

(without a lot of help from Borman). When Borman arranged to have Eastern taken over by Frank Lorenzo, well known for his less-than-positive attitude toward unions, union officials—who put a fair amount of their credit with the rank-and-file on the line working with Eastern management—were left looking more than a little silly.

24. This ignores the possibility that even if workers in the soon-to-be-closed plant will be ex-workers, closing this plant can affect management's reputations with employees at other plants it operates, with the workforce at the new plant it is opening, and possibly with suppliers and other constituents. Hence, employer concern for reputation may not be entirely absent, even in such drastic cases as this.

25. And, on the other side of the coin, the union's acceptance of what amounted to a no-strike clause for eight years provided management with the sorts of guarantees they needed, to permit large-scale investment in developing the "K."

26. Moreover, the National Labor Relations Board treats such strategic issues as "voluntary topics" of collective bargaining, which means that unions and management may bargain over them voluntarily, but it is illegal for a union to bargain them to an impasse (strike).

27. Two interesting variations on this theme: (1) In Great Britain, management historically has been so unwilling to share power with organized workers that the dominant culture is one of antagonism, as well. In Great Britain, as in the United States, this means that cooperation between labor and management is unusual. (2) In Germany, workers are represented by the unions on bread-and-butter issues and by their Works Council on broader issues concerning work practices, the strategy of the firm, and the like. And when it comes to bread-and-butter negotiations, bargaining takes place on a national, industrywide level. Little wonder, then, that management tends to see the Works Council as cooperative and the union as more adversarial. Indeed, under the spur of substantial and rising levels of unemployment, firms in Germany have very recently (1998) begun bargaining for givebacks directly with their more compliant (and weaker) works councils, which is causing tremendous controversy and legal action in Germany. For instance, see Mary Williams Walsh, "Boss' New Deal Jolts Germany's Unions," *Los Angeles Times* (Monday, February 2, 1998): A1.

28. When workers are (or perceive themselves to be) diverse, it can be harder to surmount the collective action problems that must be overcome if workers are to organize effectively. Hence, in cases where a vast majority of the workforce belongs to an industrial union (the United Auto Workers in automobile assembly or the Teamsters for UPS employees), it is not uncommon for small minorities of skilled workers to belong to their own distinct craft unions (e.g., electricians working for the Big 3 auto makers or pilots flying for UPS).

29. Other improvements in efficiency seem to be associated with managerial responses to the fact of unionization itself—that is, when a firm becomes unionized, management will sometimes respond to the "crisis" by rationalizing its general operating procedures.

30. Think of this action in terms of the signal it conveys. Unionization is presumably less costly for employers who intend, even without a union, to be fair and treat workers well, to give employees a voice in the enterprise, to be open in their dealings with labor, to offer good pay and benefits, and the like. By inviting the Teamsters to organize UPS, Casey sent a powerful signal to employees and others that he intended to be a reputable employer; otherwise, absent those intentions, he presumably would have found such an invitation to be far more costly. Note also that there are other ways in which invitations like Mr. Casey's might be competitively advantageous for

firms like UPS. For instance, if Casey believed that unionization was going to be less disruptive and costly to UPS than to many of its competitors, then by encouraging unionization in the *industry,* UPS could put competitors at a disadvantage.

31. A case study of a union decertification election reported that the company spent $10,000 on attorney fees and roughly $70,000 on management consultants in a campaign lasting more than a year, which resulted in ousting the union. With 105 union employees involved, these costs amount to more than $760 per employee in the bargaining unit, without even factoring in the enormous indirect costs, such as the diversion of management and worker effort during the campaign, long-term decrements in worker morale, increased turnover, adverse public relations, increased administrative burdens on the company after ousting the union, and the like. See John J. Lawler, *Unionization and Deunionization: Strategy, Tactics, and Outcomes* (Columbia, SC: University of South Carolina Press, 1990).

32. This is among the reasons that labor unions have recently been alarmed by trends toward telecommuting and other forms of "home work," echoing the concerns that long ago led to laws restricting textile firms from contracting with individuals to do garment piece-work at home.

33. We know of an organization whose panel for hearing corporate grievances consists of an equal (and moderate) number of management and rank-and-file representatives. A senior manager in this company, who says he is frequently asked how the company can possibly entrust important decisions to such a balanced board, responds by noting that even if management and the rank-and-file were inclined to vote as blocs, this structure requires simply that *one* of the rank-and-file members support whatever company decision or action resulted in the grievance. He says that if the company cannot make a case that persuades a single line employee and all managerial representatives, then that is *prima facie* grounds for believing the grievance is justified.

7

EMPLOYMENT, SOCIETY, AND THE LAW

While we were writing this book, a local radio station was carrying advertisements for several firms offering to handle the human resource management tasks at client companies. This wasn't an offer to integrate firms' strategies with their HR practices, or do their recruiting, or set compensation levels. Instead, one firm was offering payroll administration and compliance, which means filling out the many forms required of employers by state and national government, posting the many notices that the government says must be posted, and otherwise keeping the firm out of trouble in terms of employment law. And the advertisement offered a pretty compelling argument for why client firms should employ this service: It is simply impossible for anyone attending seriously to a real business to keep track of the constantly changing intricacies of employment law. Another company's ad went even further, offering to take on the existing employees as its own so that the current employer could be spared not simply the administrative hassles but especially the legal liabilities.

Ask most managers, and we'd bet they will find this a sad commentary on contemporary times, that such a large chunk of HRM comes down to complying with government mandates. The range of matters connected with employment into which the government intervenes is enormous, including the basic forms that labor contracts can take (neither slavery nor indentured servitude is permitted); who can work (child labor laws); the length of the work week; what wages can be paid (minimum wage laws); conditions at the workplace (health and safety legislation; privacy provisions); how benefits are administered (working especially through the tax code); who can be hired and how (laws against discrimination); who can be terminated and how; and what rights employees have to bargain collectively (see Chapter 6). And that isn't all; in Exhibit 7-1 we give a more complete and systematic list of major HR topics covered by statutes and regulations in the United States.

In the United States, the growth in lawsuits pertaining to employment has been staggering. For instance, one study reported that between 1970 and 1989 the number of employment discrimination lawsuits in the United States increased by 2166%.[1] Within one Tennessee district of the federal district court, the number of employment civil rights filings increased by 80% just between 1993 and 1996, with employment cases rising from 6.3% to 10.2% of all civil filings within that district.[2] The *New York*

- Hiring Competitors' Employees
- Employment Agreements
- Using Independent Contractors and Employment Agencies
- Employing Disabled Individuals, Minors, and Aliens
- Wages and Hours
- Provision of Time Off from Work
- Workplace Health and Safety
- Employee Benefits
  — Mandated benefits
  — Fringe benefits
    ∘ Contractual obligations
    ∘ Nondiscrimination obligations and pregnancy leaves
    ∘ ERISA obligations
    ∘ COBRA obligations
  — Stock options and profit sharing
- Employment Policies
  — Policy manuals
  — Promulgating work rules
    ∘ Absenteeism and tardiness
    ∘ Moonlighting and conflicts of interest
    ∘ Alcohol and drug use
    ∘ No solicitation/distribution rules
- Scope of Employment Laws
- Policing the Workplace; Discipline
  — Drug and alcohol testing
  — Protection of trade secrets
  — Surveillance and searches (including computer monitoring)
  — Investigation of alleged wrongdoing
- Union Activities and Collective Bargaining
- Recordkeeping Requirements
- Employee Privacy Rights and Whistleblowing Protections
- Requirements to Post Notices
- Discrimination in Hiring, Training, Pay, Promotion, Performance Evaluation, Discipline, Working Conditions
  — Gender
  — Race, color, ancestry, national origin
  — Age
  — Sexual orientation (in some localities)
  — Religion
  — Marital status
  — Handicap or medical condition
- Employee Termination and Reductions in Force

Exhibit 7-1 Main HR Topics Covered by State and/or Federal Laws and Regulations

Times reported in 1997 that federal discrimination class actions had more than doubled in the preceding four years, and that major pending cases included Glorious Foods (caterer), Motel 6, Dun & Bradstreet, and Smith Barney.[3] According to a recent article in an attorney trade publication, the U.S. Bureau of Labor Statistics forecasts a 28% increase in attorney jobs by 2005, with employee benefits, sexual harassment, and intellectual property included among the fastest-growing specialties.[4]

Foreign firms operating in the United States sometimes find American employment law perplexing and not at all consistent with what goes on back home. To take two somewhat notorious examples, Japanese conglomerate Mitsubishi and Swedish drug maker Astra both faced tremendous adverse publicity in the United States in recent years because of alleged violations of employment laws (sex and race discrimination in the case of Mitsubishi, sexual harassment in the case of Astra). After protests, boycotts, and a disrupted annual meeting, Mitsubishi agreed to provide several hundred million dollars to increase opportunities for women and minorities at its American operations. Following a highly publicized investigation (and a *Business Week* cover story), the U.S. Equal Employment Opportunity Commission announced it will seek a "sweeping and costly settlement" against Astra or else take the firm to court.

Is this simply a matter of too many lawyers and too much litigation in the United States? After all, a 1991 report by the President's Council on Competitiveness (headed by then-Vice President Dan Quayle) cited statistics indicating that the number of lawyers per capita in the United States was approximately 25 times the rate in Japan, 3.4 times the rate in England and Wales, and 2.5 times the rate in Germany. However, even though lawyers may be more numerous within the United States, employment law outside the United States is in some instances even more "intrusive." At least, one corporate employment lawyer recently observed that:

> ...most U.S. companies expanding abroad are surprised to learn that foreign employment laws are more protective of workers' rights than anything they ever have heard of in the United States. By global standards, the United States has a relatively "hands-off" approach to regulating the employer-employee relationship.[5]

Multinationals often get the worst of all worlds. For example, American courts have taken the view that U.S. companies operating outside the United States are accountable to domestic employment laws, unless complying with U.S. law would require the firm in question to violate host country laws. Companies headquartered in the United States frequently encounter complicated conflicts between the mandates of U.S. employment laws and regulations on the one hand and the business and social imperatives associated with doing business globally on the other. For instance, in one case, Saudi Arabian officials allegedly told a U.S. employer that "Saudis did not want any Jews in their country" and that there was a "paternalistic concern for the safety of Jews traveling in Arab lands" (*Abrams v. Baylor College of Medicine*, 805 F. 2d 528, 532–3 [5th Cir. 1986]). The employer consequently rejected Jewish applicants, but a court found that this violated Title VII of the Civil Rights Act. Similarly, in another lawsuit (*Fernandez v. Wynn Oil Co.*, 653 F. 2d 1273 [9th Cir. 1981]), a U.S. oil company was found to have engaged in sex discrimination when it claimed that gender was a relevant selection criterion for certain higher-level positions because key South American clients would refuse to deal with a female executive.

These introductory observations are intended to make two points (which, if you are a practicing manager, probably didn't need making): The government intrudes fairly heavily into the relationship between employer and employee, and contemporary managers are foolish not to pay close attention. A book about HRM that ignored these facts of life would paint a pretty inaccurate picture.

But what is there to say beyond this, in a book that aims at relating HRM to the strategic concerns of general managers? It makes little sense to recount here the specifics of any particular body of employment law. The laws that pertain in one country—or even one jurisdiction within a single country—often differ markedly from laws elsewhere. And the laws that pertain today may (and do) change a lot over the course of time. General managers in particular jurisdictions ought to become acquainted with their basic responsibilities and their employees' basic rights, and they should probably have specialists on hand who can advise them regarding specific matters. But to provide a global orientation to employment law would take a multivolume encyclopedia.

Rather than recount specifics, in this chapter we aim at two general tasks. First, although most managers view government regulation of employment relations as "intrusion," there are some good reasons for government intervention (to use a more neutral and, we think, appropriate word). Your attitude toward employment laws and regulations is apt to be more tolerant if you understand their bases and functions. So we will give a brief account of why governments intervene, both normatively (why they ought to) and positively (why they do). Second, although the content and scope of employment laws and regulations vary enormously from one jurisdiction to another, the presence of employment regulation has some common and important effects on the management of human resources. It makes sense to discuss those common effects and, to the extent that we can, draw some lessons about how managers can improve their responses.

THE NORMATIVE BASES FOR INTERVENTION

To understand the normative bases for societal intervention in the relationship between employer and employee, it is helpful first to set forth as a straw argument the basic libertarian position: The government (and society) has no business intervening in private transactions between two consenting adults, if that transaction does not adversely affect some third party. This is so because the transaction must be presumed to make both parties to it better off—otherwise, why would they willingly take part in it?—and social rules should aim solely at increasing the welfare of individual citizens.

Paternalism and Bounded Rationality

The first normative basis for societal intervention involves the condition that the transaction is between consenting adults, with emphasis on *adults*. The restriction of the argument to adults is shorthand for the following: The parties involved should be well informed about the terms and consequences of the transaction, and they should understand what is (or is not) in their own best interests. Only the most rabid libertarian would argue that the basic position should extend to children, who may lack the judgment needed to perceive their own best interests, or the information required to assess the consequences of the transaction, or both.

In some employment transactions, the story goes, the individuals involved are inadequately informed about the consequences of their actions, or they lack the judgment to know what is in their own best interests. For example, health and safety regulations are intended in part to protect employees who otherwise might not perceive the dangers of working in an environment with, say, free-floating asbestos particles. Laws against indentured servitude keep individuals from alienating their freedom, partly because they may not realize how badly they will be affected by such an act. Child labor laws (insofar as the child decides to seek employment) are a third example. This, essentially, is paternalism; society knows better than the individual what is good for the individual, and so it forbids transactions that the individual might undertake to his own detriment.

The term *paternalism* casts this rationale in a somewhat pejorative light; it sounds as if society is protecting individuals against their own immaturity or foolishness. An alternative to statutory restrictions on transactions among sensible people, it would seem, would be for the state freely to provide information and education but place no restrictions on individual actions. In our view, this pejorative connotation to paternalism is unwarranted. Even sensible people are not infinitely rational; they lack the ability to think through the full consequences of their actions; it can be costly (in time and effort) to become fully informed about, say, the full range of environmental hazards we may face on the job and to respond rationally to those hazards. For each of these reasons, a good case can be made that it is more efficient to regulate employment transactions, to economize on the costs of information gathering and processing.[6]

Externalities

The condition "if the transaction does not adversely affect some third party" refers to what economists call externalities. If A and B exchange money for apples, or apples for oranges, C is (presumably) unaffected. But suppose A and B enter into a transaction in which B dumps some toxic substance into a river. If C lives down river, she is adversely affected by this transaction, and thus there may be good reason for regulating the transaction between A and B.

Health and safety regulations can be justified in part by citing externalities. Suppose A undertakes some job working for B that is potentially dangerous to A. Insofar as society stands ready to support A and her family in case of catastrophic injury, A may feel that the rewards outweigh the potential personal costs to her. But Taxpayer C, who picks up the tab for the social safety net, is certainly adversely affected by A's decision. Hence C, and society in general, may seek to regulate health and safety. Similar arguments apply for child labor laws (society bears the cost of uneducated individuals), regulations pertaining to mass layoffs, and regulations concerning pension funds. The tax code can also be used in this regard; one reason that health benefits are tax-advantaged is that society has a stake in public health.

Note carefully the differences between this sort of argument and paternalism. It is paternalistic to stipulate that the workplace must be free of asbestos because individual workers cannot adequately assess the dangers of working in an asbestos-contaminated environment. But even if the individual can assess those dangers, insofar as society in general will step in to care for the victims of asbestos-induced lung cancer, we have a further argument based on externalities and the interests of taxpayers generally.

Redressing Power Imbalances and Redistributing Wealth

In some economic transactions, the parties to the transaction have vastly different amounts of economic power. The threat by a single employee to leave his job is often of much less concern to his employer than is the employer's threat to fire the employee, because the employee has a much greater share of his wealth invested in transaction-specific capital than does the employer. In the extreme, there is the case of the company town, in which there is one employer for the entire community, who controls all the housing and services. Employees can leave their jobs, perhaps, but only at the cost of relocating completely.

Just as society has an interest in redistributing wealth, to promote equity, so it is held to have an interest in redressing power imbalances. In effect, society is attempting to create a more level bargaining field. So, for example, workers are given the right to organize and bargain collectively with their employer, and employers are restrained in how and when they can fire employees.

General legislation intended to level the bargaining field will tend to be a blunt instrument, as conditions (i.e., the pitch of the pre-leveled bargaining field) will vary greatly from one situation to another. Thus, the rights of employees to organize and the limitations on what employers can do to campaign against unions may produce a level surface in one industry, only barely begin to redress the balance in a second, and give workers all the bargaining power in a third.

How does this rationale for government intervention square with the libertarian straw argument? It may be true that unfettered bargaining between consenting adults leaves each of them better off than if the bargain they wish to make is forbidden to them. But if they begin with vast differences in their bargaining power, one side (the employer) may garner most—if not all—of the value the two together can produce. By redressing the power imbalance, we are theoretically moving to a different and more equitable point.[7]

A libertarian would object to this by arguing that when governments intervene they usually increase inefficiencies. For example, libertarians argue that giving workers the ability to bargain collectively makes them a monopolist supplier of labor services, with the usual (inefficient) consequences ensuing, not to mention the corruption that is inevitable whenever you replace market-based outcomes with outcomes that depend on political processes. But a defender of this rationale responds that government intervened because the employer had too much market power to begin with. If labor markets were competitive (and, given the prevalence of long-term employment, *remained* competitive), we wouldn't need this sort of protection for employees. It is because employers are alleged to have too much bargaining power, *ex post* if not *ex ante,* that the government intervenes.

Promoting Efficiency

The libertarian objections to giving bargaining power to employees, and the defenders' response, lead to a fourth general basis for government intervention—namely, to promote efficiency in transactions. This begins with a classic justification for redressing power imbalances: To the extent that employers are monopsonistic purchasers of labor services (single buyers of a particular good from many suppliers), they will employ fewer workers than is socially efficient in order to hold down wages (just as a monopolist will sell less, at higher cost, than is efficient). Hence, power–balance redressing can promote efficiency, whether achieved by giving employees the ability to organize (on the presumption that bilateral monopoly will lead to a more efficient outcome) or through minimum wage legislation.

But there is more to it than this. Take the administration of pension funds as an example. Assume it is efficient to have pensions administered by private sources, rather than directly by the government. (The argument for this is not hard to make but is off the immediate point, so we won't bother with it here.) In entrusting the administration of pension funds to their employer, workers must worry about employers absconding with the funds or investing them unwisely, say in a leveraged buyout of the firm. To the extent that employees cannot be sure that their pensions will be managed prudently, they are less inclined to contribute to them and they will place less value on contributions by their employer, leading to inefficiencies in the savings process. The government, by regulating pension-fund administration, can provide employees with substantial guarantees that their pensions are being prudently managed, thereby increasing efficiency in savings.

Or take regulations that prevent management from instantly engaging in plant closures, to move work overseas. Recall the argument from Chapter 6 that management's ability to take such actions may undermine the basic reputation construction on which efficient employment relations are often based. By using statutes to restrain management prerogatives, a better basis for trust, and thus more efficient employment transactions, may be created. Note that management is better off in this case for being restrained (just as in the case of pension fund regulation); management would like *ex ante* to be restrained from taking certain actions that would be appealing *ex post.* Guarantees that are based on government-enforced regulations can stand in for private promises and commitment, when those private promises and commitments would be less effective.

To take one further example, the U.S. Congress not long ago enacted provisions that (in part) made medical benefits portable, so that employees who participate in a medical benefit plan that they like can take that plan with them when/if they change employers. The economics of benefits are too complex to get into here—we will discuss them more fully in Chapter 12—but the efficiency-promoting properties of portability should be clear: Such legislation will promote employee mobility, increasing the odds of good matches between employees and employers.

Protecting Inalienable Rights of the Individual

The fifth and final normative basis for societal intervention is the inalienability of certain individual rights. Some rights held by the individual—to privacy, to leave a job whenever he chooses, to work in a safe environment—may be held by society to be inalienable. That is, even if the individual himself chose to sell that right, society would not permit it. Hence, society outlaws transactions in which the individual alienates those rights.

Why does society take this position? In a sense, this mixes several of the normative bases discussed previously. To begin with externalities, it may be held to be an affront to society for an individual to have alienated his right to privacy. For instance, suppose Mr. A grants to his employer Ms. B permission to conduct a lie detector examination of A at B's will. Such a transaction may generate negative externalities for otherwise unconnected third parties.[8] It is also a matter of leveling the bargaining field; your bargaining position with your employer may be so weak that, in order to get and keep a job, you would be willing to alienate your rights to privacy. No one, the rationale goes, should be faced with this decision. And finally, there may be paternalism involved: The employee does not fully understand the consequences of alienating certain basic rights.

POSITIVE REASONS WHY SOCIETY INTERVENES

Complementing the foregoing list of normative bases for societal intervention into private labor transactions are more positive reasons why individuals seek to get through the government what cannot be accomplished through private negotiations.

The key economic term here is *rent seeking,* which means attempts by groups to strengthen their bargaining positions, so that they get a better outcome for themselves. It is hardly surprising, for example, that labor unions lobby hard for legislation that will increase their bargaining power vis-à-vis management, and the U.S. Chamber of Commerce lobbies just as vigorously against such legislation.

By defining *rents* sufficiently broadly, it is tautological to an economist that all political action comes down to rent seeking: Any action by any individual is by definition an action taken to promote his own welfare (albeit perhaps broadly defined), because economists define the individual's welfare or utility to be that which he seeks to improve by his actions. What about the (rare) case where an employer campaigns for some law that would derogate her own profits, because she feels the law is morally correct, or because it will correct some socially undesirable externality? The tautology-constructor would say that the individual is still chasing her own welfare, which (equating rents with welfare) is rent seeking. To give substance to rent seeking as a positive explanation, we have to be clear on the nature and source of the rents being sought. Two cases in particular that are interesting involve employers seeking legislation that *seemingly* hurts their own interests.

Tying One's Own Hands

Employers may seek legislation that adds credibility to commitments or promises they would like to make to their employees, but that would not be credible without government enforcement. For instance, a firm that wishes to engender trust by ensuring its employees that it will not suddenly relocate overseas might lobby for legislation that restricts its own ability to do so in the future. A firm that wants to assure its workers that they will not at some later date be subjected to lie detector examination might campaign for legislation that forbids such actions. In terms of the theory of reputation and reciprocity of Chapter 4, the employer recognizes *ex ante* that, *ex post,* she may have an incentive to exploit her employees. More to the point, the employees recognize this and take actions to protect themselves. Insofar as these actions derogate the value of the relationship to the employer *ex ante,* the employer will want to bind her own hands.

Recall the story related briefly in Chapter 6 about how Jim Casey, founder of United Parcel Service (UPS), invited the Teamsters to organize his workforce. No doubt he did this for a mix of reasons. But among them (it is likely) was the calculation that, by giving the workers representation by a strong union, Casey provided the employees with some assurance that he wouldn't be as able to exploit them ten or fifteen years down the road, after they had built up UPS-specific assets. This isn't quite the same as tying one's own hands, except insofar as by bringing a union in, the employer is compelled by labor law to negotiate certain issues. But it comes down to the same basic idea, which is that by strengthening the *a posteriori* position of employees, either by unilaterally giving them a hammer to hit you with *or* by removing a hammer from your tool kit with which you could have hit them, you can sometimes promote cooperative actions and forestall uncooperative actions by them.

Tying Everyone Else's Hands, as Well as Yours

Suppose firm A, competing with firms B through E, believes that legislation that will tie its own hands will bind much more on its rivals. That is, the best of all possible situations for firm A would be for its rivals B through E to be constrained and for A not to be, but having everyone constrained (including itself) is better for firm A than having no one constrained. In such circumstances, firm A may well lobby for the constraining legislation. For example, major chemical manufacturers are sometimes strong lobbyists in favor of tight health and safety regulations, which is often attributed to their abilities to comply with such regulations at lower cost, relative to smaller chemical firms in the industry. Or, returning to the case of Casey, UPS, and the Teamsters, suppose that Casey calculated that his recognition of the

Teamsters would encourage them to organize his rivals. If he felt that he would gain more or lose less than his rivals would from having a unionized workforce, he would then be motivated to recognize the Teamsters.

SOME LESSONS FOR THE GENERAL MANAGER

Employment is arguably the most extensively regulated form of business transaction. This is not simply the result of political rent seeking by hordes of workers and the machinations of politicians seeking the votes of those hordes; important social interests are served by some legally imposed restraints on employment transactions. And in some cases, the private interests of employers are enhanced as well.

Regardless of the causes of these restraints, general managers need to pay attention to the specific laws and regulations that apply to their operations. And multisite employers must be especially attuned to the different legal requirements in each of the localities in which they operate. Indeed, differences in the legal and regulatory environment bearing on human resource management deserve careful attention in deciding where to site facilities in the first place. Beyond this general exhortation to pay close attention, however, there are some worthwhile lessons for general managers, lessons that tend to transcend the specific content of employment law in a particular locale.

First, compliance cannot be left to the lawyers and HR specialists, or even to the lawyers, the specialists, and top management. It is important for *all* supervisors and managers to understand the legal implications of their conduct. The courts generally hold companies liable for the actions of their managers, and it takes only one loose-cannon supervisor to generate an incident resulting in embarrassing and damaging publicity, as well as the monetary costs of a lawsuit or settlement.

When seeking to determine whether an employee has been improperly treated, courts increasingly tend to scrutinize not only the explicit agreements crafted between the employer and employee but also the *implicit* contracts that develop during an employee's tenure with an organization. As we observed in Chapter 4, an employer's reputation is a valuable asset, which is created not only through formal practices and policies, but also through the informal channels by which employees learn how they should expect to be treated. But such expectations can be created inadvertently—for instance, when a manager puts an overly positive spin on what should have been a negative performance review or simply says nothing at all in the face of unacceptable performance; when an inebriated supervisor takes a subordinate aside at an office function and whispers that "there will always be a place for you at this company"; or when flowery corporate recruitment literature encourages prospective hires to expect certain benefits, perquisites, and types of treatment that the firm is not able or willing to provide. In short, the firm's implicit contracts are created every day through formal and informal communications between those in authority and those whom they supervise or manage. Because of the abundant opportunities for misunderstanding, there is particular danger in this regard in multicultural settings, where a boss and subordinate may, due to cultural differences, attach very different meanings to the same communication.

Although the data are more anecdotal than systematic, it is our impression that firms in transition—subject to rapid growth or decline; where the demographic makeup of the workforce has changed dramatically; or where recent events have created a sense of injustice among employees, whether through a contentious downsizing, changes in compensation and benefit policies, or similar unpopular actions—should be particularly sensitive to issues of compliance. Transitions of these sorts heighten ambiguity in the relationships between employers and employees, which translate into increased danger of violating laws or, at least, of facing allegations of having done so.

The complexities of employment laws mean that forgoing the assistance of HR specialists and employment lawyers is foolish. Yet powerful conflicts can arise between these specialists and general managers (both top managers and line managers) within an organization. Minimizing these conflicts is another reason to educate your cadre of general managers about the requirements of the law; when the HR department and the legal office spend their time cleaning up the messes created by ignorant line managers, the firm is unlikely to sustain a favorable reputation in the labor market or to be characterized by much cooperation and trust between the HR specialists and lawyers on the one hand and the firm's supervisors and managers on the other.

At the same time, understand that HR specialists and employment lawyers sometimes attend to their own agendas. If it is important for line managers to understand their responsibilities under the law, it can be at least as important for the specialists to understand the day-to-day tasks of those on the line as well as the general strategy (and specific HR strategy) of the organization. HR specialists and employment lawyers should be using their skills to tailor policy recommendations to the organization's strategy, technology, workforce, culture, and socioeconomic environment. However, most lawyers have little or no managerial experience or training. They are generally focused on assessing and minimizing legal risks and exposure, whereas a manager's concern is with maximizing organizational effectiveness, even if this involves taking risks and making concessions to employees that might prove injurious down the road. And in too many organizations, Human Resources is a final stop for managers who have fallen off the fast track. Such HR "specialists" have as both a mandate and a goal living a quiet life, keeping problems at bay. But the pursuit of a quiet and problem-free life in HRM can mean an unwillingness to push the envelope or to allow those on the line to push the envelope when it comes to HR practices. Indeed, the expansion of the human resource function in many organizations is directly attributable to the increasing quantity and scope of employment laws and regulations, leading some commentators to argue that this has engendered a defensive, compliance-oriented posture among HR managers, limiting their effectiveness as "strategic business partners" and in crafting innovative and effective relations with employees.[9]

Most seasoned executives advise that you cannot and should not run an organization to stay out of court. Instead, you should decide what your HRM model and philosophy is going to be, *based on the business strategy and organizational context,* and then seek to minimize legal exposures associated with that model. This speaks to the benefits of having lawyers and HR specialists who deeply understand the business and the pragmatic realities confronted by employees, front-line supervisors, and middle managers, and who are rewarded for helping to balance their own concerns with the larger concerns of the organization. United Parcel Service, for instance, has traditionally rotated even its attorneys through stints in front-line jobs and various managerial positions. Such broad career paths are more commonplace in large Japanese companies than in the United States, where few companies have gone as far as UPS, but the potential benefits of having legal and HR specialists who are intimately familiar with the business and the company's labor force are considerable.

On what sorts of issues are there conflicts between good management practice and safe HR policy? Among the most contentious issues are long-term employment guarantees; selection and recruitment based on "fit" rather than on credentials or measured ability; subjective performance evaluation, especially where it can lead to dismissal on one end and promotion on the other; voluntarily offered grievance procedures; and (in collective bargaining situations) anything that smacks of an attempt to remove the barriers between labor and management as classically defined. Employment lawyers by and large fret over these sorts of practices and will offer the opinion that they really ought to be avoided. But these practices are central to two (somewhat related) systems of HRM that have a strong record of effectiveness—namely, internal labor markets (ILMs) and high-commitment HRM. To close the first half of this book, we will study these two systems in turn, in Chapters 8 and 9 respectively. They provide excellent case studies of HR systems in action, which permit us to review and recap the basic frameworks and ideas we have advanced so far in this book.

IN REVIEW

⇒ Normative bases for government/societal intervention in employment include:
- Paternalism
- Externalities
- Redress of power imbalances
- Promotion of efficiency
- Protection of inalienable rights

⇒ Positive reasons for intervention inevitably come down to rent seeking by the parties involved. But for management, two somewhat subtle rent-seeking rationales are:
- To ties one's own hands and/or to strengthen the hands of your employees, to increase trust among the workforce and thus increase efficiency

> - To take comparative advantage (vis-à-vis one's rivals), by subjecting everyone to regulations with which the particular firm can comply better or more cheaply
>
> ⇒ Because of the enormous variation in specific laws and regulations, it is hard to offer much specific advice, but one general piece of advice warrants mention: Compliance cannot be left to lawyers and HR specialists. Top management has to be involved in framing HR-compliance policy and fitting it with general business strategy, and line managers must be fully cognizant of the consequences of their actions.

ENDNOTES

1. John J. Donohue III, and Peter Siegelman, "The Changing Nature of Employment Discrimination Litigation," *Stanford Law Review* 43 (May 1991): 983–1033.

2. From a presentation by Judge Thomas Wiseman at the 1997 American Bar Association annual meeting, Section on Labor and Employment Law; viewable online at: http://www.abanet.org/labor/97papers.html.

3. Allen R. Myerson, "As Bias Cases Drop, Employees Take Up Fight," *New York Times* (Sunday, January 12, 1997): Section 1, p. 1.

4. Marcia Coyle, "Lawyer Jobs To Increase 28% by 2005: Corporate Work Is Growing, But Incomes May Drop," *National Law Journal* 19 (February 17, 1997): A1.

5. Jordan W. Cowman, "The Rules Around the World: U.S. Companies Doing Business Abroad Must Follow U.S. and Host Country Labor and Employment Laws," *New Jersey Law Journal* 149 (August 4, 1997): 33.

6. As a matter of formal economic theory, it is difficult to analyze efficiency when parties are boundedly rational. So the formal case to support this claim is based on a model in which all parties are fully rational but subject to costs of gathering and processing information. In such a situation, it can be efficient to have one party gather information, process it, and promulgate regulations based on what she learns. As for the case where parties are less than fully rational, we must appeal to common sense and analogies to the formal argument just sketched.

7. There is also sometimes a whiff of paternalism in power–balance redress arguments: When an individual employee is desperate enough to feed his hungry family, he may make agreements that actually worsen his position overall. That is, desperation caused by a lack of power leads to less-than-rational evaluation of options, resulting in decisions that are not in the individual's best interests. Or, desperation causes the individual to take actions that may serve his interests in the immediate run but that have devastating long-run consequences (for him and/or his dependents), which he doesn't fully account for in his immediate state of despair. Hence, we do not allow the individual to make certain decisions (for instance, indentured servitude is not permitted, which is pure paternalism). And we level the bargaining field, so that desperation is no longer a strongly motivating factor that can lead the individual to agree irrationally to really bad deals.

8. Libertarians will argue that there is no reason for an otherwise unconnected third party, Ms. C, to be affronted if A allows himself to be subjected to random polygraphic ex-

aminations by B; it is none of C's business. Perhaps there is a compelling moral case against such affront, but here libertarians, who are fond of incanting *de gustibus non disputandem est* (there is no arguing about tastes), are in a bit of a pickle: If C alleges that she is indeed affronted by this, and if there is no arguing about tastes, then who is to say that she is *not* affronted?

9. See Jeffrey Pfeffer, *Competitive Advantage through People* (Boston: Harvard Business School Press, 1994), Chapter 6. In Chapter 20, we discuss at length the role of HR specialists in the organization and their relations with general managers.

8

INTERNAL LABOR MARKETS

There are obviously many ways in which workers' careers can unfold. In some lines of work, mobility takes place primarily within a specific occupation, by moving among ranks or statuses that denote one's recognized standing within the occupation or profession. Examples include college professors (assistant, associate, full professors) and carpenters (apprentice, journey status, master status). In other lines of work, individuals advance primarily by performing the same job but progressing through a hierarchy of firms, regions, or markets. Examples might include television newscasters (who advance from small towns to larger cities to the national network), baseball players (who advance through the farm system to the professional leagues), public officials, and educational administrators (e.g., university presidents).

For some workers and some kinds of jobs, however, the career unfolds primarily or entirely within a single organization. Individuals enter the organization through a small number of entry ports, advancing through sequences of jobs within the enterprise. At the limit, some organizations may hire from the external market at one level only, bringing all outsiders in through a specific entry slot and then moving people up through the organization throughout their career, screening out the undesirables along the way.

This kind of cradle-to-grave arrangement is typically referred to as an *internal labor market* (ILM). Although different authors use the ILM rubric to mean different things, the typical definition involves employment relationships characterized by some combination of:

- A contract (though not necessarily an explicit one) between employer and employee
- Long-term attachments between the organization and its workforce
- Promotion from within, except for a few designated entry ports
- Skill gradients reflecting on-the-job training (i.e., there are important skills that have to be learned on the job, which give rise to skill and promotion ladders within the organization)
- Formal rules and procedures governing employment relationships, including the assignment of wage rates to jobs rather than to individuals

- An emphasis on seniority
- Grievance procedures and due process arrangements designed to ensure fair treatment of employees[1]

Thus, the term ILM is somewhat of a misnomer. An internal labor market is actually not a market at all, but instead an administrative system for allocating labor.

Among companies displaying this broad set of defining characteristics, many variations on the ILM theme can be found. One dimension of variation concerns the criteria for determining advancement. In one Japanese auto manufacturing enterprise, for instance, blue-collar workers advance through eight job levels, with an individual's level determined by the range of job skills he or she has mastered and the degree of proficiency with which each skill has been mastered.[2] In other organizations, different advancement criteria are emphasized, such as seniority, passage of an examination (as in some civil service systems), performance, and less-formal criteria (such as loyalty).

Another dimension of variation concerns how large a fraction of the organization's employees the ILM encompasses. Some organizations go to great lengths to foster a sense of inclusiveness among their entire workforce, permitting all employees (even part-timers) to apply for internal openings and sometimes even extending benefits coverage to part-timers. In that vein, Starbucks—the rapidly growing coffee retailer—provides a very generous and comprehensive benefits package that includes stock options to all of its "partners" (employees), even part-timers working twenty hours per week, a policy that is all the more distinctive given the high turnover that characterizes its industry.[3] In other firms, there are fairly clear dividing lines between the privileged segment covered by the ILM and those who are excluded. At elite Japanese manufacturing firms, for example, ILM employment guarantees and HR practices apply to so-called school-leavers—male workers who join the firm at the end of technical school or university—and they apply somewhat to so-called mid-career men, who join the firm from a school-leaver position at a similar firm. Women, on the other hand, are frequently left out, as are seasonal and temporary employees. Indeed, an increasingly prevalent tendency is for firms to outsource their non-ILM labor, giving them a rationale for differentiating between ILM and non-ILM workers and increasing their flexibility (in terms of staffing levels and costs) by decreasing the amount of ILM labor to which they are committed.

And ILMs vary in their structural and cultural features: Some resemble stereotypical bureaucracies, appearing inflexible and unresponsive; others, such as the first-tier Japanese manufacturing firms, employ an array of HR practices that increase workforce flexibility and intrinsic commitment to the organization.[4] In this chapter we will discuss how ILMs work, as well as their strengths and weaknesses, which depend importantly on the specific context (i.e., the five factors) facing the firm.

We are particularly interested in coming to grips with the recent trend among some organizations to dismantle or transform their ILMs. These organizations have come to the view that ILMs, with long-term, insular employment relations, stifle flexibility and innovation and drive up labor costs. (Recall, for instance, our discussion in Chapter 2 of IBM in the 1980s.) A major objective for this chapter—to be complemented by our discussion of high-commitment ILMs in Chapter 9 and outsourcing in Chapter 18—is to understand the sources of inflexibility, lack of innovation, and high labor costs that are being attributed to ILMs.

Another important goal of this chapter and the following one is to examine what it looks like in practice to have in place a *system* of coherent and complementary HR policies. We'll discuss in detail in the second half of the book the various HR activities that are integral to ILMs, such as promotion and career development (Chapter 16), training (Chapter 15), and selection (Chapter 14). But in this chapter and the next, we are interested in putting some meat on the bones of our arguments in Chapter 3 about the crucial importance of internal consistency among HR practices.

FORCES LEADING TO THE EMERGENCE OF INTERNAL LABOR MARKETS

What factors give rise to ILMs? It turns out that many of the factors that favor long-term employment (surveyed in Chapters 4 and 5) also favor the development of ILMs.

Firm-Specific Skills and Knowledge

Recall that one reason given in Chapter 4 for long-term employment relationships concerned employee training. In brief, whenever the skills necessary to perform the job are obtained at the expense of the employer, then the employer will wish to amortize training costs over a longer duration of employment.

This argument is refined by distinguishing between firm-specific skills and job-specific skills. By job-specific skills, we mean skills that pertain to the particular job at the particular firm.[5] For a shipping clerk, job-specific skills would include knowledge of the shipping forms used by the firm in question, knowledge of the company's freight forwarders, and so on. These are all things that are more or less particular to the firm *and* to the job of shipping clerk in the firm. Firm-specific knowledge connotes more general knowledge about the enterprise—its billing practices, who in the purchasing department can be trusted to get something done fast, and so on. The existence of job-specific skills, and an unwillingness of the employer to train new workers in those skills every day or every week, favor having the same worker in the same *job* for a long period of time. But even if the worker leaves the particular job, the existence of firm-specific skills and the unwillingness to train new workers in them argue for a long-term attachment between the worker and firm.

One might be inclined to argue that if there are job- and firm-specific skills to be learned, then the firm should *not* use internal promotion to fill upper-level positions. The argument runs as follows: Imagine a job hierarchy with four rungs, with the top slot numbered position 4 and the bottom entry slot being position 1. If the firm promotes Employee A from position 3 to position 4, then position 3 must now be filled. If 3 is filled with Employee B, who previously held position 2, then 2 must be filled. If Employee C from position 1 fills 2, then 1 must be filled. And because position 1 is the entry port in the firm's ILM, then 1 is filled by a new employee. The firm must expend the cost of giving Employees A, B, and C the job-specific skills for their new jobs, and the new hire must acquire both job-specific *and* firm-specific skills. Thus, four sets of job-specific skills and one set of firm-specific skills must now be learned. But if the firm simply hires an outsider into position 4, and leaves A, B, and C where they are, then it must pay for only one set of job-specific skills and one set of firm-specific skills.

You probably already see the flaws in this argument, but let us be explicit. In the first place, it assumes that Employee A will be content to continue in position 3. If A seeks career advancement, and if she can advance only by leaving the firm, then the firm will lose her services and have to engage in training a replacement in firm- and job-specific skills. Second, this assumes that the firm-specific skills required for the upper-level position 4 are no more costly to obtain for a new employee than are the firm-specific skills for the lower-level position 1. This seems highly unlikely. The costs of errors and gains from successes of those higher up in the hierarchy are usually much greater than for employees in lower-level jobs. Hence, the level of knowledge required for higher-level positions is likely to be much greater and therefore more costly to acquire. Higher-level positions typically require deeper knowledge of the firm and its environment. Insofar as higher-level positions involve coordinating the actions of many subordinates, employees in those roles must have a broader base of experience with the firm's personnel. Higher-level positions also generally require making decisions that span larger pieces of the organization, so that broader knowledge is required about the firm and its activities. Employee A, by virtue of having been in position 3 (and even more by virtue of having been with the firm for a long time) may be very close to having already acquired the deep and broad firm-specific knowledge required in position 4. Thus, it will be much cheaper to train a new employee in the limited amounts of firm-specific skills needed for entry position 1 while benefiting from A's accrued on-the-job acquisition of knowledge, rather than teach an outsider all the knowledge needed for position 4.

Two variations can be played on this theme. First, the firm-specific knowledge and skills required in upper-level jobs often consist in large measure of knowledge about the firm, its operations, its personnel, its traditions, and so on. Typically, personal relationships with others in the organization (i.e., networks) become increasingly important as one moves up in the hierarchy. Skills and knowledge of this sort are often *only* obtainable on the job and after a long time. So if the firm hires from the outside for high-level positions, it may have to get by with someone who, for a while at least, lacks these skills, knowledge, and network ties. These types of firm-specific skills may be developed at relatively low cost through ILMs; where broad knowledge or networks throughout the firm are valuable, firm-specific skill development is especially enhanced by ILMs that encourage lateral rotations.

Second, on-the-job training is often imparted by co-workers. Will employees share their knowledge with a new employee, thereby running the risk of abetting a potential competitor for promotions and the like? They may not, unless the employment relationship is designed to mitigate this problem. Having a clear hierarchy of jobs, with promotion rights typically structured along seniority lines, helps ensure that senior workers do not have to fear imparting their accumulated wisdom and skill to their junior counterparts. (It also helps ensure that those lower in the hierarchy are more willing to cooperate with their bosses, or rather it mitigates the problems that might arise with Employee A in position 3 if A was constantly being passed over for promotion to position 4, which was being filled by a succession of outsiders.) Note that we are arguing here for more than just the existence of promotion from within. We are arguing as well for promotion from within using a system with formal promotion rights, in which seniority gives at least some advantage, a feature that is commonplace in ILMs.

Building Employee Loyalty: The Psychology of Escalating Commitment

Another reason for long-term employment relationships (discussed in Chapter 5) is that they may promote employee loyalty to the employer through the psychology of escalating commitment. The idea is that the longer a worker is *happily* employed by a particular employer, the greater will be the worker's commitment and loyalty to the firm. The key word here is *happily*. One could describe, for example, what has gone on lately between UPS and the Teamsters or between GM and its line workers in some of its traditional assembly plants as *escalating hostility*.

This is an argument for long-term employment only if employees will be happy and effective in continued employment. Hence, management must seek methods that keep employees happy and effective. Some means to this end—such as reliance on seniority rights for promotion, tying wages to jobs and/or to seniority (to reduce politicking), and instituting formalized grievance procedures—give us the constellation of practices that make up an ILM. By creating routes of internal advancement; articulating specific criteria for determining promotions, pay, and other rewards; and providing formal means of redress for grievances, ILMs supposedly create a superior atmosphere or climate. Recent empirical evidence attests to these effects, showing that the prevalence of ILMs is related to such outcomes as reduced grievances and disciplinary activity, greater organizational commitment, reduced turnover and absenteeism, and longer employment tenure.[6]

Incentives

The argument in the previous subsection is social psychological. Good and equitable treatment of workers over a long period of time, with opportunities for advancement, resembles a gift from the employer, causing employees to reciprocate with greater concern for the welfare of the firm. One can come to the same conclusion with an argument couched more in terms of employees' economic self-interest. When an ILM is operating equitably, the employee can be relatively sure (with guarantees underwritten by the firm's desire to maintain its reputation, say) of advancing as far as his or her skills and energy warrant. This increases the employee's desire to stay within the ILM, which means to stay with the firm, and to perform in ways that attract favorable notice. If the firm deals with malfeasance by withholding promotions or, more severely, by terminating the employee, then the employee has a self-interested incentive to perform well. This general incentive would be stronger insofar as positions higher up in the firm's hierarchy come with above-market benefits and wages,[7] because rising in the hierarchy then becomes a prize to be sought and not lost by mistakes or malfeasance.

A second argument based on incentives concerns the ability to monitor the employee. As we discussed in Chapter 4, some aspects of work—the quality of the work done, for example—become apparent only after the passage of a long period of time. Hence, incentives that effectively motivate these aspects require a long-term relationship between worker and firm. An ILM provides for this long-term relationship while simultaneously providing the employee with the opportunity for career-long growth and advancement.

Screening

Using an ILM to screen provides further efficiencies. Hiring from within provides the employer with a richer database for making staffing decisions than she has for newly hired individuals. When the employer can observe an individual's ability and effort more precisely and accurately than the market can, there are potential gains from minimizing reliance on the external labor market in hiring, limiting it to a few entry ports and then relying on internal promotions. In addition to the superior information that presumably accompanies internal job candidates, ILMs facilitate better matching of people to jobs by creating a graded distribution or hierarchy of skills among jobs within a ladder, among which employees can be moved more gradually (and safely) than would be the case if there were bigger skill gaps among positions. If the employer can link jobs into ladders of related positions, making successful completion at each rung a prerequisite for advancement to the next step, more effective screening of individuals becomes feasible, especially for the higher-level positions, where substandard performance is especially costly.[8]

This screening function may also serve to discourage employees from leaving an ILM voluntarily by worsening their outside opportunities.[9] The idea here is that because the ILM firm has superior knowledge about its own employees, those who leave an ILM are apt to be the less able. They may be workers formally told to leave, or they may be workers who are discouraged about future prospects within the ILM and thus who are encouraged to move on. In either case, a prospective outside employer must worry that an employee from within an ILM who is seeking employment elsewhere—for instance, the accountant in a top-tier firm who is sniffing around for outside opportunities shortly before an impending partnership decision—is something of a "lemon." The argument can even extend to the case of an outside employer who initiates employment talks with the employee of an ILM. In a variation of the so-called winner's curse, the outside employer must worry that the only ILM insiders that could be lured away are somewhat tainted; turning Groucho Marx's famous dictum on its head, what is being asserted here is that a club should never want as a member any individual too willing to join it. ILM employees, knowing that the outside world may draw adverse inferences from an expressed desire to move, are thus more beholden to the ILM. Indeed, the rational response from an ILM employee is to spend less time looking for good outside prospects.[10]

This process should work to lessen voluntary turnover among ILM employees, increase the incentive aspects of the ILM (because losing a plum ILM job has very dire consequences for the employee), and increase the ILM's bargaining power vis-à-vis specific employees. Note well, this all traces from the presumably superior information (relative to outsiders) that the ILM provides about the abilities of current employees. We could make a similar case for any employment situation, in that the current employer probably knows better than outsiders do how good a particular employee is. However, the informational advantage is likely to be particularly strong in an ILM for several reasons. First, ILMs tend to presume long-term employment relations, and as an employee's tenure increases, not only does the employer become better informed about that individual, but knowledge about the individual available to alternative employers is likely to become obsolete. Second, the heavy front-end investments that ILMs foster in screening, socializing, and training candidates, combined with the intention of long-term employment, provide a strong rationale for the employer to keep close tabs on employees' capabilities and limitations, to make best use of these "quasi-fixed" human assets in which the firm has invested. And finally—bringing in the idea from the previous paragraph—a prospective alternative employer will realize that the incumbent employer has these strong motivations to keep close tabs on her ILM employees, therefore viewing with increased suspicion any employee who is departing an ILM.

Staffing Economies

Even if the employer were no more capable of making informed hiring decisions among insiders than among outside candidates, limiting consideration to insiders may be efficient because it can make the search problem more manageable and less expensive without a huge downside in terms of the predictive accuracy of staffing decisions. (This is another reason why ILMs are generally better suited to guardian positions than to star roles: Although internal-only searches are less costly administratively, they obviously restrict the pool from which candidates can be drawn, reducing the chance of finding the one diamond or star hire in a mountain of coal.) There may also be substantial economies of scale in recruiting, screening, hiring, and training many outsiders for a single or a few specific entry-level positions, rather than conducting many searches for one or a few outsiders for each of many positions.

Cohort Effects

Finally, there may be desirable social effects when cohorts of entry-level hires are brought into the firm at the same time and rank. In traditional Japanese firms, for instance, each entering cohort of school-leavers exerts peer pressure on its members. Professional organizations—such as law, consulting, accounting, and investment banking firms—typically hire an annual entering class, whose members begin employment at the same time. These entry cohorts create useful support networks, may induce healthy competition, and facilitate relative performance evaluation (see Chapter 10).

CRITIQUES OF ILMS

Some observers put a drastically different spin on much of the preceding analysis, alleging that ILMs are favored because they make it easier for the firm to control (exploit?) its workforce. Having made employees dependent on the organization by making it very costly for them to leave the firm, the organization is then in a stronger position to direct the activities of employees as desired. According to this view, ILMs represent a co-optation device used by employers to get workers to buy into the business. By aligning workers' long-term interests with those of the organization, and by promulgating various bureaucratic rules and procedures governing employment relations that foster the illusion of fairness, organizations are able to placate workers and thereby reduce the costs of monitoring, disciplining, and controlling employees. Even more ominously, to the extent that ILMs raise the costs of exit for a worker, they lower the worker's bargaining power when and if conflicts arise between the worker's desires and those of a supervisor.

Some critics of ILMs also view them as a divide-and-conquer device to manipulate and control the workforce by encouraging subgroups of employees to compete with one another (for promotions, job security, and the like) and by implicitly threatening the privileged workforce through reminders that a cadre of workers willing to take their place always awaits.[11] As an example, consider the two-tiered employment systems sometimes used in air transportation or automobile manufacturing, in which new entrants into the organization are paid lower wages, have less job security, and enjoy fewer privileges and lower status than their senior counterparts. Such environments are alleged to reduce the old guard's incentives to rock the boat very forcefully.

Critics also allege that the formal rules and structures in ILMs legitimize inequalities within the workforce—perhaps intentionally—by creating a set of seemingly rational rules and categories that perpetuate unequal treatment of women, ethnic minorities, and other disadvantaged groups. The segregation of women or African-Americans into dead-end, low-paying job categories and promotion ladders seems neither capricious nor arbitrary, but instead appears to result from a rational and bureaucratized personnel system, even if the job classifications and wage assignment system are themselves arbitrary and inherently discriminatory.[12]

Another way ILMs supposedly facilitate control over employees is via the peer group. By reducing turnover, ILMs foster long-term communities of employees who share a unique history. Under these circumstances, any employee is much less likely to pursue self-serving objectives that go against the interest of his or her peers. ILMs make the peer group a more salient basis of social comparison and more potent form of social control, reducing the firm's reliance on formal controls. Critical treatments of Japanese employment systems often stress this theme.

Critiquing the Critique

Rhetoric aside, these perspectives on the ILM do not seem fundamentally antithetical to the efficiency-oriented account sketched by its supporters. What critics see as a conspiracy of control is seen by others simply as the firm economizing on the costs of labor market transactions and supervision. Recent empirical evidence suggests that the incidence and costs of disciplinary actions are indeed reduced by ILM arrangements, and that organizations with long-tenure workforce and well-developed ILMs require less intensive supervision and oversight to control employees. Unless one is prepared to argue either that employees do not understand their own true interests or that they have no reasonable alternatives to joining an ILM, it seems difficult to view the ILM as a pernicious conspiracy.

THE DIFFUSION OF ILMS

This conclusion seems all the more valid given the zeal with which workers and their unions have themselves pressured organizations to develop ILM arrangements. The origins of ILMs have been traced to various institutional actors with an interest in employment stability within the firm. Chief among these are workers' industrial unions. As we saw in Chapter 6, industrial unions tend to represent relatively unskilled workers, trying to increase the power of their membership by organizing the broadest possible constituency and by promoting a detailed division of labor (e.g., specific job titles and work rules) that creates an artificial monopoly of skills. In contrast, craft unions typically possess a genuine monopoly of skills and therefore resist any imposition of rules or procedures by employers that would interfere with the union's discretion in recruiting, training, and protecting their members. The logic of ILMs—seniority rights, formalized sequences of job titles, grievance procedures, and the like—is highly compatible with the organizing strategy of industrial unions.

Another constituency that has sometimes favored the development of ILMs is the government.[13] In the United States, for instance, labor shortages brought on during both World Wars prompted extensive government intervention in the labor market through such agencies as the War Labor Board and War Production Board. These interventions favored long-term employment relationships and the evolution of many of the personnel practices that we today recognize as hallmarks of the ILM. Centralized labor market planning required that employers (e.g., aircraft or ship manufacturers) desiring to hire new workers away from another industry justify their needs; it was seen as critical to the war effort to make sure that workers were well matched to jobs and firms and that they were stable and productively employed. Systematic personnel selection and turnover reduction thus became matters of patriotic obligation, not just economic efficiency. This, in turn, prompted firms to formalize work roles and job requirements (to match personnel with positions), develop rating and salary classification systems, formalize and rationalize promotion systems (e.g., by conducting job analyses and evaluations to determine what skills each position required), conduct market surveys to set wages, take steps to reduce turnover, institute grievance procedures to minimize labor–management conflict, and so on. These personnel practices, and other key features of ILMs, had already started to develop well before World War II in those firms and industries where technical considerations made them most attractive—specifically, in settings with a large scale of operations, high costs of employee turnover, and firm-specific skills and technologies. However, government regulations during wartime tended to apply to the economy as whole, thereby encouraging the diffusion of ILMs to other industries as well.[14]

Government intervention in employment relationships during World War II established the precedent for continued intervention afterward in such domains as Social Security, employee health and safety, and civil rights, all of which contributed to the need for organizations to further formalize and bureaucratize their personnel systems. After the war, many of the HR innovations introduced were also retained through the actions of a third constituency that had an interest in seeing such practices maintained: personnel professionals. By creating specialized organizational subunits devoted to the new functions of personnel administration (e.g., hiring, testing, job evaluation, compensation, benefits, industrial relations), the advent of ILMs broadened career opportunities and power bases for personnel specialists. Personnel professionals found new "problems" for which many of the personnel innovations adopted during wartime could serve as solutions. Instead of justifying the need for ILMs by emphasizing the need to deal with labor shortages, as they had in wartime, they focused their arguments after the war on the HRM challenges associated with absorbing soldiers back into a peacetime economy (selection, training, productivity management, etc.). In the two decades following World War II, the growth of the personnel profession far outstripped growth in the white-collar labor force in general, as ILMs became ever more institutionalized within the U.S. economy, aided in part by new government interventions in labor markets, such as civil rights and affirmative action initiatives that favored formalized selection criteria, training practices, and wage and promotion systems.[15]

The influence of unions, personnel professionals, and the government on the development of ILMs underscores the important role of key external stakeholders in human resource management. Organizations have numerous objectives in crafting employment relations, including a desire to achieve political objectives and/or gain legitimacy with various publics—such as government agencies, potential hires, labor unions, and HR professionals—by promulgating certain kinds of personnel policies. Consequently, the design of HR policies may be targeted not only to employees, but also influenced by considerations of reputation and balance-of-power involving constituencies outside the firm. Organizations may embrace various bureaucratic personnel practices, as well as the broader ILM model, in part because these policies become taken for granted socially as the way a world-class enterprise is *supposed* to manage its human resources. Such imitation is especially likely to prevail among organizations whose outputs are difficult for external constituents to measure or evaluate precisely, such as schools, hospitals, or firms building nuclear reactors, and who will therefore tend to be judged more on the basis of the structures and procedures they employ.[16]

EFFECTS AND IMPLICATIONS OF INTERNAL LABOR MARKETS

Implicit in the foregoing discussion are a number of implications about how work and employment should be structured in an ILM. The ILM converts labor from a largely variable to a more fixed factor of production. Decisions about initial screening of employees become extremely important, comparable to decisions about purchasing a piece of costly capital equipment that is expected to be in use for many years to come. Moreover, having invested in the training of employees, organizations have a strong desire to recoup those investments, making turnover reduction and performance management especially important considerations for an organization with ILMs.

Because ILMs involve long-term attachments between employees and the organization, they come to be intimate social communities. As a result of this intimacy, concerns of social equity loom very large within ILMs; by injecting a family flavor into the employment relationship, treating employees fairly becomes almost as salient in the employment context as is treatment given to siblings within the nuclear family. As we have seen, the conditions that favor ILMs are often ripe with possibilities for discontent and perceived inequity (e.g., lots of team production), so grievance procedures and due process protections tend to accompany the creation of ILMs.

Moreover, concerns about internal equity tend to produce distinctive wage systems within ILMs. Wages are typically tied to jobs, thereby eliminating inequities within job classifications and reducing squabbles to ones about job assignment rather than about wage allocations within job classifications. Also, organizations structured along ILM lines tend to display more pay compression than otherwise-comparable enterprises. Because external market considerations only shape wages at specific entry ports, the internal allocation of wages tends to be compressed to promote harmony, cooperation, and feelings of equity among employees (and between management and labor), which are presumably harder to achieve when conspicuous pay differences exist.[17]

Because of these effects on the wage structure, the existence of a well-developed ILM within an organization can have implications for decisions about how to contract for certain kinds of labor services. Within firms having ILMs, it can be difficult to carry out within the boundaries of the organization a task with a distinctly high or low market price, because equity forces will create "trickle down" or "trickle up" pressures on the rest of the wage structure. For instance, when Japanese organizations—with their well-developed ILMs and strong cultures—wish to undertake an activity (such as R&D) that would command substantially higher wages than those prevailing within the organization, they will often spin this activity off into a separate administrative and geographical entity.[18] Conversely, paternalistic employers with strong cultures and well-entrenched ILMs are increasingly discovering, as have their Japanese counterparts, that it may be prudent to outsource low-wage tasks, rather than conduct them internally, where equity pressures would drive up the wage levels. A janitorial service firm may be able to pay its janitors less and provide fewer protections and benefits than, say, Philips Electronics or Procter and Gamble would be required to offer those same laborers by virtue of internal equity pressures.

A growing body of empirical evidence confirms the theoretical claims about the efficiency-enhancing effects of ILMs. By bureaucratizing wages and job assignment, the ILM reduces opportunities for costly individualistic bargaining. The long-term attachment to the organization and promotion opportunities build commitment. The ILM favors economies of scale in recruitment (because the firm only goes to the outside market to hire in a few entry ports) and protects against initial judgment errors in hiring (you gain first-hand experience with employees before advancing them to higher positions where judgment errors would be more costly). The seniority emphasis that is often associated with ILMs[19] reduces turnover (which may be an asset or a liability, of course, depending on the context), increases perceptions of internal equity, and reduces the reticence of senior employees about sharing their knowledge with their junior counterparts. The grievance machinery associated with ILMs can provide a transactionally efficient way to resolve and contain employment disputes, ensure perceptions of equity, and co-opt workers by institutionalizing conflict (i.e., we agree to disagree within a specific domain and using a specific set of rules).

The Downside of ILMs

The advantages of ILMs are balanced by a substantial set of potential negatives.

ILMs Can Be Expensive

The point is obvious: In addition to higher wage and benefits costs, the increased overhead (particularly in the personnel area) required to sustain an ILM may represent a burden on the firm.

ILMs Can Be Inflexible

The alleged inflexibility of ILMs takes on a number of forms and has a number of sources. At the most prosaic level, firms with ILMs have converted labor into a fixed factor of production; staffing levels and, ultimately, the firm's payroll cannot easily be moved up and down to suit changing conditions in the firm's product markets. We have already noted how some firms have responded to this by outsourcing noncritical tasks, such as janitorial services or benefits administration. Other firms—notably, first-tier Japanese manufacturers—have historically used seasonal and temporary (hourly) workers who are outside of the ILM to buffer workforce demands. (Of course, this workforce strategy requires a culture in which such sharp distinctions can be legitimated.) Still other firms have adopted a strategy of tapered integration; the firm retains some competency in a number of stages of the production process and uses the extent of its taper to suit conditions. When demand for the firm's product is strong, the firm will contract out a very high percentage of the early stages of production, using its own labor force primarily to make the final product. But when demand slacks off, the firm transfers its own employees to earlier stages of production, "discharging" its outside contractors. Lincoln Electric, for example, has used this technique to great advantage; when demand for its product has been very low, it has even resorted to sending skilled machine operators out to paint fences. This strategy does not come for free, nor is it costless: The workforce must be willing to accept job reassignments, and the firm involved will sometimes be overpaying its own (over)qualified employees to undertake tasks it could have done more cheaply on the open market.

A second variety of inflexibility pertains to work methods and skills. Workers in an ILM, by virtue of having been with the organization for a long time, can come to identify the way the firm operates as the only way it *can* operate. We saw an illustration of this in Chapter 2 at IBM. Employees at IBM came to view the IBM way—honed and refined in the 1960s and 1970s—as *the* way the firm ought to be run. When conditions changed in the 1980s and 1990s, necessitating major shifts in strategic foci and basic work practices, IBM had a hard time getting its workforce to adapt.

Related to this is a form of demographic inflexibility. As conditions in the industry change, a firm may require new skills, and quickly. But in a strong ILM, with a tradition of developing human resources internally, it may be difficult to integrate outsiders with the requisite skills. There may be passive or even active resistance to individuals who didn't come up through the same, shared boot-camp experience. The story of information processing at UPS, told in Chapter 3, is directly relevant.

At the top of organizations, ILMs sometimes suffer from inflexibility in leadership. In a company that is run along ILM lines and is facing changing market conditions, the board of directors might want to shake things up by bringing in outsiders to lead the company. Or corporate management may want to shake up a division. But when promotion from inside becomes more like religion than a rule, this can be difficult to implement. Often the result is that changes occur very late— sometimes too late—when conditions reach a crisis stage. Think of IBM and the eventual hiring of Louis Gerstner from RJR Nabisco as CEO. Or consider Firestone, a major U.S. tire manufacturer. In the 1970s and 1980s, the tire industry faced a precipitous decline in demand for older bias-ply tires due to the introduction of products incorporating the new radial technology. Consequently, companies like Firestone needed to close down plants dedicated to the dying technology and otherwise radically reallocate resources. A recent study documents that Firestone CEOs groomed from within were much less likely than those brought in from the outside during this period to implement the major restructuring required by changing market conditions; and when insider executives *did* reallocate resources, they were least likely to divert resources away from the plants and divisions where they had previously been employed within Firestone.[20] The study's author attributes these findings to the powerful implicit contracts built up through the firm's employment system: The unwritten employment contract at Firestone, according to one long-time employee, was simple and widely understood: "If you did nothing wrong, you had a job for life."[21]

This problem is not unique to ILMs, of course; any enterprise with a strong culture and a tradition of recruiting top management from among the faithful can have a hard time switching directions. But as the Firestone example illustrates, the long employment tenures and promotion from within associated with ILMs can strengthen implicit contracts that make it especially difficult for internally groomed executives to implement radical changes.

The picture we have painted for ILMs vis-à-vis flexibility is fairly bleak, perhaps too bleak. James Collins and Jerry Porras, for instance, have documented some prominent cases of companies that have developed flexible and innovative ILMs, such as H-P, 3M, Wal-Mart, Motorola, GE, and Sony. Their examples suggest that one key to achieving this balance between stability and flexibility may be marrying the sort of high-commitment HR policies we discuss in the next chapter with a strong cultural emphasis on flexibility, innovation, continuous learning, and a willingness to embrace change.[22]

ILMs Can Be Insular

The strong employee identification and solidarity supposedly engendered by an ILM need not work entirely to the employer's advantage. For instance, work groups may protect their less competent members. They may develop and enforce norms and values (e.g., regarding output restriction, pilferage, or sexual bravado) that contravene managerial authority and impede organizational effectiveness. At the same time, managers may protect those who work for them and subordinates may protect their superiors. Loyalty can be a great thing, but it does tend to dull incentives: One doesn't often hear of families that discharge their black sheep, and within an ILM, employees who are merely gray sheep—not grossly incompetent, but not quite doing the job either—may last a long time.

This is a real problem for any organization that depends on loyalty—we will confront it again in high-commitment work systems in the next chapter—and there are no easy answers. Perhaps it must be accepted as an inevitable cost of developing ties of loyalty, to be weighed against the substantial benefits that such ties can bring. But there are some organizations—the military in wartime, for instance—in which ties of loyalty are strong and in which commanders nonetheless have a well-established tradition of replacing subordinates who, for whatever reason, aren't getting the job done. (In the case of the military, two things help. First, the superordinate goal of winning the war is immensely powerful. Second, sacked unit commanders are not fired, but instead moved to jobs at the rear. Although being sacked may mean that a Brigadier General will never earn another star, it doesn't mean unemployment. There are clear lessons here for more standard sorts of organizations.)

One form of insularity that deserves special mention concerns workforce diversity. ILMs can become insulated from important changes in the demography of the overall workforce. To achieve a diverse workforce, especially at the top levels of the organization, can take a distressingly long time. We will return to this issue in Chapter 16, in discussing promotion and career concerns.

ILMs Can Breed Mediocrity and Conformity

To the extent that ILMs develop compressed compensation schedules, they often cannot compete in terms of pecuniary rewards with organizations that hire and pay for star potential. Consequently, the ILM's most able members, *to the extent that they are motivated by pecuniary rewards,* may be lured away. In contrast, the least able employees, or rather those employees who are competent enough to survive but no better, have little motivation to leave. Recall from Chapter 2 the brain drain that faced IBM in the 1980s and early 1990s. But also recall from Chapter 3 how H-P has defused a similar brain drain by recruiting employees who are motivated by rewards its ILM can deliver—in H-P's case, the freedom to work at projects largely unfettered by some corporate master plan regarding product mix and what each employee "ought" to be doing.

The compensation policies of ILMs can compound this problem in other ways. With an emphasis on seniority and other rewards that accrue to long tenure to the firm, ILMs will tend to pay junior workers less than their market alternatives, whereas longer-term employees may be paid more than they "deserve." This will result in an older, more stable, and (potentially) more conservative workforce. This isn't necessarily a bad thing—in some businesses it is quite a plus—but in businesses that thrive on change, new ideas, and iconoclastic thinking, it can be a substantial negative.

ILMs Can Be Bureaucratic

To many readers, the term *bureaucracy* will conjure up a fairly dismal picture of a vast organization filled with "offices," each housing a bureaucrat who has a precise place on some mammoth organizational chart and some very precisely defined responsibilities, rights, and privileges. Getting the approval of a bureaucracy for anything is a trip into a Kafkaesque nightmare; one hundred signatures are needed, each of which requires visiting one hundred offices before the right official is found, and the hundred right bureaucrats have no interest in you, your situation, or your need for their signature.

To organization theorists, the term doesn't connote anything quite so bleak. The defining characteristics of a pure bureaucracy, roughly, are: rights, responsibilities, and privileges are vested in offices or jobs, and not (otherwise) in the people who happen to inhabit those jobs; and those rights, responsibilities, and privileges are spelled out explicitly in formal documents, such as rule books, manuals, and job descriptions. Bureaucrat X may report to Bureaucrat Y, but Y cannot compel X to do anything that runs counter to X's written-down job description, which is considerably more detailed than, "Do whatever Y says to do." (The formal definition of bureaucracy, given originally by sociologist Max Weber, goes on to identify other characteristics that were important in analyzing organizational structure and performance in the late nineteenth and early twentieth centuries but that are probably of less consequence today.)

Using the term a bit loosely, a bureaucracy is an organization characterized by "jobs," which are created independently of the individuals who occupy those jobs and governed by explicit rules for how each job should be staffed and administered. An organization is more bureaucratic to the extent that it relies on these devices. Is bureaucracy bad? Not entirely: A more bureaucratic organization is less flexible, to be sure, which generally speaking is bad. But bureaucracy can afford protection to individuals within the organization, thereby helping to foster employee trust (see Chapter 4). For instance, civil service reforms around the turn of the twentieth century made government organizations more bureaucratic and, it is commonly held, thereby less prone to political corruption.

For fairly obvious reasons of economic efficiency, bureaucracies tend to be large organizations. Size, together with a premium on explicit rights and duties and protection afforded to anyone who follows the rulebook, often promotes self-interest (albeit self-interest pursued within the specified rules) and alienation from the job (but active interest in ensuring that rules and procedures are being followed). The Kafkaesque nightmare—the tyranny of the petty bureaucrat who feels responsible only to himself and to a faithful application of the rules—isn't guaranteed by a bureaucratic form, but the two are certainly associated.

We mention all this here to make the simple point that an ILM is *not necessarily* the same as a bureaucracy. The defining characteristic of an ILM is that employees' careers are conducted within the organization; employees enter at the bottom and move up as their skills, talents, and accomplishments warrant. Even the term "moving up" is something of a misnomer. An organization without a rigid hierarchy of jobs, but where individuals spend their lifetimes moving laterally among different jobs after a suitable apprenticeship, could still be an ILM. But to provide the requisite job variety to sustain lifelong careers and to justify the entire structure, ILMs tend to be found in larger organizations. To motivate employees, ILMs tend to have a status structure through which workers ascend (even if authority doesn't always rise with status). And being large and hierarchically structured, ILMs are often (but not always) accompanied by bureaucratic rules, procedures, and documents.

One might thus expect to observe greater employee alienation in an ILM, compared to the greater family feeling of more organic, loosely structured, informal organizations. Yet ILMs can engender powerful feelings of loyalty to the firm and to co-workers. By promoting longer tenures, a richer language for communication, shared values and social ties, procedural justice, and internalization of organizational goals, ILMs may make organizations—even seemingly bureaucratic ones—appear more family-like than otherwise-comparable enterprises lacking ILM structures.

Traditional first-tier Japanese firms—manufacturers like Toyota and NEC, the major banks, trading companies, and the like—are outstanding examples. These are ILMs *par excellence* for their core workforce—specifically, male employees who come to the firm as so-called school-leavers out of technical school or the universities. Yet for the same group of school-leavers, an array of HR policies promotes extraordinary commitment to the firm and fosters a high degree of staffing flexibility. This is not only a Japanese phenomenon; some U.S. firms (such as H-P, for example) and others in Europe (such as Siemens) combine high-commitment HR practices with strong ILM features. In Chapter 9, we discuss high-commitment HR *per se,* as well as hybrids that marry high-commitment HR with ILMs.

ILMS AND THE FIVE FACTORS

Let us summarize this chapter by recasting it in terms of Chapters 2 and 3. Taking Chapter 3 first, it is clear that the ILM represents a *system* of HR practices. The starting point for identifying an ILM may be the defining characteristic of lower-level points of entry into the organization and staffing from within otherwise. However, it is essential to fill out the rest of the portrait—the formal personnel rules and procedures governing employment relationships, the assignment of wage rates to jobs rather than to individuals, the emphasis on seniority, and the grievance procedures and due process arrangements designed to ensure fair treatment of employees—because the defining characteristics complement and are complementary to these other features.

We have seen that ILMs can add a lot to the efficiency of employment relationships, but they come with substantial costs. The answer to the question *Does an ILM make sense in a given context?* brings us back to Chapter 2, because the answer obviously depends on how the five factors play out in that context. We didn't organize our discussion in this chapter in terms of the five factors, so it may be helpful to review things in these terms here:

Technology

The ILM structure is relatively favored when the technology exhibits high interdependence, task ambiguity, and long delays in measuring performance. It is generally better suited for guardian jobs than for star roles, for a variety of reasons: because of the limited sampling of the workforce associated with running an ILM; because of the compensation compression that typically is associated with an ILM; and because of the conformity that it can breed. It is strongly favored for technologies that require high levels of firm-specific human capital, which must be developed slowly on the job. It is suited less well to industries facing rapid technological change and in which obsolescence of human capital is a problem.

Environment

The interaction between ILMs and labor mobility is complex. Where labor mobility is low, especially among mid-career employees, ILMs are favored because it is relatively more costly to recruit mid-career employees. But where labor mobility is moderately high in general, an ILM structure can benefit the individual firm by restraining voluntary departures. ILMs are not favored in industries and locales where labor mobility is so high that, even with the ILM in place, the firm would lose workers in whom it has invested, especially where it is apt to lose a disproportionate fraction of its most able workers. Obviously, a host of environmental considerations already touched on in this book impinge on the level of labor mobility within a region, industry, or country, including the extent and nature of unionization, training regimes (see Chapter 15), portability of pensions and other benefits, and legal restraints on discharge and employment agreements. In terms of product markets, ILMs tend to reduce flexibility in staffing levels, so they tend to be more prevalent in industries where demand is relatively more stable or, even better for the demographics of the workforce, where demand is growing relatively steadily. The logic of industrial unionism is more consonant with ILMs than is craft unionism, and ILMs are favored in contexts where loyalty and seniority are generally valued.

Strategy

Organizations whose strategies entail rapid growth are less likely to be plagued by the potential dysfunctions and costs of ILMs noted in this chapter. ILMs also appear well suited to strategies entail a long-term, stable workforce—for instance, strategies based on quality, service, or long-term relationships with clients. The ability to sustain an ILM may also depend on the financial strategy of the firm: A number of firms that have taken a long-term orientation to their workforce have eschewed the short-term pressures imposed by the capital markets by keeping stock ownership closely held or by resisting external debt.[23]

Culture

The culture of an ILM will naturally support loyalty and cooperation as virtues. But ILMs can and do work well with cultures that are more family-like and with those that are more market-oriented. Notwithstanding some notable examples of ILMs that make a point of valuing flexibility and innovation, ILMs tend to have cultures that emphasize stability and continuity. For obvious reasons, the culture of an ILM will tend to place great value on *process* and abiding by rules, values, and conventions.

Workforce

ILMs tend to flourish in organizations having more highly educated employees. Certainly an ILM is likely to function better with employees who have the underlying skills necessary to grow over the course of a career, and the formalization and intensive communication associated with ILMs may also put a premium on some of the skills and dispositions acquired through formal schooling. The value placed on employment stability within ILMs tends to increase the average age and tenure of employees and to put a premium on characteristics that employers may associate (rightly or wrongly) with a stable work history, such as marital status, children, previous work experience, and the like. Workforce diversity can play either way: ILMs, by promoting identity with the organization, can help unify an otherwise diverse workforce—multinationals that seek uniformity among their different national divisions often find the ILM structure to be invaluable. But a workforce that is very diverse in terms of social background and basic skills can make a firmwide ILM problematic; firms may need to establish several different career ladders within the organization, and they increasingly are moving to outsource tasks that require skills, pay levels, or social mores that are wildly at variance with the predominant pattern among their "regular" employees.

IN REVIEW

⇒ Internal labor markets (ILMs) are administrative systems for allocating labor in organizations. Different authors mean different things by the term; a number of features claimed to define ILMs are listed on pages 167–8. Although firms vary widely in how they combine those features and in how inclusive the ILM is, enduring employment relations and staffing from within are integral to maintaining an ILM.

⇒ A number of factors and potential benefits lead to the emergence of ILMs:
  - Firm-specific skills and knowledge
  - Attempts to enhance employee loyalty through escalating commitment
  - Enhanced motivational (incentive) and screening capabilities
  - Staffing economies
  - Beneficial cohort effects

⇒ The diffusion of ILMs in American industry illustrates how various interest groups—the government, unions, and personnel specialists—affect organization design and HRM.

⇒ The ILM structure has a number of important effects on HRM:
  - By converting labor from a variable to a quasi-fixed input, ILMs put a premium on selection, employee development, turnover reduction, and performance management.
  - Except at entry ports, labor market pressure tends to be reduced in ILMs. For that reason—and to minimize invidious social comparisons and cater to equity norms—ILMs tend to display distinctive compensation structures:
    ○ Wage distributions are usually relatively compressed.
    ○ Wages are tied to jobs.
    ○ Rewards are often based on seniority.
  - ILMs thus often don't cope well with tasks that on the market would command much higher or lower pay than the firm's average.

> Many ILM firms have sought to handle this by outsourcing these activities or segmenting them (administratively or geographically).
>
> ⇒ ILMs can have a number of potential downsides: expense; inflexibility; insularity; fostering mediocrity and conformity; and excessive bureaucracy.
>
> ⇒ Bureaucratic organizations are not necessarily inefficient; bureaucracy can be a force for trust and efficiency and against corruption.
>
> ⇒ An ILM needn't be bureaucratic. ILMs are compatible with high-commitment HRM (which involves more organic forms of organization), as we will see in Chapter 9.
>
> ⇒ Echoing the main themes of Chapters 2 and 3:
> - An ILM is a coherent system of HR practices that complement one another.
> - A five-factor analysis can shed considerable light on the question *Does an ILM make sense in a given context?*

ENDNOTES

1. For a useful overview, as well as an interesting case study of one company's ILM, see Lawrence T. Pinfield, *The Operation of Internal Labor Markets: Staffing Practices and Vacancy Chains* (New York: Plenum, 1995).

2. Kazuo Koike, "Learning and Incentive Systems in Japanese Industry," pp. 41–65 in Masahiko Aoki and Ronald Dore (eds.), *The Japanese Firm: The Sources of Competitive Strength* (New York: Oxford University Press, 1994).

3. Dawn Gunsch, "Benefits Leverage Hiring and Retention Efforts," *Personnel Journal* 71 (November 1992): 90–7.

4. We discuss in this chapter the role of the ILM *per se* in fostering commitment, leaving to the end of Chapter 9 a discussion of the high-commitment ILM hybrid.

5. Thus, to be precise, we should use the clumsy term *job-and-firm-specific skills.*

6. For examples of this evidence, see Thomas A. Kochan, Harry C. Katz, and Robert B. McKersie, *The Transformation of American Industrial Relations* (New York: Basic Books, 1986); Ronald G. Ehrenberg (ed.), *Do Compensation Policies Matter?* (Ithaca, NY: ILR Press, 1990); Alan Blinder (ed.), *Paying for Productivity: A Look at the Evidence* (Washington: Brookings Institution, 1990); and Morris Kleiner et al. (eds.), *Human Resources and the Performance of the Firm* (Madison, WI: Industrial Relations Research Association, 1987).

7. The "market wage" here is more accurately rendered as the worker's (next best) opportunity wage.

8. Put differently, a smooth distribution of skill levels among positions within job ladders reduces the odds of enormously costly "Peter Principle" debacles. With a smoother distribution of skill levels, the extent to which any individual is in a job for which he or she is unqualified is presumably reduced, relative to what it would be if there were

bigger skill gaps among jobs. Of course, there is a concomitant possibility in an ILM of having lots of people who are all "out of their league" by a small amount. Thus, there are two ways in which ILMs are claimed to facilitate better matching of workers to jobs: better information on job candidates; and smoother transitions among jobs due to graded job ladders, reducing the incidence of catastrophic mismatches. Consequently, ILMs are better tuned (in this respect, at least) to guardian jobs than to star jobs.

9. Robert Gibbons and Lawrence F. Katz, "Layoffs and Lemons," *Journal of Labor Economics* 9 (October 1991): 351–80.

10. As we discuss in Chapter 15, a countervailing force is at work in the real world: Top-tier ILMs may provide superb on-the-job training and attract superior raw material, so that even an adverse selection from the crop of ILM employees may constitute a "good deal" for a lower-tier firm.

11. The empirical evidence in support of this argument links the development of ILMs to periods of industrial crisis and conflict, arguing that employers used ILMs to consolidate control over an otherwise potentially militant workforce and/or to forestall unionization. Thus, the early existence of ILM arrangements in such staunchly nonunion firms as Kodak, IBM, Polaroid, and the like is sometimes interpreted as evidence in favor of this "control" viewpoint.

12. See Pinfield, *op. cit.*, pp. 273–6.

13. To be precise, the U.S. federal government during the 1940s, 1950s, and 1960s favored the development of ILMs. More recent administrations have taken actions (or failed to take actions) that have hurt ILMs and favored other sorts of employment practices, such as outsourcing of labor.

14. As an illustration of how dramatic such changes in personnel administration were during World War II, surveys by the National Industrial Conference Board in 1939 report that only 17.3% of firms with 250 or more employees were conducting job evaluations in 1939. By 1946, the figure was 61.2%. In smaller firms, the same proliferation occurred; only 5.1% of firms with less than 250 employees did job evaluations in 1939; by 1946, 44.6% did. Similar increases occurred in the existence of such personnel practices as centralized employment and seniority provisions, both mainstays of contemporary ILMs. See James N. Baron, Frank R. Dobbin, and P. Devereaux Jennings, "War and Peace: The Evolution of Modern Personnel Administration in U. S. Industry," *American Journal of Sociology* 92 (September 1986): Table 1.

15. Baron, Dobbin, and Jennings, *ibid.*

16. Law firms and consultants have had a hand in diffusing these practices as well. We know of a small furniture manufacturer (fewer than 100 employees) in Southern California, in less-than-robust financial health, which faced the threat of unionization. Management retained a large and prestigious (thus, expensive) law firm to help fight unionization. The labor lawyers involved immediately created and distributed to employees a thick and glossy employee handbook, complete with illustrations and customized binding. The contents were clearly based on boilerplate text which the law firm had developed for its large and well-heeled corporate clients, and thus the small furniture manufacturer wound up with the sort of documentation and HR practices one would otherwise expect to see in a firm 20 to 50 times its size.

17. On the other hand, the fact that there are "levels" in the organization that are accessible to everyone gives some scope for wage differentiation, in comparison with less bureaucratic and more clan-like organizations.

18. See Masahiko Aoki, "Aspects of the Japanese Firm," pp. 3–43 in Masahiko Aoki (ed.), *The Economic Analysis of the Japanese Firm* (Amsterdam: Elsevier, 1984).

19. In Chapters 11 and 12, we identify some of the circumstances in which seniority rights are most likely to be emphasized. But a brief precapitulation may be helpful here: These include contexts in which employees' outputs are hard to measure directly, are influenced substantially by factors outside of workers' control, or are produced through joint (team) effort. These conditions make any output measures, particularly ones tied to individual output, highly contentious. (Notice that these contexts also tend to be highly conducive to industrial unions, which usually endorse the seniority principle strongly.) There are also some features of work settings, as we noted in Chapter 5, which exacerbate the tendency for workers to compare among themselves, thereby favoring allocation criteria that do not invite invidious comparisons and perceptions of unfairness. When workers are in close physical proximity, have a long history together, and resemble one another along social or demographic lines, social comparisons will be more likely, making it more costly for the employer to try and sustain a highly differentiated reward structure based on individual output. In these contexts, seniority represents a criterion for allocating rewards that is often more broadly acceptable to the workforce.

20. Donald Sull, *Organizational Inertia and Adaptation in a Declining Market: A Study of the U.S. Tire Industry,* unpublished doctoral dissertation, Graduate School of Business Administration, Harvard University, 1996.

21. *Ibid.,* p. 136.

22. See James C. Collins and Jerry I. Porras, *Built to Last: Successful Habits of Visionary Companies* (New York: HarperCollins, 1994).

23. Several of the companies mentioned in previous chapters as examples of a long-term attachment between employees and the firm, including Lincoln Electric and Sun Hydraulics, have undergone initial public offerings in recent years. Similarly, some of the first-tier Japanese companies that have historically operated ILMs have been relatively insulated from a preoccupation with short-term results by the financial markets, but they are now becoming increasingly vulnerable to those pressures. It will be interesting to observe these transitions to see if they serve to weaken reliance on ILMs. Conversely, some privately held, relatively debt-free companies have taken steps to dismantle key elements of their ILMs. United Parcel Service comes to mind as a prominent recent example.

9

HIGH-COMMITMENT HRM

High-commitment human resource management is a general catch-phrase we will use for an ensemble of HR practices that aim at getting more *from* workers by giving more *to* them. High-commitment HRM comes in many flavors: It is a part of *total quality management,* of *open-book management,* and of the management style of traditional first-tier Japanese firms. We have already seen some very successful examples of firms practicing forms of high-commitment HRM, such as Hewlett-Packard in Chapter 3 and Sun Hydraulics in Chapter 4. If you are a regular consumer of popular books on management, you have probably encountered high-commitment HRM being touted as the answer to virtually every HR question. But notwithstanding the gurus, it isn't a panacea. It comes with substantial costs, and it can fail spectacularly under certain conditions. It is enough of big deal in the world of management to be worthy of a chapter.

Besides being interesting and important in its own right, high-commitment HRM is a good way to wrap up the first half of this book, because it illustrates so well many of the themes we have emphasized thus far. In particular, high-commitment HRM consists of an array of different and highly complementary HR practices, which do or don't work well depending on the five factors, and that embody many of the economic and social-psychological processes we discussed in earlier chapters. And unions and labor laws, at least in the United States, can pose some impediments to high-commitment HRM that bear scrutiny.

GOALS AND MEANS

To begin our discussion of high-commitment HRM, we should be clear on the goals of this sort of HR system. Highly committed workers provide consummate effort—they do more than just the standard work-a-day work. In high-commitment HRM, however, there are three dimensions of employee effort that are particularly sought by the firm:

- Employees work for the best interests of the organization, based on a deep understanding of those interests.
- In particular, employees are flexible; they are willing to take on assignments different from their normal work if this is in the interest of the organization.

- Employees work with their brains as well as with their hands. That is, they use their own (considerable) judgment to determine and anticipate what needs to be done, and they help the organization to improve, by contributing ideas and information needed to achieve improvement.

The Means of High-Commitment HRM

How are these goals to be accomplished? There is no single one-size-fits-all array of practices, but instead a list from which organizations pick and choice. Different authors have different master lists; ours follows:

- *Employment guarantees:* Workers will not be discharged except perhaps for grave errors of omission or commission.
- *Egalitarianism in word and deed:* Distinctions among workers at different levels of the hierarchy are aggressively deemphasized. Everyone is part of one big team. Symbolic distinctions—for instance, separate washrooms, dining facilities, and reserved parking spots for executives—are eliminated or downplayed, and real distinctions (most significantly, in compensation levels) are also deemphasized.
- Emphasis on *self-managing teams and team production*
- *Job enlargement* (the job includes more tasks than is typical) and *enrichment* (the variety and challenge of tasks is larger than usual)
- *Premium compensation: efficiency wages and superior benefits*
- *Incentive compensation based on team, unit, or firmwide performance*
- *Extensive socialization and training* of employees, including cross-training
- *Extensive job rotations*
- *Open information* about all aspects of the enterprise
- *Open channels of communication:* Employees at all levels are allowed and expected to contribute ideas. Associated with this—and with the downplaying of hierarchical distinctions—are flattened hierarchies.
- A *strong culture* of egalitarian teamwork, often focused on *some superordinate goal,* such as zero defects or the organization's mission and "vision."
- *Extensive screening* of prospective employees, emphasizing cultural fit
- *Strong emphasis on ownership, both symbolic and financial (through stock)*

This is quite a long list, and on similar lists presented by other writers, you will find some items that we've decided to omit—for instance, some authors put internal staffing/promotion on this list.[1] Many organizations will implement only a few of these items. But, as we shall see, the items fit together very nicely; the complementarities are strong, so that if you elect to do some of these, you are likely to want to do others as well.

High-Commitment HRM versus ILMs

To provide a contrast with the previous chapter, it may be helpful to compare and contrast high-commitment HRM systems with the characteristics of an ILM. An ILM will typically provide some employment guarantees, but in high-commitment HRM the guarantees are meant to be virtually iron-clad. ILMs often offer above-market compensation, at least in the later stages of a worker's career; they typically offer substantial training to employees; and they often involve careful screening. (In some ILMs, screening is done during a probationary period, after which employees are eligible for employment guarantees. In such cases, the careful screening takes place after initial recruitment.) But the emphasis on teamwork, egalitarianism, cross-training, open information, and open channels of communication that are integral to high-commitment HRM systems are not necessarily present in an ILM. And there are aspects of ILMs that may not be as necessary in all high-commitment HRM systems, such as external recruitment only at selected entry ports, promotion from within along well-defined job progressions, and wages attached to jobs.

This is not to say that there are no high-commitment ILMs. There are, of course—this is nearly the defining characteristic of traditional first-tier Japanese firms—and we will explore this hybrid at some length later in this chapter.

Connecting the Goals and the Means of High-Commitment HRM

The goal of high-commitment HRM is a dedicated and flexible workforce, working with their heads as well as their hands. How is this goal connected to the long list of practices we just provided, and what are the complementarities among these practices? To answer these questions, we suggest thinking of four somewhat more concrete steps that will achieve the ultimate goal: (1) Employees must be *recruited* who are capable of and inclined to provide the sort of consummate effort sought. (2) Employees must be *trained,* to fill in general gaps in their knowledge and skills, to enhance their ability to work in teams, and to give them necessary background about their organization, its strategy, technology, and so on. (3) Employees must be *enabled*—given the information, opportunity, and authority required to provide the sort of efforts being sought. (4) Employees must be *motivated* to provide consummate effort—in particular, to be flexible and to use their heads as well as their hands.

Recruitment

An immediate complementarity between recruiting and training should be noted first. High-commitment HR firms invest heavily in training their employees. This increases the value to these firms of recruiting the "right" employees, so high-commitment HR firms devote more resources than usual to recruitment. Moreover, investments in employee training pay hefty dividends only if the workers are around long enough to make the sorts of contributions the firm seeks. Thus, one objective of recruitment in high-commitment HR firms is prospective longevity; applicants with a history of frequent job movement are avoided in favor of those whose history and (to the extent that it can be considered legally) demographic status suggests long employment spells. Moreover, high-commitment HR firms will tend to recruit in local labor markets (and thus site their facilities) in locations with lower rates of job mobility and that are stocked with employees more likely to stay on the job.

But there is more to longevity than demographic status, especially when, as is often the case, high-commitment HRM is not the norm in the local labor market. High-commitment HRM requires more of the employee than the usual work-a-day job or, perhaps more precisely, it requires different things. Interviews of personnel working in high-commitment HRM facilities reveal that these work environments are usually quite stressful. A lot of responsibility is placed on employees—and we'll see in a bit that peer pressure is usually intense—and employees therefore tend to take their work home with them emotionally. Some workers are willing to do this; indeed, many individuals thrive in this sort of atmosphere. However, some workers don't want such responsibility; they want to be told what to do, how, and when, and then be left alone. High-commitment HRM involves teamwork, and not every potential employee has the appropriate temperament and skills to be an effective team member. Employees must be able to communicate with each other and with "management." (We put management in quotes here because the culture and HR practices in high-commitment environments tend to deemphasize management as a separate function or group, promoting instead the notion that management is a collective responsibility.)

Consequently, attitude and fit count for a lot in recruiting for high-commitment HR firms. New employees who find that they don't fit—who don't like the stress, the challenges, the team-based atmosphere—are more apt to leave sooner. Indeed, given the corrosive impact that a non-team-player can have on the smooth functioning of existing teams, the firm is probably better off if misfits leave rather than nurse a grudge about "all the crazy things our employer expects us employees to do here." Compared with attitude and fit, the possession of specific skills is often of lesser importance. Given the level of cross-training and the enlarged and enriched jobs offered, few applicants are likely to possess all the skills needed anyway. Imagine having to make a hiring decision between two candidates: a star performer in his or her field who is a loner or a prima donna; versus a more modest and untrained team player who shares the organization's values, thrives in an environment where new challenges arise constantly, and loves to be part of a cohesive working group. If you pose this choice to those responsible for hiring in the archetypal company practicing high-commitment HRM, they would sign up the latter candidate without much hesitation.

Recall that when we introduced the idea of efficiency compensation in Chapter 4, we said that one of its benefits was recruiting based: An employer that offers premium wages and superior benefits will be attractive to a larger fraction of the workforce and therefore can have its pick from among a larger pool of applicants. Employment guarantees are another inducement to potential applicants. High-commitment HR firms, by offering these benefits, will get a broader selection of the working population as prospective employees from which to choose. Nonetheless, high-commitment HR firms will often consciously downplay their high compensation and generous benefits during the recruitment process. For example,

Tandem Computers—a manufacturer of high-end computers that became a wholly owned subsidiary of Compaq in 1997—is reputed to emphasize to prospective employees the exciting work and work environment it offers, without any mention of precise compensation levels. Prospective employees who ask about salary figures are told simply that Tandem is an industry leader in compensation; prospective employees who insist on getting a figure before signing on are shown the door.[2] Why? High-commitment HR organizations often find that the tangible incentives they provide are insufficient to ensure the sort of efforts they wish to elicit (recall Chapter 5 and also see below concerning motivation). Moreover, employees who are in it for the money can presumably be romanced away by another employer offering even bigger bucks, better benefits, or—in high-tech industries, at least—the lure of an entrepreneurial bonanza. Better to find employees who are motivated by the intangible (and harder to replicate) aspects of the job—the work itself, the enterprise's mission, the egalitarian team-based production style, the organizational culture, the autonomy offered, and so forth.

In this regard, these aspects of the work environment all help in the recruitment process by fostering employee self-selection. A high-commitment HRM organization, by indicating clearly what sort of organization it is, tends to attract applicants who value the high-pressure, team-oriented atmosphere that it is offering. Just as importantly, by emphasizing these aspects of its work environment, the firm discourages applicants who are ill-suited to this environment. Many of the specific practices of high-commitment HR firms appeal disproportionately to those prospective employees who most value learning, teamwork, and responsibility. Therefore, those HR practices are valuable recruiting and screening tools when it comes to finding prospective employees who value learning, teamwork, and responsibility. Note that some aspects of high-commitment HRM—for instance, egalitarianism— may be indirectly valuable in these same terms, if prospective employees who will work well in teams, say, tend to have a taste for egalitarianism. If this general idea seems circular, it is indeed, and the circularity is important. As we discuss at length in Chapter 14, it is rarely a good idea to recruit employees on the basis of a false picture of the work environment. Self-selection is a powerful and, in most cases, beneficial tool of management. But to work, self-selection requires an honest portrayal of the organization.

This is especially true for high-commitment HR firms, because they usually offer a somewhat nonstandard work environment. The recruitment process at high-commitment HR firms is often structured to emphasize these nonstandard aspects; potential recruits to these organizations are often given a heavy dose of the reigning culture and the overarching goals of the organization when coming in for "the interview." The organization is looking for employees who want to join the particular crusade it has on offer, eager and able to work well with the particular fellow crusaders who are already on board.

Training

High-commitment HRM organizations want consummate effort from their employees. However, they want more than just a consummate level of the standard effort: They want flexibility and a willingness to be self-directed and to contribute ideas. To be effective in these tasks, employees need a greater-than-usual level of skill and a much-greater-than-usual level of knowledge about the organization they work for, what it aims to do, and how it does things. Accordingly, workers are trained and cross-trained extensively, so they can fill jobs as needed, and they are also given broader forms of education so that they can understand more of the whole production process and the business context. Jobs are enlarged and enriched and production is team-oriented. This serves to promote flexibility; for instance, a ten-person team can be asked to lend a member or two when necessary and still be able to do its work. The broad education and training, combined with job rotations, also help promote a big-picture understanding of the organization among employees. Finally, the open provision of information to employees by the organization facilitates training; employees exposed to more data get a broader picture of how things—and, in particular, *they*—fit into the big picture.

Enabling

This is fairly obvious. To be self-managing and to contribute ideas, employees need information, opportunities to communicate their ideas, and the requisite authority and autonomy to be self-managing. The deemphasis on hierarchical rank also helps to enable employees by signaling to them that they are not simply subordinate drones. Job enlargement and enrichment give the individual employee greater scope for making thoughtful contributions, as does team-based production. And employment guarantees help assure the employee that what she contributes will not be used in a fashion that harms her own long-term prospects with the firm.

Motivation

An economist looks at key features of a high-commitment HRM system—the valuable employment guarantees (if the employee doesn't misbehave); the premium wages and benefits; the group-based performance part of that compensation; and the psychic benefits (to the right sort of employee) of autonomy; enlarged and enriched jobs; and training—and thinks: "Just as in Chapter 4, there is a clear *quid pro quo* offered here: The employee values all these things and wishes to preserve them; but to garner these goodies, the employee must provide the sort of labor services that the firm desires. So the employee's provision of consummate effort and her willingness to be flexible and to work with her head as well as her hands are a response to economic incentives." An economist will also look at the team-based production and group-based or organizationwide incentive compensation and see powerful peer pressure being used to combat free-riding: Employees, carefully monitored by their fellow workmates, face social sanctions as well as possible economic penalties for giving less than their all (see Chapters 11 and 13). The intensive screening characteristic of high-commitment HRM systems, in which prospective co-workers often play a central role, together with the strong culture and focus on a superordinate goal, further helps ensure that peer pressure is a salient and influential form of social control. Finally, the economist will look at the consistency between the organization's production style on the one hand and its culture and specific HR practices (e.g., pay compression) on the other hand and explain how this consistency helps employees to understand better the nature of the implicit *quid pro quo* on offer.

At the same time, in the spirit of Chapter 5, sociologists and social psychologists will look at all these "above-market" benefits and think of the norm of reciprocity and gift exchange. They will see the long-term employment relationships, the teams, the egalitarian culture and symbolism, the enriched and enlarged jobs, worker or team autonomy, the group-based or organizationwide performance compensation, and the focus on an overarching goal, and think of high levels of intrinsic motivation and internalization of the organization's welfare by employees. They will also stress how the minimization of status differences, the emphasis on group-based rewards, the open provision of information, the scope for individual autonomy, and the internalization of organizational values in a high-commitment HR system are likely to create a strong sense of distributive and procedural justice among employees.

Whether you take the perspective of an economist or that of a sociologist or social psychologist, it should be clear how and when the various high-commitment HR practices can support strong employee motivation. This is not to say that the economic and social-psychological factors all pull in precisely the same direction, however. To encourage all employees to internalize the welfare of the organization, for instance, pay-for-performance is often tied to measures of how well the firm as a whole does. Social psychologists believe the symbolism in this can promote worker identification with the organization. But an economist, looking at the same pay-for-performance scheme and applying the economic theory of incentives, will worry that the employees are inefficiently subject to too much uncontrollable risk. (We discuss this particular issue at length in Chapter 11.) In general, a balance must be struck between economic incentives and social-psychological motivating forces; ideally, the organization identifies motivational devices that work well on both sets of grounds, such as group-based rewards reflecting the performance of smaller teams.

THREE FLAVORS OF HIGH-COMMITMENT HRM

We have already observed that there is no single blueprint for a high-commitment HR system; organizations will pick and choose from our master list of high-commitment HR practices, according to their own needs, circumstances, and desires. And high-commitment HR practices are often pieces of a larger, more encompassing strategy of the organization. To give you a sense of the range of high-commitment HR systems, in this section we explore three specific flavors that high-commitment HRM takes on.

Total Quality Management

In the early 1990s, one of the most fashionable innovations in management was total quality management (TQM). TQM was (and continues to be) used as a loose descriptor for several different interrelated management techniques, including TQM as promulgated by Philip Crosby, by W. Edwards Deming, and by Joseph Juran. Frequent reference is also made to the Toyota Production System, which is a TQM system, and a host of other buzzword phrases, such as *world-class manufacturing, lean production systems,* and, in recent years, *reengineering.* There are significant differences among the various flavors and strains of TQM, but for our purposes here the similarities are more important. We place these similarities in three categories: philosophy, production techniques (excluding HR), and human resources.

TQM is a *philosophy* and style of management, in which management, workers, and even suppliers together focus on the *quality* of the organization's products and processes, measured as conformance to specifications. Defects are never tolerated and are held to result from flaws in product and process design, not from worker malfeasance. The ultimate goal is a foolproof and error-free production process, achieved by *continual and continuous* incremental improvement. Dramatic and discontinuous improvements are not rejected and may even be sought, but the emphasis is on the cumulative effect of many small improvements. TQM must be subscribed to by management and workers at all levels; it must permeate the culture of the workplace.

In terms of *production techniques,* the production process must be very carefully and rigorously documented, and quality levels (conformance to spec) must be carefully and rigorously monitored. Defects that do appear provide opportunities to improve because they provide an opportunity to understand products and processes better. To gain maximal learning advantage from defects, they should be dealt with immediately upon detection. Thus, we have the Japanese system of *Jidoka,* whereby any worker noting a defect can literally stop the entire production process, calling the defect to everyone's attention. To provide these useful opportunities to improve the process, the production process should be subjected to ever-increasing tension: "Cushions," such as work-in-process (WIP) inventory or long production runs with infrequent changeovers, hide product and process defects and should be eliminated slowly. To achieve these ends, firms often apply the Japanese system of *Kanban,* or inventory control cards, which can be slowly removed from the system in order to bleed out WIP inventory.[3] Total quality efforts must extend to suppliers, as quality problems presented by suppliers cannot be tolerated. Suppliers unwilling to accept TQM become ex-suppliers; suppliers who accept TQM are rewarded with long-term, stable relationships.

Turning finally to the *human resources* dimension: Line workers are best situated to monitor and improve the production process because they are closest to problems that arise and because they possess unrivaled knowledge about the production process. Line workers must monitor their own efforts; they must document the production process; and they must be responsible for suggesting improvements in production techniques and product designs. Accordingly, line workers should be carefully selected and then given the training and tools necessary to carry out these functions, including on-the-job training, frequent job rotations, job enrichment and enlargement, and free sharing of information. Employees must be given the authority and autonomy to make changes in the production process (workers are organized in self-managing teams; channels of communication between line workers and all levels of the hierarchy must be kept open). Workers must also be motivated to act as responsible partners (by being given employment guarantees and premium compensation, being treated with respect by their nominal superiors, etc.). Of course, all this is nothing more than a particular contextual selection of high-commitment HRM practices.

According to the gurus of TQM, the payoffs from a well-implemented effort are substantial. At the extreme we have Philip Crosby's famous (some would say, notorious) declaration that *Quality is free*; TQM will result in higher quality at the same or even lower production costs. To reconcile this with Milton Friedman's even more famous (or notorious) declaration that *There is no such thing as a free lunch*, we suggest a slight amendment to *Quality is free*: a total quality initiative is an investment in production technology that, when done well and under the right circumstances, can have a surprisingly high rate of return (or, if you prefer, short payback period, or large and positive net present value). When TQM is implemented, production costs generally do rise immediately. However, subject to good implementation and the right circumstances, costs will fall very quickly to levels below where they began, with product quality rising at the same time.

That's the story, according to TQM gurus. But is it correct? Or is TQM simply a management fad? Some careful empirical evidence in the context of automobile assembly has been provided by John Paul Macduffie and John H. Krafcik.[4] They examined returns to total quality efforts measured in terms of productivity and levels of defects, in automobile assembly facilities worldwide.[5] Within their sample were some facilities that used traditional methods, those that embraced TQM (more or less as outlined above) fully, and others that adopted only parts of the system. Among the partial adopters, some facilities embraced the production-technology part of the system (Kanban, statistical quality control, careful documentation) but not the HR pieces; others adopted the HR pieces but not the production technology aspects. Macduffie and Krafcik found that higher productivity and lower defect rates were associated with each of the two pieces of TQM, but intriguingly there was a statistically significant interaction effect as well: The plants combining both the operations and HR facets of TQM were ahead of the pack. (The effect is stronger in the case of quality than in the case of productivity, presumably reflecting the fact that discretionary efforts by automobile workers are likely to have more effect on product quality than on the time it takes to build a vehicle.).

Similar interactions have been documented in other contexts. For instance, a recent study of 97 plants in the metal-working industry reported an interaction between adopting a manufacturing strategy based on quality and adhering to a "human-capital-enhancing" approach to HRM (e.g., selective staffing, intensive and broad training, group incentives, pay-for-skill, all-salaried workforce), reflected in several metrics for assessing organizational performance.[6]

Our discussion of high-commitment HRM suggests why researchers are uncovering these interaction effects. The lean production parts of TQM aim at putting stress on the productive system so that product and process improvements can take place. High-commitment HRM enlists line workers in those efforts. It stands to reason that the returns from stressing the system in this way, in order to improve it, or from simply focusing manufacturing strategy on product quality will be enhanced if the army pursuing those improvements is broadened to include as large a segment of the workforce as possible.

Beyond such careful empirical evidence about TQM, there is a large amount of mixed anecdotal evidence, from a wide range of applications. Spectacular successes have been observed, as have dramatic failures. The anecdotal evidence suggests that the philosophy part of TQM is critical; dramatic failure is often the result of implementations by managers who don't fully embrace the program but instead put in place somewhat half-heartedly the technological and/or HR pieces of TQM. We can suggest two explanations for this mixed evidence. First—not quite to the point of this book, but worth saying anyway—quality is probably not precisely free. Unit costs generally will fall eventually from a TQ initiative, as the product/process improvements are made. But initially at least, TQM comes with overhead costs for sure and possibly with decreased productivity.[7] Top management that is sold on rosy forecasts of instant improvements in the bottom line is apt to be disappointed and to abandon ship prematurely. And second, very much to the point of this book: The HR part of TQM involves enlisting line workers and suppliers as partners, who must make a leap of faith. They must believe that management is serious and will live up to its end of the bargain. Top management that is unsure is probably not going to do well in hiding its uncertainties, and it is unlikely to get the sort of line worker buy-in that makes the system work. We don't mean to say that TQM is a confidence trick perpetrated on line workers. But confidence is certainly a key ingredient that is apt to be missing when top management doesn't manifest the sort of crusader zeal that it is trying to elicit from its workforce.

Open-Book Management

A second flavor of high-commitment HRM is called *open-book management* (OBM). It embodies many of the elements of high-commitment HRM—in particular, employment guarantees, job enrichment and enlargement, and cross-training—but most significantly, information is freely shared. Workers are trained to be able to do "bottom-line accounting"; some one-dimensional financial metric of performance is chosen (e.g., profits, unit costs), and workers are taught how to evaluate their own actions in terms of how those actions will affect that bottom line measure. And they are exhorted and empowered to take whatever steps they find worthwhile, in terms of improving performance operationalized in this fashion.

In contrast with TQM, OBM usually focuses workers' attention on bottom-line financial measures and effects, such as cash flow, rather than on quality *per se*; and it usually puts less emphasis on dynamic improvements in process and product. (Although we don't have the benefit of their wisdom, we suspect that TQM gurus such as Deming, Juran, and Crosby would find both of these aspects of OBM to be troubling. Deming, at least, is lyrical on the evils that befall an organization that focuses its attentions on short-run, bottom-line calculations.) There is much less OBM out there than there is TQM, so we can't offer much of a report card on how well it does.[8] But in terms of this chapter, TQM and OBM share: (1) the basic high-commitment HRM belief that line workers have a lot of brain power to contribute to the organization; and (2) many similar HR practices, intended to elicit from workers the fruits of their minds as well as their hands.

The Traditional Top-Tier Japanese Organizations: High-Commitment ILMs

The top tier of Japanese businesses—companies like Toyota, Mitsubishi Trading Company, Matsui Heavy Industries, Sumitomo Bank, and NEC—all employ a selection of high-commitment HRM practices, for at least some of their workforce.[9] Of course, some of them also practice TQM-like systems; indeed, a good case can be made that TQM was perfected by Toyota. And for the core workers, for whom high-commitment HRM is practiced, these firms run ILMs. These firms selectively and intensively recruit so-called school-leavers—young men finishing college (for white-collar jobs) and technical schools (for blue-collar jobs). School-leavers are employed in large cohorts or classes, and they are initially trained and oriented with their cohort. Subsequently, members of a given cohort will "watch out" for their classmates, helping them as needed, but also exerting severe peer pressure on classmates who are not upholding the reputation of the class. School-leavers rarely leave their initial employers voluntarily, largely because their employment prospects outside their initial employer are poor: Japanese are traditionally very status conscious, with status accruing from the group, rather than from individual accomplishments.[10] Thus, to leave a top-tier firm has historically meant a significant loss in status, unless the worker can move to another top-tier firm. And although the top-tier firms do hire a few school-leavers from their fellow firms, such individuals, known as mid-career men, rarely have the promotion prospects or general status of their school-leaver colleagues.

School-leavers are moved along slowly in the organization, rising through a well-defined hierarchy of positions. They are extensively cross-trained. Their compensation is strongly influenced by seniority and perhaps by overall firm performance—the concept of individual performance bonuses is essentially unknown. Formal status in the organization among school-leavers is largely based on age and seniority. But decision making is not hierarchical: Senior managers spend their time setting very general strategic directions and on managing external relationships; middle-level managers are charged primarily with managing the human resources of the organization; and hence operating decisions are left to the lower level colleagues, in a system that requires consensus before a decision is taken.

Not all school-leavers ascend all the rungs of the ladder in the organization. Involuntary departures occur at various stages. But in a variation on lifetime employment guarantees, the separated school-leaver is typically placed with a subcontractor of the parent firm. (If the subcontractor is large enough, it will itself have subcontractors to which it sends its surplus senior workers.) There is a substantial loss of status associated with such a move, but at least the employee is able to make use of his connections within the parent firm.

Note the use of male personal pronouns in this discussion of school-leavers. Women are employed by the first-tier Japanese firms, but with rare exceptions they are expected to leave upon marriage or, at the very latest, by the time they have children. And the first-tier firms have hired extra blue-collar labor on seasonal and even temporary (hourly) contracts, to supplement the permanent workforce as needed. Needless to say, the ability to adjust workforce levels in this fashion while maintaining high-commitment HRM for a core cadre of workers goes a long way toward ameliorating a key disadvantage of high-commitment HRM.

In Chapter 5, we were quite negative about segmenting the workforce in this fashion, asserting that social comparison processes would inevitably wreak havoc. The top-tier Japanese firms have avoided the problems we predicted in part by emphasizing symbolically the distinctions among the different classes of workers, down to different colored baseball caps for workers depending on their type. The larger societal culture, in which gender-based distinctions are largely legitimate, has helped sustain the differences in treatment. Unions in Japan are enterprise-based (that is, each firm has its own union), and they tend to represent the interests of the core workforce and the firm. And the general emphasis on status in Japanese society is a boon; a seasonal employee will think of himself as somewhat different from the school-leaver operating the adjacent machine on the factory floor, simply because of differences in their employment statuses.

In other societies, running a high-commitment HRM system for only a core cadre is apt to be a good deal harder to do. But there are stratagems that firms have employed toward that end. One that seems particularly effective—at least, it has been popular—is to outsource non-core tasks. That is, a firm might operate a high-commitment HRM system for its skilled blue-collar labor force, engineers, and managers, but outsource clerical, janitorial, and warehouse services. (At an extreme, we have the example discussed in Chapter 5 of U.S. high-tech firms outsourcing a portion of their computer programming needs.) We'll have more to say about this in Chapter 18.

By and large, the top-tier Japanese firms have not paid premium wages to their school-leavers. The benefits of lifetime employment and nonsalary perks (e.g., subsidized housing) are valued by the workers, but the prestige associated with working for such a firm, combined with the relative unattractiveness of outside options, has served the same purpose as premium compensation in high-commitment HRM firms elsewhere. The lack of labor mobility in Japan, at least for this class of workers, is typically cited as an important environmental factor, supporting the heavy investments Japanese firms make in their school-leavers. In labor markets where mobility is a good deal higher, running a high-commitment HRM system is likely to be more expensive.

Indeed, labor mobility for the cream of Japanese managerial ranks is reported to be rising, especially with the rise of nontraditional Japanese firms that are willing to hire school-leavers away from the elite and the increasing presence of multinationals inside Japan. Older multinationals, notably IBM Japan, largely adopted the practices of the elite firms, but more recent entrants on the scene have been less reluctant to poach from the elite. And, importantly, the status conferred by employment at nontraditional Japanese firms or foreign multinationals has been rising. With increased Westernization, there have also been increasing pressures in Japan for giving equal treatment to women and others who have historically been disadvantaged in the labor market. And the relative lack of growth recently in the Japanese economy, coupled with the cumulative effects of Japan's post–World War II baby boom, have left a demographic bulge in the ranks of school-leavers at the elite firms, a bulge that is not being entirely absorbed by growth. (This demographic bulge has in part meant a reduction in the use of seasonal and temporary workers at the elite firms.) It is not entirely clear where these forces will take the "traditional" practices of the elite firms, but it seems a relatively safe bet that the practices we have reported will have to adapt to these substantial changes in the external environment.

ONE SIZE DOES NOT FIT ALL: IS HIGH-COMMITMENT HRM FOR YOU?

High-commitment HRM sounds like a very well-integrated system of highly complementary individual HR practices, leading to an ideal workforce. But it ain't necessarily so. Even assuming your organization can achieve effective high-commitment HRM, the cost may be substantial. And getting there from more standard forms of HRM can be quite difficult.

Maintaining High-Commitment HRM: The Five Factors

There obviously are many direct costs associated with high-commitment HRM. Employment guarantees, premium wages and benefits, extensive training and cross-training, and highly selective recruitment all cost money. If high commitment came for free, it would be hard to turn down (but see further on in this subsection!). But it certainly isn't free, and those costs have to be compared with the benefits.

The benefits depend on the organization's overall strategy and can interact with its technology: Does the establishment compete in a marketplace in which quality is all-important? In service industries, is quality important and is quality-of-service largely at the unsupervised discretion of employees? Does the organization compete on cost in a setting where process improvements are available? These are all cases in which, if the answer is yes, the benefits to a highly committed workforce are likely to be considerable. But a firm is unlikely to reap as much benefit from this sort of HR model if it competes principally on the basis of cost, where the good is a commodity, and where process improvements are unlikely to be found.

And the cost–benefit ratio also can depend on the external environment and on workforce demographics. High-commitment HRM may be very costly in a setting with high levels of labor mobility. An organization with a large workforce, serving a declining market, may find employment guarantees prohibitive. An organization in a labor market with a badly trained workforce may find that the concomitant costs of internal training don't justify the returns. A firm drawing from a relatively tight labor market, where there is already a successful high-commitment HRM employer in place, may find that the cream of the local labor force has already been skimmed.

These are just examples. It is impossible to give a complete schema of when and where high-commitment HRM will lead to large benefits and/or small costs. But, as we hope these examples indicate, thinking in terms of the five factors—together with an informed view of the type of benefits you are meant to get from high-commitment HRM—will help shape a specific analysis of the basic question.

As you do this sort of analysis, remember that high-commitment HRM, even if achieved "for free," has some drawbacks. Most importantly, high-commitment HRM usually entails giving workers autonomy or, at least, a real say in the directions the firm can pursue. The beneficial aspects of autonomy are numerous, but the costs should not be overlooked. It may take a high-commitment HR firm longer to decide on what strategy to follow than it would take a traditionally run firm, although the reverse side of this coin is that high-commitment often speeds implementation because employee buy-in is higher. Recall from Chapter 3 that Sun Hydraulics, a high-commitment HRM firm *par excellence,* was concerned that employee initiatives would cause it to lose its focus. It is easier to say *no* to an employee initiative in a traditionally-run firm than it is at a Sun Hydraulics.

The point can be made best, perhaps, by recalling that in the early days of hand-held calculators in the United States, the two major players were Texas Instruments (TI) and Hewlett-Packard (H-P). H-P at that time was the quintessential high-commitment HRM firm. In contrast, TI resembled a military organization (and, indeed, a significant fraction of its managerial ranks came from the military). These distinctions were reflected in their respective product strategies and even in the products themselves: H-P went after the high end of the market, offering calculators that were beautifully engineered but, perhaps, not engineered with low-cost manufacture or marketing in mind, while TI relentlessly pursued the low-cost mass market. It is easy to see how their HR practices were reflected in the market niches they pursued. Put another way, if H-P had competed head on with TI in the mass market for calculators, the autonomy given its designers might have posed significant problems.

Or consider Nordstrom, the successful upscale retailer, which has applied many elements of high-commitment HRM in an industry notorious for high turnover and poor employee relations. The employee handbook given to new hires at Nordstrom lists the "Nordstrom rules" as follows:

> Rule #1: Use your good judgment in all situations.
>
> There will be no additional rules.[11]

Why such a sparse set of rules? The key is consistency of message. As we noted in Chapter 3, simplicity and consistency promote learning, and high-commitment HRM is all about having employees learn to take as much responsibility and initiative as they are capable. Firms like Nordstrom, which practice high-commitment HRM, are often willing to live with the occasional snafus that arise because there wasn't a rule or procedure in place that could have prevented a bad outcome, rather than promulgating rules and procedures that would stifle creativity, autonomy, and self-management.[12]

Achieving High-Commitment HRM

When your starting point is a conventionally run firm, with traditional work norms and employment practices, getting there—achieving an effective high-commitment HR system—takes more than just adopting pieces of the system. We have noted at various points in this book how and why it is difficult for an organization to alter the reputations and traditions that characterize relations with its employees (see especially Chapters 4, 6, and Appendix B). Particularly in an enterprise that has a history of low commitment, changing expectations—and providing employees with the education, training, autonomy, information, and feedback necessitated by a high-commitment HR system—are formidable tasks.

As we have seen (especially in Chapter 5), symbolism and process are crucial to communicating, reinforcing, and *shaping* expectations. Not surprisingly, high-commitment HR systems tend to place tremendous importance on symbols and processes—sometimes vivid, sometimes subtle—that reinforce a few basic messages: that employees are the masters of their destinies; that we are all in this together; that good ideas can come from anywhere; that we must continually improve; and so on. In firms that are seeking to institutionalize high-commitment HRM, top management will frequently recount a vivid story or two about an important and urgent decision that had to be taken, where subordinates came to their bosses asking what to do, only to be told that the subordinates had to decide on their own. Inevitably, the denouement of these anecdotes is that by marshaling their superior knowledge of the operational details, the employees came up with a much more creative and effective course of action than management could have concocted. Or one will hear how senior management dismantled the executive dining room and began taking lunch with the rest of their colleagues in the main eating area. It is the vividness of such parables, and the fact that they tell a story about going in a direction opposite from how things *used to be* or how they are done elsewhere, that make them such powerful tools of inculcation. Shrewd managers seeking to build high-commitment work systems not only know how to *tell* such stories effectively; they know how to design and implement the symbolic actions that later get recounted in those stories. The point we are trying to emphasize here is simple but crucial: Implementing high-commitment HRM doesn't just involve designing a cluster of HR practices; it also involves capturing employees' hearts and minds.

If you seek to capture the hearts and minds of your employees, remember that high-commitment HRM affects different employees differently. Shifting from traditional management to high-commitment HRM isn't all peaches and cream for line workers: pressure on the job often rises; new skills must be learned; and so on. For workers with the right temperament, the shift certainly has its merits, but some employees may manifest confusion, skepticism, or downright hostility. Top management may also bear costs in such a switch: loss of autonomy; the need to share information widely; loss of symbolic perks; and the like. However, there are some potent countervailing benefits available to both of these constituencies, which may help overcome their initial skepticism or opposition. For top management, creating a more efficient organization can be rewarding both emotionally and financially. And flattering stories in the business press can provide additional compensation. For line employees, the promise of greater autonomy, security, training, information, or other benefits associated with the move to high-commitment HRM may be welcome.

In contrast, you should be prepared for the possibility of facing a more acute and challenging source of resistance: first-line supervisors and middle managers. Those groups often lose when high-commitment HRM is adopted; they lose their perks, their status, and their authority, often without compensating gains. Indeed, the flattened hierarchy frequently means diminished chances for them to advance. Hence, in trying to shift from traditional HRM to high-commitment HRM, firms often find that the greatest resistance and obstruction comes from first-line supervisors and middle managers. The potential costs to organizations associated with this resistance include not only the time and money that must be spent on managing their transition—retraining and outplacing affected supervisors and managers, handling grievances, and so on—but also the potential loss of the talented middle managers, who might otherwise have gone on to fill key top management posts within the organization.

If there is a handy and simple solution to this problem, we haven't heard it. We have heard the recommendation—said as if in jest, but deadly serious behind the smile—that the only thing to do is to fire the firm's entire cadre of middle managers. This may be effective, but it can be costly given severance pay provisions. Moreover, it is hardly a great bit of symbolism for a firm that is proclaiming that it offers secure employment. This isn't to say that you should abandon any hopes of shifting to high-commitment HRM, but in deciding whether or how to do it, you should ponder what you will do with your supervisors and lower- and middle-level managers and what those actions will mean in terms of implementation of the entire scheme.

Supervisors and middle managers are not the only constituency that may pose problems for implementing high-commitment HRM. If your workforce is organized (unionized), the union may fight high-commitment HRM, both in the workplace and in the courts, at least in the United States. Unions typically see high-commitment HRM for what it is, a system that blurs the distinction between labor and management, a distinction that often is important for the union. There are cases of unions that have cooperated with high-commitment HR practices, but those cases are swamped by examples of obstruction. Indeed, the labor movement in the United States (that is, the AFL-CIO) has as a legislative objective laws that will clearly label certain high-commitment HR practices as unfair labor practices, an objective that (as we write this book) is firmly supported by the Clinton Administration.

And labor lawyers tend to look askance at some high-commitment HR practices. In part, the labor lawyers will want to steer clear of messing with the unions (assuming your firm is organized and the union is opposed). But in addition, as we noted in Chapter 7, labor lawyers are wary of anything that smells like an implicit contract, because judges often enforce implicit contracts that a firm decides it wants to break. To win over your employees, you may have to make explicit noises about employment guarantees. Making explicit noises about employment guarantees is quite high on a labor lawyer's list of things to avoid doing. And some of the more subjective elements associated with high-commitment HRM, such as screening based on attitudes and fit, are likely to generate discomfort among your labor lawyers.

The Bottom Line

Please don't misunderstand all this negative talk. We are, by and large, fans of high-commitment HRM. Managers brought up in organizations and cultures that practice traditional HRM tend to underestimate the benefits to be accrued from high-commitment systems, because they have insufficient appreciation of the talents of their workforce and the contributions that the workforce can make if moved to do so. (We cannot resist noting that an HR philosophy that advocates narrow jobs and presumes that line employees require close oversight from managers has the convenient effect of ratifying the importance of and need for managerial and staff roles.) Careful empirical work like that by Macduffie and Krafcik testifies to the potential benefits of high-commitment work systems, as do hordes of anecdotes and case studies of extremely successful firms whose success is based, at least in part, on high-commitment HRM. The sources of its success are hardly a mystery: If you will grant that line workers do have a lot to contribute by way of brains and flexibility, then the means of getting there—and the ways in which these means complement each other—follow clearly from the perspectives on the employment relationship that we've tried to develop in this book.

But high commitment isn't easy, and it certainly isn't low-maintenance HRM. It is hard work, it puts a lot of stress on line workers, it can threaten middle managers and first-line supervisors, and even when successful, it needs constant attention and, potentially, organizational overhead. If you are going to launch a high-commitment HRM effort, both you and those to whom you report had better acknowledge what you are getting into and recognize that it isn't as smooth or as easy as might be supposed from rose-tinted testimonial accounts of successes. Notwithstanding all the success stories, it certainly isn't for everybody or for every organization.

MOVING ON

This completes the first half of this book. The frameworks and basic disciplinary concepts that we need are in place, and we can now focus on the "meat and potatoes" of HRM—topics such as performance evaluation, compensation, recruiting, downsizing, and the like. Over the next nine chapters, we will be taking these topics on, one at a time. But as we've stressed constantly, we can't really take them on one at a time, because effective HRM represents a system, with pieces that fit together well. Hence, although each upcoming chapter focuses on a single topic, the discussion will often of necessity connect to material from other chapters.

IN REVIEW

⇒ High-commitment HRM seeks consummate effort, initiative, and flexibility from employees by granting them more autonomy, security, information, and a stake in the outcomes.

⇒ Characteristic features of high-commitment HR systems include:
- Employment guarantees
- Egalitarianism in word and deed
- Self-managing teams
- Premium compensation: efficiency wages and superior benefits
- Incentive compensation based on team, unit, or firm-wide performance
- Extensive socialization and training
- Enlarged and enriched jobs
- Extensive job rotations
- Open communication and information about all aspects of the enterprise
- An egalitarian culture and strong overarching goal, such as zero defects
- Extensive screening of prospective employees, emphasizing cultural fit
- Emphasis on ownership, both symbolic and financial (through stock)

⇒ The variety of high-commitment systems is illustrated by the similarities and differences among:
- Total quality management (TQM), which consists of an overriding philosophy or superordinate goal of improved quality (zero defects), a distinctive set of production techniques, and a cluster of HR practices aimed at broadening and empowering production workers.
  - Recent research in various industries suggests that productivity and (especially) quality is improved by adopting production techniques or the cluster of HR practices characteristic of TQM, but adopting the combination of the two is especially powerful.
- Open-book management (OBM), which has less of a track record to date than TQM. Though similar to TQM in many ways, OBM tends to focus workers' attention on the effects of their actions on bottom-line financial measures, rather than quality *per se*, and to pay less attention to continuous product and process improvement.
- The traditional top-tier Japanese corporations, which have—at least, until recently—managed core employees through a hybrid of high-commitment HRM and internal labor markets.

⇒ The appropriateness of high-commitment HRM in a given setting depends on the five factors. Moving to high-commitment HRM from more traditional approaches involves changing expectations and attitudes—no easy thing, often requiring symbolism and drama—and some significant costs and sources of potential resistance, including:
- Pressure and stress on employees frequently increase.

- Workers may be reticent to use the discretion they are given, or they may misuse it.
- First-line supervisors and middle managers often perceive themselves as losers in a shift to high-commitment HRM and consequently resist it.
- Unions and/or labor lawyers may oppose some high-commitment HR practices.

⇒ Understanding how and why high-commitment systems work, and their limitations, illustrates some important themes covered thus far in this book:

- High-commitment HR is a system of complementary practices, which fits better or worse depending on the five factors.
- It is vital to achieve simplicity and consistency in messages communicated through HR practices.
- In an organization that has previously adopted a traditional approach to HRM, it can be difficult to unfreeze past expectations and establish a new reputation.
- Symbolism and process play a crucial role both in achieving and then in sustaining a high-commitment HR system.
- High-commitment HR is an investment in employment relationships, and as with all investments, the payback doesn't come instantaneously or for free.

ENDNOTES

1. For a comparison of some different definitions of the HR practices comprising "high-performance work systems," see Brian Becker and Barry Gerhart, "The Impact of Human Resource Management on Organizational Performance," *Academy of Management Journal* 39 (August 1996): 779–801.

2. At least, we are told this was the pattern in the past.

3. Japanese users of these systems speak of walking across a shallow pond that has rocks on its bottom. As you walk across, you stub your toes. But if you slowly drain the pond, you will see where the rocks are and be able to remove them (or at least choose a path that avoids them). Walking across the pond is the production process. The rocks are flaws or defects in product or process. The water is WIP inventory and other cushions. Hence: Remove the WIP and cushions, and you will find and correct the underlying defects.

4. John P. Macduffie and John F. Krafcik, "Integrating Technology and Human Resources for High-Performance Manufacturing: Evidence from the International Auto Industry," pp. 209–25 in Thomas A. Kochan and Michael Useem (eds.), *Transforming Organizations* (New York: Oxford University Press, 1992); and John P. Macduffie, "Human Resource Bundles and Manufacturing Performance: Organizational Logic and Flexible Production Systems in the World Auto Industry," *Industrial and Labor Relations Review* 48 (January 1995): 197–221.

5. Their studies control statistically for various other factors that might be expected to influence the productivity or quality of an automobile plant's output, such as the age of the plant, the complexity of the model(s) being manufactured there, and so on.

6. Mark A. Youndt, Scott A. Snell, James W. Dean Jr., and David P. Lepak. "Human Resource Management, Manufacturing Strategy, and Firm Performance," *Academy of Management Journal* 39 (August 1996): 836–66.

7. And even if a TQ initiative quickly produces the desired increases in product quality and operating efficiency, financial performance may not improve and might even worsen over the short-to-medium term. For an illuminating discussion of some unanticipated side effects of a very successful quality program at Analog Devices, which resulted in diminished financial performance over the short-to-medium run, see John D. Sterman, Nelson P. Repenning, and Fred Kofman, "Unanticipated Side Effects of Successful Quality Programs: Exploring a Paradox of Organizational Improvement," *Management Science* 43 (April 1997): 503–21. One of those side effects reflected concerns about job security; for a variety of reasons, initial productivity and quality gains outstripped the organization's capacity to develop new products and otherwise stimulate demand, thereby creating pressures for layoffs, which in turn slowed TQ success elsewhere in the company and also diverted management attention from other pressing concerns.

8. As an indication of their relative diffusion to date, a search of Web pages (using Alta Vista's search engine in December, 1998) turned up more than 220,000 Web pages containing references to "total quality management" or "TQM," compared to less than 1,000 for "open-book management." For largely anecdotal (and certainly missionary) accounts of the application of open-book management, see Jack Stack (with Bo Burlingham), *The Great Game of Business* (New York: Doubleday, 1992); and John Case, *Open Book Management: The Coming Business Revolution* (New York: HarperCollins, 1996).

9. Some recent observers assert that what you are about to read is rapidly becoming dated, owing to changes in the social, economic, and cultural environment of Japan. Our description of the practices of these firms is an accurate, if oversimplified, representation circa 1985, but perhaps not as of the year this chapter was written (1998), let alone the year in which you are reading it. (We will discuss some of the reported changes and their likely effects at the end of this subsection.) But even if these descriptions are no longer entirely valid, the HR practices of these firms circa 1985 constitute an important "base case" that should be studied and understood by students of management. In this regard, a second caveat is that our discussion of these practices will be quite cursory and oversimplified and will ignore important variations among these traditional top-tier Japanese firms. For additional background, we suggest: James C. Abegglen and George Stalk, Jr., *Kaisha, The Japanese Corporation* (New York: Basic Books, 1985); Masahiko Aoki and Ronald Dore (eds.), *The Japanese Firm: The Sources of Competitive Strength* (New York: Oxford University Press, 1994); Kazuo Koike (translated by Mary Saso), *Understanding Industrial Relations in Modern Japan* (New York: St. Martin's Press, 1988).

10. As we noted in Chapter 2, according to Japanese culture, at least as of the 1970s and 1980s, it is better to be a substitute on a championship team than to be the star of an also-ran.

11. Reproduced in the "Nordstrom Department Store" case study, written by Donna Dick under the supervision of Professor Peter Capelli, Center for Human Resources, Wharton School, University of Pennsylvania, 1991.

12. Compare this with firms that practice high-commitment HRM as a part of TQM. An important objective there is foolproof manufacturing techniques: We wouldn't say that a firm that practices TQM is willing to live with occasional snafus. In this regard, you must distinguish between the manufacturing process, which is meant to be foolproof, and the process of learning and continuous improvement that leads to foolproof manufacturing. A firm practicing TQM is happy—well, *happy* may be the wrong word, but at least, not unhappy—for a line worker to stop the production line if she thinks she sees a problem, even if she doesn't ultimately find one. Getting employees to take responsibility and contribute ideas is still the key, and if "errors" are sometimes made, it's a price that must be paid.

10

PERFORMANCE EVALUATION

In the mid-1980s, American Cyanamid Company, a large U.S. chemicals manufacturer, changed the way in which it conducted performance appraisals of its workers. At roughly the same time, Merck, a large U.S. pharmaceutical manufacturer, changed its performance evaluation system. Both companies were quite pleased with how the changes worked out. Both reported general acceptance by their workforce. The interesting thing is that each adopted roughly the type of system that the other was in the process of abandoning.[1]

Before the change, American Cyanamid had a system in which workers were rated as being in one of three major categories. (These categories were further subdivided, but that is unimportant to our story.) There was a "curve" for the three categories; each manager had to rank 20% of her subordinates in the highest category, and 40% in each of the other two. This was felt to be arbitrary and inequitable; in a small group with an outstanding worker, other very good workers might have little chance of getting the highest ranking. The fixed percentages hurt cooperation among co-workers, who were essentially placed in competition with one another.

To deal with these problems, American Cyanamid adopted a system with three categories. Almost everyone was placed in the middle category; outstanding workers could be placed in the highest category, and those needing immediate improvement could be put in the lowest. There was no quota for either extreme. Ratings were done on an absolute basis by the evaluating manager, with the understanding that the percentages in the two extreme categories should be small. Employees, freed from the arbitrariness of the percentage quotas, responded very positively.

Merck, in contrast, began with an evaluation system in which there were many summary levels of performance to which an individual could be assigned (thirteen in all). Assignment was done on an absolute basis by supervisors. It transpired that most employees (73%) fell within three "upper-middle" levels, with little difference among the three levels in terms of consequences for salary. Managers would lump almost everyone together because they didn't feel comfortable making broader distinctions, and because it was difficult to live with the disgruntlement that ensued when someone was ranked markedly below the ranking given a co-worker. Employees complained that this gave them little in the way of motivation. So Merck decided to try a new system, with four levels and fixed percentages for each. Although there were some complaints, employees and management generally felt good about the change, saying that this forced managers into making distinctions, so that merit would finally be rewarded.

The businesses of American Cyanamid and Merck are not identical, but they are more alike than many. Yet here they are, going in basically opposite directions concerning performance evaluation at the same point in time, and both claiming to be making progress. How is this possible?

This is possible on at least two grounds. First, in most cases, measuring performance is a difficult and ambiguous task. When a firm is unclear on precisely how to measure performance, it often expends a lot of energy tinkering with different schemes. Also, we have in these two cases good examples of the aphorism: *Familiarity breeds contempt*. Besides being difficult and uncomfortable for both the evaluator and the person being evaluated, performance evaluation is frequently contentious, and those being evaluated quickly recognize and focus on the bad aspects of whatever system they are living with. No system of performance evaluation works perfectly—most systems have substantial flaws—so there is usually plenty on which employees can focus their displeasure. It is not improbable that sometime soon, American Cyanamid will discover the superior system of forced-percentage performance evaluation, and Merck will discover that it is better to resort to an absolute scale with few distinctions, so that each will once again improve by going to a system like the one used by the other firm. The improvement will arise not so much from the changes themselves as from the *process of change*, which serves to refocus attention on performance—what it means, what the organization values, and how to achieve it.

THE DIVERSE FUNCTIONS OF PERFORMANCE EVALUATION

The primary reason why performance evaluation is so difficult and why almost every appraisal system is flawed is that performance appraisal serves many different purposes, which are rarely well-served by the same methods of performance evaluation. The purposes for conducting performance evaluation include:

1. *Evaluation to improve job matching.* Employees must be given tasks and assigned to jobs based on their skills and abilities. Performance evaluation of workers gives their superiors a sense of what they can do and how well they do it.

2. *Communication of organizational values and objectives.* The individual employee sometimes has a poor sense of what the organization wants done. An employee may wish to satisfy the desires of the organization but cannot do so without some guidance. Performance evaluation can be a very powerful tool for showing employees what is valued and what is incidental. At the same time, performance evaluation can be a powerful means of communicating organizational culture and norms of behavior, with regard to both outcome (what is sought) and process (acceptable methods).

Note that performance appraisal systems can serve to communicate norms, values, and expectations not only to the employees being evaluated, but also to those doing the evaluation and to a number of external constituencies. Performance appraisal forms that contain explicit evaluations of community relations, compliance with ethical guidelines, meeting affirmative action objectives, environmental responsibility, mentoring, and the like convey important messages to managers and external stakeholders, including government agencies charged with oversight in these areas.

3. *Information for self-improvement.* As an extension of (2), performance evaluation can be and often is used to indicate to the individual employee where his performance needs improvement and where it is simply unsatisfactory.

4. *Training and career development.* Either through self-improvement or through more external efforts, performance appraisal can be used to guide training and career development efforts for the individual.

5. *Pay (and promotion) for performance.* Any organization that allocates pay (and other rewards, such as promotion) based on performance must measure who has succeeded. Performance evaluation provides the necessary measures. Note that this is a different point than (1) above, which did not require that better performances lead to higher rewards. "Rewards for performance" is the defining characteristic here.

6. *Information for hiring strategies, especially validation of entry requirements.* Firms use a number of screens for deciding whom to hire (see Chapter 14). The validity of those screens is often subject to question, and performance evaluation, combined with retrospective looks at an individual's employment application, can be used to refine and develop more valid screens.

7. *Validation of other HR practices.* More broadly, analyses of performance data can permit organizations to evaluate the efficacy of a variety of human resource practices. Are we reaping benefits from company or external training programs? Have we developed career paths that prepare individuals at lower levels to perform effectively at higher levels? Do changes in compensation and benefits programs have the desired impact on performance or on the ability to retain high performers and weed out low performers?

8. *Retention and reductions in force.* Organizations often need to make regular decisions about retention—for instance, if there are mandatory probation periods—as well as occasional decisions about reductions in force, for which performance evaluation data are important inputs.[2]

9. *Legal defense.* Hiring, promotion, and discharge decisions can be challenged in court. To defend itself, an organization needs a well-documented paper trail of performance appraisals that will pass scrutiny as being valid, nondiscriminatory, not capricious, and so on.

10. *Effects on those doing the evaluating.* Evaluation can also be useful for those doing the evaluating. Following up on (2), it signals to evaluators what the organization values. More directly, to the extent that managers can influence the performance of their subordinates, performance evaluation systems can serve to remind managers about what their priorities should be in hiring, developing, managing, and rewarding their subordinates. Finally, formalized performance evaluation systems may force managers to do something which most people inherently find difficult to do, especially with heavy demands on their time: give candid feedback to employees. We are not aware of any organization in which managers profess to enjoy performance appraisal or do not complain about how time consuming it is, which we take as a signal that (in part) it is forcing managers to do something they would otherwise avoid.

Obviously, these various functions of performance evaluation overlap considerably. Consider efforts to broaden performance metrics to incorporate evaluations by peers, subordinates, and internal and external customers, sometimes called "360 degree feedback." Of course this reflects a desire to provide the person being evaluated with more varied and refined feedback from specific constituencies. But other purposes are served as well: It communicates, to both the evaluator and the person being evaluated, a set of values about whose opinion matters within the organization; and it provides a sense of fate control and "voice" for the parties whose evaluations are solicited.

Yet it isn't hard to see how a system of performance evaluation that does a good job on some of the tasks listed above may almost of necessity do a poor job on others. For example, if performance appraisal is meant to signal what part an employee is meant to play in the organization and to give information that can lead to intrinsically motivated self-improvement, then multicriteria evaluations, customized to the worker's unique situation and characteristics, may be most helpful. But pay for performance must ultimately be based on one-dimensional measures of performance. These measures can be tailored to each individual's circumstances, but individually tailored criteria, when used as a basis for distributing rewards, can be contentious (see below) and are more difficult to sustain when challenged in court. Thus, firms that use pay for performance often use a single generic measure that summarizes the overall quality of employee performance, in a way that is "objectively" comparable across individuals within the organization but that may fail to capture differences in the circumstances and demands of each employee whose performance is being compared. As another example, when performance appraisal is used for salary administration, promotion decisions, and terminations, those being evaluated have an incentive to shade the data to the extent they are able, and their peers and supervisors may have strong incentives to be less than candid. But this compromises the quality of data that are obtained for purposes of self-improvement, training, validation of hiring screens, and the like.[3] In short, as we consider different forms of performance evaluation, we have to think through all the different purposes being served, as well as the multiple constituencies with a stake in the outcomes (see the section on the four constituencies, below).

CHARACTERISTICS OF DIFFERENT PERFORMANCE EVALUATION SYSTEMS

Performance evaluation systems can be classified along a number of dimensions that capture variations in their structure, content, and process characteristics. Among the most important dimensions are the following:

- *Who/what is evaluated?* Do we evaluate the individual, the workgroup, the division?

- *Who performs (and has input into) the evaluation?* Is it done by each individual's immediate supervisor? a committee of supervisors? peers, subordinates, or (in part) by customers? by higher-up managers? How much input does the person being evaluated have into the evaluation and in appealing the results?

- *Time frame: short to long.* What is the time frame over which data are collected (either formally and objectively or informally and impressionistically) before evaluations are rendered? At Lincoln Electric, for instance, performance reviews are conducted twice a year; in pure piece-rate environments, performance is essentially reviewed daily. But in professional service organizations, partners often complain that even once a year is too often to gauge their performance, given the long-term nature of their tasks and client relationships.

- *Objective/formulaic versus subjective/impressionistic evaluations.* In some cases, performance is measured very objectively, using unambiguous measures of different aspects of performance. For example, a salesperson might be scored on dollar sales, new customers developed, and increases in orders by old customers, with each of these being put on some standard scale (e.g., standard deviations from the mean performance of salespersons in the organization) and then weighted 40%, 40%, and 20%, respectively. In contrast, employees in an R&D facility might be evaluated and rated based on the subjective overall impressions of their immediate superiors.

    When objective or formulaic evaluations are used, there is the further issue of how closely tailored the formula should be to the situation of each individual. At one extreme, every similarly situated individual in the firm (say, every salesperson) is evaluated using the same rigid formula. The middle ground includes cases in which individuals are evaluated against their own previous performance; improvements are noted, but the same categories are used for each individual. At the other extreme are systems in which each individual in each period has a specially tailored set of goals and objectives. A prime example of this is management by objectives (MBO) schemes, in which each individual takes part in designing his or her set of objectives.

- *Relative versus absolute performance.* In some instances, employees are evaluated on an absolute scale—for example, sales volume, units produced per week, touchdowns scored, or dollar value of hours billed to clients. In other instances, performance is evaluated on some sort of *relative* basis, or performance is measured on a mixture of absolute and relative performance. Sometimes, the benchmark that is used is the performance of other individuals, either within the organization or outside, who are presumed to face the same productive environment and constraints and to possess similar capability levels. In other cases, performance is measured relative to the individual's own previous performance.

- *Forced distribution versus unspecified percentages.* When summary categories are used, a forced distribution (so many percent in category 1, so many in category 2, etc.) may be employed, or the percentages may go unspecified. Note that where forced distributions are used, there must be some sort of relative performance evaluation going on, even if only implicitly.

- *Multisource versus single-source evaluation.* In some systems, data are gathered entirely or largely from a single source, such as the individual's supervisor. Other evaluation systems gather performance appraisals from many sources—customers, peers, supervisors, and so on—where each source is asked to appraise those aspects of performance that the source can reasonably be expected to know about. At Lincoln Electric, for instance, the quality staff is consulted about the quality of each individual's work, supervisors of closely related workgroups are consulted about the cooperativeness of particular employees, and so on.

- *Multicriterion versus single summary statistic.* In perhaps the majority of performance evaluation systems, all the data are ultimately massaged into a single summary rating statistic of overall performance. Many dimensions of performance may enter into this statistic, but the final outcome is one-dimensional. In some other systems, there is no attempt to formulate a single statistic. In the middle are systems where there is a summary statistic that is very coarse (almost everyone is in the same category), with finer gradations made on many dimensions.

- *Fine versus coarse performance distinctions.* Related to the previous point, a final dimension concerns how fine the distinctions are among levels of performance. To take an academic example, at some universities, grades are reported as numbers, on a 0 to 100 scale. Elsewhere grades are "massaged" into broad categories like A, B, and C, with (in some cases) the majority of the group being lumped together into a single grade category.

FOUR CONSTITUENCIES OF THE EVALUATION SYSTEM

In addition to considering the multiple objectives and key dimensions of evaluation systems, we need to be cognizant of the different constituencies with an interest in the outcomes of evaluation systems. We lump the different people concerned with a firm's performance evaluation system into four groups. (Obviously, some specific individuals may belong, in different capacities, to more than one of these groups.) These are: the person being evaluated; the person(s) doing the evaluating; management of the firm in general (in their role as agents of the owners of the organization); and external stakeholders, including the government, unions, and the courts. The interests of each of these parties deserve some discussion.

The Employee Being Evaluated

Empirical research on performance evaluation suggests that the most important ingredient in programs that are successful is that those being evaluated see the system as equitable and in line with the general culture and strategy of the organization. It is also important from the perspective of those being evaluated that the system support the individual's social and organizational roles, that it neither denigrate the individual nor create role conflict, and that it respect the individual's privacy and dignity.

With respect to equity, remember to distinguish between perceptions of *distributive justice*—the results are viewed as equitable, regardless of the procedures—and *procedural justice*—the evaluation process is viewed as equitable, regardless of the outcomes. Of course, in reality perceptions of these two aspects of equity will be intertwined: An evaluation system will tend to be viewed as more distributively just if its procedures are perceived to be fair, and the procedures used are more likely to be viewed as equitable by those who view the outcomes it produced (ratings or rewards based on those ratings) as fair.

When it comes to perceptions of procedural justice, important ingredients include the following:

- Individuals being evaluated should have some impact on the process. Individuals value: (a) participation in setting the standards by which they will be judged (MBO scores very well here); (b) the opportunity to present their own case, especially when evaluations are subjective; and (c) rights of appeal, when they disagree with either the process or outcome.

- The evaluator should be seen as being informed and neutral, without any discernible biases. Insofar as the scheme is more formulaic, this becomes less important (because the evaluator is doing less actual evaluation). Put differently, when there are social conflicts in the workplace—say, the supervisor and many employees are from one social or organizational group, whereas other employees are from another group—then more formulaic systems of evaluation may be desirable from this perspective.

- The evaluator should be seen as having benevolent intentions, rather than some hidden (or open) agenda other than providing a fair evaluation. For example, when the evaluator is under pressure to reduce her staff, employees may perceive that she is using performance evaluations to justify the actions she plans on taking.

- Criteria that are used should be salient to job performance. That is, validity—or, rather, *perceived* validity—is important. When comparison rankings are used, comparisons should be fair. When forced percentages are employed, the groups over which the percentages are forced should be larger rather than smaller, so that a very good individual doesn't feel inequitably penalized by being in a workgroup with a superior performer.

- The process should reinforce the individual's social standing in the group, rather than diminishing that standing. For example, if a firm *surreptitiously* monitors the performance of its employees, the process may make the individual feel devalued, insecure, or humiliated, which would then taint the process of evaluation, no matter how favorable the results are on average.

Those Performing the Evaluation

From the perspective of the evaluators, the key questions are: How time-consuming is the process? How costly is it in terms of relations with those being evaluated and others in the organization (e.g., in terms of emotional strain)? Are evaluators properly prepared to carry out and deliver the evaluations?

In general, evaluators find performance evaluation to be a difficult and unpleasant task. When evaluations are tied to compensation and termination decisions, evaluators will frequently resist making distinctions because of the adverse consequences for those to whom they give critical evaluations. Unless checked, ranking compression—almost everyone is put into an intermediate category—or ranking inflation (like grade inflation) will take place.

If the organization wants more dispersion in employee ratings, providing a forced set of percentages may be helpful to evaluators, giving them a stiffer backbone (and something on which to blame the inevitable bad evaluations that must be given). When percentages are forced, however, one must be careful to guard against evaluators who simply give each employee his or her turn at the top rank.

In response to this, many organizations have found that it is helpful to decouple evaluations of performance for purposes of making "bread-and-butter" decisions (e.g., pay, promotions) from evaluations for feedback purposes, either conducting separate evaluation sessions at different points in the year, or else communicating the feedback at a different time of year than when the bread-and-butter stuff is announced.[4] Although more time-consuming, this practice apparently makes it easier or more comfortable for evaluators to provide candid and critical feedback to employees without being overwhelmed by their concern for the economic consequences to the person being evaluated. As we said earlier, it also makes it easier for the person receiving that feedback to hear it and accept it. But there is a potential problem here as well: Careful evaluation takes time, and unless the organization stresses the importance of the evaluation process—through culture and other means—evaluators may respond to the lack of "serious" consequences with superficiality. Those who perform evaluations ought to be evaluated themselves based on the quality of the evaluations they perform—that is, their ability to appraise the performance of subordinates. If this activity is seemingly not valued by the organization, in the sense that it doesn't turn up as part of the evaluator's own evaluation, then little attention may be paid to it.

And the evaluation of an evaluator's performance should include an appraisal of how well the evaluation is *communicated*—that is, performance evaluation should be viewed as a facet of the management and development of subordinates. In this respect, evaluators generally benefit from instruction on how to perform and communicate the evaluation, especially when evaluation is done subjectively. If they are to give feedback based on the evaluation, training in giving feedback constructively and usefully is often very valuable. Research studies have demonstrated that the most useful feedback tends to be behaviorally specific, identifying those high-leverage behaviors that *can* be improved and providing guidance on how to do so. Yet it is by no means uncommon for untrained supervisors and managers to provide feedback that is vague, focused on dispositions rather than behaviors, or focused on conditions that are difficult or impossible to change. Examples might include feedback to an employee that he or she: "lacks leadership potential," "should relate better to your people," "must be more charismatic," "should display more creativity," "fails to respect superiors," "sometimes does not inspire confidence of customers," or "doesn't seem to embody our company's values." Feedback of this type—especially if it is not accompanied with specific illustrations—does not provide the individual receiving it with much guidance as to the particular behaviors or remedial efforts that would ameliorate the deficiencies.

The Interests of Management and of Outside Constituencies

From the perspective of management, acting on behalf of the owners of the firm, the important questions are: How (administratively) costly is the system? What is the quality of information that is generated, for purposes of placement, promotion, and termination? Does the system motivate or demotivate workers? If bonuses and compensation are tied to performance evaluation, does the system lead to unwarranted wage inflation?

Finally, the more important concerns of HRM professionals, courts, unions, and the government include the *reliability* of the evaluations—ratings should not change dramatically if they were redone by the same rater shortly thereafter or by other raters from the same organization (assuming no dramatic events intervened)—and their *validity,* meaning that they are relevant to job performance.[5]

PERFORMANCE EVALUATION SYSTEMS AND THE FIVE FACTORS

Given the diverse purposes of performance evaluation, the various key dimensions along which evaluations systems can vary, and the numerous constituencies with a stake in the outcomes, it should be clear that assessing the appropriateness of a given performance evaluation system is a complex business. In fact, it is even more complex than that, because the appropriateness of a particular performance evaluation system will depend critically—as you no doubt anticipated by this point—on two other sets of influences: (1) how the five factors impinge on the organization; and (2) how well the performance evaluation system fits with other pieces of the overall HR system.

Needless to say, we can't possibly provide a complete discussion here of all these interdependencies in the abstract. Instead, we proceed as follows. We first discuss how the ideal design of a performance evaluation system is likely to depend on five-factor considerations. We won't cover all the possibilities, but we will get to a number of five-factor-related considerations. Then, we explore several practical dilemmas that organizations face in trying to design and implement performance evaluation schemes, and a few of the commonplace tactics and strategies that organizations adopt in trying to strike a balance among the different objectives and dimensions of performance evaluation that suits their five-factor context.

Strategy

Performance evaluation systems should be congruent with the strategy of the firm, helping to communicate that strategy clearly and forcefully to individuals and putting positive value on behaviors that reinforce the strategy. For example, a manufacturing firm whose strategy involves providing high levels of quality and after-sale service to customers should not reduce performance evaluation of salespersons to levels of dollars sold or new customers developed. Looking at reorder levels or surveyed measures of customer satisfaction may be much better. In the same context, a firm that emphasizes after-sale service may wish to slow down the pace of performance evaluation, so that a greater amount of relevant information can be brought to bear. Although the need for congruence between strategy and performance evaluation is obvious, it is not hard to find examples of organizations that fail to satisfy this simple desideratum. We have encountered some already in this book—for instance, Portman Hotel, and Sears' auto repair centers—and our experience is that most managers can readily (and vehemently!) identify discrepancies between the professed business strategy of their organization or business unit on the one hand, and the form and content of its performance evaluation system on the other hand.

When an organization changes its strategy, using performance evaluation to communicate the nature, importance, and salience of the change to employees can be very effective. For instance, when John Mack assumed the presidency of the Morgan Stanley investment bank in 1993, he sought to create a unified, continuously innovative "one-firm firm," with greater collaboration and cooperation across units in the service of Morgan's global clients. Mack viewed implementation of a new 360° feedback system as an important tool in achieving this organizational and cultural change and as a powerful symbol of the strategic redirection, and he took a strong personal role in championing the new evaluation system.[6]

Technology and Work Organization

Technology and work organization enter in several ways. For *guardian* jobs, we want to differentiate between acceptable and unacceptably low performance, but fine distinctions should not be made among those whose performance is acceptable; we don't want to stimulate employees to gamble on getting slightly better performance if there is a risk that this will lead to a disaster. To take a concrete example, evaluating airline pilots based on the number of on-time flights they make might encourage them to take off in marginal weather or to hurry through safety procedures. This is not a good idea. On the other hand, if the job has *star* characteristics, performance evaluation should recognize outstanding performance and treat failure as being close to on par with mediocrity.[7]

Jobs that entail high degrees of interdependence are generally bad candidates for performance appraisals that are formulaic or objective in terms of individual performance, especially insofar as this may discourage cooperation.[8] Fixed percentage rankings and other forms of ratings that are based on comparisons with fellow workers are especially dysfunctional. Group-related evaluations may work well, but only when the group is large enough to encompass most of the interdependencies. Individual evaluations in which a great deal of weight is put on cooperative aspects of the job, or where peers give part of the evaluation, can also be employed, although measuring cooperation is generally difficult and peer evaluation can be tricky (see below).

Jobs that entail a high degree of ambiguity are generally bad candidates for performance evaluation that is formulaic at any level. How do you create a formula for measuring performance when it isn't clear at the outset just what the job entails?

Jobs in which results take a long time to emerge naturally favor evaluations that emphasize long-term results and that do not tie substantial reward allocations to any narrow or short-term output measure. For example, at Japanese trading conglomerates such as the Mitsubishi Trading Company, performance evaluations for the purposes of promotion are based not only on a long period of observation, but also on performance in a wide variety of jobs, thereby providing a less noisy measure of ability and future managerial potential.[9] This approach to performance evaluation is well-suited to the jobs in question within Mitsubishi, in which success depends on building deep and extensive social relationships inside and outside the company and on having a broad understanding of the many products and services offered by Mitsubishi's trading group.

Difficult trade-offs arise when those being evaluated have the ability to manipulate or obscure the data on which performance evaluations are made. If the performance evaluation scheme is formulaic, the firm is inviting a great deal of attention to and (attempted) manipulation of the numbers on which the formula is based. For instance, a clerical worker at Lincoln Electric whose performance evaluation was positively tied to the number of keystrokes her typewriter recorded was discovered to be eating her lunch with one hand while using her other hand to punch a typewriter key as fast as she could throughout the lunch break. Another classic example concerns the unintended and undesirable effects of formal performance records within government employment service agencies, whose mission is to help chronically unemployed people find work.[10] A new supervisor imposed formal performance measures on the workforce to improve efficiency and performance. Knowing that they would henceforth be evaluated based on various output measures (such as the proportion of job applicants for whom they found jobs), the government employees tried to drive their ratios up by focusing their efforts on those job applicants having the highest likelihood of being quickly placed into an existing job opening. Consequently, the bureaucrats began overlooking the individuals on whom the agency was supposed to be focusing most: people who had been unemployed for long periods of time and were having no success finding employment. In organizations where evaluations are subjective, the person being evaluated may not be able to fudge or cook the numbers as easily and directly as in these examples. However, one can never completely escape attempts by employees to massage their evaluators' perceptions of the data so as to appear to be doing better than is actually the fact.

Related to this are cases in which workers have opportunities to do "favors" for their supervisor or where the supervisor can extract favors. In these cases (a different form of manipulation), subjective evaluation by a single evaluator is fraught with dangers; objective performance evaluation or rating by a group of supervisors is relatively more desirable.

When the job entails many different tasks or has many different aspects of performance, subjective evaluation is usually favored over formulaic evaluation. Formulas that involve fifty-seven different scaled quantities rarely achieve an appropriate balance among them. Moreover, when different aspects of the job compete with one another, formulas are often dysfunctional, especially when one aspect of the job is easier to measure than the other. For example, in a job where the quality of work and speed are both important, formulas will often lead to bang-bang incentives; the worker sacrifices quality for speed or vice versa, rather than balancing the two. This is one reason why many educators oppose merit pay for schoolteachers, arguing that any evaluation scheme that ties rewards for teachers to a precise output measure (e.g., standardized test scores) will discourage teachers from doing other, harder-to-measure things that are important in educating children (e.g., spending extra time on children with special needs). Or, to pick a sports example, a famous quarterback once allegedly negotiated a contract containing a year-end bonus aimed at minimizing the number of interceptions recorded against him. During the following season, he had very few interceptions. However, he was also sacked more times than ever before in his career and had a very poor passing record; afraid of being intercepted, he held onto the ball and, when he threw, threw only safe, very short passes.

Formulas that lead to balance can be devised, but the formula can quickly become too complex for anyone to understand, thereby undercutting its value as a tool for communicating the organization's strategy and culture. The case of Analog Devices in the 1980s is illuminating in this respect. Analog Devices, a semiconductor manufacturer, designs, manufactures, and sells precision electronic components and subsystems employed mostly in measurement and control applications. The company developed innovative bonus plans for both technical and managerial personnel that sought to achieve balance among the following: short- versus longer-run performance; high productivity and quality on mature products while stimulating the development and timely release of new products; absolute improvement as well as performance against industry benchmarks; individual contributions as well as subunit and companywide performance; and a desire for equity and consistency in the bonus schemes for management versus technical personnel while also recognizing the different success factors involved in managerial versus technical work.[11] Believing that a very precise evaluation formula would serve better to communicate the company's strategic objectives and resonate with the firm's engineering culture, the top management team developed a complex set of non-linear multivariate formulas for calculating bonuses. Over time, these formulas became so complex and in need of tinkering that their usefulness came to be questioned, especially when the stock price dove in the late 1980s, causing calculated bonus payouts to plummet. By the end of 1980s, Analog started to rethink their whole evaluation scheme.

Finally, formulaic evaluation can be dysfunctional when there is variation in desired job performance among different individuals who are in the same basic job category but doing distinct tasks (e.g., divisional vice presidents in a multidivisional company; research chemists in a pharmaceutical firm). Insofar as one can engage in MBO-style tailoring of the formula to each individual, some of the difficulties can be avoided. However, personally tailored formulas can invite feelings of inequity (the formula in division A is perceived as easier than that in division B or as better suited to the talents of some worker in division B), while uniformity in the formulas would clearly lead to inappropriate incentives for at least some, and often all, employees.

This is especially true when, in a small group, one wishes workers at the same level to perform very different tasks. For example, imagine trying to devise a formula for quality of performance for a workgroup of engineers, some of whom are expected to become generalists and others of whom are expected to specialize narrowly and deeply in a particular area. Or imagine trying to evaluate all the partners in a corporate law firm using a simple formula to measure their value to the firm. Given huge differences across the practice areas, this will be difficult to do. Easy to measure quantities, such as billable hours, may do a poor job of reflecting particular lawyers' contributions in important areas, such as: the brilliant tax or estate attorney who provides invaluable service to other lawyers in the firm by solving thorny dilemmas facing an important client; the young Turk who has been asked to help the firm build a presence in a new practice area or region; or the veteran partner who is unrivaled at business development and training young lawyers. If attorneys are all evaluated based on the same evaluation metric, and especially if those evaluations are used to determine rewards, we would quickly find an increase in requests to be assigned to the "easiest" practice areas in terms of being able to score well on the formula and a reticence to undertake the tasks whose impact on the formula is hardest to gauge.

Culture

Culture is meant to reinforce and be reinforced by performance evaluation systems, so the connections between them should be tight. If the firm has a culture of cooperation, stressing individual performance is obviously perilous. If the organization has or wishes a culture of entrepreneurship, performance evaluation should weight entrepreneurial efforts heavily; successes should be heavily weighted and failures should be discounted so that risk taking is not discouraged. If the culture is egalitarian, forced percentages are out of step. If the culture is clan-like, coarse summary rankings (you are doing okay or, in exceptional cases, not okay) may be appropriate, or, alternatively, perhaps even no summary rankings are warranted, relying instead on performance evaluations along a number of dimensions. This is because the clan-like firm can rely more heavily on intrinsic motivation and peer pressure (so summary rankings are less needed) and because the act of reducing a complex web of performance measures to a single stark statistic invokes connotations of the faceless market, not of friendship or family relations.

Of course, culture is important not only for the content of performance evaluation systems, but also for the *process*. Who evaluates performance, how, and with what kinds of involvement and input from the person being evaluated conveys important cultural messages, such as the degree of trust placed in employees, the reliance on hierarchy, and how much participation and openness are valued.

To give an example, in organizations that rely heavily on intrinsic motivation (research laboratories, for example), frequent performance appraisals, even if untied to compensation, can be quite dysfunctional. An extreme case of this was Bell Telephone Laboratories prior to the break-up of AT&T. Among the technical staff, the measure of output was by and large the Technical Report, in which the scientist reported internally on his or her work. Technical Reports were never counted, and (the story goes) employees could survive quite a while without producing any at all. Indeed, one mathematician, who was working on the four-color map problem (a mathematical problem that is at best barely connected to commercial concerns of AT&T) went several years without preparing any Technical Reports at all. At the gentle urging of his supervisor, he finally wrote a report stating, more or less, that while he had become very adept at drawing fantastically complex maps that were hard to color, he had simultaneously become adept at coloring them in, and so he had no definitive conclusions to report yet. Employees of Bell Labs told this story not to point out how poorly managed the Labs were, but—very much the reverse—as a point of pride and as an accurate reflection of the culture. The point was that the Labs insulated scientists against the bean counters by giving the bean counters very few beans to count. Management understood full well that this meant that the Labs provided sinecures for an uncomfortably large number of individuals who provided few benefits to Ma Bell. But the culture fostered a relatively healthy number of extremely valuable contributions to technology and, not coincidentally, to AT&T's bottom line.[12]

Workforce

Workforce and demographics play a number of roles. A workforce consisting of practicing engineers may favor relatively formulaic evaluations. (To the extent that this reflects the external culture of engineers, this is a factor of the *external social environment.*) When the workforce has a low rate of turnover and there is promotion from within, performance evaluation will often be viewed as more equitable by those being evaluated, because of a shared vocabulary and common understandings, social similarity, and goal congruence between the person doing the rating and those being rated. Professionals whose allegiance is to their profession rather than to the organization will have a harder time with evaluations that only look at their contributions to the organization and that are made by people who are not *bona fide* practitioners of the profession. Think of Bell Labs again. Research papers and publications may contribute very indirectly to the profits of AT&T, but they directly contribute to knowledge in the science involved. An attempt was made following deregulation to evaluate the contributions of Bell Labs employees to AT&T directly. This contributed to a minor exodus from the Labs to universities of some of the best people working there, with the exodus concentrated more in the basic sciences than in fields of applied engineering.

When the workforce is demographically diverse, the potential for bias in subjective evaluations is greater (where the biases run along race, gender, age, and disability lines). Objective measures of performance may be less biased, as long as the objective measures are *valid* indicators of performance. Yet one should also worry about biases in so-called objective performance measures. There are at least two aspects to this. First, some seemingly objective measures may be psychometrically biased against individuals with particular cultural backgrounds, education levels, and the like. For instance, one could easily imagine measures of customer satisfaction that would disadvantage individuals with certain social or cultural characteristics. Second, performance itself may sometimes be adversely affected by biases of the customer or relevant "suppliers" (including co-workers supplying work inputs or social support). For instance, an African-American salesperson, an effeminate construction supervisor, or a female corporate attorney may have greater trouble achieving performance targets if their clients, co-workers, or subordinates behave in a biased fashion.

External Environment

The external environment enters in a number of ways. Legal concerns and requirements may favor relatively more objective forms of evaluation, because lack of reliability (in the technical sense) can be deadly in front of a judge, jury, or arbitrator. Documentation of validity has long been important for EEOC (and other) proceedings. The presence of unions also typically influences both the form and content of evaluation procedures, favoring greater emphasis on seniority and skill acquisition (as defined by the union) and more formal, explicit procedures that are subject to appeal by the employee.

In some societies, social norms may work against evaluation systems that explicitly and consistently rank younger, newer employees above older employees with more years of service to the organization. In other societies, norms may favor evaluation procedures that make strong distinctions on meritocratic grounds.

Finally, the economic environment, especially labor mobility of talented workers, can play a part. A few studies have documented the unsurprising fact that in *star* technologies (e.g., sales contexts) where outstanding individual performance can be measured but is not rewarded commensurately, the highest performers are most likely to depart the organization. Thus, labor market pressures may exert discipline on an organization, pushing it in the direction of making finer distinctions among performance levels and tying reward allocations to those distinctions.

STRIKING BALANCE IN PERFORMANCE EVALUATION SYSTEMS: SOME KEY ISSUES AND TACTICS

The five-factor analysis just conducted is noteworthy for the number of times we invoke the words "don't" and "doesn't fit." It might seem that nothing will fit or work well! We reiterate that the problem is the large number of objectives and constituencies served; it isn't hard to find something wrong with virtually any performance evaluation system. So a truly ideal system, in most cases, doesn't exist. The challenge for the designer of the system is to strike the right balance among the various objectives and constituencies involved. In this section, we survey some of the more important dilemmas that are routinely encountered in this balancing act, and we present some tactics that have been employed to reconcile the dilemmas that appear. This survey isn't meant to be complete. Instead, it is intended to illustrate the kinds of critical choices you'll need to ponder after you have done a five-factor analysis, as you try to translate the "ideal" system that might emerge from such an analysis into practice.

Comparative Performance Evaluation

We noted that one method organizations sometimes employ to tackle some of the challenges associated with performance measurement is comparative or relative performance evaluation, assessing individual employees or groups relative to one another, to some externally derived benchmark, or to previous performance, rather than against some absolute standard.

The point of comparative performance evaluation is simple: It permits the evaluator to control for the impact of unmeasured environmental variables on tangible measures of performance. For example, instead of worrying about the optimal measure(s) or formulas for how well a division performed in absolute, one looks at how well it performed relative to other firms or divisions engaged in similar trade and facing similar environmental uncertainties. A salesperson is compensated not for the absolute level of sales, but instead for how her sales compare with those of other salespersons in the organization. As long as the unmeasured exogenous factors influencing performance—such as weather, interest rates, or the odds of a key supplier or customer going bankrupt—affect the individuals or groups in the comparison set in a similar manner, measuring the relative performance of the affected individuals or groups provides a (statistically) better measure of the individuals' or groups' levels or qualities of effort. (To keep from repeating the ugly construction "individual or group," we will henceforth discuss this technique in terms of one or the other singly; but almost everything to follow applies equally to individual and group comparative performance evaluation schemes.)

Besides providing a better statistical measure of how well the individual has performed, comparative performance evaluation schemes may lead to enhanced perceptions of procedural justice, on at least two grounds. First, individuals are not penalized or rewarded for things they cannot control, such as the state of the overall economy or the company's inferior product line. Moreover, the relatively formulaic nature of comparative performance evaluation may enhance the notion that performance is being measured objectively or "scientifically," at least in comparison with more subjective systems of performance evaluation.

But these advantages of comparative performance evaluation can become disadvantages, if the comparison set is not very carefully constructed:

- *The performance measures that are compared should be similarly affected by uncontrollable environmental variables, so that relative performance reflects to the greatest extent possible things under the control of the individuals involved.* Suppose, for instance, that regional sales managers are evaluated comparatively and that their company manages its advertising nationally, placing ads on national network TV shows and in national magazines and newspapers. If advertising is important and if sales regions vary in how well those ads reach potential customers, then sales managers in some districts may have a plausible case in claiming that they are being inappropriately compared to sales managers who are fortunate to have been assigned to districts where the company's advertising has better penetration. In such a case, the company may find itself facing pressure to decentralize its advertising, so that each sales manager can have control over one of the factors that is likely to influence his or her comparative standing vis-à-vis other managers.

  Or consider the case of a firm that seeks to measure the performance of its research staff. There may be good reasons not to evaluate individual members of the research staff relative to the performance of their closest peers. The firm might therefore choose instead to measure performance relative to members of other research teams within the organization, or even relative to the performance of the research staffs of competitors. The problem with this is that, in most cases, the more diffuse the comparison set, the less control there is for environmental factors. If, say, a measure of comparison is the number of patents gained, the specific research agendas of the different research staffs, set to some extent by managerial decree, may become important: Group X is "penalized" because it works in an area that is less likely to lead to many patents. This may lead to research groups arguing for a greater measure of autonomy: "If our performance is going to be measured on the basis of the patents we gain," will go the argument, "then we should control what we work on."

- *The individuals in the comparison set should be comparable, in the sense that their performances are "on the same scale."* If salespersons are evaluated based on their relative sales levels, and some salespersons are blessed with larger markets than others, those with the smaller markets will properly view the system as unjust.

- *Individuals in a relatively small comparison set are "penalized"—usually unjustly, in their view—if the comparison set contains one or more truly exceptional performers.*
- *Comparative evaluation schemes can clash with other important status norms.* For instance, a comparative evaluation scheme that consistently ranks younger employees ahead of those with greater seniority may, in some cultures, give rise to substantial status inconsistency, thereby decreasing perceptions of legitimacy for the evaluation scheme.

Some of these problems can be dealt with by constructing smaller and "tighter" comparison sets—for example, sales personnel might be evaluated only relative to others servicing similar types of customers; professional service workers are compared relative to others in the same experience cohort and practice area; research groups are compared only to other groups that deal with similar scientific problems. Of course, using smaller groups can exacerbate the third problem listed above. And constructing smaller and tighter comparison sets often means restricting comparisons to other individuals (or groups) inside the specific firm or specific business unit of the firm; we'll see some potential problems with this below.

In theory, these difficulties can also be addressed by *handicapping* the relative performance measures: To compensate for their relative disadvantages, we might give "extra credit" to: the sales manager working in an area relatively less well covered by national advertising; the research group working on a subject less prone to developing patents; the salesperson with the smaller market area; and individuals stuck in a group with an exceptional star performer. In practice, however, handicapping is a fragile and contentious process. The basis for the handicapping scheme may be disputed: The salesperson assigned to the larger and potentially more fruitful territory will point out that sales take time and effort, and she has to work harder. Or she may argue that the size of her territory is partially of her own making, as she has built up her clientele. And even if the basis for the handicapping scheme is agreed upon, the size of the handicap can be contentious. Almost every handicapping process is rife with the potential for politicking and feelings of procedural injustice by those who face the handicaps, and even by those who are advantaged by handicaps but not (in their own view) advantaged enough. In some instances, handicaps can be constructed reasonably objectively, using statistical techniques.[13] But in general, handicapping must be handled very carefully.

The smallest and tightest comparison group possible is, of course, the individual herself. Each person can be evaluated relative to a performance standard that is tailored to his or her unique abilities and productive environment. MBO works in this fashion, where the individual is involved in setting her own idiosyncratic targets. A variant of this approach—which sometimes is employed in MBO schemes—is to benchmark performance against the individual's own performance in the past, providing rewards based on *improvements* in performance over time. For instance, a division manager might be given a bonus that depends on how well costs have been contained in his division, relative to costs in the previous period.

Evaluation schemes that appraise each individual relative to his or her own unique baseline can overcome some of the difficulties associated with absolute performance evaluation or relative performance evaluation based on comparisons among individuals. However, such "self-handicapping" schemes can also create their own difficulties. One kind of problem, which we will discuss in more detail when we turn to compensation issues in Chapter 11, is called the *ratchet effect*. Suppose that employees are evaluated relative to their performance in the past, and imagine that a worker is extraordinarily successful in one period at containing costs. This will result in a high evaluation (and, presumably, higher compensation) in the current period, but it also sets a higher standard for cost containment in the future. If the worker will remain in this job, she has ratcheted up the standards by which she will be judged next time; as long as her intentions are to remain, because of the ratchet effect she may have less incentive to control costs than might be thought. Of course, there is a way to beat the ratchet effect: Workers can try to make quick improvements and then depart, rather than concentrating on long-term, sustainable improvements. But this is almost certainly *not* what the firm is aiming for with its incentive scheme.

Another difficulty with handicapping schemes concerns equity. There are no doubt some occasions in which employees will believe it is fair for a supervisor to hold a particular co-worker to a lower performance standard—for instance, a colleague whose entire family was just killed in a car crash, or who lost a finger, or who has a learning disability, or who is brand new to the job. However, appraisal systems that permit evaluators to establish a separate baseline for each person being evaluated can invite perceptions of subjectivity and bias among those being evaluated. They certainly invite ferocious politicking and the possibility of corruption.

Besides worrying about perceived (and actual) justice in comparative evaluation schemes, you have to worry about the impact that such schemes can have on the behavior of those being evaluated. We've already discussed some likely behavioral reactions:

- *Politicking and possible attempts at corruption* may occur at the time the criteria for evaluation are established or handicaps are employed. We know of no fool-proof response to this problem, but for several reasons it often helps to have criteria set and handicaps determined by a committee of supervisors: (a) it is usually harder to corrupt or influence a committee than an individual; (b) individual supervisors are less likely to be capricious or biased when they have to defend their actions in a group;[14] and (c) committees can stiffen the backbone of individual supervisors, by giving them a "cover" or excuse for decisions that are made.
- *Schemes that rely on improvements in individual performance are prone to the ratchet effect,* discussed above.

- *Those being evaluated will press for more control over environmental variables that are material to the comparison.* This isn't necessarily a bad thing (see the discussion of autonomy in Chapter 13); but the costs arising from loss of coordination must be weighed against the benefits from giving employees greater autonomy.

In addition to these, we add several other typical and sometimes troublesome reactions to comparative evaluation.

- *Those evaluated will attempt to game the system, in terms of assignments they accept, tasks they perform, and so on.* For instance, when a particular division of a firm is in trouble, it may be worthwhile for the firm to send one of their better managers to the rescue. But with ill-constructed incentive systems that engage in comparative evaluation using measures of divisional performance, asking a manager to take an assignment in a poorly performing division may be asking that manager to take a cut in compensation. The same is true when a professional is asked by a partnership to develop a new practice.

- *When the comparison group lies entirely within a single organization, the group that is competing may collude against the evaluator's interests.*[15] This sort of collusion is particularly likely when those who are in competition are socially similar to each other and different from their superiors, and when they are in close communication with one another. Stories of restrictive work-rate norms, enforced on the shop floor by social sanctions (or worse), are well known to most managers with a background in production. The somewhat pejorative term *rate-buster* was invented precisely to describe those who exceed the rate set informally by the workgroup.

- *Even if the group doesn't collude explicitly, conformity—a form of implicit collusion—may result.* Individuals who are being evaluated may seek safety in numbers, especially when the scheme penalizes relatively poor performance more than it rewards relatively good performance. Complaints are often voiced, for example, that institutional money managers are more concerned with following what their counterparts are doing than with conducting their own fundamental analysis of stocks in the portfolios they manage. (Note that this is a case of conformity among individuals who work "independently.") Such an outcome can sometimes be desirable—for instance, in guardian jobs, where "collective wisdom" is a good guide to acceptable performance. But in many cases this kind of conformity can substitute groupthink for individual judgment, impeding good performance.

- *Cooperative efforts among those being comparatively evaluated may be hindered.* Because individuals are being evaluated relative to one another, one person's improvement comes at the expense of someone else in the same evaluation pool. Organizations relying on comparative evaluation schemes use a variety of approaches to deal with the potential problem of impeding cooperation among the employees who are being comparatively evaluated. One tactic is to add a subjective assessment of employee cooperation to the measure of absolute or relative performance, to temper any dysfunctional tendency for employees to seek maximum performance at the expense of their co-workers. For instance, the large year-end bonuses for which the piece-rate employees at Lincoln Electric compete are based on an assessment of their relative productivity, but Lincoln's bonus formulas also incorporate subjective assessments of workers' cooperativeness, obtained from multiple managers within the plant. This approach can be a healthy corrective to the potential divisive effects of relative performance evaluation. However, cooperation is often harder to measure than other dimensions of performance. For reasons we discuss in Chapter 11, this can make it very tricky to devise evaluation and reward schemes that will foster the desired balance between cooperation and "sticking to your knitting" to maximize individual output. Another means of trying to preserve cooperation among potential rivals in a relative performance evaluation tournament is to offer longer-term rewards for cooperation, such as promotions, which might offset any shorter-term incentive to withhold cooperation in order to fare well in the short run.

- *Relative performance schemes may also provide poor incentives near the end of the evaluation period.* Think about a race or competition, in which the prize money is determined simply by what place you finish in. If you get very far behind or very far ahead of the rest of your competitors, there may not be strong incentives to perform at your highest level: If you are way ahead of the pack, you might simply wish to coast and protect your lead; if, on the other hand, you are dead last in the contest by a wide enough margin, you may conclude that there is no point in putting in any more effort. Yet obviously in many (if not most) settings, organizations will wish individuals to continue to strive to do their best, even if they are clearly destined to finish first or last in a relative performance contest. A good partial antidote to these problems is to avoid schemes that have the flavor of a pure tournament: To the one victor go all the spoils. Instead, rewards should be sensitive to how far in front or behind individuals are, so that finishing a "close third" yields better rewards than does a "distant third," let alone a distant fifth.[16]

- *Finally, perhaps most importantly, and going back to perceptions of procedural injustice, inappropriate comparisons may be demotivating.* An individual who perceives the firm's relative performance evaluation scheme as unjust may respond by downgrading the importance she places on these evaluations and on her status in the organization as a whole. The key challenge here—and for relative performance evaluation in general—is constructing comparison sets and criteria that are accepted as being procedurally just, while at the same time accomplishing what comparative performance evaluation is meant to accomplish: improving the ability to identify strong (or weak) individual performance by controlling for environmental uncertainty that is beyond the control of the individual.

Coarse Summary Measures: Blurring Distinctions in the Middle

We have seen that some organizations adopt a quite different approach to the problems involved in trying to compare and differentiate among employee performance, namely, to make only minimal distinctions. In the story we told in the introduction of this chapter, we mentioned how Merck's evaluation scheme—with thirteen summary levels of performance—resulted in the large majority of individuals (73%) being placed in one of three "upper-middle" levels. This is typical of schemes that use relatively coarse summary measures without forced percentages. Intel, for instance, has in recent years utilized a three-point scale, with roughly 10% of employees placed in each of the two extreme categories and 80% in the middle. Indeed, in academia, the phenomenon of grade inflation at elite institutions is notorious: Nearly everyone winds up with an A level grade. We've already given a common rationale for this sort of outcome: Managers in most organizations find performance appraisal to be difficult, uncomfortable, and time consuming. When the stakes (in terms of rewards to employees) are high, managers feel uncomfortable about giving negative evaluations, and when the stakes are low (e.g., there is no bonus pool to dole out this year or the appraisals are being emphasized purely for legal protection), managers resent the imposition on their time.

A different rationale for this pattern—one that concludes that it can be rational for organizations to evaluate people in this fashion—has been offered by Todd Zenger, and he provides some supportive empirical evidence, obtained by looking at performance appraisal and reward (pay and promotion) decisions in two Bay Area high-technology companies.[17] Zenger assumes that making distinctions among employees in the middle of the distribution is less beneficial to the organization than is making distinctions in the tails, holding fixed the costs of making the distinctions. That is, he assumes that it is important to distinguish "very good" from "superb" performance and to distinguish "poor" from "unacceptable" performance, but that distinguishing among "slightly better than average," "average," and "slightly below average" performance will produce little gross benefit to the organization.[18] Zenger argues that whether the distinctions should be made ought to reflect these gross benefits *and* the costs incurred in making them, which include invidious social comparisons that lead to perceived inequity and associated dissent.

When is it most costly to make such distinctions? Zenger claims that under the following conditions—which he suggests are quite common in organizations—the expected cost of each distinction in terms of invidious social comparisons will be highest *in the middle of the distribution*: (a) when the underlying distribution of performance is bell-shaped; (b) when the distributions of ratings and rewards in the organization are common knowledge, but performance ratings of specific employees are not; and (c) when individuals tend to overestimate their own relative performance. He argues that the more people there are who are roughly comparable to a given individual, the more likely that individual is to find someone who received unwarranted better treatment. This opportunity to see injustice is highest when there are many comparable individuals being rated (that is, when distinctions are made in the middle of the distribution) and lowest where there are few (when the rated individual falls in either tail of the distribution). Zenger is giving two rationales here where either one alone would suffice: The gross benefits of the comparison are highest in the tails, by assumption; and the social costs are lowest there, because of the likelihood of an invidious comparison being made. For these reasons, separately or in concert, the optimal pattern is what Zenger observes empirically: a policy that groups most people in the middle, rewarding and punishing only extreme outcomes.

Zenger's model also yields some intriguing predictions relating performance to turnover intentions. In a reward-the-extremes regime, the people most likely to be content are the highest performers, who are being rewarded for their achievements, and the below-average-but-not-awful performers, who have escaped the punishments meted out to the awful performers but would not gain much if their performance improved from below-average to average. Conversely, the two groups most likely to be dissatisfied and planning to leave are: the above-average-but-less-than-outstanding performers, who may believe their performance is outstanding and consequently resent not having received the rewards obtained by co-workers who were rated as outstanding; and the worst performers, who may even be forced to leave. These predictions receive some support in empirical analyses of employee turnover intentions, which might help explain why previous researchers have tended not to discover any clear linear relationship between performance and actual or intended turnover.

Objective versus Subjective Measures

As we saw in discussing the five factors, the desirability of objective/formulaic evaluation measures versus subjective/impressionistic measures hinges largely on considerations of strategy, technology, and culture. But either of these alternatives involves a number of complex considerations when it comes time to devise and implement a particular scheme. Foremost among these complex considerations are perceptions of procedural justice: An evaluation system that is purely subjective—the evaluator simply announces whether she thinks the employee's performance is excellent, good, fair, or poor—is apt to score low on procedural justice, being too susceptible to caprice and bias by the evaluator. Some basis for the evaluation should be offered. But highly formulaic systems, applied in a nonformulaic environment—different individuals face different challenges, have access to different resources, and so on—are equally apt to be seen as procedurally unjust, because they miss all the distinctive factors applying to the individual being evaluated. A compromise scheme that uses objective measures, but tailors the "formula" to the individual situation (as in MBO), invites corruption or at least politicking in the formula-setting process, and as a result can lead to perceptions of procedural injustice.

Schemes that rely on unsupported subjective judgments tend to have negligible administrative costs, but they can impose substantial emotional costs on the evaluator. Schemes that are formulaic, especially when the formula involves data that are easily obtained (say, because they are retained in the files anyway), are cheap both administratively and in terms of the evaluator, who can throw up her hands and tell her "evaluatees" (in quotes because she isn't really evaluating anyone): "It's the system."

Of course, formulaic schemes tend to score well on reliability. However, depending on the environment, they can score poorly on validity. On the other hand, schemes that rely on subjective judgments that must be documented and supported are perhaps the most costly to maintain, but they do provide evaluators with some cover when dealing with employees who are unhappy with the evaluations they received.

Evaluation by Committee and by Multiple Sources

In trying to strike the right balance here, many organizations have begun experimenting with having evaluations done by multiple sources. This can take a variety of forms: a literal committee-based evaluation process, where the committee typically includes the immediate superior of the person being evaluated; gathering input from multiple constituencies, such as subordinates, peers, and clients; or aggregating assessments obtained from multiple independent raters, all representing the same constituency. The hope is that the greater number and diversity of evaluation inputs can produce overall assessments that not only are more reliable and valid in a statistical sense, but more legitimate and informative from the vantage point of the person being evaluated.

We begin by discussing the case in which overall performance evaluations are literally produced by a group or committee (e.g., all the managers at a given level will collectively evaluate and rank the subordinates whom they manage), a practice that is quite common in both public and private sector organizations. Both from the perspective of evaluators and, in many cases, from the perspective of management in general, evaluations produced in this fashion can have significant advantages. This scheme enables other managers who have had contact with a given employee to provide input into the evaluation, providing a richer assessment than one based solely on one superior's appraisal. It enhances knowledge about others in the workforce, so that placements, rotations, and transfers can be arranged more efficiently. It can give a more uniform message as to what the organization desires; in contrast, when one group is evaluated by one manager's set of criteria and a second group by a second manager's, and when the two groups interact sufficiently to see that there are differences, the validity of the entire scheme is called into question. More deviously, evaluation by a group can give the individual supervisor of employee X some ability to lay off blame for a "poor" or mediocre evaluation of X, attributing the bad outcome to the group, and it somewhat decouples personal feedback (conducted by X's supervisor, in most cases) from summary rankings (produced in committee) that are used for compensation administration. Finally, it can enhance the quality of the performance evaluations that are done, because it encourages evaluators to take the process seriously; if managers must justify their rankings in front of others (including, perhaps, their own superiors), then presumably they will take those rankings more seriously.[19]

On the other hand, this kind of process has its potential pitfalls: It can encourage gaming (log-rolling, coalition formation) on the part of the evaluators; it can result in the systematic undervaluation of those who work for a less forceful, inarticulate, soft-spoken, or disrespected supervisor; it can help perpetuate patterns of discrimination that have a history of "social acceptability" within the organization. Furthermore, this process will work better in organizations with relatively low turnover among the managers participating in the collective evaluation process, so that they develop a shared vocabulary and body of experience with which to calibrate one another's assessments. And (of course) producing evaluations through a committee process can be terribly costly in terms of the time needed to do it right.

If it is useful to broaden the evaluation inputs for a given employee to include the perspectives of other managers, it is not too big a leap to consider broadening things even further to include input from other constituencies with whom the employee interacts, including peers, subordinates, and clients (both inside and outside the organization). In addition to the potential increases in validity, reliability, and legitimacy that such "360° feedback" systems can provide, they can be a useful symbol and tool of cultural change in organizations (like Morgan Stanley) seeking to promote more internal cooperation and communication. But there are substantial problems to confront: If evaluation by a committee sounds time consuming, 360° feedback systems are in another league. And eventually all the disparate inputs received have to be aggregated or summarized into a form that can be communicated to the employee (and perhaps used as part of the formal evaluation process), which can be a very challenging task for the person to whom it is assigned (usually, the employee's immediate supervisor). What do you do, for instance, if you have solicited evaluations of one of your direct reports from two of your own superiors, say, or from two valued clients, and you receive back two diametrically opposite reports?

But our impression is that the trickiest issue raised by 360°-type schemes has to do with the tension between performance *feedback* and performance *evaluation*. For obvious reasons, organizations implementing schemes that solicit performance information from peers, subordinates, or clients will generally want to be extremely cautious about using that information as the basis for high-stakes reward decisions (bonuses, promotions, etc.). The potential for abuse, dysfunctional competition, politicking, and all the other pathologies that can accompany performance evaluation is simply too huge. Hence, organizations generally adopt these types of systems with the intention of using them to provide performance feedback, not as the basis for formal performance reviews. For several reasons, however, things often don't work out as the architects intended.

First, as we have already noted, people tend to find it difficult and time-consuming to provide detailed performance feedback, and they often will be more inclined to do so to the extent that they believe their input will have consequences. Of course, the flip side of this coin is that we have also noted a tendency for people to be reluctant to be critical or harsh in their assessments when they know this may have severe consequences for the person being reviewed. Therefore, it is conceivable that reassuring people that their input will be used purely for developmental and feedback purposes can induce them to be more candid, especially peers and subordinates who may be fearful about bringing harm to a colleague or a superior. The difficulty, however, is that if the firm is operating a separate performance evaluation process that is used for purposes of compensation, promotion, and the like, there is the risk that the 360° system comes to be perceived either as duplicative or, even worse, as a sham, thereby undercutting its symbolic and cultural benefits and possibly producing a variety of negative effects.

A second reason why inputs solicited for "feedback" purposes often end up becoming used for "evaluation" purposes is simply that once information has been collected, it is difficult for decision-makers not to attend to it. This is particularly true given the aversion that most decision-makers have to performance evaluation: If managers wish to economize on the time they devote to performance evaluation, and they already have a large stack of data gleaned through the 360° process, we think it is fanciful to expect that they will disregard this information and carry out a thorough and independent evaluation for purposes of formal review.

SHOULD INDIVIDUALS BE EVALUATED AT ALL? SHOULD SUMMARY EVALUATIONS BE INCLUDED?

This tension between the feedback and evaluation aspects of performance appraisal that is commonplace in 360°-type systems suggests that it is worth pondering two deeper, more profound questions: Should individuals be evaluated at all? Should summary evaluations be part of the process?

It has been argued by some, most notably by W. E. Deming, that the appraisal of individual employees is almost inevitably dysfunctional. Deming asserts that such appraisals do not lead to improvements in organizational performance; rather, organizational performance is improved through refinements to the overall system or process of production, which must be the focus of attention. According to this line of thought, individual performance appraisals typically divert attention from more important tasks; they focus people's attention on alleviating *symptoms* of poor performance rather than identifying root causes, and they serve only to demotivate workers who find the evaluations unfair or inequitable. Deming argues that performance can usefully be appraised at the system level only, because it is system improvements that must be stressed. We suspect that Deming would prefer to see the parties to a 360° feedback system spending their time talking about how to work together collaboratively to improve all facets of performance, rather than filling out forms rating one another, a process that at a minimum is diversionary, illusory, and too formulaic, but that at its worse could be divisive and maladaptive.

Without going as far as Deming or others who mount similar arguments, one can legitimately ask why summary evaluations are necessary. If the point of performance appraisal is to help the individual to comprehend what the organization desires or to aid in self-improvement, then a vague, multicriterion evaluation—"You did well in sales level, but you need to pay more attention to established customers, at least as measured by repeat sales"—is often adequate and even superior to a single precise summary statistic, such as "Overall, you are a 3 on a scale of 1 to 6."

We are not asserting that multicriterion evaluation systems are a panacea, however. They have their own undesirable effects. A particularly pernicious problem with such schemes concerns getting employees to strike the desired balance across the multiple dimensions of performance being evaluated. Because of the psychological salience of deficiencies, there is a natural tendency for organizations and individuals to focus on those aspects of performance that are subpar—an eccentric and brilliant chemist, for instance, who is advised to work on her managerial and interpersonal skills. This tendency is often unfortunate because it can encourage a misdirection of efforts; a marginal hour invested by our hypothetical egghead in building her managerial human capital may not yield the same return for the firm as a marginal hour devoted to her scientific calling. Note that this pernicious effect is enhanced to the extent that anything that is below average is interpreted as being subpar: Half the people in any organization will fall below average along any dimension, and having everyone attending to their relative deficiencies can be quite dysfunctional.

A single summary statistic may avoid this problem: If performance is accurately measured as a weighted average of aspects A, B, and C, with weights (say) equal to 30%, 20%, and 50%, then the individual who can get a big marginal improvement in A for the marginal hour devoted to that task relative to what she can get in task B will be clearly motivated to spend her marginal hour in that fashion. The single statistic legitimates the individual's decision. But, as we noted earlier, rarely do linear weighting schemes accurately capture value to the organization, and complex nonlinear schemes are often too complex to be understood.

There is no one-size-fits-all cure for this conundrum, but three compromises can help in many instances. First, even when a summary statistic is computed, it is sensible to share with the individual his ranking along the different aspects of performance that go into that ranking, together with at least an informal sense of how he can improve his summary statistic. "You did well in sales level, but you were below average in attention to established customers. To move from an overall evaluation of 3 up to a 4, you can either. . ."

Second, it is often effective to establish minimally acceptable standards in each of several aspects and, if all the thresholds are met, evaluate the individual according to a weighted average of the different performance indices. This approach works well for guardian jobs, where the minimums are set at levels that avoid disasters. When jobs mix star and guardian elements and it is desirable that individuals star in different ways, it can be effective to measure performance on the basis of the *best single aspect* instead of a weighted average, as long as minimum standards are met in all aspects. For instance, think of physicians who are engaged in clinical research, teaching, and treating patients in a university hospital. There may be good reasons why a university hospital would want to have physicians doing all three of these activities, especially because of complementarities among them; that is, physicians doing applied research and teaching medical students will benefit from having an ongoing practice treating patients in their area of expertise, and doing research and teaching keeps clinicians plugged into the state-of-the-art, which is likely to improve their effectiveness in treating patients. But particular physicians may be better able to deliver star performances as researchers, others as teachers, and others still in particular areas of clinical practice, such as mastery of an esoteric type of organ transplantation that differentiates the hospital from its competitors. A hospital in these circumstances might want to adopt an assessment scheme for physicians in which they are evaluated based on the task—research, teaching, or clinical practice—that they have chosen to make their primary concentration, subject to maintaining acceptable performance at the other two tasks. (And because treating patients has much stronger guardian aspects than do research or teaching, we would expect to see particular emphasis on maintaining minimum standards in clinical practice among all physicians at the hospital.)

Third, if multicriterion evaluations are desirable on other grounds—such as providing richer and more accurate feedback, guiding corporate training efforts, or communicating multiple organizational goals—you might consider a system in which, except for truly exceptional performers, salary distinctions are not made at all or are based on seniority and rank, and promotion is detached to some extent from formal annual performance reviews. The point is to remove contention from the evaluation process to the greatest extent possible, so that evaluators are as comfortable as possible providing candid feedback and the individuals being evaluated can approach the assessment process with a relatively open and nonhostile mind.

Incentives? Legal Requirements?

Experienced managers may regard the advice just given as head-in-the-clouds stuff, on at least two grounds.

What about incentives to perform? We'll deal with this question more fully in Chapter 11, but to anticipate what will be said there: To the extent that individual performance comprises many different aspects, it may be nearly impossible to provide good direct incentives. More often than you may imagine, you can rely in these cases on intrinsic motivation, backed by the powerful (but vaguer) incentives provided through promotion prospects. Or, putting it a bit more darkly, when you can't rely on intrinsic motivation, you may be facing a managerial task too difficult for us to solve. Good luck!

What about legal requirements? Certainly to justify dismissal, a paper trail will be needed. And where (as in the United States) managers face court challenges on grounds of alleged discrimination, aren't you increasingly in need of "objective," single-dimensional measures of performance?

Where dismissal of an employee must be justified, it can suffice to produce a well-documented record of repeated warnings to address certain specific deficiencies, together with documentation showing that those deficiencies were not adequately addressed. Promotion decisions are harder to justify when the statistics make it appear that you have discriminated. But single-dimensional summary statistics will not save you here, unless you can justify their validity in measuring job performance and suitability for the next rank. You may well be better off with a multidimensional system, as long as you can document that you used those dimensions in nondiscriminatory fashion and that the dimensions used are valid and relevant to the decisions they were used to make.

SUMMARY

Performance evaluation is a tricky business, primarily because of the many functions that appraisals play. What is good for one function is sometimes quite bad for another. Performance evaluation is also difficult because the different constituencies inside and outside the organization who are affected by performance evaluations have different desiderata concerning the evaluations and the evaluation process.

In this chapter, we have seen that a "reward-the-extremes, muddle-the-middle" regime is one response by organizations to dealing with the various complexities, contradictions, and discomforts associated with performance evaluation. Other organizations are experimenting with different approaches to these dilemmas. For instance, recent initiatives involving gain-sharing, total quality management, worker empowerment, self-managed teams, and the like have fueled experimentation by some organizations with peer appraisals—in which peers evaluate one another (and sometimes even their supervisors)—and the sort of 360° appraisals by internal and external customers that we discussed. It is too soon to know how successful these experiments will prove to be, but (for instance) peer-based appraisals would seem to have potentially desirable properties on the key dimensions of distributive and procedural justice.

A different kind of adaptation to the complexities of performance evaluation is hinted at in the story with which this chapter began. We described how Merck and American Cyanamid, two reasonably similar firms, essentially exchanged performance evaluation systems and both felt better for the change. Our impression is that firms tinker with their performance appraisal systems regularly—perhaps more frequently than with any other element of the HRM system—almost invariably concluding that the revisions were a raging success, based on no hard data whatsoever.[20] Of course, this incessant tinkering may simply be the product of an HR department with too much time on its hands. And too much tinkering can be dysfunctional; a performance evaluation system that changes with every evaluation period will hardly be viewed by employees as legitimate.

However, given the complexities and multiple goals of performance evaluation surveyed in this chapter, a different perspective may explain periodic tinkering: Changing the system periodically may be an optimal dynamic strategy for performance evaluation, serving different functions better or worse at different times, to promote a general awareness of all the functions and objectives of the performance management system and to periodically redirect the attention of employees (and managers) toward the key dimensions of performance that contribute to organizational effectiveness in the current environment.

This chapter will have served its purpose if it has convinced you that there are few easy answers in the domain of performance evaluation.[21] Often the best one can do is to try to understand how the system being used helps or hinders the various functions that performance appraisal serves. Toward that end, one is led back to the five factors and our abiding concern with complementarities, so that the form and content of performance evaluation can be aligned with other elements of the HRM system and with the broader organizational context.

Throughout this chapter, we have discussed some of the tensions involved in using performance evaluation for developmental, feedback, and job assignment purposes versus as a basis for determining compensation. In the next chapter, we focus in depth on the issues involved in paying for performance.

IN REVIEW

⇒ Performance evaluation serves many diverse—and sometimes competing—functions in organizations.

⇒ There are many key dimensions to the design of a performance evaluation system, including:
- Who/what is evaluated
- Who performs (and has input into) the evaluation
- How short versus long the time frame for evaluation is
- Whether evaluations are objective/formulaic versus subjective/impressionistic
- Whether performance is evaluated in relative versus absolute terms
- Whether or not a forced distribution (or "curve") is used
- How many sources of input go into the evaluations
- Whether a single summary statistic versus a multicriterion approach is used
- How fine versus coarse the performance distinctions are

⇒ Performance evaluation systems affect and should be evaluated from the perspective of at least four different constituencies: those evaluated; those doing the evaluation; management in general; and outside constituencies, notably unions, the government, and the courts.
- From the perspective of those being evaluated, perceptions of procedural justice are paramount.
- The impact of performance evaluation systems on those doing the evaluations—especially in terms of communicating the organization's values—should be given careful consideration.

⇒ Taken together, this means that finding an ideal performance evaluation system is a nearly impossible dream. But an informed five-factor analysis can give some strong hints about what to look for in a performance evaluation system—in particular, the form and content of performance evaluation systems should reinforce both organizational strategy and culture.

⇒ In trying to strike the right balance among the various functions, dimensions, and constituencies involved in performance appraisal, firms have found a variety of tactics to be useful, each of which also has its limitations and potential pitfalls:
- Comparative performance evaluation, which enables the evaluator to control for the effects of unmeasured, environmental influences on performance
- Using coarse summary measures, blurring distinctions in the middle of the distribution and only rewarding (punishing) the extremes
- Marshaling a diversity of inputs in the evaluation process—for instance, systems that rely on evaluation committees or "360° feedback"

⇒ As you design or evaluate a performance evaluation system, there are several important questions you should ask yourself:
- Is the main goal to produce a formal assessment (e.g., for pay or promotion decisions) or to provide feedback that will aid the employee's development? Is performance evaluation (especially at the level of the individual employee) even necessary?
- Are one-dimensional summary measures of performance necessary?

⇒ Performance evaluation is a complex subject, and there are no easy answers. New methods are constantly being tried and may contribute to the art of performance evaluation. But we doubt that there is a "magic bullet" out there. And given the important role of communication served by performance evaluation, it is perhaps a good idea to change the system periodically.

ENDNOTES

1. The details are taken from Saul W. Gellerman and William G. Hodgson, "Cyanamid's New Take on Performance Appraisal," *Harvard Business Review* 66 (May–June 1988): 36-41; and Kevin J. Murphy, "Merck & Co., Inc. (A) & (B)," Harvard Business School cases #9-491-005 and #9-491-006 (1991).
2. If you view continued employment as a reward, this is a subcategory of (5).
3. We will discuss ways around these conundrums later in the chapter.
4. Another technique for defusing the loaded character of performance evaluations when financial rewards and even continued employment are at issue is to give the evaluator some cover for unhappy decisions. For example, rankings can be prepared by a committee, so that an employee's immediate superior doesn't bear all the responsibility. We discuss this specific technique later in this chapter.

5. For example, a student's performance on the sort of exam given in microeconomics, consisting of questions with precise answers, is fairly reliable. As an index of the student's ability to use economics on the job to generate insights and help guide behavior, this sort of test is much less valid.

6. See M. Diane Burton, "The Firmwide 360° Performance Evaluation Process at Morgan Stanley" and "Rob Parson at Morgan Stanley (A)," Harvard Business School cases #9-498-053 and #9-498-054 (1998). Also see Chapter 20, in which we discuss steps that Mack took to bolster the importance of HRM at the firm.

7. If it can be demonstrated that "failure" entailed some chance of great success, failure might even be evaluated ahead of conservative mediocrity, to encourage risk taking.

8 If cooperation can be measured and included in the formula, this criticism goes away. But cooperation is usually quite hard to measure objectively.

9. See T. B. Lifson and H. Takagi, "Mitsubishi Corp. (A): Organizational Overview," Harvard Business School case #9-482-050 (1986).

10. Peter Blau, *The Dynamics of Bureaucracy: A Study of Interpersonal Relations in Two Government Agencies* (Chicago: University of Chicago Press, 1955).

11. For details, see Harvard Business School cases #9-181-001, #9-181-002, and #9-183-019.

12. Note the interplay here with technology: Being a research scientist at a laboratory is inherently a star job—a very small number of discoveries and inventions can make a huge positive contribution to the organization's bottom line. The organization can't determine in advance where those discoveries will come from, and the scientists who do not make any big breakthroughs have little or no adverse effect on the bottom line compared to the huge positive effects associated with the big breakthroughs. Hence, intrinsic motivation can be relied upon more safely than in other kinds of work. For instance, compare the scientists working at AT&T to, say, physicians working in a hospital, who are also doing highly skilled work and likely to be subject to a very strong culture and a lot of intrinsic motivation. Nonetheless, given the significant guardian aspects of physicians' jobs, we would expect to see more formal controls, including more frequent performance evaluation and harsher treatment of substandard performance, than at Bell Labs.

13. For instance, in trying to "correct" for market size in evaluating salespersons, a firm may use population and per capita income in a sales region as instruments for measuring market potential, and they might then regress sales in different regions against these variables, to find the appropriate "corrections" to apply. Note that the residual variance in the regression will reflect both individual salespersons' efforts and environmental uncertainty that is common across salespersons; if the firm runs separate regressions for data at different time periods and finds that the constant in the regression changes with time, it has a good indication of common environmental uncertainty, which the handicapped or adjusted relative performance evaluation scheme can control for.

14. But be careful here! Some forms of bias, such as discrimination based on gender or race, may be exacerbated by working through committees, if those forms of bias have a history of social acceptability.

15. In theory, this sort of collusion is possible even if the comparison group includes employees of different organizations. But the logistical difficulties of arranging and engaging in such collusion make this an unlikely prospect.

16. Of course, promotion as a reward often has, almost out of necessity, a pure tournament character. We'll deal with promotion at length in Chapter 16 but, to anticipate, many of the problems we are mentioning here about comparative evaluation systems in general will be very troublesome when we study promotion in particular.

17. See Todd Zenger, "Why Do Employers Only Reward Extreme Performance? Examining the Relationships among Performance, Pay and Turnover," *Administrative Science Quarterly* 37 (June 1992): 198–219.

18. This implicitly assumes that the jobs in question have a combination of star and guardian attributes—that is, the organization gains a lot by identifying and rewarding extremely gifted performers and by identifying and coping with extremely poor performers, but the returns are presumed to be minimal elsewhere in the performance distribution.

19. If each of the managers participating has a relatively small number of subordinates, there may also be statistical advantages derived from combining their direct reports into one larger pool for purposes of ranking or evaluation. For example, if ten managers each have five direct reports, the likelihood of sizable "measurement errors" in ranking a given employee seem greater if that person is being ranked as one of five people rather than placed in a distribution of 50 people.

20. Not infrequently, firms will use employee satisfaction data gathered through climate surveys to validate or assess their performance appraisal system. Though by no means irrelevant, it is not clear to us that such survey responses represent a valuable—much less, *the* most valuable—gauge for evaluating the performance evaluation system. As we have noted, there are many important functions of performance evaluation, not all of which are necessarily consistent with improving employee perceptions and satisfaction. A high degree of satisfaction among the worst performers in an organization may not be a virtue! Moreover, climate surveys do not incorporate the responses of people who have exited the organization, whose departure may reflect an important deficiency in how performance is evaluated and managed.

21. But there are a few. For example, decoupling salary/compensation administration from performance appraisal for feedback is often not utilized when it might be advantageous to do so.

11

PAY FOR PERFORMANCE

When a driver in the United States needs a new windshield for her car, the procedure often runs as follows.[1] The driver calls her insurance company. The insurance company calls the regional dispatch center of a windshield installer (a typical region is something like the San Francisco Bay area), which assigns an installer from a "branch office" to the job. The installer puts the appropriate windshield on his truck, drives to where the car is, and installs the windshield. The installer is an employee of the windshield company, and industry practice is that installers are paid according to the amount of time they are on-call or on-a-call—the installer punches a time clock upon arriving at his "branch" in the morning, punches out upon leaving, and is paid a set wage rate per hour worked (with adjustments made for overtime, holidays, etc.). Each installer's job performance is monitored—how long on average it takes him to complete a service call; the rate of breakage of glass he installs—and installers who fail to clear relatively low performance hurdles are discharged. The job is not very highly skilled, and turnover among installers is substantial. The industry is fairly competitive, with several large national chains as well as smaller local companies competing on the basis of price and quality, measured largely by response time.

Safelite Glass is the largest installer of replacement automobile glass in the United States. Until recently, Safelite compensated installers as described in the previous paragraph. Then, in 1994 and 1995, Safelite moved to an incentive compensation system, hoping that this would improve their productivity, a powerful competitive weapon in this industry. In the system they implemented, installers would be paid each week the maximum of: the amount they would have made according to the old, hourly wage rate system; or a fixed amount per job completed times the number of jobs completed. The amount paid per job completed, the so-called piece rate, was set at a level so that an installer completing an average number of jobs in a week would be better off under (and would be paid according to) the old hourly wage formula. But the piece rates were set so that an enterprising installer, who completed jobs with dispatch, could do a lot better than under the old scheme.

Management's reason for implementing this new compensation system was first and foremost to increase worker productivity. They were worried that installers knew the minimum number of windows they had to install per week to keep from being fired, and that installers were thus keeping output at close to that rate. Indeed, an installer thinking about leaving the firm in a month or so might slow down his work rate still further. The hope was that by making pay responsive to work rate, installers would be motivated to work faster.

The scheme worked, even better than Safelite initially dreamed. Average productivity per worker, measured by number of windows installed per week, rose a whopping 44%. This dramatic rise came from two sources: Workers who changed from the old scheme to the new increased their productivity by around 20%. And turnover among the firm's most productive workers fell dramatically, so that Safelite's workforce became increasingly more productive.

What was the bottom line for Safelite? Of course, if turnover falls, Safelite saves on training and recruitment costs. But what about direct labor costs? After all, Safelite was paying each worker at least as much under the new system as it would have paid under the old.

Actually, unit labor costs *fell*. Safelite rolled the scheme out gradually in different localities, making it possible to compare unit costs for areas with the new compensation scheme against costs in comparable areas still using the old scheme. Under the old scheme, the average labor cost per window installed was $44.43, while with the new compensation scheme, average labor cost was $35.24 per window. The reason: Average compensation per worker rose, but productivity per worker rose even more. In fact, Safelite was guaranteed that there would be no rise in cost per window, because the firm set the piece rate for each window installed at a level below its pre-incentive-scheme cost per window.

It isn't hard to see why worker productivity rose: Workers now had a tangible incentive to work more than at the minimum acceptable rate. The turnover effect is a bit more subtle: Because workers could only improve their compensation under this scheme, their level of satisfaction with the job would rise. (You might ask whether satisfaction could fall for installers who work alongside a very fast— and thus well compensated—installer, through a process of social comparison. For reasons we will discuss later, this is a case in which that effect is unlikely to be significant.) Hence, employees would be less likely to leave voluntarily. And note well that the rise in satisfaction is going to be highest among those installers who work the fastest, because they are the ones who can take greatest advantage of this scheme. Sure enough, turnover rates among Safelite's faster workers dropped the most.

This story illustrates the powerful impact that compensation can have on job performance and, ultimately, the competitive strength of a company. This is hardly surprising, as compensation is usually one of the most salient and immediate concerns of employees and employers. The topic of compensation is huge and diverse, and although we will go on about it at length, we will barely do justice to it. Because of the enormous number of topics to discuss under the rubric of compensation, we have (somewhat artificially) broken our discussion into two chapters. In this chapter, we deal primarily with issues connected with paying individuals or groups based on measures of performance. In Chapter 12, we will take up a host of other issues related to the design of compensation systems, including the form that compensation takes (which includes a discussion of benefits), the determination of compensation levels and dispersion, and the provision of information to employees about compensation outcomes.

Our discussion of pay for performance comes in three parts. We begin by describing the economic theory—*agency theory*—of pay-for-performance systems.[2] We next balance this economic perspective by recalling important social and psychological considerations from earlier chapters. We then integrate the two perspectives in real-life contexts. To let you know where we are headed: You probably know from the popular business press that pay for performance attracts a lot of commentary, both favorable and unfavorable. Some commentators write as if it is the answer to all workforce problems, while others see it as a sure ticket to an unmotivated, unhappy, and unproductive workforce. It is neither of these. Rather, it is a fairly delicate set of motivational tools that can be powerfully effective in one setting and utterly dysfunctional in another. It should be used with circumspection and in view of the five factors and the need for consistency among HR practices. It worked at Safelite because Safelite's strategy, technology, culture, workforce, and environment all fit it very well. Understanding why it fit the five factors at Safelite—and why it may be a very poor fit elsewhere—is our main objective.

Before getting started, one more word of background is appropriate. Because compensation is such an important issue, it has spawned a number of named "systems" which, like patent medicine, are sold as somewhat off-the-shelf answers to the question, How should the firm manage compensation? Exhibit 11-1 gives a brief recap of some of the more prominent of these named systems. We won't be getting too deeply into the details of any of these, but we will mention these terms at times in this chapter and the following one; when you encounter them in our discussion, a quick look back at the exhibit may be in order.

THE ECONOMIC THEORY OF INCENTIVES

In basic economics, labor is a commodity no different than apples or cold-rolled steel. The employer buys whatever amount of labor services she desires at the going market price of labor—if you look in the early chapters of textbooks on labor economics, you'll find simple models where w is the market wage rate, l is the amount of labor services purchased by the employer, and, therefore, wl is the wage bill.

It is clear that w is the amount of money paid per *unit* of labor purchased, but what are the units in which labor is measured? In the real world, we normally find labor services measured by time, so that w is a wage rate per hour, say, or per day or year. But there are cases in which labor services are denominated in something closer to the fruits of labor; $l = 10$ doesn't mean 10 hours, but instead the labor needed to assemble 10 of whatever the employer is assembling, or 10 trucks unloaded, or 10 post holes dug.

In the early chapters of labor-economics textbooks, the distinction doesn't matter. A definite relation between hours of work and post holes dug or trucks unloaded is assumed; digging a post hole takes, say, 45 minutes, so $l = 12$ *post holes*

Efficiency wages: Economics fancy-talk for the idea of paying above-market wages, in order to obtain a wider selection of applicants, to reduce turnover, to provide incentives to workers (to avoid dismissal), and to create a gift-exchange relationship.

Gainsharing: Incentive programs in which groups are given rewards (bonuses) according to cost reductions and/or productivity increases. Almost always based on objective performance criteria that reflect gains from previous performance. Group performance is stressed, where the relevant group can be the shop, the factory, the division, or even the entire operation. Gains are shared with the hourly workforce as a matter of principle.

Improshare: A form of gainsharing that focuses on the productivity of direct labor alone, where performance improvements are measured by the quantity of direct labor in output. The idea is that direct labor cannot control, and thus should not be responsible for, anything except its own efficiency in production.

Management by objectives: A scheme of worker evaluation (often, but not invariably, tied to incentive compensation) in which goals and targets for each worker are set by agreement between the employee and his or her superior, taking into account the needs of the organization and the particular situation facing the employee. Generally plagued by high transactions costs (goals and targets are generated on a case-by-case basis), and so is usually reserved for managerial workers. Very flexible and potentially fair, but the flexibility is a weakness and a potential source of inequity: Since there are no objective rules about how goals get set, politicking can be ferocious.

Pay for skill: Schemes in which wage/salary increases are tied to the acquisition of skills deemed useful by the employer. Skills are acquired by employees at their own pace. Weaknesses: (1) Provides incentives for awhile, but as employees top out, having gained all the skills that bring pay increases, they may lose motivation to perform. (2) Paying for skills makes less sense in cases where workers have no opportunity to use those skills. Firms are sometimes put in the position of paying for skill acquisition and credentials that have little to do with the worker's job.

Scanlon plans: A particular form of gainsharing, characterized by the following features: (1) The "group" is the entire organization. (2) There is a long period of education and training before the program begins, so management and workers are aware of what is involved. This usually culminates in a secret ballot on whether to participate, in which a vast majority of workers and managers must agree to take part. (3) Heavy emphasis on management training and buy-in to the program. (4) Heavy emphasis on ongoing communication (progress reports, war stories) and exhortation to participate and make progress. (5) Emphasis on the need for a permanent shift in worker attitudes and culture. (6) A system of "improvement" committees is created, empowering workers to analyze, make suggestions, and even implement suggestions that will lead to improved performance.

Scanlon plans (and the closely associated variant, Rucker plans) are much more than simply gainsharing incentive plans; they are philosophies of management, in which workers are treated in egalitarian fashion and empowered to take control of their workplace. In a sense, Scanlon plans can be seen as a system for bringing to the workplace the superordinate goal of achieving *gains in the formula,* which is meant to fire everyone up. The cost reduction and/or productivity improvement aspect of the Scanlon plan is meant more as a focus of the new culture than as a serious freestanding incentive device (which is just as well, given the obvious ratchet effect).

Exhibit 11-1 A glossary of compensation-related terms (with commentary).

and $l = 9$ *hours* are the same thing. Of course, the wage rate depends on the units: $8 per hour is the same as $6 per post hole.

But reality isn't so simple. Different employees dig post holes at different rates, so buying 9 hours from employee A is different from buying 9 hours from employee B. In addition, and more to the immediate point, employee A can choose how hard to work; 9 hours of his time can result in 12 post holes or 15 or 3. Labor hours come in an infinite variety of "qualities," and when those introductory textbook chapters denominate labor by the hour, they intend something like "$l = 9$ hours of time digging post holes at a rate of one post hole every 45 minutes."

In later chapters of modern texts on labor economics, this problem of units is implicitly recognized when the issue of incentives arises. The question is, If the employer pays the worker by the hour, how does she guarantee that the worker will choose to work at the agreed-to rate? If the connection between time worked and work done is completely under control of the worker, the problem disappears: The employer can say that she is paying, say, $10 per hour for 9 hours, as long as 12 post holes are dug. Or she can say that she is paying $7.50 per post hole, as long as the digging takes no more than 9 hours.[3] But what if the time to dig a post hole isn't clear? On average post holes may take 45 minutes to dig, but the soil might be filled with rocks or unusually soft in a particular locale. What happens if the employer reappears after 9 hours, finds only 6 post holes dug, and hears as an excuse that the soil was rocky, there was a layer of hardpan 12 inches down, and the pickax that was provided broke and had to be fixed? In practice, she will ask to see the rocks, check the hardpan, and inspect the pickax, but suppose all she can observe is the number of post holes dug. What then?

The Basic Model of Agency Theory

Agency theory, the *principal–agent model,* and the *economic theory of incentives* are three names for the same thing: a collection of models created by economists to answer this question. We discuss the basic model in this subsection and elaborations following that.

The basic model begins with the supposition that the connection between time and effort exerted by the worker and the fruits of his labor services is not entirely under his control. The employee can influence the amount of work accomplished, by exerting himself, but he can't control output entirely. Supposing he is on the job for a set length of time, we let e denote the effort he chooses to exert over that period of time, and we suppose that the amount of work done x has a probability distribution that is affected by e; think for now of the case where e is one-dimensional, and larger values of x are more likely the larger is e.[4]

In these circumstances, the employer probably wishes to pay on the basis of x—so much per post hole dug—whereas the employee prefers to be paid according to hours worked. The employer is unhappy paying by the hour, because then the employee has no incentive to exert himself; the employee is unhappy being paid per unit of x that is produced, because then he bears the risk of rocky soil, an ax breaking, and so on. (The conflict is more symmetrical if the amount of output is influenced both by the effort exerted by the employee and by some simultaneous and independent decision by the employer, such as the quality of shovels and pickaxes provided. Complicating the story in this fashion takes us away from basic agency theory, to more advanced variations.)

There are three implicit assumptions in what was just asserted, which are the foundations of the basic model of agency:

1. The employee is averse to effort. That is, he will choose as low a level of e as he can and still get paid, if he is paid on a per-unit-of-time basis.

2. The employee is averse to risk. If the employee were risk neutral—if he valued risky compensation according to its expected value—then he wouldn't object to being paid based on x, as long as his expected compensation was in line with market wages. The issue of incentive compensation is trivial in this case; compensation is set so the worker bears all the risk and thus completely and efficiently internalizes the consequences of his choice of effort. Incentive compensation becomes more interesting when, based on first principles, the employee and employer should share the risk, rather than the employee bearing all the risk.[5] Indeed, in the standard model it is assumed that the employer is risk neutral, so that on grounds of risk-sharing efficiency alone, the employer should bear all the risk as long as the employee is risk averse. And then the trade-off is: The more risk we load on the employee, the more he internalizes the consequences of his choice of effort level, and the more efficient an arrangement we have in terms of motivation. But the more risk we load on him, the less efficient the arrangement is in terms of risk sharing.

3. The parties cannot contract on the level of effort e. If they could, and if the employer were risk neutral, then the efficient outcome would be to pay the employee a wage that depends only on e, leaving the employer to bear all the risk. Note that this is essentially the "solution" employed in practice in some cases, namely when the employer utilizes some technology to monitor the level of effort exerted by employees, with the threat of dismissal hanging over workers who are found to be exerting themselves insufficiently. But this solution is fraught with problems. Monitors are costly. It is potentially risky—for instance, what if the monitors conspire with the employees against the employer's interests? And in some cases, this solution is simply technologically impossible, or at least prohibitively expensive. So incentive compensation or pay for performance, where the agent's pay depends on the level of output x, may be the answer.

In Appendix C, we analyze a formal model of this sort of situation. The objective of this analysis is to find an optimal compensation scheme for the employer, where an optimal scheme is one that gives the employer the highest expected profit net of compensation paid (assuming she is risk neutral), subject to the constraint that the employee must be given a compensation package attractive enough to get him to accept the job. For now, we eschew the formal analysis, summing up what the analysis tells us:[6]

- The optimal compensation scheme for the employee will typically involve him getting more compensation the greater is x. But, at the same time, he will not bear entirely the risk of the venture: He will be guaranteed a base wage, even if $x = 0$.

- In general, the completely optimal compensation scheme is a complicated function of x. But if we restrict attention to more realistic and simpler compensation schemes where the employee is paid a base wage of B and a bonus of b per unit of x produced, we typically find that B is greater than zero and b is smaller than the "full" value of a unit of output to the employer.

- In some instances, the value of the services provided to the employer may not be known when it comes time to pay off the employee. For example, the branch manager of a bank may decide on loans to make, and it will take years to discover whether those loans perform well or not. In such cases, incentive payments can and should be made on the basis of any observable variable that is statistically related to the value of the services provided. For example, a branch manager might have her compensation based on the quality of a randomly selected sample of loans that she makes, where the quality of one of those loans is determined by independent examiners.

- Other things held equal, incentive compensation works better the better (less noisy) the compensation-linked variable is as a signal about the employee's level of effort e.

- In the economic theory of incentives, most models posit that compensation is the motivator. That is, in formal models (of the type discussed in Appendix C), the employee likes money and dislikes effort, and the employer motivates higher levels of distasteful effort by offering higher levels of income for better outcomes. There is nothing in the formal theory, however, that mandates that compensation is the only motivator. Promotion, power, autonomy, the esteem of co-workers, and the ability to remain employed—to enjoy the work atmosphere, to maintain enjoyable social relations, to keep one's children in the same schools—are all tangible things that employees value to varying degrees. Thus, any and all of these can motivate employees. (There are also intangibles—such as pride in one's work, interest in the work itself, and the psychological need to justify to oneself actions taken previously—that go into the creation of intrinsic motivation. These intangible motivators are left for later sections of this chapter.) Because this chapter is about compensation, we focus on compensation as a motivator. But as we will note later in this chapter, when *applying* these ideas, the employer must consider the net effect of all the motivators, including intrinsic motivators. And specific problems accompany specific motivational devices, particularly promotion, which is dealt with at length in Chapter 16.

Variation #1: Screening and Sorting

The basic model of agency theory, as well as all of the other variations we are about to discuss, focus on what economists term *moral hazard* effects of incentive compensation. In plain English, the question is how to get a specific worker to act as the employer wishes. But incentive-compensation packages can also serve a *screening* and/or *sorting* function.

We can illustrate with the case of Safelite. Suppose that, in this context, each individual installer could completely control his or her rate of output, measured as windows installed per week. Then, according to agency theory, there is no incentive problem: Safelite offers the worker a weekly salary if the worker installs the "right" number of windows. (Of course, it is important that Safelite can measure work output; obviously, that is possible in this case.) But what is the "right" number of windows? It is whatever number is efficient in terms of value added to Safelite versus the cost to the specific employee of effort.[7] And therein lies the problem: The value added to Safelite of an installed windshield doesn't depend on who installs the windshield, but workers differ in how much the effort of installing costs them. Some workers are simply more able; they can install windshields more quickly, because of, say, better finger dexterity, or whatever. And workers differ in how much the effort costs them psychologically; one installer may have a greater distaste for working up a sweat than another, even if the two can do the job just as quickly. The point is that Safelite, ideally, would tailor a contract to each worker, reflecting individual workers' personal abilities and costs of effort.

However, Safelite doesn't know *a priori* which workers have high ability or a low distaste for effort. So to sort out workers along this dimension, it might offer to the workers a menu of contracts: The worker can have $150 a week if he is willing to install five windows a week, or $175 for six, or $205 for seven, and so on. Then workers who are quick with their hands or who don't mind hard work will select more windows for more pay. This sort of menu-of-options and worker self-sorting may sound a bit strange—does anyone really do it?—but in fact it is precisely what pay for performance accomplishes. Safelite, if it sets a piece-rate of $30 per window, effectively offers to its employees "$150 for five windows or $180 for six or . . . take your pick." And by offering a floor, Safelite is simultaneously offering insurance that is valuable for workers who don't (contrary to what we are assuming momentarily) completely control their rate of output.

This is all about self-sorting among Safelite employees, according to their diverse tastes for effort and abilities to work. But it extends to a further screening function, involving prospective employees. Safelite would like a selection from the population of prospective employees: It wants to employ individuals who, because of their tastes or abilities, require relatively less compensation per window installed.

Someone who is willing to work hard looks at Safelite's pay-for-performance scheme and says: "That's for me. I can get ahead there, relative to XYZ Window Installers." And that person applies for a job at Safelite instead of at XYZ. Someone who doesn't plan to take advantage doesn't care whether he works for Safelite or XYZ (or in some other form of manual labor that doesn't have pay for performance). Even assuming that Safelite gets a random draw from everyone who applies for a job with them, they will wind up with more of the hard-chargers who only apply to them and not to XYZ. And, finally, Safelite is more likely to retain the hard-chargers, who are happier to be there than at available alternatives, given the hard-chargers' relative desire to make more by working harder and Safelite's willingness to provide the opportunity to do so. Note well: Safelite doesn't want to select the hard-chargers simply because they are hard-chargers. It wants them because—as it discovered—it can pay them less per window installed, saving on its net labor costs (and saving on training costs as well, through better retention).

Because of the important role this sort of screening plays in recruitment, we leave a formal discussion of it until Chapter 14. (It will also play an important role in Chapter 16, where we discuss promotion and retention.) For now, we will emphasize the moral hazard, single-employee aspects of incentive compensation. But you should not be misled by our emphasis here; an important role of pay-for-performance systems is to widen the range of compensation-for-effort choices available to employees, to accommodate a diversity of employee tastes in making this choice.[8]

Variation #2: Rewarding the Type and Quality of Effort

The basic principal–agent model assumes the employee is effort averse, and the point of incentives is to get the employee to exert himself. For some classes of work—Safelite installers, perhaps—this may seem a reasonable assumption. But in other cases—say, a teacher, a physician, or a plant manager at Honda Motor—it isn't so clear that workers need to be motivated to take effort *per se*. Employees will fill their working time with some mix of activities, activities at which they will work quite hard without specific extrinsic incentives. The employer's problem is to motivate them to choose the particular mix of activities that the firm would like to have done. Very few people complain, for instance, that the problem with elected government officials is that they aren't doing *anything*; rather, the complaints seem to be that they are doing the *wrong* things!

Incentive schemes that reward only one activity or one particular class of activities can have unhappy effects. For example, an incentive scheme that rewards a salesperson based on the dollar volume of sales may cause the salesperson to devote too much energy to repeat sales and not enough to developing new clients. When some activities in the employee's mix of activities are directly rewarded and others are not, then the employee is being given a not-very-subtle signal and the direct incentive to ignore the latter and concentrate on the former.

It is rare, of course, that an organization will reward one aspect of job performance and completely ignore another. A firm that wishes to motivate its sales force to increase its client base might offer its salespersons a higher commission for sales to new clients than for sales to established clients. But multicriterion incentive compensation can involve a delicate balancing act: Will higher commissions for new customers cause the sales force to ignore after-sales service inquiries from old clients? More generally, when an employee is meant to attend to a number of different tasks or different aspects of the same task, the employer faces the problem: If incentives are to be provided, (how) can they be designed so that the employee will balance his attention among the tasks in precisely or even approximately the way the employer wishes?

An important insight into this question is provided by the analysis of Holmstrom and Milgrom.[9] Suppose that some of the tasks to be undertaken by the individual are connected fairly directly to meaningful observable measures of performance, whereas others are not. (The degree of connection compounds both uncontrollable influences on output levels and measurement errors concerning outputs.) To take an example, imagine the plant manager of a manufacturing plant, who is charged with: keeping production rates up; keeping machines in good repair; finding and implementing process improvements; and developing the human capital of her subordinate managers. Suppose that the manager is willing to work hard but has a budget of effort or time that she must divide among these four tasks. It stands to reason that it is relatively easy to measure how well the plant manager does on the first two of these tasks, with measures that are not subject to too much "noise." It is harder for the plant manager to affect directly the number of process improvements at her plant. And in anything short of a multiyear time horizon, it is likely to be quite difficult to measure adequately how she does in developing her staff's human capital.

According to the theory developed in the previous subsection, the firm could motivate her fairly effectively along the first two dimensions, but it would have a harder time with the third, and a very much harder time with the fourth. Should the firm use incentives that give her large rewards for good performance along the first two dimensions? If it does, it must choose whether to accompany these incentives with strong incentives for the latter two. If it doesn't offer strong incentives for the latter two dimensions, the strong incentives to attend to the first two will mean a (mis)allocation of time away from the latter two. To balance her allocation of time among the four, it will have to provide strong incentives to attend to the latter two. But because she has relatively little control over observables, this will introduce a lot of uncertainty into her compensation; if process improvements and human capital development strongly influence her compensation, then notwithstanding her level of effort along these dimensions, her compensation will be strongly influenced by things she can't control, such as technological breakthroughs. If the employee is substantially risk averse, this is not attractive either: Taking these effects into account, the firm will (optimally) provide only weak incentives along the first two dimensions. In Chapter 13, we will return to this issue in the context of job design, extolling the virtues of bundling together in one job tasks that are relatively easy to measure accurately (so that strong explicit incentives can be employed) and bundling in another job tasks with a noisier relationship between efforts and outcomes (and relying, for this job, on weak incentives and intrinsic motivation).

Variation #3: Benchmarking and Tournaments

The basic agency model contends that incentives lack power and efficiency when the employee has little control over the measures on which his compensation is based, or alternatively when the employee can control certain measures of performance but those measures give a noisy indication of the value-adding efforts provided by the employee. If a division manager is rewarded on the basis of how well his division does—measured by the division's earnings—and if those earnings are largely outside of the control of the manager, then little will be gained from the incentive system. The division manager might, on the other hand, have a lot of control over the cost of manufacturing goods his division produces. But a lower cost of manufacture may not necessarily correlate with higher corporate profits; indeed, actions taken to lower cost-of-manufacture—for instance, reducing the variety or quality of output, refusing rush orders—may mean lower corporate profits. This, essentially, is the multitask problem in slight disguise.

As we discussed in Chapter 10, the impact of uncontrollable environmental variables on tangible measures of performance can sometimes be controlled by *comparative or relative evaluation.* To provide incentive compensation for a division manager, we might measure performance of the division *relative* to other divisions in the firm or other units in other firms that compete in the same basic market. Or we might compensate a salesperson based on how her sales compare with those of other comparable salespersons in the organization. The idea is that although the division manager may be unable to control her absolute level of performance, because she can't control economywide variables, those same variables affect the performance of her "peers," and her division's *relative* performance gives a better idea how well she herself did. The salesperson may have had a very strong year because of the economy as a whole, or because her firm has introduced a great new product; because these same factors affect the entire sales staff, the relative performance of a particular salesperson gives a better indication how she herself did. When performance is measured relative to others outside one's own organization, the term *benchmarking* is used. When compensation depends on how well A does relative to fellow employees B, C, and D, we say that the firm is using a *tournament* compensation scheme; although to be precise, in a true tournament, A's compensation will depend solely on her ordinal ranking relative to B, C, and D.

In Chapter 10, we noted several potential adverse effects and limitations of using comparative evaluation—namely, collusion among those being evaluated; conformity; stifling cooperation; encouraging demotivating comparisons; discouraging people from taking on challenging, risky, or relatively unattractive assignments; and not adequately factoring in differences in relative ability or "endowments." We add here that these adverse effects are stronger the more salient are the relative performance measures, and tying wages to these measures certainly increases their salience. Notwithstanding these adverse effects and limitations, comparative evaluation for purposes of motivation is very widely used, although the reward at stake is more often promotion—and thus future compensation, as well as power, perks, status, influence, and authority—than immediate compensation.

Variations #4 through #6: Multiperiod Effects

Long-term employment, especially in a firm with a strong internal labor market, adds some interesting dimensions and complications to incentive compensation systems.

The Ratchet Effect

Consider incentive schemes that reward participants for *improvements* in their individual or group performance. For example, a division manager might be given a bonus that depends on how well costs have been contained in his division, relative to costs in the previous period. This is often manifested as a *gain-sharing* program, in which gains over a period of fixed length, measured relative to some base-level performance, are shared between the workers and the firm. As we noted in Chapter 10, a problem with such schemes is the so-called *ratchet effect*: If a worker takes extraordinary effort in one period to contain costs, this results in higher immediate compensation, but it also sets a higher standard in the future. The worker shares in the gains with the firm for a single period, but for that period only; afterward, the gains are assumed by the firm.[10] Moreover, *if* the worker will remain in this job, he has ratcheted up the standards by which he will be judged next time; as long as his intentions are to remain, because of the ratchet effect he may have less incentive to achieve gains than might be thought. As we observed in Chapter 10, the ratchet effect could also encourage employees to seek quick improvements (to pocket fast money) and then depart, rather than concentrating on long-term, sustainable improvements.

Time and Hurdle Levels

Incentive schemes are sometimes constructed in which rewards to the individual depend on achieving certain hurdle levels of performance. That is, compensation depends discontinuously on the achievement of some numerical goal. For example, a salesperson's bonus may depend on whether he surpasses some level of sales, and/or his average commission percentage may jump discontinuously as certain sales figures are exceeded. When effort is spread over time, such schemes can fail to achieve the desired ends. For example, a worker whose performance near the end of the evaluation period is far from the next hurdle will have little incentive to work hard. In contrast, employees who are close to a hurdle will have strong reasons to want to kill themselves (or others!) trying to make it, even at the cost of hurting performance in the future or undertaking dysfunctional actions, such as bilking a valued customer in order to make a quick sale. The salesperson far from the next hurdle may "bank" sales for the next period, while the salesperson close to the next hurdle may try to accelerate sales.

This can be particularly true of comparative schemes, where a prize is given, say, to the best cumulative performer over some period out of a set of employees. In such cases, if one employee builds up a substantial lead over the others, then all may decrease their efforts; those who are behind slow down because there is little chance that they can catch up, and the leader slacks off because those behind have slowed down. (When running a tournament compensation scheme for some stretch of time, issuing interim reports on who is ahead and by how much can build excitement and, if the race is tight, a lot of effort. But those near the back of the pack or even mired in the middle may have little incentive to push ahead.) In general, the worker's ability to shift the level and nature of effort as time passes makes schemes that evaluate performance over a period of time somewhat tricky.

Linear incentive schemes, such as giving a salesperson a fixed commission based on sales, are remarkably prevalent in the real world. Doubtless this reflects, in part, the simplicity of such schemes and their ability to motivate employees robustly (i.e., they work for all sorts of employees, in all sorts of situations). But, in addition, a strong theoretical case has been made for linear incentive schemes, based on the sort of dynamic considerations mentioned here. Roughly, when the outcomes of employee efforts are time separable (the value added in each week depends only on efforts expended in that week), to keep the pressure of incentives steady over a longer accounting period, the firm will want to keep a steady rate of reward for marginal contributions, translating into linear incentive schemes.[11]

Tying Workers to Firms

As we noted in Chapter 4, there are a number of reasons why firms wish to decrease voluntary turnover. Hence, an important aspect of motivation can be encouraging the employee to remain. We'll make two relatively cursory comments here. First, you may recall from Chapters 4, 8, and 9, that efficiency wages—compensation higher than what is available in the local market—can reduce voluntary turnover. (Of course, efficiency wages can also have other desirable effects.) Second, for a variety of reasons, firms will often be particularly eager to reduce voluntary turnover among workers with greater seniority (e.g., the firm's investment in the human capital of more senior workers is relatively greater; more senior workers tend to be more stable and provide good role models for other workers). A method for increasing retention of more senior workers is to have compensation rise with seniority; if an employee is promised a valuable reward—such as disproportionately high wages, access to stock options, or a pension—if he remains for ten or twenty years with his current employer, he will be decreasingly inclined to quit the closer he gets to that reward.[12]

Variation #7: Group Incentive Schemes

In the literature of agency theory, there are also variations on the basic model in which incentive compensation is provided to a group, which (in various models) either shares the compensation according to some rigid scheme—for instance, equal shares, or in proportion to base income—or, more speculatively, divides up the compensation according to some internal bargaining process. Group incentive schemes are best discussed after we remind you of some noneconomic forces that affect compensation schemes, however, so we leave this topic until later.

NONECONOMIC CAVEATS

The economic theory of incentives is built up from the standard economic model of human behavior. Roughly but fairly accurately put, employees within economic models are greedy, slothful, and concerned entirely with ends and not means. There is no need to recapitulate Chapter 5 in its entirety, but it may help to remind you of some noneconomic facts of life that soften this fairly harsh picture and that are particularly germane to compensation and motivation:

- Employees will evaluate compensation systems and their own compensation in terms of the fairness of the outcomes and the process by which their performance was evaluated and rewarded; *distributive* and *procedural justice* will be considered.

- They will engage in *social comparisons*; it won't necessarily matter how well each did on an absolute scale, but rather how each did relative to his peers. (We recall an eminent labor economist who, while doing his stint as chair of his economics department—one of the best in the world—remarked in somewhat mystified fashion that his best-paid colleagues seemed particularly concerned not with how their annual raises compared with inflation, but instead how they stacked up with the raises earned by their other highly paid colleagues.)

- Compensation should be consistent with and even reinforce *social status*. Japanese firms are able to maintain very steep wage–seniority profiles in part because in Japan seniority *per se* confers social status. In hierarchical U. S. enterprises, compensation that doesn't correlate strongly with position in the organizational hierarchy can be problematic.

- Compensation should be consistent with the organization's *culture*. For instance, incentive compensation leading to enormous cross-sectional or temporal variation in wages might be entirely acceptable in organizations with a "market-like" culture, as long as those who get more are viewed as having earned what they get. The same compensation systems may be woefully inappropriate, however, for an enterprise that otherwise promotes a familial culture.

- In addition to external motivators—compensation, promotion, power and perks, retention, the esteem of peers, and positive social relations with peers—*intrinsic motivation* can play a powerful role. And extrinsic incentives can dull intrinsic motivation, when employees attribute their efforts to the pursuit of extrinsic rewards instead of inner satisfaction.

The force of these social processes can be ambiguous. Perhaps most importantly, the force of distributive justice is not always clear. Compensation is distributively just, by and large, if it conforms to the norm of equity—individuals should be paid according to how much they contribute. But what is "contribution?" Is it effort exerted or profits generated? Perceptions on this vary according to circumstances and, in given circumstances, can vary among observers.

To take a stark caricature, suppose a firm has two salespersons, Jean and John, who work two different territories. Jean consistently sells 20% more than John. Should Jean be paid more? For most people, the just answer to that question depends on the answer to the question, Why does Jean outperform John?

Suppose the reason is that Jean's territory is simply better than John's. To keep matters simple, suppose as well that this is not to Jean's credit or John's blame: Jean has been assigned to a territory that has always produced more sales than has John's (where territories are, say, metropolitan areas, so their integrity must be maintained on administrative or technological grounds). Suppose John works just as hard as Jean. Should Jean be paid more? We suspect that most people—and you—will find that the balance of equity in this case is to pay John the same as Jean.

Now suppose that the reason is that Jean simply works harder at sales than John. Jean puts in more hours, spends more time on the road, and is more available to her clientele. This case also seems clear-cut; most people—including you, we suspect—would probably agree that the equitable thing is to pay Jean more, perhaps even 20% more.

But now—to muddy the waters—suppose Jean puts in more time because John has a family, and one of his children has been stricken with a disease that takes time and attention away from sales. Or suppose that Jean is a particularly gifted salesperson; there is no doubt that John tries just as hard, but Jean is simply better at it and so racks up more sales. Suppose in particular that Jean's particular gift is that she used to be on the professional golf tour, and her clients buy more from her because she will then reward them with a round of golf, or with tickets to local tournaments, procured through her contacts. We're not confident we can predict your opinion about what is equitable here. Moreover, we suspect responses will systematically vary with the respondent's culture. For example, we expect that U. S. respondents would be more inclined to say that the balance of equity in all these cases supports greater compensation for Jean than would, say, Danish respondents. (We haven't run a systematic survey; this is just a guess based on crude impressions.)

The issue here is important. If people can disagree on what equity means even when it is clear why performance levels differ, the disagreements can only become sharper to the real-life extent that differences in performance cannot be easily attributed. When Jean sells 20% more than John, Jean is more likely to attribute this to her hard work and unique, job-relevant skills; John will probably claim that Jean benefited from a mixture of luck, advantage in assignment, and/or advantage due to "irrelevant" characteristics. Equal pay for the two will result in Jean feeling badly treated; 20% more compensation for Jean will leave John feeling ill-used.

And this matters. Jean or John might leave for another employer if either feels ill-used. But there is often a gap between the value to an employee of the current job and the value he or she could command via the next best alternative, a gap that is of increasing size as time passes and the employment relationship matures. (Go back to Chapter 4 on this point.) The unhappy salesperson might leave, and then again, he or she might stay on, feeling somewhat bitter, or disillusioned, or alienated—but in any case, feeling demotivated.

As we discuss the important design elements of a compensation system throughout the rest of this chapter, we will keep returning to the point that an important characteristic of the system is that employees feel it is equitable or legitimate. As we do this, remember that: (1) perceptions of equity are somewhat culturally driven; (2) even within cultures, there are bound to be disagreements; and (3) by and large, the "losers" in terms of compensation are more likely to attribute inequity to the system. Exhorting you to design a compensation system that is perceived as fair is much easier than actually doing it. (And that's why we think it is entirely equitable that you'll no doubt be earning so much more than us!)

BONUSES OR RAISES?

To illustrate how noneconomic forces can complicate "economically simple" questions about pay for performance, and because it is important in its own right, we turn next to a simple question: If you are going to reward employees based on performance, should the rewards take the form of a bonus (paid immediately) or a raise in base pay?

If the definition of pay for performance is stretched to include systems in which employees' raises reflect past performance, then pay for performance is much more prevalent than one might initially think. The idea that one gets raises for a job well done is fairly common because of its ties to promotion: Workers are promoted for having done well, and promotions to new jobs usually entail higher wages. Promotion as a general topic is left for Chapter 16, so for the time being we will focus our discussion on discretionary permanent raises in base pay given in each period, independent of promotion, depending on how well the individual performed in the preceding period.

If employees were perfectly rational beings who could compute net present values with ease, the differences between bonuses and pay raises would come down to two economic issues: (1) Who can do better investing the money—the firm or the individual? (2) When will the employee cease employment with this employer? To explain, suppose the employee is due a bonus of \$100,000. Suppose as well that the employee will stay with this employer for precisely 20 years more and has a pure rate of time preference of 5% per year, meaning that \$1 given to the employee today is the same as $\$(1.05)^N$ given to the employee N years from now.[13] Then to give the employee \$100,000 today is, from his point of view, equivalent to giving him twenty equal payments of \$8,024, the first in a year from now, one in two years, . . . , and one twenty years from now. We can give him the bonus or a raise in base pay, starting for next year, of \$8,024, and he doesn't care, one way or the other. The firm might care, however, depending on its opportunity cost of capital: If it can realize, say, 6% per annum on funds it invests internally, then the "raise" scheme costs it less money.[14]

But all this supposes that the employee will last precisely twenty years more with the firm. In reality, the employee's tenure with the firm is probably uncertain. We can adjust the amount of the raise to give the employee the same expected net present value as an immediate bonus of $100,000, but this would ignore several further considerations. First, to the extent that the employee's tenure is uncertain and outside of his control, risk aversion on his part may lead him to undervalue the raise; the raise will have to be increased to leave the employee whole. But the impact of risk aversion isn't so clear: If the employee is worried about dying before leaving the firm, a permanent raise, like an annuity, gives the employee a fixed amount of money for the rest of his life. In most cases, annuities are valuable (above their expected net present value) to their owner on insurance grounds. So the annuity effect could lead to a smaller permanent raise being equivalent to the immediate bonus. At the same time, the employee's tenure with the firm is not entirely outside his control: If the raise is indeed permanent, it provides a reason for the employee to remain with the firm—better to get the raise for more periods than less. This increases the firm's hold on the employee, which in general is good for the firm (except insofar as the firm might want the employee to leave but be unwilling to fire him, in which case a severance agreement might be helpful). The employee, realizing this "lock-in" effect, might insist on a larger permanent raise to offset the damage done to his mobility and his bargaining position vis-à-vis the firm.[15]

Notwithstanding all these personal finance calculations, employees aren't perfectly rational. In particular, they engage in social comparisons, comparisons that don't always pay attention to events in the distant past and that don't take into account net present value calculations.

Suppose, for instance, that our meritorious employee, who is due a $100,000 bonus, has a $100,000 base salary. Seated at the desk next to him is a second employee performing much the same tasks, also with a $100,000 base salary, but not entitled to any bonus. If the bonus is paid out to the first employee as it is due, we might presume that he and his neighbor understand the justice in these bonuses: The reason for them is close at hand and salient in the mind of each. But now suppose we pay out bonuses in the form of permanent raises. In the second year, the salary of the bonus-earning employee jumps to $108,024. Fifteen years down the line, the two are performing precisely the same, and yet the first is earning 8% more than the second. The second, having forgotten about events fifteen years ago, is likely to see injustice. Indeed, suppose the second employee only arrives eight years after the extraordinary contributions of our meritorious employee. Then she will not have been present to observe any of those contributions. It can be explained to her that her colleague earns 8% more than she does, even though they do the same job, because of events that took place nearly a decade before she arrived, but: (1) sometimes these explanations aren't given; and (2) even if they are, they aren't always accepted completely. Hence, as time passes, the second employee will see injustice. In fact, it is even possible that the events that led to the higher salary for the first employee will become a blur in his mind, and he will (mistakenly) decide that he is currently contributing more to the company.

Now add a third employee, seated at a desk on the other side of our first employee. The same year as our first employee is due $100,000 in bonus, so is the third. They both have base salaries of $100,000. But the third employee is two years from retirement, not twenty. So to give the third employee an NPV of $100,000, his raise must be $53,780. Any bets on how the first employee will perceive this?

And there is one final point to make about perceptions and bonuses versus raises. Go back to our example, and forget for the moment about social comparisons. Imagine our meritorious employee having saved the firm, say, $200,000 by dint of extraordinary effort, in a firm where the norm is that the employee and the firm share this sort of savings 50–50. The employee then learns that his salary has been raised $8,024. He can do the math—$8,024 is not half of $200,000. Of course, this is the wrong calculation: the NPV of twenty years of $8,024, discounted at 5% per annum, is $100,000. So if he does these calculations, he understands.[16] But do you work out the impact on your lifetime income of a given raise in your base salary? Do you correctly perceive that, if you are twenty years from retirement and your neighbor will retire in five years, and you each get the same dollar raise in your permanent salaries, you were just given a reward around three times larger than your neighbor received, assuming a rate of pure time preference of 5%?[17] We don't routinely do these kinds of calculations on our own compensation—and we wrote this chapter!—so we suspect you don't either.

In this story, we are doing nothing more than playing on the imperfect perceptions of the workers. But those perceptions are important, and compensation schemes that look the same on a spreadsheet may be perceived very differently. Suppose, for example, that instead of giving the meritorious employee permanent raises in his base pay, the firm allows him to "bank" his bonuses in a managed portfolio that grows at some specified rate per year, allowing him to make withdrawals at his own discretion—say, up to some certain size—and providing full vesting to him or his estate after ten years of service. Some of the details are changed, so this is not quite the same as paying out in terms of a permanent raise in base salary, but in many ways it mimics the raise-in-salary strategy. (To the extent that the portfolio's returns are tied to returns of the firm, there is a problem in risk diversification to worry about; see part [1] of endnote 14.) But because of how things are *named,* the perceptual problems mentioned above are much less likely to arise.[18] A new employee can hardly complain that her co-worker, who has the same base wage as does she but who has been with the firm for a decade more, has more "savings on account" with the firm. The worker with twenty years left and the worker with two years left until retiring both get the same contribution to their "bonus account" for the same contributions. And the employee due a $100,000 share of the $200,000 he saved the firm gets $100,000 posted in his "bonus account."

Notwithstanding the merits or demerits of this particular scheme, there has been a long-term secular trend, at least in the United States, to use bonuses instead of raises. To summarize: (1) Onetime bonus payments are generally more salient to the workforce; workers' attention is gotten more easily by them. (2) When differences in current base pay result from events in the distant past, workers may perceive inequities. (3) When job tenure is uncertain, a risk-averse employee will value more highly (in terms of expected utility) an immediate bonus, compared to a permanent raise whose expected NPV, taking into account the probability of quitting, equals the bonus amount.[19] In addition: (4) Insofar as it is perceived as illegitimate for subordinates to make more than their superiors, placing incentive payments into the base wage can be contentious. That is, workers tend to see base wages as a reflection of permanent value to the organization, whereas onetime bonuses are seen as a more legitimate way to reward onetime contributions. (5) With the leveling of marginal income tax brackets, there is less incentive for income-spreading through time.

Having noted the long-term trend toward bonuses and away from raises in base pay, we should note that very recently there has been something of a counterreaction against bonuses. The issue is, once again, employee perceptions. When using bonuses, the employer must be careful that workers don't come to view annual bonuses as entitlements. This is particularly true when bonuses serve simply to bring total compensation up to or near market standards. Bonuses, to be framed as such by employees, should be compensation that really is a bonus—above a base wage or salary for the worker that even without a bonus represents reasonably competitive compensation in the appropriate labor market. And even when base compensation is at or above market levels, a long unbroken history of paying bonuses can lead workers to view them as an entitlement. Lincoln Electric, which provides base compensation (using piece-rates) that is at or above local market levels, ran into this problem recently. Lincoln generates annual bonuses for workers, above their piece-rate pay, that typically are quite substantial. (Bonuses equal to annual base pay have not been uncommon.) The bonus pool is tied to Lincoln's earnings, and when recent management decisions led to some lean times for the firm, management decided to omit the bonus. The reaction from workers was predictable; because it wasn't their fault that Lincoln had fared poorly, and because the bonuses had come regularly in the past, they felt that something they deserved had been taken away.[20]

GROUP INCENTIVE SCHEMES

So far, we have talked almost exclusively about individual-based pay for performance: The bonus or raise given to an employee depends on how well, absolutely or relatively, he or she did. But when meaningful measures of performance aggregate the actions of a number of employees, it is natural to resort to group incentive schemes, in which individual compensation depends on how the group as a whole performs. Indeed, many off-the-shelf gainsharing systems, such as Improshare and Scanlon Plans, are group incentive schemes.

The Free-Rider Problem and its Resolution

Economic analysis of group incentive schemes begins with the free-rider problem: The individual member of the group bears fully the personal costs of her efforts but shares the gains from those efforts, in terms of improved performance and hence increased compensation, with members of the group. If she behaves self-ishly and trades off only her own benefit against the personal cost of her efforts, she will underperform, relying instead on the efforts of her colleagues. The employer can control this by increasing the extent to which the group reward responds to measures of group performance, but this generally increases the risks to employees, who must then be compensated for bearing this risk. The larger the group, the more severe the problem becomes.

Four somewhat intertwined factors ameliorate this grim picture:

1. At least for small groups, it is natural to assume that group members can monitor each other's actions more cheaply and efficiently than the employer can. This may be true, for instance, on technological grounds, because of proximity to other members of the group. This by itself is of no consequence, but it becomes important if . . .

2. . . . the interaction among group members is repeated and rewards are provided to members of the group that depend on the group's performance. Then, just as in Chapter 4 (and especially in Appendix B), the members of the group may enter into a cooperative scheme of working harder for the common good, under the threat that all will go back to acting selfishly if some slack off. Of course, the ability of group members to monitor one another is key to this type of cooperative scheme, which is the link back to point (1).

3. Reinforcing this is the possibility of social sanctions, imposed by members of the group on any members who do not work hard for the common good. Members in workgroups share time together, time that often extends to off-the-job social activities, and they are usually better able to enforce meaningful social sanctions on each other than can the employer. Once again, it is the combination of this factor with the first that ameliorates free-riding: Members of the group have the ability to tell who among them is slacking off, and then—through the threatened breakdown of future cooperation or through the immediate imposition of social sanctions—they can effectively discipline slackers.

4. In addition, whether through natural bonds of kinship or through the psychological process of escalating commitment, members of a work-group are likely over time to internalize each others' welfare, irrespective of any threats of future noncooperation or social sanction. To the extent that this occurs, even without the ability of group members to monitor each other, we will see effort levels by members of the group that come closer to balancing the privately borne costs of effort with the groupwide benefits that accrue from increased effort.

Of course, you probably recognize what is being described in (1) through (3) as good old common-sense *peer pressure*. We are merely describing in economic terms how peer pressure works.

These four factors, taken together, can be very powerful. Indeed, even if an employer has available good measures of individual performance, it may be worthwhile to resort to group incentive schemes, just to take advantage of the relatively greater ability that groups have for internal monitoring, as long as peer pressure (or internalization of the welfare of the group) can be relied upon to conquer the free-rider problem.

This analysis suggests that the longevity, size, and composition of the group all matter. For longevity, the argument is short and sweet: Longevity is a *sine qua non* for the sort of collusive, cooperative equilibrium suggested in (2); longevity of membership is likely to heighten the impact of social sanctions pointed to in (3); and internalization of the welfare of others (point [4]) often arises because of escalating commitment. On all three grounds, it is better to have groups that can remain together unless and until they decide to separate. (Allowing dysfunctional groups to disband is, of course, important as well.) As for group size and composition, these are each sufficiently complex to warrant separate subsections.

Group Size

The direct effect of group size is pretty clear: As groups get larger, they generally lose the ability to engage in meaningful internal monitoring, they are apt to find it harder to reach a cooperative equilibrium, social sanctions will be harder to enforce, and internalization of welfare of the group is less likely to occur.

Group size matters in another way, on economic grounds. Although it is not a law of nature, it is typical that as the group gets larger, measures of performance for the group incorporate more and more extraneous-to-effort uncertainty.[21] Work teams are measured according to their output and costs, divisions according to divisional profits, and entire firms according to their bottom lines; yet as the group gets larger, its performance reflects the impact of completely extraneous factors, such as the state of the economy or the entry of a foreign competitor. It is also the case that meaningful relative performance measures are generally harder to devise the larger is the group, because there are fewer other groups that share a similar environment. Thus, on grounds of efficiency in risk sharing, group-based incentives for larger groups tend to be less efficacious.

But this isn't the end of the story. In Chapter 9, we asserted that firms that practice high-commitment HRM will often use group-based incentive compensation, and they emphasize employee ownership of the entire enterprise through the use of stock ownership plans and the like. From the perspective of agency theory and risk sharing, this is mysterious on several accounts: (1) The free-rider problems (when it comes to affecting the performance of the entire firm in a nonnegligible way) are ferocious. (2) Employees have a lot of human capital tied up in the fortunes of their employer; they should diversify their financial capital holdings into other industries. By the same general argument, basing compensation on the performance of the firm subjects employees to all sorts of risks they can't control. (3) And employees in a firm that practices high-commitment HR are being asked to undertake a large number of tasks, some of which are quite concrete, but others of which are very ambiguous, with measures of performance that are at best very noisy and at worst virtually nonexistent. For multitask jobs that mix such disparate tasks, agency theory recommends very weak pay for performance and increased reliance on intrinsic motivation.

The mystery isn't hard to resolve, however, as long as you aren't too addicted to the economic principle that individual preferences are given and unalterable. Precisely because it is hard to provide good extrinsic motivation, high-commitment HR firms want their employees to internalize the welfare of the firm. And the *symbolic* content of ESOP plans and bonuses based on the firm's annual income figures can be quite powerful—it takes a market relationship, in which the employee is paid for a set of services provided according to the market wage for those services, and replaces it with a team-member relationship in which the employee shares in the successes (and, unhappily, sometimes the failures) of the team/firm. This symbolism is heightened when everyone in the organization is on the same "plan," albeit perhaps on different scales: Treating everyone the same in terms of the form of incentive compensation lowers perceptions of differentiation.

The lesson here transcends high-commitment HRM. The economic arguments against rewards based on large-group performance take no account of the symbolic content of such reward systems, which can powerfully affect the extent to which the individual internalizes the welfare of the entire organization. Where such symbols can activate powerful internalization processes—which depends on the workforce, organizational culture, and to some extent on the external social and economic environments—and where internalization is particularly valuable on strategic and technological grounds, the economic arguments against basing rewards on firm-level performance are generally outweighed by the noneconomic effects of this sort of pay for performance.

Group Composition

Both to heighten internalization of others' welfare and to improve the efficacy of social sanctions, social homogeneity of group membership is desirable. Indeed, it would seem that allowing groups autonomously to form and break up as necessary would be nearly ideal: People would choose to be with their friends, and this would promote the efficacy of social sanctions, increase the likelihood of a cooperatively collusive equilibrium being reached, and encourage internalization of the group's welfare by individual members. But things are not so simple, for several reasons.

First, to the extent that group members are socially dissimilar from others in the organization, or even just socially dissimilar from their "bosses," a dysfunctional us–them atmosphere may be created. This can lead in turn to a within-group equilibrium that works against the interests of the firm—for instance, fostering norms of restricted output; lack of cooperation among groups; concealment of information; unwillingness to discipline group members who underperform; and norms that tolerate mild corruption (petty theft, for example).

Other social and technological concerns must be weighed as well. In particular, to the extent that within-group diversity on ethnic, racial, gender, or other grounds is socially desirable, self-forming groups may pose a problem. On grounds of skill mix, talents, attitudes, and experiences, the employer may wish to form groups that combine workers of different ages, educational backgrounds, and family statuses, among other factors. Self-forming groups are unlikely to fulfill this sort of wish. And groups that are largely self-formed but then are mixed by the forced inclusion of a member of some underrepresented group can lead to scapegoating and the like.

Besides forming on the basis of friendships, groups will naturally form on the basis of abilities, at least insofar as compensation is tied to group performance. Outstanding performers will want to be with outstanding performers, and after they form their own groups, the very good (but not outstanding) performers will band together, followed by the good, then the mediocre, and finally the poor performers. Whether such a pattern of "within-group homogeneity, between-group heterogeneity" in terms of abilities is good for the organization is complex and depends on the firm's technology. In two extreme cases, however, the answer on technological grounds is straightforward.

First, consider a case in which it takes a team of high performers to get outstanding group performance, but groups as a whole are "stars." In this case, it is desirable to have teams that are internally homogeneous but heterogeneous in ability across teams (i.e., within-group homogeneity and between-group heterogeneity). This is because homogeneous groups composed of low-achievers won't hurt much, while homogenous groups of high-achievers will give spectacular results for the organization. Think, for example, of research teams that require one member from each of several specialties—the team that gets all the stars is likely to produce something outstanding, while the teams that are filled with less brilliant performers are unlikely to get anywhere and, at the same time, are unlikely to cause any damage as they spin their wheels.

Conversely, think about a setting in which teams are guardians, and individual members of teams are stars—that is, a poorly performing group is a disaster for the firm, but one solid member of the group can substantially make up for all her teammates. Here, within-group homogeneity combined with between-group heterogeneity could be disastrous, because the team with all the low performers could wreak tremendous havoc. By maintaining homogeneity across groups—rationing the individual stars among the groups to pull all the groups up—the organization is likely to experience no worse than mediocre performance from all the groups.[22]

These are the two easy cases for the question of within- versus between-group homogeneity. Answers are, however, quite unclear for the other cases: where members of the group are stars (respectively, guardians) in their effects on the group, and groups are stars (respectively, guardians) in their effects on the organization.

To complicate matters further, the specific technology will influence the extent to which self-forming groups will yield within-group homogeneity in terms of ability (see endnote 22). The best we can do here is to warn you to watch for these considerations, when contemplating group-based production with or without autonomously forming groups.

The Division of Rewards Within the Group

Saying that members of the group should be rewarded according to group performance leaves unanswered at least one key question: Should rewards be given to members of the group according to some fixed formula (such as *equal division,* or *divide group compensation in proportion to base pay*)? Or is the group given an overall reward—a bonus, say—which must be apportioned to members of the group through a consensus process? In some organizations, supervisors are called upon to apportion bonus pools according to their subjective sense of the value of the different workers in the group. Occasionally, the group members themselves must decide how to divide the total award. In theory, having the group divide the reward is very attractive, if one can trust the group to solve the division problem efficiently and equitably, because this increases the power of the group over the individual, heightening the power of peer pressure. But the phrase *if one can trust the group to solve the division problem efficiently and equitably* hides a multitude of potential problems. Politicking, back-scratching, and logrolling are all natural in such settings and can be quite destructive of group cohesion. And of course management must also balance the potential benefits of involving group members in reward allocations against the risk of losing a valued individual team member who feels unfairly rewarded by his or her colleagues. We have no particular insights to offer on these questions, except one that is obvious: If rewards are going to be divided "locally," management should keep an eye on the process.

Legitimacy

Group-based performance measures raise important issues of legitimacy. If there is homogeneity within groups and heterogeneity between groups in terms of abilities, individuals "stuck" in a group with mediocre or poor performers may see injustice. On the other hand, if within-group heterogeneity is high, high-fliers in a group may be upset at having to "carry" their colleagues who are less able, ambitious, or energetic, particularly if the group-based rewards are divided equally.

Also, the process of social comparison can become more invidious. If an employee is rewarded individually, he is most likely to compare his situation with socially similar workers, which generally means workers in the same work environment. If rewards are given to the group, group members will look for similarly-situated groups. If rewards are given to the division, comparisons will be made with what was given to other divisions. But as the unit becomes larger, objectively appropriate comparisons will be harder to come by. An individual employee is likely to find others in his work unit who face similar challenges, have similar abilities, and so forth. If the firm is equitable in how it treats employees, adverse conclusions are unlikely to be drawn. But finding a "matching" work group is harder (because there are fewer of them, and because different groups face objectively different circumstances), and finding a "matching" division is harder still.[23] Management can choose a formulaic reward structure (e.g., the bonus pool for each division is 25% of its earnings), and members of a division that is facing a particularly challenging competitive environment or that is engaged in expanding its market share will see injustice—why weren't their special circumstances recognized? Or management can make subjective adjustments that it believes are entirely equitable, and live with the unhappiness of employees in Division Z who perceive that Division Y is unfairly being given advantages, because the CEO used to work there or has her protégé there.

Rewarding Individuals versus Teams

Emphasizing teams and teamwork has become, in some circles, almost a religious dogma in recent years. We discussed some efforts along these lines in reviewing high-commitment work systems (Chapter 9). In concluding this discussion of group-based incentive schemes, we wish to underscore an important point reflecting the emphasis we have placed throughout this book on alignment and consistency: *The choice between a job design and reward system organized along individualistic versus group-based lines may be less important than ensuring that the job design and reward system are aligned with one another and consistent with other HR practices.* Empirical work bears this out. Ruth Wageman recently studied more than 800 Xerox repair technicians working in 152 teams. Some teams consisted of technicians that performed their work more or less independently; other teams worked as a highly interdependent unit; still others reflected a hybrid model, combining individualistic and group work.[24] With permission from Xerox, Wageman was able to assign these teams to different reward conditions: one in which rewards and feedback were provided to the team as a whole; one in which rewards were contingent on group and individual performance (hybrid); and one in which outcomes were entirely individual-based. Wageman found that pure individualistic and pure group arrangements—both in terms of task interdependence and outcome interdependence—consistently outperformed the hybrid teams, based on company performance data, which included customer satisfaction evaluations and hard measures of repair time and costs, as well as attitudinal data solicited from the employees. Furthermore, although the pattern wasn't perfect, in general Wageman's results suggested that effectiveness was highest when there was congruence between the amount of task interdependence and the extent of outcome interdependence; that is, either both tasks and rewards were individualistic or they were both group-based.

These results serve to underscore the importance of aligning reward systems with technology, a point not infrequently overlooked in companies that embrace "teams" but either transform work to make it interdependent without altering selection and reward systems, or else move to group-based evaluations and rewards but continue to adhere to an "individual contributor" model. As Wageman notes:

> Work design shapes individuals' preferences, their behavior, how they experience their rewards, and the impact of those rewards on their performance. Not all work, perhaps, permits as much choice about how tasks are designed as was the case for the service technicians in this study. But whenever cooperative behavior is critical to excellent task performance, it is most essential to create real task interdependence and then support the task design with interdependent rewards.[25]

Wageman's findings also suggest why group-based rewards might sometimes be so contentious (because the tasks aren't very interdependent in the first place) and why in some highly interdependent settings it may be valuable to involve the team members themselves in allocating rewards, to reinforce their collective identity and responsibility.

THE CASE AGAINST PAY FOR PERFORMANCE

Agency theory, it seems, gives a clear-cut rationale for pay for performance. Pay for performance is necessary to get workers off their duffs and to drive the lazy workers away. And it works: At least, the case of Safelite provides strong empirical confirmation.

Even so, the popular management press is full of articles with titles such as "Why Incentives Never Work" and "Pay for Performance and You Won't Get It."[26] When you get past the attention-grabbing titles, the arguments made in these articles seem to us to come down to five general points: Pay-for-performance schemes are too blunt an instrument, resulting in misalignment of incentives; they load uneconomically large amounts of risk on the worker; they often have problems with perceived legitimacy; they can breed inflexibility; and they can dull intrinsic motivation. Following our discussion in Chapter 5, there is no need to reiterate the last point. But the other four are worth some elaboration:

Misalignment of Incentives

Misalignment of incentives usually comes down to a problem of workers choosing to do the "wrong" thing. The variations on the basic model of agency that we gave illustrate many of these problems:

- When workers have several tasks to perform, incentive systems have a hard time getting the balance right. Attention and effort will be given to those activities on which the employee perceives that he or she can have the biggest impact in terms of compensation. The perception of a large impact, in turn, depends on two considerations: Does the reward system take significant account of this or that measure of performance? And how much control does the individual have over the performance measures—how noisy is the relationship between efforts and performance measures?

Incentive systems typically are keyed to tasks that are measured easily and relatively noiselessly; things that are harder to measure are given short shrift because they are hard to measure well. But no matter what the reason, if a task is not formally recognized in a worker's incentive pay, he or she has less incentive to pay attention to that task. This problem can be particularly vicious in service industries where it is hard to monitor the quality of service given; service can suffer, unless the server is motivated by tip income or (more effectively) by the desire to build a personal clientele who will reward the server with repeat business.

- Misalignment also results from dynamic effects: For several reasons—administrative cost, to provide reasonable measures of performance along some dimensions, and to keep the scheme from consuming workers' attention entirely—review periods may be kept fairly long. But then workers have the incentive to play games with the review system, as a review deadline approaches.

- And, as we noted in Chapter 10, comparative evaluation or tournament schemes can cause substantial misalignment: Employees have some motivation either to hurt the efforts of co-workers, to engage in undue conformity, or to collude among themselves against the employer.

But misalignment isn't simply a matter of value-neutral responses to a given set of economic incentives. When a firm engages in pay for performance, it is signaling to employees—perhaps unintentionally, but nonetheless strongly—what it seemingly wants. When the organization explicitly rewards efforts at task A, it is sending a fairly strong signal that tasks B and C, not explicitly rewarded, are less important. When it rewards quantity, it is signaling that quality is less important. When it makes compensation more salient, it signals that "pushing the envelope" to get more compensation is okay. Let us be clear here: Most managements that engage in pay for performance would be aghast at the suggestion that they are sending these signals. But in at least some external environments, those signals are going to be received, whether or not they were intentionally sent.

In Chapter 2, we cited one particularly vivid example of incentive misalignment, concerning Sears Auto Centers, which once put its mechanics on a commission system. The mechanics were rewarded by different amounts of money for different tasks performed (e.g., brake jobs, wheel alignments, tune-ups). The problem with this, discovered by state and local law enforcement officials working undercover, was not so much that the jobs were done in slip-shod fashion, but that mechanics would tell clients that their cars needed work that in fact was not required. Sears discovered the problem and abandoned the scheme, but not before they were required to pay substantial fines and penalties.

And lest you think this problem arises only in blue-collar settings, recently the U.S. Congress has been investigating the performance of the Internal Revenue Service (IRS) and has found that "suggested quotas" imposed by management on individual tax auditors led to fairly abusive treatment of some taxpayers. Top managers of the IRS are—for the record at least—suitably aghast that this should have happened. Perhaps they really are aghast, but they shouldn't be surprised.

Controlling the Risk Loaded onto Employees

The point about loading excessive risk on employees needn't be developed further; it is the main point of agency theory. But we might reiterate that a standard weapon for fighting this problem—comparative performance evaluation—comes with its own set of problems. As just noted, tournaments can promote unhealthy rivalry, undesirable conformity, or worker attempts to collude against the employer. (When the comparative evaluation is done relative to an external benchmark, the problem of conformity remains, but the other two problems are usually largely absent.) And as we discussed at length in Chapter 10, tournaments and benchmarking schemes will be viewed as inequitable if they don't take into account uncontrollable factors that lead to differences in performance outcomes. But efforts to surmount those difficulties through elaborate, subjectively determined handicapping schemes are often rife with politicking and viewed as illegitimate on those grounds. And schemes that base rewards on improvements in individual performance raise the specter of the ratchet effect and the corresponding individual response to seek short-term improvements and then depart.

Problems with Legitimacy

Legitimacy is a potential concern not only with schemes that employ comparative evaluation, but whenever a scheme either doesn't take account of special circumstances or does so subjectively. The standard story here concerns rewarding division managers in a large corporation based on how well their divisions do. Imagine such a scheme being used by a firm with an important division that is in trouble. Top management may want to send one of their most talented managers to tackle the problems facing this division. But is the manager to be rewarded: (1) strictly on the basis of how the division does, making it a very unattractive assignment, at least for a while; (2) on a subjectively "adjusted" basis, sparking cries of favoritism and encouraging politicking; or (3) based on "objective" improvements in performance, which gives the division head an incentive to find quick fixes that are motivated by the formula more than by concern for the long-term problems of the division and then to move on to another division or job, before the quick fixes become problems?

Inflexibility

The argument that pay-for-performance systems can be inflexible begins with the obvious observation that such systems rarely are perfectly tuned to their environment. The specific measures used, the comparisons made, the scale of rewards offered—indeed, *all* aspects of the actual system—are based to some extent on guesses as to what is appropriate and legitimate. Sometimes these guesses are proved wrong. And sometimes, even if the system put in place is effective when it is put in place, the underlying technology, environment, workforce, or even the strategy of the firm changes, calling for changes in the system. The difficulty is that the workers who are being paid for their performance will not necessarily attribute pure and impartial motives to the changes. Even if the adverse effects on compensation are only temporary, while employees adjust to methods changes, workers may balk. But to the extent that the changes hurt them over the longer term by worsening their compensation formula, employees will suspect, perhaps with justice, that management is playing games with them. And they may play games in return. This, of course, is just a high-level version of the ratchet effect. Management, in turn, may be reluctant to implement changes—to avoid ratchet-effect problems and even more to avoid the political costs involved in a change—even sometimes when the changes might leave the firm (and employees) better off.

WHY IT WORKED AT SAFELITE: THE FIVE FACTORS AND PIECE-RATE PAY

In response to all these caveats and potential criticisms, adherents of performance-based pay point to examples such as Safelite. The question is, Why is pay for performance working so well there?

Not surprisingly, we think the way to address this question is through a five-factor analysis. But to generalize a bit beyond the specific case of Safelite, we will conduct a five-factor analysis of piece-rate pay in general. This gives us more opportunities to see benefits from and problems with pay for performance, of which piece-rate compensation is one of the most common and important examples.

In a pure piece-rate system the employee is paid a fixed amount, the piece rate, for each piece or particular task accomplished. Piece rates are commonly used for repetitive tasks. In the garment industry, for example, one employee might be paid $1.07 for each shirt cut from a bolt of fabric, while another employee might receive $1.31 for each shirt sewn from the pieces cut by the first. A salesperson paid on a straight commission basis might be said to be on a piece-rate system, where the piece is the dollar's worth of goods sold. For reasons we shall discuss, in some cases, a modified piece-rate system is employed: The employee might be paid a base wage plus a certain amount per item produced, or—as in the case of Safelite—the employee might be guaranteed some minimum level of compensation per period.

In practice, the piece rate for a particular completed task in an industrial setting is usually set by industrial engineers, who attempt through time-and-motion studies to determine how many pieces N a standard employee, working at a standard pace, can produce in one hour. A standard hourly wage rate W for the employee will have been set, taking into account the wages paid in the local labor market as well as firm-specific factors, such as a policy of paying efficiency wages, a policy of wage compression, and so on. Then the piece rate for the task will be set at W/N, so that a standard employee, working at a standard pace, will make a standard wage.

Advocates of piece-rate compensation will often employ an analogy. Imagine a firm that sources, say, steel rods from two different suppliers, one of which is more efficient than the other. We would hardly expect the firm to pay the second, less efficient, supplier more per steel rod than it pays the first. The cost of producing steel rods is the business of the supplier, not the client firm, which simply wishes to source its steel rods as cheaply as possible.[27] By simple analogy, piece-rate compensation is the obvious compensation system to employ because it ensures that the purchaser (i.e., the employer) pays for what she gets—namely, labor services sufficient to complete a specified task. But labor is not quite the commodity that steel rods are, which is where our five-factor analysis will begin.

Technology

Most of the problems encountered with piece-rate pay are technological in origin, so this will occupy much of our discussion. Piece-rate pay is ideal when the technology is simple: There is no ambiguity; there are few or no discernible quality differences in how the job is done; workers are foot-soldiers; employees can't adversely affect the capital equipment they work with; neither training nor cooperation among workers is a serious concern; and there is little extraneous uncertainty connecting worker inputs with the level of output.

Safelite does pretty well on most of these dimensions. There is no ambiguity in the task: The old, broken windshield is removed and a new one inserted; the proper windshield for a given car is specified in a manual; calls are handled serially. Quality problems can arise—the new windshield might pop out or crack while being installed—but quality problems generally appear immediately and are apparent. And, at Safelite, installers aren't paid the piece rate for windshields they install poorly.[28] One might worry that in a service business like Safelite's, workers are guardians. But the "customer" here is the insurance company more than it is the individual car owner needing the windshield, and insurance companies have a large base of experience—one or two bad performances by Safelite will not unduly compromise Safelite's reputation. There seems little in the way of capital equipment that gets used. Installers generally work alone, and training is minimal. And although there is some extraneous uncertainty affecting the input–output connection—workers can be idled if no calls come in to a particular location for awhile—the base-wage guarantee that Safelite employs insures installers against long periods of enforced idleness.

In piece-rate settings more generally, task ambiguity is killing. Quality problems can be killing, unless quality can be monitored reasonably easily and a problem can be traced back to the responsible culprit, who then usually corrects the problem, paying a penalty (or at least going uncompensated for the botched work). Note in this regard that at Lincoln Electric, which makes extensive use of piece rates, workers must "stamp" their work to identify themselves, so that the necessary traces can be made when quality problems arise; a worker responsible for a quality problem is required to redo the work on his or her own time.

Maintenance of capital equipment can be a problem when piece rates are employed, insofar as workers abuse machinery in pursuit of higher output rates. Consequently, in some cases workers are required to purchase their own tools, and in other cases the individual worker is required to pay for consumables such as drill bits. Where a substantial amount of cooperation is needed, piece rates generally do poorly. And even when employees work largely independently—think of clothing manufacturing and the individual worker at his or her sewing machine—training new workers can be problematic, due to the opportunity cost this imposes on the trainer's piece-rate earnings. A standard practice is to have, on each shift, a "lead" worker who is responsible for helping less-experienced workers and whose compensation is based on (or supplemented for) time spent training, supervising, and the like.

Even when workers work independently, their efforts can be linked when production is sequential, because one employee can be starved of work if the person "upstream" is underperforming. This constitutes extraneous and uncontrollable uncertainty in the compensation of the downstream individual, who is ready and willing to work, but has nothing to work on. Lincoln Electric exhibits a common response to this problem: They maintain work-in-process inventories as buffers between work stations that are larger than would otherwise be economical.

In service industries generally, the source of uncertainty at Safelite—random fluctuations in the incidence of service calls—can present a problem to piece-rate systems. Where it is feasible, service industries will resort to queues of clients (the hospital emergency room) or to scheduling-in-advance systems (the barber shop). Safelite's insured-pay scheme is another common response. Yet another is to pay workers when they are idled at a rate that depends on their "normal" rate of output of work. Another tactic is to maintain an inventory of miscellaneous, "rainy day" tasks that can occupy the downtime, such as deferred maintenance or courtesy calls to customers.

Piece-rate compensation (and pay for performance more generally) can be problematic for stars, although one must be careful about what makes the job a star job. For a single individual who rarely gets a very big win for the organization, and who must be motivated to take the risks necessary to get that win, pay for performance is enormously risky. Consider how much uncertainty confronts a laboratory scientist whose salary depends substantially on how many patents she herself writes, making due allowance for the value to the firm of those patents. Thus, risk-sharing considerations militate against pay for performance in that case. But in some contexts, "stars" can perform their miracles repeatedly; someone who gets a big win is likely to do so again, and the firm's problem is to find the very rare individual who can do this again. For such star roles (and technologies), pay for performance can be very useful, although more as a screening device than a motivational tool.[29]

Guardian jobs are somewhat better suited to outcome-based rewards, as long as it is easy to identify the disasters and who caused them. For these sorts of jobs, the obvious and common compensation scheme is to reward the individual or team whenever a disaster is avoided and/or penalize heavily for disasters. But when disasters are hard to monitor or slow to manifest themselves—quality in many service industries is a good example—then piece-rate-type schemes become problematic.

There is one final technological consideration worthy of mention: How rapid are method changes? Piece-rate systems are generally inflexible to methods improvements. Once a piece rate for a particular task is set, it is usually hard to reset on administrative grounds. This is typically built in as part of the piece-rate system, to protect workers against the ratchet effect (see the discussion in the preceding section on flexibility).[30] A related issue is that if the technology changes in ways that increase the value of (re)training employees, a strong piece-rate system can provide disincentives for employees to receive such training; they pay for this training through reduced opportunities to earn money. We don't know how the Safelite system and its workers will respond to changes in the piece rate that are driven by technology, or by management attempting to ratchet things up on workers. It no doubt helps that, when it comes to installing windshields, technological advance has not been rapid.

Strategy

Piece-rate systems emphasize speed and efficiency. They can lead to neglect of quality, unless it is easy to monitor. (In some service industries where there are high rates of repeat services for the same server, this problem is ameliorated by the server's desire for a loyal clientele.) Thus, piece-rate systems mesh well with strategies for which low-cost production and speed of provision are important. Safelite qualifies on both grounds, because the industry is competitive, and nonprice competition largely comes down to getting a windshield installed in a car quickly.

Workforce

Safelite has a workforce that is very well suited for piece-rate compensation. Employees are not diverse along dimensions that would lead to problems of legitimacy. Imagine, for example, that Safelite's workforce had a large component of workers with long tenures with the firm, workers who (because of their advanced age) are no longer able to pop windshields in very quickly. If Safelite had had such a workforce, the introduction of the piece-rate system, leading to higher pay for less-senior, more "agile" workers, would have been likely to generate ill-will.

Culture

Piece-rate systems work best in organizational cultures that place a premium on individual effort and that legitimize rewards for hard work and/or skill. They typically work poorly in family-like cultures, or in cultures dominated by professional norms that denigrate speed and quantity of output relative to the quality, challenge, elegance, thoroughness, creativity, or subtlety of the work done. Again, Safelite is a winner on all counts.

Environment

Economic environments that support low-cost strategies—in a word, competitive industries—tend to go well with piece rates. Social norms that support the idea that individuals who work hard or are agile deserve greater rewards go well with piece rates. Social norms of ethical behavior can ameliorate problems of unethical or shady behavior caused by misalignment of worker incentives. The economic environment at Safelite is certainly conducive to piece-rate—we saw this already to some extent under the heading "Strategy."

Unionization is another feature of the environment that is likely to bear on the feasibility of piece rates. Unions have tended to oppose the imposition of such schemes, fearing exploitation and their use as a tool to "divide and conquer" the workforce. In addition, in some locales the legal environment affects the ability of an employer to run a pure piece-rate type system. For instance, in the United States, minimum wage laws specify a floor below which compensation cannot fall.

PAY FOR PERFORMANCE?

Moving beyond the specific context of piece-rate pay, what is the bottom line for pay for performance more broadly? It should be obvious that the answer to this question is neither *It's good* nor *It's bad*. Like most things in the complex world of HRM, *It depends*.[31] In general, pay for performance is less likely to be effective:

- The more complex the technology
- The more ambiguous the tasks
- The more the culture emphasizes cooperation
- The more the strategy centers on hard-to-measure quality or emphasizes innovation
- The more tenuous the connection between inputs and outputs
- The more one can rely on intrinsic motivation of the workforce
- The more workforce diversity and/or technological diversity will encourage perceptions of inequity or illegitimacy in a pay-for-performance regime
- The more the general social culture, and the specific culture of the workforce, militate against "crass monetary distinctions"

This isn't a complete list, of course. But it makes our point—an informed five-factor analysis of the specific work environment is called for, bearing in mind the economic rationales for pay for performance, the other social forces that work against or for it, and the general categories of problems it can present.

The generic response to poor outcomes in HRM—in the United States, at least—is to assume that the problem is motivation and the cure is compensation. But the problem may not be motivation. Among the other HR levers to pull are job design, recruitment and retention, training, and assignment and promotion policies—

in other words, the topics of Chapters 13, 14, 15, and 16. And, of course, there are non-HR levers to think about, such as strategy and technology.

But suppose the problem is indeed motivation. Even so, the answer may not be compensation or, at least, it may not be compensation *per se*. You may do a lot better using other motivational techniques, such as promotion prospects (but see Chapter 16 first!), activating peer pressure, increasing workers' identification with the firm, and emphasizing intrinsic motivation by, say, providing opportunities to grow or to take on new challenges.

In *The Soul of a New Machine*,[32] Tracy Kidder describes how young engineers (hardware designers and microprogrammers) at Data General Corporation, who were involved in the design of a new minicomputer, worked ridiculously long hours for very little pay. What motivated them to work so hard? Kidder is clear that peer pressure played an important part, as did the inherent fascination the engineers had with their tasks. But he also describes how Data General used "pinball effects" to motivate the engineers: Their reward for building a successful machine—attained by working extraordinarily hard for low pay—was to be permitted to do it again, to build another, prospectively even "sexier," machine. Of course, this motivator fits perfectly with the process of attribution that leads to high intrinsic motivation: The engineers must attribute their efforts to their love of the work, inasmuch as their pay is clearly inadequate to motivate such Herculean efforts. And because it is love of the work that spurs them on, the firm will give them the opportunity—if they succeed—to do again the thing they love. That is, Data General controls access to interesting work, and it rewards success with more opportunities. We don't want to oversell this point; Kidder is equally clear on how these engineers suffered from burnout. And, twenty years later, the culture among computer-engineering types is increasingly driven by economic motivators (everyone gets rich and buys at least a Porsche after the IPO). But for the time that Kidder writes about, when firms like Data General controlled the access of engineers to projects of this sort, this is a textbook case[33] of how to use rewards other than compensation to motivate individuals, in a way that works with instead of against intrinsic motivation.

The point is simple: The formulation *pay for performance* is too limited and limiting. Think instead of *rewards for performance,* and think accordingly in terms of the full spectrum of rewards that employees value or can be induced to value.

A final thought will take us to the next chapter. We've put a lot of emphasis on the dysfunctional atmospherics that pay for performance may engender in some settings. (We emphasize *may*; for some organizational cultures, in some social and economic contexts, and for some production technologies, pay for performance fits remarkably well.) But this is not intended to imply that money is irrelevant. It isn't. People expect to be paid and take it very much amiss when the paycheck is missing. At the same time, there is a huge difference between monetary rewards and monetary attributions. Some organizations have found very ingenuous ways of taking advantage of the power of monetary rewards in cases where they are feasible and appropriate, while at the same time ensuring that employees retain a strong sense of pride and psychological ownership in their work. For instance, recall that earlier in this chapter we mentioned how Lincoln Electric Company—which has achieved enormous notoriety by using piece-rate compensation successfully for nearly a century—has workers put an individualized stencil on each machine. This enables quality problems to be traced back to the source and reworked by the responsible employee on his or her own time. But also note the subtle psychological impact of having workers stencil their identities onto the products they produce, just as the members of the now-famous team that designed the Apple Macintosh did by stenciling their names inside the computer.

In short, in thinking about whether to employ a scheme that pays for performance, you should be thinking not just about the mechanics of such a scheme, employing the theory we covered in this chapter, and about the appropriateness of such a scheme based on the five factors and its consistency with other HR practices. You should also be thinking about how explicitly you wish to encourage employees to *focus* on rewards for performance and to attribute their behavior to the pursuit of those rewards, especially bearing in mind that explicit calculations require formulas, and formulas in a complex world often miss some important things.

This brings us, in turn, to the topics of the following chapter. Setting aside pay for performance, what other criteria exist for allocating rewards and when are they appropriate? How should the *level* of compensation be set? How much *dispersion* in compensation levels should be built into the pay policies of a firm? What *form* should financial compensation take—should it be mostly money in the pay package, or perks and benefits, or shares in the enterprise? How much *information* should workers be given about the distribution of compensation and about specific compensation levels? We address these questions in Chapter 12.

IN REVIEW

⇒ Compensation is an enormous and important topic. In this book we divide it into two chapters: this chapter, on pay for performance; and Chapter 12, on "everything else."

⇒ Agency theory, also known as the theory of incentives and principal–agent theory, gives the theoretical take on the subject from the point of view of economics.

- The simple form of the theory assumes employees are averse to effort and risk, and that employer and employee can't base compensation on actual employee effort expended.
- Thus, to the extent that tangible measures of output reflect effort expended, tying compensation levels to output can help motivate employee effort.
- The basic trade-off is: Strengthening the tie between compensation and output makes the worker (inefficiently) subject to more risk, insofar as she can't control output levels entirely. But weakening the tie reduces her motivation to work hard. Relatively efficient incen-

tive compensation, therefore, is based on measures of output that most accurately reflect the employee's efforts and that don't depend on uncertain factors outside the employee's control.

- A number of variations on the basic model explore:
  - Using incentive compensation to screen and sort among prospective employees.
  - The (mis)use of incentive compensation when effort is multidimensional. The key point here is that when some aspects of effort can only be measured noisily, incentive compensation is rarely effective overall: It either causes the employee to focus on a few aspects of her job or it subjects the employee to excessive risk.
  - Using relative performance as the basis of compensation. This can be effective, but it is subject to many qualifications (discussed in Chapter 10).
  - Multiperiod effects—the ratchet effect, hurdle levels, and using compensation to bind workers to firms—which all complicate the story.

⇒ The agency theory perspective should be tempered by a host of psychological and social processes, including social comparison, the effects of social status (and the dangers of status conflict), the symbolic character of compensation in reinforcing (or derogating) organizational culture, intrinsic motivation, procedural and distributive justice, and cognition and perception (illustrated by our discussion of pay raises versus bonuses).

⇒ Group incentive schemes can work powerfully when groups can solve the free-rider problem by peer pressure and individual members internalize the group's welfare.

- Solving the free-rider problem is often aided by some degree of stability and homogeneity in group composition.
- From the perspective of economics, limiting group incentives to smaller groups seems sensible, because usually in larger groups the free-rider problem is exacerbated and measures of output are subject to more uncontrollable uncertainty. But there are rebuttals that emphasize the symbolic content and effects of incentive schemes that tie compensation to organization-level performance.
- How to form groups, and whether to allow them to form autonomously, is a complex issue turning, among other things, on the technology of (group) production and the relationship between group-level outcomes and organizational outcomes.
- Giving groups autonomy to distribute rewards internally is, in theory, a powerful way to enhance peer pressure. But in practice, this can be a dangerous system to follow.

⇒ The case against pay-for-performance systems generally turns on five points: These systems misalign incentives; they put too much risk on employees; they have legitimacy problems; they are inflexible; and they can kill intrinsic motivation.

⇒ Notwithstanding these concerns, pay for performance can be a powerful tool in the appropriate circumstances, as a five-factor analysis of piece-rates illustrates.

- Piece-rate compensation generally is most effective in technologies that have low levels of ambiguity, easy-to-observe quality, low levels of worker interdependence, and a low pace of methods changes. It can be effective for guardians and foot-soldiers, but is usually ineffective with star jobs.
- Piece-rate compensation fits relatively well with general business strategies that emphasize speed and efficiency.
- Workforce-related considerations generally revolve around problems of legitimacy, tracing back to workforce diversity.
- Piece rates mesh with cultures that emphasize rewards for individual effort.
- Piece rates work relatively well in economic environments that support low-cost strategies and where social norms and culture support rewards for those who deliver "the goods." Unions tend to oppose piece rates, and some other legal problems can arise.

⇒ In many contexts, pay for performance is too narrow a concept:

- You should think more broadly in terms of *rewards for performance,* considering the full portfolio of rewards that the organization can provide to its employees.
- In considering pay for performance, keep in mind the basic question: How much do you want employees focusing on pay as their main source of job motivation?

ENDNOTES

1. We are abridging and simplifying from Edward Lazear, "Performance, Pay, and Productivity," mimeo, Stanford University (1997). The full story is extremely interesting, and we heartily recommend the original article.

2. In the Safelite story, the new compensation system improved both the performance of individual workers and, through retention (and, eventually, selection), the average quality of workers. Agency theory concerns the impact of pay for performance on a single worker. We will briefly discuss as well the impact that pay-for-performance systems can have on the selection and retention of workers, although much of our discussion of this topic—which economists call market screening—is reserved for Chapter 14.

3. In this example, it seems natural to suppose that the latter piece-rate way of doing business is superior, because the employer is really only interested in getting her post holes dug and not in how long it takes. But if we were thinking of, say, the framing of a house, both the amount of framing done and the time it takes to complete could be consequential to the employer.

4. We will try in this section to give nontechnical readers a feel for how agency theory works—what is assumed and what conclusions are reached. To do this, we will simplify in places and avoid technical niceties—for instance, regarding optimal risk sharing with nonsmooth utility functions, monotone likelihood ratios, optimal wage discrimination schemes of various orders, and so forth. We apologize to economists whose proprieties we offend. This is also a good place to recall that we are describing economic theory in this section and not reality. Factors such as intrinsic motivation, social comparisons, and a taste for distributive justice are ignored in the basic model of agency. Later in this chapter, it will be our (relatively more difficult) job to blend such things into the general story. For the time being, at least, we also apologize to noneconomist readers who are offended by these omissions.

5. According to the economic theory of risk bearing, this is so whenever the employee is risk averse—that is, he values a risky gamble at less than its expectation.

6. In fact, in the appendix you will find a very simple version of basic agency theory. The conclusions we draw here are based on more general analyses of the problem; they are consistent with the analysis in the appendix, but they go beyond the very simple model studied there. These conclusions do, however, depend on some technical assumptions that we will not bother to give here. The appendix suggests some further reading for those interested in the whole story.

7. More precisely, it is the number of windows such that the marginal value to Safelite of another window installed matches the dollar-equivalent marginal cost to the employee of installing that window.

8. Lest you think this is exclusively a blue-collar or manufacturing sector phenomenon, we mention in Chapter 14 a similar menu-of-options approach used by Sapient Corporation for its mid-level information technology consultants.

9. Bengt Holmstrom and Paul Milgrom, "Multi-task Principal–agent Analysis: Incentive Contracts, Asset Ownership, and Job Design," *Journal of Law, Economics, and Organization* 7 (1991): 24–52.

10. Suppose a firm announced that it was willing to share cost savings that arose from employee suggestions, giving 20% to the employee and 80% to the firm. An employee makes a suggestion that saves the firm $100,000 per year. Assuming the firm will operate for a long period to come and discounts cash flows at, say, 10% per year, this $100,000 savings year after year amounts to $1 million in net present value. So does the employee get an immediate bonus of $200,000? Or does the employee (and, after her demise, her estate) continue to receive $20,000 per year for the firm? In most cases, we suspect that the employer passes on $20,000 in the first year only (2% of its eventual gain), subsequently asking the rhetorical question, *What have you (the employee) done for me this year?* Note that in the ratchet effect, the employee's treatment is worse still, insofar as she has to exert effort to make the $100,000 savings. Having gotten her $20,000 the first year, she is expected to continue to put in the extra effort needed for no additional pay, because she has set a new standard for herself.

11. A more complete discussion of this idea is in Paul Milgrom and D. John Roberts, *Economics, Organization, and Management* (Englewood Cliffs, NJ: Prentice-Hall, 1992),

Chapter 7. The precise argument is quite complex; if you are ambitious (and able to tolerate fairly hard mathematics), see Bengt Holmstrom and Paul Milgrom, "Aggregation and Linearity in the Provision of Intertemporal Incentives," *Econometrica* 55 (March 1987): 303–28.

12. For a theoretical analysis related to this point, see Edward P. Lazear, "Why Is There Mandatory Retirement?" *Journal of Political Economy* 87 (December 1979): 1261–84.

13. You might pose two questions here. First, what about inflation? Inflation or other things that change the real value of money complicate the story without adding anything substantive, so for the balance of this subsection, we'll assume that the value of money stays constant—there is no inflation. To adapt these calculations to the reality of inflation, simply assume all dollar values given are inflation-adjusted. Second, what about the individual's abilities to invest the money? We will assume that the employee's outside savings–investment possibilities are impounded in the 5% figure.

14. And in such a case, it does better still by paying out the lump sum of $[(1.05)^{20} \times 100,000] = \$265,330$ in twenty years. There are three things to say about this. (1) If there is uncertainty in rates of return from money invested by the firm, this subjects the employee to a lot of risk, and risk that is probably correlated with the value of his human capital. Some discount for this should be applied. (2) See the next paragraph in the text: The effect described there would be heightened by such a lump-sum payment. (3) If the firm can do better than the employee investing money—which is what the story is asserting—then the firm might want to let employees reinvest their bonuses, and any other money they care to, in the firm's activities. Indeed, some money management firms allow this. For instance, employees at Long-Term Capital Management (LTCM) in Greenwich, Connecticut were allowed to plow their bonuses back into the firm's main "fund." It should not go unsaid—especially in light of the current troubles confronting LTCM—that attention to (1) above is particularly pertinent in the case of money management firms, where the value of the employee's human capital is very closely tied to the performance of the fund that he or she helps to manage. Note also that this sort of scheme has all sorts of tax implications; we won't pursue those implications in this book, but we explore other aspects of this general scheme in the text below.

15. There is a subtle point lurking here: Suppose the firm pays bonuses or gives pay raises in part to promote longer job tenures: That is, the firm wishes to engage in efficiency wages, but only for employees who contribute more. The permanent raise scheme then has a problem. Suppose there are two employees A and B. For some reason, A is much more likely to depart voluntarily than is B; to have something concrete to think about, imagine that B's family lives in the area, so B is rooted to this job, or A has a spouse who is having problems finding employment in the area. If A faces the prospect of having to depart regardless of the salary he is being paid in the future, then in the shorter run, permanent raises are worth less to him than are immediate bonuses, compared with B. Hence A is more likely to depart in the short-run as well; the permanent raise scheme gives more value to those employees for whom it is less necessary, from the perspective of reducing voluntary turnover.

16. The employee may rightly be worried that raises are not permanent, in the sense that his salary will "regress to the mean" if his contributions don't continue to be extraordinary. That is, the firm may *claim* to be giving him a permanent raise in base salary but then diminish his raises in the future to the extent that his salary is out of line with the salaries of colleagues. So the perceptual bias we are referring to on the employee's part here may be quite rational.

17. As you answer these questions about your own perception, be sure to include the impact of inflation. If, for example, you and your neighbor both get a raise that just matches the inflation rate, you both got the same raise—namely, none at all. It is "merit raises" over and above the rate of inflation that are at issue here.

18. Indeed, perceptions of and reactions to a compensation system that is concerned only with *current* compensation can change simply depending on the language in which the system is framed. Consider a commission (bonus) scheme for a salesperson which pays the individual $50,000 in base pay, plus $10 per unit sold. Compare this with a scheme in which "base pay" is set at $150,000, but the salesperson has a quota of 10,000 units; if she sells more than 10,000 units, she gets $10 per unit sold, but she also pays a penalty of $10 per unit for every unit less than 10,000 she manages to sell. So, for instance, if she sells only 7,000 units, she must pay a penalty of $30,000, lowering her compensation to $120,000. We know of no systematic evidence on the point, but we would bet that many individuals would find the second scheme, with its notion of penalties and quotas, more aversive than the first, simple bonus scheme. Of course, some simple algebra will show you that the two schemes are exactly the same: If X is the level of sales, $50,000 + 10X = (150,000 - 100,000) + 10X = 150,000 + 10(X - 10,000) = 150,000 - 10(10,000 - X)$.

19. This is ameliorated by the annuity effect, if any.

20. Zachary Schiller, "A Model Incentive Plan Gets Caught in a Vise," *Business Week* 3459 (January 22, 1996): 89–92.

21. We have to be careful here: To the extent that the group can solve the free-rider problem and to the extent that the idiosyncratic risks facing each individual within the group are statistically independent, the effect of size runs precisely the other way: Members of the group, in essence, share in each other's risks. (For instance, equal bonuses to members of a research group, based on the number of patents received by the group, would insure members of the group to some extent against purely personal risk in the research process, as well as encouraging cooperation. And, as long as the lab facilities are configured appropriately, it is easy to imagine that members of research group could adequately monitor each others' work habits.) What is asserted in the text is that if meaningful measures of group performance increasingly reflect extraneous-to-effort *systematic* risk—probably the more relevant case empirically—then on risk-sharing efficiency grounds, large size is problematic for effective group-based incentive schemes.

22. And note that in this kind of setting, there is less of a technological rationale for all the stars to want to form together into a homogeneous group. Stars won't want to be dragged down by the lower performers with whom they work. But if there is little upside from having stars in a group except to prevent disasters, and if a single star in a group is sufficient to achieve this, then in this setting teams could form among heterogeneous workers (e.g., a group of friends, one of whom is a star) without substantial adverse consequences for group performance.

23. Readers with good memories may recall our discussion in the previous chapter (based on a model by Zenger) of why organizations might only reward the extremes and minimize the distinctions they make among individuals in the middle of the reward distribution, to reduce invidious social comparisons. Zenger is thus suggesting that it may sometimes be a virtue to reduce the opportunities individuals have to make comparisons. Isn't that true for groups too? Zenger's conclusion, applied to group-level outcomes, is that the incentive system should reward workgroups similarly unless they

perform remarkably well or remarkably poorly. In an organization that does this consistently—where the consistency of this policy legitimates the fact that distinctions in the middle are not made—such a policy will mute invidious comparisons. But this system moves us away from pay for performance, by and large.

24. Ruth Wageman, "Interdependence and Group Effectiveness," *Administrative Science Quarterly* 40 (March 1995): 145–80.

25. *Ibid.*, p. 173.

26. One of the more recent, high-profile tracts in this genre is Alfie Kohn, *Punished by Rewards* (Boston: Houghton Mifflin, 1993).

27. We are ignoring issues of strategic sourcing of factors of production here, of course.

28. Installers are not responsible for the cost of the broken windshield when there is a quality problem, perhaps because windshields can be defective in manufacture, outside the installer's control. This potentially gives Safelite workers insufficient incentive to be careful in installation, although the cost to them in lost time (having to go back to get another windshield and returning to reinstall) is pretty large. In any case, it seems that there was even less incentive to take care in the old, wage-based system, because the incentives provided by making the worker redo a botched job have actually *lowered* the amount of rework that Safelite installers now do. See Lazear, "Performance, Pay, and Productivity," *op. cit.*

29. Compare with the discussion of RE/MAX in Chapter 14.

30. In industries and technologies characterized by strong experience curve effects (so that workers become more productive over time as they gain experience with a new technology), the dilemma is particularly acute: If the piece-rate holds, workers' compensation goes up over time as they gain mastery; if the piece-rate is adjusted down, however, workers may feel punished by their own successes. And how *should* the piece-rate be adjusted? For instance, should employees be rewarded or punished if they adjust more rapidly to a new technology than management anticipated?

31. For an overview of the evidence, based on both scholarly research and practitioners' experiences, see George T. Milkovich and Alexandra K. Wigdor (eds.), *Pay for Performance: Evaluating Performance Appraisal and Merit Pay* (Washington, DC: National Academy Press, 1991).

32. Boston: Little, Brown (1981).

33. Well, *now* it's a textbook case!

12

COMPENSATION SYSTEMS: FORMS, BASES, AND DISTRIBUTION OF REWARDS

This chapter picks up precisely where Chapter 11 left off. Setting aside questions of pay for performance, we study the questions: What determines the level, basis, distribution, and form of compensation? How much information should be provided to employees about the distribution of compensation within the organization? What are the consequences for the firm and for other aspects of HRM?

THE BASIS FOR PAY: TASKS, STATUS, SKILLS, SENIORITY

If compensation is not tied directly to performance, what might and *should* it be tied to? To answer these questions, consider how wages and salaries are set in many organizations. Perhaps the most common approach involves something like the following. The firm looks at compensation rates in the local labor market for similar jobs or for jobs with similar skill requirements. Some adjustment will take place according to the firm's experience. If positions are hard to fill, the firm might raise compensation; if there is a long queue of applicants, firms might lower pay rates (or, at least, not move them up with inflation). Sometimes a firm will adjust the rates upward in an attempt to broaden the applicant pool or reduce turnover—that is, the firm will pay efficiency wages. Of course, all this is subject to negotiation with a union if the job in question is covered by collective bargaining. Equally *of course,* it is clear that such a procedure leads to a rough-and-ready approximation to wages set by the economic slogan *supply equals demand*.

Hay Points and Job Evaluation

A variety of seemingly more "scientific" approaches to wage setting involve formal job analysis and evaluation. These methods begin with a systematic analysis of the underlying attributes and demands of jobs. Each of the jobs being studied is characterized in terms of various common dimensions and distinctions, such as the types and complexity of knowledge required, number of employees supervised, amount of capital overseen, type and unpleasantness of working conditions, and so on. These measures are then used to put all the jobs on a one-dimensional scale of "value." This can be done in a number of ways. To take two examples: (1) The measures may be scaled and then subjectively determined weights are used to compute a weighted average, where the weights reflect what is important to the firm. For instance, a firm whose culture emphasizes HRM might choose to weight heavily the number of employees supervised. (2) In other cases, a statistical technique such as linear regression is used to fit wages paid to a sample of jobs, either within the firm or in the relevant external labor market, using the job characteristic measures as explanatory variables. The result might be, for instance, that each additional worker supervised is "worth" $152 in a supervisor's monthly pay packet.

When a technique like (1) is used, the result is an abstract measure of each job's value to the firm. The firm then can determine an average wage it wishes to pay (based on local market conditions, the desirability of paying efficiency wages, and so on) and the amount of dispersion in wages it wishes to have (see later in this chapter), assigning wages to specific jobs based on this value-to-the-firm measure, so that it gets the distribution it desires. Or it might consult local market conditions to peg wages for two (or more) benchmark positions, filling in wages for other jobs based on the value-to-the-firm measure. Of course, when a technique like (2) is used, the result of the analysis is, for each job, an estimated "appropriate" wage, although the firm may then choose to increase or decrease the wages it will pay, to change its overall position in the wage distribution of the local labor market.

Compensation consulting firms, such as the Hay Group, are particularly sophisticated at these techniques and have large proprietary databases that enable their clients to compare pay rates to a wide variety of possible benchmarks. These firms are often called in as consultants when an organization wishes to reorganize or rationalize its wage/salary levels. In fact, because of the preeminence of the Hay Group in this field, a standard scale for measuring the "value" of a job is known as the *Hay points* of the job.

The objective of these techniques is primarily rationalization of the firm's pay structure. According to the norm of equity, employees believe they ought to be paid according to their contributions to the organization. Essentially, a Hay system appears to employees to be an objective method for finding appropriate compensation levels, thereby lending legitimacy to the firm's wage structure and heightening perceptions of procedural and distributive justice. Moreover, jobs whose characteristics are relatively rare in the local market, for which direct evidence on appropriate pay is lacking, can be priced out "equitably" by these methods. Note that perceptions of justice will depend on the firm's overall culture: Techniques that follow the rough lines of scheme (1) are more in tune with organizations whose general culture is less market-driven, while scheme (2) probably has greater appeal to firms that value precision and project a general culture of listening to the market (although see below).

Economists usually sneer at attempts to tie appropriate wages to positions based on an artificial scale of value. Wages, according to economics, should reflect conditions of demand *and* supply. The sort of scale constructed in schemes such as

(1) *might* capture something of what is important in the demand for labor services, but it misses the supply side. Schemes that estimate weights from wage data—that is, schemes like (2)—potentially come closer to impounding both demand and supply factors, but they still miss the impact of factors omitted from the job analyses. Suppose, for instance, that this sort of analysis led to the conclusion that driving trucks and typing manuscripts are equally "valuable" and so should command the same pay. What if, for some inexplicable reason, driving trucks is more fun, holding pay equal, so no one wants (at these equal wages) to type reports?[1] What should someone with a report that needs to be typed do? Economists presume that the answer is *pay more to get the report typed,* an answer so compelling to the person needing typing services that more pay will inevitably be offered. Or suppose, in a full-service law partnership, legal assistants are paid uniformly. A partner who defends common criminals and whose assistant spends much of his time going to and from the county jail will have a harder time finding a competent assistant than will the partner who represents movie stars in contract negotiations, and whose assistant spends time hobnobbing with the clients. Economists presume that the first partner will find some way to increase the compensation of her assistant, to compensate for the relatively less desirable job characteristics. In other words, the economist's religious belief in market forces leads him to the view that if Hay points are used to value and thus price jobs, the prices so derived will survive only to the extent that they are close to market prices. Otherwise, market forces will take over and push them to where they ought to be.

Is the stereotypical economist's belief in market forces justified? The answer is something of a tautology. If competition in the labor market is strong—if workers are highly mobile and well informed, and if neither side of the market acts collectively or colludes—then any attempt to use a Hay point system or something similar will be eaten away by market forces, to the extent (which may not be large) that the Hay point system doesn't result in wages that match market conditions. But the condition *If competition in the labor market is strong* is not there just for show. Jobs are rarely identical and, as we saw in Chapter 4, when an employee's tenure with the employer increases, more and more relation-specific assets tend to build up, weakening further the force of competition in dictating wages. You might choose your brand of toothpaste to save a few cents (and, if you don't, someone on the margin will), but it is much less likely that someone would choose one employer over another on account of a few extra dollars a week in compensation. And *changing* an employer based on such minor differences is less likely still. To the extent that labor markets aren't perfectly competitive, procedural and distributive justice in salary–wage administration become important for promoting good relations in the workplace, and a Hay-type system, with its gloss of objectivity, can promote feelings of justice. Indeed, the effect might well be circular: To the extent that employees value equity, an administered wage system that promotes feelings of equity *on that account* may be better protected from market forces.[2]

Hay-type systems can have a dark side in terms of perpetuating discrimination: Job characteristics can be chosen in ways that replicate a pattern of discrimination in the local market. For instance, jobs may be categorized as clerical versus administrative, or as indoor versus outdoor, in ways that match patterns of discrimination by gender. If local labor market wages reflect gender discrimination, then estimates of the "value" of these characteristics based on regression analysis will support the notion that (to take the obvious cases) administrative jobs should be paid more than clerical jobs, and outdoor work paid more than indoor work. Furthermore, evidence indicates that organizations are more likely to create unique job titles for white males, whereas women and people of color are more likely to be grouped into larger, less-specialized job categories. Some scholars have argued that this has the effect of tending to insulate white males more from market comparisons, because their job classifications are more idiosyncratic and thus harder to peg to the external labor market. Moreover, some studies have shown that when market wage data are gathered for a subset of benchmark jobs and then used to determine the relative wages among the remaining jobs within an organization, the pay of female-dominated job titles tends to be pegged to the pay of the female-dominated benchmarks, perpetuating discrimination.[3] And critics have argued that past inequalities are perpetuated by the common practice of conducting separate job evaluation and benchmarking studies within different occupational groups—for instance, separate studies for blue-collar versus white-collar clerical positions, or for managerial versus nonmanagerial jobs, rather than a single study that embraces the full range of positions within the organization. The claim is that by conducting studies that only compare, say, managerial (or blue-collar) jobs to other jobs in that same occupational family, inequities associated with privileged treatment of one group—such as managers or skilled blue-collar workers, who tend to be male—may be masked.

Believing that jobs dominated by women tend to be systematically devalued in organizations and that women have limited opportunities to redress this inequity by shifting to male-dominated jobs, some feminists advocate a policy of *comparable worth,* whereby employers are required to calibrate the worth of jobs according to objective standards and ensure that gender (or race) composition has no direct bearing on pay. Opposition to such a policy comes, predictably, from those who believe that such a large-scale system of legislatively mandated and administered wages would introduce large-scale and irremediable imbalances between supply and demand, and that no matter how noble the intent, this cure would do more social and economic harm than good.[4] In addition, some feminists who support the intent oppose the particular solution, worrying that—given the discriminatory features of job evaluation and wage benchmarking systems summarized above—comparable worth might simply institutionalize and justify inequitable treatment of female-dominated jobs or reduce the incentive for young women to enter occupations previously dominated by men.

Status Within the Organization

There are some cases—especially in star roles, such as sales, professional athletics, and surgery—in which it is viewed as legitimate to pay a nominal subordinate more than his or her nominal supervisor. No one quibbles with paying a top athlete more than his coach, or a star surgeon more than the director of her hospital. This legitimacy is often market-based or, at least, market-excused; the extraordinary compensation is legitimate because this is what it takes to retain the individual.

But with these exceptions noted, superiors are generally paid more than their subordinates. This promotes status consistency (see Chapter 5) and generally confers legitimacy both to status distinctions and to the compensation system. But it raises some substantial problems, to which we will return in Chapter 16, when we discuss promotion.

Seniority

Firms will often pay higher wages to more experienced workers based on their seniority, either in terms of chronological age or, more often, tenure in the job or organization. This tendency for earnings to rise with age and seniority is well-established empirically, though the magnitude of the age–experience premium varies considerably across settings.

Numerous explanations have been offered for these rising age– and seniority–earnings profiles. For instance, in some societies, especially those of East Asia, age confers status, and rising age–earnings profiles are (then) rationalized as a manifestation of status consistency. But the data do not indicate a substantially greater age or seniority wage premium in, say, Japan than in the EC or the United States.[5] In settings governed by collective bargaining, unions will generally favor contract provisions that reward the most politically powerful members within the union, who are often the older, more senior employees. As we recounted in Chapter 6, the data do suggest a greater emphasis on seniority (in wages *and* in other work rights) in unionized settings, at least in the United States.

Older workers and/or workers with greater seniority may be more valuable to their employers. Their skill level is usually greater and they are more stable workers (lower absenteeism and quit rates). Or, looking at the other side of this coin, firms may be providing inexperienced workers with on-the-job training, which will benefit the employee by raising his pay in the future, in this job or in others. The classic case of this is the apprenticeship system, in which a trainee works for very low wages—perhaps below the value provided by the worker—to learn a trade. (We will discuss training in general and apprenticeship in particular in Chapter 15.) However, the slope of observed age–earnings profiles seems too high and persists for too long for these to be entirely adequate explanations.

Other explanations stress the role that such wage patterns can play in motivating and screening workers. As we noted in Chapter 11, rising wage profiles can serve as a dynamic incentive device by which firms seek to reduce turnover. Employees are paid less than their value to the firm early in their careers but later are paid more than what they produce for the firm. In a sense, the firm is "saving" some of the employee's early earnings, releasing those savings to the employee later in life. An employee who quits the firm before retirement would forfeit a portion of his or her accrued savings; this ties the employee to the firm more effectively than if the age–earnings profile were flatter and reflected current contributions to the firm. In a related fashion, rising wage profiles will be more attractive to prospective employees who believe they are more likely to remain with the firm long enough to harvest these "savings." Put the other way around, individuals who are highly mobile are on that account alone less likely to apply for and take a job where rewards are received after long tenure. Thus, organizations with these pay policies will attract an inherently more stable workforce.

Allied to these explanations are several that are more social-psychological in nature. In a variant of gift exchange, workers who have just joined the firm may be thought of as initiates into the "clan," whereas those who have high tenure have become full-fledged members. There is substantial symbolic appeal to the notion that the gifts given by the firm in the form of premium compensation should go more to those whose long service has established their loyalty to the enterprise. And because compensation confers status, at least to some extent, a firm that rewards longevity will promote the status of its more senior workers. This has a positive impact to the extent that the organization wants its more senior workers to be "leaders" in the workforce.

The practice of rewarding chronological age or longevity has some drawbacks, however. Insofar as the worker faces some uncontrollable uncertainty about his or her tenure in the job—for example, the worker's spouse may get a good job in another location—this injects a degree of uncertainty into the employee's compensation that isn't necessary. In other words, although such arrangements may have positive incentive effects, they may be suboptimal in terms of risk. And because these rewards are delayed and, therefore, somewhat contingent on the employer's continued good will, they place employees in an increasingly poor bargaining position vis-à-vis their employers. Employees who appreciate either of these effects will demand higher average wages, averaged over the life of their employment, to compensate.

Indeed, the willingness of workers to delay receipt of their rewards decreases as average tenures in a particular job become shorter. The shortened tenures can result from: voluntary turnover, as worker mobility increases; less-voluntary turnover (for example, as the need for two-earner families to find suitable employment for both parties rises); and involuntary turnover, caused for instance by the recently fashionable practices of downsizing and reengineering (see Chapters 17 and 18). Recall our discussion in Chapter 9 of the changing environment facing elite Japanese firms. These changes include increasing status associated with working for firms that don't adhere to the time-honored HR system of the first-tier Japanese firms and that are willing to raid the elite firms for their best young workers. This is putting substantial pressure on the elite firms to raise the wages of younger workers, pressure that is growing with the rise of two-earner families and the increasing difficulty first-tier firms are having in making credible their promises of lifetime employment.

Finally, in some contexts, offering wages that increase with tenure can hurt the firm directly. Where skills and/or knowledge obsolesce quickly, it makes little sense to promote low turnover among more senior workers or confer status on those who, increasingly, are "out of it." For such firms, rewards given here-and-now for work done here-and-now make greater sense.

Pay for Skill, Knowledge, and Credentials

Firms increasingly are paying explicitly for bundles of skill or knowledge that employees acquire during their employment. A worker entering employment is given a base wage that will be increased formulaically as the worker demonstrates the ability to carry out certain tasks. Teachers and other professionals are often paid more if they acquire credentials through off-the-job study or successfully complete certain training programs. The direct rationale for such pay policies is clear: A more skillful or better trained employee is more valuable to the organization, and paying for skills, knowledge, or credentials gives employees a motivation to obtain the valuable skills and knowledge. But do not overlook less direct rationales: Such pay policies can promote worker retention because they give employees a chance to grow on the job. They attract workers who are more likely to grow on the job and who, in consequence, are probably more flexible and "trainable." And they confer status on more skilled and knowledgeable employees.

High-commitment HR firms are often particularly strong advocates of skill- or knowledge-based pay, because they want to give employees the incentive to be able to do more, thus to be more flexible and to understand better the workings of the entire firm. Japanese auto assembly firms, for example, practice this sort of system for their school-leaver blue-collar workers. It is a system that meshes well with a strategy predicated on innovation and with an organizational culture that emphasizes human potential and learning new things. It is also generally viewed as a legitimate basis for pay, at least insofar as the skills that are acquired are connected to the tasks carried out by workers.

A recent study by Murray and Gerhart of the implementation of a skills-based pay program in one plant provides some compelling evidence of how adopting such programs can benefit the bottom line.[6] The authors focused on an assembly facility within a large American manufacturing company that adopted a skills-based pay plan. They assessed the impact of the program by conducting statistical analyses of cost, quality, and productivity outcomes before and after the plan was adopted and, for some outcomes, by comparing the treatment facility to a matched control facility within the same corporation. Their time-series analyses controlled for a number of factors that might be expected to affect quality and productivity outcomes, such as equipment changes, wage rates, and periods in which layoffs, quality task forces, and just-in-time processes were implemented in the treatment or comparison facility. Despite the fact that wage rates grew in the treatment facility as workers ascended the skill ladder, after adoption of the skills-based pay system the facility experienced significantly higher productivity (variable labor hours per part declined by 58%), 16% lower labor costs per part, and superior quality outcomes (scrap increased by 66% at the control facility, but only by 12% in the treatment site).

But, as Murray and Gerhart concede, pay for skill or knowledge is not without problems and challenges, at least as generally implemented. Workers can "top out" fairly quickly; after a few years in the organization, all the skills have been learned, and the motivation and excitement that come with progressing is gone. Workers sometimes become motivated not by acquisition of new skills or knowledge *per se,* but rather by the money this brings in; the acquisition and use of new competencies, which can be a source of substantial intrinsic motivation, is objectified, where the object is money. To deal with the topping-out problem, firms will sometimes increase the list of competencies for which it is willing to pay, by adding capabilities that will seldom be used by the worker, leading to an "overqualified" and (more to the point) overpaid workforce. Moreover, firms that have experimented with pay for knowledge and skill have found that this is a case where complementarity and consistency among HR practices is crucial. The value of paying for skill or knowledge is enhanced through job redesigns that create real opportunities to use the knowledge and skills the employee has developed; changes in recruitment and selection practices; new performance management techniques; HR information systems that provide an up-to-date inventory of the skills and competencies possessed by the workforce; employment security to reassure workers that they will not be discharged once they move up to the top of the pay hierarchy; and the like.

Salaries or Wages?

Employees who aren't paid by piece-rates or some other very direct form of pay for performance are usually paid based on time on the job. The rate of pay per unit of time may depend on job title or seniority or the skills acquired, but nonetheless the wages are expressed as so much per hour or so much salary per month or year. In general, the distinction between wage versus salary compensation is this: Individuals who punch a time clock or whose time on the job is closely monitored earn wages by the hour; those whose schedules are less intrusively monitored earn salaries.

The traditional distinction is clear. Salaries are paid to those for whom managing their own time is an important aspect of the job. Wages are paid to those who find their workday controlled to a much greater extent by management. Of course, there are exceptions to this rule: Members of craft unions—the pressmen who run the large printing presses of newspapers, for instance—are typically paid wages, but they also have (through their shop steward) a great deal of task autonomy and control over their working hours.

In the United States, the hourly versus salaried distinction is institutionalized within the Fair Labor Standards Act (FLSA), dating back to 1938. Individual states have their own statutes in this domain as well. The FLSA mandates that all "nonexempt" employees be paid on an hourly basis, at or above the federal minimum wage, and be eligible for overtime pay of at least 150% of their regular wage rate for hours worked in excess of 40 per week. These rules apply unless pay is not reduced for periods of absence *and* the position meets one of various exemptions defined in Department of Labor regulations. Interpretation and enforcement of the FLSA are quite complicated and the subject of considerable legal activity, but the main exemptions to these requirements involve: (a) jobs whose duties are primarily executive or managerial, with at least half the employee's time spent on management of two or more full-time employees; (b) administrative positions in which the occupant exercises discretion, independent judgment, and authority to carry out (nonclerical) office work relating directly to management policies and general business operations (e.g., HR specialist, marketing analyst, purchasing agent); or (c) professional positions requiring advanced knowledge in a field of science or learning and the consistent exercise of discretion, judgment, or innovation (e.g., lawyers, physicians, artists).

As you might imagine, in today's economy the boundary between nonexempt and exempt positions has become increasingly difficult to pinpoint, so much so that numerous employers have faced costly legal problems for failing to comply with the FLSA.[7] What was initially a fairly straightforward traditional distinction between those who commanded and those who followed orders, based on the technology of work, may to a large extent now reflect social, historical, and legal influences. The murkiness between nonexempt and exempt positions becomes particularly evident as firms experiment with new forms of organization that intentionally seek to blur the distinctions among the categories of owner, manager, and worker (see Chapter 9). Especially among firms practicing high-commitment HRM, there has been a move toward putting wage earners "on salary." (Movement in the opposite direction—people previously on salary moving to hourly wages— can arise in the context of outsourcing; see Chapter 18.) It is clear that the symbolic character of the change is the primary driver here; if a firm wishes to promote a one-big-team culture, blurring distinctions between "labor" and "management," this is a very nice note to hit. Moreover, in high-commitment HR settings, it is generally desirable that individual workers (and, even more, teams of individuals who previously were all closely supervised wage-earners) become autonomous and self-directed, characteristics typically associated with salaries instead of wages. Finally, wages and the time clock that almost inevitably accompanies them make time-on-the-job highly salient to the employee—one works to see the seconds and minutes fly (or crawl) by—which is bad for a firm seeking to enhance intrinsic motivation and greater feelings of psychological ownership. But bear in mind that the desire to create a less hierarchical, more empowered organization is not sufficient to exempt an employer from the complicated wage and hour regulations and record-keeping requirements associated with the FLSA and its counterpart statutes at the state level. We underscore that this is a legally sensitive area; informed expert legal advice is strongly encouraged.

Ranges and Levels

We close this section with a brief discussion of a very common form of wages: Each job is classified, and each job classification comes with a range of wages, often broken into a discrete number of steps. Hence, the assistant to the VP for Marketing is an Administrative Assistant III, who happens to be on Step 4 out of six steps within that grade. The job is an AA-III because of certain criteria that are met: amount of independent work done, amount of work that is delegated out, responsibility for (say) maintaining the calendar of the boss, and so on.

We live with such a system at Stanford University, and based both on our personal experience and more systematic analyses of such systems by others, we can note the following advantages. As in any "scientifically determined" system of wages or wage ranges, there is some perception of procedural justice. By having wages attached to the position, workers are less apt to spend a lot of time politicking for a raise. And the steps act as a mild form of pay for performance.

But there are obvious corresponding deficiencies. Instead of politicking directly for a raise, workers politick for step increases. The steps often become rewards for seniority; workers expect to progress at a certain pace, and a supervisor who doesn't satisfy those expectations does so at his or her own peril. As an employee advances toward the mandated pay ceiling for the position, pay raises are likely to decline in percentage terms, creating perceptions of injustice. And once a worker is "maxed out" at the highest step in a job classification, the only two options for progression are to get the job reclassified or look for a job in a higher classification. The supervisor, worried that valued employees will depart in order to "advance," is often ready and willing to aid in the efforts for job reclassification.

In recent years, many organizations have sought to get out of the trap of having to promote or reclassify employees into a different job classification simply to justify a pay increase, believing that the politicking, proliferation of job titles, and paperwork for managers and HR professionals that this requires is detrimental. The following chapter on job design begins with an example of one such company—British Petroleum—that has moved to streamline its system of job titles and moved to a system of "broadbanding," which permits greater pay differentiation within a given job class. But recall some of the material from the previous two chapters—for instance, our discussion of relative performance evaluation and of the rationales for coarse performance distinctions in Chapter 10; and the sections of Chapter 11 that deal with bonuses versus wage increases—and you'll be able to anticipate some potential costs that come with broadbanding.

DISPERSION, COMPRESSION, AND INFORMATION

In principle, the norm of equity is cardinal: Workers should be paid according to their contributions to the enterprise. In practice, it is probably more ordinal than cardinal: If X contributes more than Y, X should be paid more than Y. But if X contributes twice as much as Y, it isn't necessarily required that X be paid twice what Y gets.

Consequently, to the extent that firms are insulated from market pressures, they can influence the amount of dispersion or compression in their wage structure. For instance, Ben & Jerry's, "hippie" ice cream makers, had a rule that the ratio of the salary of the highest paid employee to the lowest should never exceed 7:1.[8] More generally, organizations like Ben and Jerry's that have a family or clan-like culture usually find that wage compression relative to market-based differentials enhances the culture; equity in a family is more "to each according to his needs" than "according to her contributions," and who has the right to say that a white-collar executive has forty or fifty times the needs of an unskilled worker? Firms that practice high-commitment HRM also tend to compress wages, because of the symbolism that everyone is on the same team, and to break down symbolic barriers between management and workers. And in many societies, certainly Japan and most of Europe, the sort of compensation dispersion observed in U.S. firms is viewed as more than illegitimate; a commonly heard word is *obscene*.

The extent to which firms seek to restrict variation in rewards is likely to depend not only on the societal context, institutional forces (such as unionization[9]), and organizational culture, but also on the organization's strategy, technology, and workforce. Rampant distinctions in status and other rewards among groups are particularly likely to be dysfunctional when quality is important and cooperation among disparate groups is essential to produce it, and when there is a high degree of social and/or task interdependence among employees. Consistent with that conjecture, a study of 102 business units in North America and Europe (primarily U. S. manufacturers) found that organizations with narrower pay differentials (between top executives and line workers and between top executives and first-level managers) were viewed by customers as having significantly higher product quality relative to competitors, even after controlling for differences across the business units in unionization, size, workforce composition, market share, and technology.[10] To cite another body of research, studies of university faculty have demonstrated that—all else being equal—wage dispersion tends to reduce collaboration and job satisfaction. Furthermore, tendencies to compress wages are strongest in those academic settings in which collaboration is most important (e.g., joint research), where social comparison processes are most rampant (e.g., public as opposed to private universities), and where social ties among individuals are most extensive (e.g., colleagues reported more social contact with one another outside of work).[11]

Compressing wage distributions has a price, however. The firm may wind up underpaying its best performers, who might then pick up and leave, or overpaying its worst. Insofar as the firm needs a range of skill levels, from executives to skilled labor to semi- or unskilled labor, either it underpays those on the top, getting the reverse of efficiency wages, or it overpays on the bottom. Indeed, some firms facing this dilemma have sought to manage it by outsourcing both at the bottom and top of their labor needs: Bring in outside legal consultants instead of maintaining an in-house legal office, say, and at the same time, outsource custodial services and warehouse operations. We will discuss outsourcing at some length in Chapter 18.

A related "design" decision concerning compensation is, How much should employees know about it? Should the firm make known its distribution of wages? Should it attach names to particular data points within those distributions, so the compensation of specific individuals can be identified and compared? A certain level of transparency is required by law. In the United States and Canada, for instance, publicly traded firms must list the annual compensation (including stock and option grants and the value of certain other benefits and perquisites) of their five most highly paid executive officers, as well as other information pertaining to compensation of corporate officers and directors. In Germany, the Supervisory Committee, which includes labor representation, will know of (and, indeed, set) top management salaries. In a setting with organized labor present, the details of the union contract are generally accessible to the rank and file. In public sector organizations, individuals are usually able to ascertain the compensation of any employee.

But in many firms, the norm and practice is that individuals keep information about their personal compensation levels to themselves. In Chapter 4, we were lyrical about the openness of information at Sun Hydraulics. But compensation is the exception. Compensation levels are set by . . . well, we can't tell you how, because this is one thing that Koski and the management of Sun do not discuss explicitly. They just do it, and the norms of the organization hold that it is kept quiet.

Though a lot has been written about pay secrecy, the conclusions are ambiguous.[12] It is clear that managers are likely to make less marked pay distinctions when the distribution of pay is common knowledge. On the other hand, insofar as some information about relative standing is necessary for employees to perceive distributive and/or procedural justice, the absence of such information can create unfavorable perceptions of the pay system. In short, there are compelling arguments on both sides of the pay openness versus secrecy debate.

In many settings, it is not an issue of *whether* employees will have some information about the pay distribution, but only an issue of what kinds of information, how detailed, and whether the organization provides the information or allows workers to get it by gossiping. And whether there is active gossip or not, studies show that people tend to assume that differentials are larger than they actually are and to assume that they fared worse in relative terms than they actually did. (This latter tendency, at least, could result from selective revelation of salaries by co-workers. If I'm pretty sure I'm well paid, I brag. If I suspect I fared poorly, I keep my mouth shut and listen with envy. The point is that the cases about which there is gossip will be skewed toward higher pay levels, at least if individuals in the organization have any clue as to how they stand relative to the distribution.) To the extent that this is true, official revelation of the distribution is probably going to improve matters. The downside, of course, is that those who suspected they were paid less than the median now *know* that they were. And there is an issue of atmospherics here; see two paragraphs hence.

In addition, the issue of openness or secrecy about pay and other sensitive HR matters is a pretty strong litmus test of the organization's real values in some fundamental areas: Are employees trusted? Is openness and honesty valued? Are monetary rewards a big deal or are other forms of motivation and reward more valued?, and so on. This needn't be decisive; our sense is that employees at Sun Hydraulics feel trusted and work in an environment where honesty and openness are valued, except when it comes to compensation. But the general level of employee trust at Sun—in the founder (Koski) and the upper echelons of management—is quite extraordinary, so they may be able to play their cards close to the vest when it comes to compensation without engendering undue suspicion. If you haven't built up this kind of trust and want to, secrecy about pay may send the wrong signals.

Cutting against this is the obvious point that making information about salaries or the salary distribution public makes it *salient*. Indeed, such data are sometimes salient to the point of absurdity. Our employer, Stanford University, annually publishes in the university newspaper data about faculty salary distributions by rank, years of service, and area (Arts, Social Sciences, Physical and Biological Sciences, Business, Law, etc.). The data are cooked; indeed, some of the cooking is so blatant that it is publicly acknowledged. For example, the Economics department—whose faculty are paid more than professors in the other social and behavioral sciences—is lumped in with the physical and biological sciences on the grounds that, well . . ., it just fits better there. University professors, by and large, are meant to be fairly sophisticated folks, who understand about cooking numbers. (At least, our colleagues in the Business School ought to know about these things.) But when these data are published, faculty office doors close and, we imagine, the Accounting office gets a lot of phone calls from faculty who long ago forgot exactly what they are making this year and now feel the need to know, "What is my base salary, precisely?"

So where does this leave us on the issue of pay secrecy? We suggest that it is a useful exercise for all organizations and managers, if they are inclined to withhold information regarding the distribution of salaries, to ponder *why* they are doing so. More often than not, an important source of the reticence has to do with managers' concern that openness about pay will unleash a torrent of complaints, requiring awkward and unpleasant conversations with disgruntled subordinates, and whetting employees' appetites for information about other sensitive topics. Our own impressions are: (1) This is not necessarily true. Public sector organizations as well as partnerships, for instance, have to deal with the realities of open salary information, and many HR professionals and managers can attest to the fact that keeping information secret doesn't immunize an organization from complaints! (2) If open information about pay unleashes a torrent of complaints, this strongly indicates that employees either do not understand or do not embrace the organization's performance appraisal and reward allocation systems. The problem here is deeper than, and different from, secrecy about compensation levels. (3) Managers are paid, among other things, to have the occasional awkward and unpleasant conversation. (4) There are a number of fairly compelling anecdotes about companies making dramatic turnarounds through practicing "open-book management" (see Chapter 9), which suggests that an appetite by employees for increasing amounts of information about the enterprise need not be a bad thing. In short, there is potentially much to be learned—about what is valued, about how employees view various aspects of the HR system, and about what motivates managers—from an organization candidly assessing why it provides or withholds particular types of information regarding compensation.

In the final analysis, of course, the case for or against openness regarding compensation depends crucially on the five factors. The desirable amount of openness and information sharing will reflect the technology (interdependence, measurability of tasks, etc.), workforce (occupational mix, demographic heterogeneity, average tenure level, etc.), culture (value placed on openness and self-management, salience of money), and external environment (unionization, legal issues concerning privacy, social norms, etc.). In addition, the organization's system of governance (partnership, public/private, etc.) and strategy may enter the equation. Based on a careful five-factor analysis, we would counsel that an organization or manager make three decisions *before* choosing how much information to release concerning compensation: How much differentiation should exist in pay? How much salience should be attached to pay versus other rewards, including noneconomic rewards? How important a value is openness in general within the enterprise? By making more information available to employees about pay, it will generally be harder within most organizational cultures to differentiate rewards as much across individuals or subunits. Increasing the availability of information about compensation will tend to make compensation more salient and to increase its association with status in employees' minds. Furthermore, given the importance we have placed on consistent cultural messages underpinning an HR system, openness about salaries is likely to be most sensible in an organization which values and encourages openness in general; otherwise, there is the danger that employees will have abundant information about the distribution of pay outcomes, but little or no information about the functioning of the organization to use in calibrating the salary data.

THE FORM OF COMPENSATION (INCLUDING BENEFITS)

Compensation is more than just money paid in the form of wages, salaries, and bonuses. If we really want to stretch the definition, we could include intrinsic or psychic compensation, such as status, independence, power, and so on. For the present we don't want to stretch the definition quite that much, but there remain other important forms of economic compensation. Top-level executives will often be compensated with equity or with options to purchase equity; some firms extend this to line workers through stock-ownership plans (where the compensation part of the program is that stock can be bought at below-market rates). Managers and professionals will be given perquisites, such as a company car, an expense account, and the like. In some organizations, perks will be extended to all workers—all employees of airlines are entitled to cut-rate travel, for instance; and perhaps most significantly, firms compensate their employees with benefits, such as contributions to health care, personal insurance, pensions, and so on.

We've already had our say in Chapter 11 on employee stock ownership programs (ESOPs). But to reiterate: Purely in terms of risk diversification, these programs rarely make economic sense. But the proponents of ESOPs contend that the economics of risk diversification are heavily outweighed by the symbolic effects and the tendency for stock ownership to encourage workers to internalize the firm's interests—workers, who work for top management, own the firm and top management works for the owners, hence everyone is on the same "level." The argument makes a lot of sense, especially when ESOPs are part of an overall high-commitment HR strategy, complementing policies that permit the organization to take maximal advantage of the symbolism and internalization.

TABLE 12-1   Percentage of Full-time Workers Receiving Various Employee Benefits in the United States, 1994–5

	Small Private Establishments, 1994	Small Independent Businesses, 1994	Medium and Large Private Establishments, 1995
Paid Time Off:			
Holidays	82	80	89
Vacations	88	86	96
Personal leave	13	11	22
Funeral leave	50	42	80
Jury duty leave	58	51	85
Military leave	17	11	44
Sick leave	50	44	58
Family leave	2	2	2
Insurance:			
Sickness and accident	26	24	44[a]
Long-term disability	20	14	42
Medical care	66	62	77
Dental care	28	23	57
Life insurance	61	54	87
Retirement:			
Defined benefit pension	15	9	52
Defined contribution pension	34	29	55
Types of plans:			
Savings and thrift	17	12	41
Deferred profit sharing	13	13	13
Employee stock ownership	1	1	5
Money purchase pension	5	5	7
401(k) plans with employer contribution	20	15	45
Other Benefits:			
Flexible benefits plans	3	1	12
Reimbursement accounts	19	11	38
Child care	1	1	8
Unpaid family leave	47	37	84

Source: U.S. Bureau of Labor Statistics (http://stats.bls.gov/ebshome.htm). Data for small establishments (fewer than 100 employees) are for 1994; data for medium and large establishments are for 1995. Employment in small establishments represented about 55% of total private nonfarm employment. Small independent businesses are those small establishments that are not part of larger businesses.

[a]Definition of this item changed in 1995; the figure shown here for medium and large establishments is for 1993, the most recent date when a definition comparable to that used for small establishments was employed in surveying medium and large establishments.

As for executive stock options or grants of equity to upper-level management, these are usually rationalized as pay for performance; the executive is given an ownership stake in the organization so that she will better attend to the interests of equity holders, or she is given stock options that will be worthless unless she improves (or maintains) the value of equity. The general topic of executive compensation is extraordinarily controversial at the moment, and we have little to add to this controversy, so we simply steer clear of it, except to make one obvious point. Firms that pay their top managers extraordinary amounts can run into problems if they simultaneously are seeking to implement a teamlike culture (or high-commitment HR), or if they are in the midst of programs of downsizing and/or outsourcing, citing financial pressures as an excuse. (We'll have a bit more to say about the general level of top management pay in Chapter 16, when we discuss promotion.)

In terms of dollars, except for the really extraordinary option packages given lately to some U.S. top managers, the action in terms of noncash compensation concerns benefits. So that is the focus of most of this section.

The Prevalence of Benefits and Perquisites

We begin with some data describing how prevalent (and valuable) benefits and perquisites are. Data describing the prevalence of benefits and perks for U.S. employees are shown in Tables 12-1 and 12-2. Table 12-1 reports information on the percentage of full-time employees in different work settings who are covered by various employee benefits. The table underscores not only that employee benefits vary considerably by size of firm, with large enterprises generally providing much more comprehensive benefits,[13] but also that there is considerable variation in how institutionalized particular benefits have become. For instance, despite considerable ballyhoo lately in the business press, access to such benefits as employee stock ownership and employer-subsidized child care is still quite limited. Moreover, Bureau of Labor Statistics data (not in Table 12-1) indicate that the availability of benefits varies markedly across employee categories. For instance, within medium and large enterprises, 15% of professional and technical workers have access to employer-subsidized child care, while access to these benefits is virtually *nonexistent* among the other occupational groups in these establishments.[14] In contrast, some employee benefits, such as medical care and various types of paid leave, are commonplace across most work settings and available to the vast majority of full-time employees.

Table 12-2 summarizes the monetary cost of these benefits, showing variations across different types of occupations and work settings. The aggregate costs are really quite striking. It is worth noting that the average hourly cost of benefits for civilian workers in the United States ($5.47 in March 1998) exceeds the legally mandated federal minimum wage ($5.15, as of September 1, 1997). Even in those settings providing the least extensive perquisites—such as small enterprises, service occupations, and the nonunion sector—the absolute cost of benefits is considerable, representing at least one-quarter of total payroll expenditures.

TABLE 12-2 **Benefits Costs in the United States, March 1998**

	Hourly Benefits Cost	% of Total Compensation
U. S. civilian labor force	$5.47	27.7%
White-collar occupations	$6.32	26.5%
Blue-collar occupations	$5.55	31.1%
Service occupations	$2.90	26.3%
State/local government	$8.10	29.7%
Unionized employees (private sector)	$8.22	34.8%
Nonunion employees (private sector)	$4.58	25.7%
Private sector establishments with:		
1–99 employees	$3.91	24.6%
100–499 employees	$4.85	27.7%
500 + employees	$7.78	30.4%

Source: U.S. Bureau of Labor Statistics (http://stats.bls.gov/news.release/ecec.nws.htm).

Why Don't Smaller Firms Provide as Many Benefits?

Both these tables show clearly that smaller firms are less likely to provide benefits. Why is this? In part, size is correlated with some other factors that clearly are at work. For instance, unions generally pursue benefits for their members—recall the union–voice story of Chapter 6—and smaller firms are generally less likely to be unionized. But a more direct effect is probably most responsible: Benefits administration comes with substantial overhead costs. There are economies and advantages to the employer of providing benefits as opposed to giving the money directly to employees (see below). But there are costs as well. The major cost is restricted choice for employees. In addition, there are costs of administration to worry about. Some administrative costs rise with the number of employees. But as the employment rolls grow, fixed administrative costs can be increasingly amortized over the employee base. Thus, the bottom line (advantages less costs) for benefits is more likely to work out in favor of providing benefits, the larger is the organization.

A related explanation that is sometimes heard is that small firms are less likely to have formalized HR systems or an HR Department, which would (in most cases) take charge of designing and administering benefits. This, in large measure, is the fixed-cost argument at one remove: Smaller firms are less likely to have HR departments primarily because they are less able to amortize the fixed costs over their smaller workforce.

As we discuss in Chapters 18 and 20, independent HRM contractors have become increasingly commonplace in recent years, playing the economic role of managing the HR function (e.g., compensation and payroll, government compliance, benefits administration) for smaller firms. A fairly new innovation, the professional employer organization (PEO), extends this role even further, serving as the formal employer and manager of record for individuals who have an enduring assignment/relationship with one of the PEO's client companies.[15] In other words, the PEO is the employer and HR manager for most or all of the individuals who, on a daily basis, show up to work at your firm. Near the top of the list of advantages that PEOs are claimed to provide for employers and employees are superior quality and reduced costs of benefits (and of benefits administration). In addition, from the employee's perspective, the benefits may be more portable, as workers unhappy with or discharged from one assignment can move to another client firm within the PEO's portfolio without any change in benefits coverage or eligibility.

To a very large extent, the existence and growth of these various types of HR contractors is rationalized by the economies-to-scale notion at work in the previous two paragraphs; by managing HR matters (and/or serving as the employer of record) for multiple firms, these contractors are better able to amortize fixed costs. It is reasonable to conjecture that as contractors playing the role of HR manager for multiple organizations become more prevalent in the economy, benefits coverage at smaller firms will increasingly come to resemble benefits coverage at larger firms, at least insofar as the explanation for the lower coverage is fixed costs.

Economies in Firm-Procured Benefits and Perks

On strictly economic grounds, one might question why a firm should include benefits and perks in its compensation package. If employees can purchase the benefits or perks as cheaply as can the firm, why not just give the money spent on the benefits to the employee and let the employee choose how to spend it? (Cafeteria-style benefits programs, discussed further on, do some of this.) There are at least two sets of reasons why this argument doesn't hold water. First, there are reasons why the firm may be able to purchase benefits or perks at lower prices or higher quality than individual workers can. Second, giving compensation to employees in the form of certain types of benefits or perks can change the employees' behavior and quality of work, to the advantage of the firm. (The second set of reasons is stretched to include the value of benefits in screening for a particular sort of job applicant; see Chapter 14 and below.)

Perhaps the most obvious way in which firms have an economic advantage in purchasing certain benefits and perks is that the purchase is tax-advantaged. To take an example, if the firm contributes to a pension fund, this is not taxed at the outset, nor are any accrued earnings taxed. Eventually, workers must pay taxes on their pension payments; however, insofar as this smooths the individual's income stream, it can be a tax-reducing device.[16] And some perks are tax advantaged, although, in the United States at least, there has been a long-term secular trend toward diminishing if not totally closing these tax "loopholes." For instance, consider an employee who, absent a corporate membership, would pay a monthly membership of $100 to a local gym. Even if the employer weren't able to use its market power to negotiate a better deal for its employees than the $100 retail rate (see below), employees would still prefer a corporate membership paid for by a $100 monthly reduction in gross pay rather than paying for the gym membership directly.

This is because the salary reduction is in pretax dollars, whereas the $100 monthly payment to the gym would (presumably) not be tax-deductible; consequently, the advantage is especially large for employees in higher tax brackets.

A second savings arises from a combination of economies of scale and the exercise of market power in purchasing certain benefits. Insofar as the purchase of different forms of savings or health care involves knowledge, the firm can employ a benefits officer who will specialize in this knowledge and, through the purchase of benefits, put this knowledge to use for all employees. When a firm goes to a health care provider to purchase health care for all of its employees, the per capita administrative costs—collecting fees, obtaining names and information, and so on—are dramatically reduced relative to having each individual employee deal with the health care provider. At the same time, because the firm is going to purchase a large amount of health care, it may be better able to negotiate a good price by exploiting its market power.

Finally, when an individual purchases health care, health insurance, life insurance, or an annuity (which is to some extent what certain forms of pensions represent), the problem of adverse selection obviously arises. The provider or insurance firm must worry that people who know privately they are sick will be more likely to purchase health care, health insurance, and life insurance—and to purchase more of them—than those who are well, and they will be less likely to purchase annuities. When the firm purchases some of these things for all of its employees in a block, the adverse selection problem usually is greatly reduced.

Note well, each of these rationales for employer-provided benefits gives a reason for extending benefits coverage to members of employees' families (in the first case, to the extent allowed by the tax code).

Impacts on Productivity (Through Employee Motivation, in Particular)

A second set of justifications for employer-provided benefits and perks concerns their impacts on productivity, through *screening* (helping the firm attract and retain more able employees) and *motivation* (helping to elicit superior performance). One fairly straightforward story is that employer-provided health care, especially when it comes from a health maintenance organization (HMO), is simply an investment by the firm in the maintenance of its human capital. Employees who become sick will be unable to work as well as those who are healthy; the firm—insofar as it gains some surplus in the employment of the worker—bears some of the cost of this. Being gruesome about it, if the employee dies, the firm loses its investments in having trained the employee. Thus, the firm wants to make it cheaper and easier for the worker to stay healthy and to seek health care when symptoms first appear, rather than when they become severe. Taking this a step further, a worker with sick family members and large medical bills to pay can be distracted on the job or forced to moonlight. Both of these can adversely affect the quality of work provided; better for the firm to provide insurance against these things.[17]

Pensions and other retirement benefits are often cited as an incentive device in two respects. First, to the extent that pensions do not vest fully in the employee, or to the extent that pension benefits and contributions rise with tenure at the firm, this gives employees a powerful incentive to remain with the firm. This, in turn, lessens voluntary quits, saving on training and turnover-related costs, and acting as a discipline on employees, who don't wish to give management any grounds for discharge. A related rationale for compensation systems with delayed benefits (such as pensions) is that they are relatively more attractive to relatively more stable workers, thus acting as a screening device for a valuable type of employee. Recall that both these rationales were also advanced earlier in this chapter for seniority-based compensation in general, so they are incomplete as explanations for compensation in the form of pensions *per se*. But, pensions and retirement benefits—especially defined-benefit forms of pensions—give the firm a lever with which to induce retirement of workers, which can be especially important as enforced retirement becomes illegal.[18]

As for perks, some types—such as a company car and driver, or use of an executive jet—can be rationalized as enhancing productivity. A top executive might choose to drive herself to work, but the value to the firm of her output in the back seat of a company car outweighs the cost of the car and driver, even taking into account the "cost" of forcing this choice on her rather than giving her the money. Company planes facilitate easier travel, in conditions more conducive to working while traveling. And some of these items are status symbols, with a positive impact on the attitudes of customers and suppliers.

Benefits and perks can also be particularly powerful symbols of gift exchange, moving the employment relationship from one with purely economic connotations to something more along the lines of a kin or friendship relationship. Salary, wages, and even bonus payments all have the connotation of an economic exchange, in which (according to certain social norms, at least) each party should attempt to extract for itself the best possible (narrowly selfish) deal. Some forms of benefits and perks are of an entirely different flavor and can cause the worker to respond with reciprocal gifts or by internalizing the welfare of the organization. As examples of benefits that are strongly symbolic of gifts, consider gift packages distributed at Christmas and Easter or on other holidays, or bottles of wine given out on the employee's birthday, especially when employees observe that these gifts are personalized to the employee rather than generic. Benefits that are intended to meet special personal needs of employees, such as parental leave or carseats for newborn children, have particularly strong connotations as gifts, because they are not given out uniformly but instead to members of the corporate "family" that have special needs. Note that especially insofar as benefits are intended to have the connotations of a gift, extension of benefits to family members is a very logical symbolic action to take.

To give one further example, we know of a case in which a very strong-culture firm provided a group of executives with a certain number of hours of personal financial management counseling, rather than giving them the cash equivalent with which to purchase those services (or something else). Why not give the executives the dollar value of the services with, perhaps, the phone number of a good financial planner, in case the recipient might choose to purchase financial management counseling? According to the Director of Benefits for this company, who insisted on providing the gift of services, rather than cash: "We felt the financial services were more of an ego thing."

The idea of benefits as gifts is intended to foster positive associations between employer and employee. On other social grounds, benefits are sometimes given to prevent negative associations. When most employers in an area, or even just the leading employers, add dental insurance to the benefits package, for instance, employees at other firms are likely to conclude that they are similarly entitled—if their employers don't add dental benefits, employees may decide that they are being mistreated, reacting accordingly.

Thus, the psychological leverage associated with providing benefits is likely to depend on whether the employer is a pioneer in providing this perquisite or instead perceived to be simply matching the competition. Consider, for instance, the difference between being the first firm in your industry to offer full benefits to employees' domestic partners—a move that involves not only financial costs but also potential negative reaction in some quarters—versus being one of the last in the industry to do so, perceived by employees either as having been dragged kicking and screaming all the way or as having made a cold, crass cost-benefit calculation. Along the same lines, in discussing gift exchange and reciprocity in Chapter 5, we said that the psychological impact of a gift depends on how needy the recipient is, how much the gift is tailored specifically to the individual recipient, how deep the donor's pockets are perceived to be, and whether the gift is perceived as being given for ulterior motives. This suggests some obvious factors that are likely to influence how much a firm's benefits package and its process of administering benefits promotes goodwill among the workforce. In addition, culture—both outside and inside the firm—will obviously affect the psychological significance of a particular benefit. In Great Britain, for instance, company cars have traditionally been viewed as an important perquisite for management, more than in some other countries.

Other Rationales for Benefits

There are several other rationales for providing benefits that don't fit neatly into either of the two preceding categories but which deserve mention nonetheless. First, firms sometimes act paternalistically, arguing that workers would not utilize the additional cash as wisely as the benefits. For instance, the firm might want to ensure that employees consume a certain amount of health care rather than spend the corresponding cash compensation on general consumption items. Second, providing specific kinds of benefits may help a firm attract specific kinds of workers and distinguish itself in the labor market, relative to simply providing equivalent cash compensation. A firm that is known for providing ample child care and family leave benefits, for instance, may be more effective in telegraphing what kind of workplace it is and in attracting particular kinds of employees than if it simply gave workers as salary the per capita cost of these benefits.

Finally, benefits can sometimes be used indirectly to deliver extra compensation to groups favored by management.[19] For example, if the firm wishes to offer extra compensation to workers with families, it can extend health care or educational benefits to family members. If management wishes to increase the compensation of men over women and is prevented from doing so by antidiscrimination laws, the firm can offer benefits packages that are, in subtle ways, relatively favorable to men. For instance, the health care benefits offered may be generous in providing for cardiac rehabilitation, alcoholism, or the treatment of smokers' ailments, but not for, say, infertility; or more generous with regard to military and educational leaves (likely to be more common among men) than dependent care leaves (more common among women).[20] Finally, management may wish to channel extra compensation to itself, especially in ways that are less direct and quantifiable than through salary, such as automobile allowances, subsidized housing loans, and club memberships. The key in all this is (lack of) transparency and the norm of equity: Management may wish to provide extra rewards to a particular group or class; benefits and perks often provide a means of doing so without being as obvious about it, or even, in some cases, in a form that seems legitimate and equitable.

Cafeteria Benefits

An increasingly popular scheme for structuring employee benefits is the so-called cafeteria approach. Employees are given a "budget" of funds for purchasing benefits and a list of available benefits with internal prices. The head of a young family can spend more of the benefit budget on child care or life insurance; a young single worker could spend more on educational programs or recreational and travel-related activities; and a middle-aged employee might spend more on vision care or purchase "elder care" coverage, anticipating a parent in failing health.[21] Some care must be taken in designing these schemes to satisfy tax authorities, but it can be done.

The main advantage of this sort of scheme should be clear: If benefits in general reduce workers' discretion concerning how their compensation will be spent, cafeteria plans give back at least some of that discretion. The economic motivations for benefits—tax efficiencies, efficiencies of scale in procurement and administration, market power, reduced problems of adverse selection—all continue to apply, as do some of the employee-response motivations: Because the firm controls the list, it can direct expenditures at least somewhat; and employees can use some of this money to meet critical needs.

Note, however, that some of the economic motivations may be diluted to some extent under a cafeteria plan. For example, economies of scale may be reduced somewhat by virtue of employees choosing to allocate benefit entitlements across various benefit categories or, within a particular category, among various providers, such as different HMOs. And cafeteria plans may exacerbate adverse selection problems by giving employees the ability to allocate benefit budgets into particular categories—for example, health care, dental care, vision coverage, legal services—based on private information. Furthermore, cafeteria benefit systems may also transform benefits administration into something more clearly economic in character, potentially harming the gift-exchange effects that the employer sought to create.

COMPENSATION—THE BOTTOM LINE

It should be clear from what (and how much!) we've had to say in the previous chapter and this one that the topic of compensation is enormously complex. Indeed, although we have not made a scientific survey, it seems likely to us that more has been written about compensation than any other topic in HRM. This is entirely natural; compensation is usually the most salient reward for working and thus will be of enormous concern to everyone involved. Despite the number of pages we have devoted to the topic in this chapter and the last one, we have barely scratched the surface of the relevant theory and evidence bearing on the design and administration of compensation systems.

This is a domain where simplistic takeaways are particularly hard to come by and likely to be misleading, but we think there are several important implications of what we have had to say about compensation that bear summarizing here. The first issue an organization needs to consider in thinking about compensation is how much it wants to rely on direct, shorter-term economic incentives, versus longer-term economic rewards—for example, promotion or stock ownership—or nonmonetary forms of motivation. We spent considerable time reviewing the factors that made pay for performance effective at Safelite Glass, noting how organizations confronting different strategies, technologies, workforces, cultures, or environments could expect very different consequences of adopting a scheme like Safelite's. Because paying for individual or group performance may prove to be problematic or even dysfunctional in some settings, we spent some time at the beginning of this chapter reviewing some other ways in which organizations allocate compensation and the circumstances under which these may be appropriate.

Second, throughout this book we have urged managers not to lose sight of the powerful social and psychological forces that motivate people and that influence their reactions to any reward system. This has led us to put strong emphasis on the *processes* by which performance is evaluated and rewards are distributed in an organization, which are likely to have a profound impact on perceptions of distributive and procedural justice. In this chapter, we have placed particular emphasis on the degree of pay dispersion maintained and the amount of information provided to employees about the reward distribution. We suggested that these are two other crucial design decisions that an organization should ponder, employing a comprehensive five-factor analysis.

Reflecting back on some of the organizations whose reward systems we have thus far examined in this book—such as Safelite, Lincoln Electric, Portman Hotel, IBM, Sears Auto Centers—underscores the importance of aligning reward systems with the five factors. Equally important, we have seen how the difference between effective and ineffective compensation systems hinges on closely aligning an organization's reward practices—the form, bases, distribution, and openness of reward allocations—with the other elements of its HR system. In deciding on a particular reward system, a firm will want to be sure that it can attract and retain employees who are well-suited to its particular system of evaluating performance and allocating rewards. We take up this topic in Chapter 14. An organization will also want to consider the anticipated longevity of employment and the sequence of activities that it expects employees to carry out over time. This, in turn, will shape the degree to which it relies on training and promotion, two of the most important nonpecuniary "rewards" that a firm can give to workers. Training and promotion are more than rewards, however. Training improves the firm's human capital, and promotion is an allocation device for getting more able workers into more important slots in the organization. Thus, training and promotion are complex topics in their own right, so we devote a chapter to each one: training in Chapter 15 and promotion in Chapter 16.

As we noted toward the end of Chapter 11, there are often numerous ways of organizing a given activity that can be equally effective. For instance, recall the highly interdependent teams of Xerox repair technicians, versus the more individualistic, "independent contributor" model that other technicians followed, both of which worked quite well according to a variety of metrics. Similarly, in examining the HR systems of technology start-ups later in this book (Chapter 19), we will see that founders of flourishing companies often championed quite different HR blueprints for their organizations, even within the same narrow industry niche, suggesting there are multiple routes to survival and success. Consequently, creating an effective reward system seems to depend less on finding "the one best way" than on ensuring that the reward system and jobs are designed in tandem, to be consistent and complementary (in both the technical and cultural senses discussed in Chapter 3). Consequently, we turn next to the topic of job design and its relationship to other elements of HRM.

IN REVIEW

⇒ Compensation can be based on a number of factors other than on-the-job performance:
- Perhaps most frequently, compensation is tied to hours worked, where the wage rate is set by a rough analysis of market compensation for similar jobs.
- More "scientific" systems for valuing jobs and setting pay involve statistical analyses of compensation within the local job market or the firm (*job evaluation*), analyzed against objective characteristics of the job (based on *job analysis*).
  ○ When labor markets are very competitive, these systems will be eroded by market pressures. But they can persist in less than perfectly competitive labor markets and can even resist market pressure when they have value in promoting perceptions of both distributive and procedural justice.

- ○ Job analyses and evaluations along these lines are sometimes criticized as perpetuating patterns of discrimination.
- Compensation levels are often set so as not to cause status conflicts.
- Seniority- and tenure-based pay is prevalent for various reasons, including social norms, union influence, increasing value of an employee over the career, "repayment" for training or below-market pay earlier in employees' careers, turnover reduction, and fostering gift-exchange by disproportionately rewarding the most loyal employees.
- Pay for skill and knowledge is also employed, especially in high-commitment HR systems. Such systems can work well, although they are not without problems.
- Traditionally, the distinction between salary and wages concerned the extent to which the employee controlled his own time and work calendar. In the United States, at least, the distinction has acquired legal standing.
  - ○ High-commitment HRM, which seeks to downplay differences between worker, manager, and owner, has pushed firms toward all-salary work structures, which (once again, in the United States, at least) can cause legal headaches.

⇒ The amount of dispersion or compression in an organization's salary structure should fit well with the five factors.

⇒ The amount of information given to employees about the firm's salary levels and distribution trades off two important and competing values: openness of the organization and feedback on results, which favor disclosure; versus a desire to keep compensation from being overly salient.

⇒ Benefits are an important part of compensation; in the United States (in 1998) benefits cost firms around 28% of their direct payroll.
- One set of rationales for employer-provided benefits involves transactions costs and economies of scale: tax advantages; administrative savings; market power; and reducing adverse selection problems.
- Employer-provided benefits also positively affect employee behavior: providing employees with goods or services that generate positive externalities for the organization; providing incentives not to quit and to avoid being fired; and promoting gift-exchange effects.
- Cafeteria benefits plans—in which employees can tailor their benefits packages to their own tastes—capture some but not all of the advantages of more-directly-provided benefits (in addition to having the advantage that they can be tailored to individual tastes).

⇒ In designing compensation schemes and setting compensation practices, firms must consider how salient to the employee they wish to

> make immediate tangible rewards; other forms of reward should be weighed carefully.
>
> ⇒ Managers should not lose sight of the important social and psychological forces that affect how employees react to their compensation (and to rewards more generally). Process, procedural and distributive justice, and symbolism all play an important role, which managers ignore at their peril.

ENDNOTES

1. Of course, it is more likely that some people will prefer driving while others prefer typing. The more realistic, less extreme scenario is, say, that the firm finds it hard to find enough qualified clericals at the going wages, whereas truck driver candidates form long queues at the employment office.

2. The frictions that impede a competitive market outcome may emanate from the employer as well as from the employees, and may also be driven by processes of social comparison. For instance, consider hospital nurses. Registered nurses were in short supply in the United States for many years, and many interesting solutions were attempted, such as making working hours more flexible, providing various benefits, entreating nursing schools to increase their supply of students, shifting tasks to nurses and nursing assistants with less training, and so on. After a shortage lasting roughly two decades, it has only been recently that wages for nurses have improved significantly, with the gratifying (for economists) response of more supply. But economists can be less gratified that it took hospitals so long to figure out that increased wages should be attempted.

   Why the inertia? Gender discrimination is one obvious explanation. Relatedly, we suspect that "social status" was at work. Registered nurses occupied a definite position in the wage distribution at hospitals beneath doctors (and above nursing assistants, LVNs, and orderlies), and hospitals were loathe to disrupt the pattern, worrying that members of other professions would cry foul. In other words, hospital administrators were willing to live with a shortage of RNs if the alternative was to break relative wage patterns. Other commentators believe that hospital monopsony power was a cause; with only a few hospitals per geographical area, and nurses unwilling to move great distances for small increases in wages, it is conceivable that hospitals implicitly colluded to keep RN wages down.

3. In other words, a female-dominated job title is more likely to have its pay pegged to the market wages of a female-dominated benchmark position than can be explained simply based on how similar the job demands are. For some suggestive evidence, see William P. Bridges and Robert L Nelson, "Markets in Hierarchies: Organizational and Market Influences on Gender Inequality in a State Pay System," *American Journal of Sociology* 95 (November 1989): 616–58.

4. For some efforts to assess how comparable worth has performed in practice, see Lynda J. Ames, "Fixing Women's Wages: The Effectiveness of Comparable Worth Policies," *Industrial and Labor Relations Review* 48 (July 1995): 709–25; Paula England, *Comparable Worth: Theories and Evidence* (New York: Aldine de Gruyter, 1992); Morley Gun-

derson, *Comparable Worth and Gender Discrimination: An International Perspective* (Geneva: International Labour Office, 1994); Shulamit Kahn, "Economic Implications of Public-Sector Comparable Worth: The Case of San Jose, California," *Industrial Relations* 31 (Spring 1992): 270–91; Mark R. Killingsworth, *The Economics of Comparable Worth* (Kalamazoo, MI: W. E. Upjohn Institute for Employment Research, 1990); Robert T. Michael, Heidi I. Hartmann, and Brigid O'Farrell (eds.), *Pay Equity: Empirical Inquiries* (Washington: National Academy Press, 1989).

5. For data that span both blue- and white-collar workers in Japan, the EC, and the United States, see Kazuo Koike, *Understanding Industrial Relations in Modern Japan* (London: Macmillan Press, 1988).

6. Brian Murray and Barry Gerhart, "An Empirical Analysis of a Skill-based Pay Program and Plant Performance Outcomes," *Academy of Management Journal* 41 (February 1998): 68–78.

7. For instance, Nordstrom, the large retailing company, was sued by the United Food and Commercial Workers Union, representing its sales personnel, and eventually forced in the early 1990s to pay roughly $20,000,000 in back pay and fees for failing to conform to state and federal labor standards. Salaried sales personnel at Nordstrom were not being paid overtime for record-keeping, writing thank-you notes to customers, and other "preparation" tasks they were conducting outside of normal working hours. See Charlene Marmer Solomon, "Nightmare at Nordstrom," *Personnel Journal* 69 (September 1990): 76–83.

8. When, owing to growth, Ben & Jerry's felt the need to hire an outside CEO, they publicly and somewhat ceremoniously declared that this principle was no longer applicable. Indeed, they dressed things up in market garb to legitimize this action, asserting that the need to hire an outside CEO, who had managerial abilities beyond those of Ben and Jerry—who had been running the firm—meant that they had to pay more.

9. Recall the arguments in Chapter 6 regarding why unions (especially outside the United States, and, within the United States, particularly the craft unions) often favor restricting differentiation among their members, to preserve collective solidarity and political clout among the membership. Some authors argue that unionization also serves to lower pay dispersion among *nonunion* workers, because nonunion employers will seek to avoid the threat of unionization by raising the wages of those workers who are otherwise most likely to unionize—namely, the lowest-paid ones. For empirical evidence consistent with this argument, see Lawrence M. Kahn and Michael Curme, "Unions and Nonunion Wage Dispersion," *Review of Economics and Statistics* 69 (November 1987): 600–7.

10. Douglas M. Cowherd and David I. Levine, "Product Quality and Pay Equity Between Lower-level Employees and Top Management: An Investigation of Distributive Justice Theory," *Administrative Science Quarterly* 37 (June 1992): 302–20.

11. For empirical evidence, see Jeffrey Pfeffer and Nancy Langton, "Wage Inequality and the Organization of Work: The Case of Academic Departments," *Administrative Science Quarterly* 33 (December 1988): 588–606; and "The Effect of Wage Dispersion on Satisfaction, Productivity, and Working Collaboratively: Evidence from College and University Faculty," *Administrative Science Quarterly* 38 (September 1993): 382–407. Economists have also developed formal models that propose efficiency rationales for these empirical tendencies; for examples, see Edward P. Lazear, "Pay Equality and Industrial Politics," *Journal of Political Economy* 97 (June 1989): 561–80; David I. Levine, "Co-

hesiveness, Productivity, and Wage Dispersion," *Journal of Economic Behavior and Organization* 15 (March 1991): 237–55.

12. For good overviews, see Edward E. Lawler III, *Pay and Organization Development* (Reading, MA: Addison-Wesley, 1981); Edward E. Lawler III, *Pay and Organizational Effectiveness: A Psychological View* (New York: McGraw-Hill, 1971).

13. Other data from the same government surveys identified a number of other benefits enjoyed by significant numbers of employees (especially professional and technical workers) in medium and larger establishments, but which are very rare among smaller enterprises, including severance pay, adoption assistance, fitness centers, employee health and wellness programs, job-related travel accident insurance, and educational assistance (both job-related and non-job-related). See Bureau of Labor Statistics, "Employee Benefits in Medium and Large Private Industry Establishments, 1995," Table 3, viewable online at: http://stats.bls.gov/special.requests/ocwc/oclt/ebs/ebnr0003.txt.

14. *Ibid.*

15. The National Association of Professional Employer Organizations, the industry's trade association, defines a PEO as an organization providing "an integrated and cost effective approach to the management and administration of the human resources and employer risk of its clients, by contractually assuming substantial employer rights, responsibilities, and risk . . . through the establishment and maintenance of an employer relationship with the workers assigned to its clients" (http://www.napeo.org/ind-definition.htm). The NAPEO estimates that roughly two to three million Americans in 1998 were co-employed in a PEO-type arrangement, working for one of the nearly 2500 PEOs that now exist in the United States (http://www.napeo.org/ind-questions.htm).

16. Why should the government and, ultimately, society, get involved in compensation to this degree by tax-favoring certain items? The quick-and-dirty answer is a mix of paternalism (workers wouldn't be sensible enough to save for the future or buy health insurance) and externalities (given social safety nets that are maintained by the general public, private incentives to save and insure are lower than the social incentives).

17. The notion of workers being forced to moonlight also gives a partial explanation for benefits intended to help the employee meet extraordinary, temporary expenses, such as college tuition for children.

18. In *defined-benefit* pension plans, upon retirement the individual receives an amount that is tied to her compensation, such as 75% of her average salary she earned over her last three years of employment. In contrast, in a *defined-contribution* plan, the employer contributes to the individual's personal retirement fund while the individual is employed (usually tied to her salary or wages); upon retirement, the individual draws from this personal retirement fund. Thus with defined benefits, there is a stronger incentive to retire early and begin drawing the benefits for a longer period of time; with defined contributions, early retirement simply depletes the personal retirement fund more quickly.

Why not just offer a "retirement bounty" to induce retirement at a particular age? Such things can be concocted in ways that placate the lawyers, but firms (in the U.S., at least) must be careful to avoid being perceived as forcing employment. The employer cannot, for instance, say that retirement is not mandatory at age 65, but wages will be cut in half each year the employee works past this age. Offering a retirement bounty that diminishes with chronological age may be legal, but it might fail to pass muster if an employee sued. Also, the employee would be compelled to pay taxes on the bounty the year it was received.

For an excellant review of the many theories of what pensions do and accompanying empirical evidence, see Alan L. Gustman, Olivia S. Mitchell, and Thomas L. Steinmeier, "The Role of Pensions in the Labor Market: A Survey of the Literature" *Industrial and Labor Relations Review* 47 (April 1994): 417–38.

19. We wish to say, as clearly as possible, that we are reporting a practice here and not advocating it. In some cases this use of benefits seems ethical to us; in other cases, the practice is reprehensible. Please note that we by no means condone all the examples we are about to give.

20. An especially subtle discriminatory effect in benefits is that survivorship benefits for surviving spouses generally favor men over women, owing to gender differences in life expectancies.

21. Related to these plans are schemes where employees can forgo some fraction of their income and then spend what was forgone on health or child care. These schemes are motivated purely by tax avoidance.

13

JOB DESIGN

Not too long ago, the Exploration Division of British Petroleum, one of the world's largest oil companies, jettisoned their traditional job classification system. Their old job descriptions were replaced by a more flexible set of grids or skill matrices that describe the particular bundles of skills and levels of performance applicable to different families of jobs. An article co-authored by BP's head of human resources outlined the rationale for this change:

> A job, as we have been trained to think of it, is a set of static, predetermined duties created by management and evaluated by the human resources department, which also assigns salary levels to it. . . . People are hired or promoted according to how well they fit this job description. This, unfortunately, is an old, industrial-engineering construct—one that ignores the obvious differences in the way people think, grow, communicate, and approach their work. It also ignores the fluidity of business and technology needs. . . . If we want to unlock the potential of both individuals and the organization, we need to change the way we design, allocate, and talk about work. Organizations that fail to do this are in danger of following the dinosaur into oblivion.[1]

British Petroleum is hardly alone in this view. Many organizations nowadays are focused on empowerment, flattening hierarchies, and broadening the scope of employees' duties, dismantling many of the traditional boundaries that have existed among jobs and between the categories of manager and worker. As organizations redesign jobs to give employees a wider range of tasks to perform and more responsibility or decision-making authority, they grapple with the broader implications of these changes for other domains of human resource management, such as selection, training, performance evaluation, compensation, collective bargaining, and career development.

This chapter provides a brief analysis of job design. We don't focus on job design in the narrower sense of the term as it is used in the field of Production and Operations Management. There, the subject of job design arises in the context of an assembly line (or similar technology), involving issues of line balancing: Given a temporal sequence of tasks to be completed and an amount of time required to do each one, the job designer seeks to break the tasks into groups of close to equal total length (respecting the temporal sequence of tasks), and the cycle time of the line is then set to be the maximum of these totals.

Instead, we will be discussing job design issues at a somewhat broader and more conceptual level, more along the lines of the experiment being conducted at British Petroleum and so many other organizations. Specifically, we will be looking at the following job design parameters:

- *The level and breadth of job content.* This includes both issues of *job enlargement* (many tasks impounded in the job, all at the same basic level) and *job enrichment* (the tasks impounded in the job vary "vertically" in the sense that a line worker might also be involved in materials flow, scheduling output, and so on).

- *Variability over time in task assignment and extent of rotations.* Do workers stay with the same tasks forever (or until promoted), or is there frequent rotation of tasks? How much cross-training goes on? How much lateral transferring goes on?

- *The specific mix of tasks given to the individual worker or group to do at any one time.* In particular, we will focus on the measurement properties of different tasks, as we did in the chapters on performance evaluation and compensation.

- *Individual or team.* Is each individual given a mix of specific tasks, or are tasks given to a team or group, which then governs itself concerning who does what?

- *Level of autonomy.* How much autonomy is the individual worker or team given to decide what to do, how to do it, and when to do it?

The boundaries between the different design parameters can be pretty fuzzy. For example, we interpret job enlargement narrowly, to mean an increase in the number of tasks assigned to the employee to be done more or less contemporaneously. This is distinct from increased over-time variability in task assignment, where the individual carries out more tasks as time progresses but for short time periods (say, a day or a week) may have a relatively narrow set of tasks. For instance, a worker who tightens the same four bolts on cars that pass by on an assembly line—month after month, year after year—has a narrow and low-variability job. If the worker is instead asked to tighten eight bolts and install seat covers and hubcaps, her job has been broadened. If she is asked to tighten four bolts for one month, four other bolts the next month, to install seat covers in the third month, and hubcaps in the fourth, her task-assignment variability has been raised. The distinction is fuzzy because the relevant time period—hourly rotations in tasks?, or daily?, or monthly?—isn't clear. Especially when it comes to job enrichment— where the employee tightens eight bolts, installs seat covers and hubcaps, and does material procurement and quality control testing—the notion of doing the tasks contemporaneously presents problems; typically, the enriching tasks of material procurement and quality control testing will not be done contemporaneously with tightening bolts, and so on.

We won't go through all the other fuzzy boundaries in this set of design parameters. The one example suffices to make the point: Although conceptually we treat these as distinct parameters, in the real world they naturally run into one another.

Organizations vary markedly in their use of formal *job titles* and other symbolic markers of distinction (or sameness) among bundles of tasks, so in this chapter we will also examine how their use complements or supplements job design levers for accomplishing various objectives.

We will evaluate these job design parameters in terms of the following objectives for job design:

- *Technological efficiency.* Are the tasks performed efficiently in terms of level of output per unit of labor input (adjusting for the cost of labor inputs)?
- *Flexibility.* How flexible is the organization in adjusting to both temporary and more permanent changes in its external environment?
- *Explicit extrinsic incentives.* To what extent can (must?) workers be given explicit, extrinsic incentives that will lead them to act in the fashion desired by the organization?
- *Intrinsic motivation and commitment.* To what extent are workers intrinsically motivated to perform well? To what extent does the job design encourage or foster commitment to the organization?
- *Social aspects.* Does the job design foster positive peer pressure and discourage negative peer pressure? Are social comparisons fostered or defused? Do workers benefit from positive social interactions on the job?

Many of the issues we will be discussing in this chapter have arisen already, most notably in Chapters 9 and 11. We will reiterate points made before, but we will try to be brief.

Before we proceed, a word on how the notion of *job design,* the topic of this chapter, relates to the concept of *technology,* as defined in Chapter 2 ("The Five Factors"). The two concepts overlap considerably, but they aren't quite the same. One difference comes in the attitude we take to them. We have treated technology as an exogenous factor, with which HR policies either do or don't fit. Job design, in contrast, is treated as an important HR lever. Of course, this distinction is only one of attitude; in Chapter 2 we exhorted you to think of the five factors as being drivers of *and driven by* HR concerns, not as a one-way street. But those exhortations aside, we have for the most part tended to regard the five factors as exogenous drivers of HR policies. So, to some extent, this chapter is about the (HR) endogenous pieces of technology.[2]

But thinking of job design as the HR-endogenous piece of technology isn't entirely accurate, either. The two overlap, to be sure. But some aspects of technology—the extent of observability, for example—may be largely or completely uncontrollable and thus not part of a job design. And some aspects of job design—for instance, the amount of task variability over time and the use of job-design symbols such as honorific job titles—are related to but more than aspects of the technology of work; these are HR levers that interact with the other four factors.

THE LEVEL AND BREADTH OF JOB CONTENT

The notion that labor-force specialization enhances technological efficiency is at least as old as the discipline of economics. In *The Wealth of Nations*, with which economics as a discipline began, Adam Smith goes on at some length regarding the advantages gained in pin manufacture by having one worker cut lengths of wire, a second make pin heads, a third join the head to the body of the pin, a fourth put a point on the pin, and a fifth collect the pins into bundles ready for sale. Smith doesn't mention—but probably takes as obvious—that it is efficient as well to have another party keep accounting records, still another sell the pins to retailers (who in turn sell the pins to consumers), and yet another specialize in sales to industrial customers of manufactured pin products.

By creating highly specialized jobs that are extremely limited in scope, one takes advantage of increasing manual dexterity that comes from repeating a given task over and over, as well as taking advantage of specialized knowledge (such as how to keep accounts, proclivities of specific customers, how best to make a pin head, and so on). And, to the extent that these skills can (or must) be learned, one economizes on training costs. Furthermore, in a highly developed labor market, one may also economize on labor costs by optimally matching workers of differing wage rates to the specific tasks for which they are trained. (The alternatives would involve either potentially overpaying workers doing a bundle of tasks by aiming too high in compensation, or else paying too little, thereby running the risk of attracting only mediocre talent.)

A countervailing force is that some tasks are *complementary* in production: Doing one makes the other easier. This is especially the case when the complementarity is knowledge-based—that is, when knowing what is happening in the sphere of one task can aid in performing other tasks. For example, bundling together sales and service can be sensible (especially for technical products); knowledge about the needs of a client that is useful in making a sale can also help in providing services to that client. An executive secretary carries out a number of different tasks—typing, dictation, maintaining the boss's calendar, and so on—that are bundled together at least in part because of the knowledge base that cuts across them. Universities usually expect faculty both to do research and to teach, predicated on complementarities assumed to exist between teaching and research functions.

An important variation on this theme (discussed extensively in Chapter 9) involves process improvement efforts by employees. If employees possess knowledge that can be used to improve the overall production process, management should create conditions conducive to obtaining this information. In some cases, employees will be able to employ such information fruitfully only if they have a broader understanding of the production process, gained by broadening the scope of the job and enriching the job so that workers understand different facets of the production process.

Job enlargement and enrichment can potentially increase organizational flexibility, both in the short term and the longer term. In adapting to short-term changes, the workforce is more malleable; workers with experience doing a wider range of tasks can be redeployed to perform urgent duties. And workers who self-select for enriched and enlarged jobs are likely to be more capable of and interested in "growing" over time in the skills they acquire and employ, and thus more likely to be able to shift more or less permanently to new tasks as longer-term business conditions warrant.

Combining multiple tasks into a single job generally complicates explicit, extrinsic incentives. We went on at length about this in Chapter 11 and needn't repeat the detailed arguments here, but in brief, it becomes harder to get the right balance in extrinsic incentives the more things there are to balance, especially when the different tasks vary in how well results can be measured.

On the other hand, job enrichment is generally held to improve intrinsic motivation. Workers who contribute more broadly to a final product—who are less of a faceless cog in a huge machine—are more apt to identify with that product and to reflect pride in its quality. For the appropriate sort of worker, job enrichment fights against the proverbial assembly-line ennui and boredom; the job becomes more interesting and commands more attention and pride.[3]

Mixing social aspects with intrinsic motivation, job enlargement and enrichment usually promote a wider circle of acquaintances for the individual worker, increasing the worker's identification with the entire enterprise, rather than just his or her own smaller group of peers. In this respect, job enrichment and enlargement probably foster positive peer pressure and defuse negative peer pressure—there is less of an us-versus-them mentality. But the impact on social comparisons is at best mixed and possibly, on balance, negative; the wider the circle that the individual worker travels in, the greater the opportunity to find social comparisons that leave the employee feeling unjustly treated. Thus, these job design parameters are complementary to an evaluation regime in which most individuals are doing "alright" and a reward system that doesn't make many conspicuous distictions.

On balance, then, the tradeoffs in job enlargement and enrichment primarily come down to these: Narrow jobs are better on basic technological grounds and for explicit incentives. However, the more the firm depends (or can depend) on employees working with their minds, the less valid is the technological efficiency argument, and indeed it quickly starts to run the other way. Broader jobs are generally better for promoting flexibility and intrinsic motivation and commitment. But the social dimensions of job enlargement and enrichment are critical to their effects and can vary enormously across settings, depending particularly on the workforce and the external social environment.

In particular, before implementing job enlargement and enrichment, three caveats deserve emphasis:

1. Several paragraphs above, we wrote, "For the appropriate sort of worker, job enrichment fights against the proverbial assembly-line ennui

and boredom . . .". The phrase *for the appropriate sort of worker* is there for a reason. Enriched or enlarged jobs are not to everyone's taste. There are employees for whom expanded scope and responsibility is not at all desirable. An organization whose employees have self-selected this work setting because of the unchallenging jobs on offer will find it very difficult to change to a high-content, high-commitment regime.

2. The process of enlarging or enriching jobs (or increasing the variability of workers' responsibilities over time) often leads to demands for greater tangible rewards, to compensate for the harder assignment. Similarly, job enlargement and enrichment often lead to increased demands for worker autonomy. In other words, job enrichment innovations often produce a taste for *even more enrichment* among employees. If you engage in job enlargement or enrichment, you should be prepared to meet these demands one way or another. So you should consider whether you are prepared to grant employees more autonomy (see below).

3. As we noted in Chapter 9, job enrichment efforts can be subverted by middle and lower-level managers, who often perceive a threat to their role as coordinators of narrow-scope workers and their monopoly of knowledge about the bigger picture.[4] Efforts to enrich line workers' jobs typically involve a simultaneous and fairly profound redefinition of the jobs of supervisors and managers in the organization. In place of a focus on monitoring, discipline, and routine administration, supervisors focus on training and development activities, procuring resources from throughout the organization, linking their team to the rest of the organization, and the like. Effecting this transition in management styles and job design for supervisors is often one of the trickiest aspects of job enrichment interventions: The literature on job design innovations suggests that job enrichment schemes are much more likely to be successful in organizations that begin with (or adopt) organic, flexible, decentralized structures than in mechanistic bureaucracies.

OVER-TIME VARIABILITY IN TASK ASSIGNMENT AND EXTENT OF ROTATIONS

Job enlargement and enrichment mean, essentially, increasing the number and breadth of tasks performed by the individual at a given moment (or over a very short time frame). In this section, in contrast, we have in mind varying the tasks performed by the individual over longer time frames. Thus, much of what we had to say about job enlargement and enrichment applies, *pari pasu,* in this case. In particular, in terms of flexibility and intrinsic motivation and commitment, variability over time in task assignment is usually a winner.

But there are several differences. First, the explicit incentive problems associated with jobs that combine multiple tasks can be reduced to the extent that the "review period" for administering extrinsic incentives is smaller than the time frame over which the individual rotates among tasks. For instance, consider a case in which an employee rotates jobs every twelve months but receives incentive pay based on three months' worth of performance. Then the incentive formula can be changed whenever the mix of assigned tasks changes, to achieve the desired balance of efforts. And if the time it takes to descend the relevant learning curve(s) is short relative to the cycle of rotations, then any objections to job rotation based on the costs of learning and adjusting to new duties are minimal.

In some cases, however, the relevant learning curves must be descended rather slowly, especially where deep and specialized knowledge is required for consummate performance. This will limit the extent to which it is sensible to vary workers' task assignments over time. Put differently, in some technologies and for some strategies, having a workforce that consists largely or entirely of jacks-and-jills-of-all-trades is much worse than having specialists. A large full-service law firm is a good example: Having lawyers who specialize in tax law, others who specialize in litigation, and still others who practice labor law, is nearly a necessity. In grooming someone for a managerial role in a law firm, you might want to expose that person to a sample of the different specific practices in the firm. But you certainly wouldn't want to run every attorney through all—or even a sample—of the different practices. Many organizations that rely on a highly specialized professional or technical workforce deal with this by segregating professional–technical from managerial–administrative job ladders, enabling depth and specialization to be attained in the former versus more breadth in the latter. (And to the extent that the firm's strategy and culture emphasize the quality of professional work, with authority and respect given to those who are the most skilled or deeply knowledgeable, it may pay to have those on managerial–administrative job ladders win their spurs at the outset in some more specialized role.)

The appropriateness of frequent lateral transfers will also depend on the types of relations with customers, clients, and constituents mandated by the organization's strategy, technology, and culture. Frequent lateral transfers can function poorly in service organizations whose strategy emphasizes very stable relationships between clients and their servers. Particularly if the company transfers employees most frequently when they show real promise, as part of a career development strategy, then customers may perceive that the less able is the individual who handles their account, the longer they are likely to be stuck with that person. In contrast, when the firm's success depends on highly interdependent efforts from different parts of the organization or on transferring knowledge acquired in one part of the enterprise to other parts, then lateral rotations can be an important ingredient in achieving the necessary organizationwide coordination and learning. Note that in some service industries, the firm may wish to *discourage* stable client–server relationships; the relationship sought is between the client and the firm, to prevent an individual employee from departing with "his" list of clients. This gives yet another strategic rationale for lateral transfers. Or in some cases, the firm may rotate employees across tasks, subunits, or locales that differ in their appeal to ensure some equity in job assignment, or it may use frequent transfers to ensure that overly strong bonds do not develop among groups of co-workers. (Club Mediterranee, the French operator of Club Med resorts worldwide, cites both of the latter two rationales for why it rotates its thousands of young GOs or *Gentils Organisateurs*—who serve and entertain guests—among its resorts as frequently as every six months.)[5]

It perhaps goes without saying that frequent job rotations are not to everyone's taste, just as with job enlargement and enrichment. If you are considering an increase in job assignment variability, you should think hard about how your workforce is going to react to this. And you should also think about the training costs that will be entailed; job designs that involve a lot of lateral transferring and cross-training can be prohibitively expensive in environments with a lot of labor mobility.

An important special case of job designs with task variation over time concerns organizations that are built around some core function or set of tasks, where broad exposure to that activity is necessary to provide adequate technical understanding of the "core" and instill the right values, so that other areas of the organization can be effective in supporting its core. A good example is United Parcel Service. Without denigrating the importance of local and regional sorting/shipping centers, or the information systems department of UPS, the heart and soul of UPS is the package car driver in those chocolate-brown trucks—the person who picks up from and delivers to specific clients. At UPS, then, everyone—lawyers, accountants, information system specialists—takes at least an abbreviated tour of duty in the brown trucks, as something of a boot-camp experience, to get a dose of the "brown blood" that is meant to flow in the veins of every UPS employee. This sort of stint in the culturally and technologically central function of the organization can play an important role in acculturating specialist employees and in teaching them what the organization is about.

THE MIX OF TASKS

It is often the case that a single worker's list of job responsibilities will contain a mix of different tasks. The length and breadth of this list is affected by the sorts of considerations that we have already discussed, but in this section we want to take a closer look at what sorts of tasks are likely to mix well or poorly.

A first consideration—related to technological efficiency—is that some tasks fit together well because they are accomplished based on common information or skills. We have already mentioned the example of sales and after-sales service, especially for products that are tailored to the individual client: Knowledge of the specific needs and tastes of the individual client cuts across the two tasks, and so a firm in this sort of situation might combine the two tasks into a single job.

The same example illustrates a second point. For some bundles of tasks, individual measures of performance for each task are unavailable; instead, available measures of performance compound the employee's efforts on all the tasks in the bundle. For instance, the level of repeat sales to a particular client reflects both the initial sales effort—did the client have a good purchasing experience?; was he sold the right product?—and subsequent service. In such cases, especially when the firm relies on extrinsic incentives based on measures of performance, the case for a job that includes both sales and follow-up service is clear. Or let us take an example from manufacturing. For some products, poor quality, indicated by lack of conformance to the product's specifications, could be due to malfeasance on any one of several tasks during the production process. In such cases, it makes sense to bundle the tasks together into a single job, so a single worker is responsible for conformance on all the tasks and can be rewarded (and monitored) accordingly.

Next, imagine a situation in which there are a variety of tasks to be done that must be bundled together into a smaller number of jobs. (Suppose, for instance, that no single task provides full-time work for an employee.) Suppose as well that for each task, a measure of performance on that task is available, but these measures are somewhat noisy, some more than others. What do we mean by *noisy*? The firm seeks a measure of the quality of efforts expended by the individual employee. Suppose we have a very precise measure of performance in terms of the bottom line for the firm—say, the dollar value of an order placed by a customer after a salesperson's call—but this measure compounds the efforts of the salesperson with uncontrollable environmental variables. This is one case in which we say that we have a noisy measure of performance. We also have noise when the performance measures available only roughly reflect the efforts of the particular employee and the outcomes for the firm. But in a case where we have a very good indication of *what* the specific employee did and *how well,* even if this gives only a rough sense of what the outcome will be for the firm's bottom line, we say that we have a fairly precise measure of performance for that employee's task or set of tasks.

Now suppose that the measures of performance for the different tasks being done by the employee vary in how noisy they are. In other words, for some tasks, we have fairly precise measures of performance, while for others there is a lot of noise. For the reasons we discussed in Chapter 11, if a worker is given a job that combines precisely measured and noisily measured tasks, then the firm cannot provide strong extrinsic incentives for any of the tasks. Strong extrinsic incentives for the noisily measured tasks will subject the worker to substantial risk. It is a maintained assumption that individual workers are fairly risk averse, so this will mean that the worker will require a compensating increase in average rewards. And if strong extrinsic incentives are provided for the precisely measured tasks but not the noisily measured ones, then the worker is motivated to neglect the noisily measured, weakly motivated tasks altogether.

Thus, if we have an array of tasks that vary in the precision with which performance can be measured, if we must bundle some of those tasks into jobs, and if we want to rely on extrinsic motivation for the precisely measured tasks, jobs must be designed that put only precisely measured tasks into a bundle. For any job that includes noisily measured tasks, intrinsic motivation will have to suffice (at least, for risk-averse employees).[6]

Of course, this last prescription of how to bundle tasks into jobs can run up against some of our other prescriptions. For instance, a plant manager may be responsible for cost of goods manufactured, for maintenance of the plant's physical capital, for obtaining process improvements, and for developing the human resources of the plant's workforce. Performance on the first two tasks is, relatively speaking, precisely measurable; performance on the latter two is much less so. So the preceding paragraph advises you to split the plant manager's job into two: Have a "day-to-day" plant manager who attends to day-to-day costs and routine maintenance, and have another "big picture" plant manager who deals with process improvements and human capital development. One might, indeed, be able to split off from the plant manager's job responsibility for routine maintenance of the physical plant. But, especially for plants that embrace ideas such as TQM, the connections between day-to-day operations, process improvements, and human capital development are tight. For instance, if the "big picture" manager wants to cross-train workers and the day-to-day plant manager sees this as hurting bottom-line performance for months to come, it will take someone with responsibility for both sets of tasks—a real plant manager or Director of Operations Management—to decide what is to be done.

Mixing Stars and Guardians

When the terminology of *stars* and *guardians* first arose in Chapter 2, we mentioned that it is usually difficult to provide appropriate guidance and incentives to jobs that have both aspects. The reason, which we can now explain more fully, is based on the premise that in many cases the worker is faced with a choice between a safe course of action, which promises mediocre (or acceptable) outcomes with very high probability, versus a risky course of action, which can give either very good or very bad outcomes at the individual level. For a guardian's job, one wishes to structure extrinsic incentives to discourage gambling; the differences in reward between a good and a great performance are kept low, while the "rewards" for a truly bad performance are dire. One also wishes to develop a culture for these jobs that discourages gambling. For instance, an airline presumably does not want to encourage pilots to attempt daring, novel, or creative ways of landing a jumbo jet. On the other hand, explicit incentives for a star should avoid heavy penalties for failure; the dominant culture should accept failure and emphasize success.

As long as the job design entails either a clear star or a guardian pattern, incentive design is relatively straightforward. But when the job mixes these patterns (e.g., as in many managerial roles), incentives are much harder to get right. In fact, in Chapter 2, we suggested that in jobs having a mixed star–guardian profile, there would be a strong tendency for the guardian aspects to outweigh the star elements. One justification for this prediction is that losses tend to loom larger than gains in most people's thinking—that is, a loss of K units measured in, say, sales, dollars, or company image is usually perceived as more of a loss than a gain of K units is perceived as a gain. To the extent that employees (and the people who manage them) think this way, we would expect the guardian elements of jobs having a combined star–guardian profile to dominate.

This is a common problem in organizations seeking to create a more entrepreneurial culture in what has traditionally been a very conservative industry. For example, a few years ago this concerned the senior management of John Hancock, a large diversified financial services organization involved in investment and commercial banking, various forms of insurance, investment management for institutional and individual investors, venture capital, pension fund administration, and the like. Hancock's many subsidiaries and divisions faced a deregulated and increasingly competitive business environment that put a premium on innovation, risk-taking, creativity, and other attributes for which stars can make a big difference. Yet these lines of business are still characterized by very significant guardian elements, such as preserving the company's reputation for prudence and financial solvency. Hancock's leadership was frustrated that despite their intense efforts to communicate and reward a more entrepreneurial spirit, mid-level and even senior managers in this organization remained risk averse and oriented toward the status quo. Put differently, the mid-level managers continued to be more concerned about not screwing up the guardian parts of their roles than about hitting it big on the star dimensions. What makes this situation ironic is the fact that this company's mainline business includes *insurance.* The dilemma of the mixed star–guardian profile is that of providing credible career "insurance" for failed star efforts in a context where everyone knows that particular guardian failures could be catastrophic for the organization (and, thus, for the individual). If one can distinguish between the individual's efforts for the star dimensions and her guardian-dimensions efforts, and if the latter can be measured fairly precisely, then appropriate extrinsic incentives can be designed. But if efforts along these two sets of dimensions cannot be distinguished—something that is especially hard to do when it comes to the amount of time allocated to each—a job design that mixes star and guardian roles will present substantial problems. Reliance on intrinsic motivation and social rewards are likely to be the most successful means of motivating employees.[7]

TEAM (VERSUS INDIVIDUAL) JOB DESIGNS

It is currently quite fashionable, especially in high-commitment work environments, to assign sets of tasks to teams or groups of employees rather than to individual workers. The team is often self-governing, in the sense that it determines internally (possibly subject to some oversight) how the tasks should be accomplished.

We can distinguish two somewhat different ways in which teams can be granted autonomy. In the first, a team is assigned a specific task or list of tasks to do but granted autonomy over how to accomplish their assignment (as opposed to being closely controlled). In the second, the team has broader autonomy, receiving only very general guidelines about its charge, with team members left to decide on their own what to do on a day-to-day basis as well as how to accomplish their work. In this section, we focus on the first sort of team design—for instance, a team that is told to build a particular car with particular specifications, but then left to decide among its members who will perform which assembly operations. Issues that arise in the second sort of team-based job design (e.g., where the team would decide which cars to build) are discussed in the next section, on autonomy. And we will return to closely managed teams at the end of this section.

We discussed teams at length in Chapters 10 and 11 (especially), so much of what we have to say is review. But, to review and extend:

- Team-based job designs may be imperative when an overall task to be done requires close cooperation among a number of individuals who have different skill bases or roles to play, and where there is a great deal of ambiguity about what should be done and when. Standard examples include research on a scale too large for any single individual, or the development and design of new products. A team-based job design may also be required when the firm wishes to rely on explicit, extrinsic incentives, and the number of "informationally related" tasks is too large for a single individual to tackle.

- Even if it is unnecessary on technological grounds, a team-based job design can be technologically efficient whenever the firm can rely on internal monitoring and peer pressure or internalization to motivate workers.

- A countervailing effect concerns work restrictions enforced or enhanced by the group. If a task is given to an individual, he or she may be subject to peer pressure to slow down output. When the task is given to a team, this effect is magnified, because the individual is physically constrained by the group concerning how fast he or she can work.

- Teams may also protect members who misbehave or fail to perform adequately. They can lead to an us-versus-them mentality, especially where the team is socially homogeneous and quite different socially from management or from other outsiders.

- To the extent that teams produce something tangible and "whole," individual pride in and identification with the product can be increased, thereby enhancing intrinsic motivation. Think of assembly-line versus team-built automobile assembly. Imagine a worker responsible for tightening nuts onto four particular bolts on each of an endless stream of half-built cars that slowly moves past, hour after hour, day after day. That employee may understand that a car is the end product of her efforts and those of her peers, but she is unlikely to have much emotional attachment to her four bolts. In contrast, a team of workers who together assemble entire cars are apt to be much more attached to the specific cars they have assembled, leading to increased quality and care in the assembly process.

- To the extent that team-based job designs naturally increase the content of work done by any individual, the advantages and disadvantages discussed under job enrichment and enlargement apply. In particular, in high-commitment environments where the employer wants employees to contribute ideas for process and product improvements, team-based production increases the individual's knowledge about the whole production process, leading to higher-quality ideas, which reflect the realities of a larger slice of the production process instead of the worker's own (smaller) slice.

The effect of a team-based job design on flexibility is unclear. Teams are generally held to increase flexibility for reasons similar to those given earlier in our discussion of job enlargement and enrichment: Teams promote a greater range of skills among their members (through informal on-the-job learning, at least, and often through the team's own internal system of task rotation), which means that teams have more flexible human resources to deploy. But teams also build up their own internal social equilibria, and getting a team to shift the content of its work can be difficult when this involves breaking the established order in the team. Thus, teams may be inflexible to some changes.

A particularly clear instance of such inflexibility involves changes that require introducing into the team a new member who provides specialized skills that the current team members lack. The new member can have a hard time "fitting in," especially one who is socially different from the existing team members (with the effect heightened to the extent the team was socially homogeneous). A lot of time may be lost and wheels spun as the team finds a new equilibrium. This is one reason why many organizations creating self-managed teams have team members play a major role in hiring or selecting new members, to ensure compatibility with and commitment to new team members.

The issue of diversity within a team can be troublesome, even beyond the problems incurred when a new (and different) member must be added. Especially when the team's overall task is innovative and technical, it may be necessary to include within the team a mix of varying background skills, educational levels, or social groups. The mix required may make heterogeneity in norms and social backgrounds not only inevitable but desirable. Yet research on group behavior suggests that homogeneity of team members is often an asset, particularly with respect to communication, interaction, and mutual trust. Where homogeneity is not feasible because of the required mix of tasks, and especially where the "differents" make up a small part of the team membership (in particular, where one "different" is put together with an otherwise homogeneous group), those that are different can find themselves locked out of the social and political order of the group, subjected to scapegoating, or even worse.

When heterogeneous teams are required—on technological grounds, under the spur of external social and legal pressures, or simply because management believes that this is the right thing to do—management should consider various alternative means for creating strong group cohesion. Common approaches along these lines include: identifying an overriding external objective (e.g., "a man on the moon by 1970," in the case of NASA in the late 1950s and early 1960s); building *esprit de corps* by invoking a common enemy (as Nike did in using Reebok as a unifying corporate threat); intensive socialization; and symbolic stripping away of preexisting differences.

There are some final caveats to make here, just as there were in discussing job enrichment and enlargement. First, self-managing team members generally believe that they are doing a harder job and deserve to be rewarded for it. In addition, granting team members discretion over *how* they do their tasks often whets their appetite for more control over *what* tasks they will be doing. So the next section of this chapter, on autonomy, becomes germane. Second, first-line supervisors and middle managers often lose power and authority when team-based job designs are instituted. Resistance from these groups should be expected. At a minimum, they will need training on how to change their role from "commander" to that of "advisor" or "coach."

Third, we have discussed teams that are internally self-managing. But we don't advocate that management take a complete *laissez faire* attitude toward teams. Management retains responsibility for ensuring that individual members of the team are not scapegoated or otherwise unfairly treated. Particularly concerning the division of tasks among members of an autonomous work group, management must be concerned with whether internal equity will be achieved. On the other side of this coin, although the strong social ties that often develop among workgroup members can be of enormous value, they can sometimes make it difficult for group members to allocate rewards and punishments in a way that is commensurate with contribution. After all, if it is hard to withhold rewards from a subordinate, it is even harder to do when that person is a teammate. Thus, although a relatively light-handed style of management is called for, the hand should not be so light as to be nonexistent.

What about extremely heavy-handed management of teams? At the extreme, we have closely managed teams, where a representative of management directs the specific efforts of the team members. The point of teams that are closely managed in this sense is almost entirely social—the appropriate social comparisons can be encouraged, and to the extent that strong social ties are formed among the team members, team members may be counted upon to help each other as needed. Also, to the extent that these social ties are valuable to the individual employee, the employer—by controlling the employee's access to these social ties, at least during work hours—gains a lever with which to discipline or threaten the worker. But the social aspects of small workgroups can be delicate to manage. A social order among team members can emerge that impedes change; an us-versus-them mentality of the team members vis-à-vis their supervisor in particular and management in general may result. Closely managed teams miss many of the advantages that internally autonomous teams can have, while possessing a number of the disadvantages. Except where concerns for internal equity are paramount, allowing teams the freedom to internally manage themselves seems to us the better strategy.[8]

AUTONOMY

Teams are usually given some autonomy over how to conduct their tasks, with management often deciding what tasks are assigned to the team. A further job-design decision concerns granting autonomy to teams or individuals regarding the set of activities to be done. When should employees or teams be given the autonomy to decide what to do on a day-to-day basis?

From the perspective of the employer, granting autonomy to individuals or to a group makes sense only insofar as the group or individual given the autonomy has interests that are more or less aligned with the employer's. In some cases, this alignment of interests may be present naturally. In other cases, the organization will need to encourage alignment of interests by relying on intrinsic motivation—inculturating employees, providing interesting and challenging work, building commitment through symbolic actions—or by offering more tangible extrinsic incentives, running the gamut from peer pressure to more formal rewards for performance (as long as there are favorable conditions for using formal incentives, such as the presence of accurate measures of inputs).

The basic case for autonomy goes back to considerations raised in Chapters 2 and 4. When the specific tasks needing to be done are ambiguous or when the individual or team has the best information and expertise concerning what to do, then broad autonomy concerning both *what* should be done and *how* is almost mandatory. For example, highly specialized professionals (lawyers, doctors) essentially tell their employers (clients) what they will do on behalf of those employers. And individuals engaged in basic research direct their own efforts, subject to very broad guidelines and infrequent review. But examples run more broadly: UPS, for instance, expects its package car drivers to do what it takes to satisfy individual clients. The package car drivers have broad autonomy, subject to *ex post* review, in which they are asked to explain why some extraordinary action *seemed* the best way to satisfy a client. The key here is on-the-spot information and the need to react quickly to unusual circumstances.

Flexibility might be enhanced by granting autonomy. For the clearest case, consider a single employee, whose actions are only very loosely bound to the actions of others in the organization technologically, and whose interests are closely aligned with those of the employer. Then, in an uncertain or ambiguous environment, allowing that individual to decide on the spot what to do will of course raise flexibility of response. This, in essence, is the case of the UPS package car driver.

But at the other extreme, when the individual's or team's efforts are closely bound to the efforts of many others—when coordination is crucial—then autonomous individuals or teams must *all* be convinced that a particular change is meritorious before it can be effectively implemented. Because it is the rare effort from which all parties involved benefit (or benefit equally), extended horse-trading may be needed to get unanimous consent from a large number of autonomous entities. In this situation, autonomy may impede flexibility.

Autonomy on the job, particularly regarding the choice of tasks, can raise commitment, as the employee feels more in control of the work environment and work processes. For this reason, high-commitment HR systems generally involve substantial grants of autonomy, to increase intrinsic incentives and commitment. But the usual caveats apply: Autonomy is not to everyone's taste. Individuals granted autonomy generally believe that their job has become harder and therefore that they deserve more compensation. And granting autonomy to lower-echelon employees can adversely affect those who used to control them; resistance and subversion from supervisors and middle managers can be a problem.

JOB DESIGN AND THE EXTERNAL ENVIRONMENT

The design of jobs does not take place in a social vacuum. The image of a job designer who bundles tasks into jobs on behalf of the owners of the firm may be a pleasant one for managers to hold, but it really isn't accurate. Social, legal, and economic pressures from the workforce and from society have many effects on how jobs are designed. Here we briefly summarize some important examples of these effects.

Job designs have been profoundly affected by organized labor. Recall from Chapter 6 the main tendencies here. Industrial unions have tended to advocate more narrowly defined jobs. The logic is one of attaining monopoly power for relatively unskilled workers by creating artificial monopolies through extreme task specialization. Craft workers, in contrast, possess a natural monopoly of skill, and therefore craft guilds and unions historically have resisted vigorously any efforts to subdivide or specialize their work in ways that would undercut workers' power and the ability of the union to dictate job content, training requirements, or occupational certification.

The same craft logic applies to work that is socially regarded as professional in character. Professionals often strongly identify with a broader occupation and resist efforts by organizations to intervene in the specification of job responsibilities. Because professionals are increasingly employed in large bureaucracies, we do observe more task specialization and a gradual narrowing of professional jobs. Owing to the strong occupational identity of professionals and their taste for autonomy, efforts to narrow or specialize professionals' jobs or to usurp their autonomy will usually be resisted by individuals and their unions or professional associations. Moreover, professionals are supported by a broader normative order, whereby people are more willing to grant autonomy to professionals because of their occupational certification, high social standing, and the like.

In addition to occupationally derived interests in how jobs are designed, workers may have economically and socially derived interests as well. We have noted in several contexts that pay and other entitlements in organizations tend to be allocated to jobs (and to job titles, which isn't quite the same thing—see below), rather than to individuals. When this is the case, individuals develop especially strong interests in how their jobs are designed and labeled. This is true, for instance, when white males observe women or ethnic minorities moving into their job or occupation. There is a large and diverse literature showing that the perceived value of an occupation declines as women and ethnic minorities move into it.[9] This suggests that whatever their social interests might be, white males in a specific job or occupation may perceive strong economic interests in resisting the entry of women or people of color into their domain, which could drive down the perceived value of the work and thus the wage rate as well. Hence, they may seek the creation of job designs that impede the entry of women or people of color— for instance, jobs that include a few tasks requiring significant upper-body strength to exclude women.

SYMBOLS AND JOB DESIGN: JOB TITLES AND OTHER ATMOSPHERICS

Although not part of the design of the job itself, job titles and other symbols of job design can be used by employers and by others to accomplish a variety of aims.

Take the sort of situation discussed just above, in which white males may be resisting the entry into "their jobs" of women or people of color. Research shows that the tendency to proliferate detailed job titles within a line of work increases as the employees doing that work become more heterogeneous with respect to sex and ethnicity.[10] Within the organizations studied, these job title distinctions re-segregated the workforce along race and sex lines, and the differences among job titles also translated into differences in prescribed pay rates, which served in turn to disadvantage women and nonwhites and to reinforce the advantage of white males. Similar findings have been reported in case studies of occupations in which women have started to make inroads in recent years.[11]

Management can use job titles to achieve its aims, as well. For instance, we have already noted that social comparison often takes place among similarly situated peers. Within organizations, "similarly situated" often equates with rank and job title. To reduce invidious social comparisons, organizations sometimes find it useful to create bureaucratic distinctions between groups whom they wish to differentiate.[12] This can favor certain kinds of institutionalized distinctions that might not seem warranted purely on task-related grounds. In two-tiered employment systems, for instance, there are usually separate titles used to describe the higher- and lower-tier workers, who are performing tasks that are nearly or even precisely identical. Firms that outsource some of their labor, say, to maintain labor flexibility, will sometimes use job titles and physical separation to differentiate between their core employees and the supplementary work force of temporaries. Indeed, Japanese automobile assemblers use different-colored baseball caps to distinguish between school-leavers, seasonal, and temporary employees who work side-by-side on the assembly line. In some medical schools, there is a separate set of formal job titles to differentiate clinically oriented faculty members—those who see patients—from those who primarily do research. Similarly, in some educational institutions, separate titles distinguish teaching faculty from researchers, such as Professor of Human Resources Management (Teaching) versus Professor of Human Resources Management (Research). These distinctions have been used to support differential treatment or entitlements between the two groups, such as different teaching loads, who can vote on faculty promotion cases, who is authorized to serve as a principal investigator on sponsored research projects, and so forth. Different job titles aren't simply cosmetic but rather shape the identities, interactions, and social comparisons among the faculty members involved; as evidence, note that one of the strongest arguments levied against such dual systems of late is that they balkanize faculties.

Another purpose of formal roles in organizations—in addition to creating an optimal division of labor—is to symbolize things internally and externally. Thus, when organizations exist in a highly differentiated environment, they may wish to subdivide jobs and job titles so that they correspond to specialized "chunks" of the environment. For instance, a marketing-oriented organization may create separate job titles for customer service personnel subdivided by market, region, type of customer, and the like (e.g., Peripherals Marketing Manager: Financial Services, versus Peripherals Marketing Manager: Governmental Sector). Often, the duties involved here do not vary appreciably across the different segments; rather, the distinctions in job titles exist either to legitimate differential pay across segments or to symbolize to internal and external constituents a heightened sensitivity to particular segments of the environment.[13]

JOB DESIGN OR CAREER DESIGN?

We have, in large measure, discussed job design as it relates to a snapshot in time. That is, we've discussed what tasks are bundled together for one employee (or team) to attend to in a relatively short time frame, how much autonomy that individual or team might be given, and so on. The one notable exception to this has been our discussion of job rotations; we were explicit there about how job rotations can broaden the perspective of the employee, making her a better generalist when the time comes for her to be a generalist.

Especially when we get to job designs that are based on such long-run considerations, we have shifted from job design as the term is usually used to "career design." A large, full-service law partnership has "jobs" in litigation, corporate law, and tax, and it has "jobs" in managing the partnership. The job of manager—as much a *career* as a current job—has implications for the short-term job design of employees who are being groomed for managerial roles. For instance, those being groomed may rotate through a number of different legal specialities, to gain a broader perspective on the connections among the different specialties within the partnership. Or, to take an example we will discuss at length in Chapter 20, when designing the job entitled Divisional Head of Human Resources, the organization might structure the job so it can be filled by general managers rather than by HR specialists, in the belief that it is important for top managers, as part of their career development, to have a thorough grounding in HR. Our point is that in thinking about job design, it can pay to think more broadly about career design.

An excellent example for seeing this consideration at work (and for illustrating several other themes of this chapter) concerns the career and job designs of commissioned officers in the armed services.[14] We begin with relevant pieces of the five factors.

The objective of the armed forces is not only to win wars that are fought, but even more to project power and competence so that the wars are unnecessary. The technology of warfare is remarkably complex, involving many different functions and tasks. There is a high degree of task ambiguity in many instances, much uncertainty about outcomes, and a very high degree of interdependence, both at the level of the fighting unit and more globally. Officers have mixed star–guardian roles (the term foot-soldiers is ironic, and certainly doesn't apply to commissioned officers)—a risky attempt to wreak havoc with an enemy's supply lines or formations, if it ends badly, may leave a devastating hole in one's own defenses. The culture is very intense, with a strong sense of "membership" and mutual aid.

Thus, turning to job design, teams are employed extensively. Moreover, there are teams within teams—in the army, there are companies, battalions, regiments, and so on. In general, a team is assigned particular tasks and (in the field and at sea, at least) left with a lot of autonomy concerning how to carry out those tasks. This grant of autonomy is natural on at least two grounds. First, mixing technological factors with the vastly uncertain and dynamic environment, success depends crucially on making on-the-spot decisions, based on real-time information, and implementing those decisions instantly. Indeed, the premium on quick decisions and implementation gives rise to a very special sort of team: Decisions are taken (perhaps after consultation) by a single commander, who orders the implementation of his or her decision.[15] The "commander" in a particular situation is specified by a chain of command for that situation: On a ship, the captain is in command unless he becomes incapacitated, in which case the Executive Officer takes over, and so on.

Second, ensuring implementation by subordinates of the command decisions mixes compulsion (it helps to be an employer having the power to court martial and imprison team members who decide not to go along!) and internalization of the welfare of other team members. In the latter respect, empowering the team to make decisions that affect its fate—at least, about how to accomplish tasks that are given to the team—capitalizes on processes of commitment and on local information about the psychological and physical state of the team and its members that the team leader (commander) possesses.

To understand the design of jobs and careers for commissioned military officers requires that we bring in another factor, which mixes technology with environment: The team leader and his senior staff are subject to sudden . . . shall we say . . . incapacitation. The chain of command specifies which officer takes over next (with some defaults in case the entire chain disappears). The point is that even fairly junior officers may be thrust suddenly into important command positions. These officers must therefore be generalists to some extent; they must appreciate the many interdependent pieces of a complex technology. This gets us to the issue of job design versus career design: Commissioned officers are frequently rotated from one short-term job or posting to the next, so that when and if the moment comes for them to take over, they are as ready as possible. Of course, as the technology has become more complex and specialized, it is increasingly difficult for any one individual to have all the required experiences. Thus, career trajectories can and do follow different patterns for different branches of the armed forces—for example, army officers rarely get posted on ships. Even within a single branch of the armed forces, there is some specialization. In the U.S. Navy, for instance, naval aviators, surface ship officers, and submarine officers do not "mix."[16]

Because of the mix of star and guardian roles for officers that is virtually mandated by military technology, the military faces a difficult incentive problem. Of course, it relies very heavily on intrinsic motivation and peer pressure; *esprit de corps* was not a term coined in investment banking. But the incentive problems are far from solved, and consequently the armed forces do a lot of screening and performance evaluation, to find those officers whose natural mix of prudence and initiative best match the needs of command. This is also another reason for granting unit commanders autonomy in how tasks will be accomplished: It provides opportunities through observation to acquire information about the command and decision-making capabilities of junior officers.

This example not only illustrates a number of the basic themes of this chapter, but it also underscores our main point—that job design in the narrow sense of what an employee does today or this week can be influenced by career design. Is the "job" of a particular commissioned officer in the Navy to serve as the weapons officer on a destroyer? Of course, a particular mix of tasks and duties is assigned to whoever is the weapons officer. These tasks and duties are affected by the considerations we have discussed throughout this chapter. But a broader conception of the individual's job is that he is a line officer in the Navy, training for eventual command and the (unhappy) possibility that "eventual" means *tomorrow*. To accommodate that broader conception, the tasks and duties assigned to the "job" of weapons officer are broadened considerably.[17] And when it comes to issues such as the duration and variety of postings, the Navy certainly thinks along those broader lines.

This brings us full circle to where this chapter started, with the innovative program of job redesign at British Petroleum. At BP, job paths have been redefined to correspond to different levels of achievement in an array of basic skills. There are general management positions and specialist positions, and there is some opportunity for individuals to move from one to the other. But the point is, BP's innovative system is very similar to the military's hoary system of rank—not so much in terms of the notion of command, but instead in the idea that to carry out a particular posting, the employee must have particular levels of competence in various skills. Thus, job design is not conceptualized as "What tasks go with this posting?" Rather, it concerns the skills (levels) that are needed to meet the series of challenges that are expected in due course to accompany this posting. Just as with our example of the military, this is driven by a more career-oriented view at BP of designing jobs, which stresses the dynamic trajectories of employees throughout their careers, rather than focusing on the specific mix of tasks to be done today. For many organizations, particularly those that run ILMs or depend on high commitment, it is a very sensible way to conceptualize things.

WRAP-UP

Beyond this most important takeaway—that one should conceive of job design broadly—this chapter discussed a number of important job design levers in terms of a set of desiderata. As a review, it may help to think the other way around: For each of the desiderata, what are the impacts of the different HR job design levers?

- *Technological efficiency* is traditionally held to arise from narrowly defined jobs. But especially where there are informational complements, broader and richer jobs can be more efficient, and variation in job assignment may be warranted. When choosing particular tasks to mix, specific informational complements are worth watching for.

- *Flexibility* is enhanced by job enrichment and enlargement and by frequent job rotations, because these attract and help promote a more widely skilled and flexible workforce. Teams have ambiguous effects on flexibility. Autonomy also has ambiguous effects on flexibility; the key variable here is often the degree of coordination needed to achieve a particular change. In particular, the more coordination among autonomous individuals or groups that is required, the less flexible the system will be by virtue of autonomy.

- *Extrinsic incentives* are harder to design for broad jobs than for narrow jobs, when breadth is measured in terms of the number of tasks in the job per review period. If a job must mix many tasks, tasks that are matched in terms of "observability" of employee efforts should be bundled into a single job. Where the available measures compound several tasks and extrinsic incentives will be used, those tasks should be bundled together; and as the set of these tasks grows, a team-based job design is called for. Teams that are able to solve the free-rider problem can function very efficiently under team-based incentive systems.

- *Intrinsic motivation* is generally held to improve when jobs are enriched, when frequent task rotations are employed, for team-based job designs, and when autonomy is granted. But in all these cases, the workforce must have a basic taste for the innovation; these innovations aren't for everyone. Workers expect more rewards the more "complex" their jobs become. Supervisors and middle managers are often resistant. And each one of these methods for improving intrinsic motivation is likely to trigger demands for others.

- Inappropriate *social comparisons* can be triggered by broader job designs and by frequent task rotation. Team-based designs have complex *social impacts,* some beneficial to management and some not. Job titles and other symbolic parts of a "job design" can have powerful *social effects*; indeed, they are often a response to social pressures, both from within and from outside the organization.

Our overview of job design issues has emphasized the importance of aligning job design with the other elements of an organization's HR system, particularly the procedures used in recruiting and staffing. Team-based job designs, for instance, are likely to alter not only the attributes sought in hiring new employees (greater emphasis on interpersonal and communication skills, a willingness to learn, tolerance for ambiguity, and self-monitoring capabilities), but also the *processes* by which the organization recruits and selects personnel (more reliance on hiring through informal networks of current employees, greater involvement of team members in screening, hiring, and training of recruits). Accordingly, we turn next to the topics of recruiting, screening, and selecting employees.

IN REVIEW

⇒ We consider the following elements of "job design," broadly defined: level and breadth of job content, over-time variability in task assignment, specific mix of assigned tasks, use of teams, and the level of autonomy granted to individual workers or teams.

⇒ We evaluate these in terms of their effects on technological efficiency, flexibility, ability to craft explicit extrinsic incentives, intrinsic motivation and commitment, and social relations.

⇒ Enriched and enlarged jobs:
- Typically decrease efficiency, although complementarities among tasks (especially based on shared information) can dull or even reverse this effect.
- Increase organizational flexibility, though both screening and training effects.
- Complicate explicit incentives, because it is hard to balance incentives among the many diverse tasks impounded in the job.
- Generally increase intrinsic motivation.
- Have ambiguous social impacts: The employee's circle of acquaintances is usually widened, which can create invidious social comparisons but also foster positive peer pressure.

⇒ Increasing variability over time in task assignment has many of these same impacts:
- Narrow and specialized jobs are warranted where deep knowledge bases are required to execute specific tasks, training costs are high, or on-the-job experience is obtained only very slowly.
- When job duties vary over time, the problem of balancing explicit incentives across diverse tasks may be less severe if performance review periods are shorter than rotation cycles.

⇒ Team-based job designs:
- Can enhance extrinsic incentives when members can monitor one another efficiently.
- Generally enhance intrinsic motivation.
- Can enhance flexibility, but when flexibility demands changes in a team's composition or status order, groups may resist change.
- In the same vein, granting autonomy to teams or individuals can accentuate positive or negative outcomes: helping well-functioning individuals and teams to perform even more flexibly and effectively; exacerbating any problems arising from scapegoating, the abuse of individual team members, lack of sharp individual incentives, and the like.

⇒ The following guidelines should be considered in deciding which tasks to impound in a single job:

- Efficiency is enhanced by bundling tasks that depend on common information or skills.
- When measures of performance compound efforts at several different tasks, effective extrinsic incentives may require bundling those tasks into a single job. (As the set of these tasks grows, a team-based job design may become necessary.)
- Structuring effective extrinsic incentives for a bundle of tasks is tricky when the tasks differ in how well performance can be measured.
- Star and guardian roles differ in the best ways to recruit, evaluate, and motivate personnel, so bundling star and guardian tasks together poses a formidable challenge.

⇒ "High-commitment" job designs typically have three consequences that warrant careful attention:
  - Employees believe their jobs are more difficult and hence that rewards should rise.
  - Enriching jobs in one respect tends to raise employees' appetite for other job design innovations.
  - The power and authority of supervisory personnel and middle-level managers is often challenged, as their own job designs evolve from "commander" to "coach."

⇒ Job design, including the creation of symbolic distinctions among positions, is not simply a rational planning process. It also reflects social, legal, and economic pressures, including the influence of organized labor, the cultures of professional groups, and employees' social and economic interests.
  - Job titles play a particularly powerful role in shaping social comparisons and can be used strategically by management to foster or discourage specific comparisons.

⇒ As workers' job duties become broader and more varied, "job design" and "career design" of necessity become closely linked, to design employment trajectories that leverage the multiple competencies that employees have acquired.

ENDNOTES

1. Excerpted from "Job Descriptions for the 21st Century," by Milan Moravec and Robert Tucker, copyright June 1992. Used with permission of ACC Communications Inc. *Personal Journal* (now known as *Workforce*), Costa Mesa, CA. All rights reserved.

2 In the same way, to some extent Chapter 14 ("Staffing and Recruitment") concerns the HR-endogenous aspects of the workforce. We've more or less continuously discussed HR-endogenous aspects of culture. And whenever we discuss siting a facility to take

advantage of this or that aspect of the local labor pool, we are looking at the HR-endogenous aspects of the external environment.

3. The same motivational claims cannot necessarily be made for job *enlargement*. If a job consists of a single highly boring task, adding a second stultifying task to the job duties may not provide much intrinsic motivation, though it may relieve a bit of the monotony.

4. See, for example, Janice A. Klein, "Why Supervisors Resist Employee Involvement," *Harvard Business Review* 62 (September–October, 1984): 87–95.

5. Of course, there are other strategic reasons for the rotations. For instance, repeat business and word-of-mouth referrals are critical to Club Med's strategy, and GOs who have worked in other resort villages can help cross-sell by enticing guests with descriptions of other Club properties. Mixing GOs by nationality also provides a multicultural environment for guests that meshes with the Club's desired global image. Offering opportunities to visit far-flung lands no doubt also helps Club Med in its efforts to keep costs competitive (i.e., it pays relatively low wages, offering travel opportunities as an alternative form of compensation). And, anticipating material on screening to be discussed in Chapter 14, the willingness of a prospective GO to move frequently from resort to resort signals attributes that the company desires in its service employees; material on the Club's Web site (http://www.clubmed.com/ClubMed/Jobs/go2.html) aimed at potential recruits proclaims that "a good G.O. is by definition eager to meet and work with people from many cultures. . . . Only if they're genuinely curious about other cultures can G.O.'s learn to communicate with [guests] on their own terms." Club Med is hardly the only organization to foster such an itinerant culture. Some readers may be old enough to remember when employees of IBM Corporation claimed that the acronym stood for "I've Been Moved."

6. What about direct monitoring of job performance for jobs that include noisily measured tasks? To the extent that cost-effective monitoring is possible, this is an alternative. But the distinction is more semantic than real—if cost-effective monitoring of worker performance is possible, we would say that performance on this task is precisely measurable, where the measure is the report of the monitor.

7. The star–guardian mix creates challenges along other dimensions as well, and we will revisit this mix in Chapters 14 (staffing and recruitment) and 16 (promotion and career concerns).

8. Of course, this takes as given that team members have internalized the organization's goals and possess the information and resources (including training) necessary to manage themselves effectively. If these conditions are not satisfied, then the management involved has been derelict in establishing the preconditions for a team to work effectively.

9. See James Baron and Jeffrey Pfeffer, "The Social Psychology of Organizations and Inequality," *Social Psychology Quarterly* 57 (September 1994): 190–209.

10. See David Strang and James Baron, "Categorical Imperatives: The Structure of Job Titles in California State Agencies," *American Sociological Review* 55 (August 1990): 479–95.

11. See Barbara Reskin and Patricia Roos, *Job Queues, Gender Queues: Explaining Women's Inroads into Male Occupations* (Philadelphia: Temple University Press, 1990).

12. Of course, such bureaucratic distinctions between groups are most effective when they are reinforced or buttressed by other mechanisms for heightening intergroup bound-

aries, such as limited contact (through distinct shifts or work locations), differences in social composition of the groups, and so on.

13. Taking this a step further: In Chapter 12, we proposed the example of a law firm whose client base ran from movie stars to street criminals, suggesting that a legal assistant who interacts with the movie stars might—according to economic theory—have lower wages than one whose job includes frequent visits to the county jail because of a compensating differential (i.e., the movie stars provide psychic compensation to the first legal assistant, whereas the second needs some extra money to compensate for visits to the jail). But we think it more likely, in fact, that the first legal assistant gets to hobnob with movie stars *and* gets higher wages, to fit her social status as legal assistant to the movie-star counselor. To legitimize this double advantage in working conditions and wages, the law firm might resort to categories such as Executive (or Senior) Legal Assistant versus Legal Assistant.

14. Armed forces are complex organizations, and our description here is something of a simplification of general trends. Also, we draw almost entirely from the "job design" used by the armed forces of the United States. We suspect that most armies and navies are structured similarly, but one can imagine important differences under varying circumstances (e.g., an army that depends on conscription and very long periods of mandatory reserve duty, as in Switzerland and Israel, might differ significantly). As a final caveat, even within the U.S. armed forces, some commissioned officers specialize. In the Navy, for instance, there are engineering specialists and supply officers, in addition to line officers. We are giving a simplified description of the career design for a line officer.

15. In exceptional cases—such as the use of nuclear weapons—some measure of consensus is required. And there are limits on what can be ordered.

16. Consequently, the chain of command on a ship does not necessarily respect rank: A submarine that is carrying a high-ranking naval aviator is not commanded by that aviator if the captain and exec of the submarine are incapacitated, on the very good grounds that the aviator's experiences are inappropriate for commanding a sub. But if the submarine's crew and its aviator guest are somehow marooned on an island, the aviator, being the ranking officer, takes command. And command does not pass to specialist engineers or supply officers, regardless of their rank, if (more junior) line officers remain to take command.

17. In particular, every officer on a ship takes turns standing watch as Officer of the Deck, in which capacity he or she is in charge of "driving" the ship while the captain is doing something else (e.g., sleeping). To do this, the officer must be briefed on the operational situation as well as the status of all shipboard systems. That is, although weapons officers have primary responsibility for the weapons systems—responsibility that they will exercise in critical situations unless incapacitated or forced by circumstances into a more senior role—their job also entails preparing for sudden command responsibility.

14

STAFFING AND RECRUITMENT

Organizations often expend substantial resources trying to hire employees who are well suited to the positions that need to be filled. New employees may be subjected to a probationary period (more about this later), but there are often substantial costs associated with hiring, training, and discharge of unsatisfactory employees, and those costs rise the longer it takes to discover that an employee is unsatisfactory. For example, a study conducted at Merck & Co., the pharmaceutical company, estimated that their costs associated with employee turnover, including disrupted work relationships and the transactional costs of getting employees on and off the payroll, are between 150% and 250% of the employee's annual income.[1] Even for jobs involving less specialized knowledge or network interdependencies than the workforce at Merck, turnover costs can still be enormous. For instance, in 1989, 119,000 sales jobs turned over in the retail network of the Merchandise Group of Sears, Roebuck and Co. With an estimated cost of $900 to replace and train a new sales associate, the annual turnover cost amounted to more than $110 million, representing 17% of the Merchandising Group's income that year. Even more important, Sears' own customer surveys revealed a strong negative relationship between store turnover and customer satisfaction.[2]

Careful decisions made at the outset concerning whom to hire can therefore be quite important. Dimensions along which an employee can "fit" a job or organization include (but are not limited to): particular skills or talents that the employee possesses, including interpersonal and communication skills, whether innate or acquired through education and training; the taste for particular sorts of work that the job entails or rewards that the firm emphasizes; and fit with the culture and social norms of the organization. Mechanisms exist to select along all these lines. In this chapter, we outline *some* salient theories of employee selection that can be found in the literatures of economics and other social sciences. The chapter is organized around four questions: (1) What sort of workforce does the firm want? (2) How does it encourage the right sort of people to apply? (3) How does it judge applicants? (4) What legal limitations are there on this process? After giving some answers, we focus on some important process considerations relating to staffing and recruitment.

WHAT SORT OF WORKFORCE DOES THE FIRM WANT?

We won't have a lot to say about this, because in many ways we've said it all before. But there are two important points to make here. First, the quality and qualities of workers should fit with the firm's strategy, culture, technology, and environment. Toys "R" Us, because of its strategy as a large-volume, low-cost, no-frills retailer, probably doesn't want to attract the same sales personnel as does FAO Schwarz or Learningsmith, two retailers that emphasize high-quality toys and educational items sold by knowledgeable sales personnel. A firm that offers lifetime employment and realizes this objective by shifting employees from one line of work to another as needs arise should put greater emphasis on general skills and flexibility than should a firm that does not move workers around very much. An organization that hires clericals in a local labor market with very high demand for skilled clericals will, on the basis of cost effectiveness, hire a different sort of clerical worker (and design the job accordingly) than the same organization would if the market for clericals were not very competitive. And so on. In all our discussions to date about fit between the workforce and the other four factors, we were to some extent discussing the sort of employee the firm should be pursuing.

Diversity

The second point is in some sense a particular case of the first, but one that deserves particular mention. It concerns the level of diversity in the workforce. There are compelling social reasons (and, in some jurisdictions, legal requirements) for maintaining a workforce that is as demographically and socially diverse as the general population. At the same time, organizations may face external economic pressures to increase *or* decrease diversity. Customers and clients may resist dealing with certain types of individuals, or they may insist on it. And for internal reasons, organizations may find that diversity is helpful or problematic.

One case for diversity is that it broadens the perspectives the firm can bring to bear in specific decisions. Insofar as the firm is able to choose among alternatives with some discernment, then having more diverse viewpoints represented will widen the set of alternatives considered, leading on average to better decisions. Diversity can also help the firm to reach out to and then serve a broad clientele. An American firm, for example, that wishes to extend operations or sales to the Far East, South America, or virtually anywhere in world, may find invaluable resources in the ethnically and racially diverse population of the United States, giving it a competitive advantage over firms that recruit from more homogeneous populations. Particularly in transactions involving trust, ambiguity, and intensive communication, some similarity between an employee and the external constituencies with whom he or she interacts can be an asset.

On the other hand, that same argument can cut the other way. Whereas diversity may be an asset externally in relating to heterogeneous constituents, it may be a liability internally in some instances. Spontaneous trust will usually be stronger between socially similar individuals, and in cases where the individuals share a social environment beyond the workplace—most dramatically, in family businesses—the ability to punish bad behavior with social sanctions is increased, which in turn increases trust. In particular, an organization with a more interdependent technology may find itself favoring a relatively more socially homogeneous workforce.[3]

Thus, private organizations benefit in some ways from a diverse workforce, but diversity can also have (private) countervailing disadvantages. Society, on the other hand, generally has a strong preference in hiring and staffing that is nondiscriminatory.[4] Consequently, a private organization may face societal pressure to become more diverse than it finds privately optimal.

Organizations that wish to realize the benefits of diversity, both for themselves and for society, can blunt some of the costs by screening for alternative forms of homogeneity or, alternatively, by creating them "artificially." For instance, recruiting students who attended similar educational institutions or majored in the same subject or served in the military or have the same off-work hobbies may produce some of the same benefits of homogeneity, while still permitting a labor pool that is heterogeneous on racial, ethnic, gender, and other lines.[5] And exposing new recruits to similar formative experiences and socialization can often create the same types of bonds that usually exist *a priori* among individuals who are homogeneous along racial, ethnic, or other dimensions.

ENCOURAGING THE RIGHT APPLICANTS

Once the firm decides what types of workers it wants, both in terms of their average qualities and the amount of dispersion sought around those averages, it must find ways to select among applicants. But this formulation—the firm chooses from a set of applicants—doesn't do justice to an important part of the process, namely *encouraging* desirable people to apply. Some firms, seeking candidates for at least some positions, have found proactive searches to be somewhere between useful and essential. At the extreme is the use of headhunters, which we will discuss at the end of this section. But less extreme forms of soliciting applications from qualified candidates should also be part of the formulation.

For example, firms that pay premium wages and provide premium perks (relative to local labor market conditions) find that, among other benefits, this encourages a larger applicant pool. These other benefits include reduced turnover and a more committed workforce, whether out of fear of losing a plum position or because of the norm of reciprocity. These are the most often cited justifications for premium wages and benefits. But there are the recruiting benefits to consider as well. Insofar as the firm is able to select intelligently among its applicants, a larger applicant pool is *per se* a good thing. However, for several reasons, offering premium wages and benefits also often results in an applicant pool that is better on average: (1) If applicants are drawn to some extent from other firms, and if more able workers are apt to be better paid elsewhere, then it may take a premium package to attract their attention and application. (2) If the firm is known to be able to select intelligently from among its applicants, and if the premium wages and benefits attract some very qualified workers (say, by the process described in [1]), then less able applicants have less incentive to apply, knowing that they are less likely to land the job.[6]

Applicant Self-Selection Through Reputation or Job Characteristics

In many cases, it is as much in the interest of the employee to fit a job as it is for the employer, because the employee suffers when the fit is bad and the situation must be either endured or rectified. This is especially true concerning fit with the organization's culture. Thus, in many instances, the organization can benefit from worker *self*-selection if the organization can make known to potential workers the conditions of the workplace or job. A good example concerns the Lincoln Electric Company. We noted in Chapter 3 that the conditions of employment at Lincoln are so well known within the surrounding community of Cleveland that hard-working, industrious children reportedly will sometimes come home from school with report cards that read that "Joanie is a Lincoln Electric sort of child." As a result, applicants for employment at Lincoln will have a very good idea about what the job entails and what it takes to fit the culture and compensation system at Lincoln. Similarly, it is not hard to imagine that Sun Hydraulics has a strong general reputation both among hydraulic engineers internationally and among skilled metal workers and the like in the Sarasota area, so that substantial self-selection takes place there as well. The United Parcel Service also benefits from self-selection; many of its entry-level workers (entering as package car drivers) are previous part-timers who worked during a school holiday at a sorting hub and found that they enjoyed the feel of the place.

General reputation can be complemented or supplemented by the exact terms of employment, especially when those terms are markedly different from other organizations in the industry. In Chapter 2, we mentioned the real estate network RE/MAX and its distinctive compensation system for its agents. The industry standard is that agents split their commissions with the agency for which they work, perhaps with a base wage to supplement commissions and insure against dry spells. RE/MAX, in contrast, allows agents to keep all of their commissions, collecting from them a fixed amount per month for office and clerical services that are tendered. This is clearly a compensation system that favors hard working, talented, and aggressive agents; and thus the compensation system attracts this sort of real estate agent.[7] In the language of market signaling and screening (see below and in Appendix D), working for RE/MAX is a signal to potential clients that the agent is hard-working and aggressive; someone with a house to sell who wants this sort of agent knows that RE/MAX has a stable of them.[8]

An example with a different flavor is a firm that is known to pay slightly sub-standard wages, but that is known to make up for this with greater worker autonomy, less hierarchy, and so on. (We're thinking here of Sun Hydraulics.) Workers attracted to this firm might be those who are less concerned with pay and more concerned with the quality of projects available and particular sorts of working conditions, who are just the sort of worker the firm desires. Note that the relatively low wages act as a self-selection device, screening out those for whom monetary compensation is extremely important, or at least more important than those qualities (such as a desire to exercise independence) that the organization finds especially valuable.[9]

Co-worker Referrals

Many organizations rely on current employees for referrals. Sometimes employees are even rewarded financially for such referrals. Referrals are in part a selection device—current employees may have good information about the qualities of the candidate that might otherwise be unavailable to the employer. But for now, we wish to focus on three other aspects of co-worker referrals. The first two are simple: Hiring through such informal channels can result in savings on search costs, advertising, and the like. And current employees have a very good understanding of the requirements of the job, the culture at work, and other aspects of the job, and are therefore likely to provide this information to the friends and acquaintances whom they recommend. Thus, the worker-self-selection effect mentioned in the preceding subsection is at work; one can trust that the referred party has a good understanding of what the job entails and has therefore passed a self-selection test. Consequently, we expect that individuals who find a job through a personal contact with someone already working in the organization should be more satisfied, productive, and likely to remain. In general, research on the topic confirms those expectations.[10]

The third aspect is that, on several grounds, co-worker referrals can be desirable hires *per se*. A social tie to an existing employee provides a ready-made avenue of socialization, training, and social support for the new hire. (Note that there may also be positive effects on the attitudes and behavior of the person who *made* the referral.) The co-worker responsible for the referral presumably will also have a reputational stake in the success of the person whom he or she referred, providing an additional reason to provide assistance and support to the new hire. Finally, we would expect a new employee who enters an organization with a preexisting tie to a current employee to have an easier time becoming assimilated socially within the workgroup. There is a strong psychological tendency toward balance in social relationships, whereby the friends of our friends become our friends. (It is difficult to like and respect someone while simultaneously disliking or disrespecting that person's friends.) Accordingly, the new hire is likely to form positive relations with the other people with whom the "sponsor" has positive relations within the organization. Co-worker referrals seem likely to be particularly valuable to organizations that hire primarily based on attitudes, values, or organizational fit, such as Southwest Airlines or Toyota.[11]

There is, however, a darker side of co-worker referrals. By relying on personal referrals of existing employees, organizations are more likely to reproduce themselves socially, which could hamper efforts to diversify the workforce along particular dimensions. Furthermore, the prevalence of preexisting social relations among co-workers need not be an unqualified positive; it could facilitate undesired collusion, for instance, or generate uncomfortable role conflicts (e.g., if the new hire ends up ultimately as the supervisor of the person who "sponsored" her application for employment). And, of course, employers will want to bear in mind that there are many reasons why a referral is made; to engage in caricature, one will wish to be appropriately wary of an employee recommending a sibling-in-law or the nephew or niece of the employee's spouse.

Personnel Search Organizations

An interesting phenomenon in the realm of staffing and recruitment is the personnel search organization: a firm that acts as broker, bringing prospective employees and employers together. To discuss fully the brokerage function performed by such search firms would take another chapter (at least), but it may be worthwhile to mention several economic functions played by such organizations: (1) One rationale for personnel search organizations is that they specialize in the task and thus have a presumably superior technology for locating individuals to fit particular jobs. At the very least, they have a wide information base to call on.[12] (2) In Chapter 8, we argued that an advantage of internal labor markets was that close experience with employees could provide employers with a wealth of useful information on which to base promotion decisions. But a disadvantage that comes with this is that employees may be motivated to engage in influence activities, taking actions designed to make themselves look good (and competitors look bad). By enlisting a personnel search firm, one may be able to reduce influence activities. (3) When we discuss promotions (Chapter 16), we will note the problems posed for organizations by the "losers" in the promotion contest. Losing *per se* may be demotivating, but having a third party involved in the decision may help to defuse responsibility from being attributed by the losers to the organization they (continue to) work for. This may be especially true when an outsider is brought in over the heads of insiders. (4) Conducting negotiations somewhat at arm's length may serve either the employer's or prospective employee's need for confidentiality.

SELECTING AMONG THE APPLICANTS

Having obtained a pool of applicants, the next step is to select among them. There are several means for doing this.

Probationary Periods

Sometimes the most valid screen that can be applied is to hire the worker for some probationary period, to gauge his or her level and quality of performance on the job itself. In a sense, internal labor markets (ILMs) use this practice to an extreme degree, where one's performance for several years at lower-level jobs is used as a test of suitability for higher-level jobs. As we have already noted, the ILM structure is especially prevalent when the higher-level jobs have a strong guardian character. Also, this sort of probationary period is useful when the firm wishes to hire nontraditional workers or employees whose credentials and qualifications are hard to ascertain. Thus, this can be useful as part of an effort aimed at increasing workforce diversity (but see point [5] below).

A number of problems with the use of probationary periods are worth noting:

1. Insofar as the purpose of screening is to avoid training, search, and replacement costs, probation can be a mediocre solution. It may lessen search costs, insofar as the firm is more willing to gamble if it can discharge those who work out poorly. However, search costs usually don't fall to zero, training costs often remain high, and there is the prospect of having to replace the candidate at the end of the probation period.

2. A "rat race" phenomenon naturally ensues.[13] To some extent, effort and ability are substitutes in job performance. Employees who are on probation will know that they are (at least in the United States, there is a legal responsibility for the employer to disclose this), and they may be motivated to work especially hard during the period of probation. Once the probationary period is over, however, the worker may slack off enormously. If everyone has the same ability and desire to employ effort as a substitute for skill, then this isn't a large problem, as the more able will still win in any comparative evaluation. But people vary in their ability to put out spurts of effort and in their distaste for such bursts of effort. The result is then a bias in favor of those who are relatively more able to sprint over the probationary hurdle and those for whom such sprints are relatively less distasteful.[14] Also, the existence of such "rat races" early in one's career with a particular firm may send a powerful message inspiring a sense of fear, subordination, and expendability, undercutting attempts by the firm to encourage intrinsic motivation or gift-exchange effects.

3. Related to the rat race phenomenon is the fact that probationary periods may result in very high levels of counterproductive politicking and influence activity. We will discuss this in greater detail in Chapter 16.

4. The longer the probationary period, the more costly it is to the employee to be discharged at or near the end of the period. Thus, the higher must be the compensation offered at the outset. When the costs of discharge are very high and the individual is risk averse, the amount of compensation that must be offered can be enormous. Hence, the system will tend to select for those who are less risk averse or who have better fallback opportunities on the outside, neither of which is necessarily beneficial. At the same time, it sometimes becomes hard for superiors to make tough discharge decisions, especially when personal attachments and considerations become strong.[15] These problems can be ameliorated if the organization can find ways to cushion a decision to discharge someone at the end of their probation (e.g., by providing counseling services or severance pay).

A related effect concerns the costs of discharge to the employer. At least in the United States, employees can and sometimes do sue over wrongful discharge. Declaring at the outset that the job has a probationary period attached affords the employer some measure of protection against such suits, but the longer the probationary period, the more (in general) the courts insist on careful end-of-period evaluation and on due process for the individual.

5. When probation is used to widen the pool of applicants, discharge decisions that appear discriminatory can occur. Suppose, for example, that a firm filled with Ivy League graduates decides to broaden its ranks by taking on some employees who were educated in the French *Grandes Ecoles*. All new employees, whether from the Ivy League or the Grandes Ecoles, are subject to a six-month probation. Suppose that the standard for surviving probation is such that most new employees survive (because, for example, good screening is possible at the outset). Now, suppose that there is no difference in the *average* performance of Ivy League and Grandes Ecoles candidates, but that there is greater *dispersion* in the performance of Grandes Ecoles candidates. This might arise if, for instance, the firm has a harder time reading Grandes Ecoles transcripts or letters from Grandes Ecoles instructors than it does with the Ivy League, because it has had far more experience with the Ivy League. Then, even if the averages of the two populations are the same, the greater dispersion in the Grandes Ecoles candidates will mean that more of them will fail to make the grade, and it will look as if the firm is discriminating against Grandes Ecoles probationees. In the United States, at least, if graduates from the Grandes Ecoles are disproportionately members of a protected class,[16] the use of a probationary period can open the firm up to legal challenges. (This phenomenon is related to statistical discrimination, which is discussed more formally below.)

With all these potential drawbacks, why use probationary periods as a screening device? We can think of two related reasons. First, the firm may have little choice. The data available at the time of application may be insufficient to make an informed judgment as to the applicant's suitability for the job; only time on the job will tell the employer what she wants to know. Universities typically put new faculty through a seven-to-ten-year probationary period, because it takes that long in many cases to be sure about the relevant qualities of the individual. Second, in cases where the employee has a better initial sense about his fitness for the job than does the employer, probation can discourage unfit applicants from applying. By raising the stakes for the employee if discharge takes place (see [4] above), the firm creates a useful self-selection mechanism. (Notwithstanding the theoretical possibility of this second reason, it is usually the first—no other effective screen being available—that leads to the use of probation.)

Credentials

Employers will sometimes rely on employees having obtained certain credentials before offering employment. At least three rationales can be provided for this:

1. The organization that offers the credential is particularly skilled in its selection process, and employers free ride on those skills. For example, a theory sometimes advanced regarding MBA degrees from premier business schools is that all the value added comes from the admissions process. Having survived the competition to gain admission to Harvard or INSEAD, say, the student is certified as a good potential manager. Insofar as this is true, there is little reason to bother with the (according-to-this-theory) irrelevant education and tuition. We might expect potential employers to offer jobs to newly admitted students, if they could get hold of the admission lists.[17] Schools, in response, should keep tight control over their admissions lists, so that they can obtain the student's tuition, as their payment for performing this brokerage function.

2. By obtaining the credential, individuals signify that they possess desirable talents or skills that are acquired in the process of obtaining the credential. An MBA education might actually be useful, for instance, because of the specific knowledge conveyed, or perhaps because of the values and work ethic inculcated while pursuing the degree. Alternatively, the value of the education might come from the network of contacts that students build while in graduate school.

3. By obtaining the credential, individuals signify that they possess desirable *inherent* talents or skills, which are signaled by the possession of the credential. For example, an employer may not feel that the education attained by getting a high school diploma is of any particular use on the job, but the employer may view applicants who obtained their diploma as more apt to be diligent or to accept authority or to be trainable than are applicants who didn't graduate high school. The idea, in other words, is that having, say, a high school diploma correlates with desirable skills and traits, even if education itself doesn't produce any of the desiderata.

There have been substantial debates about whether educational credentials in particular reflect specific competencies (e.g., reading, reasoning, etc.) relevant to job performance or instead reflect how an individual will fit into an organization (e.g., interactive style, deference to superiors, willingness to comply with rules). Another hypothesis is that credentials do not correlate with any requisite job skills except for an ability to learn, which will be important to an organization that plans to impart necessary job skills itself. It has also been argued that organizations choose more highly educated workers for reasons other than screening; the educational makeup of an organization can help enhance the organization's reputation in the eyes of key constituencies (including clients). These ideas lead to some predictions about the settings in which we might expect to see the greatest reliance by organizations on educational credentials in screening. Educational credentials should be emphasized most (in hiring and pay allocation) in settings where: information and communication play important roles; workers are highly interdependent; monitoring is difficult; external evaluations of the competence of the workforce are important; training is intensive and internal labor markets are well developed (as the employer will want to make sure to select the right workers to invest in for the long haul); or there is rapid social and technological change (because in such circumstances the employer will tend to fall back on more general assessments of worker ability, lacking well-developed alternatives). The research evidence is generally consistent with these predictions.[18] Similarly, evidence suggests that differences in the systems of control used in educational institutions tend to map to differences in the control systems of organizations that recruit from those institutions. For instance, the more autonomous, intrinsically oriented control systems of elite educational institutions are claimed to correspond closely to the elite jobs to which graduates of those institutions are destined, whereas harsher, more authoritarian, rule-based control systems are used in lower-tier educational institutions that prepare students for jobs in more bureaucratic office and factory settings.

Market Signaling and Screening

Suppose that having a high school diploma is an indicator, albeit an imperfect one, of the individual's willingness to submit to authority, and suppose that this is viewed as a desirable trait for a new employee. Then employers might reasonably choose among job candidates based on whether they have a high school diploma.

Suppose further that this is generally the case—that is, employers in an area view a high school diploma as a desirable signal about the qualities possessed by the individual, and so they give preference to high school graduates. (We are not ruling out the possibility that a high school diploma is viewed positively because employers believe that a high school education provides useful skills. But neither are we insisting that this is the only reason a high school diploma might be viewed positively.)

If this is well known in the community, then individual high school students, despite resenting the discipline imposed by vice principals and physical education teachers, might nonetheless stay in school to obtain the valuable credential. That is, if a high school diploma is useful in getting a job, and if this is well known by prospective dropouts, it can change the quality of a high school diploma as a signal. Getting a diploma is no longer such a strong signal of willingness to submit to authority (but dropping out *before* graduation is a stronger signal of unwillingness to submit). Indeed, it is possible that the signal loses all meaning because everyone chooses to endure high school, so as not to be stigmatized as a truly rotten apple. Those who are really willing to accept authority and wish to indicate this to prospective employers might then have to resort to more onerous demonstrations of their willingness to obey (e.g., enlistment in the armed forces). The point is that as parties sending a particular signal come to understand how that signal will be used, they may change their behavior regarding the signal, and the meaning of the signal thereby changes. A signal, to be sustained as a signal, must be so distasteful or costly for some group that will be disadvantaged for not sending it, so that even taking that disadvantage into account, members of the group will choose not to send the signal, living instead with the consequences.

This idea is the beginning of the economic theory of market signaling (and the closely related theory of market screening), developed initially by A. M. Spence.[19] If you have never encountered the theory of adverse selection and market signaling, now might be a good time for a quick overview of the abstract theory (which we provide in Appendix D). Assuming some familiarity with the basic theoretical formulation, we proceed here to an illustrative application related to the job market.

Imagine a completely fictitious world in which "investment bakeries" seek to hire individuals who possess a single skill: the ability to work at all hours of day and night, even in a state of advanced sleep deprivation. Such individuals are invaluable to investment bakeries, and they are willing to pay a very large amount of money to lure such people into their employ. The amount of money is so very large that literally everyone in society wishes to get one of these jobs, even though only 1% of the population is really qualified to do so. Because of the costs of training and turnover, bakeries must know in advance that the people they hire are from the 1% who can stand up to the physical demands of the job, and bakeries are unable to ascertain this through direct observation or from medical examination. In this society, there is a Famous East Coast BAking School (hereafter, called FECBAS), which specializes in providing MBAs (Masters of Bakery Administration) to its students while giving them absolutely no useful knowledge. None of the education imparted at FECBAS is of any use whatsoever in a productive sense. But FECBAS does provide a signaling device. The heart of the two-year FECBAS MBA program is the first-year core, a trip into the pits of hell, in which students must work all hours of the day and night, even in a state of advanced sleep deprivation. Since the FECBAS core curriculum is only a year long and has no academic merit whatsoever, any member of the population can survive it. But it is extremely distasteful to everyone. The key is that although this program is distasteful to everyone, it is comparatively less distasteful to the 1% of the population that investment bakeries would like to identify. That is, for any member of that 1% of the population, two years at FECBAS (including a year in the core) followed by a job with an investment bakery is preferable to a more normal job, whereas for the other 99% of the population, the job with an investment bakery is insufficient compensation to make up for two years at FECBAS. Hence, the 1% of the population who can stand the FECBAS program go there to signal that they are in this 1%, and they get jobs as investment bakers in consequence. "Education" at FECBAS is a pure signal sent by the 1% in order to distinguish themselves from the masses, and the signal works because even though everyone dislikes the FECBAS program, this 1% dislikes it relatively less.

Note well, if suddenly the demand for investment bakers were to increase, leading to an increase in their salaries, FECBAS would have to redesign its core curriculum, to make it even more distasteful and onerous. Otherwise, the increased salaries (and the old core) might attract to FECBAS people outside of the 1% that investment bakeries wish to attract. The more attractive the payoffs from sending a given signal, the more onerous or costly the signal must be to the group that is *not* supposed to send it, to get the same signaling value out of it.

Also note that if we were to replace FECBAS with the Famous East Coast BUsiness School (FECBUS) and investment bakeries with investment bankers, this is a different theory of MBA "education" than the one we advanced earlier. In both cases, the (entirely fictitious!) story is that MBA education is of no productive value. But in the earlier story, the admissions office of FECBUS did all the work, selecting the best students, aided perhaps a bit by the unwillingness of somewhat less-qualified students to pay the application fees. In the FECBAS story we are telling here, however, the students completely sort themselves out, based on their relative ability to withstand the FECBAS core curriculum, an ability that is correlated (perfectly in our story, but, more generally, positively) with the characteristics desired by employers.[20]

This is a rather too-colorful rendition of the idea that education may be a signal of latent ability or motivation, sent consciously by the more-able members of the population. Education in general does provide productive skills, but if at the same time it is relatively less onerous to obtain for those who are inherently more able, then those who are more able may use education as a signal of their ability. And, in a signaling equilibrium, they may be overinvesting in education, insofar as education has signaling value beyond its direct benefits in increasing the productivity of the student.

Three comments on the theory are in order:

1. In models of market signaling, it is assumed that employers are able to decipher the signals that are being sent. In reality, signals will be noisy, and employers will have to assess (statistically) what they entail. When a small fraction of the population is sending a particular signal and thus reliable data are scarce, disentangling the meaning of that signal may be difficult. For cases in which employers are relatively risk averse about the individual being hired, this may make such signals ineffective. Indeed, when the sample size becomes zero, employers have no data to read. So when signals are sent that are not part of the general equilibrium, employers must come up with some hypothesis as to what these signals mean, a hypothesis that needn't bear any particular relationship to the truth.

    This has two consequences: First, it allows for the existence of many different signaling equilibria, based, so to speak, on custom and not necessarily on economic efficiency.[21] Second, it can lead to self-generating discrimination: If members of a particular group never send a particular signal, then employers might not know what to make of the signal. If employers respond cautiously, this causes members of the group to stop trying to send the signal, which means there is no data for employers to process. For instance, never having encountered a deaf FECBAS graduate, a prospective employer might be inclined to conclude (wrongly) that a deaf graduate's MBA has no signaling value because the two years at FECBAS couldn't have been that onerous for a deaf person, relative to students who had to listen to their professors. Concerned that this is how employers might respond, deaf individuals might not pursue a FECBAS MBA, thereby perpetuating the status quo.

2. *Signaling* is used by economists to describe a situation in which a party holding private information sends some signal to an uninformed trading partner, expecting that this signal will communicate the private information and understanding what inferences will be made and what consequences will ensue. Hence, a more able individual signals this to employers by getting an MBA, because a less able individual couldn't stand the pain of the program.

Screening is used to describe closely related phenomena, whereby uninformed parties in the market offer the informed party a menu of choices, and the choice from this menu by the informed party communicates information. In the job market, a lot of screening takes place. Recall RE/MAX, for instance. The notion was that RE/MAX, by offering an unusual and particularly risky compensation scheme, would attract only hard-working, aggressive, and talented real estate agents. Note that in this case, RE/MAX itself is not offering a menu of compensation schemes and using a potential employee's choice as a signal of that person's traits.[22] Rather, in this case, by offering a compensation scheme that differs so markedly from the traditional compensation formula that other real estate companies utilize, RE/MAX is able to screen for the particular array of traits that it desires in its workforce. Another example from the employment context concerns cafeteria benefits plans. Although seldom recognized (and no doubt likely to be contentious), an employer could presumably make inferences about employees' characteristics and propensities by exploiting information on how individuals choose to allocate benefit dollars from among a menu of choices. Consider, for instance, the employee who allocates a large proportion of her benefit dollars to the company-sponsored legal insurance plan, versus another who allocates a big chunk to the company's educational reimbursement program.

3. Our discussion has focused on market signaling by employees being considered for employment by firms. But we also have had (and will have) occasion to discuss ways in which organizations might send signals to potential employees. Imagine that we have two employers, one of whom is more willing and able than the other to treat employees well. (For instance, the benevolent employer might have a sweeter disposition or perhaps a bigger savings account that makes her more able to refrain from discharging people when times turn bad.) If you are the benevolent employer, and you want to attract workers to your employ based on that fact, how do you effectively signal your character to potential employees? The answer is, *You take actions that would be too costly for a malevolent employer to take, but that are not as costly for you, if they result in potential employees identifying your benevolence.* Recall the example of Jim Casey in the early days of UPS inviting his employees to join a union. Or think of organizations that provide assurances of employment security of the sort experienced by workers at Lincoln Electric or Sun Hydraulics.

Job Interviews

A common way to evaluate job candidates is through an employment interview or a series of interviews. Psychologists and sociologists have studied the reliability and validity[23] of job interviews in great depth, and their conclusions are somewhat devastating. Job interviews are neither reliable nor valid in general. Moreover, they are subject to substantial cognitive and evaluative biases, including in-group bias (i.e., favoring those who are socially similar to the interviewer, especially when the interviewer is part of the organization's dominant group), improper discounting, anchoring on initial impressions, and so on. Some studies have shown that the evaluation given a candidate depends strongly on the quality of the preceding candidate(s): the better those that preceded, the worse on average the current candidate does. In many studies, biases of the interviewer about the nature of the job, or preconceptions held by the interviewer about the characteristics of an ideal candidate, proved to influence specific evaluations. (For example, women are scored poorly when interviewing for a traditionally male job, and vice versa.) Interviewers can have a significant impact on the responses given by the interviewee, through both verbal and nonverbal actions.[24]

Research has also shown that there are better and worse interviewing styles. A very common finding is that unstructured interviews are particularly unreliable and invalid; reliability and validity rise substantially when interviewers follow a set script in the interview, which allows for more direct comparisons of candidates and somewhat defuses anchoring on initial impressions. Panel interviews, in which the interviewee faces a panel of interviewers simultaneously, tend to give better results. Interviews that involve a simulated decision-making exercise tend to work better (when the job calls for decision-making). Interviews can be most useful for assessing communication and interpersonal skills and (sometimes) general intelligence, and they are least useful for assessing specific analytical skills.[25] Interviewers do a better job when they rate the individual along a number of different scales and combine scores mechanically or by formula than when they try subjectively to integrate the different aspects into a single overall evaluation. Training of interviewers can be effective in increasing reliability and validity and in reducing interviewer influence on the interviewee's answers.

It is important to recognize that job interviews are often not only about the employer collecting information about prospective employees, but also about *dis-*

seminating information to potential hires. In other words, the job interview is often where an organization creates its first impression on individuals who will eventually become employees, and where it begins to communicate its culture. For that reason, the process of the interview can be very important. This is doubly true for organizations that serve the public and rely extensively on public image, because every job interviewee is also a potential customer.

An extensive body of research has examined how the expectations communicated during applicants' initial contacts with the organization affect their subsequent job attitudes and behavior once hired. This work documents fairly convincingly that so-called "realistic job previews," which communicate the good and bad things about the job and the organization, are better in the long run than hard-sell efforts that ultimately produce disappointment and disillusionment. Realistic job previews have been shown to facilitate self-selection and to result in greater job satisfaction, higher performance, stronger organizational commitment, reduced ambiguity and stress, and lower turnover.[26] Such previews are most effective when they provide accurate and credible information from multiple sources concerning a variety of aspects of employment, especially things that employees feel they wouldn't otherwise have easily been able to find out. Their effects also seem to be strongest among employees or job applicants who were otherwise already inclined to view the job situation favorably. Note that in addition to helping employees form more realistic expectations and facilitating self-selection, realistic job previews may also cause employees to perceive the employer as honest and therefore as more credible and deserving.

Direct Testing and Evaluation

Recognizing the potential legal and managerial downsides of credentials and interviews, some organizations rely instead on more direct measures of job-related ability or aptitude. There is a large industry of firms that devise and administer psychometric and physical tests to job candidates to evaluate their fitness for particular jobs. The most prevalent users of these tests include organizations that invest the most in training (because hiring mistakes are more costly), which are not unionized, and which have well-developed personnel departments.[27]

Of course, no psychometric test will indicate perfectly whether the individual is suited for a particular job, because no test gives results that are perfectly correlated with job performance. So all such tests (and, more generally, all forms of evaluation) are somewhat *indirect* tests of the relevant variables. The key to successful application of such tests is to find tests whose scores correlate to the greatest possible extent with eventual performance and that are least subject to cognitive or other biases in application. Although this should seem obvious and straightforward, it is disturbingly easy to find instances of screening tests that have gained widespread use despite convincing data to support their job-related validity. An example in this connection might be the Myers-Briggs personality inventory, which is widely used by companies for selection and career development decisions and yet has received low marks in an independent comprehensive evaluation of the evidence.[28]

Recalling our earlier discussion of signaling and screening, we can suggest one plausible and more subtle rationale for the use of direct tests in the absence of evidence of their job-related validity, namely, where their use may play a signaling or screening function. For instance, one might argue that there are jobs for which the willingness of potential employees to submit to blood or urine or personality testing provides information about their tendency to submit to authority and accept the organization's rules and values, even if the blood or urine or personality test results themselves are not terribly diagnostic.

An intriguing example along these lines is Cognex Corporation, a Massachusetts-based publicly traded manufacturer of high-tech machine vision systems, computers that "see" and can be used to automate a wide variety of manufacturing processes. The company's charismatic and flamboyant founder, Dr. Robert Shillman—a former MIT professor, to whom all "Cognoids" refer as "Dr. Bob"—has created a very strong corporate culture, including a variety of distinctive symbols, celebrations, and rewards, trumpeted proudly on the company's Web site, including the corporate salute (adopted from the "Three Stooges" of TV and movie fame).[29] Shillman believes that the company's success has depended and continues to depend most fundamentally on adherence to the ten corporate values that he champions (customer first, excellence, perseverance, enthusiasm, creativity, pride, integrity, recognition, sharing, and fun). Shillman is also a fervent believer in graphology (handwriting analysis) and requires all applicants for managerial employment at Cognex to submit to a handwriting analysis. He uses the characteristics of their writing to rate prospective employees for creativity, perseverance, work ethic, and intelligence. Not surprisingly, the practice has been somewhat controversial and has received considerable attention from the media. In a *Boston Globe* article reporting on the practice, the company's HR director defended the use of the handwriting test as follows: "We want to know whether an applicant . . . can fit into our corporate culture."[30] In other words, one might regard applicants' willingness to take the test and to view it as legitimate as a signal of their likelihood of sharing Shillman's values and fitting into the strong culture he has created.[31]

Statistical Discrimination

No credential or signal or test is perfect, in the sense that it identifies perfectly the characteristics desired in the employee. There is always some residual uncertainty about how desirable a particular prospective employee is. Thus, when it comes to comparing two candidates for a given job, there is always the chance that the wrong person will be chosen, based on rational decisions that take into account all the data. Such errors cannot be avoided. But in some cases, the statistics involved (and the dynamics set up by the use of the statistics) lead to discrimination against a group of individuals, based on their membership in a group that is objectively unrelated *a priori* to desirable job characteristics. The term *statistical discrimination* is used to describe this sort of effect. Because of the quite substantial impact that statistical discrimination has had, as well as the potential legal problems it can cause employers, we want to spend time being precise about two forms it can take.

Differences in Group Averages

Suppose an employer wishes to select employees who are more accepting of authority. Suppose further that we could measure "acceptance of authority" on a one-dimensional scale. Break the entire population into two groups, those with high school diplomas and those without. Assume, as we did earlier, that the group with high school diplomas will, *on average,* be more accepting of authority, and so one should select from among high school graduates. Let's flesh this out in Figure 14-1. On the horizontal axis we have the dimension for "acceptance of authority" and we see in Figure 14-1 two probability densities, one for the population of individuals who have their high school diplomas, and the second for individuals who don't. As drawn in Figure 14-1, the distribution of those with diplomas is shifted to the right along this scale; that is, on average, those with diplomas are more accepting of authority than those without. But possessing a diploma is not a perfect indicator of acceptance of authority; in particular, there are some people without the diploma who are higher on the "accepts authority" scale than others with diplomas. (That is, the two densities overlap.) The conclusion, then, is that one has a better *chance* at getting high acceptance of authority if one chooses a high school graduate. But this is no more than a statement of probability; there are some high school dropouts who are better suited for the job along this dimension than some high school graduates.

Now imagine that the two groups are people with blue versus brown eyes (in place of high school graduates versus nongraduates), and the scale is one of "willingness to remain on the job." Suppose that the employer will invest substantially in the training of new employees and so wants to hire employees who are higher in their willingness to remain. The argument given for high school diplomas then becomes: This employer should hire blue-eyed people, everything else held equal.

And if, instead of blue-eyed and brown-eyed people, we have men and women, we have a case of *statistical discrimination by sex;* the employer rationally discriminates in favor of men, in order to maximize the probability that the employee will remain on the job for a long period of time. Put aside, for a short moment, your objections to the assertion that women *on average* remain on the job for less time. The point is that if you grant this hypothesis, then we have discrimination that is perfectly rational economically. The employer is simply using the statistical measures of valuable traits that are available. It is no different than an insurance firm rationally charging men a higher premium for life insurance than women of the same age for life insurance, on the grounds that men are more likely to die sooner. Of course, one can object to the hypothesis that the distribution of "willingness to remain" for men is different from the distribution for women. (Indeed, one can marshall considerable evidence *against* the proposition that women are more prone to work interruptions than are men.) But in this regard note two things:

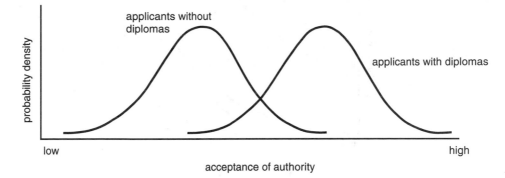

FIGURE 14-1 Two densities of "acceptance of authority."

- "Willingness to remain" is not completely exogenous here. Believing that women have a statistically smaller willingness to remain, employers may take actions that endogenously validate this hypothesis—for instance, failing to promote women or to offer them as many opportunities, which lowers the value of the job to women in general and thus raises the likelihood that they will depart. This might be a society-wide phenomenon, or it might be limited to particular industries. That is, if women are discriminated against in one industry in this fashion, those women whose willingness to remain is high within the population of all women may seek employment in other industries, where there are fewer barriers to their advancement. Thus, in the sectors that discriminate the most, the women who remain are, from the point of view of this measure, an adverse selection of the population as a whole, containing a higher fraction of the "less willing to remain."

- The ability of individuals to process data is far from perfect and is subject to cognitive biases. Such biases could lead to the perception of differences in distributions when none exist. For example, a female executive might depart from a job for family-related reasons. If there are few women in executive positions, one such incident might be overprocessed by others in the organization, and the fact that the departure is due to family reasons may reinforce initially held prejudices. Put differently, the incident may seem more salient because it reinforces prejudices initially held. The actual time lost per male executive on leave because of alcoholism therapy or recovery from a heart attack may exceed the time lost per female executive on maternity leave, but because of the larger number of male executives in most organizations, the extent of men's leaves may seem less salient and therefore weigh less heavily in personnel decisions.

Differences in Group Variances

A somewhat different form of statistical discrimination concerns the amount of residual variance in the predicted level of performance, given a statistic that predicts performance. To reiterate, no test statistic will be a perfect indicator of even-

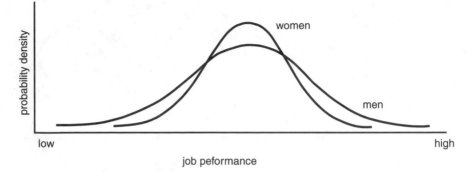

Figure 14-2 Two densities of "performance on the job."

tual performance; therefore, given any set of data about an individual, there will be some residual uncertainty about the "truth" for that individual. Now imagine you are trying to fill a position that is particularly critical to the organization and, moreover, a position in which bad performance is more costly than symmetrically good performance is beneficial (i.e., the position has a guardian character). This causes you to be risk averse concerning the level of performance; given two candidates whose estimated average performances (based on data) are the same, but where the first is from a group with lower residual variance than the second, you rationally choose the first.

Imagine now that the populations of men and women have different *a priori* distributions for "performance" on the job. The two distributions have the same mean, but they have different variances. In particular, the distribution of men along this scale has higher variance. (See Figure 14-2.) The same test result by a man and a woman (or, more precisely, test results that lead to the same *ex post* average estimated level of performance) will lead to more uncertainty about the man's performance than the woman's; this is a simple matter of Bayesian inference. Accordingly, if you have two candidates whose average estimated levels of performance are identical, and if you are filling the sort of position outlined in the previous paragraph, you should rationally discriminate against the man.[32]

This implicitly assumes that the test statistic gives the same likelihoods for men and women. That is, a man and woman with the same underlying abilities would have the same distributions of scores. But with many tests, especially those with culture-based features, it is inappropriate to assume that members of different groups who are identical regarding the desired characteristic will have identical distributions of scores. One must determine how to "score" the tests, based on observable differences such as race, sex, and other surrogates for social background. Normally this is done empirically: For each group, we gather data on the distribution of test results and (subsequent) levels of performance along the desired dimensions. However, the process of gathering evidence will not always proceed evenly. In particular, when it comes to certain tests and (subsequent) tasks, a history of discrimination may lead to a situation in which we have a lot more data about, say, white men than we do about women or people of color. As a simple matter of statistics, then, we can have more faith in our interpretations of test results for white men than for other groups, which means that the residual variance for white men will be lower, in cases where the average estimates of skills are identical. This is true even if the "underlying joint distributions" are identical across different groups; until we have enough data about all groups, we won't know this, and we will rationally assess higher residual variance for groups about which we have less data.

This shows how statistical discrimination can be self-reinforcing. Our initial uncertainty about Group A favors hiring from Group B, which provides a larger sample within Group B (and thus more precise information about the underlying joint distribution of abilities and test results for Group B), which then increases the statistically based advantage of Group B candidates. In addition, it can be riskier, in these circumstances, for members of Group A with a given level of ability to pursue jobs where there is much room for uncertainty in measurements of performance, because As will be disadvantaged relative to Bs in competing for such positions. Instead, rational As, facing such statistical discrimination, will gravitate toward more routine or easily evaluated lines of work. Specific occupations or subunits can become "ghettos" in organizations for risk-averse members of disadvantaged groups seeking to minimize the negative informational effects associated with their rarity in the organization.

We mention this here to emphasize that some forms of discrimination may be economically or statistically rational from the point of view of statistical inferences from test or biographical data concerning a candidate's skills and traits, even when there is no true difference between the favored and disadvantaged groups. We hope it is clear that this explanation is in no way intended to defend or endorse such discrimination. Moreover, the "rationality" of this kind of statistical discrimination is based on a specific information-theoretic argument (or set of assumptions)—namely, that no cheaper or more effective screening technology exists that would enable the employer to make better screening decisions, or that the gains to the employer from making superior decisions are not sufficient to motivate the use of some alternative technology. California employers in the 1970s used physical-lifting requirements of jobs as the basis for preferring men for positions as yard workers and assigned women to particular clerical and low-level manufacturing positions requiring finger dexterity.[33] Given how easy and inexpensive it is to measure such abilities directly, this kind of statistical discrimination appears less rational than it does pernicious.

VALIDATING STAFFING AND RECRUITMENT METHODS AND OTHER LEGAL CONCERNS

In recent years, legal challenges have made test validation an increasingly salient concern. Employers must be able to document the predictive value of any screening device or staffing method that may have an adverse impact on a particular segment of the labor force (i.e., a protected class) or on a specific member of a protected class.

Sometimes, sex, national origin, or other distinctions may be the direct basis for an employment decision. The law permits two defenses for such decisions. One involves establishing that the criterion used (e.g., sex, national origin) is a *bona fide occupational qualification* (BFOQ). The BFOQ exception stipulates that "it should not be an unlawful employment practice for an employer to hire an employee . . . on the basis of religion, sex, or national origin in those certain instances where religion, sex, or national origin is a bona fide occupational qualification reasonably necessary to the normal operation of that particular business or enterprise." The second defense rests on a claim of "business necessity," which involves showing some overriding business purpose—for instance, safety or efficiency—that makes a specific discriminatory practice defensible. The practice in question must not only directly foster safety and efficiency but also be essential to those goals.

Courts have construed both of these exceptions very narrowly. For instance, it is not acceptable to claim that sex or religion is a BFOQ simply because customers have a preference for specific types of employees. Employers have in some cases successfully defended preferential hiring practices using the BFOQ defense in cases where specific physical characteristics are required (e.g., actors, models, rest room attendants) or where the purpose of an enterprise involves a distinct national heritage (e.g., an Indonesian "theme" business in the United States) An example of a successful business necessity defense is a lawsuit brought by a minority candidate applying for a pilot job at United Airlines, who claimed that United's requirements of 500 flight hours and college degrees were discriminatory. A trial court held that given United's enormous training costs and the health and safety risks involved in hiring unfit pilot candidates, United's rigorous selection standards were essential to the efficient and safe running of the airline and therefore justifiable, notwithstanding potential adverse impact on minority job candidates.

The more common allegation of discrimination in hiring or promotion concerns a requirement or personnel technique that hinders members of protected classes from employment opportunities in a less explicit manner. In these cases, something about the way individuals are selected (i.e., a criterion or technique used in the selection process) works to the disadvantage of members of a legally protected class. For instance, selection criteria involving height, military service, upper-body strength, hair color, or a college degree from an elite institution could all potentially be illegal.[34] In such cases, the legal burden is likely to fall on the employer to document the validity of the employment practice in question.

Validation involves trying to assess how well a particular trait, attribute, characteristic, or personnel method used actually predicts relevant dimensions of job performance. This is a complex business, and obviously there are some settings in which validation is extremely difficult. For instance, on many jobs, it is extremely difficult to measure performance accurately and reliably. (Think, especially, of a guardian job, in which we would expect to see all incumbents performing above threshold most or all of the time.) It may be possible to isolate predictors for specific outcomes—for instance, to show that men or candidates hired through referrals by current employees exhibit lower rates of absenteeism than women or people hired as "walk-ins." However, unless the employer can demonstrate that absenteeism is a very significant dimension of the job in question, such validation evidence may still not convince a court. In some jobs, the requirements may be so idiosyncratic or the number of job incumbents so small as to make statistical validation studies impossible to carry out. In particular settings, the employer may lack the data with which to conduct a validation study or there may be no variation among applicants or employees on the dimension(s) in question. For instance, if a consulting firm has always recruited at Harvard and Stanford, it may have a hard time determining whether individuals hired from less prestigious MBA programs would perform just as well.

Courts are generally sensitive to these difficulties associated with predictive validation efforts. Accordingly, they often will permit the use of so-called content validation, which involves demonstrating that the selection techniques and criteria used measure the knowledge, skills, and abilities used on the job better than any available alternative. This approach generally involves conducting a detailed job analysis of the position in question, breaking the job down into its component tasks and responsibilities, and demonstrating how proficiency on the most important of these is captured by the selection criterion or technique employed. Courts may also permit employers to avail themselves of relevant studies done in other organizations. For instance, imagine a relatively small manufacturing firm that administers intelligence tests to candidates for production jobs. It might not be feasible for this firm to have conducted its own comprehensive predictive validation study, but if it can point to relevant studies conducted elsewhere (e.g., within the military), that evidence might be deemed probative.

Note that validation involves not simply demonstrating that some attribute or selection technique is *correlated with* performance but also that it is *necessary* to achieve satisfactory levels of performance. For instance, employers often place substantial weight on candidates' previous relevant experience in making hiring or promotion decisions. Even if the amount of prior experience were associated with measurable job performance, it might nonetheless prove unlawful to use prior experience as a selection criterion. In some circumstances, such a criterion will have an adverse impact on women, people of color, or other groups who have only recently gained entry into an occupation or industry. If members of protected classes have less experience than white males but are capable of performing a given job satisfactorily, it may be illegal to screen for that job based on previous experience, especially if there are readily available forms of training that could be provided to ameliorate the disadvantage in experience.

The same argument applies to other types of experience that employers might wish to favor in personnel decisions. Suppose, for instance, that a toy company only hires people with school-aged children into product development or consumer research positions. This will almost certainly discriminate on the basis of marital status (and perhaps age). Even if the company could demonstrate that people with school-age children have a better handle in general on what kinds of toys will sell, it would have to demonstrate why it is not possible to bring nonparents "up to speed" quickly and inexpensively. Similarly, although it is entirely acceptable for an employer to state during an interview that the job might require special demands, such as frequent travel or work outside of normal business hours, employment lawyers advise against inquiries to applicants about any barriers they might face in meeting those demands, such as dependent care, spouse's career, transportation problems, church attendance, and the like, all of which could be construed as discriminatory. In the same vein, with the passage of the Americans with Disabilities Act, employers have recently become highly sensitized to the potential for legal problems arising from screening methods that could have the effect of discriminating against those who have physical challenges (e.g., use of laboratory or psychological tests; requiring information on medical, insurance, mental health history, or on interruptions to prior employment). In some jurisdictions, newly enacted regulations have also required employers to review recruitment and selection methods to ensure they do not wittingly or unwittingly discriminate on the basis of actual or perceived sexual orientation (e.g., by inquiring about family or living conditions, HIV testing, etc.).

This discussion underscores the importance of distinguishing very carefully between an attribute that may *favor* someone for a job versus an attribute that is *required* for a job. Employers must be very careful in specifying job requirements so as to ensure that these are not unduly restrictive, not only because of the legal consequences, but also because of the risk of bypassing talented people by imposing overly restrictive requirements. In this regard, there is some evidence to suggest that employers may be more lenient in waiving officially posted job requirements for certain privileged segments of the workforce. For instance, one study of formal promotion ladders in a large sample of California firms documented a common pattern: A specific low-level position was monopolized by women at the bottom of the organization and that position was listed as requisite experience for promotion to the next level; yet all occupants of the next highest position would be men. Apparently, men were able to substitute alternative qualifications or experiences for those supposedly required and obtained within the firm's internal labor market, whereas women rarely had this option.[35]

To pass legal muster, however, an organization must do more than have policies and processes that produce nondiscriminatory selection decisions, where "selection" pertains not only to hiring but also to decisions regarding promotion, transfer, reclassification, retention, admission to training programs, and the like. Courts have also identified fundamental privacy rights that must be attended to when employers solicit information on current employees or applicants for employment for purposes of making selection decisions. Organizations in the public and private sectors have not infrequently faced legal challenges from employees and labor unions regarding the use of various background inquiries (including medical and credit histories) and testing procedures (e.g., drug, urine, hair, and blood testing; personality testing; "honesty," "integrity," and lie-detector tests) in selection decisions. Where potential invasions of privacy are involved, courts weigh the magnitude of the invasion against the organizational and public interest served by the screening practice. Needless to say, the particular fact situation, including the type of screening methods at issue and the legal context of any such challenge, will be crucial to the outcome. But in general, courts have been most likely to uphold the use of such screening procedures when: (a) they are employed sparingly, in particular job classifications where poor selection decisions carry significant costs or risks (e.g., airline pilots), rather than being applied across-the-board; (b) the use of these screening procedures is known in advance to employees or applicants affected, rather than done on a surprise basis; (c) the methods used have been extensively validated for the jobs and organization in which they are being used, by presenting statistical evidence that screening in this particular manner significantly enhances productivity or performance or significantly reduces the incidence of bad outcomes; (d) the employer is able to demonstrate that there are no superior screening technologies available at reasonable cost that would be less intrusive; (e) the screening techniques used are applied uniformly to all similarly situated employees (e.g., medical tests are not administered solely to applicants or employees for a job classification who happen to be physically challenged, or male, or above the age of 50); and (f) employers make provision for treating sensitively and confidentially any information gathered through selection procedures that intrude into employees' private lives (e.g., restricting access, storing files in secure remote locations, etc.).

Because the recruitment and selection process is generally where new hires form initial expectations regarding how they can expect to be treated, firms must worry not only about the legal implications of their screening procedures for those who are *not* selected, but also for those who *are*. Anyone who communicates with potential employees should understand that vague promises made at a job interview might become legally binding obligations. Loose talk about promotion practices, job assignments, and the like should be avoided. And all employees who take part in recruitment and selection—especially those who deal face-to-face with potential employees—should understand the rules that bear on nondiscrimination, privacy rights, and so on. These are not just legal nuances that the company's lawyers and HR specialists need to understand, especially as organizations increasingly are involving a broader cross-section of their employees in the recruitment and selection process (e.g., allowing self-managed teams to do their own hiring) and placing more emphasis on hiring for values or "cultural fit."

SOME ADDITIONAL PROCESS CONSIDERATIONS

The processes by which new employees are selected and recruited can be quite important for reasons that go beyond such legal considerations. An important part of the recruitment process is communication *from* the firm *to* the prospective employee about the work environment, the job and what it entails, the organization's culture, and so forth. Indeed, in our discussion of job interviews, we offered the opinion that the job interview is possibly more valuable as a job *preview* than as a device for selecting among applicants. And we noted that a sizable benefit associated with recruiting via referrals from existing employees was that the prospective employee probably would have a fairly accurate picture of the job.

Successful recruitment practices result in employees who are well matched with their employers, so honest communication is almost always the best policy. Thus, members of the organization who conduct job interviews or communicate with prospective employees should be careful to paint an accurate picture. But beyond this, it should be understood that the recruitment process itself sends signals to prospective employees. Are lie detector or urine tests administered? Are background checks undertaken? Is the candidate interviewed by his or her prospective superior? by an HR functionary? by the team of employees with whom he or she would prospectively be working? by a panel that includes clients or customers? Are first names used? In the interview, is the focus on the candidate only in conjunction with the job in question (specific skills and training, experience, etc.), or is the focus on the "whole person" (e.g., hobbies, interests, etc.)? Do interviewers refer to the organization in the third person ("they") or first person ("we")? How demanding is the application process? How selective is the process? All of these send powerful messages to potential hires about the organization and what it values. An important first step in having employees who fit in with your corporate culture is to have a recruitment process that matches that culture.

Recognizing the power of expectations that are established during an employee's initial recruitment into the organization, we offer several important cautions that should be attended to in trying to "romance" an individual who has been selected as the preferred candidate to accept employment:

- A short-run strategy of painting too rosy a picture to a prospective employee is rarely a good idea. Promises made (explicitly or implicitly) are rarely forgotten, and if they are broken, the employee may sue. Sometimes the courts will enforce such promises as binding commitments. And in many jurisdictions, very severe penalties are imposed if an employer is found by the courts to have engaged in fraudulent misrepresentations in the recruitment process. But suppose the employer doesn't fear the courts, in the belief that either the employee will not seek judicial relief or that the courts will not grant it. And suppose that the employer believes that the employee, once lured into employment, will not depart because of the sunk costs that are involved in finding a new job and relocating. Even in these circumstances, painting too rosy a picture may not be worthwhile, if it results in an employee who is embittered and no longer trusts the employer.

- What about promising the moon and meaning it, especially for an ideal candidate for an important position? "Pulling out all the stops" to get a particularly desirable candidate for a job is a slogan that the candidate's prospective colleagues can often be heard to use, frequently in hushed tones around the water cooler or its local equivalent. But when and if the candidate becomes a colleague, processes of social comparison will kick in, and sweetheart deals made to lure the candidate quickly turn into precedents that "ought" to be applied to one and all. (Perhaps this is why the slogan is so widely and so quickly embraced!) In other words, one must be mindful of the fact that how a new hire is treated and what he or she is promised has potentially huge implications for the remainder of the workforce.[36]

Because of the legal and other dangers associated with having "amateurs" take part in the recruitment process, HR staff will sometimes try to keep the process firmly under their own control or at least to minimize the participation of line managers and workers. There is some measure of safety in this practice. But this is safety that comes at a high price, especially in organizations where workers are tightly interconnected, where team-based job designs are used or peer relationships are important, or where the culture emphasizes teamwork and cooperation. Allowing those on the line to choose among candidates can be dangerous in terms of discriminatory outcomes. But imposing new recruits on a team can be equally disastrous. Allowing line managers and workers to take a real part in the recruitment and selection process builds a feeling of commitment to the new recruit, so that the new hire is more quickly and successfully integrated into the work environment. Indeed, if the new hire represents a significant diversification in terms of, say, race, gender, or occupation, then participation of incumbent workers may be an important cooptation device, getting them to buy into the general policy of increasing diversity. Of course, this means that participating line managers and workers will have to be taught what they can and cannot do and say. And hence some risks will be run. But the alternative is typically much worse.

WHAT NEXT?

Having attracted a workforce that is suited to its strategy and tasks, an organization must ensure that employees have the requisite skills, knowledge, and orientations to be successful, not only at their entry position, but for subsequent assignments they may receive later in their careers. Accordingly, we turn next to the topics of training (Chapter 15) and promotion (Chapter 16).

IN REVIEW

⇛ Staffing and recruitment are critical parts of HRM because recruitment is costly and correcting selection mistakes is often costlier still.

⇛ Desired workforce attributes depend on the other four factors and the firm's general HR philosophy.

⇛ Organizations can encourage the "right" applicants through:
- Offering premium wages and conditions, thereby attracting a larger, more able applicant pool
- Self-selection, which is a powerful tool for finding applicants who "fit"
- Referrals from current employees, which often have beneficial ef-

fects (including on the referrer) but can also reproduce the existing workforce

- Judicious use of personnel search organizations

⇒ Selection among applicants is achieved in many ways:

- Probationary periods can provide excellent information, but they can also be costly, carry significant legal risks, and give rise to a rat race.
- Credentials can be useful selection devices on at least three grounds: (1) skills/training acquired with the credential may benefit the organization; (2) an applicant's ability to obtain the credential may signal desirable characteristics; and (3) the credential-granting body may perform a valuable screening function.
- The value of a credential as a signal of employee quality depends in part on whether job applicants recognize how the credential will be used.
  - ○ Signals work insofar as sending them is less costly for those with the desired characteristic than for those who lack the characteristic.
  - ○ As the payoff from sending a signal rises, the relative cost of sending the signal for those without the characteristic must also rise, if the signal is to retain informational value.
  - ○ A vicious circle can arise: When a particular signal is rarely seen, it can't easily be interpreted, and so to send it is a risky venture and (thus) it is rarely sent.
- As a screen, job interviews are only sometimes reliable or valid.
  - ○ They are subject to numerous cognitive and evaluative biases.
  - ○ They are generally better as employment screens when: the interview follows a script; panels of interviewers are used; and summary evaluations are created formulaically from evaluations along several specific dimensions, rather than being created impressionistically.
  - ○ Interviews generally score poorly as an evaluation tool but can be valuable in communicating information about the job to applicants.
- Direct testing and evaluation can be useful. However, recognize that tests can engender "rational" statistical discrimination (i.e., a tendency to favor members of a particular group because of how that group tends to score *on average*), and be particularly wary of any test whose validity is not firmly established.

⇒ The benefits to society of a diverse workforce are particularly large, whereas potential costs are largely borne privately. Society may therefore pressure an organization to seek a more diverse workforce than it would seek on its own.

- In seeking to foster diversity, organizations can enlist a number of techniques for creating or achieving alternative dimensions of similarity among employees.

⇒ Many legal concerns intrude on the process of recruitment and selection.
- Recruitment and selection criteria must, at least in some jurisdictions, be justified, especially when they seem to have a discriminatory impact.
  - The criteria involved in justifying a technique or device that has an adverse discriminatory impact are quite strict. For example, a screen with discriminatory consequences can be justified if it is *essential* to legitimate business concerns, but not if it simply fosters those concerns.
- Recruitment and selection methods must also respect the privacy rights of job applicants.
- Courts may construe promises made orally to job applicants as enforceable. By the same token, off-hand remarks can be taken as evidence of discrimination or as a violation of the applicant's privacy rights. Hence, when allowing "nonexperts" to participate in the recruitment process, brief them carefully on what they can (and cannot) do and say.

⇒ Three final process concerns connected to recruitment are:
- Despite the legal dangers just cited, there are real benefits from having nonexperts intimately involved in recruitment, including securing their commitment to new recruits, accelerating the integration of new hires into the organization, and coopting employees into recruitment goals and efforts of the organization.
- Painting overly rosy pictures for job candidates can be dangerous and self-defeating.
- New hires frequently activate social comparison processes. Pulling out all the stops for a desirable candidate can engender perceived inequity, requiring costly and contentious negotiations with veteran employees.

ENDNOTES

1. Joseph P. Bacarro, "The Hidden Cost of Employee Turnover," *Grant Thornton Benefits and HR Advisor,* Grant Thornton, 1992; Leonard A. Schlesinger and James A. Heskett, "The Service-Driven Service Company," *Harvard Business Review* 69 (September–October 1991): 71–81.

2. Schlesinger and Heskett, *ibid.*

3. As we have noted previously, homogeneity at the level of the workgroup can also sometimes be *dysfunctional* to the organization, especially when members of the workgroup are socially very homogeneous, but differ from their supervisors and the workforce of the organization generally. For an overview of existing research on these is-

sues, see Kathy Williams and Charles O'Reilly, "Demography and Diversity: A Review of 40 Years of Research," pp. 70–140 in Barry M. Staw and L. L. Cummings (eds.), *Research in Organizational Behavior,* Vol. 20 (Greenwich, CT: JAI Press, 1998).

4. In a mixed economy, society has some interests in technological efficiency of private firms; if diverse workforces compromise efficiency somewhat, society's interests in workforce diversity are also mixed. But many of the social costs from discrimination are borne by society generally; the case for workforce diversity is very much stronger at the level of society as a whole.

5. Selection based on hobbies outside the workplace may sound silly (and one would need to be careful to steer clear of the potential legal landmines involved—see below). But firms can (at least) *encourage* the formation of similar avocations through some of the benefits they supply or subsidize, such as a company-sponsored health club, athletic teams, paid time off to work for schools or particular charitable organizations, etc.

6. It doesn't quite fit the story of premium wages and benefits, but note how less able students are discouraged from applying to premium universities because they understand that the competition will be tougher. Insofar as universities perform something of a screening function for subsequent employers—a role that many business schools, at least, are thought to play—there can be a bit of a vicious circle here: FECBUS, a fictional Famous East Coast BUsiness School, attracts more-able applicants because it is known by employers to provide an excellent selection, hence its graduates get good job offers. But the strengthened competition for admission means that less-able applicants have less incentive to apply, which makes the prophecy that it can select good students easier to fulfill. Note that the vicious circle, to keep revolving, depends on an admissions office with some capability of differentiating among applicants in terms of their quality. Otherwise, the less-able applicants would not be deterred by the application costs from applying simply by virtue of there being more-able applicants in the pool.

7. There is another, somewhat more subtle, form of signaling that may operate here. Regardless of the compensation scheme employed, we presume that working in an office environment full of hard-charging, aggressive real estate agents is likely to be less pleasant for those who are not themselves aggressive hard-chargers. Hence, given RE/MAX's reputation for hiring such agents, the mere willingness to work with such colleagues signals an agent's aggressiveness and work ethic.

8. How does RE/MAX benefit from the provision of this signal? It capitalizes on the reputation that it confers on its agents by charging premium amounts for the clerical services and office space that it provides. An aggressive agent has three choices: (1) work for RE/MAX and pay handsomely for these services, but gain instant recognition for being aggressive; (2) work for a traditional agency, get some compensation insurance, but lose the instant recognition and a fraction of the commissions earned; or (3) work independently, paying less for clerical help and for office space than is charged by RE/MAX and keeping 100% of commissions earned, but depend on one's own (local) reputation for aggressiveness. Young and aggressive agents will see the RE/MAX option as best. Older, more established (but still aggressive) agents might opt for the third choice, if they have the desired local reputation.

9. Recall here our discussion of recruitment at high-commitment HR firms in Chapter 9, particularly the way compensation reportedly was deemphasized in the recruitment process at Tandem Computer.

10. The advantages held by "connected applicants" in the application process are documented by Roberto M. Fernandez and Nancy Weinberg, "Sifting and Sorting: Personal Contacts and Hiring in a Retail Bank," *American Sociological Review* 62 (December

1997): 883–902. Fernandez and Weinberg also provide citations of relevant studies of the effects of network-based hiring on worker performance and behavior.

11. See Gary Dessler, "Value-based Hiring Builds Commitment," *Personnel Journal* 72 (November 1993): 98–102.

12. Headhunting firms find this to be a double-edged sword. It is true that they often have a broad database to draw on, but insofar as they work with two firms that otherwise compete, they could be accused (and even guilty) of using information acquired through a search conducted for Firm A in placing someone at Firm B. Indeed, they might think to raid Firm A to satisfy Firm B's needs. Consequently, to maintain good relations with their clients, search firms often build "Chinese walls" such that information gained in a relationship with one firm cannot be used in a relationship with a competitor, and they sometimes will have policies not to raid the ranks of a client, at least not too soon after they make a placement.

13. See George A. Akerlof, "The Economics of Caste and of the Rat Race and Other Woeful Tales," *Quarterly Journal of Economics* 90 (November 1976): 599–617; and Bengt R. Holmstrom, "Managerial Incentive Problems: A Dynamic Perspective," pp. 209–30 in *Essays on Economics and Management in Honour of Lars Wahlbeck* (Helsinki: Swedish School of Economics, 1982).

14. Compare with the discussion of market signaling below.

15. Note that some forms of influence activity and social maneuvering can be used by savvy probationary candidates to raise the costs of a discharge decision. In universities, as a consequence, tenure decisions are often really made at the university level and not the department or school level, to blunt the impact of any influence activities and (thereby) to reduce their frequency.

16. A protected class is a group which has historically been subject to discrimination, and which is therefore protected by certain laws against discrimination. Because the French are not a protected class, we would have to change the story, replacing (say) the Grandes Ecoles with the Seven Sisters (colleges that primarily educate women) or colleges with a heavy representation of African-Americans.

17. In fact, something like this, if not quite so bold, once took place at the Stanford GSB, when a major consulting firm tried to lock up new admits for summer jobs during the first-year orientation period.

18. For instance, see Yinon Cohen and Jeffrey Pfeffer, "Organizational Hiring Standards," *Administrative Science Quarterly* 31 (March 1986): 1–24.

19. See *Job Market Signaling* (Cambridge, MA: Harvard University Press, 1974).

20. Thus, if the FECBUS story of sharp-eyed admissions officers is correct, the admissions staff should get all the money. In the FECBAS story, the rewards should go to whoever administers the punishments in the core (i.e., the faculty.) Also, the stories have different predictions about how large should be the queue of applicants to the programs, although the predictions are a bit murkier than may be apparent in less stark versions of the stories.

21. For a general discussion of this point, see Appendix D. For a theoretical treatment, see Spence, *op. cit.,* or David M. Kreps, "Out-of-equilibrium Beliefs and Out-of-equilibrium Behavior," pp. 7–45 in Frank Hahn (ed.), *The Economics of Missing Markets, Information, and Games* (Oxford: Oxford University Press, 1989).

22. However, it is not hard to find cases of companies utilizing such a "menu" approach to induce screening. For instance, Sapient Corporation, based in Cambridge, Mass., is

a leading provider of information technology solutions, known for their novel fixed-price, fixed-time basis of bidding on contracts. In pursuing this strategy, Sapient extensively emphasizes teamwork. The firm permits its mid-level IT consultants to select between two compensation plans: one which is more individualistic (base pay and individual bonus), and the other involving slightly lower base pay but greater upside potential, in the form of a team bonus that reflects project results.

23. Recall that reliability is a measure of whether the conclusions of one interviewer are stable over time (assuming no change in the characteristic being measured) or match those of other evaluators. (The former kind of reliability is called "test-retest," whereas the latter is called "inter-rater.") Validity concerns whether the evaluations produced by job interviews are at all predictive of the performance desired of individuals on the job.

24. For a detailed survey, see Richard D. Arvey and James E. Campion, "The Employment Interview: A Summary and Review of Recent Research," *Personnel Psychology* 35 (Summer 1982): 281–322.

25. A somewhat famous case concerns an interviewer who, in court, claimed an ability to judge manual dexterity by watching the hands of the interviewee during an oral interview.

26. For instance, see Steven L. Premack and John P. Wanous, "A Meta-Analysis of Realistic Job Preview Experiments," *Journal of Applied Psychology* 70 (November 1985): 706–19.

27. Cohen and Pfeffer, *op. cit.*

28. See Daniel Druckman and Robert A. Bjork (eds.), *In the Mind's Eye: Enhancing Human Performance* (Washington, DC: National Academy Press, 1991).

29. See: http://www.cognex.com/about/index.html.

30. Diane E. Lewis, "Prospective Employers Looking for the Write Stuff: More Hirers Seeking Clues in the Slants, Loops, and Undotted I's of Applicants," *Boston Globe* (January 26, 1997); also see John Goff, "Method in the Madness," *CFO* (January 1997), viewable on-line at http://www.cfonet.com/html/Articles/CFO/1997/97JAcogn.html.

31. Of course, we hasten to point out that even if such a handwriting test is useful in screening applicants along this dimension, that would not ensure that Cognex could survive a legal challenge to its use—say, on the grounds that it discriminates against certain demographic groups. Presumably there are other ways in which Cognex could screen applicants along this dimension at least as effectively and inexpensively (see the discussion of test validation below).

32. On the other hand, if the job has star-like characteristics—if the idea is to maximize the chances of finding someone in the extreme right-hand tail of the distribution—then in this instance you would rationally choose the candidate with the higher residual variance, everything else held equal.

33. William T. Bielby and James N. Baron, "Men and Women at Work: Sex Segregation and Statistical Discrimination," *American Journal of Sociology* 91 (January 1986): 759–99.

34. The practice need not adversely affect all members of a protected group to be found unlawful.

35. James N. Baron and William T. Bielby, "Organizational Barriers to Gender Equality: Sex Segregation of Jobs and Opportunities," pp. 233–51 in Alice Rossi (ed.), *Gender and the Life Course* (New York: Aldine, 1985).

15

TRAINING

Imagine you are Vice President for Human Resources at a large British chemicals firm. One of your best chemical engineers, a chap aged 35, has submitted to you a request for "sponsorship" at something called the Sloan Program at the Stanford University Graduate School of Business.[1] Upon investigation, you discover two things: As a career-enhancing step for the individual, the program makes some sense. And it is going to cost your firm a bundle of money. Specifically:

- The program lasts for ten months, from September until the following July. (This will mean that your employee will be away from his post for approximately 11 months.)

- Successful participants (which is virtually all of them) receive a professional Masters degree—not an MBA, but a Master of Science in Management.

- The program admits a cohort of about four dozen students a year, with slightly more than half the participants being based outside the United States. Participants usually have ten to fifteen years of business experience, with an age distribution of 30 to 45 or so. It is a general management program, with courses in subjects typical to a general management MBA curriculum. Participants primarily take required courses together as a cohort, but they have some opportunity to take elective courses in the MBA program as well.

- Your employee has a degree in engineering and wishes to broaden his knowledge of management in general, so that he can move from a specialist track into general management in your organization. He tells you he has investigated numerous alternatives, including taking a regular MBA degree, attending an evening and weekend MBA program over a period of several years, or taking part in a shorter, general-purpose program in Executive Education. However, he believes that a year-long degree program is a good compromise in terms of getting a deep understanding of general management issues and functions versus the time it will take. You have made inquiries and have discovered that this program gets generally favorable reviews for the quality of instruction and also for the breadth of experience and range of contacts obtained through interaction with the other participants.

- It won't be cheap: The program insists on participants being sponsored by their employers. To quote from Stanford's Sloan Program Brochure:

> Sloan candidates should have the full endorsement of the top management of their organizations, including agreement to pay full tuition and maintain the participant's salary during the program. Sloan candidates should be planning to return to management positions in their sponsoring organizations. Some organizations have agreements with Sloan candidates requiring a minimum period of service to the organizations after the program.
>
> Employers also are expected to provide reasonable costs for relocating the Sloan Fellow and his or her family or Partner. Sponsoring organizations also generally reimburse the Sloan Fellow for the cost of study trips, which are an integral part of the program.

Tuition (for 1998–99) is $50,500. The study trips, textbooks, and study materials cost around $11,500. The current salary of this employee, plus contributions for health insurance, pension, and contributions to Social Security total $114,000 (approximately).[2] The individual drives a company car, which costs an additional $7,800 per annum, and he asks that he be reimbursed up to this amount for local transportation expenses in California. He also requests relocation expenses to and from England for himself and his family (spouse, two children), which will be on the order of $15,500. The employee, who has investigated the rental housing market around Stanford, has asked as well for a housing subsidy (because his salary of $114,000 will not go very far in the Silicon Valley, and his spouse will be forced to take a year's sabbatical from her job, due to her being ineligible to work in the United States). Contacts with the Sloan Program office indicated that a "decent three-bedroom house in the area" will run to about $40,000 for the eleven-month period. (No, we aren't kidding!) You do the math, and come up with a cost to your firm of around $240,000.[3]

Can it possibly be worth it? There are two ways to think about this question. First, can it be worth $240,000 in general to get this sort of education? Figuring about 30 years left until this employee retires, and assuming a 5% per-annum real cost of capital, the program would have to generate a real (inflation-adjusted) increase in the engineer's "value" of $15,600 per year. This, we contend, is not outrageous.

But is this worth it to your company? Suppose that you take up the hint from the Sloan Program's catalog (quoted above) and craft a set of so-called golden handcuffs for your employee: If he leaves your firm in the three years following his return from the program, he will owe you a pro-rata share of total expenses.[4] Suppose these handcuffs work, in the sense that the individual returns to your organization at his old salary and works diligently for three years. At the end of that period, however, you have to worry that he will make the following observations:

- By virtue of the training received, he is worth a lot more to your company.
- But he is also now worth a lot more to a lot of companies. The training he

got at Stanford was general-purpose human capital, in the sense that it can be employed in all sorts of jobs, for all sorts of employers.

- Moreover, there should be little question that he possesses those skills. After all, he now has a diploma from Stanford to show to alternative prospective employers.

- He doesn't wish to make threats, but he gets calls from headhunters all the time. Perhaps you can see your way, therefore, to give him a raise to reflect his appreciated value to your firm. And, because he does get those phone calls, perhaps a fair split is that his raise should equal, say, 90% of his appreciated value to the firm.

Indeed, even if he doesn't ever make these arguments, the MSM degree and his experiences in the Sloan Program will make him more attractive to other firms, and you may want to raise his salary preemptively.

Now go back and redo the math. Even in our rosy scenario—in which he dutifully returns for three years, during which you get 100% of the gain in his value—if you only get 10% of the value thereafter, the rise in his value to your firm must be $60,000 per year to recapture the $240,000 expense (at a 5% annual real cost of capital). And, as you probably can imagine, this is a rosy scenario in several respects. We believe that most Sloan participants expect (and get) a raise immediately upon returning to their sponsoring organizations. Golden handcuffs that forgive a third of the debt for each of three years of service are optimally broken after the first year.[5] And for reasons that we discussed in Chapter 8 (on ILMs), the value added of a general management education is apt to increase through time, so that much of the value added by the program is likely to accrue after the three years of handcuffs.

So, how do you explain to your chemical engineer that he should think about something a bit less costly—perhaps a subscription to some management periodicals . . . ?

Notwithstanding the calculations and arguments we have just given, the Stanford Sloan Program fills up classroom seats year after year. Indeed, some firms sponsor students every year and send more than one participant per year. More generally, firms spend substantial sums of money improving the human capital of their employees. Most of the training provided isn't as fancy as the Stanford Sloan Program, but the price tag is nonetheless impressive: According to a 1994 survey by *Training* magazine, private-sector organizations in the United States spent $50 billion on formal training programs.[6] Indeed, non-U.S. companies tend to spend considerably more on training. Consider Table 15-1, which summarizes data comparing automobile plants worldwide in the quantity of new hire and ongoing training provided to production workers.

Please note the formulation here: The firm spends on the training, and the employee gets his or her human capital improved. If the individual employee stays with the firm, and if he or she doesn't capture the value added through raises, then the firm may well benefit from its investment; this is a present-value calcula-

TABLE 15-1   Training in Automobile Plants Worldwide

Plant Ownership/Location	Training Hours: First 6 Months for New Workers	Training Hours per Year: Workers with 1+ Year(s) Experience
Japanese/Japan	364	76
Japanese/North America	225	52
U.S./North America	42	31
U.S./Europe	43	34
European/Europe	178	52
Newly Industrialized Countries	260	46
Australia	40	15

Source: John Paul MacDuffie and Thomas Kochan, "Do U.S. Firms Invest Less in Human Resources? Training in the World Auto Industry," *Industrial Relations* 34 (April 1995): 156.

tion, as in any capital budgeting exercise. But workers can and do depart, taking their human capital with them. And even if the worker doesn't depart, the threat of doing so may force the employer to pay more, because of the skills and talents the newly trained employee has acquired. So the more general question, and the focus of this chapter, is *Why do firms train workers?* And, as we examine *why,* we will also address *How should this be done?*

WHY DO FIRMS TRAIN WORKERS?

To answer the question *Why do firms train workers?* we follow an approach that economists call Human Capital Theory, in which the simple answer is, *Firms train workers (and pay for the training) if doing so enhances the firm's profits.* The firm, in deciding whether to invest in the human capital of an employee, computes three (expected) net present values: the cost C of the training; the gross benefits B that will accrue to the employer if the employee gets this training; and the increase in salary S that must be paid to the employee by this employer because of this training. The training will enhance the firm's profits—assuming the firm pays the full cost of the training—as long as $B - S$ exceeds C.

Suppose that B exceeds C—that is, the training costs are less than the gross benefits to the current employer of the training. There are two polar cases to keep in mind:

1. If $S = 0$, then of course C is less than $B - S$ and the firm is happy to pay for the training. Moreover, because the worker is not going to collect anything (in the form of wages) by virtue of the training, unless there are psychic benefits that accrue, the worker isn't going to be willing to pay *any* part of the training costs.

2. If $S = B$, then the firm isn't going to be willing to pay any positive amount. But the worker, who gets benefit $B = S$, which is greater than C, will be willing to foot the entire bill, assuming he can finance the

training out of savings or by borrowing. (We assume that training must be paid for up front, whereas the increased wages only accrue through time.)

Between these two polar cases are cases in which S is positive but less than B—that is, the firm will have to raise the employee's wages, but not by as much as the gross benefits from the training. Then, under the maintained assumption that B exceeds C, and assuming the worker can finance training if it makes sense on a net-present-value basis, the training can be financed: The worker is willing to pay up to S, whereas the firm is willing to pay up to $B - S$.[7] Thus, the "total willingness to pay" is the sum of these, or B, which exceeds C. But be sure to note that in this case there is some indeterminacy regarding who pays how much—only C has to be paid, and the total willingness to pay is B.[8]

The question before us is, What factors influence the values of B, C, and S? A large and diverse set of factors must be considered, and we tackle them in the following three categories: factors that affect the benefits gained from the training (B); factors that affect the extent to which the firm can appropriate those benefits ($B - S$); and factors that affect the costs of training (C).

THE GROSS BENEFITS FROM TRAINING

Three fairly obvious factors in this category are: the length of time the employee can be expected to work with the firm; the skills that the employee has before undergoing training; and the extent to which the skills provided by the training complement other skills the employee already may have. Perhaps less obvious are the gift-exchange aspects of the training and the impact of training on recruitment efforts. Least obvious are the external effects of the training: signals to other employees; signals to customers and suppliers; and general reinforcement of the organizational culture.

Factors that Affect Tenure

In most cases, the training is paid for up front, whereas B is a net present value (as is S). As with any investment, the number of "years of service" that can be expected is important. Thus, an investment in a worker's human capital is more likely to be worthwhile if the employee has many years of service remaining. Consequently, it is rare to find firms investing heavily in the human capital of workers close to retirement. But matters aren't as simple as that, because the employee retains an inalienable right to pick up and leave. The key question for the employer is, How long can the employee be expected to remain with this organization? Consider the following factors that bear on this:

- *Family status*: A very young employee who has yet to put down roots may have a shorter expected duration of employment than a middle-age employee with a family and kids in school.
- *Local levels of job-market and locational mobility*: In a close-knit, rural community, where families tend to stay for generations, training is a better bet

(on these grounds) than in an urban setting. (When setting up plants in the United States, why did the major Japanese automobile manufacturers pick such locales as Smyrna, Tennessee and Marysville, Ohio, instead of a suburb of Detroit? Here is one reason.)

- *HR practices that prolong employment spells and cut down on voluntary turnover* can be important complements to training. Such practices—for instance, wages rising with seniority and pensions that vest only after enough years of service—were discussed at length earlier in the book (in Chapters 4 and 12, in particular), and we will have more to say about them in the next chapter. Perhaps the most significant complements to training are HR practices that: (a) screen prospective applicants carefully for fit and likely employment stability; (b) give employees opportunities to broaden themselves and their role within the firm; and (c) provide employees with career-long opportunities. Firms that maintain an ILM do relatively more training than do other firms, and with little wonder: These sorts of firms do relatively better in retaining and using the skills their workers acquire.

The Worker's Preexisting Skills

The value to the firm of training provided to employees depends on the *improvement* in those employees' productivity. So, of course, firms must consider the level of skills that workers bring to the job. If prospective employees possessing critical skills are sufficiently scarce, it may pay for a firm to provide those skills through training, even if there is a great risk of losing a trained employee (to another employer, say) in the short-term. To put it in the language of finance, when the flow of value from the training is very high, the payback period for the cost of the training is very short.

An illustrative example is provided by the case of the world-renowned Oriental Hotel in Bangkok, Thailand, now part of the Mandarin Oriental Hotel Group. The Oriental routinely finishes at or near the top of surveys ranking the world's finest hotels. Given a shortage of local employees trained to provide the extraordinarily high levels of service that The Oriental seeks, the hotel has found that it must provide extensive basic employee training, notwithstanding the fact that other luxury hotels in Bangkok routinely raid the Oriental's staff. This is not to say that the Oriental—or, more generally, a firm that finds it necessary to provide "basic training" (because of the local labor pool's lack of crucial skills)—must suffer this sort of raiding without response. In such cases, there are often good strategies available for lowering the costs of the training or raising its expected payback, and we will examine some of these strategies later in this chapter.

Complements to Other Skills

The value engendered by giving an employee particular skills often depends on other skills that the employee has or may come to possess. You can't usually look at specific skills in isolation; you have to consider the whole package the employee will possess.

Take the British chemical engineer, for example. What is the value to his firm of sending him off to Stanford? Couldn't the firm do better by hiring an MBA from Stanford or elsewhere who already has the sort of general management training that the chemical engineer will come to possess, after a year at Stanford? After all, the MBA will have the same training, and she will probably have paid for it herself.

Of course, the answer here is No. At least, it is not clearly Yes. His general skills as a chemical engineer may make him a better general manager for a chemicals firm; to replicate him, the firm may need to search (at least) for an MBA with a background in chemistry or chemical engineering. But even more, this chemical engineer has presumably worked for this firm for a while, and he is likely to have acquired human capital that a new recruit would lack, such as a network of acquaintances in the company and knowledge about the firm's plants and products. That very specific knowledge is unlikely to be immediately replicable in an MBA recruit. This isn't to say that the firm can't hire a newly minted MBA with a background in chemical engineering and then, through time, give that individual the firm-specific human capital assets that this engineer already possesses. But the costs of that specific training (measured especially in time) must be factored in. Indeed, to the extent that the graduate of an MBA program will be unwilling to spend time learning the fine-grained technicalities that this engineer already has, the bundle of skills he will have after an MBA-like program may not be replicable at any (reasonable) cost. If—and this is the big if—this *bundle* of skills is particularly valuable to the firm, then the training investment may be worthwhile.

Or consider training investments made by firms initiating a TQM program. Often a first step in such programs is to train line employees in both communications and team-participation skills and in process-control techniques. These are valuable skills for any employee. But it is the extent to which they complement other human capital the employees have *and will come to have*—as their jobs are enlarged and enriched, and as they learn more about the firm's entire production process—that really gives these skills value.[9]

A related point concerning training (such as the Stanford Sloan program) that isn't focused or tailored for a particular employer is that employees are likely to attend selectively to parts of the training they receive, based on whatever is most salient to their work situation. Consequently, employers may find it advantageous to pay for untailored training for their own employees, rather than hire the average individual who has gone through that training. For instance, the hypothetical chemical engineer in our story is likely to be more attentive in class when issues arise concerning occupational health and safety, accounting for environmental liabilities, and business-to-business marketing, or when (in Operations) continuous-flow process technologies are examined, if (as seems likely) these topics are especially salient to his employer.

Eliciting Consummate Performance Through Commitment and Gift Exchange

So far, we've been focusing on fairly tangible and objective factors that influence the value of training. But equally important are some less tangible effects of training that affect employees' behaviors and attitudes.

In an employment relationship, a worker has a lot at stake. Employees develop all sorts of relation-specific assets that tie them to their employer. If an employee is going to make these investments in an ongoing relationship with her employer, she seeks some assurance that the employer will employ her gainfully, will put her skills to good use, and will not take advantage of her. This was the main theme of Chapter 4, which emphasized balance of power and reputation as the main forms of assurance given by the firm to workers.

Employer-provided training can contribute to a balance of power in the employment relationship. When the firm trains the employee—a better phrase in this instance might be *invests in* the employee—the employee understands that the firm is putting things at risk too. The firm has given the worker something of value, which the worker can walk away with. The training is a bargaining chip that can be used by the employee to keep the firm honest. By providing the training the firm has in essence signaled its good intentions for the future. Consequently, the employee can more comfortably make investments in her relationship with the firm, thereby making the relationship more efficient (and thus more valuable to the firm).

For instance, suppose the British chemicals firm wishes to assign our hypothetical chemical engineer to a brand new plant, in a role dealing mainly with technical matters. The firm is convinced that the plant is important to its future and wants the engineer to gain expertise there. But the posting will be personally expensive for the engineer—it means, say, six months away from his family. The engineer seeks assurances that the firm is not simply trying to exploit his technical capabilities at this start-up. An expensive course of study at Stanford, conducted at the employer's expense, sends a strong signal that the firm's intentions really are to move the engineer into management, just as he desires. Indeed, an employee looking for assurances that his current employer intends to advance his career will read the most positive message into precisely those forms of education and training that are expensive for the firm to provide and most closely tailored to the sort of advancement he seeks.

Closely related to the commitment signaled by offers to train prospective and current employees are the psychological or gift-exchange aspects of training. Notwithstanding the economic benefits that accrue to the firm, employees will often regard training as something of a gift and, through the psychological mechanisms discussed in Chapter 5, reciprocate with gifts of their own, including the gift of consummate effort on the job. Of course, the firm can affect the employee's perception of training as a gift: Training that is personalized to the employee, given willingly and with frills added on, and that is expensive for the employer, will seem more like a gift than training that is standardized, given grudgingly, bare-boned, and inexpensive.

Screening Through Training

All the benefits from training discussed so far concern the impact of training on the performance of a given employee. A more subtle effect of having a well-articulated and publicized training program concerns the selection of employees. Recall from the last chapter that the general working conditions and employment practices offered by an organization will influence the tendency of prospective employees to self-select. So, for instance, we said in Chapter 9 that high-commitment HR practices will attract a workforce that is suited to those practices—workers who crave the responsibilities, teamwork, and opportunities to learn and grow that high-commitment HRM provides. In the same way, training programs will attract employees who desire training; in many cases, those employees will be individuals who seek to grow in the job, who value the acquisition of skills, who are generally curious, who are ambitious and aggressive, and so on. Not every employer will find this selection of job applicants to be advantageous. But many will, and for those who do, publicizing the opportunities available for training will improve the quality of the applicant pool.

Having said this, we must note that training programs may attract workers who want to acquire skills and to grow, who are generally curious, and who are ambitious and aggressive, but who don't necessarily feel the need to remain with your organization once they've been trained. Indeed, if training appeals to the ambitious and aggressive, you may be screening for employees who are more inclined to leave for better opportunities. We've already remarked that training programs—that is, investments in human capital—are complementary to HR practices that prolong employment spells. We reiterate that point here, with the further remark that the best HR complements to training are often those that prolong employment spells of the employees who are attracted by the training opportunities in the first place—for instance, the maintenance of an ILM, job designs that provide ample opportunities to use the skills that are learned, rewards that increase with employment duration, and opportunities to exercise judgment on the job.

Spillovers, Direct and Indirect

We have so far discussed ways (some perhaps somewhat subtle) in which training enhances the value added by the employee who is being trained. But in assessing the overall value added from training, a firm or manager also needs to consider potential third-party effects. An obvious third-party effect is direct spillovers—for example, a clerical worker sent to a course to master the fine points of a word-processing package shares what was learned with co-workers. This sort of spillover will often happen informally, but it can be enhanced by conscious efforts of the employer: A general culture of cooperation can be provided; the trained employees can be identified and asked to give informal seminars on what they have learned; or team-based job designs can be employed.

Another subtle but potentially important spillover effect of training is that it can prompt a form of "rat race" among employees. Suppose, for instance, that from time to time a consulting firm selects its most talented secretarial staff to go through courses on advanced computer skills (e.g., use of PowerPoint and Access). Suppose further, as is often the case, that the pay and advancement opportunities for these staff members are a function of the status of the consultants for whom one works. Then an up-and-coming staff member will want to master those skills, even if he or she has not been selected to receive them as part of the firm's training program, because *not* having those skills will be a major disadvantage in trying to get ahead. In such circumstances, the company's true "return on investment" from having trained a select segment of the secretarial staff is likely to be much greater than simply the enhanced productivity of secretaries who went through the training program themselves.

Sending Signals to Others

Training often sends signals to others—other employees, and other constituencies generally—signals that can be valuable to the firm.

Take the example of our British chemical engineer. Suppose he is a pioneer in moving from a technical specialty track in the organization to a general management track. If the organization wishes to encourage other talented specialists to consider this sort of career move, then sending the chemical engineer to the Sloan program may be regarded as a highly visible signal. Of course, the value of this signal can be enhanced by specific actions—when he returns from Stanford, the firm may wish to have him meet with selected specialists in whom the firm is interested; or it may publicize his career plans in a company newsletter. But the point is simple: If the firm wishes to proclaim that this is an important and viable career path for its employees, one that it is willing to support, it has to signal this support with facts. Sending the engineer to Stanford is a fairly vivid signal.

The same logic may apply to *prospective* employees. Young engineers graduating from university and considering a range of employment possibilities, or a mid-career engineer making a similar choice, may wonder whether moves from specialist roles into general management are possible. Sending our friend to Stanford is a signal that they are. More generally, current and prospective employees, looking for indications of what sort of firm they are dealing with, will often construe a general program of improving employees' human capital as a clear and credible signal of the firm's commitment to its workforce. In effect, this is the same point as made in the subsection on commitment and gift exchange, although that was keyed to the specific bilateral relationship between the firm and the employee being trained; here we are looking at the signal received one step removed.

Other constituencies, such as customers or suppliers, may also infer valuable signals about the intentions and values of an organization from its training activities. A potential industrial customer who seeks to work with suppliers having a highly trained, well-educated workforce will be reassured by a program of training offered by the potential partner, reassurances that can lead to investments in an efficient supplier–vendor relationship (that, in turn, benefits the firm providing the training).

Reinforcing Culture

Third-party signals can be very specific—for example, about the training the firm provides. Or the signals may be more general and diffuse—such as about the firm's commitment to its workforce and about its values. On the very diffuse end of the spectrum are messages that reinforce organizational culture.

For instance, a popular buzz-phrase these days is the "learning organization," used to describe organizations with a strategy—reinforced by workforce, technology, and especially culture—for continuously adapting and improving. The cultural aspects are important; to improve and advance—to learn—becomes an overriding goal of the organization. Organizations seeking to foster this sort of culture will probably reap important symbolic benefits from training workers generally; if the organization wishes to advance and improve, this should be evidenced by employees who are given (and expected to take) opportunities to advance and improve personally. And of course, if an organization's leadership is credible in espousing the superordinate goal of continuous learning, this should increase the willingness of current and prospective employees to receive training, as they will perceive a greater chance of being able to apply the skills and knowledge acquired.

Or to take a less trendy example, research labs and other knowledge-intensive organizations often strive to foster an academic culture, whereby information is shared freely and status accrues to the well-versed and intelligent. Those values mesh well with the strategy and technology (ambiguous tasks, star roles) of research labs and can also be an important recruiting device for labs that compete with universities for talent. For such organizations, a broad program of free training for employees resonates well culturally. For example, in its heyday, Bell Telephone Laboratories, now part of Lucent Technologies, had an incredible education program for its technical staff. Courses were offered by scientists for their peers—the "course catalog" would have been the envy of virtually any university—and if an employee found an interesting topic not covered by some internally offered course but being taught at one of the nearby universities, the Labs would generally pay tuition and give work-release time. To do a cost-benefit analysis of these programs was regarded as . . . well, impolite. The Labs were not in the business of making money for AT&T, but rather of advancing knowledge, like a university. And if Ma Bell made a few bucks in the process of funding all this advancement in knowledge, that was just a fortuitous spin-off. At least, those were the dominant atmospherics in suburban New Jersey, at the Labs. (The bean-counters and top management at AT&T Corporate Headquarters in New York City might have been forgiven for looking at things slightly differently, but they generally had enough sense to be circumspect about it when interacting with the scientists and engineers from the Labs.)[10]

In short, training can be used to send messages to third parties (particularly, other employees) about the organization's culture and strategy. Although this point is obvious, we feel confident in asserting that it is overlooked with remarkable frequency, inasmuch as few organizations devote much effort to articulating for employees how the particular training programs that are sponsored reinforce specific aspects of corporate strategy and culture. In many organizations, it is not difficult to find dimensions of strategy or culture that are described by top leaders as absolutely pivotal (e.g., teamwork, ethics, diversity, learning) but that receive little or no emphasis in company education and training programs. Conversely, it is not challenging to find specific training activities being emphasized in many organizations that seem to bear little connection to *any* important strategic or cultural theme (at least as employees perceive things). If one views training as an important tool by which management communicates its strategy and values to employees, then those who design the training programs should articulate clearly to trainees how their training relates to and supports those broader themes. This involves little added cost but has the potential to increase markedly the returns from training.[11]

THE ABILITY TO APPROPRIATE THE RETURNS TO TRAINING

The previous section was essentially about a host of factors that affect B, the gross benefits to the firm from training the employee. But the firm doesn't necessarily appropriate all those benefits. Workers who become more skillful by virtue of training they receive are often paid more after the training. Thus, in the basic calculation, the firm doesn't compare the cost of training C with B, but instead with $B - S$, the net present value of training benefits, *net of additional salary that must be paid to the employee.*

Firm-Specific and General-Purpose Human Capital

The seminal analysis of $B - S$ is due to Gary Becker, the father of Human Capital Theory (and recipient in 1992 of the Nobel Memorial Prize in Economic Science for this work, among other things).

Becker begins by assuming that labor markets are competitive but with firms holding the balance of bargaining power when they deal with workers. Workers take the best offer made to them, and firms compete aggressively with each other for workers. A firm is willing if necessary to pay a worker up to the amount that the worker is worth to the firm (in terms of value added). But a firm that values the worker most highly only needs to pay the worker the amount the worker is worth to the employer who values the worker next-most-highly. That is, if employee X is worth $100,000 per year to firm A, $80,000 per year to firm B, and no more than $80,000 to any other firm, then firm A will offer X a salary of $80,000 (or perhaps $80,001), just enough to outbid firm B, and X will take this offer. (This assumes, of course, that there aren't any nonmonetary attractions of firm B that outweigh the salary differential. Obviously, if employment at firm A were, say, life-threatening and employment at firm B were not, firm A might need to offer considerably more than $80,001 to attract X.)

Under these assumptions, Becker proposes two polar types of human capital that correspond to the two polar cases that we noted at the start of our analysis: $S = 0$ and $S = B$. Suppose the training results in an increased value for the worker only at his current place of employment. Becker calls this the case of *firm-specific* human capital. Typical examples are things like: becoming inculturated in the values of the firm; mastering proprietary software; making a network of contacts inside the firm; and acquiring knowledge of the specific products and production processes of the firm.[12] Even if the worker gets this training, his wages are unaffected, because his value to the next-best employer is unchanged. Thus, in this case, $S = 0$, and the firm will be happy to purchase the training (as long as $B > C$).

The other polar case is training that improves the value of this employee to all employers equally. The sort of example that is typically cited in this case is general education, such as at the Stanford Sloan Program. For this so-called *general-purpose* human capital, $S = B$, because the improvement in value B applies as well to the employee's next-best employment situation, and his wages will have to pushed up by this amount to keep him employed at his current firm. Thus, according to our earlier analysis of the case $S = B$, the firm should be unwilling to pay for this training—the employee must pay (and will do so, assuming he can finance the training). Precisely this sort of financing arrangement is used for human capital investments like standard MBA degrees; at least at Stanford, most MBA students have resigned from their previous jobs and are themselves paying for the education, using personal and family savings, spousal income, and in many cases borrowing against future earnings.

Incidentally, observe that nothing prevents S from exceeding B.[13] This could happen when some training improves the value of employees to their present employer, but at the same time improves their value *even more* to other companies with which that employer competes in the labor market. For instance, imagine a bank employee who masters a technology that her employer intends to use, such as Web page design and security. Suppose that same technology has become even more critical to a competitor's strategy, for instance because it intends to make a bigger push in Internet banking. Or think of a scientific or technical employee who was recently trained in a new body of knowledge with which her employer is experimenting—such as voice recognition—but that happens to be integral to a rival firm's strategy. Becker doesn't offer a name for this, but something like "competitor-specific human capital" would seem appropriate.

Perhaps more typically, we have intermediate cases in which S is positive but less than B—the training is good for other potential employers but is best suited for the current employer. In these cases of mixed firm-specific, general-purpose human capital, the theory's predictions about who pays and how much remain somewhat ambiguous.[14]

When applying Becker's ideas, a measure of care is called for. The term "general-purpose human capital" means skills and knowledge that are worth *the same* to other employers, which is a lot more than saying that it is human capital that is somewhat valuable to all employers. Complementary training and knowledge, which we discussed above, become important here. The young British chemical engineer, going off to Stanford for general management skills and a MSM degree, would seem to be getting a nonpareil example of general-purpose human capital. But by virtue of the store of knowledge this individual has built up about his specific employer—his network of contacts in the firm; his knowledge of the products, processes, and plants of this firm—it is likely that his newly acquired skills as a general manager will be more valuable to his current employer than they would be to an alternative employer. If general management skills complement his preexisting firm-specific human capital, then under Becker's definition, the training he will receive at Stanford is not entirely general-purpose human capital. The same sort of caveat applies to many of the other factors we discussed in the previous subsection; complementary training to be given later, signals to the individual and to third parties, and reinforcement of a general culture all are factors or effects that may impart some firm-specific character to training that on its face might seem to involve plain-vanilla, general-purpose human capital.

It should also be carefully noted that Becker's analysis is anchored in the assumption of a competitive labor market. But employment relations reflect a host of labor market imperfections, as we discussed in Chapter 4, which make the market less than perfectly competitive. In the rest of this section, we summarize several of the more important departures from a world of perfect competition, which complicate matters and affect the basic analysis regarding how much of the benefits from training the employer can capture.

Giving Skills that Can't Be Used in a Reasonable Alternative Location

Suppose a blue-collar worker in rural Tennessee is trained in process control by his current employer. If that worker is rooted in the local community, with family and lifelong friends nearby, it is somewhat irrelevant that those skills might be valuable to automobile assemblers located in and around Detroit, Michigan. This employee is unlikely to move to Detroit for anything short of a fortune. The question is, How valuable are those skills to other employers in the immediate area? Depending on how rural this part of Tennessee is, the answer may be that these skills cannot be used by any other nearby employer. Here is a second training-motivated reason why Japanese car manufacturers located assembly plants in places like Marysville, Ohio and Smyrna, Tennessee, when they came to the United States intent on giving their workers much more training than is typical in U.S. plants (see Table 15-1).[15]

The point is: Just because the skills are useful to some other employer, somewhere in the world, doesn't mean that they will cause the worker's wages to be bid up. Looking at the skills themselves isn't enough to evaluate the critical difference $B - S$. And employers may be able to take strategic actions (e.g., by how they move employees geographically and where they site facilities) to minimize the salary increases that must be given to employees who possess skills that are in principle valuable to another employer.

Hidden Skills and the "Lemons" Problem

As we noted earlier, an organization providing training in general-purpose skills must worry that the trainees will use that training as leverage by threatening to walk away with what they have just learned. However, the credibility of such a threat will depend on how much prospective (outside) employers can discern about the worker and her newly acquired skills. In a hypothetical perfectly competitive labor market, if the employee obtains skills that raise her value to other employers, those other employers know this.[16] But, in real life, prospective alternative employers may be unaware of the skills that are acquired or unsure what those skills are worth. And because the value of skills depends in part on the basic abilities and work habits of the employee (and possibly those of her co-workers), the prospective employers may be unsure about how valuable the skills are for the particular worker.

Imagine a form of training that improves the value of all workers who are trained by amounts that differ for different workers. The current employer, having provided the training and then having been able to watch its impact, knows who is who. However, an outside employer, seeking to raid the current employer, does not. If the outside employer offers wages appropriate for the "average outcome" of this training, and if the current employer selectively chooses which employees to fight to retain and which to let go, then the outside employer will garner an adverse selection, winding up with a disproportionate share of the "lemons" among employees who received the training.[17] This can mean that the current employer is able to retain a substantial fraction of the value of the training, even if, for a given employee, the training is as valuable for the outside employer as for the current employer.[18]

There is a twist to this general line of thought that bears mention, however. We noted in Chapter 4 that current employers will often have an advantage in retaining employees, owing to the adverse selection problem an outside raider faces. To put it anecdotally, if a large German chemical firm wishes to locate a facility in England or otherwise raid our British chemical firm, it may have trouble determining *ex ante* who are the really bright and talented chemical engineers with managerial potential. But if the British firm sends a particular employee to Stanford's Sloan Program, it has just publicly certified this individual as a real star—not everyone gets to go to Stanford. So now it is clear who the German firm should try and steal. The moral: Selective training for the best and the brightest, just as with early promotion, may result in certification to the outside world that this is someone worth stealing.

Inertia, Especially Loyalty

In a hypothetical perfectly competitive labor market, the increased wages that must be paid to a freshly trained worker reflect the increase in that worker's value to the employer that values him next most highly. The firms bid for workers, and the worker goes to whoever pays the highest wage. Labor markets in the real world aren't always so price driven, however. In Chapter 4 we noted that as time passes, employees increasingly establish employer-specific assets that incline them to stay put at their current place of employment. Moving one's family, requiring one's spouse to find new employment, losing old friends and coworkers, and simple loyalty can all be at work here. If financial terms are equal and one is happy at the old job, the employee is likely to stay—the raiding employer has to beat the terms of the current employment relationship by enough to overcome all those sunk-cost investments and inertial forces.

Our emphasis for now is on loyalty, the least tangible of these inertial forces. One hears less and less frequently of the soccer star who stays with the (say,

Colombian) club side that first saw his talent and then raised and trained him, even though big bucks and a spot in the Italian First Division are on offer. Similarly, corporate lawyers frequently discuss nowadays whether their profession has witnessed a precipitous decline in loyalty, compared to the days when corporate lawyers felt an abiding commitment to the firms in which they had been trained and promoted to partner.[19] But if such loyalty in soccer or corporate law is less frequent (in part because Italian First Division teams and top-tier law firms can offer a lot more money and in part because it is perceived less and less as a mark of loyalty and more as a mark of . . . *stupidity* to pass up such a golden opportunity), in less stratospheric realms loyalty is a real and abiding factor. This is gift exchange again, but now the employee responds to the gift of training with a willingness to remain, even in the face of an attractive outside offer, which enables the employer to appropriate greater returns from the training investment.

Will the Firm Necessarily Underwrite Firm-Specific Training?

To this point we've been giving various arguments for why firms might be observed providing training that on the surface looks like general-purpose human capital. To give equal time to the other side, we want to ask, Will firms necessarily purchase training that is purely firm-specific (and economical)?

Becker's argument that they will do so stems from the assertion that for purely firm-specific human capital, wages are not raised ($S = 0$). Thus, as long as $B > C$, the firm provides the training. But the assertion that $S = 0$ for firm-specific human capital—that the employee gets nothing back in the form of higher wages—depends crucially on the assumption that the firm holds all the bargaining power vis-à-vis the worker. At least in some labor market contexts, however, the firm and the employee are on more equal bargaining terms. An employee who is worth $100K to her employer and $80K to her next-best opportunity might be willing and able to say, "Pay me $90K, please, or I walk." If the firm retorts: "If you walk, you won't get more than $80K," the employee's rejoinder is: "But when I walk out the door, $100K of value added for you walks with me." We aren't saying that the employee will win this argument. Whether she does depends on many factors, such as whom the firm can find to replace her and how quickly. But the idea that she will simply accept an offer of $80,001 is quite extreme.

Now suppose that, for $6,000, the firm can provide her with training that will increase her value to $110,000. This, of course, meets the test of economy—the value added of $10,000 is more than the $6,000 cost. And suppose this training is purely firm-specific. If her bargaining leverage is such that she recovers 50% of her "excess value added" to her employer, she would take back $5,000 of the valued-added of $10,000. And the firm, anticipating this, would do better not to invest in the training.

This story may seem a bit fanciful, but there are real data behind it. Firms practicing high-commitment HRM often provide substantial training and socialization (in skills, culture, etc.) to their employees. Employees—at least the sort of employees who do well in high-commitment HR systems—generally like training; it is good psychic compensation. One can argue that this is, at least in part, general-purpose human capital. But even when the firm faces few (local) rivals for the sorts of skills it provides its employees, it is likely to find that employees expect a raise to be tied to this type of skill acquisition. As we noted in Chapter 13, job enlargement and enrichment tend to raise workers' standards of entitlement, so it seems reasonable to expect that the acquisition of new skills and knowledge would also cause workers to expect their rewards to be upgraded. The employees may enjoy this sort of training and be deeply grateful to the firm for it, but the point is that they have also advanced up the social ladders of status and skill symbolized by virtue of this training, and they feel that they ought to be compensated for this. It isn't hard to imagine that if the additional compensation isn't forthcoming, at least some of the personal satisfaction the employees get from learning new things and the gratitude they feel to the firm for providing these skills will go out the window, together with a lot of the benefits the firm can obtain from these skills. Proponents of high-commitment HRM claim that the benefits accruing from this sort of training so dramatically exceed the costs, that even including the costs of the higher wages, the investment is worthwhile. But the notion that the firm captures 100% of the enhancement of firm-specific human capital is based on a fairly stark (and, we think, often less than fully accurate) model of the labor market.

Implicit Collusion to Minimize Raiding

To appropriate a greater return from training, firms in a particular labor market may collude. In its most explicit form, we have the case of transfer fees among soccer clubs: When a rich club in the Italian First Division goes hunting for a midfielder from, say, the Colombian First Division, they will negotiate a fee for the Colombian club intended, at least in part, to compensate for the training the midfielder received. But this is more blatant than usual. More common are implicit agreements among enterprises not to raid each other, as among the elite Japanese firms in the 1970s and 1980s (see also the discussion of medical interns and residents below).

In theory, one might also see explicit or implicit agreements among organizations to maintain a given level or standard of training, or to prevent raiding, so that when and if transfers occur, they occur for better reasons than to snatch someone else's trained workers just to save on the training costs. Real-world examples of this are not terribly common, but we can mention several. For instance, organizations promoting regional economic development, such as Joint Venture in California's Silicon Valley, may encourage dominant companies to maintain a high level of investment in worker training so that the region can continue to compete effectively against other locales for knowledge-intensive employment. During wars (e.g., World War II) government agencies sometimes prohibit firms from raiding the labor force of other employers without obtaining prior approval, requiring employers to justify in the process why the reassignment would be in the national interest during wartime. Stretching the point a bit, unions and other market-wide employee organizations can be powerful forces in promoting some degree of uniformity in training. Whether through pattern bargaining or through informal insistence on comparability in contracts, unions often bargain so that industry members look alike when it comes to training. (Indeed, craft unions, with their origins in skilled-craft guilds, often take over the training function entirely.) Professional associations and licensing bodies often impose similar mandatory requirements for continuing education and training. For example, most state bar associations—the state-level professional organizations that regulate and certify attorneys—mandate specific minimum amounts and types of continuing legal education that attorneys must complete to remain in good standing with the Bar. (Bar membership is required to be able to represent clients, receive malpractice insurance, and the like.) Interestingly, in our home state of California, the state Court of Appeals recently ruled that the State Bar's mandatory continuing legal education program is unconstitutional, and the case is currently on appeal before the California Supreme Court.[20]

THE COSTS OF TRAINING

A final set of factors to consider concerns the costs of training and, especially, actions firms can take to lower these costs.

Many forms of informal training occur on the job, while the worker is producing, and result in little or no diminution in worker value added. On-the-job training can sometimes take place nearly effortlessly and virtually incidentally, if employees are provided with the information needed to accomplish this training. Indeed, proponents of high-commitment HRM sometimes assert that the cost of such training is negative, in the sense that workers display greater intrinsic motivation if they are simultaneously learning.

Moreover, firms can rely on formal or informal mechanisms to maximize the "on-the-cheap" spillover effects on other employees from having trained one worker. These mechanisms include having newly trained employees demonstrate what they have learned in seminars for their colleagues and building computerized knowledge databases that can be accessed by other employees.

On-the-Job Training and Apprenticeships

Not all on-the-job training is costless, of course. On-the-job training frequently requires taking time away from other productive activities. And for some skills, learning on the job is about the only effective way to learn, at least beyond a certain point. Think, for example, of a young machinist who may have learned the basics of handling a metal lathe in high school or technical school but who learns lots of fine points and tricks from her experiences and from watching her more senior colleagues. Who pays for this?

A common labor market response in this sort of case is apprenticeship, whereby a worker seeking to learn certain skills (on the job) works for a period of time at wages below what a fully trained worker would get, because part of the apprentice's compensation is received in the form of training. Minimum wage laws will sometimes permit officially sanctioned apprentices to make sub-minimum wages. The question is, How low will the wages of an apprentice be?

Assuming competition among apprentice employers, the apprentice will be paid at least the net value of what he produces while he is learning, where net value means net of the cost of instruction (in terms of the time and effort devoted to training the apprentice by other employees, the materials required, etc.). It may be entirely sensible for the employer to pay more than this if the apprentice is developing firm-specific human capital or ties that will bind him to the firm at which he is apprenticing.

But can apprentices be paid *less* than the net value of what they produce while learning?[21] From the point of view of the apprentice, it certainly can be sensible to undertake an apprenticeship on these terms. That is, apprentices stand ready to work for less than the immediate net benefits they provide, if the alternative is to forgo the training altogether. If the enhancement in future wages is sufficient (by enhancing one's human capital in ways that will provide higher wages subsequently, whether with the current employer or with someone else), and if financing can be found, then apprentices may be willing to work for free or even to pay for the privilege of the training. Whether this is necessary, however, depends on whether employers offering apprenticeships can keep from competing with one another to raise apprenticeship wages. It takes apprentice employers who operate collusively or, at least, noncompetitively in the apprentice labor market.

For example, it is widely accepted that medical interns and residents are paid far less than what they "give back" to the hospital to which they are attached, even net of the costs of their training. Indeed, in the United States, hospitals are paid handsomely by the government for providing this education to residents, in addition to getting the value of the residents' services. The cartel is maintained by a number of interconnected factors: strictly limited allocations of board-certified residencies at each hospital; the prestige hierarchy of residencies at different hospitals (i.e., a residency at Mt. Sinai Hospital in New York is perhaps not as desirable as one at Massachusetts General, but is much more prestigious than one at Mercy General in Podunk, making wage competition more difficult); and variously explicit agreements among hospitals.[22]

Prestige Apprenticeships and Training Institutes

The example of medical internships and residencies raises an important set of issues about training and its costs and benefits. In many professions—examples include medicine, law, consulting, accounting, investment banking, and university teaching—there is a fairly clear hierarchy in apprenticeships. That is, interning at Mass General, clerking for a Supreme Court Justice, being an associate at McKinsey or Arthur Andersen or Salomon Smith Barney, or being an assistant professor at Harvard University, is viewed by most people in the respective industries as outstanding on-the-job training.[23] Because of the prestige associated with these apprenticeships, the wages that (according to economic principles) ought to be paid to the apprentice are low, relative to the wages paid at less prestigious apprenticing organizations. We are convinced that in most if not all of these cases, the apprentice is paid less than what she generates in value added. But one doesn't tend to see Mass General paying less for its interns than Mercy General, or Harvard paying less for assistant professors than Midwest State. Why not? And what are the benefits to the Mass Generals of this world for maintaining their prestige?

Needless to say, these are complex questions. But some pieces of the answers can be given. For one thing, social status and status consistency are at work. Because an internship at Mass General is higher in status than an internship at Mercy General, interns at Mass General expect they will be paid no less (and probably more); to do otherwise is to invite invidious social comparisons.[24] At the same time, the prestige of an internship at Mass General depends in part upon the excellent training available there (which in turn depends on the clinical faculty who teach there), but it also depends on the quality of the interns who go there. Mass General attracts the best interns in part because . . . it attracts the best interns.[25] If Mass General tried to exploit its reputation temporarily by lowering the wages it pays to its interns, it might drive at least some of the people it wants to attract to other hospitals, thereby lowering its reputation relative to more far-sighted rivals.

As for the returns to maintaining a prestigious apprenticeship program, the ability to attract outstanding individuals is of direct benefit to other parties involved. In the for-profit examples, such as consulting, accounting, and law, this means an ability to charge clients higher fees. For nonprofit examples, such as hospitals and universities, this can mean the ability to attract better senior colleagues and secure external funding (which, in turn, increase the attractiveness of the institution for apprentices).

There is another advantage of a prestige apprenticeship program that applies fairly generally (but not in the case of Supreme Court clerkships). Recall the adverse selection problem discussed earlier; an enterprise wishing to raid the labor force of a competitor must worry that it will get an adverse draw of employees. This is probably true in the cases of these prestige apprenticeship suppliers: The quality of associates hired away from Salomon Smith Barney is probably lower than the quality of those who remain. But because of the quality of training provided, the status conferred by having been trained at one of these institutions, and the concomitant attractiveness of the training for potential trainees, the adverse selection problem is not so great as to prevent raiding. Competitors below the first tier may simply be unable to provide commensurate training or to do so at reasonable cost; certainly they do not attract such good raw material on average. In these cases, it may be preferable for the second tier to hire away personnel who have already received training at a top-tier institution, even taking into account the risk of adverse selection and the need to pay a wage premium in the process.

But if raiders are getting an adverse selection, then the prestige institutions are getting and keeping the cream. To maintain an outstanding training or apprenticeship program means that you get the first and best shot at the top people in the program, which in many instances will already be a selection of the best people available.

This basic idea can be applied more widely than just to the case of professional employees in such fields as law, accounting, and medicine. Recall the example of the Oriental Hotel in Bangkok, which found, given the local labor pool, that it had to train its recruits, only to find some of those it trained being bid away by rival hotels. The Oriental responded in a way that some other training-intensive firms have done—namely, it got in the business of selling the training, by opening up a school for training hotel employees. By training more individuals, the Oriental was able to spread the fixed costs of training over a wider base. But they benefited in other ways as well. The Oriental's training program is well known for its quality; graduates are eagerly sought by other hotels, and so people aspiring to work in this industry queue up to get into the Oriental's program. Thus, the Oriental attracts into its school the best people seeking a career in this industry, from which it is able to skim the cream of the graduates.

Enlisting Public Support

Firms whose strategy or technology requires greater reliance on more highly trained workers in a particular local job market may lobby local governments to spend more on public education and training. One useful strategy is to "subsidize" public education and training efforts in ways that push them in directions where the employer wants them to go. We are hardly surprised to learn, for instance, that the Japanese auto companies that moved into places like Smyrna, Tennessee and Georgetown, Kentucky quickly became actively involved in helping shape local curricula and donating money and capital equipment to the public schools.[26] Quite apart from the generic public relations benefits derived from these activities, they help provide some welcome human capital for the firms, with the local community sharing the cost. (Of course, the returns from such donations are higher because of the relatively rural nature of the communities involved. Similar donations to public high schools in Detroit, Michigan by, say, the Ford Motor Company, may well take place. But we doubt that Ford can capture as much of the returns in Detroit as Nissan can in Smyrna. Note, however, that even in Detroit, if Ford sends instructors into local technical schools to "help out," it can gain some valuable information about—and build ties with—prospective employees.)

On the legislative side, firms that will benefit from a better-trained workforce may seek tax incentives for providing training to workers. Often these incentives are granted, and for reasons that go beyond simple political rent-seeking. Government-run training and retraining schemes have a harder time selecting those candidates who will benefit most from the training; firms, with superior information about their employees, can do better on these grounds. Similarly, those who attend government-run training programs often have a hard time finding appropriate post-training employment; in contrast, firms, who often plan to use the workers they train, have less of a problem with this. This is not to say that private-enterprise-based training schemes are perfect; in particular, they have on occasion been used to facilitate and perpetuate discrimination based on age, disability, race, and gender. But there are social advantages to them.

Under some circumstances, firms can also utilize legislation and regulations regarding training and vocational certification as a strategic weapon vis-à-vis competitors. Suppose you run a high-commitment firm and have structured employment to maximize the returns on investments in human capital (e.g., intensive screening, long-term employment, seniority-based rewards, broad job designs). You potentially stand to benefit if you can impose—for instance, through legislative enactment of a training tax or more stringent regulations regarding vocational certification—those same training costs on competitors who are either unable or disinclined to structure employment relations along the same lines, because they will incur similar costs but reap fewer benefits from the training. For instance, Southwest Airlines, which operates a distinctive high-commitment HR system, may stand to benefit if it could persuade federal regulatory agencies to raise the amount of continuing education and training required of pilots, mechanics, and flight attendants for all carriers in the industry. In other words, even if you are unable to alter the direct costs of providing a form of training, it may be feasible to enlist third parties (particularly the state, but also unions, professional associations, etc.) to impose equal or higher costs on rivals.

MAKING AND EVALUATING TRAINING DECISIONS

We have suggested that training is not an expense, but instead is an investment in the human capital of employees. Unfortunately, as numerous commentators have observed, managers' mindsets and accounting tools too often bias them toward treating financial and physical capital as more "real" than the intellectual capital embedded in their employees. That perspective, in turn, may lead to an underinvestment in human capital.

There has been a lively debate in recent years about whether the financial markets place sufficient value on intangible human assets,[27] prompting much discussion within the accounting, financial standards-setting, and regulatory communities about implementing reporting standards that more accurately reflect the value of nonfinancial assets, including human capital. To be sure, financial markets can put substantial value on intellectual capital (and other intangibles, such as customer goodwill). For instance, in late September 1998, the most recent quarterly balance sheet for Microsoft Corporation reported total assets of roughly $19 billion, but the company's market capitalization at that time was more than $270 billion. In contrast, balance sheets for the U.S. Big Three auto makers—GM, Ford, and Chrysler—reported combined assets of $527 billion, but those firms had a combined market capitalization less than half of Microsoft's (around $125 billion). And there are plenty of examples of high-technology start-ups that achieve substantial market capitalization on the basis of zero sales and very little physical capital. But the question remains whether the financial markets always do a good job evaluating the value of human capital. And there is little question that financial statements as currently prepared do a lousy job of capturing the economic value embedded in a firm's labor force.

Given the difficulty of accurately measuring the value of human capital and, correspondingly, of measuring the costs and returns associated with investments in human capital, there is ample potential for managers to make suboptimal training decisions. We will have more to say about this issue in the last chapter of this book, concerning the role of the HR function. But here we wish to underscore several fairly straightforward, yet nonetheless important, implications of the fact that the returns on investments in human capital are harder to quantify than returns on other sorts of investment.

First, the increasingly strong pressure that so many organizations face for documenting bottom-line results, particularly over the short-term, is likely to bias managers away from making investments for which the precise payback is harder to calculate or whose payback period is longer. This may bias managers against investments in human capital, relative to other forms of investment, and it may also bias them toward investing disproportionately in training programs having the fastest and easiest-to-document payback. It is not uncommon, for instance, for corporate training departments to evaluate training programs by sending surveys to the employee who was trained (or perhaps to the employee's supervisor) shortly after the program, asking for an evaluation of what was learned in the program that the employee has been able to use in the intervening period. Moreover, to the extent that companies view training as a cost or employee benefit, rather than as an investment, their training budgets often tend to lag financial performance, being reduced when times are tough. Needless to say, this is hardly likely to encourage managers to undertake costly investments in human capital that may, over the long term, be crucial to returning the organization to sustained profitability.

Note that hard performance-based measures on their own aren't necessarily a sound basis for evaluating investments in training either. If candidates are selected into training programs based on a record of past performance that is distinctly better or worse than average, for instance, then one will need to be careful in trying to make any inferences about the effectiveness of the training simply by comparing the performance of those who went through the training against those who did not. Even measures of performance *improvement* may be problematic, for at least three reasons. First, there may be floor and ceiling effects; if the most talented employees, for instance, are selected into training programs, there may be less room for seeing immediate performance improvements than is possible among employees whose performance is average. Second, some forms of training may actually be expected to diminish performance over the short-term by requiring the employee to descend a new learning curve. Third, one needs to be concerned that any observed performance improvements following training may simply represent Hawthorne effects.

Obviously, the appropriate means of evaluating any particular form of human capital investment will depend enormously on the specifics of the employee, the type of training, and the organization and its context. But several useful suggestions and caveats can be noted here. First, there is the obvious point to make about the limitations of evaluating training programs simply by soliciting evaluations either from those who went through the program or those who were responsible for designing and/or delivering the training. Second, we expect it generally would

392 · Chapter 15: Training

be quite beneficial to have an explicit, MBO-style discussion with the employee *prior to the training* regarding: (a) how the training being contemplated contributes to the organization's strategy; (b) how it contributes to the employee's professional and career development; (c) what the expected byproducts are from the training; and (d) what metrics are appropriate for evaluating the effectiveness of the training received. Note that (d) should include a discussion of the constituencies whose input is relevant in evaluating the impacts of training—peers, subordinates, superiors, customers (internal or external), suppliers, and so on. For instance, a manager undergoing a training program on "managing effective teams" might agree with her boss in advance on a set of metrics and milestones by which the efficacy of the training is to be evaluated—time-to-market and quality performance of the product development teams this manager oversees, as evaluated by the boss and other informed parties (such as the quality office); indicators of team cohesiveness and conflict; 360°-style assessments from subordinates; or possibly client satisfaction data. Although this hardly seems controversial or profound, our impression is that such explicit discussions occur fairly infrequently.

Another step an organization can take that may enhance its return on human capital investments is to pay explicitly for the skills and knowledge employees acquire through training. We noted earlier that when firms increase their workers' firm-specific skills, they often find they must increase wages commensurately—in other words, training often begets a pay-for-skill program. (A general discussion of the benefits and costs of paying for knowledge and skill is found in Chapter 12.) Of course, this aspect of training, even when the skills are purely firm-specific, goes into the Costs column on the balance sheet. And when pay-for-skill is formalized as such, calling attention to the financial payoffs that employees receive from acquiring new knowledge and skills may undercut any gift-exchange benefits that might otherwise accrue. But formalizing pay-for-skill can have a subtle and somewhat countervailing benefit: When the employer must explicitly pay for knowledge and skills that employees acquire, there is increased discipline on the organization and pressure to answer the questions: (a) Why are we providing these particular competencies?; and (b) Are employees using their newly acquired knowledge and skills to the fullest? Another side benefit of systems that pay for skills and knowledge is that they tend to encourage the formalization of information systems that catalog and track employees' competencies, if only for purposes of determining when individuals qualify for competency-based pay adjustments. By furnishing a comprehensive and up-to-date portrait of the knowledge and skills possessed by employees, such information systems can assist managers and HR professionals in trying to utilize employees' human capital to its fullest and maximize the organization's return on its investments in the labor force.

Finally, an additional way of seeking to evaluate training impacts that is sometimes underutilized is experimentation. For a variety of reasons—inertia; vested interests of training departments (and those who have gone through a particular training program, who have an interest in believing that it was a good experience); and the "network externalities" associated with having multiple employees go through the same training program—an organization will often settle on one approach for imparting specific skills. The organization will have the training delivered by one particular provider, using one specific technology, in one format, and so on. Although this is understandable and potentially even beneficial in some respects, it limits the extent to which the firm can identify the relevant aspects of the training that add or detract value. Even when it is desirable for groups of employees to go through a common training experience, there are often natural experiments that can be conducted to vary the particular form and content of training received by subgroups, so that analyses can be conducted after the fact to assess the efficacy of these different "treatments." Similarly, this mode of experimentation might extend to manipulating systematically the post-training assignments given to trainees, in order to look for interactions between the kinds of training that employees are provided and the sorts of job designs, career tracks, and compensation schemes utilized.

DESIGNING TRAINING PROGRAMS

A similar set of issues needs to be thought through carefully by those responsible for delivering training concerning how to design training programs, and by general managers in deciding what form of training to provide to a given employee. Among the dimensions along which training programs can vary are:

- On-site versus off-site
- Provided internally versus by an external vendor
- Organization-specific versus participants from multiple organizations
- Vocational training focused on particular job competencies (e.g., a seminar on "Spreadsheets for Beginners" or "What Is Sexual Harassment?"); through more general professional training (e.g., "Managing Teams" or "Introduction to Competitive Strategy"); to education and training focused more on personal human and intellectual development (e.g., "Achieving Work–Family Balance" or "Theories of Human Learning")
- Individuals versus groups/teams as the recipients of the training

We expect that you can readily identify some of the cost–benefit trade-offs that need to be weighed here. For instance, training conducted on-site is less disruptive, can be conducted more on a just-in-time basis, and may enable employees to apply what they are learning immediately. Training that is organization-specific and done internally is easier to customize to the business needs of the particular client, but with the obvious trade-off that training programs designed by external parties or involving participants from other companies may provide more opportunity to learn from other organizations (i.e., from the other companies sending participants, as well as from the accumulated knowledge of the vendor providing the training). Training aimed at specific vocational competencies can be utilized more quickly and is likely to have a quicker payback, but it also is likely to depreciate in value more quickly.

But the main point we want to emphasize, which often receives less attention from those who design and purchase training, concerns the *symbolic benefits* sought through training. To the extent that one views much of the value of training as stemming from its effects on motivation and loyalty through a process of gift exchange, this may have implications for the form of training one wants to provide, just as we noted (in Chapter 12) that it affects the form that employee benefits should take. We would speculate, for instance, that employees are generally less likely to view training as representing a gift—that is, as a discretionary investment in the employee by the firm that should be reciprocated through enhanced loyalty or effort—when it is: (a) provided by a subunit of their company; (b) provided on-site; (c) organization-specific; (d) narrowly vocational in orientation; and (e) mandatory.

Clearly, there are many other dimensions along which training programs can vary, and these too should be examined not simply in terms of their direct cost–benefit trade-offs, but also for their symbolic implications. For instance, there has lately been excitement within the training community about the prospects for using the Internet and corporate intranets, CD-ROMs, videoconferencing, and other technologies to deliver training to employees in ways that are seamless, just-in-time, and minimize disruptions to workers' normal work schedules. These technologies may prove attractive in terms of reduced cost and increased effectiveness of delivery, but it is also important to ponder their symbolic, motivational, and interpersonal effects, relative to more conventional forms of training. And where the firm is explicitly providing the training in part to seek gift-exchange benefits, it should explicitly seek to measure those impacts in evaluating the efficacy of the training—for instance, by focusing on effort, output, turnover, satisfaction, employee hiring referrals, suggestions, cooperation, continuous learning, and other indicators of discretionary effort and loyalty.

LESSONS FOR THE BRITISH CHEMICAL FIRM

Let us now return to the problem posed at the start of this chapter. If you are head of HR at this British chemical firm, what do you take away from the general discussion, to employ in this particular case? We think there are several important lessons.

To begin with, a hard look at the resume of this engineer is warranted. You want to screen on at least three grounds. First, and perhaps most obviously, is he a viable candidate for a general management position in terms of capabilities (e.g., communication and people skills), and is there time for him to make a career along this track in your organization? Second, do the competencies he would acquire through the training complement skills he already has as an engineer? Will he bring more to the table as a general manager because of his technical background and, in particular, because of his technical background with *your firm*? This speaks to two issues: Would it be equivalent in terms of gross outcomes (but easier and cheaper) just to hire an MBA (perhaps, with a chemical engineering degree)? Obviously not, if this individual has a firm-specific background that makes him especially valuable. But will the gross outcomes be close enough so that, net of the costs, hiring an outsider is more cost effective? And (if not), will this firm-specific background help you get value out of this training that other potential employers interested in his services will be unable to derive?

Third, to the extent that it is permissible under law, you may want to consider his level of attachment to your firm and your locale. Has he a network of acquaintances in the firm? Are some of them social friends? Is he married? Does he have children? Is he British to the core (unless you have overseas facilities to which you might want to post him)? We do not want to encourage discrimination here, and we are perilously close to doing so. But the idea behind these questions is not, Is he an old boy? Rather, it is an attempt to see how likely it is that he will take your education and depart.

Another piece of advice is: Don't be stingy when it comes to the budget. In this particular case, this is to a large extent a gift, not simply the purchase of a bundle of skills. You may well want to make it a gift with strings attached (see the next point). But assuming good intentions on all sides, dressing it up as a gift, with personal touches, is a good idea. For example, can you tap any personal acquaintances or people in the company to make suggestions about schools for his children?

And as you are crafting this as a gift, think of touches that will bind the individual to your firm. For example, consider flying the whole family back to England for Christmas and Spring Break. (Make sure the children get to visit their old schools and friends, in particular.) We are told that this sort of home–leave travel allowance is fairly prevalent among participants in the Sloan Program and, as long as "home" isn't going to suffer too badly in comparison with sunny California, it makes sense as a device for maintaining social and personal ties that bind. Or, to give another example (that we haven't heard of any firms using), offer an allowance to pay for phone calls back home, perhaps up to some limit, and assure the individual that this allowance is there so the family can keep in touch with friends and not so that he can keep in touch with what is going on back at the plant.

Are golden handcuffs—which bind the employee to return, say, for a few years—a good idea? We made light of them early in the chapter, when we pointed out that if the true value added of the Sloan Program education is primarily going to come long after the handcuffs have come off, then the handcuffs don't do much to protect your investment. But this isn't quite right: There are substantial costs of relocating, and a large hurdle has been surmounted if you get the individual back home, the spouse back to the old job, and the kids back to the old school and to old friends. (This, obviously, has less relevance for a multinational that plans to move the individual around.)

Next, we advise thinking long and hard in advance about how you would best use the graduates of this sort of training program and discussing extensively with the chemical engineer (and his manager) how his stint in the Sloan Program is expected to further his personal development objectives and reinforce (or perhaps help change) the strategy and culture of the company. The employee who returns ready and able to use new skills, but who is sent back to his old job or discouraged from applying the learning acquired during the training program, is apt to become disgruntled, at the very least. We alluded to the fact that the Sloan Program has some sponsors who send students fairly regularly—perhaps not every year, but fairly frequently. Based on the testimony of these sponsors, regular participation enables them to take increased advantage of each individual who goes to the program, particularly because the "graduates" in their organization form a network.

More broadly, you should consider whether your company has in place a set of HR policies and practices that are likely to maximize the return on the substantial investment you are considering making in this chemical engineer: compensation and benefit systems that encourage longevity of employment; job designs and career development strategies that will create ample opportunity for this engineer to put to good use what he will learn at Stanford; formal or informal practices that may facilitate the transfer of what he has learned to co-workers; and so on.

We could go on with further tips on how to optimize your company's use of the Stanford Sloan Program, but (of course) this is not a specific problem you are likely to face. So we'll stop here. The point we've tried to make is that whether you will recoup an investment in the human capital of your employees, an investment accomplished through training, depends at least in part on how well you can "fix" and then use the individuals in whom you are considering investing. It makes little sense to say that a form of training comes at a cost C, with gross benefits B but increased wages S, and then to compare $B - S$ with C. These quantities are all endogenous, and *how* you conduct the training program can have a lot of impact on what the outcomes will be.

TAKEAWAYS

As we noted early in this chapter, if measured by dollars spent, training is a big deal in HRM. From our perspective—viewing labor as human capital in which the firm should willingly invest—this is entirely appropriate. Indeed, like other commentators, we believe that in the United States (at least), it is not enough of a big deal.[28]

Obviously, firms that train extensively benefit most when this activity is complementary to other HR policies, most notably policies that ensure appropriate screening of employees and that prolong employment and reduce voluntary turnover. Nearly as obvious is the connection between training and HR policies that allow the individual to grow in terms of what he or she does—training fits rather neatly with broad, flexible job designs and with reliance on internal promotion. And training fits well with technologies that demand employees who work with their heads as well as with their hands—the *technological* connection to high-commitment HRM and to elaborated forms of high-commitment HRM such as TQM is clear.

We doubt that this comes as a big surprise to you. So we have tried instead to emphasize some points that are perhaps less obvious but that we think are equally notable and important. These revolve around the social and symbolic aspects of training. Most employees, as a matter of human nature, like to see their competencies grow, and they are grateful to organizations and managers that help them to learn, to accomplish more, and to have a richer and more interesting existence. Training—or, to use a term that is more evocative of the ideas we are propounding here, *education*—is a very powerful lever in this regard. Training signals to the employee the firm's commitment to her. If appropriately presented, it is generally received as an important gift, triggering loyalty and gift exchange. Because it enhances understanding and accomplishment, it enhances intrinsic motivation; this gives a second reason why it is typically integral to high-commitment HRM. It has powerful third-party effects, through its impact on other employees, through the culture of growth that it helps sustain, and through its impact on suppliers and customers.

We cannot and do not advocate that every employer offer every employee every form of education that might be proposed. There are economic limits to the returns you can expect from investing in your employees' human capital. But our analysis leads us to believe that those limits are typically less severe than you might think, because of the social and symbolic content of training and the benefits that are thereby entailed. And those limits become less severe still, the better designed the training process is to milk the social and symbolic content.

As we noted, training is highly complementary to a work environment in which individuals can progress. And in many if not most work environments, progression for the individual means promotion—a rise in the organization chart, accompanied by more power, greater responsibility, a bigger office, more perks, and a bigger paycheck. So we turn next to promotion, where we'll see that equating "progression" with promotion can be fraught with dangers for an organization.

IN REVIEW

⇒ Firms train employees if the net benefits accrued—the difference between the value added from the training and the additional amount that must be paid to the employee—exceeds the costs of the training.
  • The value added and the amount that must be paid back to the employee are both net present values. The costs of the training can also be a net present value, but in general the costs of training are expended up front.

⇒ The gross value added from the training is affected by:
  • Factors that impact on the employee's tenure with the firm, including demographics, local job market conditions, and the firm's HR practices
  • The employee's preexisting skills and how the training in question might complement those skills

- The impact of the training on employee effort and loyalty, because the training improves the employee's bargaining position vis-à-vis the firm
- Spillovers to other employees, both direct (the newly acquired skills are shared with co-workers) and indirect (by signaling to others and by reinforcing the organization's culture)
- The impact the training program has on recruitment

⇒ The share of this value added that is retained by the firm depends on the general bargaining strengths and proclivities of employee and employer. Specific factors to consider include:
- The extent to which the training develops firm-specific versus more general-purpose human capital
- Whether a substantial "lemons" problem exists for other employers who might seek to lure the employee away
- The degree of employee inertia, particularly loyalty engendered by the training

⇒ When evaluating the costs of training, keep in mind:
- On-the-job training can sometimes be relatively cheap, and apprentices can sometimes be employed for less than the value they provide the organization.
- Outstanding training programs can be leveraged by turning them into general training institutes, which both amortizes the cost of the program and gives the organization the ability to skim the cream of trainees.
- Public support can sometimes be enlisted to help defray the costs of training.

⇒ When designing or evaluating training programs, carefully bear in mind:
- Cost–benefit calculations concerning human capital investments may be distorted because important benefits are intangible or long-term in nature.
- Additional benefits of training arise through symbolic effects and impacts on third parties.
- Systematic experimentation with the design of training programs, criteria for selecting whom to train, and post-training assignments can help identify and maximize the value-added features of training activities.

ENDNOTES

1. Several disclaimers are in order. We are about to describe a program at our place of employment, so biases are certainly possible. Also, the Sloan Program we are about to describe is not unique to Stanford. In particular, MIT and the London Business School

each have similar Sloan Programs, and many institutions offer similar programs. We are describing our own program because it was relatively easy to get information about it. More generally, this chapter is about training, an activity and industry to which we are both devoted. Hence, general professional and emotional biases are possible. We believe we have given an objective account of training in this chapter, but there is little doubt that the conclusions we reach are favorable toward activities we perform. So, *caveat emptor.*

2. Our estimates of compensation costs are based on the assessment of several British HR specialists, whom we asked to help value the total compensation package for our hypothetical engineer. We have translated their answers from pounds sterling into dollars using the exchange rate of £1 = $1.70 in effect as of this writing.

3. Sponsored participants are meant to be released from duties at the sponsoring organizations for the program period, and so we have included as an expense the individual's salary. A more precise calculation would run as follows. Suppose that the individual, on the job, generates benefits to the organization equal to V and costs it C in salary, pension, etc. Suppose a replacement generates value V' and costs C'. And let E be the extra expenses incurred by sending the individual to Stanford. Then the "incremental cost" to the organization of sending the individual to Stanford is $V - V' + C' + E$, this being the reduction in value $V - V'$ generated plus the wages that must be paid to the replacement plus the incremental costs. Note that C does not figure in this calculation, since the organization pays C in both instances. Thus, to do the accounting properly, we would have to speculate on how valuable the replacement is (relative to the Sloan program participant) and how much the replacement will cost. Rather than do this, we've assumed that $V - C = V' - C'$, so that the incremental cost $V - V' + C' + E$ is $C + E$.

4. Such golden handcuffs are employed by some sponsors; we do not know the numbers, but our rough guess is that perhaps a quarter use this sort of restraint on sponsored participants. But, in the United States at least, there are questions about the enforceability of this kind of agreement. To lower participant mobility (as a "service" to sponsors), Stanford does not permit Sloan Program students to use the Career Planning/Placement services provided to MBA students. We should also note that although sponsorship is typical, it is not universal; our uninformed estimate is that around 5% of the participants will be self-sponsored, often because they come from companies which they themselves founded.

5. There are some assumptions to go with this assertion that we won't bother you with.

6. As quoted in Arne L. Kalleberg et al., *Organizations in America: Analyzing Their Structures and Human Resource Practices* (Thousand Oaks, CA: Sage Publications, 1996), p. 158. Compare this figure with a total number of employees in the private sector of around 95 million in 1994, according to the Current Employment Statistics compiled by the U.S. Bureau of Labor Statistics (available from their Web site at http://www.bls.gov.ceshome.htm).

7. This isn't quite accurate. The employee's willingness to pay for training depends on how that training will affect her lifetime earnings, and not only the earnings with her current employer. So, for instance, a young lawyer might be willing to pay quite handsomely (or, equivalently, take a vastly reduced level of income) for a short-term clerkship that will improve her earnings in her next and subsequent jobs. Also, once we begin to consider the incentives for individuals to invest in their own human capital, we have to confront uncertainty about future earnings and individual risk aversion. And if we are interested in the economic efficiency of private-sector training, we should

ask if the training will be provided if the gross benefits for the current firm and *all subsequent* employers exceed the costs. Complete accounts of human capital theory wrestle with all these issues. Because we are interested here only in the provision of training by the current employer, we will not.

8. Some numbers may help: Suppose that $B = \$100,000$ and $C = \$20,000$, so there is a net benefit (after training costs) of $80,000. If $S = \$10,000$ (i.e., 10% of the gross benefit is recovered by the employee in the form of higher wages), then the employee cannot be asked to contribute more than $10,000 toward the cost of the training. But even if the firm paid the whole $20,000, it would be getting an economical deal. So the worker's share of the cost could be anything between $0 and $10,000, and both sides are better off. What deal they strike within that range is a matter of their relative bargaining strength.

9. And to realize the value, the firm must complement all this training with HR and operations practices that give the employee the motivation and opportunity to use the knowledge she acquires. Revisit Chapter 9 if this isn't clear.

10. We are told that the education program persists, but things nowadays are more focused on specific and immediately relevant topics and skills. Note that this change in HR policies can be rationalized as a response to the changed competitive (economic) environment. When the Bell System (AT&T, Western Electric, the operating companies) was a regulated and protected monopoly, there were increased opportunities to profit from fundamental technological advances made in the Labs; hence, it made sense to promote work on "basic science" there. But in the deregulated, competitive world of telecommunications that has resulted from the breakup of the Bell System, profits from "basic science" are much harder to garner.

11. Based on a recent survey of more than 1,000 companies and in-depth case studies of training in 7 firms, Watson Wyatt, the HR consulting firm, concluded that "companies that link employee skill development to business strategy have 40 percent higher total shareholder return (TSR) than companies that do not" (http://www.watsonwyatt.com/home/homepage/us/pres_rel/FEB98/hcinvst-tm.htm).

12. Although these examples are typically cited, please understand that they may not be entirely firm-specific. Another organization—a supplier to the current employer, say—might pay higher wages to someone who has contacts within the current employer. And for a wide variety of reasons, ranging from the desire to benchmark to industrial espionage, competitors might pay for knowledge about the work systems and products of the current employer.

13. Thus, in a sense, general-purpose human capital is not really a polar case.

14. In fact, Becker's model of the labor market removes the ambiguity, because it assumes that the firm has all the bargaining leverage. The firm will raise wages by S and offer to pay max $\{0, C - S\}$, or perhaps a few dollars more, for the training; the worker will pay min$\{S, C\}$.

15. Back in Japan, the Japanese automobile assemblers have invested heavily in the human capital of their core workforce of school-leavers, relying instead on a labor market (for school-leavers at elite firms) that strongly discourages voluntary quits. Compare the two reasons for the rural siting decision in the United States that we have given in this chapter. First, there are few alternative employers in and around Smyrna, Tennessee who can use the skills that Nissan gives to its workers, so Nissan is better able to appropriate the returns from that training. This depends on a local labor force that is anchored in the immediate area. (And Nissan's benefits policies presumably help

keep them anchored there—for instance, the firm's health center and 75-acre recreation park, which includes a driving range and numerous other athletic facilities; discount vehicle leasing and maintenance programs for employees; an on-site financial center; and the like.) Second, for the same basic reason, Nissan has selected workers who are unlikely to quit voluntarily, to take any job elsewhere, which increases the number of years that Nissan can expect to appropriate these benefits. Somewhat conversely, the lack of many other major employers in the area means that it will be harder to hold onto workers with a spousal-employment problem or to move two-salary families into the area.

16. That is, it is an *assumption* of competitive markets that all parties have access to all relevant information. Of course, that this is an assumption means that many markets that otherwise seem competitive do not fit the economist's definition.

17. For a more general discussion of this "lemons" problem and issues related to adverse selection, see Appendix D.

18. For an argument along these lines, as well as some supportive empirical data based on German apprenticeships, see Daron Acemoglu and Jörn-Steffen Pischke, "Why Do Firms Train? Theory and Evidence," *Quarterly Journal of Economics* 113 (February 1998):79–119. See also our remarks in the next section concerning cream-skimming by the Oriental Hotel in its training institute.

19. For a good example of a firm struggling to cope with these issues, see John J. Gabarro and Andrew Burtis, *Brainard, Bennis & Farrell,* Harvard Business School case 9-495-037.

20. A lawsuit was brought by a 73-year old attorney whose name was removed from the list of active Bar members for failing to prove that he was in compliance with the minimum continuing legal education requirements. The rationale for the Court's ruling (in *Warden v. State Bar of California,* 1997 WL 114436; Cal. Ct. App. Mar. 13, 1997) was that the program denied the plaintiff equal protection because certain categories of Bar members (retired judges, state officers and elected officials, full-time law professors, and federal and state government lawyers) are exempt from the continuing education requirement, and the Court did not find the rationales for these exemptions compelling.

21. In Chapter 12, you may recall, we discussed wages that rise with seniority, where the employee is underpaid relative to his contribution early in his career and then overpaid as he grows older. The employee is willing to be underpaid early on, in this story, because the firm can convincingly promise that his wages later on will compensate. This sort of scheme provides one explanation for why we might see very low apprenticeship wages. But we wish to provide an alternative (and reinforcing) explanation here—an explanation that is consistent with post-apprenticeship wages that never rise above the employee's immediate contributions to the firm—and so we ignore for now the alternative rationale for low wages early on that we advanced previously.

22. Hospitals have in the past competed vigorously for the best interns and residents, but this competition was on the basis of date-of-signing, rather than wages. The competition to sign interns and residents early became so severe that the hospitals explicitly cartelized the process, creating an administered system for matching MDs to residencies. The Antitrust Division of the U.S. Department of Justice looked into this system, but was convinced that the matching system on its own was pro- rather than anti-competitive. (This judgment is controversial, in our view.) The Department of Justice has reportedly been reluctant to delve too deeply into the matter of cartelized wage-setting, because of a reluctance to get into anything that might smack of meddling with

who is qualified to be a given kind of specialist. (The power of the American Medical Association to lobby is quite significant.) The DOJ is not entirely absent in this matter: They did, for example, get a consent decree in 1996 that stopped family physicians from engaging in various anti-competitive practices, such as agreeing not to try to steal one another's residents or offering higher salaries. But the prohibition against explicit agreements does not necessarily preclude implicit wage-fixing. For a technical account of the matching process, see Alvin E. Roth and Marilda A. Oliviera Sotomayor, *Two-Sided Matching: A Study in Game-Theoretic Modeling and Analysis* (New York: Cambridge University Press, 1990). For a more general account of nonprice competition in this sort of market, see Alvin E. Roth and Xiaolin Xing, "Jumping the Gun: Imperfections and Institutions Related to the Timing of Market Transactions," *American Economic Review* 84 (September 1994): 992–1044.

23. We have chosen one example from each category and do not mean to slight the other high-prestige places to apprentice.

24. But note that a Supreme Court clerkship *does* pay less than employment as an associate at a major corporate law firm, and salaries for assistant professors in Harvard's economics department are generally lower than for their colleagues in the Harvard Business School. Presumably, there are some compensating differentials at work here, which reflect differences in the work contexts and job demands, and not simply differences in institutional status. Our claim is that the differences in work context and job demands are likely to defuse the sorts of invidious comparisons and status inconsistency that would otherwise arise if, say, a Supreme Court clerk made less than her counterpart clerking at an appellate court or a rookie in the Harvard economics department made less than a new hire in Midwest State's economics department.

25. Recall from last chapter the theory of the prestige MBA that gave all the credit to an admissions office that could separate wheat from chaff.

26. For instance, Nissan North America's Web site promotes the company's extensive contributions to nonprofits that support health and human services, education, and other community activities in and around Smyrna, Tennessee, where its manufacturing facilities are located. It also proudly publicizes that "as it upgrades and replaces its PCs, [Nissan North America] is donating the used computers to public and private schools in its home county of Rutherford. Approximately 1,200 computers will be cleaned, serviced and handed over in the next three years" (see http://www.nissan-na.com/2.0/2-3-2-b.html). Toyota's web site describing its facility in Georgetown, Kentucky notes that: "A new high school and much more was made possible by the more than $30 million that will be given to the Scott County school system over 20 years in lieu of tax payments on property exempt from taxes. Toyota donated $1 million to create a Georgetown community center, $2 million to expand the University of Kentucky Library System and $1 million to help build a new Kentucky History Center. Toyota has also contributed more than $6 million to a variety of Kentucky organizations, including the . . . Governor's Scholars Program" (http://www.careermosaic.com/cm/toyota/toyota4.html). Predictably, Toyota's dominance in the regional economy has precipitated a cascade of similar actions by employers competing against Toyota for skilled labor. For instance, the *Lexington (Kentucky) Herald-Leader* recently described how companies in Elizabethtown, Kentucky, who were losing skilled labor to Toyota in Georgetown (roughly an hour's drive away), banded together to contribute money and computers to local schools, and even designed the curricula of specific courses at the local technical school and community college to produce workers possessing the skills needed by the town's rapidly

expanding manufacturing sector. (See Bill Bishop, "Business Thrives with Cooperation," *Lexington Herald-Leader,* June 1, 1997, viewable online at: http://www.kentuckyconnect.com/heraldleader/news/060197/fbishop.html).

27. For instance, see Jeffrey Pfeffer, *The Human Equation* (Boston: Harvard Business School Press, 1998), Chapter 9.

28. Again, consult the illustrative data in Table 15-1. But remember that labor market mobility varies markedly across countries, and—concerning the differences in training for Japanese firms in the United States vs. U.S. firms—the Japanese firms have chosen consciously to locate their facilities so that the resulting labor force is less mobile. Although Table 15-1 is provocative, by itself it doesn't prove anything.

16

PROMOTION AND CAREER CONCERNS

Promotion, like performance evaluation, performs a number of different functions. These include providing incentives, sending signals to third parties, on-the-job training, placement, and screening. We begin by taking each in turn.

- *Incentives:* Promotion is usually desirable to the employee, because it typically brings higher compensation, internal and external status, greater levels of authority and autonomy, more interesting challenges, power, and the like. To be sure, not every employee desires promotion. There are employees who are more than content to stay in a "lower-level" job, especially if they are well compensated, to keep doing something they like or to avoid duties that they would not find particularly appealing. But, by and large, workers view promotion as a means to desirable ends. And thus, by rewarding good performance with promotion, organizations motivate employees.

    Promotion as an incentive device has some considerable advantages, because promotion decisions are usually based on relatively long track records. Offering promotion opportunities can advance organizational goals in two ways: (a) by encouraging employees to do things with longer-term payoffs than might otherwise be in their narrow self-interest (for instance, help recruit women and minorities to the organization or train neophytes); and (b) by discouraging employees from doing things in the short run that might be in their interest, such as distorting this year's sales figures. This is why many effective organizations—such as Lincoln Electric—that tie rewards to current output balance this with strong reliance on internal promotion, which discourages employees from trying to game the reward system for short-term gain.

    Indeed, promotion as an incentive device may loom so large in some employees' minds that attempts to provide additional shorter-term financial incentives may be ineffective. In the early 1990s, Citicorp offered massive option bonuses (worth on the order of $210,000,000) to one hundred key employees, to motivate extraordinary effort. At the end of the period covered by this program, Citicorp's CEO, John Reed, asked the individuals involved to write down how these financial incentives had affected their behavior over the period in question. From the data he received, Reed concluded that the options had done virtually nothing to add motivation or alter behavior, particularly taking into account the huge amounts of money involved.[1] We are not entirely surprised by this. Although Citicorp had recently filled a number of high-level executive posts from the outside, most of the senior personnel involved were groomed through the firm's long-standing promotion-from-within regime. Consequently, these 100 "high-leverage" individuals had already been carefully selected and developed to have goals and abilities that are closely aligned with the bank's strategy. Furthermore, these senior employees presumably were already strongly motivated by prospects for continued advancement in the firm, which we expect is all the motivation it takes to exert themselves on behalf of the bank.[2]

- *Signaling to others the characteristics that the firm desires:* Employees may be unclear about what sorts of behavior the firm desires, what skills are sought, what sorts of decisions are in the firm's interest, and so on. The promotion of a particular employee typically sends strong signals to others about what the organization values, so that others can mold themselves according to the pattern that has been rewarded by promotion.[3] Indeed, our experience is that employees often read "signals" into such decisions that the person(s) making the promotion decision did not intend to send, whether we are considering line workers trying to divine why a peer was selected for a coveted lead-worker position, divisional managers vying for a senior management post and looking for clues as to which division is in favor, or untenured professors searching through the tea leaves in the tenure decisions made by their senior colleagues.

- *On-the-job training:* In many jobs, the employee must have deep knowledge about the firm and its strategy, environment, workforce, technology, and culture. These things take time to learn, and this type of learning is often most effectively done on the job. In many cases, the amount of firm-specific knowledge along these lines that is required for a job increases the higher the job is in the hierarchy. Hence, as we noted in our discussion of internal labor markets (ILMs) in Chapter 8, employees will start out in lower level positions and be promoted as their expanding base of knowledge makes them suitable for higher-level responsibilities. This effect is reinforced by the use of promotion ladders in ILMs to obtain information about the talents of particular employees before placing them into critical jobs, a practice that we saw is especially prevalent in technologies dominated by guardian roles.

- *Placement:* Different jobs in a firm require distinct skills and talents, and promotion is often used to match individuals to jobs. This is especially true in cases where managers are hired in at some entry level and given a variety of assignments over their first few years to see where they fit the best. Once that has been determined, they are promoted into a position of responsibility that matches their interests and skills.

- *Screening:* Relatedly, thinking back to Chapter 14, firms can and do use promotion ladders as screening devices, by which employees signal important information about their abilities, interests, and intentions. For example, many high-tech firms that hire top-flight scientific and technical personnel offer a choice of two career ladders—one leading to senior technical roles and the other leading to senior management positions. In making an early choice between these ladders, employees provide clear and useful information to the firm about where their motivations lie, enabling supervisors to craft assignments, rewards, and training accordingly. If firms wish to screen employees along such dimensions as risk aversion, tolerance for ambiguity, or generalist versus specialist, an effective means of doing so can be to craft distinct promotion ladders that vary along these dimensions and then rely on employee self-selection as a disclosure mechanism.

SERVING TOO MANY MASTERS?

It hardly needs saying, but these functions of promotion do not always coexist compatibly. In an organization in which status and compensation are strongly correlated with rank, managers who are performing well in a particular slot will still want to be promoted to a higher position, even if their value to the company in the higher position is not as great as their value where they are. An example along these lines occurred in the early years of Au Bon Pain, a chain of French bakery restaurants concentrated primarily on the East Coast of the United States.[4] Prior to the advent of the company's "Partner/Manager Program," which gave store managers a stake in the profits generated by the site they were managing, store managers sought advancement either by movement to larger stores or by moving into corporate management, even if their potential contribution to the company was greater by remaining attached to their current store location. Viewing their post as store manager as a way station on the road to managing a larger store or moving to corporate headquarters, some managers were "underinvesting" in their stores and in their people. Imagine a store manager with her eyes on an upcoming promotion opportunity, who would need to use some of her own store budget for property improvements or community relations or employee training, where the returns from such investments will not be realized for some time to come. How likely do you think she would be to make those investments, relative to someone intending to remain as store manager for a long time? Thus, despite what we said earlier about promotion potentially leading to a longer-term outlook, the strong desire for rapid promotion can actually lead to a vicious cycle of short-termism and underinvestment when the employee doesn't intend to be in his or her current post long enough to reap the benefits. Notice, by the way, that the same problem can arise where employees are being rotated among assignments, rather than promoted up a hierarchy. Indeed, if employees are given a number of lateral transfers to see where they perform best in the organization, they may have some incentive to underperform in areas that they would like to avoid.

Another conflict regarding promotion is that the desire to select and reward someone with outstanding talent may work at cross purposes with "sending the right message," if the individual has behaved in nonstandard ways. Conversely, when selecting from among a group of candidates for promotion, attention to sending the right message may lead one away from awarding the promotion based strictly on merit or who is best suited for the job. To illustrate these dilemmas, consider an organization wishing to reward loyalty and seniority but also wishing to signal its commitment to diversity. The organization may well find that women or people of color have, on average, lower seniority than white males. When the enterprise adheres to a seniority-based promotion policy, its commitment to diversity may be called into question; when it promotes "nonstandard" candidates (i.e., talented women and people of color who have not been in the firm as long or who have ascended through unorthodox career trajectories), the implicit or explicit contract regarding seniority-based promotion may be called into question.

A final example of the dilemmas that can accompany a strict promotion-from-within regime concerns the pressures this can create to move people up the ladder prematurely. When an organization grooms individuals for top-management positions internally by bringing them up through the ranks, promotion decisions at a particular level may be skewed in favor of someone young enough to have a chance at making it to the top, even if that person seems somewhat less qualified for the particular promotion. We once heard the CEO of a prominent Wall Street trading and investment banking firm state that because of the energy and stamina required to run his organization, as well as the firm's corporate culture, nobody could be expected to do his job effectively far beyond their mid-50s. A tenure of 10 years was probably ideal for someone in that job, he thought, implying that the typical CEO would take over the reins in his or her mid-40s. He believed that about 10 years of developmental assignments within the company were required to gain the knowledge and breadth of perspective required to lead the firm effectively. Thus, he had begun scouring the cohort of people who are potential candidates to be groomed for the top job through such developmental assignments, and most of these people are in their early to mid-30s. Assuming that the typical MBA graduate is 28 to 30 years old upon leaving business school, this career model implies that someone joining this firm straight out of business school will have worked there no more than five to seven years before top management decides whether to include them in the select cohort to be groomed for the most senior posts.[5]

UNHAPPY CONSEQUENCES OF THE PROMOTION PYRAMID

Promotion can be a useful motivational device, it can be used to send appropriate signals to the workforce, and it can give the firm levers for training, screening, and appropriately placing its employees. As we've noted, however, these goals may not be compatible. Moreover, promotion may have a number of unhappy consequences for the organization beyond those to which we already alluded above, which result from these incompatible goals.

Promotion as an Incentive Device

Because employees value promotion, it is often intentionally used as an incentive device. We've noted some positive aspects of this, but there are negative aspects as well. Promotion is generally discrete: One either makes the grade or not. We noted when discussing compensation (in Chapter 11) that discrete incentive systems have bad dynamic properties; they can encourage frenzied activity as the deadline approaches when someone is near the threshold, and they can promote coasting or slacking as the deadline approaches and the individual is comfortably over or well below the threshold. When promotion is competitive—only one or a few of a larger group will be promoted—these effects can intensify. If one person is clearly in the lead, others slack off, and this gives the leader further incentive to coast.

Of course, promotion is not always so discrete. In some cases, promotion rewards can be graded by time—one is either promoted quickly or slowly. Nonetheless, insofar as there are those who will not make it over the hurdle, as they come to realize this they lose the incentive to continue to perform, unless some other form of incentive is put in place of the (now) dwindling chance of promotion.

Promotion as a Tournament

Many of the potential dysfunctional consequences of promotion arise because promotion resembles a tournament, with only a fraction of the people at any level being advanced to the next level. This happens because most organizations resemble a pyramid, with fewer and fewer positions at higher and higher ranks. The pyramid shape is there for completely understandable reasons. Those in higher ranks will often direct the actions of their subordinates, and even in organizations with a more bottom-up approach to decision making, those higher up in the organization will coordinate, evaluate, and manage their subordinates. Each of these functions—direction, coordination, evaluation—is often efficiently performed by one individual handling several nominal subordinates; hence, the pyramid shape. Moreover, if you view the compensation paid to an executive as a fixed cost, to be amortized over the span of the executive's control, then increasing the span—which increases the taper in the pyramid—allows the firm to spend more on the single executive, thereby, one hopes, recruiting and retaining better executives.

The fact that promotion resembles a tournament has its good points; one is naturally forced into comparative evaluation, which in some contexts is entirely appropriate and forces some discipline on whoever is doling out rewards. But all the bad things about tournaments that we discussed in Chapters 10 and 11 also apply to promotion. Most notably, promotion competitions can strongly discourage cooperative efforts among the rivals for a particular promotion. Moreover, the competitors may engage in *influence activities* of various sorts. They might take actions that are intended to make themselves look better (and their rivals worse) in the eyes of those who decide on the promotion. It may be unproductive if employees spend their time trying to generate truthful information that casts themselves in a good light. But worse than that, employees may suppress important information that reflects poorly on themselves or that reflects well on rivals, or they may try to misrepresent information to their own advantage. And worse still, they may try to ingratiate themselves personally to the decision-makers who control the promotion. Whenever compensation for or evaluation of one person is done by others, these sorts of influence activities may be present. But the tournament-like nature of promotion in a pyramid, where some must be left behind and where the reward is discrete, can greatly increase the level of influence activities.[6]

An interesting innovation that speaks to some of these concerns is the team-based "On The Move" approach to promotion utilized by Rohr Inc., an international aerospace supplier.[7] After an extended process of developing and "prequalifying" employees for promotions, which involves the HR department and the employee's team leader and manager, promotional candidates go before an interview committee that includes a representative of HR and three or four occupants of the job that the employee is seeking. Membership on the committee is for one quarter only and is staggered, ensuring that interviewing responsibilities are shared evenly among peers and that there is an experienced member on the committee. If the promotional candidate passes this peer interview, then he or she is placed into a qualified file to be considered for the next open position, which will be filled according to plant-wide seniority.

Notice that such a system has the potential to reduce some of the dysfunctional behaviors to which we referred above. Given how the interview committees are constructed, a person interested in being promoted to job X has an incentive to get along with everyone who is already in that job (or who might be in the job when their interview comes up), because any of the people currently in job X may end up being members of the peer interview committee. Of course, this should cut down on influence activities targeted toward a single individual. Peers are less likely to be bamboozled by attempts to make one's own record look good and are more likely to have access to any unflattering facts about the candidate than are third-party evaluators. Cooperation is enhanced insofar as the peer evaluations tend to value cooperative behavior. Furthermore, once the interview committee approves a candidate for promotion, we would expect its members to become committed to ensuring that the promotional candidate succeeds when and if she does garner the promotion; after all, they were responsible for certifying the person as worthy of promotion. By involving future co-workers in the process of selecting their peers, this also facilitates more cooperative relationships among people who otherwise might view their co-workers as competitors in future promotion contests, while also increasing the perceived fairness of the promotion process among all parties.

The system has some potential weaknesses, however. If the prequalifying screen is anything more than *pro forma*, self-serving influence activities will still go on, and other forms of influence directed at the prequalifiers will take place. (This may be mitigated if peers can perceive such activities and disapprove of them.) The seniority-list approach may also mean that the best available candidate won't get the job, at least for a while—a really talented individual far down in the queue may even be motivated to seek employment elsewhere. Thus, this system is probably best suited for filling foot-soldier or guardian-like positions, where the firm can be relatively happy with any qualified individual in the slot. Finally, one worries that unpopular but qualified candidates will fail to win peer approval—the system fits best in situations of high interdependency, in which cordial relations among co-workers are relatively more important, and in which "rocking the boat" is not a particularly valued activity.

Dealing with the Losers

Organizations that emphasize promotion as an incentive device and have a culture in which promotion confers status often face acute difficulties in dealing with the "losers," that is, employees who are passed over for a particular promotion. We put "losers" in quotes to emphasize that these people have not necessarily failed in any absolute sense; their failure is purely relative to those who were judged to be worthier of promotion. These may be very talented people who are excellent resources for the organization. Indeed, it may be sensible for the organization to retain an individual in a lower-level job at which he is superb, rather than promote him to a position in which (it seems) he might be less valuable. The trouble is that the individual involved may not see things this way. Relative failure is often perceived as failure, plain and simple, and those who fail to be promoted are often regarded as losers by themselves and by those who are not yet in the same boat. The workforce can become divided into those who still have the blessing of the organization and who continue to have rising prospects versus those who have lost the organization's blessing. The first group may shun those in the second, to avoid being seen with losers; the second group often comes to resent the first. Of course, those who have lost in a promotion contest often lose their commitment to the organization (something like gift–exchange in reverse): Their interests and attention go elsewhere and, sometimes passively and sometimes actively, they can undermine their bosses and resist their directions. The contributions that the "losers" could make may be lost to the organization, as their commitment and attention wane.[8]

At the same time, those who are passed over but remain with the organization represent a block to future aspirants. They hold positions that others below them could fill on the way to the top. People in fast-track positions who don't progress to the next level may have to be moved into a role that is less critical, not because they won't do a good job where they are (which, depending on their level of commitment and motivation, they might do), but because their position is needed as training ground for someone who still has possibilities for moving up.

Up or Out?

Some organizations deal with these problems quite severely, by adhering to an up-or-out system. Those that lose in a promotion contest give up not only their future opportunities but their current jobs as well. For example, in many large Japanese companies, retirement age has traditionally depended on rank. Those who don't attain higher rank must retire at an earlier age (although they often retire to some subsidiary or client firm of their original employer).

A system of up-or-out solves the problem of what to do with the losers, but it has at least four substantial drawbacks:

1. Those who are not promoted may be quite capable of making valuable contributions to the organization in their current position. Often they hold a great deal of firm-specific human capital, including effective col-

laborative relations with co-workers, which is wasted in an up-or-out system. For this reason, an increasing number of law firms and other professional organizations have created "permanent associate" slots that enable them to retain talented individuals who add value to the organization even if they are not suitable for partnership. Of course, to the extent that the promotion contest creates desirable incentive effects, one needs to be worried about diluting these by providing the fall-back option of attractive "consolation prizes" for losers in the tournament, especially where those consolation prizes become something of an entitlement.

2. Although firms with up-or-out systems will usually explain to new hires how their system works, it still can be very harsh to banish loyal employees who happen not to make the next grade. Especially when job opportunities are not abundant in the general labor market, this can pose a substantial hardship on the employee. (The departure of individuals who do not survive the up-or-out screen can also be disruptive and traumatic for those who make the cut, due to task and social interdependencies they have developed over time with colleagues who now must involuntarily depart.) For all these reasons, up-or-out is certainly not very conducive to a family- or clan-like culture.

3. By increasing the penalty for failure, the firm increases the level of influence activities that employees will engage in to avoid discharge, and it may decrease the level of cooperation that employees will give to fellow competitors.

4. When promotion decisions are made on the basis of "new needs" of the organization, those passed over may rightfully complain that an implicit contract they had with the organization has been violated. When they lose their jobs as well, the merit of this complaint is increased substantially. For instance, consider a law firm that lures a partner away from another firm to build a practice in Admiralty Law, bringing in some of that partner's junior associates as well as part of the deal. But suppose the partner in question departs or dies before the associates come up for partnership review, or suppose the firm decides that it was a strategic error to move into the admiralty area. If the associates involved excelled at doing what they were hired to do, is it fair to deny them a partnership because of events over which they had no control?

An alternative to up-or-out is a system in which people stay at a given level, always in competition for promotion to the next level. This will tend to ameliorate loss-of-commitment problems, but it won't solve them:

• Being passed over for promotion with no opportunity to make the grade (as in an up-or-out system) may be worse than being passed over but retaining later chances. However, the latter outcome can nonetheless be demotivating enough to be of concern to the organization.

- In this type of system, the employee who fails to make a particular promotion still represents a barrier for lower-level workers; if it literally is the case that no one is ever discharged, then vacancy chains (caused by someone's retirement or voluntary departure) are one-person wide at every level. That is, when one person is promoted, only that person's position must be filled, and then the slot of the person promoted into the second position, and so on. Given a pyramid shape to the organization, most opportunities for advancement will be caused only by someone's retirement; without overall growth in the workforce, this can result in a workforce whose average age increases rapidly. There is nothing inherently wrong with this, of course. However, if rewards are positively correlated with seniority or age—or if mastery of new knowledge and skills is important and tends to be greater among younger, more recently trained cohorts—then the "graying" of the workforce can put an organization at a competitive disadvantage.

- In some cases it is not realistic for someone who is passed over to have a fair chance at subsequent promotion. Especially when the chain of positions leads to the top of the organization, someone who falls off the fast track doesn't have enough time to make it to the top. (Recall the investment bank example mentioned earlier in this chapter.) Imagine having to choose a VP from between two candidates: One of them has failed in this promotion before and will (therefore) retire as a VP if promoted; the second candidate is much younger and could make it to the top if promoted now. Even if the first candidate were almost surely a bit better qualified for the job, the organization might (rationally!) favor the second person because she might someday be a candidate for a top position.[9] This will be understood by the first person, who therefore sees falling off the fast track as a huge impediment to future promotion, no matter what the organization says about second and third chances.

To deal with these problems, firms will sometimes provide a second track for those who, at some level, have fallen off the fast track. This second track may lead to higher-level staff positions, for example. Lateral movement of losers can be used in some cases to stave off boredom in a particular job. Especially at the higher reaches of management, those who "fail" may be given special troubleshooting assignments or assignments at headquarters that emphasize their acquired wisdom but that remove them from the actual levers of power; they become advisors to the boss, as a consolation for failing to become the boss. Depending on the organizational culture, these maneuvers can be somewhat successful. But in any organization in which promotion provides powerful incentives through the acquisition of status, power, compensation, and so on, dealing with those who lose in promotion contests is usually a serious problem.

Demographics

The demographic composition of the workforce, both in terms of age profile and ethnic, racial, and gender composition, can exacerbate promotion-based problems.

Owing to changes in the growth rates of the firm (or unrealistically rosy predictions of growth that led to hiring binges), the firm can acquire a bulge of employees of roughly comparable age at a particular level. These bulges increase competition at the level of the bulge and block those at lower levels. Changes in retirement age laws have had the effect of stretching out careers, thus blocking promotion ladders. Either willingly, or to comply with social, political, and legal pressures, firms have set out to diversify the racial, ethnic, and gender composition of their ranks, which has put a strain on promotion ladders and procedures.

Career Concerns

Firms with strong ILMs and cultures that emphasize advancement must be concerned that employees will seek to structure their careers with a view toward advancement to the top, perhaps to a fault. The willingness to accept a particular position may come to depend not on the inherent interest the position holds or the amount that can be accomplished for the firm in the position, but instead on the perceived value of the position in building a career. Moves that are thought to lead to dead ends will be resisted, whether they are lateral moves, moves to staff positions, or moves to positions that have not in the past been stepping-stones to advancement.

This can be particularly troublesome for a firm that—because of changes in strategy, say—wishes to restructure the route to the top. For example, in a firm in which marketing has been paramount and the path to the top has been largely via positions in domestic marketing, changes in the competitive environment may make international marketing or production more important. Those being groomed for the top may therefore be given assignments in these previous "backwaters," assignments they will resist and try hard to get out of. A few years ago, Chrysler Corporation announced the promotion of James Holden, a career sales and marketing executive at Chrysler (and, previously, at Ford) to vice president of Corporate Personnel, hardly a job that has traditionally been a stepping-stone to the top of the Big Three. If Chrysler really believes that HRM is of great strategic importance (and therefore that understanding HRM is a prerequisite for making it into very senior management positions), they will want to work hard to ensure that Mr. Holden is a big hit: Presumably every up-and-coming auto industry manager who is asked to broaden himself or herself by considering a rotation through an HR assignment will be watching Mr. Holden's career with keen interest.[10]

Individuals who are concerned largely with career advancement may also take actions that will reflect well on themselves in the short-run. Those who are stalled may seek outside offers, either with serious intent or simply to put pressure on the current boss. Where the labor market permits, employees who are impatient to advance may seek advancement by jumping from one firm to the next. Where the organization provides a fast track, most ambitious employees will want to be on it; the organization must either deny it to some of its employees, which can be demotivating, or provide it to all, which can be enormously inefficient with respect to job assignments. (Indeed, if being on the "fast track" is purely relative, then if everyone is fast-tracked, no one is.)

Promotion Purely for the Sake of Promotion

A final adverse effect of promotion is that in some settings, it becomes an end in itself. Employees strive not to reach some absolute level, but to keep moving upward, always looking toward the next hurdle.[11] When advancement in and of itself becomes an ingrained value, those who fail to advance are particularly demotivated. And even those who advance may at some point find themselves stalled for a period of time. This is especially true as higher and higher ranks are attained, because: (a) there are fewer and fewer positions left within the organization to aspire to; (b) the amount of knowledge and experience required before one is ready to advance often increases the higher up the ladder you go, implying increasing waiting times between promotions; and (c) the luck of the draw may be such that none of the incumbents vacates those positions for a while. This can lead to an inefficiently large incidence of jumps from one firm to another or to workplace politics (for instance, undertaking influence activities with one's boss's boss, in order to accelerate one's own promotion). And it can lead to employees who suddenly find themselves without a hurdle to surmount, which can be demotivating at least and perhaps even disorienting to someone whose motivation in the past has always been to jump the next hurdle.

Promotion as an end in itself, and the expectations this can engender in employees, can have particularly disastrous consequences in organizations that find they must make changes in rates of promotion, because of, say, demographic pressures, organizational decline, or a shift in strategy or technology (e.g., to a TQM system with a greater reliance on lateral movement and cross-training). Recall that we cited some research evidence in Chapter 5 to suggest that those U.S. and Japanese firms that have the strongest ILMs exhibit the most job dissatisfaction by employees, although workers in these firms still report relatively high levels of commitment to the organization. One explanation for this stems from the notion that, in these organizations, mobility prospects for employees are clearest and most salient. Employees will be aware of the *possibilities* that are open to them, and most employees, when they measure their progress against the fastest of the fast tracks, will find themselves failing to measure up. This can lead to personal dissatisfaction with one's own position, without necessarily translating into a lack of commitment to the organization.

WHY IS RANK TIED TO COMPENSATION, STATUS, AND OTHER REWARDS?

Many of the problems associated with promotion arise because workers strongly desire to be promoted. Of course, insofar as promotion is being used as an incentive device, it's crucial that promotion be something that employees value. But many of the reasons for using promotion as an incentive device—particularly, the long-term evaluation inherent in the system—could be achieved through other incentive devices, such as increased salary or bonuses decoupled from rank but determined only after long-term evaluation. And many of the conflicts among the different roles promotion may play would be defused if promotion were not so strongly desired by employees.

The desirability of promotion may arise simply because of a general desire to "advance," or because higher rank typically brings with it increased status, power, and autonomy. But promotion is especially desirable when rank is positively associated with compensation and other tangible perks and rewards. Indeed, the status given to high rank may be due in part to the fact that high rank generally carries with it high material rewards. Many of the problems associated with promotion could be mitigated if this link could be broken, so it is clearly germane to ask why this positive association exists. Here are a few answers:

- One reason for this link is, of course, the existence of strong social norms that a hierarchical superior ought to be paid more than (or no less than) a subordinate, either to maintain his or her superior status or because those higher in the organization naturally contribute more to its well-being.

- A more economic explanation for the tie is a simple market-based story: As one goes up in the hierarchy, there are fewer positions of this sort available (less demand), but the supply of qualified individuals is smaller still.

- A different economic explanation is predicated on the notion that the cost to the organization of a sudden and unplanned vacancy is greater the higher up a job is within the hierarchy. This could be because those higher up make more critical decisions, because they coordinate across more functions, or because filling these positions either from inside or outside is more disruptive to the organization. As long as this is so, when the firm has a good employee sitting in a higher-level position, the firm will want to take steps to decrease the likelihood of turnover. One way to do this is to pay more for higher positions; for an employee weighing other prospective offers of employment or facing personal reasons to move, the greater the pay, all else being equal, the lower the likelihood that she will move.[12]

- We're fairly sure it won't surprise you to learn that compensation is generally positively associated with rank. But what may surprise you is that the effect gets much stronger at higher ranks. Empirical work has demonstrated that average percentage pay increases for moves between higher ranks are greater than the average pay increases for moves at lower ranks.[13] That is, a promotion from plant manager to group VP might bring a 20% increase in salary and benefits, the promotion to senior VP would bring a larger percentage increase, and the (final) promotion to CEO might bring a salary and benefits increase on the order of 100%.

    Why is this? One hypothesis is that this is required to provide continued incentives for advancement. A promotion at a lower level carries with it the immediate raise in compensation and status *and the chance for further raises*. The final promotion is just that, the final promotion, so the full burden of incentives must be carried by the value of this promotion.[14] Another hypothesis is that financial controls on salary and benefits for top management are not very strong, because these salaries and benefits are set by compensation committees of Boards of Directors. The individuals who sit on these committees are often quite close socially to the firm's top managers and possibly use their own high pay as a benchmark in setting pay for high-level executives in the companies on whose boards they serve, thereby leading to a self-perpetuating system.[15]

IS THERE A SOLUTION?

The main point of this chapter is, roughly, that although promotion as a motivation device has its virtues, it is often a rather clumsy way to provide motivation and incentives to employees. Using promotion as a motivational device clashes with its roles in job placement and on-the-job training, and it can have dysfunctional effects both on the participants in the race for advancement and on those who are passed by. It might seem, then, that the solution is to create a culture in which promotion is not so important to the individual employee, by decoupling compensation from it, by giving greater status to those lower in the organization (or, at least, by deemphasizing status distinctions), by promoting greater autonomy at lower ranks, and so on. These are all very fine ideas, and many organizations have been moving in this direction. But before these approaches are adopted, one must consider to what extent they are consistent with the external environment, with the sorts of employees whom the firm seeks to attract and retain, and with the firm's strategy and its technology.

It is often impossible to decouple rank from power or autonomy in the organization (although the coupling is less of a problem in organizations that operate in a bottom-up manner), and, as we have noted, there are good economic and social reasons why status and compensation are generally tied to rank. But, in *some* cases at least, the ties can be broken or weakened. Often the key to doing this is some sort of objective or semi-objective external measure of performance or status. This can work especially well with employees who come from a profession in which the external market can establish the worth of individuals.

In universities, for example, star researchers and teachers rarely covet administrative positions, yet they retain high status and their compensation is typically greater than for those higher up in the (administrative) hierarchy. In technical organizations, such as R&D labs, design centers, or engineering firms, status and pay are often awarded to those employees who are most masterful at the technical skills required by the job. In traditional Japanese firms, age confers a good measure of formal status, and informal status often accrues along meritocratic lines. Firms that use bonus systems, especially those based on an objective formula, frequently compensate the very successful stars (e.g., salespeople) more highly than their titular bosses.

In other cases, the link between rank and rewards such as status, compensation, and autonomy can be deemphasized, if not entirely broken. This is especially true in firms that resemble clans or that are driven by some external, superordinate goal, because these sorts of organizations, as we have seen, often have relatively low pay dispersion and low levels of status distinction to begin with.

Finally, seniority can be used in some instances to decouple compensation from rank in the organization (as long as rank is not seniority-based). In Japanese manufacturing firms, it is common for older blue-collar workers to earn considerably more than younger white-collar workers, even though the latter are the nominal supervisors of the former. Adopting a system of future compensation for current contributions (or, equivalently, current compensation for past contributions), *when it can be understood and accepted by the workforce,* will often work.

WHAT NEXT?

In the past three chapters, we have discussed successive stages in the career "life cycle" of an employee: recruitment and selection, training, and promotion. In tranquil times, retirement and a gold watch frequently came next. But the story sometimes ends another way, with termination. This is particularly germane of late, when firms are exhorted by the business press and capital markets to become "lean and mean" in response to turbulent and intensely competitive business conditions, by downsizing the workforce and outsourcing part of the work to be done. So we turn next to these two related sets of practices.

IN REVIEW

⇒ Promotion serves a number of different purposes: It provides incentives; can send signals to third parties; gives the organization the ability to provide on-the-job training and then assign individuals to positions of increased responsibility as they become prepared; places individuals in positions appropriate to their talents and skills; and allows the firm to screen for desirable characteristics.

- As an incentive device, promotion has the advantage of often being based on (relatively) long-term performance.

⇒ These different purposes often conflict with one another, however, and the promotion pyramid can have some unhappy consequences:

- As an incentive device, it is discrete, and so suffers the usual problems of discrete incentive schemes.
- Because it is usually a tournament scheme, it can undercut cooperation and encourage wasteful influence activities.
- "Losers" pose many problems: They can become demotivated and they can stand in the way of those employees who are still rising through the organization.
  - Some organizations deal harshly with the losers, with an up-or-out system. But this can waste valuable human capital (especially of

the firm-specific variety), be viewed as unjust, be organizationally wrenching, and exacerbate behavior such as influence activities by raising the stakes involved in the promotion decision.

- Strict reliance on promotion from within can wreak havoc with organizational demographics, which in turn can exacerbate the aforementioned problems.
- Excessive emphasis on promotion can foster behavior that is driven more by career concerns than by helping the organization.
- Individuals may become solely motivated by the desire to continue jumping promotion hurdles, which can lead in turn to low job satisfaction or worse, especially when all the hurdles have been jumped.

⇒ Rank is tied to compensation because:
- It reinforces social status distinctions.
- It is economically driven (in the "thin" labor markets toward the top of organizations, there is small demand but even smaller supply of suitable individuals).
- It protects against the loss of key personnel.

⇒ Given the numerous difficulties associated with strict promotion-from-within systems, there are good reasons for organizations to consider deemphasizing the value associated with attaining higher rank.
- It may pay to decouple tangible rewards (including autonomy) from hierarchical position.
  - This may be more feasible in professional labor markets, where external standing can provide an alternative basis for status, and when other extrinsic or intrinsic rewards can substitute for promotion in encouraging the long-term behaviors sought by the organization.
- Where it is not possible to decouple compensation from rank, it may still be possible to decouple status from hierarchical position, using age, seniority, skill, or knowledge as the basis for status.

ENDNOTES

1. Presentation to Human Resource Management core course, Stanford Business School, April 9, 1996.
2. We assume that the long-term incentives provided by promotion were aligned with the short-term incentives provided by these bonuses. Note that even if this is so, so that the bonus program was "unnecessary," it may still have had some symbolic value. This was a period during which Citibank was restructuring and reviving itself, and the shorter-term incentives, even if unnecessary for motivating the 100 or so "high-leverage" individuals for whom they were intended, may have signaled both to these hundred and to others that this was an extraordinary period at Citibank, not a period of business as usual.

3. However, as we will see below, sometimes the signals can be *too* strong, so that employees will try to avoid positions that don't conform to their notion of the right trajectory to the top.

4. See Bruce G. Posner, "Compensation: May the Force Be with You," *Inc.* 9 (July 1987): 70–5; and W. Earl Sasser and Lucy N. Lytle, *Au Bon Pain: The French Bakery Cafe— The Partner Manager Program*, Harvard Business School case 9–687–063.

5. And, anticipating this, the firm is probably more inclined to hire younger rather than older MBAs.

6. Moreover, as the value of the "prize" available (e.g., through a bonus plan or promotion scheme) increases, employees may become motivated to take actions that are so risky as to be potentially harmful to themselves or to others. A colorful example of this type of effect is provided by recent empirical research on professional automobile racing. Specifically, researchers found that an increase in the spread of prize money at NASCAR races (i.e., a bigger gap between the purse for first place and second place, between second and third place, etc.) produced more unsafe driving and a greater number of accidents. See Brian Becker and Mark Huselid, "The Incentive Effects of Tournament Compensation Schemes," *Administrative Science Quarterly* 37 (June 1992): 336–50.

7. See Frank Rodgers, "A Team Approach to Promotions at Rohr Inc.," *Personnel Journal* 71 (April 1992): 44, 47.

8. For a very good description of these processes, see Rosabeth Moss Kanter, *Men and Women of the Corporation* (New York: Basic Books, 1977), Chapter 6.

9. Consistent with this argument, empirical research has tended to confirm strong "halo" effects in career outcomes, whereby success or failure in promotion contests early in the career is decisive for the person's subsequent career accomplishments. Of course, different explanations for this effect include the presence of an unobserved characteristic that is important to promotion, or a desire by the managers who promoted a particular individual to justify that earlier decision with further promotions (i.e., promotion as a self-fulfilling prophecy).

10. As of this writing Mr. Holden's career at Chrysler seems to be flourishing. After his posting in Personnel, he was assigned as Vice President, Quality, Capacity and Process Management; then promoted in 1996 to Executive Vice President—Sales and Marketing; and then in 1998 his duties and titles were expanded to Executive Vice President—Sales and Marketing and General Manager—Minivan Operations. He is now (1998) one of the top executive officers in the company, responsible for directing all the activities of Chrysler Corporation's U.S., Mexico, and Canadian sales, fleet, and marketing organizations; the Mopar parts operations; communications; Chrysler de Mexico; and minivan platform operations.

11. Some recent psychological work suggests that in many instances, an individual's level of satisfaction is determined not simply by the absolute level of the individual's accomplishments, or by the fact that the individual is progressing, but by the *rate* at which the individual is progressing. (See Christopher K. Hsee, Peter Salovey, and Robert P. Abelson, "The Quasi-acceleration Relation: Satisfaction as a Function of the Change in Velocity of Outcome Over Time," *Journal of Experimental Social Psychology* 30 [January 1994]: 96–111.) So, for instance, an investor's satisfaction depends not only on the amount of wealth she has accumulated, or on the fact that she is accumulating more, but on whether the rate of accumulation is being maintained or increased. In the context of promotion, this suggests that people who are moving up the organizational hierarchy will be sensitive to whether they are being promoted as

rapidly as previously. Because in most organizations (with a pyramidal structure), the rate of advancement is likely to slow down over time, this psychological work suggests that dissatisfaction is likely to result.

12. To flesh this story out, we imagine that all employees have firm-specific human capital, which means that their value to the firm is on average higher than their next-best-alternative value, but that there is some chance that they will have very high value to someone else, who is willing to share that surplus with them. The firm then considers how much of the rents from this firm-specific human capital to share with the employee, giving up relatively more when it would be more costly to lose the employee in question.

13. Richard A. Lambert, David F. Larker, and Keith Weigelt, "The Structure of Organizational Incentives," *Administrative Science Quarterly* 38 (September 1993): 438–61.

14. If you like this so-called "tournament" hypothesis, consider some further empirical implications. When intermediate promotions occur at a younger age, the rise in compensation shouldn't have to be so large, because the person still has more time to compete for the ultimate "prize" as well as more years of employment ahead to enjoy that increment in base compensation. This hypothesis also implies that percentage increases in compensation associated with promotions should be higher, all else being equal, in organizations that bring some personnel in from the outside than in organizations that rely strictly on ILMs. This is because the existence of more potential competitors for a promotion (i.e., outsiders) necessitates a larger "prize" to induce participation in the tournament.

15. For some suggestive evidence, see Charles A. O'Reilly III, Brian G. Main, and Graef S. Crystal, "CEO Compensation as Tournament and Social Comparison: A Tale of Two Theories," *Administrative Science Quarterly* 33 (June 1988): 257–74.

17

DOWNSIZING

As we began drafting this chapter,[1] the following stories were making business headlines:

- Kimberly-Clark Corporation, manufacturer of personal care products, announced a layoff of 5,000 employees or 7% of its workforce, as part of a sweeping corporate restructuring program aimed at eliminating high-cost excess production capacity.

- Eastman Kodak announced it was cutting 10,000 jobs, roughly 11% of its workforce, as part of a $1 billion restructuring program to be implemented over two years. Only two months earlier, Kodak had eliminated some 200 of its top 1,000 management positions and announced it would eliminate 10% of its sales and administrative staff. This latest round of job cuts, the largest by any American company in 1997, came on top of 40,000 jobs that Kodak had already cut since 1983.

- In the same week as the Kodak announcement, four other publicly traded U.S. companies announced significant layoffs. Waste Management, Inc., the world's leading provider of waste management and disposal services, responded to pressure from dissident shareholders by announcing a sweeping reorganization that trimmed 20% of corporate and support staff (roughly 1,200 jobs) to save $100 million annually.[2] Kemet Corporation, an electric components manufacturer, cut 1,000 jobs in North and South Carolina by transferring capacitor production to a plant in Mexico. Fashion designer Donna Karan International announced layoffs of 285 employees, about 15% of its workforce. Underwear manufacturer Fruit of the Loom trimmed 2,900 jobs in Louisiana and Kentucky as part of an effort to control costs and inventories, after having cut 4,800 jobs less than three months earlier.

- That same week, General Motors announced it would take a charge of as much as $3 billion in the fourth quarter of 1997 for plant closings and "asset impairments." Although no specific plant closings or layoffs were announced, some reports predicted layoffs of 42,000 jobs.

- Also during that week, the *Wall Street Journal* reported that IBM began sending layoff notices to hundreds of its North American employees, as part of a restructuring of its sales and distribution division aimed at making it able to respond more quickly and effectively to customers. The layoffs came only weeks after IBM had begun offering voluntary job buyouts in an effort to cut costs.

- Apparel manufacturer Levi Strauss announced layoffs for 6,395 U.S. workers. Shortly after this announcement, the *San Francisco Chronicle* reported with much fanfare that Tom Tusher, who had retired the previous year as president and chief operating officer of the company, had received $105.8 million from cashing out accumulated stock options he received when the company took itself private in 1985.

- The global financial services giant Citicorp (now part of Citigroup) announced it would eliminate 9,000 jobs worldwide over the next 12 to 18 months, though 1,500 new positions would be added, for a net reduction of 7,500 positions. Citicorp indicated that the layoffs were intended to help in standardizing and consolidating its operations and technology worldwide.

Several things are particularly noteworthy about these announcements. First, this spate of large-scale layoffs flies in the face of claims by many observers that the wave of downsizings, which commenced in the 1980s and persisted through the early 1990s, has abated. Indeed, the above-listed job cuts were announced in the midst of an extraordinarily buoyant labor market: The 4.7% unemployment rate announced for October 1997 represented a twenty-four-year low. In an article announcing these layoffs, the *Washington Post* wrote: "American workers, noting the record profits that companies have been posting the past few years and, until recently, the ever-upward rise in their stock prices, might wonder why downsizing is back in the headlines after an apparent hiatus."[3]

Equally noteworthy are the names of some of the companies announcing these layoffs. Eastman Kodak was one of the companies that first experimented in the early 1900s with innovative employee welfare practices, including employment security, which provided the model of high-commitment HR later emulated by many blue-chip U.S. companies, as well as by first-tier Japanese companies following World War II. As the *New York Times* reported, "Kodak . . . was once known as the 'Great Yellow Father' in its hometown of Rochester, New York, because of its paternalistic employment practices."[4] Levi Strauss is another company that has frequently been honored and emulated for its benevolent treatment of employees. In years gone by, General Motors and Citicorp in many ways exemplified the model of stable corporate hierarchies, depicted in William Whyte's 1950s classic *The Organization Man,*[5] in which employees could expect to build lifelong careers. And we have already discussed IBM's long-standing tradition through the late 1980s of employment security (see Chapters 2 and 8).

WHY DO FIRMS DOWNSIZE?

Why do firms downsize? What are the objectives? Some of the downsizing craze may be pure herd behavior; if everyone else seems to be doing it, you should also. Some of this herd behavior may be induced by the financial markets (see below). In other (and, we hope, fairly rare) cases, downsizing is a managerial response to inane incentives—for example, a division chief is told that her performance will be assessed based on *per capita* sales or earnings, where the denominator in the *per capita* calculation is full-time equivalent regular employees. Thus, the manager is given an incentive to cut regular employees and replace them with outsourced labor, even if the outsourced labor is (not too much) more expensive.

But in many cases some serious and substantial reasons are given. The layoff announcements given above illustrate a number of the chief objectives that companies cite:

- Cut costs, especially overhead.
- Increase adaptability: Speed up decision-making, foster entrepreneurship, ease adaptation to the business cycle, and so on. Efforts to trim management layers are often particularly focused on this goal.
- Enhance a focus on the company's core competence by eliminating peripheral and superfluous positions and activities.
- Increase productivity.
- Shift some or all of an activity previously done in-house to external parties (that is, by *outsourcing*), to neutralize "political" behavior by an entrenched subunit, spread risk on high-risk projects, and help get knowledge and skills from the outside transferred inside the organization.
- By doing some or all of these things, improve shareholder equity, under the assumption that the market responds positively to initiatives undertaken by firms to get lean, mean, and focused.

Presumably companies have always wanted to achieve these objectives, so what is driving them to do so more ferociously now? Among the more common rationales given are:

- Competition has intensified and is now on a global scale.
- Product life cycles have decreased, putting a premium on faster response and shorter cycle times.
- Increasingly diverse customer needs mandate more agile organizational response.
- Escalating benefits costs (particularly for health care) and legal liabilities have made labor more expensive, favoring a less labor-intensive, more capital-intensive strategy.
- Innovations, improvements, and cost reductions in information technology have led firms to automate tasks previously done by administrative functionaries and generally reduce the need for human labor.
- Increased capital market discipline through hostile takeovers and other means has focused top management on short-run, bottom-line performance, which often can be improved more easily by cutting costs, particularly labor costs, than through other means.

- Managers are responding to a new and not necessarily rational belief on the part of both private and institutional investors that downsizing is a palliative for companies whose performance is sluggish or worse. Insofar as this explanation applies and the belief is the product of market psychology rather than rational analysis, we have herd behavior at one remove, where the herd is the investing public, believing based on fairly limited evidence (see below) that downsizing is in fact a profit- or profitability-enhancing strategy.

- In the case of downsizing that is tied to outsourcing, the growth of contracting services and various labor market intermediaries—temporary agencies, leasing firms, and the like—has made it easier for firms to meet their labor needs by relying on third-party providers. Moreover, the rampant competition among such providers enables firms purchasing their services to impose stringent quality standards. Many labor supply firms will provide "guarantees" that anyone they place will be acceptable to the client firm, whereas such guarantees are neither easy nor inexpensive to obtain if the client firm hires a regular employee for the same activity.

- Finally, some commentators argue that outsourcing has become cheaper and thus more attractive because a larger segment of the labor force desires more flexibility and variety in their lives than the traditional long-term attachment of an individual to an employer affords.

THE EFFECTS OF DOWNSIZING

The objectives listed above are all quite reasonable, and the rationales for why downsizing might recently have acquired greater appeal seem plausible. But what effects do downsizing programs actually have?

Effects on the Firm's Bottom Line

Because downsizing has been both prevalent and controversial, a fair bit of empirical research has been conducted trying to find its effects on firms' bottom lines, both in terms of operating profits and financial market performance. The research evidence to date is mixed, to say the least. A recent survey of over 1,000 companies by Watson Wyatt, a consulting firm, found that only one-third of companies that had downsized saw profits increase after the layoff as much as expected; fewer than half reported that the cuts reduced expenses as much as expected; and only a small minority reported a satisfactory increase in shareholder return on investment as a result of the layoff.[6] Similarly, a 1997 survey of HR managers in large U.S. companies by the American Management Association (AMA) found that companies that had eliminated jobs in the 1990s were slightly more likely than other firms to report short-term profit increases, but they were also somewhat more likely to report profit *declines* afterward.[7] The AMA report also found no relationship between the short-run reductions in operating expenses attained through downsizing and longer-run profitability. Nor have efforts to identify the impact of corporate layoff announcements on accounting numbers or stock market returns produced consistent or overwhelming findings. Although some econometric studies have uncovered modest positive effects of white-collar downsizing on financial performance, in general the studies suggest the financial effects of downsizing in the short- and longer-term are negative.[8]

One reason why researchers may have found little demonstrable effect of downsizing *per se* on long-term financial performance is that the layoffs themselves, as well as the cost savings they produce, are often transient. In an article decrying the "binge and purge" staffing practices of large U.S. corporations, *Mother Jones* magazine cites several studies documenting that headcount reductions achieved through downsizing tend to be fleeting: "The Wyatt study discovered that the majority of managers refill some positions within two years. The AMA study showed that of 1,003 companies, the average workforce at the 501 companies that downsized in 1994–95 shrank by a meager 1.1 percent, even though these companies laid off nearly 7.7 percent of their employees."[9] Hence, without being accompanied by significant *permanent* changes, layoffs may simply produce short-lived cost reductions.

Other recent studies suggest similarly that it is not employment cuts *per se,* but how they are implemented that may determine the long-term effect on financial performance. Examining changes in employment levels among companies listed in the *Standard & Poor's (S&P) 500* between 1981 and 1992, Wayne Cascio and his colleagues recently reported that firms that engaged in pure employment downsizing did not show significantly higher returns than the average companies in their respective industries.[10] In fact, their overall returns were worse than companies with stable employment, but this was due to industry differences.[11] However, those firms that combined job cuts with asset restructuring (divestitures, plant closures, etc.) displayed higher returns on assets and higher stock market returns over the subsequent two years than typical firms in the same industries.[12] In the same vein, other studies have reported that downsizing companies experience superior performance (reflected in operating performance and excess stock market returns, both in the short-run and over periods as long as several years after the layoff) only when the job cuts are combined with significant restructuring, strategic changes, or changes in organizational structure. This effect is especially pronounced among firms that were experiencing deteriorating performance relative to their industry prior to implementing the layoffs.[13] In other words, downsizing seems to have the potential to enhance long-run performance only when it is part of a more fundamental change in an organization's strategy, structure, culture, and/or work arrangements.

Nor is it clear that downsizing boosts productivity. A study by the National Bureau of Economic Research on productivity growth during the 1980s, when downsizings were commonplace, found that plants that increased employment as well as productivity contributed almost as much to overall productivity growth in the 1980s as the plants that increased productivity *at the expense of employment*.[14] Productivity trends were found to be attributable to differences between companies, not to changes in the staffing practices of individual companies observed over time. Furthermore, the American Management Association study found that achieving quality and productivity improvements in conjunction with downsizing depended significantly on the amount of training activity in which firms engaged following the job elimination (see below).

Employee Morale and Attitudes

The evidence concerning the effects of downsizing is clearest and most consistent regarding employee morale and attitudes. Not surprisingly, the effects here are largely negative, manifested in distrust, demotivation, loss of valued employees, stress, and overwork by the stayers. For instance, the American Management Association study reported that among firms implementing job cuts in the 1990s, HR managers reported these immediate and longer-term effects:[15]

- 69% reported a decline in employee morale within the first year, with 28% reporting diminished morale persisting even longer.
- 42% reported increased resignations and voluntary departures within the first year, with 27% reporting an increase lasting beyond one year.
- 36% reported increased employee turnover within the first year, with 23% reporting a continued increase in turnover beyond one year.
- 13% reported increased disability claims within the year following the layoff, with 8% reporting a persistent increase in disability claims beyond the first year after the layoffs.

This last finding has been corroborated by other studies. A newsletter on employee benefits explains the relationship this way:

Typically, fewer workers means more work for the survivors of downsizing. The remaining workers face larger workloads and longer hours. Often, they're not trained to perform these new tasks and many feel overwhelmed by the new situation. Also, the remaining workers often feel demoralized and stressed out. The so-called lucky employees who didn't lose their jobs are forever looking over their shoulders, fearing they're going to be next to get the ax. This anxiety may translate into disability claims for illnesses which are difficult to diagnose and treat such as chronic fatigue syndrome, fibromyalgia and stress. . . . [From] audits of organizations across Canada, Watson Wyatt has concluded that recently downsized organizations may have a significant increase in disability claims, particularly the difficult to diagnose and treat claims.[16]

Downsizing in Work Environments that Emphasize Creativity

Downsizing appears to be particularly disruptive in work environments that thrive on creativity. Recent research looking at employees before, during, and after a layoff suggests that the job insecurity wrought by downsizing is detrimental to the creative process and to risk taking. Moreover, downsizing diminishes the stability of workgroups and their speed and effectiveness in communicating, which are important for the success of creative work.[17] The evidence suggests that these adverse effects do abate somewhat over time, but that there are nonetheless enduring negative effects after the layoffs have been completed. The disruptive effects of layoffs on creative teams highlight the important point that in interdependent work settings, layoffs result not only in the loss of specific employees, but also the loss of another valuable asset: the working relations built up between each of those employees and the co-workers and external constituents with whom they interacted.

Who Leaves: Downsizing and Workforce Quality

Although we know of no comprehensive and careful empirical evidence that speaks directly to the issue, theory, anecdotes, and casual empirical evidence suggest that firms that downsize do not always shed their least able employees, or even a representative sample of employees. Instead, sometimes some of the most able employees go.

The reason this happens is linked to the process of downsizing. Many firms, when implementing a downsizing program, attempt to reduce the size of their workforce first through voluntary attrition. To motivate employees to leave voluntarily, severance pay is offered and outplacement services are provided. Of course, not all employers are so generous when they downsize, but firms that have maintained a familial culture are especially likely to try to rely on voluntary quits and to offer generous terms for the leavers. The problem is that those who choose to leave are more likely to be those who believe they can get a good job elsewhere, which will tend to be the better employees.

You might think that to control this phenomenon, it is sufficient that the firm retreat from voluntary quits, instead selecting those workers who will get the proverbial pink slip. To some extent, this does control the problem. But it isn't a perfect control. For one thing, downsizing programs have an unhappy tendency to be repetitive: The firm sheds some workers today, claiming that this is it; but a year or so later, the firm is undergoing yet another wave of downsizing. (A survey of nearly 1,200 companies in June 1997 by the American Management Association revealed that 40% had cut jobs in *three or more* calendar years since 1990.[18]) If employees anticipate this, even those who aren't told to leave may wish to get out while the getting is good. The stayers will be polishing their resumes and quietly putting out feelers on the job market. Of course, the better the employee, the more likely that those quiet efforts will bear fruit in the form of an outside job offer, and hence the nonvolunteer downsizing program may result in some voluntary quits, which will tend to be concentrated among the more able.

And, at the same time, those who are told to leave may have unwittingly influenced their own termination decision. We can explain this with an anecdote. Our Silicon Valley neighbor, Apple Computer, has been going through wave after wave of downsizings. The severance terms for those who are let go have been quite generous. But as Apple's performance continued to sink, employees became increasingly concerned that the good terms on offer would, in later downsizings, be changed, and not to the advantage of those let go. At the same time, job opportunities in the Silicon Valley have been excellent for good people; Apple's woes had not generally been shared by the computer industry. Thus, one would find employees of Apple who *wanted* to be terminated sooner rather than later, while both the severance benefits and the local job market were good. (This is not just a reflection of something distinctive about Apple. We have heard similar confessions from employees at other high-tech companies that have recently been implementing layoffs, such as Silicon Graphics.) And these employees have some ability to influence their own termination decision; we know of at least one individual who refused a restructuring reassignment that would have protected him against termination, in the (fulfilled) hope that this would lead to his termination. Because the more able workers are more likely to be willing to try their luck on the job market, such processes will lead to the same adverse selection processes that arise with voluntary quits.

Downsizing and Society

Critics of downsizing (and the outsourcing trend that fuels some layoffs) argue that not only are the effects on the bottom line seldom as rosy as management expects, but that job loss has profound negative consequences for the displaced employees and their families, consequences that add to the social costs of downsizing. They cite research showing that unemployment and job loss are related empirically not only to long-term wage loss and employment insecurity,[19] but also to a wide range of other outcomes, including criminality, drug and alcohol abuse, domestic violence (of spouses and children), separation and divorce, declines in objective and subjective health, depression, suicide, and children's well-being (e.g., self-esteem, mental health, and school performance).[20] There obviously are also quite massive potential economic effects on communities and the public at large.

Those who defend downsizing argue that the social impacts are primarily *positive,* at least in the long run. For instance, layoffs promote superior matching of workers to jobs and increased dynamism and risk taking in the economy, thereby fueling economic growth.[21] Moreover, defenders of downsizing argue that new job creation has more than compensated for the jobs lost through layoffs and outsourcing. And they argue that in the competitive global environment, if domestic firms (be they in the United States, Western Europe, Southeast Asia or wherever) don't "wake up and smell the coffee," those firms will not remain competitive. The government will then have to choose between protection—an economic and social disaster in the long run—or letting the firms sink, causing even more massive layoffs and dislocations.

THE MORAL FROM THE DATA

We certainly aren't able to settle the question, How costly (if at all) to society is downsizing? But even given the problems inherent in empirical research on this question (see endnote 11), the data given earlier about bottom-line impacts of downsizing ought to give you pause if you are considering such a program for your enterprise. Though the data do not speak with one voice, they indicate that downsizing is likely to work better when it is part of a well conceived general strategy of restructuring the firm and its workforce. This can include spinning off pieces of the organization that have diverted managerial attention from core competencies, or a well-constructed program of outsourcing non-core tasks (see Chapter 18). Or it could consist of efforts to reengineer the firm or change its culture, such as redefining jobs and work processes, redefining measurement and reward processes, employing techniques of high-commitment HRM, and emphasizing new strategic priorities—such as quality or customer focus—to energize employees and to provide an overarching goal.

Why does downsizing tend to work better when it is part of a broader initiative? There are two linked explanations that can be offered for this. The first and more straightforward explanation is that while firms may become bloated in terms of their workforce, the bloat is unlikely to be evenly distributed. Downsizing programs that go beyond layoffs and pursue underlying organizational problems or try to exploit real opportunities are more likely to address the *real* problems or successfully exploit the *real* opportunities. And the improvements thereby obtained are likely to be longer-lived than are those resulting merely from reducing headcount. When management thinks it has some idea of what it *should* be doing besides simply firing folks, it is more likely to know what it *is* doing.

The second, related explanation concerns the reaction of the survivors to the downsizing campaign. In general, downsizing can and often does have a devastating effect on relations between survivors and the firm. A constant theme in this book has been that consistent HR practices, acting through the firm's reputation, help promote efficient and effective labor exchanges. Another theme has been how "generosity"—especially generosity that is unstinting when times are tough—can pay for itself through the psychological process of gift-exchange. And especially in the context of ILMs and high-commitment HRM, we have seen how employment security in particular plays an important role in getting the best out of employees.

If employment continuity has served firms well in all these respects, it follows that layoffs and downsizing that unravel implicit contracts and otherwise sour the atmosphere have the potential to serve some firms poorly. When downsizing serves a purpose—when there is a rationale for it that can be offered to and accepted by employees—then it stands a much better chance of not being disruptive or, at least, of being less disruptive and poisoning. For instance, if downsizing comes largely from the elimination of layers of middle managers as part of converting to a high-commitment HR system, with ample assistance provided to the displaced middle managers, or if it is part of a program of enhancing the firm's focus on its core competencies, then the effort is more likely to make more sense to employees. And it is thus more likely to make economic sense by virtue of the fact that employees will accept it and adjust.

Employees aren't dumb. If they see management that responds to increased competition or changed conditions with nothing more intelligent than exhortations to get mean and lean, they are unlikely to respond very well, especially when the management ranks are untouched by the layoffs. If, however, there is some sense to management's actions—and employees are likely to understand what is sensible, what isn't, and what is simply reactive downsizing—then the workforce is more likely to accept and adjust. Put differently, laying people off amounts to an admission that a firm's old way of doing business is no longer well-suited to the current or impending business environment. But layoffs on their own don't help the employees who are left behind understand or implement a *new way* of doing business that is better suited to the company's strategy and context. One is reminded here of the admonitions that physicians and nutritionists routinely give to would-be dieters: Rapid weight loss seldom produces satisfying long-term results unless it is accompanied by changes in lifestyle, eating habits, and exercise.

Obviously, we don't mean to imply that simply coupling downsizing with *some* broader managerial initiative is going to have a positive impact. Our hypothesized explanations for why the data look as they do depend on the broader initiative being sensible for the firm involved and being *perceived* as such by the workforce. Coupling downsizing with some broader initiative makes sense when the broader initiative addresses the firm's *real* problems or opportunities.

And we freely admit the possibility that the real problem may simply be that the firm has too many workers. There are organizations that, after years of sloth induced by a lack of competition, have become swollen with redundant (and possibly overpaid) workers. Longitudinal studies of organizations confirm that the increases in staff—particularly administrative staff—that accompany growth are seldom counterbalanced by commensurate reductions in headcount during periods of decline.[22] For such bloated organizations, downsizing *per se* may be what is needed. But if this is so, management ought to have a no-holds-barred look at how the organization became bloated and whose interests this served, concluding that review, if appropriate, by having someone in management visibly walk the plank. If management says to employees, "We screwed up, now you pay," it shouldn't count on harmonious relations with the workforce in the future. And for a randomly selected firm in need of some workforce reduction, we are willing to bet that more than just downsizing is called for.

MUST YOU DOWNSIZE?

We have suggested that downsizing almost inevitably imposes substantial psychological costs on the workforce. It comes with some social costs for the community, at least in the short term. And the available evidence on its bottom-line impact isn't clear. So the question *Must you downsize?* should be pondered carefully.

Of course, the costs and benefits of downsizing depend on the particular circumstances of the organization. If downsizing seemingly works best when tied to a plan for restructuring or repositioning, then the extent to which management has a good sense of what it is doing and why is crucial. But beyond this, we can draw on the five factors and complementarity considerations to speculate on how costly the effort is likely to be.

Family-like cultures, in which employment has been cast as a social bond rather than a stark exchange relation, are likely to suffer relatively more from downsizing. Firms that depend on good relations with the surrounding community and that loom larger in the local labor market will also find downsizing to be more costly. Firms in a tight labor market will face a stronger adverse selection problem in terms of who departs, although a tight labor market will mitigate the damage to those who depart and thus on the community and on the psychological state of the survivors.

Technology and work organization also figure prominently. Where tasks are interdependent, downsizing tends to be more disruptive, both economically and socially. Particularly when a firm's culture and technology emphasize cooperation across units, downsizing strategies that explicitly or implicitly pit different segments of the organization against one another in struggling to retain employees can be extremely destructive. One common solution to this problem is simply to mandate "across-the-board" layoffs, with each business unit being given a fixed percentage of headcount or payroll that must be trimmed. But, as we'll see in the next section, this kind of approach has substantial problems. With respect to business strategy, organizations that seek competitive advantage from continuous improvement or by transferring knowledge gained in one product, service, or division to another part of the firm will tend to suffer most from the knowledge losses wrought by downsizing.

As for complementarities with other HR policies: If an organization has relied on secure employment, promotion from within, employee investments in firm-specific training, and the like, layoffs can certainly be expected to undercut workers' confidence in the employer's representations about future prospects. Organizations with seniority-based protections built into their HR systems may stand to gain less economically from downsizing, because the layoffs will disproportionately hit workers with lower seniority, who are presumably making less money.[23] And obviously the cost implications of a layoff will depend substantially on the benefits plans an employer has adopted—for instance, its health and pension plans and obligations for continued coverage that may be mandated by law, collective bargaining agreements, or company policy. In other words, in thinking through whether a layoff makes good business sense, an employer needs to be assessing both the impact of past HR practices on the costs and benefits of a layoff, and the impact of a layoff today on the kinds of HR practices the firm will be able to implement in the future.

We don't mean the preceding to be anything like a complete list of factors that affect the cost of downsizing; it is just a selection of some important factors. And against these costs and the benefits to be accrued, you have to consider alternative actions the organization might take to address the problems or to meet the new circumstances that have led you to consider downsizing. Wage cuts, hours adjustments, job transfers, and reassignment of work across plants are all alternatives to be considered. Especially when it comes to layoffs that respond to short-lived changes in economic conditions, such alternatives can be quite cost-effective.

Notice also in this regard that four important factors may bear on a firm's ability to avoid downsizing: (a) its inventory policy; (b) the extent of uniformity in its operations (including HR policies) across work sites; (c) the extent to which it has cross-trained workers; and (d) the extent of vertical integration. One strategy taken by many high-commitment organizations to minimize layoffs is to respond to temporary downturns by producing for inventory or by redeploying workers to other tasks, such as deferred maintenance. For instance, Lincoln Electric at one point responded to slack demand by sending production line workers outside to paint fences and buildings. One of the things the workforce did at Sun Hydraulics during the recession of the early 1990s was to grind out the catalog they'd been trying to produce for so long; the fact that workers knew the products and that there were employees knowledgeable about desktop publishing made this feasible. Obviously, running a just-in-time production system will limit the option of producing for inventory, and running an HR system in which workers have very specialized skills will limit options to redeploy employees temporarily.

Another strategy sometimes used is to reassign work across work sites, to smooth out fluctuations in demand. This will be easier to do in a firm that is vertically integrated with a variable taper; then the taper can be adjusted, with workers deployed downstream when demand is strong and upstream when it is slack. Of course, a firm's ability to reassign work across sites will be easier to the extent that the firm has uniform operations and HR policies in its different work sites. If a firm is running a high-commitment system in one site and a "high-control" system in another, it is harder to imagine how it could respond to a cyclical downturn by shifting work or workers from one of the sites to the other.

HOW TO DOWNSIZE IF YOU MUST: PROCESS CONSIDERATIONS

If after due consideration of all these issues you are still set on downsizing, then you should consider ways in which you can attenuate (or might unwittingly exacerbate) the psychological costs for workers and reputational costs for your organization. Indeed, you should be thinking about these things as you debate whether to downsize at all. The key here is the *process* of downsizing.

Perhaps the most important way to attenuate the psychological costs is implicit in what we said above about the "moral from the data": By tying downsizing to a broader and sensible change initiative, a firm gives its workforce a sensible and credible reason for why this pain must be inflicted, a vision of what sort of better future beckons after the suffering is over, and a broader purpose around which the survivors can rally.

The research literature, as well as assessments from practitioners who have lived through downsizings, suggest some further conditions that can help minimize the adverse effects of layoffs on the attitudes and work performance of stayers:[24]

- The process should be well understood by workers: *There should be extensive communication before, during, and after.* Although this seems self-evident, companies that have downsized consistently report that it doesn't get the attention it deserves. For instance, in a survey of HR executives by the Wyatt Company in 1991, 79% said they most often used letters and memos from senior executives to communicate with employees about restructurings, but only 29% percent of respondents found these communications to be effective. The study concluded that such impersonal approaches to communicating with employees on such a sensitive subject were easier for senior managers to use but ineffective at addressing many of the employees' concerns.[25]

- Because of the enormous costs imposed by layoffs, *it should be clear to employees that you have given due consideration to alternatives* of the sort discussed in the last section. This doesn't mean that you have to try every alternative first. But downsizing, if not necessarily a last resort, certainly shouldn't be perceived as the first thing you thought of and then decided to try. And to the greatest extent possible, employees who will be affected by the downsizing—if it comes—should be coopted into the process of analyzing alternatives.

- *The process should be perceived as embodying distributive and procedural justice.* Both communication and a willingness on the part of management to avoid downsizing are a good start in this direction. Employee input should be solicited and incorporated into the planning process. When the layoffs come, there should be fair and clearly stated criteria to determine on whom the ax will fall. Those terminated should have the right to appeal the decision.

- *The process should be kind to the leavers.* In particular, there should be maximum advance notification and generous buyout, severance, and outplacement benefits. This is more than simple benevolence; the stayers will grieve less and be more ready to adjust and adapt if their former colleagues and (perhaps still) friends are well treated. The need for this, of course, depends on the pre-layoff culture and implicit contracts at the firm. If the firm had a dog-eat-dog, highly competitive culture, it can probably get by with less than is advisable for companies that previously had employee-welfare, clan-like cultures, like Eastman Kodak and Levi Strauss.

  On balance, we believe that kindness to the leavers is a good idea, and the existing evidence supports that view. But we hasten to reiterate a point we made earlier: The greater the employer's largesse, the more one must be concerned about inducing "voluntary" departures that will be drawn (adversely) from the more able employees.[26]

- *There should be support services for the "survivors."* Perhaps the best support service available is a good sense of where the firm is headed after the layoffs are done. When the survivor's new role is less ambiguous, she is more likely to adapt and move on, presumably because she will find it easier to envision and control her worklife after the layoff. In addition, when the downsizing is accompanied by reengineering and redefinition of roles and tasks, intensive retraining and resocialization of the survivors is likely to be critical, both so that the survivors know what is now expected of them and have the competencies to succeed in the new milieu, and so that they understand the firm's commitment to the new way of doing business.

The American Management Association's recent (1997) large-scale survey of corporate experiences attests to the crucial impact of training activities following a downsizing on the outcomes an organization experiences.[27] They found that a year or more after implementing job cuts, firms that had increased their training activities were more than twice as likely to report quality improvements, 75% more likely to see gains in worker productivity, and 60% more likely to increase operating profits, compared to firms that did not increase training following layoffs.[28]

Notwithstanding the desirability of these general practices, the 1997 American Management Association survey data also reveal that it is still only a minority of firms that increase training budgets and training activities following layoffs; and that there has been a decline in certain post-layoff services being provided by companies, such as outplacement assistance, extended severance pay, extended health coverage, and job retraining. Some of this decline in outplacement assistance no doubt reflects the improved labor market prospects for discharged workers in the last few years. However, the AMA survey also reveals a decline in firms' use of some practices that reduce or eliminate the need for layoffs in the first place, such as demotion, downgrades, transfers, and early retirement incentives.

Interestingly, the AMA survey data also indicate that firms are becoming much more selective in providing outplacement assistance. In 1995, 44% of firms providing such assistance offered it to all workers whose jobs were eliminated; only 31% did so in 1997. It is worth pondering the distributive justice implications of such a trend, which seems to reflect increasing stratification or differentiation in the treatment afforded to various subgroups of employees. Those who have lived through downsizings generally observe that widespread layoffs increase dramatically the real and perceived interdependencies among the surviving workers, who usually face the challenge of doing more with fewer resources to drawn on. And it is worth noting that the two most frequent rationales given for layoffs by the firms surveyed by the American Management Association are organizational restructuring and reengineering of business processes, both of which often involve an increased reliance on teams and a desire to strengthen shared companywide values. We certainly should not overinterpret one small piece of data and what appears to be only a moderate trend, but the apparent tendency to be more selective and restrictive in providing outplacement assistance highlights an important point: In deciding on what treatment will be given to those who are laid off, management needs to think carefully about the symbolic and cultural effects their actions will have on the organization that remains. Persuading the survivors that "we must all be rowing with the same oar" may prove much tougher to do when groups (occupations, subunits, seniority cohorts, etc.) have been treated differently during the downsizing process.

Massacre or Drip-Drip-Drip?

A process issue that deserves careful thought in contemplating a downsizing concerns the choice between dramatic, swift cuts versus a more gradual, less wrenching approach. Unfortunately, this is another topic where the paucity of systematic research limits our ability to offer strong advice. The advantages of a gradual approach are apparent: The firm may be unsure how deeply to cut, and a onetime massacre runs the risk of cutting too much. Of course, the psychological costs may be attenuated by a gradual approach. Local labor markets may be better able to absorb the discharged workers if they are discharged gradually, which in turn may ameliorate the adverse impact on the local economy and community. On balance, however, those who have suffered through downsizings tend to believe that a "get it over with in one fell swoop" approach is superior (at least, for the firm) to a process that drags on.

The responses of companies surveyed by the American Management Association suggest some plausible reasons for thinking this is right. For instance, those data indicate that a number of the dislocative effects associated with layoffs—such as increases in disability claims; post-downsizing turnover; and declines in morale, productivity, and the quality of customer relations—abate considerably after the first year following the downsizing. Conversely, a number of the beneficial effects—such as increases in quality and productivity—do not manifest themselves for some time following the layoffs. This suggests that a protracted process, in which it is presumably more difficult for employees to identify a discernible end to the layoffs and associated structural changes, may simply delay or prolong the adjustment period of up to a year or more that frequently seems to follow workforce reductions. By moving boldly and rapidly, companies may minimize the long-term psychological damage and also perhaps achieve a more pronounced and rapid increase in shareholder equity. Although this conjecture seems sensible, recall the survey finding cited earlier in this chapter: Of the nearly 1,200 companies surveyed by the American Management Association in mid-1997, 40% had cut jobs in *three or more* calendar years since 1990.[29]

Across the Board or Targeted Layoffs?

When structuring a downsizing program, firms often must decide whether to implement cuts across the board, with every unit shedding a fixed percentage of its employees, or concentrate the cuts in specific units. The costs of targeted layoffs are clear: They lead to internal political activity aimed at redirecting the ax at some other target. When our own university engaged in a large-scale "repositioning" some years back, which entailed the first significant layoffs in its long history, many of the staff support areas that had been targeted for the largest cuts spent enormous quantities of time in jurisdictional disputes and trying to document their workloads by creating forms, databases, and other devices intended to demonstrate to the university administration how much service they were providing. Such political campaigning is apt to be particularly ferocious and disruptive when a firm's culture and technology emphasize cooperation and collegiality. In an attempt to head off such efforts, and also simply to avoid hard and painful decisions, management may—we believe, too often will—take the seemingly easy route of equally shared pain and across-the-board cuts in employment levels.

This route may seem easier for management, but it has real dangers for effective downsizing. For one thing, although a "share the pain" strategy of equal, across-the-board cuts may have some appeal as being distributively just, there can be significant perceptions of distributive injustice by units that are performing exceptionally or that have through disciplined efforts kept their headcount down and thus should be reduced less. Management doesn't want to anger any of its workforce, but demotivating these units in particular is an especially bad outcome. Across-the-board downsizings will also tend to score low on procedural justice because of the arbitrariness and inflexibility of the targets. Appeal mechanisms that allow special pleading, which would increase perceptions of procedural justice, invite just the sort of politicking and internal competition that the across-the-board strategy is designed to preempt. In addition, this sort of downsizing strategy, if it is anticipated in the future, may (perversely) lead unit-level managers to try to pad their payrolls, in anticipation of an across-the-board cut to come later. For organizations with a strong clan-like culture—and especially if emotional bonds and task interdependencies are more intense *within* units than *across* units—this "spread the pain" strategy will do just that: Everyone will feel intense loss of friends and colleagues, as opposed to having concentrated the pain in a few units. Finally, across-the-board downsizings have the same reactive odor as does downsizing alone (without some accompanying restructuring initiative): It signals to workers that management doesn't really have a well-thought-out plan for the future.[30]

Layoffs, Seniority, and Age

Another issue that often arises when downsizing is contemplated is how to handle seniority claims. In unionized settings, this is often mandated by the contract, with seniority typically serving as a strong protection against layoff. But outside those settings, management has to decide whether to target more senior or less senior employees or to be seniority-neutral in distributing the pink slips.

There are conflicting forces at work in this issue, and thus no easy answers. To the extent that senior workers are, by virtue of their seniority, more highly paid, the firm gets more economic bang-for-the-buck by terminating more senior employees. In settings where the knowledge base and technology change rapidly, recent hires may be more in tune with important new developments, giving another reason to discharge more senior workers. But potential claims of age discrimination (in locations where there are laws against age discrimination) must be attended to. Consequently, when a firm decides it would prefer to prune selectively from its more senior workers, early retirement programs, carefully crafted to avoid any adverse selection and appearance of age discrimination, may be more desirable. Layoffs targeted at older workers are also unlikely to appear procedurally or distributively just.[31] Organizations with a culture that emphasizes loyalty will obviously have an especially difficult time with targeting senior workers, as will organizations that depend on slowly developed firm-specific human capital. But targeting the young can be dangerous, in the United States at least: Because women and people of color are (usually) concentrated in the lower-tenure ranks, firms that protect seniority rights and discharge the most recently hired workers can face claims of adverse impact by sex and race. And nowadays you don't avoid lawsuits by protecting women and people of color; reverse discrimination lawsuits are increasingly likely to follow.

In short, downsizing represents a potential legal minefield, and the relevant case law is still evolving rapidly. In recent years, courts have made it clear that age discrimination statutes protect workers from discriminatory treatment, including layoffs, based on age *per se*—that is, where the employer's actions are based on discriminatory and unfounded notions about the capabilities of workers as a function of their chronological age. Of course, wages frequently rise with seniority, and seniority in turn is frequently correlated with age. Consequently, a downsizing motivated purely by cost-cutting considerations—say, a firm with a high tenure workforce, whose wages were no longer competitive vis-à-vis newer, younger competitors—is likely to result in layoffs concentrated among older, higher-wage workers. Is this illegal?

Our (nonexpert) reading of the relevant case law is that the answer is: *No, not necessarily, but you have to have done your homework* (see below). For instance, in one recent case, a 62-year-old employee was fired by his employer, a paper manufacturer, after nine years of service, apparently just a few weeks short of the ten-year anniversary on which his pension would have vested. The United States Supreme Court ruled that the employer's conduct, although potentially illegal under pension law, did not represent age discrimination unless the plaintiff could demonstrate that it was age *per se* that had motivated the firing. The Court concluded that when personnel decisions are motivated by factors other than age, the problem that prompted age discrimination legislation—inaccurate and stigmatizing stereotypes about older workers' productivity and competence—disappears. "Because age and years of service are analytically distinct, an employer can take account of one while ignoring the other, and thus it is incorrect to say that a decision based on years of service is necessarily 'age based.'"[32]

Recently, the Supreme Court in our home state of California reached a similar conclusion, failing to overturn an appellate court ruling in favor of Loral Corporation. Loral terminated most of the staff in a California facility that it had recently purchased from Ford Aerospace. The only employees who did not find work with another division of the company were over forty years of age, and one of them brought suit. Loral claimed that their higher salaries were the basis for the terminations. The Court found for Loral, ruling that "employers may indeed prefer workers with lower salaries to workers with higher ones, even if the preference falls disproportionately on older, generally higher paid workers." In their opinion, the panel of appellate court justices wrote colorfully:

[We] are not unmindful that the image of some newly minted whippersnapper MBA who tries to increase corporate profits—and his or her own compensation—by across-the-board layoffs is not a pretty one. Even so, neither Congress nor the state Legislature ever intended the age discrimination laws to inhibit the very process by which a free market economy—decision-making on the basis of cost—is conducted and by which, ultimately, real jobs and wealth are created.[33]

Documenting and Rationalizing Layoff Decisions

If you are contemplating a large-scale layoff, labor lawyers counsel extreme caution, deliberation, and documentation, especially in contexts that are covered by collective bargaining or advance notification requirements, where there is potential for discrimination claims, or where managers may wittingly or unwittingly have given employees an impression that their employment was secure.[34] But as we noted in Chapter 7, it is generally unwise to permit legal concerns to *drive* HR decisions, and in the arena of layoffs there often are generally few options that organizations face that are immune from the risk of litigation (e.g., by older workers if seniority is emphasized in a layoff, or by women and people of color if less senior workers are affected disproportionately).

Consequently, the starting point of any downsizing campaign needs to be a careful assessment of its appropriateness and the dimensions along which layoffs should be structured. Of course, we recommend the five factors and complementarity considerations as good organizing principles in doing that assessment. For instance, what is the role of seniority in your organization's past, present, and future, given the enterprise's strategy, technology, environment, culture, workforce, and the array of HR practices and policies in place? Will impending developments make seniority more of an asset or a liability? To what extent can the organization use layoffs as one tool within a broader organizational change initiative?

If such an analysis leads management to decide that layoffs are appropriate, whether seniority-based or otherwise, then the lawyers will want the homework and the paper trail to begin in earnest. Ideally, to convince relevant outsiders of the business necessity of layoffs in situations like this, management will want to have the following sorts of information and documentation: (a) how the organization's wage structure, seniority distribution, and staffing ratios compare with relevant benchmarks (including before the downsizing); (b) empirical relationships between the company's hiring, compensation, and career development practices on the one hand, and important business outcomes on the other (e.g., if layoffs are to be concentrated disproportionately among more senior employees, evidence of demonstrable negative relationships between seniority and important outcomes); (c) where layoffs are done selectively within a business unit, evidence that demonstrates that the company's performance management system is valid (see Chapter 10) and provides a defensible and legitimate basis for ranking employees in terms of layoffs; and (d) documentation of having fully explored the feasibility of reassigning workers or lowering the compensation of employees who would otherwise have been laid off.

Having done this kind of homework is likely to make your labor lawyer sleep better at night. Indeed, your labor lawyers, ever in pursuit of a better night's sleep, are likely to suggest some additions to our list. But such documentation is good for more than a court of law. We believe that firms that downsize invariably confront some form of influential "jury," whether in a court of law or on the evening news or around water coolers as employees (or prospective employees) gossip about what management is up to. Consequently, the lawyerly advice that you be able to document and defend the layoffs is sound advice whether or not the risk of litigation is high. The kinds of evidence that increasingly are needed in legal proceedings—to help convince a court that a downsizing that might adversely impact a particular group is defensible for business reasons—will also be crucial in demonstrating distributive and procedural justice and thus in minimizing the psychological and reputational damage of the layoffs on survivors and prospective employees.

Dealing with the Community

Another set of thorny process issues concerns the impact of downsizing on the local community. Downsizing, especially focused layoffs by large corporations (that lead, say, to the closure of an entire facility), can have devastating impacts on a local community. As extreme examples, there are cases of rural communities simply disappearing after a local lumber mill or mine is closed.

These considerations obviously have to be weighed in management's decisions about where and how to cut. And this is more than a matter of ethical behavior. A firm that devastates one community may "get away with it" in terms of that community's ability to strike back. But the firm can substantially harm its reputation, particularly insofar as the firm has explicitly emphasized positive community relations as a matter of corporate policy. For example, Waste Management—one of the companies we mentioned at the beginning of the chapter that recently announced layoffs—extols the virtues of responsible corporate citizenship on a section of the firm's web site outlining the company's Good Neighbor Policy.[35] This policy expresses eloquently how the fortunes of a company, its employees, and the community in which it operates are connected, and how a responsible company must understand and balance the needs of the community with those of its employees and with its own business agenda. Waste Management, in this Policy, pledges itself to precisely this sort of good corporate citizenship.

It is easy to understand why such a corporate responsibility creed is important for a company like Waste Management, whose business activities (including toxic waste management) have such serious potential effects on the physical environment. But to be perceived as credible in its commitment to the community, a company like Waste Management will have to be especially careful and selective in implementing layoffs, given the values it has publicly articulated.

If downsizing is necessary, what can be done? Roughly put, a firm that is downsizing in a way that will materially harm a local community should give due consideration to doing what it can to help that community, just as it considers what it should do to help its downsized ex-employees. Facilities may be redeployed. Workers at a facility may wish to "buy out" the facility and run it themselves. It may be possible to help attract a replacement employer. (Re)training can be subsidized. We reiterate: Such costly attempts to attenuate the impact of a downsizing decision are more than just conscience money for a firm, and more than just a way for top management of the corporation to be able to sleep better at night, although they are certainly that. Corporations carry reputations as employers and as corporate citizens, and while it is hard to put "community goodwill" on your balance sheet, it is an asset that pays returns and that requires investment to maintain.

CONCLUSION AND COMING ATTRACTIONS

Layoffs are among the most important and anxiety-producing things that a manager must confront. They have profound implications not only for the employees involved, the manager, and the organizational unit implicated, but also for the broader community within which the enterprise is located. The jury is still out on the long-term economic and social consequences of downsizing, used by firms to lower costs, increase productivity, and enhance flexibility in the competitive world economy. Unfortunately, there is a shortage of solid research evidence to guide managers in making decisions about whether and how to downsize. This shortage doesn't reflect lack of effort and interest, we hasten to add, but instead the inherent difficulties in finding good controlled data.

Consequently, we've had to rely on some suggestive data and the general theories of the employment relationship that we've developed in this book. If we've got it right, we are led to conclude that process concerns matter a lot: The *how, who,* and *why* of downsizing may be at least as important as the *how much* and *when* in determining the effects on the labor force and on organizational performance. In particular, downsizing seems to work best as part of a well-thought-out plan for restructuring, reengineering, repositioning, and generally rethinking what the organization does and why. To engage in downsizing is either an admission of previous mismanagement or an acknowledgment that something—in the environment, the organization's strategy, its technology—has changed. Management should be clear in its own mind, and probably also with employees, on which it is. And it should be clear about what permanent, structural changes are going to be made to avoid previous problems or meet new circumstances.

One structural change that often accompanies downsizing is outsourcing. The firm decides that there are certain tasks, which in the past have been done primarily by its regular employees, that would be done better, faster, or more cheaply by outsiders. Those who used to do the work are downsized. (In annual surveys of downsizing activity by firms over the last few years, the American Management Association reports that between one-fifth and one-quarter of firms that are downsizing list "outsourcing and contracting" as among the rationales for their layoffs.[36]) This coupling of downsizing and outsourcing is sometimes done in a completely ineffective fashion: Work previously done by insiders is outsourced to more expensive independent contractors, who happen to be the very same workers who were just laid off, now hired back as consultants, potentially raising eyebrows not only inside the organization but outside as well (including tax and regulatory authorities). But outsourcing can have real economic benefits, and it can play a constructive, if somewhat dangerous, role in a downsizing campaign. So we turn next to the human resource dimensions of outsourcing.

IN REVIEW

⇒ Firms downsize for a variety of reasons, including cost cutting, increased flexibility and adaptability, enhanced focus, enhanced productivity, as part of organizational politics, to broaden skill bases (by using outsourced labor), and in hopes of improving shareholder equity.

⇒ Recent upsurges in downsizing are often attributed to intensified competition, decreased product life cycles, escalating costs and legal liabilities associated with employees, falling costs of substitutes (including outsourced labor), and increased discipline from capital markets, which seem to endorse downsizing.

⇒ Existing evidence about the effects of downsizing suggests the following conclusions:

• The impact on the firm's bottom line (in terms of both operating profits and financial market performance) is mixed and largely transitory.

• Employee morale and attitudes suffer, which can be especially costly in environments that emphasize creativity.

• It may not be the least able employees who leave. Instead, some downsizing programs unwittingly encourage the more able and valuable employees to depart.

• Downsizing can have a substantial negative effect on the local community, although some commentators argue that these effects are temporary and, if avoided, lead to far worse consequences down the road.

⇒ The overall moral from these data is that downsizing works best when tied to sensible restructuring of the organization's work practices, because:

• Organizations that restructure are more likely to be addressing the real problems and opportunities they face.

• Morale among those left behind is likely to be higher if management projects a clear vision of what the problem has been and how things will get better, than if they merely downsize reactively to "cut fat."

⇒ Organizations that contemplate downsizing should first contemplate alternatives.

⇒ If you must downsize, process considerations become very important. There are no easy answers in how to downsize, but the following should be kept in mind:

• Communication with employees is critical.

• Employees should be coopted into the process as much as possible, and it should be made clear that alternatives were considered.

• Distributive and procedural justice should be carefully attended to.

- Both the leavers and the survivors should be supported, the former with "services" and the latter with training and a sense of where the downsized organization is headed.
- On balance, one large round of terminations is probably better than wave after wave.
- On balance, targeted layoffs seem a better bet than uniform, across-the-board layoffs.
- Layoffs that target (or that favor) more senior workers have advantages and disadvantages on both legal and organizational grounds.
- Consider thoroughly the interests of the communities involved, what you can do to mitigate the impact of the layoffs, and whether it isn't in your organization's interest to be a "good citizen" of the affected locales (to protect your reputation as such).
- Legal considerations should be attended to carefully, though they cannot and should not be determinative. Careful planning, rationalization, and documentation may be an important "cover" in the face of lawsuits.

ENDNOTES

1. In mid-to-late November 1997. And the trend hardly seems to have abated since then. For instance, data from the U.S. Bureau of Labor Statistics indicate that mass layoffs (i.e., those involving 50 or more workers from a single establishment) actually increased by about 5% in the first half of 1998, relative to the same period in 1997. Nearly 840,000 workers were affected, a 14% increase over the number of workers to cease employment during the first half of 1997 due to mass layoffs (see http://stats.bls.gov/news.release/mmls.nws.htm).

2. *New York Times,* November 16, 1997, p. BU-2.

3. Tim Smart, "Ax and Ye Shall Receive?: Companies Are Aiming for Growth in New Round of Layoffs," *Washington Post* (November 13, 1997): E01.

4. Claudia H. Deutsch, "Kodak Will Layoff 10,000 Employees," *New York Times* (November 12, 1997): A1.

5. New York, Simon and Schuster, 1956.

6. Summarized at: http://www.disgruntled.com/corp2.html.

7. Summarized at: http://www.amanet.org/survey/97survey.htm#4.

8. For a review, see Nitin Nohria and Geoffrey Love, "Adaptive or Disruptive: When Does Downsizing Pay in Large Industrial Corporations?," unpublished manuscript, Harvard Business School, 1996.

9. Excerpted with permission from "The Wages of Downsizing," by Alan Downs, in *Mother Jones* magazine, (July/August 1996): 26–31, © 1996, Foundation for National Progress.

10. Wayne F. Cascio, Clifford E. Young, and James R. Morris, "Financial Consequences of Employment–Change Decisions in Major U.S. Corporations," *Academy of Management Journal* 40 (October 1997): 1175–89.

11. Of course, controlling for industry is only partially a control for possible contributing factors, so that all these results need to be taken with a grain of salt. To illustrate with a single example, Apple Computer has been downsizing a lot in the last few years. It has also shown some pretty poor financial results (at least until 1998), relative to the computer industry as a whole. Of course, these are not unrelated: The classic omitted variable here is the rise of Microsoft's Windows operating system. As Windows has driven the market share of the MacOS and Macs into the nether regions, it has led to Apple's poor financial performance and the waves of downsizing. We ought to be looking at data about how a firm fares with versus without downsizing; unhappily, the data don't come to us neatly packaged to answer this question.

12. Cascio et al., *op. cit.* Interestingly, the authors found the opposite pattern with respect to employment growth: The growing companies most likely to outperform other firms in the same industry were ones that engaged in pure employment growth, whereas firms that grew in conjunction with adding new assets (new plants, acquisitions, etc.) displayed inferior performance relative to the industry baseline.

13. Dan L. Worrell, Wallace N. Davidson, III, and Varinder M. Sharma. "Layoff Announcements and Stockholder Wealth," *Academy of Management Journal* 34 (September 1991): 662–78; Nohria and Love, *op. cit.*

14. Martin N. Baily, Eric J. Bartelsman, and John C. Haltiwanger, "Downsizing and Productivity Growth: Myth or Reality?," CES Discussion Paper 94-4 (Washington: U.S. Bureau of the Census, 1994).

15. American Management Association, *Corporate Job Creation, Job Elimination, and Downsizing: Summary of Key Findings, 1997* (New York: American Management Association); viewable online at: http://www.amanet.org/survey/97survey.htm.

16. Jane Auman and Brian Draheim, "The Downside to Downsizing," *Benefits Canada* (May 1997), viewable online at: http://www.benefitscanada.com/Content/managed/mc13_feature.html.

17. Teresa M. Amabile and Regina Conti, "Changes in the Work Environment for Creativity During Downsizing," unpublished manuscript, Harvard Business School, 1997.

18. American Management Association, *op. cit.*

19. See Ann Huff, "Persistent Effects of Job Displacement: The Importance of Multiple Job Losses," *Journal of Labor Economics* 15 (January 1997): 165–88; and the studies cited in Steven Pearlstein, "Downsizing's Impact on Jobs Begins Showing Up in Studies," *Washington Post* (March 21, 1996): B9.

20. For some illustrative evidence, see: Ralph Catalano, "A Model of the Net Effect of Job Loss on Violence," *Journal of Personality & Social Psychology* 72 (June 1997): 1440–47; R. L. Leeflang, "Health Effects of Unemployment: II. Men and Women." *Social Science & Medicine* 34 (February 1992): 351–63; Anthony H. Winefield, "Employment Status and Psychological Well-being: A Longitudinal Study," *Journal of Applied Psychology* 75 (August 1990): 455–59; Loring P. Jones, "The Effect of Unemployment on Children and Adolescents," *Children & Youth Services Review* 10 (Number 3, 1988): 199–215; Ronald C. Kessler, "Intervening Processes in the Relationship between Unemployment and Health," *Psychological Medicine* 17 (November 1987): 949–61; Brian Graetz, "Health

Consequences of Employment and Unemployment: Longitudinal Evidence for Young Men and Women," *Social Science & Medicine* 36 (March 15, 1993): 715–24; David Dooley and Ralph Catalano, "Recent Research on the Psychological Effects of Unemployment," *Journal of Social Issues* 44 (Winter 1988): 1–12; Ronald C. Kessler, James S. House, and J. Blake Turner, "Unemployment and Health in a Community Sample," *Journal of Health and Social Behavior* 28 (March 1987): 51–9; M. Harvey Brenner, *Mental Illness and the Economy* (Cambridge, MA: Harvard University Press, 1973).

21. For example, see John Cassidy, "All Worked Up," *New Yorker* (April 22, 1996): 51–5; George Gilder (and others), "Does America Still Work?" *Harper's* (May 1996): 36–47.

22. John H. Freeman and Michael T. Hannan, "Growth and Decline Processes in Organizations," *American Sociological Review* 40 (April 1975): 215–28.

23. More on seniority and the process of downsizing in the next section.

24. For general discussions of this topic, see Joel M. Brockner, "Managing the Effects of Layoffs on Survivors," *California Management Review* 34 (Winter 1992): 9–28; David M. Noer, *Overcoming the Trauma of Layoffs and Revitalizing Downsized Organizations* (San Francisco: Jossey-Bass, 1993); Wayne F. Cascio, "Downsizing: What Do We Know? What Have We Learned?" *Academy of Management Executive* 7 (February 1993): 95–104.

25. The Wyatt Company, *Restructuring—Cure or Cosmetic Surgery?: Results of Corporate Change in the '80s with RXs for the '90s,* 1991.

26. One general way to be kind to leavers is to structure the layoffs so that those who are terminated are not tainted by the process. Earlier in this chapter we suggested that firms should not rely on voluntary layoffs but instead choose who will go. But if you follow this advice, you should understand that this may compromise the ability of the leavers to find employment elsewhere; prospective employers may draw the (rational) conclusion that those who got the pink slips were, in the eyes of management, the employees that the firm could most easily do without. Downsizings structured so as to reduce the taint of being in the laid-off group—for instance, if governed by seniority, or if aimed at all employees in a given locale or all personnel working on a given project—may be kinder to the leavers in this respect at least. (See Robert Gibbons and Lawrence F. Katz, "Lemons and Layoffs," *Journal of Labor Economics* 9 [October 1991]: 351–80.) This isn't to say that you should, after all, use voluntary layoffs, or that you should use layoffs targeted at entire workgroups or project teams instead of across-the-board cuts (see later in this section). But this tainting effect is one more important thing to keep in mind as you choose how to proceed.

27. American Management Association, *op cit.*

28. *Ibid.* (http://www.amanet.org/survey/97survey.htm).

29. *Ibid.*

30. And across-the-board downsizings heighten the tainted-by-dismissal phenomenon discussed in note 26.

31. Indeed, within at least some cultures, layoffs targeted at *less* senior workers would score better on grounds of justice.

32. *Hazen Paper Co. v. Biggins,* 507 U.S. 604 (1993), viewable online at: http://supct.cornell.edu/supct/html/91–1600.ZS.html.

33. *Marks v. Loral Corporation* (1997), 57 Cal.App.4th 30 (July 25, 1997), viewable online at: http://www.voltz.com/emplaw/cases/marks_mod.html.

34. For an example of such advice, see Rebecca D. Eisen, "Dealing with Downsizing: What to Do Now to Prepare for a Possible Layoff," viewable online at the Web site of Brobeck, Phleger & Harrison LLP: http://www.brobeck.com/sslitle/88.htm.

35. Viewable (1/20/99) online at: http://www.wastemanagement.com/wmxlnk/gn.html.

36. American Management Association, *op. cit.* (http://www.amanet.org/survey/97survey.htm#3).

18

Outsourcing

Profiles of "the new economy" and the changing nature of work are ubiquitous these days. These accounts invariably emphasize two significant trends: (1) increasing focus by companies on core competencies, relying on third parties to handle an ever-growing fraction of tasks so as to be lean and flexible in the face of rapid change; and (2) the rise of what the business periodical *Fast Company* recently dubbed the "free-agent nation," an increasing trend toward independent, autonomous forms of work instead of long-term attachments to organizations through traditional employment relationships. An Internet search conducted in October 1998 unearthed some 888,000 Web pages containing references to outsourcing, about 41,500 for "core competence" or "core capability," and about 31,000 for "contract(ing) out." By way of comparison, searches for the Chicago Bulls basketball team and actor Tom Cruise yielded approximately 29,000 and 22,000 hits, respectively, suggesting that outsourcing and contracting are at least as prevalent on the Web as some prominent icons of popular culture.[1] The popular press and scholarly literatures are replete with discussions of the contingent workforce, flexible employment practices, the rise of part-time and temporary work, and the managerial, financial, and legal implications of various forms of outsourcing.

There is widespread consensus that these trends have been on the rise, with organizations increasingly relying on individuals to carry out necessary tasks who do not have a regular employment relationship with the enterprise. But it is easier to identify these trends than to offer precise evidence of their magnitude, in part because of a lack of clarity and consensus in definitions of the phenomenon. (We do summarize some evidence in the following section.) Consequently, it is useful to begin by distinguishing two different means by which an organization can seek to enhance flexibility, if it has decided to forgo a traditional employment relationship to accomplish a given task.

One approach is to *outsource* the task completely; another strategy is to rely on some form of *contingent labor,* such as a temp, leased employee, or limited-duration hire brought on board for a specific project. The distinction here largely concerns the role of the firm's managers in directing the actions of workers. If you outsource a task entirely to another firm—which we will refer to as an *independent contractor* arrangement, recognizing that the contractor may be an individual, acting as a self-employed consultant—you are buying an end product; the details of how that product is produced are left to others. A good example is when a firm contracts with a landscape contractor to landscape and then maintain the grounds surrounding its building. Or consider the relationship between a firm and its outside legal counsel. Management of the client firm can make suggestions to the landscape contractor or outside counsel, suggestions that are taken more or less seriously depending on the contract and the contractor's desire to see the relationship renewed. But it is the supervisors of the contractor who tell the gardeners and lawyers what to do and when. In contrast, when a firm hires someone on a fixed-duration project basis or has a worker furnished by a labor contractor—a temp agency or an employee leasing firm, say—the firm is buying the labor services of the worker, to be directed by the client firm's own managers and supervisors. When a temp shows up, he asks "What do I do?" And he expects fairly detailed instructions in response.

There are four preliminary remarks to make here. First, it should be noted that individuals who go to work for a firm that provides outsourcing services to your organization may very well have a standard sort of employment relationship, though not with your enterprise. There has been a tendency in discussions surrounding "the search for flexibility" to lump together subcontracted work with contingent work, and to assume that both provide disproportionately "bad" jobs. But it is not at all clear that being employed full-time in a firm that does outsourcing is qualitatively inferior to being employed full-time in one of the firms that is a client to the outsourcing company, or that being an independent contractor is inferior to having a traditional employment relationship. For instance, a 1997 government survey revealed that female full-time employees of contract firms earned average wages almost identical to those earned by full-time women in traditional employment relations, and the male employees of contractors actually earned *higher* wages—$685 per week, compared to $578 for their counterparts employed in traditional employment relationships.[2] Nor were the average earnings of independent contractors below those of individuals working in a traditional employment relation. Employees of contractor firms *were* slightly less likely to be covered by employer-provided health and pension benefits, but on balance their conditions of employment did not appear to be woefully inferior to those of individuals working full-time in a traditional employment setting.[3] We return to this issue below in discussing what an organization that relies on outsourcing or contingent labor can reasonably assume about the motivations of the individuals carrying out tasks on its behalf.

Second, we should note at the outset that the issue of what tasks to outsource brings us quickly to topics pertaining to the boundaries of the firm, including vertical integration—should an automobile assembly firm make its own spark plugs, engines, tires, or steel?; should the firm retail its cars or work through independent dealers?—and long-term customer/supplier relations. These questions involve, but go well beyond, HR concerns. To do full justice to them would take many chapters and, probably, an entirely different book. We are going to take a relatively narrow view of outsourcing in the discussion to follow, keeping to HR concerns. We think the HR concerns are vitally important—in setting the boundaries of the firm, you ignore them at your peril—but at the same time, as a general manager or entrepreneur contemplating an outsourcing decision, you will need to integrate other issues with the HR concerns, such as strategic sourcing and entry or mobility barriers.

Third, it is worth emphasizing up front that there is a continuum of possible relationships, between the (relative) extreme points of, say, a clerical temporary (someone employed by a temp agency or leasing firm, who is directly supervised by managers in the client firm) versus the employees of an outside contractor supplying groundskeeping services. Moreover, temps are sometimes engaged on terms that are anything but temporary; a firm that contracts for security workers (but directs their own security services) may "employ" at one remove the same individual for periods measured in years. And employees of independent contractors can be part of the family. For instance, Japanese car assemblers often send surplus employees to their captive parts suppliers; those former employees will remember old loyalties both to former co-workers and to the parent company. We will proceed in this chapter to treat these two alternative arrangements (as alternatives to each other and to using one's own *employees*) discretely, speaking of *outsourcing the tasks to an independent contractor,* and *relying on contingent labor or temps.* But in specific examples, you will have to deal with mixed cases and with cases that vary according to important dimensions such as how temporary the assignment is, and how psychologically independent the person doing the work is from the client organization.

Finally, although outsourcing is very often tied to downsizing—eliminating regular employees and assigning the tasks they used to do to an outsourcing entity or to contingent workers—"greenfield" outsourcing is also worthy of examination: Given a set of tasks to be done and an organization that is unconstrained by the baggage of past employment practices, which tasks should be done by the firm's own employees, and which by outsiders? We spend the bulk of this chapter on greenfield outsourcing because it allows for a more systematic development of the issues. We return to the connection between outsourcing and downsizing at the end of the chapter.

THE RISE OF OUTSOURCING AND CONTINGENT LABOR: MORE DATA

There can be little doubt that both ways of pursuing flexibility—outsourcing activities altogether versus relying on nonstandard forms of labor supervised by the client firm itself—are becoming more commonplace. Studying more than 1,000 plants in the U.S. metalworking and machinery sector, for instance, Harrison and Kelley found that in the mid-1980s, 57.4% of enterprises "usually" outsourced some part of their machining operations; it seems likely that this fraction has, if anything, only increased in the intervening years.[4] One (admittedly incomplete) indication of the trend in outsourcing and contracting out is provided by looking at growth within the business service sector. Between 1991 and 1995, for instance, the gross domestic product of the U.S. economy as a whole increased by 22.8%,[5] whereas receipts of firms in various business service sectors grew astronomically: 87% in "personnel supply services"; 61.3% in "computer programming, data processing, and other computer related services"; 54.7% in "security systems services"; and even 29.2% in "building cleaning and maintenance services, not elsewhere classified."[6] Using data from the U. S. Bureau of Labor Statistics for the 1980s, Richard Belous calculated that the total civilian labor force grew by 14% between 1980 and 1988; in contrast, his analysis produced the following estimates of the growth of outsourcing and contingent employment during that same period: temporary workers, 175%; part-time workers, 21%; business services, 70%; and self-employment, 19%.[7]

Given this extraordinary increase in the amount of outsourcing and contingent employment, and the intensity of positive and negative claims about its effects, there is surprisingly little hard evidence about the determinants and consequences of organizational outsourcing decisions. With regard to financial results, the existing studies are equivocal. Perhaps the most comprehensive study was conducted in 1993 by Coopers & Lybrand, involving 400 rapidly growing companies with revenues between $1 million and $50 million. Half used outsourcing, reporting average savings of 7.8% over providing the same services in-house. (About a third of the firms said they broke even and 4% reported that they lost money.)[8]

THE BOTTOM LINE

Which tasks should be outsourced, which should be assigned to contingent workers, and which should be given to the firm's own employees? To begin with the bottom line, outsourcing (of either variety) is relatively less appropriate for tasks:

- That are core activities, critical to the strategy or technology[9]
- That are highly interdependent technologically, locationally, or socially with core tasks
- That depend (for any of a variety of reasons) on workers internalizing the firm's welfare
- That require high levels of firm-specific human capital or access to proprietary information
- That are (temporally) open-ended
- That involve workers who are similar socially to the firm's regular employees

Outsourcing is relatively better suited to tasks:

- That require workers who don't fit well (in terms of culture, compensation scheme, etc.) vis-à-vis the organization's core employees
- In areas where the organization lacks expertise and cannot (comfortably) afford to maintain expertise
- Whose supervision would divert managerial attention from core issues

These bottom-line recommendations arise from three sets of differences among the alternative means for accomplishing tasks—regular employees of a firm, contingent workers, and employees of an independent contractor—that must be considered. We refer to these considerations as *transactional, social,* and *administrative* and take up each of them in turn.

Transactional Considerations

By transactional considerations, we mean the stuff of Chapter 4: the ability of the organization and the employee to form a long-term and flexible relationship, which can be adjusted to meet contingencies as they arise. It is virtually axiomatic that the relationship between the firm and its own employees has the potential to score highest in these terms, a potential that is realized when the relations between the firm and its employees are positive and constructive. Regular employees, if they feel that they have a future with and stake in the firm, will be more likely to invest in developing relation-specific assets, such as developing networks inside the firm, building close social relations with co-workers, and so forth. They are more willing to be redeployed and to accept temporarily onerous assignments if they think doing so will build up credit that they can draw on later, whether in the form of nicer assignments or a greater chance of promotion. Their duration of employment is apt to be longer; in part this is endogenous to the process—one hires temps to meet peak loads (see below)—but it also reflects self-selection processes. A clerical who chooses to work for a temp agency rather than working full-time in a standard employment relationship is more likely to be someone whose personal circumstances or tastes will lead to greater turnover. And because the anticipated duration of employment is longer for regular employees, it is easier to fashion incentives for tasks that are open-ended or whose outcomes will only arise after a considerable period of time. Longer (expected) spells of employment also mean that regular employees are better targets for training efforts, and that they are more likely to "soak up" the sorts of firm-specific human capital—for instance, networks of contacts in the firm—that require long periods on the job or with the firm.

The implications are clear. Obviously, you can't enslave or indenture any worker—not your employees, not a contingent worker, and not the employees of an independent contractor. Human capital can always pick up and leave. But the firm's own employees, because they are more likely to be around longer and to be more adaptable, represent better human capital for the firm's core competencies— the critical skills the firm needs to have (and to keep) if it is going to be profitable. Where firm-specific human capital is important, own-employees are better. In particular, tasks that require good working relationships with other workers or knowledge about who knows what inside the firm—a common feature of tasks that score high on interdependence—are best left to your own employees, as are tasks that are temporally open-ended or that can take years to come to fruition.

Empirical evidence on these points can be found in a study of engineers and engineering technicians in a large aerospace company in Southern California in the late 1980s, which designed and manufactured sophisticated equipment for air and space craft and which employed a substantial number of temps and independent contractors.[10] According to the study's author, when regular employees worked alongside contractors, the most interdependent tasks got shifted onto regular employees because supervisors felt they could not depend on contractors still being around when/if problems surfaced. Consequently, contractors were concentrated in the easiest-to-monitor and least open-ended, least interdependent assignments.

Of course, the HR policies of the firm for its regular employees play a role here. The value of having regular employees doing tasks that are sensitive in these ways is enhanced to the extent that regular employees do in fact stick around. In part, this will depend on local labor market conditions. But it will also depend on whether the firm offers employees career-length opportunities or short-term jobs; for firms that operate an ILM for their regular employees, these effects will be particularly strong.

With contingent workers and the employees of independent contractors, there is an alternative to the contractual flexibility that a firm has with its own employees: The firm can deal with the worker indirectly, by negotiating with the enterprise supplying the labor, whether a leasing firm or independent contractor. If the firm has a long-term relationship with the contractor, it may be possible to fashion a flexible yet long-term arrangement with the employees of the contractor—for instance, insist that the contractor assign a particular employee or team to the client firm in a long-term relationship or else risk losing the business. But this adds a layer of bureaucracy between the firm and the person(s) performing the work. There may be some alignment in the interests of the contractor and the firm, but that alignment is unlikely to be complete. For instance, it is hard to imagine that a client firm would provide general-skills training for contingent workers or employees of independent contractors or would "promote" or otherwise redeploy these sorts of workers; at least, it seems likely that the client firm would have to share any surplus gained from such training or redeployment with the enterprise that supplies the labor. And although a long-term relationship with a labor supply firm or independent contractor might allow the client organization to craft appropriate incentives for the contractor to undertake tasks that are open-ended or take a long time to come to fruition, the contractor will still have to find a way to pass these incentives on to its own employees. Depending on how permanent and flexible the relationship is between the contractor and its own employees, this can be a challenge.[11]

In some cases, however, it may actually be easier to craft longer-term incentives for contingent labor and/or employees of contractors than for own-employees. We have in mind the case of employees who work in technical specialties such as information services or legal services, where those services are used on an ongoing basis by a client firm but are not central to its activities. In such a case, the client firm will find it difficult to provide the specialists with career-length promotion ladders, so that working for the firm in one of these specialized capacities may out of necessity be something of a dead-end job. In comparison, contractor organizations that provide these services or that supply specialist contingent labor may have a clientele that is sufficiently large and diverse so that they can craft and maintain good (promotion-based) incentives for their employees, economically provide career-advancing training to their personnel, and the like.

Another sort of contracting difficulty arises anecdotally in the *Harvard Business Review* article, "When Outsourcing Goes Awry," in which the author describes the (we hope, apocryphal) story of a hospital that outsources its anesthesiology services.[12] The labor contractor that now stands contractually between the hospital and the anesthesiologists faces cash flow problems and allegations of cooked books (concerning incentive compensation for the anesthesiologists), and the hospital director faces a crisis: The anesthesiologists threaten to withhold services if he doesn't break his contract with the labor contractor. But the hospital director has no legal standing to do so. Indeed, the labor contractor in the story threatens the hospital director with a lawsuit if he breaches their contract or otherwise interferes in the contractual relationship between the contractor and the anesthesiologists. The motivation for this particularly silly bit of outsourcing was to economize on administrative costs (about which, see below). But for a hospital, there are few activities that are closer to the core than anesthesiology. The contracting loss of control that accompanies outsourcing this labor relationship is glaring.

Contractual concerns are especially important to firms whose strategies are based on continuous improvement of products and processes or involve the transfer of knowledge and know-how gained in one product, service, or division to other parts of the organization. These firms can suffer when outsourcing is done indiscriminately: If every element of production is interconnected, outsourcing even seemingly minor activities can limit the ability of core employees to have the kind of fully integrated understanding of products and processes sought as part of a TQM program. As *Business Week* put it, "[Some consultants] worry that if too many aspects of production, marketing, or distribution are handled outside the company, its ability to respond to changes in the marketplace could be undermined."[13] Of course, if long-term relations can be built with those to whom you have outsourced, this can help alleviate this potential problem. Recall that in many TQ campaigns, an important feature is that suppliers must be made part of the effort, with "rewards" realized in the form of an ongoing supplier–customer relationship. This, presumably, can extend to labor contractors as suppliers of labor services. But the extra contracting costs that will be entailed should not be ignored.

There is one caveat to make. Although we firmly believe that traditional employment relationships are more flexible in many ways than is either sort of outsourcing, there are some inflexibilities built into traditional employment. Most important, perhaps, is that traditional employment relations are flexible because they are long-term relationships. But this implies that traditional employment leads to less flexibility in terms of staffing levels. To put it baldly, it is a lot easier to match labor supply to the need for labor services if the workers involved are contingent workers, or if the relationship between the organization and the service provider is market-based.

Social Considerations

Being an employee of a firm confers social status; it entails "membership." This is important for processes of social comparison; an employee is generally more likely to compare herself to another similarly situated employee of the same organization than she is to a contract worker or, even more, to the employee of an outside contractor. Such comparisons are often important for purposes of inference about the implicit contract between the employee and the firm. How the boss treats a fellow employee is read by colleagues as an indication of how they can expect to be treated; how contingent workers or employees of outside contractors are treated, in contrast, is not so germane.[14] This brings us back to Chapters 3, 4, and 5 and notions about consistency of treatment, where here we have in mind consistency across individuals at a given point in time. And through various social and psychological processes, "membership" promotes attachments and thus internalization of the welfare of others. An employee of a particular organization is generally more likely to display loyalty and concern toward other employees and toward the enterprise itself than is a contingent worker or the employee of an independent contractor.[15] Of course, this depends on the organizational culture; but if we envision a continuum from arm's-length market relationships to kinship/friendship bonds, employees are almost always closest to the kinship/friendship pole, followed by contingent workers, and then employees of independent contractors.

This array of social distinctions leads to five sets of related considerations, involving legitimization of distinctions, trust and cooperation, internalization of the welfare of the organization by workers, intrinsic motivation, and dealing with dysfunctional relationships. We take each of these in turn:

Legitimizing Distinctions

By outsourcing a particular task entirely and, to a lesser extent, by using contingent labor, a firm may have an easier time legitimizing differences in treatment between those who carry out that task and the firm's regular employees. This is because social comparisons are attenuated and consistency of treatment is less of an issue. Where distinctive treatment is desirable—for instance, in terms of wages and benefits, employment guarantees, degree of autonomy, or training offered—outsourcing of either type can play a role.

For instance, the organizational culture of large paper manufacturers, with a delicate continuous-process technology in the middle of the production process, stresses adherence to established rules and procedures. One could imagine these firms integrating backward into logging. And, in fact, there is something to this: The biggest firms own and selectively harvest their own forests. But because loggers don't fit well within a culture that demands careful adherence to rules, the large paper manufacturers typically bring in contract labor or independent contractors to log the timber.

It is important to note that outsourcing can play a role in making or sustaining social distinctions, but it is neither necessary nor sufficient to do so. We discussed at length in Chapter 3 the span of consistency in HR practices and the devices available to an organization for making distinctions among employees. Moreover, merely imposing distinctions among regular employees, contingent workers, and outside employees does not preclude social comparisons. Social comparisons can and will take place across these boundaries if there are few other social

454 · Chapter 18: Outsourcing

distinctions or if the individuals involved must interact frequently because, say, their work is interdependent. Note that the external social environment will be important here. In Japan, for instance, distinctions in status and treatment between regular employees and contingent workers that are supported by differences in gender or schooling are legitimate; such distinctions would encounter greater resistance in the United States. Moreover, the employer can take steps to undergird the distinction between regular employees and contingent workers, such as placing the two groups in different working conditions. Indeed, physical separation can be quite significant; assigning contingent workers to a different facility or to shifts when the regulars are not around will make social comparisons and (in)consistency judgments more difficult. On these specific grounds (for example), warehouse operations, janitorial services, and nighttime security services are all excellent candidates for outsourcing.

As an aside, it is worth reiterating from Chapter 5 that organizations have some ability to influence the sorts of social comparisons that individuals can and do make, not only internally but externally as well. One fairly obvious means of manipulating external comparisons is through wage surveys and other benchmarking instruments that enable or even encourage regular employees to compare their treatment to personnel in other organizations. And sometimes, when a firm's regular employees must work closely with employees from contractor organizations and the client firm has a very strong culture and distinctive HR system, the client will insist that contractors have personnel policies comparable to its own, which will both facilitate collaboration between the two workforces and ensure that the client firm is not perceived by its own employees as straying from its values.

One other point concerning the making of distinctions should be noted. For organizations that rely very heavily on kinship notions, outsourcing to make distinctions is a two-edged sword. For such organizations, it is relatively more valuable to clarify the distinctions that are going to be made, and outsourcing provides a clear and discrete boundary. But the idea that tasks for the "family" should be carried out at all by nonmembers is somewhat alien to the culture, unless those tasks are clearly and distinctly peripheral to tasks carried out by members. In contrast, in an organization whose culture emphasizes competition and independence, outsourced labor will resonate better. Indeed, in such firms, we sometimes see flexible labor brought in to perform (nearly) the same tasks as the core workforce, to put pressure on the core.

Trust and Cooperation

To the extent that you rely on close cooperation and trust among workers—for instance, when work is highly interdependent, or when team-based job designs are employed—and to the extent that this cooperation is based on social bonds that form between workers, outsourcing, which creates social differences, is a bad idea. For example, in the study of the large aerospace firm cited earlier,[16] regular employees in work units using more contract laborers reported less organizational trust.

Internalizing the Welfare of the Organization

It is, we believe, nearly inevitable that contingent workers and the employees of independent contractors are going to be less concerned with the welfare of the company that is using their services than are the client firm's own employees. The former are generally less permanent; escalating commitment has less of an opportunity to take hold. They are generally less affected by gift–exchange processes, particularly insofar as the firm treats them distinctively *worse* than it does its own regular employees. Even in cases where their pay is higher, the fact that contingent employees are obtained "in the market" will lead to attributions that their high wages simply reflect market conditions. And indeed, their status as outsiders gives them less reason to identify with the firm for whom they happen to be toiling today.

This is of little concern for tasks that are easily monitored, where quality is not a great issue or is easily assessed, or where good extrinsic incentives can be provided. But it is of greater importance when the technology involves ambiguous tasks, when outcomes are harder to measure, where monitoring is difficult, and so on. To take a very specific example, when the work requires access to proprietary information, the use of contingent workers and employees of independent contractors usually involves greater risk. This is not to say that your own employees might not defect with important information, or that temps will blab your secrets all over town. But common-sense prudence suggests that organizational secrets are best kept by workers who are more closely tied emotionally and, in the long run, economically to the organization.[17]

Intrinsic Motivation

Although regular employees are usually more likely than contingent workers and contractors to internalize the welfare of the client company, the picture concerning intrinsic motivation is less clear. One might suspect that it is considerably easier to screen for and encourage intrinsic motivation to excel among regular employees than among contingent workers or outsourced labor. And there are certainly instances in which that prediction seems reasonable. For instance, the laundry, cleaning, and commissary personnel in a world-class hospital may derive special gratification from knowing that their hard work contributes to the delivery of first-rate medical services, whereas they might not feel such lofty motivations as employees of outsourcing companies that provided those specialized services. But we know of no clear evidence or theoretical rationale to suggest that regular employees are *necessarily* more (or less) prone to intrinsic motivation; it is likely to depend a great deal on the circumstances. To the extent that you rely on intrinsic motivation to obtain consummate effort, contingent workers and outside contractors may do just as well as your own employees. In some settings, contingent workers and outside contractors are just as likely to find the work itself fascinating, take pride in their craft, or embrace some superordinate goal, as are your regular employees. In fact, they may be even *more* motivated along those lines inasmuch as: (a) the

456 · Chapter 18: Outsourcing

greater variety and shorter average duration of their assignments may reduce boredom; and (b) working for a contractor organization that specializes in their craft or calling—for instance, software development, accounting, or law—may entail a stronger identification with that craft than would exist working as a full-time regular employee in some peripheral backwater within the client firm. The study we cited earlier of regular employees and contractors in the aerospace company found that the outside contractors were actually *more* willing to go beyond minimal job requirements than were the regular employees.

Indeed, even in outsourcing companies whose employees carry out seemingly menial tasks, inspired management has sometimes been able to fashion compelling visions and highly energizing cultures focused on those tasks, creating levels of intrinsic motivation that would seem hard to achieve among individuals carrying out those same tasks as regular employees of a client. A vivid example of this is ServiceMaster, the multi-billion-dollar outsourcing concern whose businesses include facilities maintenance, residential and commercial cleaning services, pest extermination, furniture repair, home inspection services, and management services for health care. Their corporate Web site summarizes the company's objectives:

> To honor God in all we do; To help people develop; To pursue excellence; and To grow profitably. . . . Realizing that facilitating the development of every employee to their fullest potential would result in a greater quality of work, training at all levels became a cornerstone of the ServiceMaster approach. ServiceMaster is committed to empowering people to serve by providing them with thorough training, and by developing and equipping them with tools and systems to do the job right.[18]

We believe that imparting such a vision and achieving these stated objectives might be considerably more challenging for someone managing these same service activities within, say, a large financial services institution or manufacturing company.

Dealing With Dysfunctional Relationships

To the extent that regular employment does smack more of a familial bond, there may be a greater role for contingent and outsourced labor when those bonds have begun taking the form of a dysfunctional family. To put it differently, sometimes the strong bonds that develop between firms and employees (or among employees) become dysfunctional. Suppose an organization has a particular employee, task, or subunit that is problematic (behaving counterproductively, receiving excess wages, resisting change, etc.) and is linked technically, socially, or culturally to other areas of the enterprise. In such circumstances, a pure outsourcing solution may be desirable to try and alter this equilibrium and minimize the contagion of these problems elsewhere in the organization.

Administrative Considerations

The employer must manage the employee, which includes negotiating with him (or his representative) and assigning him. The employer must also recruit, train, and compensate the employee. Contingent workers often must be directed by the client, but other administrative costs are usually the responsibility of the labor contractor. Employees of outside contractors impose no direct costs on the firm.

Of course, in lieu of some of the administrative costs that the client firm avoids by retaining a labor contractor, it must pay a fee or mark-up to the contracting company that supplies the contingent worker(s), which covers the contractor's costs of hiring and managing its own personnel (and presumably includes some profit as well). The client firm pays the same sort of mark-up if it elects to outsource the activity entirely to an independent contractor; the contractor's billing rate includes a charge (usually with some overhead tacked on) for the costs incurred by that contractor in administering its workforce. And, in addition, any savings by the client on direct administrative costs (in terms of dealing with workers) are reduced by the costs the client incurs in administering the relationship with the organization that is supplying contingent workers or contracted services. The point isn't that hiring workers through a labor contractor or buying services from an independent contractor avoids administrative costs entirely. But it is often the case that a labor or independent contractor can discharge the administrative tasks associated with workers more efficiently.

The relative administrative efficiencies of labor supply firms or independent contractors may be mundane, but they are often very important, presenting some of the best reasons for using outsourced labor:

- Outsourcing can economize on administrative costs for tasks requiring skills that are infrequently used by the firm or that present a substantial peak-load problem. Outside contractors and agencies supplying contingent workers can manage and deploy human capital efficiently by moving the human capital where it is needed, when it is needed. A small firm that only occasionally needs someone with talents as a Web site designer, for instance, might wish to hire a temporary IT professional with those skills (if the firm wishes to have a stronger hand in the design of its Web site) or an independent contractor who designs Web sites (if the firm is willing to leave most of the design decisions to the professional). Start-up firms often find it economical to contract out payroll preparation and HR-related government compliance to firms that specialize in providing these services to small firms. An architectural firm preparing a bid for a major project may wish to hire temporary draftspersons to meet the short-run needs of the bid.[19]
- Outsourcing labor can be a good idea for workers whose position in the labor market is one with which the firm has little contact. For example, a firm that consists primarily of professionals—individuals with postgraduate degrees—may need one or two clericals or a receptionist. Even if these needs are permanent and ongoing, it may be sensible to have the workers supplied by a temporary personnel supply agency or leasing firm, which can more economically search for, recruit, and handle such workers.
- Outsourcing can make sense for tasks that management doesn't wish to manage, because the activities either are thought to be beneath manage-

ment's concerns or require special knowledge that management lacks. Note that insofar as this is the rationale for outsourcing, it is the *task* (rather than the labor) that should be outsourced, contracting with an enterprise that will take responsibility for overseeing the activity (rather than relying on a labor contractor to supply contingent workers). Typical examples concern janitorial and landscaping services on the "bottom" of the spectrum, and outsourcing information technology (IT) on the top. (We will consider the case of outsourcing IT in detail a bit later.)

OUTSOURCING TO AVOID LEGAL LIABILITIES

An "administrative" reason sometimes cited for outsourcing—usually in hushed tones and not for attribution—is to avoid headaches that arise from legal responsibilities to employees. In the United States, for instance, certain categories of employees cannot be dismissed at the will of the employer; they can sue for wrongful termination. The employer bears some responsibility for the health and safety of its employees. The employer must negotiate in good faith with the selected representative of the workers, if they organize and choose a representative. The employer must respect some aspects of the privacy of its employees. Employers may not discriminate along a number of dimensions when it comes to hiring, promoting, firing, or (generally) in the treatment of workers. And so on.

The question is, How much of this liability does the employer avoid if, instead of employing a worker, it contracts with a labor contractor to provide a contingent worker to do the same job? How much does it avoid by hiring an outside contractor to do the work? There are a number of different scenarios in which this could be important; we provide three examples:[20]

1. Suppose the employer can duck legal liability for discrimination against women in promotions or for hiring undocumented aliens, by hiring through a labor or independent contractor. If liability stops with the contractor, then the limited liability of a contractor could protect the employer against large damage awards or criminal prosecution.

2. Suppose that the firm "hires" clericals through a temp agency and subjects them to a three-month "probationary period." During this period, the clericals remain nominally employees of the temp agency that sent them to this assignment. If a clerical doesn't work out, the firm informs the agency that the person's services are no longer needed—it was a temporary position after all—and the on-probation employee is terminated with no muss and no fuss. If the person does work out, however, he is quietly put on the regular payroll. (To make matters dicier, suppose the client firm does not feel compelled to inform probationees that they are on probation, by virtue of the fact that they are, after all, legally just temps.)

3. Suppose a firm procures its maintenance workers through a temp agency. If the workers at the temp agency vote to organize themselves

into a union, the firm might be able legally to avoid dealing with the union by finding another temp agency with nonunion labor. It couldn't refuse to deal with a union if the workers were its own employees. This, in turn, will have a substantial impact on the ability of temps at the original agency to organize; why vote for a union if it means that you will lose your job?

Employees of independent contractors are, by and large, the responsibility of the contractor. There are some notable exceptions to this legal principle, however. For instance, if the employees of an independent contractor work at a facility of the client's firm, the client retains liability for maintaining a work environment that is safe, free from harassment, and so forth. For competitive reasons, personnel supply companies and outsourcing firms will usually indemnify the client against damages arising from the negligent acts of the individuals they employ or assign, but that does not prevent a court from finding the client firm to be jointly and severally liable, particularly if there is a long-standing association between the client and the contractor. Courts have in some cases held a client firm liable for misdeeds conducted by the employee of a contractor working on the client's premises—for instance, when a contractor's employee sexually harasses an employee or customer of the client—arguing that because of the nature and longevity of the assignment, the client firm had (or should have had) knowledge of the behavior by the contractor's employee and should have taken steps to prevent it. Also, the courts have taken something of a hard line on the use of the title Independent Contractor, particularly when an employee supplied by a contractor works on a regular basis inside the client firm, taking direction from personnel who are employees of the client firm. The legal definitions must be met (in the opinion of the court)—sham transactions that label someone an independent contractor (or the employee of an independent contractor) in order to duck tax or other liabilities have been rejected by the courts and relevant regulators. Legislation is currently under consideration by the United States Congress that would clarify, for tax purposes, the distinction between employees and independent contractors and create the presumption of an employment relationship unless a set of eight requirements is met. (At present, the Internal Revenue Service has a set of 20 criteria that are used to determine employee versus independent contractor status under the common law.)[21]

As for contingent workers and the firm's legal responsibilities to them, the water is muddier still. The courts frown on sham transactions, to be sure. If, for instance, your maintenance workers in the United States are conducting a NLRB unionization election, you almost surely can't have one of your vice presidents quit, start a temp agency, take over all your maintenance workers, and then (you) threaten that you won't deal with this temp agency if its workers organize. The NLRB and the courts are going to see through this scheme. And we wonder how the courts would react to the "recruiting strategy" described above of hiring through a temp agency, with an undisclosed probation period. But even if it is accepted that the worker is not your employee but instead a contingent employee of a labor contractor, it isn't clear from legal precedent what your responsibilities are.

This is an area of evolving legal precedent; if the potential legal distinctions between employees, contingent workers, and the employees of outside contractors make such strategies appealing to you, you would be wise to take good legal advice. And we hope that you will consider the ethics of such strategies as well.

There is one other point to make about legal liability. The record on contingent workers and outsourcing suggests a positive correlation between reliance on their services and catastrophic service failures in some contexts. For instance, various studies have suggested that outsourcing of maintenance activities in the petrochemical and airline industries played a role in producing major disasters (explosions and crashes, respectively).[22] A number of contributing causes can be hypothesized. For reasons noted above, outsourced workers are sometimes less well-trained, less well-motivated, or of lower quality. Furthermore, these outcomes underscore the pitfalls in relying on outsourcing where there is a high degree of task interdependence among employees or difficulty in immediately monitoring task performance. Whatever the causes, though, where reliability or workplace safety is important, this adds to the costs of outsourcing. And the additional costs grow directly with the firm's liabilities (legal and otherwise) for maintaining reliable service or a safe work environment.

TWO MIXED CASES

To summarize broadly, outsourcing labor makes sense on three grounds: administrative cost savings; the desirability of making distinctions among workers; and (in some cases) the superior ability of the contractor to craft longer-run, promotion-based incentives. But outsourcing often entails a significant loss of transactional flexibility,[23] making it inappropriate for core tasks. And it works against processes by which the worker internalizes the welfare of the organization for whom the tasks are actually performed.

Though we have identified a number of factors that bear on decisions concerning whether and how to outsource a specific activity, two broad considerations seem critical: (a) the degree to which the task is strategically important for the firm, that is, whether it is a core competence; and (b) the degree to which the activity displays high technical or social interdependence with tasks done by regular employees.[24] Figure 18-1 provides a simplified diagnostic tool for thinking about whether and how to outsource a particular activity. Clearly, tasks that are strategically important and highly interdependent—for instance, the above-mentioned example of anesthesiology for a hospital—are bad candidates for outsourcing. Conversely, tasks that are strategically unimportant and only loosely connected to the other tasks of the firm—groundskeeping services or logging timber are good examples—are better candidates for outsourcing. For such tasks, the efficacy of an outsourcing arrangement depends primarily on the cost savings and flexibility (broadly defined) that the client firm realizes.

But what about cases that are mixed on these two dimensions? Consider first those activities that are not core competencies but that are highly interdependent with other key tasks, depicted in the lower right-hand cell of Figure 18-1. Recall,

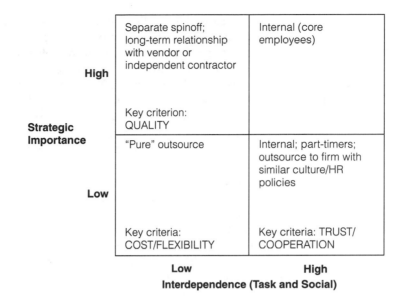

	Low	High
High	Separate spinoff; long-term relationship with vendor or independent contractor Key criterion: QUALITY	Internal (core employees)
Low	"Pure" outsource Key criteria: COST/FLEXIBILITY	Internal; part-timers; outsource to firm with similar culture/HR policies Key criteria: TRUST/ COOPERATION

Strategic Importance

Interdependence (Task and Social)

Figure 18-1 When and how to outsource activities: A diagnostic.

for instance, the Portman Hotel, which we discussed in Chapter 3, in which "personal valets" (PVs) were supposed to deliver unrivaled and uncompromising "Asian-style" service to a well-heeled clientele. The PV tasks were certainly strategically important and highly interdependent with virtually every other segment of Portman's workforce. But what about the maids and other personnel providing the lower-value-added services in guestrooms? Given Portman's strategy and the way the hotel chose to organize, we would argue there were strong technical and social interdependencies. To deliver seamless high-quality service, all the employees who serve guests must cooperate. By delivering substandard service, the maids as a group certainly have the capacity to undermine the efforts of the PVs, whose performance is critical to the Portman strategy. Furthermore, recall that the hotel's management had espoused a very inclusive culture and faced potential resistance from militant unions that represent hotel employees in San Francisco. These factors argue against either treating the maids as a completely different "class" within the Portman labor force or outsourcing this activity in a purely arm's-length way. Rather, we suggest that for activities that are highly interdependent but not strategically important, the firm will generally want to utilize insiders or a form of contingent labor that resembles regular employees (part-timers or the services of an outsourcing vendor that has HR practices and a culture similar to the client firm). Because of the acute interdependencies with key tasks in the organization, the firm contemplating outsourcing should be especially concerned about the potential effects of outsourcing on trust and cooperation. Put differently, the client firm outsourcing under these conditions should be willing to pay a fairly significant premium to ensure that trust and cooperation are not undermined among employees performing the core tasks.

The other mixed case, depicted in the upper left-hand cell of Figure 18-1, concerns tasks that are strategically important but not highly interdependent with other key activities in the organization, either in terms of workflow or social relationships. Examples here might include garment design for a clothing manufacturer, the lobbying function in a heavily regulated firm, or the R&D lab in a pharmaceutical company. Insofar as these activities are not highly interdependent with other parts of the organization, there may be some reasons to consider outsourcing them—for instance, to tap a more diverse portfolio of talent than the firm could afford to retain on its regular payroll (e.g., by using multiple suppliers), or because it would be controversial to pay the market wage to an insider carrying out this activity, or because the organization's needs change so rapidly that outsourcing makes it easier for the firm to avoid having to make bets on given individuals who may turn out to have obsolete skills. However, because the activities being conducted are strategically important, the same sort of reputational benefits realized through long-term employment are likely to be valuable to the firm, suggesting that long-term relations with the suppliers of contract services may come to supplant long-term relations with employees for carrying out these tasks. In particular, when it comes to activities such as the creation of new technologies or the management of relations with specific important clients—activities in which the human capital involved is the valuable strategic asset—firms that outsource these tasks must have some means for capturing the rents generated by this capital.

Whatever form outsourcing takes, a firm that outsources strategically critical tasks should attend carefully to the *quality* of the services being provided by outside providers. This is not to say that cost or flexibility are unimportant, but simply that the firm should be willing to pay a cost premium to ensure work of the highest quality, given its strategic importance, just as it should be willing to pay something of a cost premium to ensure work that does not undermine trust and cooperation for tasks that are highly interdependent.

THE CASE OF INFORMATION TECHNOLOGY

A very interesting—and, for many organizations, increasingly salient—example of these issues concerns information technology. A number of firms, some as big as Eastman Kodak, have pursued strategies of outsourcing information technology (IT).[25] Several different rationales are offered for this, but the typical rationales mix two factors. First, the organization desires to differentiate IT personnel from regular employees. IT professionals sometimes command off-scale compensation (including, increasingly, stock options), and they often expect nonstandard treatment, such as an ability to work strange hours, wear beards, bring their pets to work, or wear nonstandard attire. Companies with strong cultures sometimes discover that IT pros don't fit in and have little desire to do so; their loyalties are to their work, not to an organization. The second rationale is that the organization's management (particularly in smaller firms) feels that it is unable to stay on top of developments in IT or maintain up-to-date expertise in-house, given the dizzying pace of change and the complexity of the underlying technologies. Top management also sometimes worries that its IT professionals can use their command of arcane knowledge to carve out and then pad a cost-ineffective empire. Hiring an outside IT vendor, it is asserted, will give the firm access to cutting-edge developments, obtained from a vendor with little incentive except to deliver the best and most cost-efficient IT services. This sort of rationale figured strongly, for instance, in Kodak's decision to outsource IT. Needless to say, if management is outsourcing IT on these grounds, it had better be confident that the IT vendor won't take advantage, given that the decision to outsource essentially represents an admission by the client firm that it knows less about how to manage IT than the contractor does. The client must rely, then, on the IT vendor's interest in an ongoing relationship, which depends on management's ability to judge end results; or on the IT vendor's interests in maintaining a general reputation for being a conscientious supplier, which depends on other parties' abilities to judge the end results.

But these rationales for outsourcing IT potentially run up against the interdependence and strategic importance considerations discussed in the previous section. If IT is used, say, primarily for data processing—preparing payroll and the like—then there is no countervailing issue. (Indeed, EDS and H. Ross Perot made quite a lot of money providing just this sort of computer service.) Increasingly, however, IT is highly interdependent with other activities in the organization. In many cases, it is strategically important. And the rapid pace of change in what is available makes it difficult for clients and providers to agree on what level of service—especially, how frequently things should be updated—is contractually appropriate. Perhaps for these reasons, IT outsourcing, which has been fashionable, has recently faced something of a backlash. A recent *Information Week* article quotes a study by Deloitte & Touche Consulting Group, which asserts that IT outsourcing often fails to satisfy clients, when it comes to moving to new technologies or on basic provider knowledge.[26]

Recall from Chapter 3 that precisely such considerations figured in UPS's decision to build an in-house IT capability. UPS viewed its ability to respond to customer information requests and its own ability to track packages accurately—both of which would depend heavily on IT—as key competitive weapons in the future. And for IT to work at UPS, it would have to be integrated seamlessly into every aspect of their complex operational network and be deployed willingly by package car drivers working autonomously around the globe, the heart and soul of UPS's regular employee workforce.

Whereas UPS came largely down on the side of in-house IT, in other instances an outsourcing strategy makes perfect sense. The administrative cost savings can be substantial, and IT professionals will not fit so well as employees within some organizations. There are significant tradeoffs here, and there is no clear consensus on the cost-effectiveness of outsourcing IT, precisely because cost-effectiveness will depend on specific circumstances. This was precisely the point of Figure 18-1: An organization in which IT was less strategically important, or in which technical, social, and institutional forces (e.g., unionization) did not create such strong inter-dependencies across segments of the workforce, might well reach a different decision than did UPS.

OUTSOURCING AND DOWNSIZING

This completes our discussion of "greenfield" outsourcing. What about outsourcing tied to downsizing? From the previous chapter, recall that the connection between the two arises because many downsizing campaigns include outsourcing as a part of a company's strategy to divest itself of tasks previously done in-house. Indeed, in some cases (usually involving lower-skilled personnel), the individuals who last week were regular employers of a firm find themselves out of a job, but referred for possible employment to the outside contractor to whom the activity has been outsourced, albeit under worse terms of employment. In other cases, especially where the workers are highly skilled professionals, they are out of a job and then hired back by their previous employer as independent contractors or consultants, possibly on *better* terms than before. In an article entitled "More Downsized Workers Are Returning as Rentals," the *New York Times* reported in late 1996 on a government study, which found in 1995 that 17% of contingent workers had had a "previous different relationship" with the company that now retained their services; the fraction exceeded 22% for individuals currently working as self-employed independent contractors.[27]

As we've indicated, there are cases in which outsourcing makes sense. And for some organizations, this particular sort of outsourcing, of tasks formerly conducted in-house, lies well within the *makes-sense* category. Organizations can and do grow into doing tasks that: (1) dilute worker and management focus; (2) pad the payroll with workers and skills that are not really needed on a full-time basis; or (3) either compromise the consistency of HR practices or, in pursuit of consistency, extend HR practices uneconomically to groups of employees for whom those practices are ill-suited. In such cases, intelligent decisions to outsource activities or workers, which of course entails downsizing, make excellent economic sense. The ideas developed earlier in this chapter apply. But some cautions are in order.

When outsourcing is done to differentiate between the outsourced workers and regular employees, if there was and remains a lot of interaction between the two groups, and if the outsourced workers are former employees, the tactic is of dubious value. If A and B were co-workers last year, any sense of social similarity that they may have developed will not be easily dissipated simply by changing the name of B's employer. This is exacerbated when the organization involved has a familial culture to begin with.[28]

When outsourcing results in former employees working under markedly worse conditions for a labor contractor or as independent contractors, some resentment and ill will is natural. For some jobs—those where the quality of work either is not a major issue or is easily monitored—this may not be a problem. But where the quality of work is important and hard to monitor (in service functions, for example), a resentful workforce is unlikely to provide much in the way of quality efforts.

Outsourcing that turns former employees into consultants can make substantial sense if the employee-turned-consultant was underworked previously and can be employed as a consultant for a fraction of her time, supplementing her consultant fees with other opportunities that do not reflect a conflict of interest. This scenario is not unreasonable, but in some cases the outsourced-employee-turned-consultant phenomenon is the result of organizational higher-ups directing subordinate managers to downsize, leading those subordinate managers to play accounting games that cost the firm more but make the managers look like they've done what they were told to do.

Some firms have lately been experimenting with an alternative to outsourcing in this sort of case: Group a set of activities previously done in-house into a freestanding "shared service center," sometimes housed in an administratively separate entity, which charges business units within the enterprise for its services. In certain cases, this unit may even sell its services on the open market. For example, IBM has attempted to apply this approach with its "Workforce Solutions" HR consulting entity, which combined several functions previously done through the corporate HR function into a freestanding consulting unit.[29] Or a multimedia production company spun off as a separate business by a large on-line service provider such as America Online might sell its creative services to other businesses. This can help compensate for temporary dips in the demand for the unit's services by the parent company. Furthermore, the creativity and cost competitiveness required to bid successfully for outside business exacts a healthy discipline on the unit, which may improve its performance for the parent.

SUMMARY AND COMING ATTRACTIONS

In many ways, the issue of outsourcing goes to the very heart of our approach to HRM, because it is fundamentally about the relationships—economic, social, psychological, and legal—between employers and employees, as well as among employees. In a comparative way (that is, comparing employee-ship to other forms of transacting for labor services), it brings together most of what this book has been about. Hence, this chapter has not sought to introduce new concepts, but rather to show how some of the ideas developed throughout this book can help inform your thinking about an important set of issues with which contemporary organizations are grappling.

We have noted throughout this book how history and custom within organizations often make it difficult and costly to alter employment relationships. The trends toward downsizing and outsourcing discussed in this chapter and the preceding one presumably reflect efforts by contemporary organizations to overcome those inertial forces and realign themselves with dramatically changed business environments. The fact that companies like Kodak, IBM, and Levi Strauss—who helped pioneer high-commitment HRM—are among the organizations making headlines by announcing large-scale layoffs may reflect some of the inflexibilities and rigidities associated with internal labor markets, employment security, and high-commitment work systems that we noted in earlier chapters—inflexibilities in how different workers are treated, in workforce levels, and the like. This raises an obvious and important question, especially for those interested in creating their own organizations: Are there ways to build an organization and design its HR system from the outset that minimize these inflexibilities and rigidities? Where does inertia in an organization's employment system come from? When and how can it be overcome? To examine those concerns, we turn next to the topic of human resource management in new enterprises.

IN REVIEW

⇒ Organizations nowadays are increasingly relying on outsourcing to meet their labor force requirements, by hiring "temps" from labor contractors, purchasing specific services from independent contractors, and employing a host of strategies intermediate between these two.

⇒ In deciding whether to rely on traditional labor or outsourced labor, three sets of differences between traditional employees and outsourced labor should be attended to:

- Traditional employment relations are generally more flexible transactionally, although outsourced labor usually affords greater flexibility in staffing levels.
- Traditional employment relations usually confer "membership" in the organization. Hence, outsourcing can be used to legitimize distinctive treatment of workers. But outsourced workers are less likely to exhibit trust or be cooperative, and they are less likely to internalize the welfare of the organization. (It is unclear which form is best in terms of intrinsic motivation.)
- Outsourcing labor can sometimes promote administrative efficiencies, especially for types of labor that are atypical for the firm.

⇒ The bottom line is that outsourcing is generally a bad idea for activities that: are part of the organization's "core"; are closely linked spatially, technologically, or socially to core activities; depend on workers internalizing the organization's welfare; require high levels of firm-specific human capital; involve proprietary information; are open-ended; or involve workers who are socially similar to regular employees. Outsourcing is usually a better idea for jobs that require workers who don't fit within the culture of the organization or whose skills and other attributes make them atypical for the firm, and for tasks the oversight of which would divert management attention from core activities.

- In outsourcing tasks that are highly interdependent with core activities, maintaining trust and cooperation with regular employees carrying out those core activities is paramount. Consequently, it is often advantageous in such cases to make use of contingent workers (part-timers or temps) who resemble or are compatible with the client's workforce, or to retain contractor firms whose cultures and HR practices are similar to those of the client.
  - In outsourcing tasks that are strategically important, quality and the ability to monitor results are paramount. It is often beneficial in such cases to spin off a separate organizational unit to handle such tasks; or to develop long-term relations with the labor suppliers or independent contractors involved, so that they have incentives to develop firm-specific knowledge and to maintain quality.

⇒ Some organizations have chosen outsourcing in an attempt to avoid or minimize legal liabilities. If you are thinking of outsourcing for these reasons, take good legal advice; it isn't as simple or straightforward as you might think.

⇒ When outsourcing is tied to downsizing, further considerations arise.
  - "Assigning" former employees to an independent labor contractor or service provider and then "hiring" them back as outsourced labor can be contentious, particularly when the former employees remain closely tied to regular employees (which will make it less legitimate to treat the two groups differently).
  - An alternative to the downsizing/outsourcing combination, especially for employees who are "underworked" in the organization, is to enable those employees to provide services to external clients, as well as internally.

ENDNOTES

1. The specific searches were conducted on October 13, 1998 and employed the Alta Vista search engine to search web pages created or last modified in the preceding three years, requiring an exact phrase match to: "outsourc*"; "core competenc*" or "core capabilit*"; "contrac* out"; "chicago bull*"; and "tom cruise" (where the asterisk denotes a wildcard search and matches included upper- or lowercase letters). Limiting the search to Web page *titles* yielded roughly the same pattern.

2. U.S. Bureau of Labor Statistics tabulations, viewable on-line at: http://stats.bls.gov/news.release/conemp.toc.htm, particularly Table 13. For the interested reader, that Web site also provides tables describing differences among workers in different types of employment arrangements with respect to age, education, type of work, industry, and the like, which are not controlled in these simple wage averages.

3. *Ibid.*

4. Bennett Harrison and Maryellen R. Kelley, "Outsourcing and the Search for 'Flexibility,'" *Work, Employment & Society* 7 (June 1993): 213–35.

5. Bureau of Economic Analysis, "Summary National Income and Product Series, 1929–96," *Survey of Current Business* (August 1997): 148.

6. U.S. Bureau of the Census, *Service Annual Survey: 1995* (BS/95) (Washington: U.S. Department of Commerce, Bureau of the Census, 1997), Table 4.1.

7. Richard S. Belous, *The Contingent Economy: The Growth of the Temporary, Part-time and Subcontracted Workforce* (Washington: National Planning Association, 1989), p. 16. For more recent descriptive data, see Lewis M. Segal and Daniel G. Sullivan, "The Growth of Temporary Services Work," *Journal of Economic Perspectives* 11 (Spring 1997): 117–36.

8. Sana Siwolop, "Outsourcing: Savings Are Just the Start," *Business Week* 3475 (May 13, 1996): 24.

9. In determining how critical a given task or activity is, among the factors to be considered are: whether the task provides competitive advantage (by contributing significantly to customer perceptions about what differentiates the organization); whether the task is one that can be applied across multiple business units of the enterprise; and whether the task is one that is hard for others to imitate.

10. Jone L. Pearce, "Toward an Organizational Behavior of Contract Laborers: Their Psychological Involvement and Effects on Employee Co-workers," *Academy of Management Journal* 36 (October 1993): 1082–96.

11. Having said all this, we must note that extraordinarily tight relationships between firms are possible—such as between Japanese auto assemblers and their networks of subcontractors—so there are no absolutes here. Our assertions here reflect typical conditions, but we don't doubt that there are counterexamples. Though we know of little hard data, both scholars and managers seem to believe that continuity in the personal relationships among the individuals who broker these interorganizational relationships contributes significantly to their effectiveness, suggesting that long-term employment relations may be important for the employees who play that brokerage role.

12. Richard Peisch, "When Outsourcing Goes Awry," *Harvard Business Review* 73 (May–June 1995): 24–37.

13. Siwolop, *op. cit*.

14. But remember that we are discussing outsourcing decisions *de novo* here, that is, without the historical baggage of a previous employer–employee relationship. Later in this chapter, we will discuss outsourcing tasks that previously were done internally and, to take the most extreme case, turning your own (former) employees into the employees of an outside contractor. Your remaining employees will certainly draw inferences from such changes in status about what might happen to them. Perhaps the best and most accurate way to put this is that social connections cannot be sundered simply by reconfiguring who is the legal employer of record; once a connection is made, it is not so easily unmade.

15. For some supportive evidence on contingent workers in Singapore, see Linn Van Dyne and Soon Ang, "Organizational Citizenship Behavior of Contingent Workers in Singapore," *Academy of Management Journal* 41 (December 1998): 692–703.

16. Pearce, *op. cit*.

17. However, we reiterate a point made in the previous subsection—namely, in some cases, especially technical specialties, independent contractors and labor contractors may have

an advantage over the client firm in crafting long-run incentives based on promotion ladders and the like.

18. On-line at: http://www.servicemaster.com/story.htm.

19. This administrative efficiency of outsourcing is, of course, closely related to the transactional efficiency we mentioned earlier; viz., it is generally easier to match staffing levels to needs with contingent workers or with independent contractors than with regular employees.

20. We are not endorsing these three stratagems. Indeed, we find each to be ethically troublesome, to say the least.

21. The criteria used by the Internal Revenue Service to determine independent contractor status (explained in Revenue Ruling 87-41, 1987-1 CB 296) are: (1) Does the principal (the party whose tax return is under consideration) provide instructions to the worker about when, where, and how he or she is to perform the work? (2) Does the principal provide training to the worker? (3) Are the services provided by the worker integrated into the principal's business operations? (4) Must the services be rendered personally by the worker? (5) Does the principal hire, supervise, and pay assistants to the worker? (6) Is there a continuing relationship between the principal and the worker? (7) Does the principal set the work hours and schedule? (8) Does the worker devote substantially full time to the business of the principal? (9) Is the work performed on the principal's premises? (10) Is the worker required to perform the services in an order or sequence set by the principal? (11) Is the worker required to submit oral or written reports to the principal? (12) Is the worker paid by the hour, week, or month? (13) Does the principal have the right to discharge the worker at will? (14) Can the worker terminate his or her relationship with the principal any time he or she wishes without incurring liability to the principal? (15) Does the principal pay the business or traveling expenses of the worker? (16) Does the worker furnish significant tools, materials and equipment? (17) Does the worker have a significant investment in facilities? (18) Can the worker realize a profit or loss as a result of his or her services? (19) Does the worker provide services for more than one firm at a time? (20) Does the worker make his or her services available to the general public? For items 1-15, an affirmative response means the worker is an employee; for items 16-20, a "yes" answer means the worker is an independent contractor.

22. For instance, see James T. McKenna, "Third-Party Shops Face Safety, Legal Reviews," *Aviation Week & Space Technology* 145 (November 4, 1996): 90; James B. Rebitzer, "Job Safety and Contract Workers in the Petrochemical Industry," *Industrial Relations* 34 (January 1995): 40–57.

23. Except for flexibility in staffing levels.

24. To gauge technical interdependence, you should consider such factors as how central the task is within the workflow and how much spatial proximity is required. In assessing social or cultural interdependence, consider how much the firm and societal culture stresses egalitarianism; how much formal and informal information sharing there is; how homogeneous the workforce is; and what legal, political, and institutional forces (e.g., unions) inhibit or facilitate differentiated treatment of distinct groups of labor.

25. Kodak, it should be noted, decided to outsource IT after previously doing this in-house; its IT employees were "assigned" to one of three IT vendors that Kodak selected. The Kodak case is quite interesting and is well worth pondering in depth. See Lynda M. Applegate and Ramiro Montealegre, *Eastman Kodak Co.: Managing Information Systems Through Strategic Alliances,* Harvard Business School case 9–192–030; and Lynda

M. Applegate, Herminia Ibarra, and Keri Ostrofsky, *Digital Equipment Corporation: The Kodak Outsourcing Agreement (A,B),* Harvard Business School cases 9–191–039 and 9–191–040, respectively.

26. Bruce Caldwell with Marianne Kolbasuk McGee, "Outsourcing Backlash—Many Companies Aren't Getting What They Wanted from Their Outsourcing Deals," *Information Week* 650 (September 29, 1997): 14.

27. Louis Uchitelle, "More Downsized Workers Are Returning as Rentals," *New York Times* (December 8, 1996): 1, 34.

28. The case of IT outsourcing at Kodak presents an interesting inversion of this problem. Kodak's IT workers were meant to be absorbed by the three IT contractors that Kodak dealt with: IBM, Digital, and Businessland (see *Eastman Kodak Co.: Managing Information Systems Through Strategic Alliances, op. cit.*). In fact, Kodak, as a caring employer, laid a great deal of importance on the fact that these three employers had the same sort of familial, caring HR system. But one wonders how the three contractors felt about their new employees, who remained resident in Rochester, often with a spouse who continued to work for Kodak. The thought that there might be some divided loyalties involved cannot have escaped the notice of the three contractors, leading to some interesting HR questions about how to manage the new employees.

29. Regina Connell, "Corporate Strategies: Learning to Share," *Journal of Business Strategy* 17 (March/April 1996): 55–8.

19

HRM IN EMERGING COMPANIES

Imagine that you are considering starting your own firm. You've been contacted by a college acquaintance—a brilliant biology student—who tells you that while in graduate school she developed a procedure in the lab that she believes has considerable commercial potential. This classmate makes it clear that she has little interest in or expertise at managing people, and she wants you to join her in founding a company in which you will handle the management chores and she will be responsible for developing the technology and product applications. You've always wanted to get in on the ground floor of such an entrepreneurial venture, and you are convinced this acquaintance has the sort of brilliance that could lead to tremendous success. So you decide to think hard about her offer.

Needless to say, there are lots of things you'd better start thinking about concerning product development, financing the venture and managing cash flow problems, and (perhaps somewhere down the road) production and marketing. Included on your list of things to think about—and we hope, after having read this far in this book, *at or near the top of your list*—should be the human resource practices you plan to adopt in founding and staffing this organization. This is particularly true given the critical role that attracting and retaining talented people is likely to play in a science-based venture such as this.

But even if you have no interest in ever building your own company or working in a start-up, we think there are some very good reasons, both pedagogical and practical, for looking at human resource management in young emerging organizations. First, one can be led considerably astray when the theory, research, business press articles, and managerial testimonials available to guide you are all based exclusively or primarily on the experiences of relatively large, long-lived organizations, as is true in the domain of HRM. There is simply much more information available about the HR practices and performance of established enterprises than there is about new ventures, and many popular and influential management books have sought to derive broader insights and principles by examining the characteristics of companies that have remained successful over long periods of time. Those studies can be illuminating, but they have some drawbacks from both a scholarly and a managerial vantage point.

From a scholar's perspective, the danger in drawing inferences from long-lived or seemingly successful organizations is that one typically lacks information on the enterprises that have *failed* over the same period. One suspects, for instance, that the vast majority of successful firms have had male chief executives, and a large number no doubt have had mini-blinds[1] on their office windows. But one would be reluctant to conclude that these characteristics contribute to organizational success, particularly because it is quite likely that most firms that *failed* over the same period also were led by male CEOs and had mini-blinds on their windows.

From a managerial and policy perspective, studies of leading-edge HR practices in well-established corporations are also of limited value. Even if such studies can cast light on effective HRM in other large corporations, they are of less help to the entrepreneur wishing to draft an HR blueprint for a new organization or for the manager striving to achieve excellence in a smaller, emerging enterprise. Moreover, the vital role that small, young, rapidly growing organizations play in generating new jobs within the economy has been widely noted,[2] which underscores the importance of understanding human resource management in emerging companies for those concerned with employment policy and economic development.

There is another important reason for looking in some detail at the evolution of HRM within young emerging organizations: It provides a powerful lens for examining some of the topics and themes that have occupied us throughout this book. We have emphasized the path-dependent character of employment relations—that is, the powerful and enduring effects of early events on the subsequent evolution of HRM. We have stressed the importance of crafting personnel policies that are closely aligned with the organizational context and that display strong internal consistency and complementarity. And we have noted how organizations can benefit by structuring employment relations that leverage the cognitive and cultural "baggage" or expectations that employees bring with them from other social roles and experiences. Examining the birth and early evolution of employment practices in new organizations can provide important insights into all of these processes.

This chapter is somewhat different from others in this book. It reviews and interprets *one* set of research evidence bearing on human resource management in nascent organizations, providing more details about research design and a lot more of the primary data than has been the case in earlier chapters. (We'll try to keep the statistical mumbo–jumbo to a minimum or, at least, to the endnotes.) Words like *tentative* and *suggestive* are invoked fairly often. The reason for this is that the topic of this chapter—HRM in emerging companies—is less well researched than the topics of other chapters. We can't redact from many different studies to offer broad-brush conclusions. So we'll do what we can, which is tell you what the data are and then offer our own interpretations.

This does provide one added benefit. We've drawn many broad conclusions throughout this book, and although we've tried to provide references to the original conceptual and empirical research that underlies our conclusions, we haven't always been explicit about how the conclusions were generated from the data and from allied conceptual frameworks. This chapter takes you a lot closer to the process of research that was used to produce the ideas in this book, giving you (we hope) a better appreciation of that process. We believe this is useful because the capacity to digest and critically evaluate management research is a valuable skill for the would-be general manager or entrepreneur.

A SOURCE OF DATA ON HRM IN NEW ENTERPRISES: THE STANFORD PROJECT ON EMERGING COMPANIES

Until recently, there was little in the way of systematic research on the human resource practices and policies of emerging companies. However, a research project in which one of the authors has been involved, the *Stanford Project on Emerging Companies* (SPEC), has recently gathered comprehensive information on the founding conditions and early histories of roughly 170 firms in the Silicon Valley's high-technology sector.[3] The sample consists primarily of companies in the following industries: computer hardware and/or software; semiconductor devices, manufacturing equipment and testing instruments; telecommunications and networking; and medical devices and biotechnology. The sampled firms, which were first visited in 1994–95, had ten or more employees by the beginning of the study period and (with a few exceptions) were founded since 1984. Founders were asked (through surveys and face-to-face interviews) to recount: the details of the founding; their own professional background; the role of external partners and stakeholders; and whether there was a clear organizational model or blueprint in creating the enterprise (and, if so, where it came from). Founders were also asked to report on the organizational structure and HR practices at the firm's inception and to identify the timing and nature of major organizational changes or milestones. The CEO in 1994–95, who was one of the original founders in about 60% of the firms, was asked to provide detailed information on the firm's then-current strategy, structure, and business environment. The senior executive with primary oversight over human resource matters was surveyed and then interviewed at length, providing extensive information about the firm's past and current employment practices. These interviews were supplemented with documents that record the history of the firm, its organization, and its personnel practices (e.g., initial business plans, personnel manuals and reports, annual reports, 10K forms for public firms, newspaper articles, press releases). These disparate sources of information were transcribed and converted into formats amenable to computer analysis, and the sample of firms is being tracked and revisited over time to obtain updates on the business environment, top management team, corporate strategy, financing, organizational structure and performance, and human resource practices.

The project is ongoing—data continue to be collected, coded, and analyzed—and (at the time this book was written) it is too soon to provide "final results," let alone answers to many key questions.[4] Although 170 detailed company histories may sound like a large sample (and represents an ambitious undertaking, especially considering the range of information gathered), the number of factors and dimensions involved when one examines firms' HR practices and policies and their connections to strategy and environment, both statically and dynamically, is staggering. One hundred and seventy firms will not be a large enough data set to settle many contentious issues or to determine causation in many instances. Nonetheless, the data collected and analyzed so far provide valuable—albeit preliminary and tentative—insight into some strategic issues of HRM that have preoccupied us throughout this book.

FOUNDERS' BLUEPRINTS FOR HRM

The first analyses to emerge from SPEC concern how those who created organizations *conceived of* employment relations. The SPEC researchers examined the premises and conceptions held by the founders, rather than just looking at differences in early HR practices. The researchers suspected that when organizations are still very young and small, they might vary less in their specific HR practices than in the founders' premises and conceptions concerning HRM, which subsequently become institutionalized in organizational structures and practices. Accordingly, the founders were asked whether or not they had a particular "organizational model or blueprint in mind when [you] founded the company." (The CEOs were asked a parallel question about the present.) Roughly two-thirds of the founders interviewed gave responses suggesting they had some sort of organizational model, with almost half expressing a very clear blueprint, sometimes citing a specific organization as an illustration of what they wanted their firm to look like (or *not* to look like). Others strongly opposed having a clear organizational model, arguing that a company should become successful before it committed to any particular blueprint.

Three Dimensions

From their interviews, the researchers concluded that founders' images regarding employment relationships varied along three underlying dimensions: the primary basis of organizational attachment (what binds employees to the firm and/or the work); the primary criterion to be emphasized in selecting employees; and the primary means for controlling and coordinating work. Along each of these dimensions, in turn, they found that founders' responses tended to fall into one of several distinct categories or subtypes:

Basis of Attachment

Founders articulated three different bases of attachment, which the researchers called *love, work,* and *money.*[5] (1) Some founders wanted to create a family-like feeling and cultivate strong emotional bonds with employees that would inspire superior effort and increase retention of highly sought employees, thereby avoiding the frequent turnover of key personnel that plagues many Silicon Valley start-ups. What binds the employee to the firm in this model is *love*—a sense of personal belonging and identification with the company. (2) Many firms in the SPEC sample pursue cutting-edge technology, and many founders envisioned that employees would be motivated primarily by the desire to work at the technological frontier. Recognizing this, these founders emphasized providing opportunities for professional development through interesting and challenging *work* as the basis for attracting, motivating, and (perhaps) retaining employees. According to this model, employees weren't expected to display loyalty to the firm, the boss, or even co-workers *per se,* but instead to the project. (3) Finally, some founders stated that they regarded the employment relationship as a simple exchange of labor for *money*; employees would be bound to the organization through the incentives provided by salary, equity shares, and other forms of tangible compensation, or by the fear of job loss.

Selection Criterion

A second dimension concerns the primary basis for selecting employees. (1) Some founders seemed to conceive of jobs within their firms as bundles of tasks, seeking employees to carry out particular bundles effectively. Time and money tended to be the primary concerns here, so the focus was on selecting employees whom founders could bring on board and get up to speed as quickly and inexpensively as possible. In these cases, the founders envisioned selecting employees with the specific *skills* and experience needed to accomplish some immediate task(s). (2) Other founders focused less on immediate and well-defined tasks than on a series of projects, often not yet even envisioned, through which they expected employees to move over time. Accordingly, their focus was on long-term *potential*. (3) Finally, another group of founders primarily stressed values or cultural *fit*. Like the previous group, these founders were concerned about the longer-term, rather than specific shorter-term personnel needs, but they focused primarily on how prospective hires would connect with others in the organization.

Basis of Coordination and Control

The third dimension concerned the principal means of controlling and coordinating work. (1) Some founders intended to invoke *professional control.* These founders took for granted that workers were committed to excellence in their work and could do an outstanding job because they had been professionally socialized to do so. (2) The most common means of control anticipated was extensive reliance on informal *organizational norms,* exercised by peer groups or via organizational culture. Unlike professional control, which emphasizes autonomy and independence, control through organizational norms emphasizes inculturation. (3) A third group of founders stated that they intended to control and coordinate work personally, through *direct oversight.* (4) Finally, some founders espoused a more traditional view of control as being embedded in *formal procedures and systems.*

Organizational Models in Young Technology Companies

Each founder's model was thus assigned to one of 3 × 3 × 4 (attachment by selection by control) *organizational blueprints.*[6] Looking at the data, the researchers found that 57% of the companies clustered into just five blueprints, corresponding to what they term "pure type" employment models. These five pure types are shown in Table 19-1:

- The *engineering model* involves attachment through challenging work, control via organizational norms, and selection based on specific task capabilities. Some observers claim that this is the default blueprint for a high-tech Silicon Valley start-up,[7] and indeed this was the most common founding employment model in the SPEC sample, evident in 32.5% of the firms.

- The *commitment model* relies on emotional or familial attachments of employees to the organization, selection based on cultural fit, and control via organizational norms. Of the 154 companies in the sample, 7.1% of the founders interviewed espoused the pure commitment blueprint.

- The *star model* embodies attachment based on challenging work, relies on autonomy and professional control, and selects elite personnel based on long-term potential. This profile was present in 8.4% of the companies at founding.

- The *bureaucracy model* involves attachment based on providing challenging work and/or opportunities for development, selecting individuals based on their qualifications for a particular role, and formalized control.[8] Relatively few founders (5.2%) embraced the bureaucratic model in the early days of building their companies.

- Finally, the *autocracy model* refers to employment premised on purely extrinsic motivations, control and coordination through close personal oversight, and selection of employees to perform prespecified tasks.[9] Only 3.9% of founders espoused the autocratic model.

How different are these five different organizational models? Note that except for the contrast between engineering and bureaucracy, each contrast between two

TABLE 19-1   Five Pure-Type Employment Models in Emerging Technology Companies, Based on Three Dimensions

DIMENSIONS			EMPLOYMENT MODEL
Attachment	Selection	Coordination/Control	
Work	Skills	Organizational norms	ENGINEERING
Love	Fit	Organizational norms	COMMITMENT
Work	Potential	Professional	STAR
Work	Skills	Formal	BUREAUCRACY
Money	Skills	Direct	AUTOCRACY

Source: James N. Baron, Michael T. Hannan, and M. Diane Burton, "Building the Iron Cage: Determinants of Managerial Intensity in the Early Years of Organizations," Harvard Business School, Division of Research Working Paper 98-064, 1998.

pure models involves differences on at least two dimensions. (Engineering and bureaucracy differ only in terms of the locus of coordination and control—organizational norms versus formal controls.) This is not a very precise metric of difference, but it does support the notion that these are substantially different HR organizational designs.

Beyond these five "pure" types of organization, the SPEC researchers have attached labels to some of the 31 other possible blueprints. When an organization blueprint differs from pure type "X" in one dimension and is different from all other pure types in at least two dimensions, this organization is called a "nearly pure type X"—or, for shorthand, a "quasi-X"—organization. For instance, an organization whose founder envisioned basing attachment on love, selecting based on fit, and utilizing direct control represents a quasi-commitment-type company: It differs from the pure commitment type in terms of control (only), and is substantially different (i.e., on two or more dimensions) from the other four pure types. (Such an organization suggests an autocratic "cult" variant on the commitment model.) Of the 154 organizations, 6.5% were quasi-commitment firms (5 possible blueprints), 1.3% were quasi-star organizations (4 possibilities), 2.6% were quasi-autocracies (4 possible blueprints), and 0.6% were quasi-bureaucracies (2 possible blueprints).

When an organization differs from more than one pure type in one dimension only (and it isn't itself a pure type), the SPEC researchers call it a "hybrid." For instance, an organization that bases attachment on love, selects for skills, and controls via organizational norms is a commitment–engineering hybrid; it differs from a pure commitment organization because it selects for skills instead of fit, and it differs from a pure engineering organization because it bases attachment on love instead of work. Of the 36 possible blueprints, 8 are hybrids. It is perhaps worth remarking that of these 8, 7 are hybrids of engineering and some other form(s). Thus, informally, the engineering model seems to be a "compromise," located between the other pure types, which tend to be quite distinct from each other.

After removing the five pure forms, the quasi-forms, and the hybrids, eight organizational blueprints remain out of the thirty-six possible combinations. These eight are each different from all of the five pure types in at least two dimensions.

Now, let us return to the data on 154 Silicon Valley high-tech start-ups, each classified into one of these thirty-six categories, according to the founder's blueprint for the firm. These data are striking in two (related) ways. As noted above, the engineering model is the most popular, with 32% of the firms in this category. And fully another 28% of the founders envisioned a hybrid–engineering blueprint— that is, one that differed from the engineering pure type in only one dimension (not including pure bureaucracies). Yet there is also considerable popularity of the other four pure types and quasi-types. In contrast, none of the eight "anomalies" (i.e., those blueprints that are two or more dimensions different from each of the five pure types) is very prevalent; in fact, only *two* of the 154 founders' models fall into one of these eight residual categories. (Both of these firms combined money as the basis of attachment, formal controls, and selection on the basis of fit.)

This suggests two basic conclusions, both consistent with our primary emphases throughout this book:

1. There is no single, obvious best blueprint for HR in high-tech start-ups. Or, at least, there is substantial disagreement among the 154 firms in the sample concerning how to proceed, even among founders intending to pursue similar strategies within the same industries.

2. The three dimensions underlying founders' models are far from independent. To take two glaring examples: A founder who envisioned love as the basis of attachment (19% of the entire sample) was twice as likely to embrace normative control than was a founder who envisioned money as the basis of attachment (73% of founders intending to base attachment on love also planned to control via organizational norms, versus 36% of those planning to base attachment on money). And of founders who intended to select on the basis of potential, over half (52%) assumed that coordination and control would be achieved through professional socialization of the individuals hired, compared to fewer than 7% of all other founders.[10]

What explanations can be offered for these patterns? The second result is easily rationalized by one of the main themes of this book: the value of consistency and complementarities among dimensions of human resource management. Recall that in Chapter 3 we identified three bases for consistency among HR practices: technical complementarities; cognitive or perceptual congruence, which facilitates learning; and congruency with broader social or cultural norms (which also helps to convey expectations and facilitate learning). The SPEC founders' HR blueprints for their start-up organizations seem to evidence all three bases of consistency.

For instance, consider a founder emphasizing control and coordination through organizational norms and seeking emotional bonds to the company itself (rather than attachment based on the specific work assignment), perhaps in order to create common overarching goals among differentiated subunits. Here there would be a clear technical complementarity with selection mechanisms that screen for values and cultural fit, as is found under the commitment model. The very fact that many founders were able to articulate such a clear blueprint for how they intended to manage human resources is suggestive of the second rationale we offered for consistency—namely, the benefits of having a simple, coherent, and internally consistent image of the employment relationship to communicate expectations and entitlements to employees.

Finally, we suggested that both the firm and its employees may benefit when the organization's employment practices and policies resonate with rules, values, and codes of conduct that employees have experienced in other social settings. Notice that the various pure-type employment blueprints jibe with models that prevail in other social contexts. Indeed, the five names are fairly evocative of the characteristics.[11] It is almost certainly not a coincidence, for instance, that the star employment model, which is espoused particularly by founders of firms developing medical technology or pursuing research,[12] corresponds so closely to the model that underlies academic science, from which many of the founders and key scientific personnel sought for these start-ups are recruited. The commitment model draws instead, as we have noted, on familial imagery, encouraging employees to view their associations with the firm in similar terms. The engineering model, arguably the default within Silicon Valley, resonates with the socialization that engineers receive in professional school and is well suited to the Valley's highly mobile labor force, placing more value on "cool technology" and technical contribution than on organizational loyalty or elite credentials. The bureaucratic model is readily familiar to most employees from encounters with bureaucracies in numerous contexts. And the austere, no-nonsense autocracy model communicates a very powerful and consistent message that employees are certain to have encountered somewhere else before: "You work (for me, the founder), you get paid (by me)—nothing more, nothing less."

As for the first broad pattern, what explains the fact that such diverse blueprints for employment relationships are adopted at the outset by such a relatively homogeneous sample of organizations? Most theories of organizations imply that enterprises engaged in the same activities and utilizing the same resources should organize and manage their human resources fairly similarly. Admittedly, the firms in this sample are doing different things—searching for biotechnological breakthroughs, fabricating computer components, writing software, and so on. But they are fairly similar in their technologies, certainly relative to the economy as a whole. Moreover, the researchers encountered startling diversity in founders' employment models even among start-ups within the very same industry, competing directly against one another.[13]

Note also that the SPEC study, by design, controls for a number of the factors that one would expect, based on theories reviewed in this book, to influence the design of employment systems. For instance, all the companies are headquartered in Silicon Valley, representing a single labor market and regulatory regime. They are all relatively young, small companies engaged in technology-related pursuits. Most of the founders have worked previously in other ventures within the Valley and are therefore well aware of what the prototypical Silicon Valley start-up is "supposed" to look like. Indeed, sometimes the very same established company—such as Hewlett-Packard, DEC, IBM, Apple, or Oracle—was cited by one founder as a model to be emulated and by another as a blueprint to be avoided at all costs. Founders occasionally cited models emanating from very different industries, such as the software company entrepreneur who cited Ben & Jerry's (ice cream) as his inspiration.

These findings thus underscore that there is no consensus "best way" of building human resource systems in emerging high-tech companies. Moreover, there are abundant examples in the SPEC sample of firms that seem to have been quite successful—*thus far,* at least—applying very different organizational models within the same competitive niche. SPEC has not yet progressed to the point of identifying systematically how (if at all) bottom-line performance differs as a function of organizational models, and it is possible that the researchers will discover through their ongoing studies some best way, measured by success (survivability or profitability) of the organization. Some designs might be very risky—entailing small chances of great success, large chances of failure. But the data, so far, don't allow any such general conclusion about how the founder's model influences eventual economic success. The data have shown, however, that the initial blueprint has important consequences. The SPEC researchers have identified some strong relationships between the founder's model and subsequent organizational developments, and we summarize some of those relationships below.

THE FOUNDER'S CHOICE OF MODEL

What factors influence the founder's early choice of a model? Obvious candidates include the founder's tastes and prior experiences. For instance, recall Sun Hydraulics from Chapters 1 and 4. This very unconventional organization—clearly the creation of its founder, Robert Koski—reflected his strong conviction that traditional organizational forms limited the contributions of workers. Ben & Jerry's (ice cream) clearly reflected the attitudes and tastes of Ben and Jerry, who could not be imagined running a classic bureaucracy. The tastes and experiences of other stakeholders may be influential as well. For instance, some preliminary evidence from SPEC suggests that firms that received venture capital very early in their history were somewhat more likely to have been founded along bureaucratic lines and to become more bureaucratic over time; this association is consistent with the perspective (discussed in Chapter 8 in connection with the diffusion of internal labor markets) that organizational structures and HR practices are selected in part with an eye toward satisfying important external gatekeepers.[14] The SPEC team is currently exploring this issue in depth, examining the role of founders, their biographies, prior relationships (if any), and ties to external partners (such as venture capitalists, lawyers, and consultants, and the like) in shaping the organizational blueprint.

Alignment of HR Models with the Founder's Intended Business Strategy

Another possible causal factor is the founder's intended business strategy. Throughout this book, we have emphasized the importance of aligning human resource practices with business strategy. The SPEC project provides evidence suggesting that entrepreneurial founders were indeed attentive to strategic alignment in crafting their blueprints for the HR system. The researchers classified firms into categories describing the *dominant strategic focus,* based on content analyses of interviews with founders, supplemented in some cases by other sources (e.g., newspaper articles and industry analysts' reports, business plans, etc.). These sources were used to discern the means by which founders planned to succeed against competitors in the product market. Founders' responses along these lines tended to cluster into five main categories:

- *Technological Leadership.* These firms seek first-mover advantages by winning a technology race. The emphasis here is on revolutionary technology; often, this involves gaining a crucial patent or patents. This strategy is illustrated by one interview transcript, which noted: "[The founders] had found a technical solution that worked for a problem that the world didn't even realize they had."[15] Among firms in the SPEC study (that could be classified according to the founder's HR model), roughly 50% were coded as belonging in this category, which is hardly surprising given the high-tech industries involved.

- *Enhancement of Existing Technology.* These firms seek to create a product or product line similar to those of other companies, but employing some general modification to the technology to gain competitive advantage. Distinctive competencies can include system integration (e.g., of software and hardware), superior quality (in terms of dependability or availability of features desired by customers), and the like. Interview transcripts representative of this strategic emphasis noted: "[T]hey knew that there was a market for optical character recognition and they wanted to outperform their existing competitors on accuracy and speed. It was a 'me-too' approach." "[Our] competitive advantage is [in] providing *both* hardware and software expertise ..... [Our] product is the most feature-rich in the industry." Just under 20% percent of the firms fell into this category.

- *Superior Marketing and/or Customer Service.* Firms in this category seek competitive advantage by developing or capitalizing on superior relations with customers, achieved through custom design of products, nonstandard methods of sales or distribution, or simply by developing superior capabilities in marketing, sales, branding, and/or customer service. Some illustrative examples: "We're pretty sharp at understanding our customers' requirements before they even knew they had them. We foresee requirements, invest in them, and then deliver a product that people want." Another company's strategy consisted of "creating a second label . . . creating a strong second source to Microsoft [by offering] superior sales and marketing." Another company's founders "[built their] own distribution system, which almost none of [their] competitors has." Often this strategy entailed creating products that respond directly to customers' idiosyncratic needs, frequently working interactively with customers toward that end. Within the SPEC sample, 13.6% were classified as having strategies driven by marketing, sales, and/or service.

- *Technology–Marketing Hybrid.* Another 10.4% of the start-ups combined a marketing–service focus with an emphasis either on enhancing an existing technology or on technological leadership.

- *Cost Minimization.* Firms pursuing this approach seek cost advantages through superior production techniques, economies of scale, and the like. For example: "[The firm] began as an IBM PS/2 clone maker. . . . [They] knew they could build systems more cheaply than IBM." "The founder was frustrated at his previous company with the cost of [personal computer motherboards] and knew they could be produced more cheaply." Only a small number of firms were classified as having a pure cost strategy, but several others combined an emphasis on cost minimization with some other focus (generally marketing or service) and were classified by the researchers into this category as well, resulting in a total of 7.1% of the companies.

The SPEC sample is not large enough to draw robust conclusions about the correlations between the various employment blueprints and the five different business strategies. But some of the observed correlations between founders' strategies and employment models are certainly suggestive. For instance, founders pursuing a cost-minimization strategy were much more likely to view the employment relation as a purely economic exchange (i.e., attachment based on money): Of the SPEC firms for which the founder's model and strategy could be coded, only 22 founders (14.3%) espoused attachment based on money; yet of the 11 firms put into the cost-minimization category, seven founders (64%) viewed money as the primary basis of attachment. (Of course, an obvious explanation is that founders who were cost-oriented would also be more likely to expect that employees would be money-oriented.) To cite another example, only about 11% of the SPEC firms embraced formal control in their founding model, but 46% of the cost-minimizers did so.

Predictably, the star model was most prevalent among founders championing a strategy of technological leadership: 80% of the star and quasi-star firms pursued technological leadership (versus 46% in the rest of the sample). Read the other way around, whereas 16% of firms competing through technological leadership embraced a star or quasi-star blueprint, only 4% of companies pursuing a different strategy were founded along star lines. Indeed, not a single company pursuing either a hybrid or cost-minimization strategy was founded along star lines. One founder, drawing on the scholarly distinction between "theory X" (industrial engineering, Taylorism) and "theory Y" (humanistic) management philosophies, provided a clear rationale for why the star model does not mesh well with a strategy predicated on cost minimization:

> I set out to build a Y-type company, not an X-type. I wanted people who believed in the technology and were self-motivated. I realized after starting, however, that the reality of a bootstrap environment is that you can't afford the people who fit a Y environment. You have to settle for lower salaried people and drive them X-style. This "settling for less'" is also driven in part by greed. I simply don't want to give up the [stock] options it would take to get a high caliber person.[16]

The engineering model seems to be fairly robust across different business strategies. It was found in roughly 37% of firms planning to be technological leaders and 37% of those intending to enhance existing technology, and in approximately 33% in the marketing and marketing–hybrid categories. (Only one firm out of eleven planning to pursue a cost-minimization strategy used the pure engineering model.) This general popularity of the engineering model is not surprising if, as we have suggested, it is the default or otherwise-taken-for-granted conception within the Silicon Valley technical community.

Finally, the data reveal a positive correlation between pursuing a marketing–service strategy and relying on the commitment or quasi-commitment blueprint at founding. Of the 21 firms pursuing a marketing strategy, 33.3% embraced commitment or quasi-commitment blueprints, compared to only 10.5% of the rest of the SPEC sample, an association that is likely to arise by chance only five times out of a thousand. The association makes good sense: Firms that plan on sustaining competitive advantage through long-term cooperative relations with their customers and clients presumably put a higher premium on long-term cooperative relations with their employees as well. These firms depend critically on the relationships that develop between their employees and the firm's long-term customers; those relationships represent valuable firm-specific investments, which are costly to replace and which the firm therefore seeks to protect by binding employees to the firm long-term. Those relationships also represent costly firm-specific investments to employees, creating an interest on their part in long-term attachments.

Other Interactions with Strategy

The five types of strategy identified by the SPEC researchers capture important differences in the strategies of these firms, but of course there are other aspects of strategy that, we believe, may be closely tied to the HR philosophy of the firm. Two important ones are: (a) scalability—the ability of the firm to expand its workforce quickly and openly, whether to import knowledge and technology from other firms or to meet the needs of rapid expansion; and (b) matching (or mismatching) the strategies and policies of already existing competitors. The SPEC data don't give us a quantitative hold on how these aspects of strategy interact with the HR blueprint chosen by the founder, but we can speculate (based on theoretical concerns) on what sorts of interactions we might expect to see.

Concerning scalability, firms founded along commitment or star lines may be able to do a better job at retaining their valuable human assets, but of necessity they will have to be more selective. Consequently, when founders anticipate issues of scalability, we might expect to see greater reliance on the engineering or bureaucratic model early on. The trade-off here, of course, is that these latter blueprints may not involve handcuffs that are as binding on employees, but they may facilitate the firm's efforts to appropriate human assets from other sources.

As for the strategies and policies of already existing competitors, sociologists have emphasized the tendency for organizations in a given population to evolve similar structures and practices, arguing that cultural and normative forces, the interests of key stakeholders (such as venture capitalists, lawyers, and personnel professionals), and sheer imitation foster the spread of standard models for organizing (see Chapter 8). However, in some circumstances there are presumably sound competitive reasons for founders to behave in precisely the *opposite* manner, departing from convention and seeking to build an organization founded with a distinctive blueprint. Late entrants into an industry, firms with limited resources, or firms that wish to minimize the likelihood of employees departing to competitors may be impelled to adopt organizational models that are at variance with what is standard in that sector. For instance, if one is seeking to compete with a well-established competitor who long ago embraced a commitment model, there may be real dangers in trying to emulate that blueprint. Because the competitor has already derived a first-mover advantage by screening the labor market, the newer entrant faces a more acute adverse selection problem, particularly insofar as employees willing to sign on to the only (or the first) commitment firm in an industry or region are signaling more useful information about themselves than are employees who are willing to sign on to the twentieth commitment firm in the same setting. These considerations underscore that in their organization-building efforts, founders need to pay close attention not only to their own business context (i.e., the five factors), but also to the organization-building activities of their labor market competitors.

CHANGES IN THE HR BLUEPRINT: INTERVIEWS WITH CEOS

As we noted earlier, in addition to interviewing founders about their recollections of founding conditions and initial HR assumptions, the SPEC team interviewed the (then-current) CEO in 1994–95 concerning organizational assumptions, policies, and conditions. (The average firm was just over six years old at the time of these interviews.) The analyses of these data by the researchers are ongoing and the results we will report here are tentative. Moreover, there are some obvious possibilities for potential bias in the retrospective reports. In particular, when the CEO is the founder, there may be a tendency to remember "how it was" as "how it is," whereas a CEO different from the founder may have a self-serving interest in believing (and thus reporting) that things have changed from the original blueprint.[17] But even taking into account the tentative and incomplete nature of the analysis of the data and these biases, some interesting patterns emerge.

Inertia and Punctuated Equilibrium

Out of 153 firms for which both the founder's and CEO's HR blueprints could be coded, 76 (or 49.7%) displayed no change whatsoever in the basic organizational blueprint (i.e., which cell of the $3 \times 3 \times 4$ matrix they were in).[18] Examining the three dimensions separately, 80% percent retained their locus of attachment, 82% percent retained their basic selection criterion, and 63% percent retained their locus of control. We have made a lot of noise in this book about inertia in basic HR premises and policies, and although an average interval of six years is not a long time, it is a length of time over which a lot changes, especially for newly formed technology companies in intensely competitive and rapidly changing environments. We find this to be fairly persuasive evidence of inertia. Of course, a lot of this inertia is self-generated by strong-willed founders who choose an organizational blueprint and stick with it. But even so, we think a caution to entrepreneurs is in order: Choose your founding blueprint well, because it is likely to last.

Moreover, the data suggest a pattern of inertia characterized by what biologists call "punctuated equilibrium." The idea in a punctuated equilibrium is that it is the *system* (or ecology) that is in equilibrium; when one piece of the system or ecology changes, other pieces are much more likely to change as well. In terms of basic HR principles, there are two reasons we expect to see this sort of pattern. First, insofar as complementarities exist among the different dimensions, then when one dimension changes others may naturally be changed as well to take advantage of the opportunities for complementarities (or to avoid the disadvantage of badly aligned, noncomplementary pieces). Second, as we discussed in Chapter 4, one reason for organizational inertia is that expectations are difficult and expensive to unfreeze; people are often confused by change, we might expect turnover to rise (more on this later), and so forth. These types of costs associated with change are, to a significant extent, incurred if *any* substantive change is made. So once one change will be made, it may be less expensive and psychologically disruptive to consider additional simultaneous changes. (Anyone who has moved to a new residence has probably experienced first-hand how this seems to open up for consideration all sorts of issues and decisions that are much less likely to garner your attention had you stayed put.)

The SPEC data support the notion of punctuated equilibrium. If dimensions changed independently, we would have expected 3.6% of companies to have changed their assumptions regarding both attachment and selection (given the marginals on changes in each dimension listed above); yet in fact 7.2% changed both. Under independence, just under 7% would have changed on both the selection and control dimensions, whereas in fact 9.2% changed both. And—most strikingly of the paired changes—under independence, about 7% would have changed on both attachment and control, whereas 13.1% of the sample actually changed along these two dimensions simultaneously. As for organizations that changed all three dimensions, under independence we would expect to see only 1.5% changing all three; in the data, three times this many (4.5%) changed all three.[19]

What Changed? The Rise of Bureaucracy

Looking at specific changes, one fairly clear pattern is that formal means of coordination and control became much more prevalent among the CEOs' blueprints than among the founders' blueprints. Among the 153 firms for which both the founder's and CEO's models could be characterized, formal controls were espoused by only 17 founders (11.1%), compared to 51 of the CEOs (33.3%).[20]

Why do we think this is happening? We can think of several related rationales. First, as organizations age, they tend to grow in terms of the size of their workforce. Informal controls can work quite well, but as we've discussed, they work best in smaller groups. As the group gets larger and (one assumes) more diverse, there is increasing value in spelling things out through formal rules, regulations, and procedures, particularly because with the passage of time an increasing fraction of the organization's members are newcomers who weren't around in the founding days. Second, very young organizations, populated by a small group of co-workers, often lack the time needed to codify procedures. As time passes, there is increasing opportunity to codify how things are done. Thus, because both the value of formalizing things and the opportunity to do so increase with the passage of time, observers of emerging organizations would expect to see an increased reliance on formal rules and regulations.

Consistent with these conjectures, it appears that the firms that altered their HR blueprint toward reliance on formal means of coordination and control were, on average, older than the rest of the sample.[21] Indeed, if one conducts a statistical ("logistic regression") analysis predicting which firms have a CEO blueprint embodying reliance on formal controls, holding constant whether formal controls were part of the founder's blueprint, age is a statistically significant predictor. Holding age constant, there does not seem to be a clear effect of labor force size or growth.[22]

Two other factors also have a moderate positive effect on the tendency for firms to migrate over time toward formal means of coordination and control: replacing the founder and receiving venture capital (VC) backing. Among organizations whose founders did not initially emphasize formal controls, 45.1% of companies with a nonfounder CEO altered the blueprint by 1994–95 to embrace formal controls; among organizations in which the current CEO was a founder, only 17.3% had evolved in this fashion. Firms receiving venture capital were also more likely over time to incorporate an emphasis on formal controls in their organizational blueprint. Of companies whose founding blueprints had not emphasized formal controls, those receiving VC backing by 1994 were almost three times as likely to evolve their blueprint to embrace formal controls than firms that did not receive venture capital (32.9% versus 11.6%, respectively). This effect of venture capital is consistent with the above-mentioned tendency for bureaucratization to emerge in part to send signals to external gatekeepers that one has adopted an "appropriate" way of doing business. This pattern of results is quite similar to what the SPEC researchers have recently found in studying the rate at which the firms formalize and bureaucratize their structures over time (e.g., formalize their employment policies and proliferate specialized roles within the senior management group): In those analyses, age, growth, receiving venture capital, and going public were among the more important predictors.[23]

We gain additional insight into these firms' increased emphasis on formal means of coordination and control by considering interactions with the other two dimensions of the employment model. With reference to the notion of punctuated equilibrium, of the 76 firms that changed along at least one dimension, 45 changed along exactly *one*. Of those 45 single-dimension changes, nearly half (22) involved (only) the CEO embracing formal control, which had not been emphasized in the founder's blueprint. To be sure, it changes the culture of an organization to move from informal, organic control to a formal system of rules and regulations. The change is less profound, however, when the formalization or codification doesn't transform organizational practices but instead only spells out existing practices. To the extent that the increased emphasis on formal controls we observe simply reflects codification of existing practices rather than a real change in how things are done—a natural consequence of increasing age—then this type of formalization would not entail costs of change as great as those that accompany "real" changes in procedures. And, therefore, such "natural" formalization would be less likely to occasion a wholesale rethinking of the entire array of HR practices. The fact that these natural-results-of-aging changes are included in the sample (and in our assessment of changes in blueprints) makes the evidence we documented above for punctuated equilibrium all the more compelling, because we observe dramatic evidence of punctuated changes despite the fact that a number of these seemingly more "cosmetic" changes in blueprints are included in the data.

Looking still more closely at the interactions, there were only eight pure bureaucracies evident among the founders' blueprints (5.2% of the sample), compared to 27 (nearly 18%) among the CEOs' blueprints. Most of these twenty-seven firms were originally conceived along engineering or quasi-engineering lines: Of the twenty-seven, five had been pure bureaucracies at their inception, twelve were founded as pure-engineering firms, and eight were initially hybrids between engineering and some other type, leaving only two firms that switched to bureaucracy and that were unrelated to the engineering model at the time of founding. Another frequently observed pattern of change in blueprints involved firms that had been engineering hybrids at their founding—combining engineering with another model, based on the founder's responses—migrating to a pure engineering model, according to the CEO's responses to the SPEC interviewers. Nine of the 13 companies that switched to the pure-engineering model fit that profile.

At the risk of overprocessing the data, these findings suggest the following basic story: As emerging firms mature, at least within the first six years or so, many retain their initial HR blueprints (roughly half did so within the SPEC sample). Of those that changed blueprints, many made small changes that involve an exchange between bureaucratic and engineering patterns of HR, with the formalization of rules and procedures playing the biggest part. (Scholars have noted the affinity of engineers and engineering cultures for formal systems and procedures.[24] Perhaps the prevalence of the engineering blueprint at founding in this population partly reflects its malleability and robustness to the diversity of organizational transitions that a young technology company may confront in its formative years, including the transition toward bureaucracy.) Finally, the remaining observed changes are more dramatic episodes of punctuated equilibrium, usually involving a significant rethinking and retooling of the organization's HR blueprint along multiple dimensions.

Some Shifts That Didn't Take Place

It is also interesting to note that several models—particularly, the pure-form star and commitment blueprints—were almost never adopted (i.e., switched to) subsequent to the founding of the company. These models seem to entail building commitments and expectations that are more difficult to instill within an ongoing enterprise. It is not hard to see why this might be the case. As we have noted elsewhere in this book, establishing a reputation as an employer dedicated to a high-commitment HR model is difficult and potentially costly. But it is even more difficult once one has already established a reputation to the contrary. Similarly, sustaining a star system as a firm ages and grows more complex is certainly difficult: As the firm grows and becomes more complex, the value added by the stars may diminish, or at least be harder to pinpoint and defend; technical stars are often brought in by a connection to the founders or key early employees, who may depart; and so on. And *shifting to* a star system after having pursued a different model is likely to be even more contentious. Furthermore, the SPEC researchers found some quantitative and qualitative evidence suggesting that the original founders play an especially critical role as catalysts for launching a technology company along either commitment or star lines. In commitment-model firms, it is usually the founder(s) whose values and beliefs form the basis for the organizational loyalty that is the centerpiece of the HR system. In the star model, the cadre of key scientific or technical personnel (i.e., the stars) is often recruited through the personal networks of the founder(s).

The Impact of the CEO

Which companies were most likely to change their HR model? Not surprisingly, firms in which the current CEO was a founder were much less likely to have changed their employment model.[25] In the SPEC sample, about 40% of the CEOs in 1994–95 were nonfounders. Of this 40%, over three-quarters had changed to a different blueprint (i.e., shifted to a different category out of the 36 possible). In contrast, among the 60% of SPEC firms in which a founder remained as CEO, just 35% changed to a different blueprint. We have already noted that replacing the founder increased the likelihood that formal control became incorporated into the firm's blueprint. But replacing the founder didn't just promote minor, cosmetic changes in the HR blueprint: Firms in which a founder was no longer CEO were roughly twice as likely to change their HR model sufficiently to move into a different category of the typology in Table 19-1.[26] Not surprisingly, given the affinity of new CEOs for formal control, a consequence of replacing the founder–CEO was to increase the chances of a firm migrating toward the pure bureaucratic model: 27.3% of firms whose CEO is not a founder were characterized as present-day pure bureaucracies, versus 13.1% of the firms whose CEO was a founder. (Moreover, among firms that were not *founded* as pure bureaucracies, 26.4% of companies whose CEO in 1994–95 wasn't a founder had evolved into bureaucracies, compared to only 10.1% of firms still led by a founder.)

Of course, the logical rationale for this result is that nonfounder CEOs are likely to be professional managers, brought in to make the organization look more businesslike, which includes the institution of formal rules and such. Moreover, CEOs from outside the founding team are frequently brought in by investors precisely with the mandate to rewrite some of the implicit contracts that might have existed previously between the firm and its employees, especially in firms initially embracing a commitment or star model. Put differently, both change in the HRM model and a change in CEO may reflect "troubles" at the firm, whether economic, technolog-ical, or involving personnel. If both of these are caused by and thus statistically cor-related with unobserved difficulties, then they will be correlated with one another.

Other Factors That Increase the Likelihood of Changing the HR Blueprint

Firms pursuing a strategy based on marketing or service (or a hybrid marketing–technology strategy) were significantly less likely to change their employment model over time, even after controlling for age, size, CEO succession, receiving venture capital, going public, and the founder's initial blueprint. As we have noted, such strategies seem to presume continuity of employment, because the firm's strategy relies on employees to broker long-term relations with customers. Not surprisingly, older firms in the SPEC sample were more likely to have changed their model. A small number of the SPEC firms had existed in some prior form before their cur-rent incarnation (e.g., spinoffs that had been created through a merger of subunits from two preexisting companies); as one might expect, these ongoing entities were somewhat less likely to change their HR model over time than were enterprises having no prior history.

We have already reported on several factors leading to the specific institution of formal controls. Not surprisingly, those same factors tend to predict adoption of the full bureaucratic model: Age and size both tend to favor a shift toward the bu-reaucratic model.[27] A transition toward the bureaucratic model was also more likely among firms that had a nonfounder CEO and among those founded along engi-neering lines. Firms founded according to the commitment model were least likely to move in this direction, followed by firms founded along star lines. Firms receiv-ing venture capital were also more likely to evolve toward the bureaucratic model.

CONSEQUENCES OF FOUNDERS' HR BLUEPRINTS

As we noted earlier, when interviewing entrepreneurs, the SPEC researchers em-phasized that they were after the founder's blueprint and underlying assumptions concerning the type of organization being built. One might therefore imagine that the blueprint thus identified was little more than rhetoric or wishful thinking, with-out serious consequences for the actual practices put in place and the evolution of the organization. But the SPEC data indicate otherwise: The founders' blueprints have had a profound effect on the day-to-day practices of their organizations. In-deed, the SPEC data indicate that the founder's blueprint better predicts some pre-sent-day practices than does the blueprint espoused by the present-day CEO (see below). Thus, we have some dramatic support for a point we've emphasized throughout this book: Organizations and, in particular, their HR systems exhibit substantial path dependence. Early decisions and actions shape subsequent out-comes in ways that the architects of organizations may not have envisioned or ad-equately anticipated.

Staffing the HR Function and Formalizing Employment Relations

The SPEC researchers have been particularly attentive to how firms in the sample handle HR and when HRM shifts from an informal task to a formal function in the organization. Data used to indicate this shift include the date of appointing the first full-time HR employee, that individual's credentials (e.g., someone with professional HR training and prior experience versus a clerical employee who functioned informally as the "company mother"), the creation of an HR department, and the formalization and codification of HR rules (e.g., in employee handbooks).

The sample of firms shows enormous variation in these domains. About 40% of these companies had yet to hire a full-time HR employee by the time they were visited in 1994–95. Among the companies that completed HR surveys (which tended to be somewhat older, larger, and more HR-intensive), 72% had one or more full-time HR employees (the median number was 1, although the range was from 0 to 56!). Among companies that had ever hired a full-time HR employee, the median firm was 3.75 years old and had about 65 employees when that person was brought on board. Again, however, the variations were enormous; for instance, at the time the first HR person was hired, the companies ranged in age from 0 to 10 years and they ranged in size from 1 to 440 employees. Within the SPEC sample, by 1994 the median firm had 1.47 HR employees per 100 employees (mean = 2.03), but the range was extremely broad: from 0 to 33.

Turning to the impact of the founder's general HR blueprint: In general, the SPEC team found that commitment- and star-model firms took HR "more seriously" early on. Star firms in particular seem somewhat more likely to have named an experienced HR professional as the first full-time HR manager, and on average they hired this person and created a formal HR department earlier. This pattern may reflect the paramount importance of recruitment, selection, and retention functions for young firms built around a star model.

The researchers found that commitment-model firms also tended to formalize employment relations and codify HR practices earlier than average (see "Specific HR Practices" below). Interestingly, however, when the SPEC researchers analyzed the extent of employment formalization by 1994–95, firms founded along bureaucracy lines had become among the *most* formalized, whereas firms founded along commitment lines were among the *least* formalized. In other words, commitment firms apparently undertook basic organization-building and (limited) employment formalization activities earlier on, providing a foundation for creating a strong culture and system of informal controls that enabled those firms to economize subsequently on the amount of formal policies and procedures required. Conversely, in bureaucracy-model firms, the early steps to formalize the employment relationship were followed by even more such formalization.[28]

The fact that commitment firms were fastest to create such formalized HR policies may seem counterintuitive, given their emphasis on inculturation and other informal means of control rather than formal organizational structures and policies. But this is counterbalanced by the fact that they wound up being among the least-formalized organizations. The early organization-building activities on the part of firms whose founders espoused a commitment model seem to reflect a strong dedication to the role of human resources in guiding the firm's early evolution, manifested in more attention early on to management of employment relations. These data are also consistent with other recent studies suggesting that—depending on the context and supporting organizational arrangements—particular facets of bureaucracy and formalization can be either coercive or enabling, part of either a control-based or a commitment-based approach to HRM.[29]

Specific HR Practices

Specific HR practices established early on were tied to the founder's general blueprint. Commitment-model firms were faster to develop HR information systems, adopt background checks of prospective employees, develop various policies and documents aimed at internal communication and socialization, provide in-house training, tie compensation to accumulated knowledge and skill, and share corporate profits or efficiency improvements with the workforce through profit sharing or gain sharing, relative to otherwise-comparable firms (in the same industry, with the same head count, at the same age) whose founders embraced a different HR model.[30] These findings suggest that, having created an organization with the intention of forging long-term relations with employees, management went to greater lengths to screen prospective hires, orient them to the organization, and provide for employees' social welfare.

Firms following a star model were, like commitment-model firms, relatively quicker to create a central HR department and to hire their first full-time HR employee. But they embraced a different sort of HR: These firms focused on HR practices designed to facilitate selecting, differentiating, rewarding, and retaining the firm's stars (and justify this to external partners and investors). Specifically, firms that began with a star model were more likely and faster than otherwise-comparable companies to develop intellectual property (noncompetition) agreements and utilize stock option grants. They were also faster to implement standardized forms for evaluating performance, which may result from their focus on rewarding and retaining star performers. That focus might also explain several other results for star firms. For example, they implemented affirmative action plans at the highest rate; perhaps the imperative of identifying and recruiting the most talented individuals, whatever their gender or ethnicity, is nowhere stronger than in organizations embracing the star model. This might also explain their higher-than-average rate of developing human resource information systems.

Another rationale for the early development of standardized performance evaluation forms and affirmative action programs in star organizations concerns the origins of their founders. We have noted that star firms are often crafted on the model of academia; we suspect that they tend to be founded and staffed, at least early on, by academics. Academics are often great believers in the ability to measure performance (at least, they embrace examinations!), and of course affirmative action is both commonplace and viewed as legitimate in universities and colleges. The same sort of rationale may explain several findings regarding star firms that are otherwise less intuitive, such as their faster adoption of companywide electronic mail and companywide meetings. In colleges and universities, there is typically a great deal of reliance on e-mail, and regular seminars and meetings ensure dissemination of the latest research results to colleagues.

Firms that embraced the engineering model seemed inclined to emphasize stock options and nonmonetary recognition awards, both of which seem to be part of the engineering culture. Moreover, relative to firms espousing the commitment model, they were more likely to eschew activities that systematize employment relations and HRM (organizational charts, job descriptions, HR information systems), particularly practices aimed at facilitating equity, consistency, and a shared identity throughout the entire workforce (profit sharing and gain sharing, affirmative action plans, suggestion systems, company-sponsored social events). In other words, consistent with our description of the engineering pure type, there was less evidence of a "corporate" focus in the evolution of HR activities in firms that embarked with the engineering model. After all, engineers value "cool technology," not cutting-edge management philosophies.

Uniformity of Treatment

An important variable in crafting an HR system concerns the extent to which employees are treated uniformly (see Chapter 3). The SPEC data suggest that the uniformity or consistency of treatment sought across employees is correlated with the founder's HR blueprint. In enterprises embracing a star or bureaucratic model, employment practices appear to be tailored to particular work roles or in some star firms even to specific key individuals. In firms embracing a commitment model, however, HR practices promote stronger emphasis on consistent and equal treatment throughout the workforce; employment practices and organizational governance seem to be tailored not to the exigencies of specific work roles or subunits but instead to the needs and interests of the "family" as a whole. The engineering model seems to be intermediate between these two extremes. Of course, all this is entirely consistent with the general nature of star- and bureaucracy-model firms on the one hand and commitment- and engineering-model firms on the other: Star organizations are built around the notion that contributions—and hence rewards—are individually based; bureaucracies seek to codify (and thus clarify) differences in treatment across positions; engineering firms rely relatively more on teamwork and (implicitly derived) team spirit; and commitment organizations take the team concept to the extreme of everyone being a team member.[31]

Of course, the degree of uniformity in the treatment of employees is apt to face evolutionary pressure as a firm matures. Fairly uniform treatment is easier to achieve in the early years because start-ups are more homogeneous than older, larger firms with respect to their tasks and personnel, thereby enabling founders to craft a single employment system or governance regime that envelops most or all employees. Growth in the scale, complexity, and heterogeneity of an organization's tasks and employees is likely to favor more differentiation in the employment practices utilized, undercutting the applicability of any single blueprint to the entire workforce. (This process underlies some of the explanation given above for the increasing prevalence of formal controls in these firms.)

Assuming this is true, an interesting and unresolved question is whether specific business strategies and employment models are more or less flexible in coping with this transition. It seems reasonable to suppose, for instance, that firms in which the employment relationship is initially conceptualized and structured along star or bureaucratic lines might be able to cope with these pressures toward internal differentiation more easily than firms that adopt the commitment model at their inception. Thus, the SPEC finding of less uniformity in treatment of employees within the star and bureaucratic forms may reflect the greater flexibility those blueprints entail on this dimension.

Taking this a step further, an interaction with strategy may be present. It seems reasonable to suppose, for example, that firms pursuing a strategy of technology leadership view key technical personnel as their major competitive asset, adopting particular HR policies and practices designed to attract, nurture, and retain those individuals, while displaying less regard for individuals engaged in other domains of activity (e.g., manufacturing or marketing). In contrast, firms seeking to enhance an existing technology are likely to need to coordinate their technical core more closely (and more quickly) with other functional areas of the firm, which may push them in the direction of adopting employment policies that are more consistent throughout the organization. If these suppositions are correct, we would expect that the star and bureaucratic forms are better suited to (complementary with) strategies of technology leadership; as we have noted, we see this correlation reflected in founders' choices within the data.

But don't overprocess this theoretical analysis. There may be particular types of firms, plying particular strategies and caught in particular circumstances, for which the evolutionary pressures push in the opposite direction—that is, toward *more* consistent treatment among different segments of the organization over time. For instance, companies founded around a strategy of technology leadership may find, once their initial success attracts the attention of competitors, that they need closer integration between technical personnel and those employees engaged in manufacturing or marketing the firm's products, and that this is impeded by an organizational culture and HR system that has traditionally treated non-technical employees as second-class citizens.

Managerial Intensity

Among the project's most intriguing findings to date is the relationship between the founder's initial HR blueprint and the rate at which full-time managerial and administrative specialists are added over time to oversee and coordinate activities. One of our recurring themes throughout this book has been that employment models based on implicit normative controls (including peer pressure), gift exchange, and long-term commitments encourage employees to internalize the firm's welfare, enabling organizations to rely more on employee self-management to achieve desired ends. Consistent with that claim, the SPEC researchers found that companies whose founder(s) espoused a commitment model added fewer managers and administrators over time than did otherwise-similar companies, especially those founded according to the bureaucracy model.[32] Roughly six years after their founding (on average), enterprises founded along bureaucracy lines had considerably more managerial and administrative specialists than all others (particularly relative to companies founded along commitment lines), even after controlling statistically for the size of the company's workforce and its rate of employment growth, the industry and business strategy, the occupational and gender mix, public versus private status, change in CEO, and a host of other characteristics.

The magnitude of the effect is striking—approximately 169% more full-time managers and administrators at the same (nonadministrative) workforce size for firms with the bureaucratic model than for otherwise-similar firms that started with a commitment model. This is a huge difference. For instance, consider two firms— each having grown to 500 nonadministrative employees by 1994–95, and differing only in having been founded along bureaucratic versus commitment lines. The SPEC team's estimates imply that the former has 215 full-time managers/administrators, compared to 80 in the latter.

CHANGE, TURNOVER, AND ORGANIZATIONAL UPHEAVAL

Throughout this book we have emphasized the enormous power that HR systems can have and why it may be difficult for organizations to alter their ongoing HR practices and philosophies. Recall, for instance, the rancor and dissent experienced at Cisco Systems, the computer networking company, when management attempted to make a seemingly trivial change in the provision of soft drinks, causing employees to question whether the premises and values underpinning their employment relationships with the firm were being altered (see Chapter 5). One piece of evidence from the SPEC research consistent with this claim is the finding that employee turnover rates were considerably higher (on average, roughly twice as high) among firms that had changed their HR model, relative to firms that had not. This difference holds up even after controlling statistically for industry, business strategy, employment and growth rate, organizational age, the firm's initial occupational composition, the founder's HR model, whether the CEO was a founder, and other factors that might be expected to influence turnover rates.

These results reflect preliminary analyses, which are still ongoing as this chapter was being written. Among the unresolved issues is whether changes in the employment model (or in other features of a start-up firm) *cause* increased turnover. Note that for firms characterized as having undergone a change in the HR models espoused by the founder versus the current CEO, the SPEC researchers did not necessarily know *when* this change occurred, which leaves the issue of causation up for grabs. Indeed, one can easily spin stories that have causation running the other way: In businesses in which human capital plays a crucial role, an organization that suffers dramatic turnover is in trouble. That trouble may lead to changes in the HR blueprint of the firm, in an attempt to save the organization. To try and unravel these issues, the researchers' ongoing investigations exploit information on the timing of top management changes and other key events in each firm to try and determine whether these are triggers for increased turnover.[33] In any event, issues of causation notwithstanding, the correlations in the data suggest at least an *association* between changing the premises that underpin employment relationships and significant increases in turnover. This is all the more striking given that labor shortages and managing employee turnover were consistently reported as among the most critical key challenges faced by these technology companies during the time period spanned by the SPEC study.

The dislocating effects of changing HR systems are also suggested by another datum reported by the researchers, who found that "in SPEC firms that had changed their HR model, the current CEO was somewhat more likely to cite 'organizational and management concerns' and/or 'legal issues' when asked an open-ended question about the major challenges facing the company, compared to CEOs in firms where the HR model had remained stable."[34] This is another indirect indication that altering the premises that underlie employment relationships imposes a hefty toll on organizations.

CONCLUSION AND (THE FINAL) COMING ATTRACTION

We wish to reiterate that the SPEC project is an ongoing venture. Many interesting issues—most particularly, links between HRM and organizational performance—remain to be studied. And although this data set is considerably larger than most sources of information on these topics, the number of relevant dimensions of HR philosophies and practices is even larger, particularly taking into account the need for emerging companies to evolve rapidly as they grow and face new and different external and internal challenges. We cannot claim that the SPEC study "settles" anything. And if you are in the happy position of the person at the start of this chapter—charged with organizing a start-up—you are going to have to rely on your own analyses and intuitions concerning how best to proceed in the HR domain. The SPEC data do not give a clear and unambiguous answer to the question *What's best?*

But the preliminary research findings from the SPEC project are quite consistent with some of the major themes of this book. We hope that three messages in particular are clear.

First, the fact that the researchers could identify a small number of distinctive HR blueprints among the companies they studied suggests the importance of consistency and complementarities among HR practices. Founders tended to develop coherent and internally consistent philosophies of how to manage employees, reflected in bundles of interrelated HR practices that emerged early in their companies' lives. And consistency or coherence is not simply technological, but reflects—indeed, may be primarily informed by—broader patterns of social interaction.

Second, we saw that variations in these models, at least at "birth," were related systematically to differences in the business strategies founders intended to pursue, underscoring the alignment theme we have emphasized throughout this book. To be sure, we don't yet fully understand the roots of some of those connections. But some of the connections are becoming clearer. For instance, we suspect that data on how HR principles interact with an organization's ability to differentiate among employees, joined with theoretical analyses of how valuable or detrimental such differentiation is in pursuing particular business strategies, will help improve our understanding.

Third, the SPEC data suggest that founders' early choices regarding human resource management have had significant and enduring consequences for the organizations they created. For instance, the demonstrated tendency for firms founded along bureaucratic lines to become more administratively top-heavy over time, relative to otherwise-comparable firms whose founders espoused more HR-intensive models, seems likely to have significant effects on how organizations function and on their cost structures. This intriguing result suggests a long-term tradeoff between investing in HR policies and practices at the outset that attract, motivate, and bind high-quality employees to the organization versus investing in administrative and supervisory capacity to direct and monitor workers' efforts. In particular, the pattern of HR institutionalization in commitment-model firms—earlier, but then lighter—suggests how early and appropriate sorts of policies and rules may help avoid top-heavy bureaucratic structures down the road.

Research on emerging companies also holds promise for improving our understanding of the role that the human resource function plays in different organizational contexts. Among the SPEC firms, there was enormous variation in the size, timing, origins, and influence of the human resource function. Some founders believed that HR issues were so important that one of their first acts was to hire a professional HR person as part of the top management team. Other executives espoused the view that "HR is too important to be left to HR people." Still others viewed HR as a necessary evil (at best) or an unproductive cost item at worst. Some skeptical founders or CEOs eventually came to believe in the strategic importance of human resource issues, but only after initially regarding the HR function as a lowly one and initially selecting as head of HR their personal assistant or the clerk who handled payroll. Within the Silicon Valley, there are a number of firms that serve as HR independent contractors, specializing in clients that are high-tech start-ups. And some firms in the SPEC sample are clients of those independent contractors.

If you believe that HR is a crucial concern of general managers (and by now, we certainly hope that you do!), then you should conclude that these early choices concerning how to handle HR will prove very important to the firms involved. Notions of path dependence suggest that early steps in defining and staffing the role of HRM within a company may prove almost irreversible. (This topic is currently being examined by the SPEC team, as they analyze how the longer-term evolution and impact of the HR function on these companies reflects early decisions by founders and top managers about how to organize and staff the function.)

We have written this book with the general manager in mind. We believe it is vital for general managers, and not simply HR specialists, to understand and be involved in crafting the relationships between the firm and its employees. But given both the legal demands of managing employment and the detailed decisions that must be made, HR specialists in some form or other—whether employees of some independent contractor, or regular employees off in some cost center, or central members of top management—are probably going to be a part of the picture. In the next chapter, we conclude this book with a discussion of the role we think those HR specialists should play.

IN REVIEW

⇒ Reasons to study HRM in emerging companies include the following:
- Small companies are important to the economy; many believe that they are the ultimate engine of economic growth and growth in employment.
- Regardless of the merits of this contention, the subject of HRM in emerging organizations is of natural interest to (potential) entrepreneurs and to those who will work closely with entrepreneurial ventures.
- Most of what we know (from careful empirical study) about HRM is drawn from studies of large, established companies, which may be of limited validity in other contexts.
- If emerging companies are different from established companies in terms of HRM, studying the differences will help us to establish and refine general principles of HRM.

⇒ The SPEC interviews with founders:
- Classified each firm by the founder's "blueprint" for HRM, in a $3 \times 3 \times 4$ array concerning locus of employee attachment, selection criteria, and the primary basis of coordinating and controlling work.
- Found that of the 36 possible blueprints, the data "clustered" into five pure types, along with several variations on those five types and a few hybrid forms. These clusters suggest the existence of complementarities in HRM.
- Discovered correlations between the founder's blueprint and intended business strategy.

⇒ Interviews with CEOs, subsequent to founding:
- Demonstrated both inertia in HR practices and the phenomenon of punctuated equilibrium; when a substantive change in the HR blueprint was made, it tended to be accompanied by wholesale changes.
- Found a general tendency toward increasing formalized control and bureaucracy.
- Found that changes in top management tended to accompany changes in the HR blueprint.

⇒ The firm's initial HR blueprint—specifically, the founder's espoused model—had substantive consequences for the evolution of HR practices in these firms.

> • Perhaps the most provocative finding was that commitment-model firms tended to formalize HR practices (and set up formal HR functions) somewhat earlier than firms embodying other models, but subsequently they were able to economize on HR bureaucracy and administrative overhead.
> • Changing the HR blueprint appears to be dislocating, reflected in higher turnover rates and greater concern expressed by CEOs about impending organizational, management, and legal issues in those companies in which the HR model had changed over time.

ENDNOTES

1. For those readers whose knowledge of interior decor is limited, mini-blinds are a type of window covering containing small louvered slats.

2. For example, see U.S. Small Business Administration, "New Census Data Highlight Small Firms' Job Creation Role," Office of Advocacy News Release 97–32, viewable online at: http://www.sba.gov/ADVO/press/97-32.html. For useful reviews of this literature and the critiques that have been leveled against it, see Steven J. David, John C. Haltiwanger and Scott Schuh, *Job Creation and Destruction* (Cambridge, MA: MIT Press, 1996); Bruce A. Kirchhoff and Patricia G. Greene, "Response to Renewed Attacks on the Small Business Job Creation Hypothesis," Foundations of Entrepreneurship Research 1995 (*Proceedings of the Fifteenth Annual Entrepreneurship Research Conference*), Babson College–Kauffman Foundation Center for Entrepreneurial Studies, Babson College.

3. This chapter relies heavily on James N. Baron, M. Diane Burton, and Michael T. Hannan, "The Road Taken: Origins and Evolution of Employment Systems in Emerging Companies," *Industrial and Corporate Change* 5 (No. 2, 1996): 239–75; Michael T. Hannan, M. Diane Burton, and James N. Baron, "Inertia and Change in the Early Years: Employment Relations in Young, High-Technology Firms," *Industrial and Corporate Change* 5 (No. 2, 1996): 503–36; and M. Diane Burton, *The Evolution of Employment Systems in High Technology Firms,* unpublished Ph.D. dissertation, Department of Sociology, Stanford University, 1995. For additional details regarding the SPEC study, including how the firms were sampled, consult those references.

4. SPEC is maintaining a Web page, which will provide links to their most recent analyses and data. The current URL is http://www-gsb.stanford.edu/research/programs/SPEC/index.html, or it may be accessed through either the "Corporate Relations" or "Research Partnerships" sections of the Stanford Business School Web site at: http://www-gsb.stanford.edu.

5. The terminology of love, work, and money (and the other terms the SPEC investigators use to characterize the organizational blueprints) are the researchers' inventions, created after the data were collected and analyzed. Founders were not asked to pick among love, work, or money (or any other set of forced choices) as the sole basis of attachment they envisioned. Instead, the founders were asked open-ended questions during the interviews, and the SPEC investigators, based on content analysis of interview transcripts, assigned each conception of attachment to one of these three boxes.

It goes without saying—but we'll say it anyway!—that one should worry about biases in the coding process and about a forced choice of one and only one of several boxes in each of the three dimensions. The SPEC researchers have worried about these potential biases too, conducting analyses to try and gauge their magnitude, which appears to be minimal. (For discussion, see Baron, Burton, and Hannan, "The Road Taken," *op. cit.*; and James N. Baron, Michael T. Hannan, and M. Diane Burton, "Building the Iron Cage: Determinants of Managerial Intensity in the Early Years of Organizations," Harvard Business School, Division of Research Working Paper 98-064, 1998.)

6. For a small number of the firms that agreed to participate in the study, the researchers could not characterize the founder's model for one reason or another, such as an inability to interview the founder. This leaves a subsample of 154 companies for which the founder's model could be characterized in this fashion.

7. For instance, see AnnaLee Saxenian, *Regional Advantage: Culture and Competition in Silicon Valley and Route 128* (Cambridge, MA: Harvard University Press, 1994).

8. Though we sometimes tend to view bureaucrats as alienated, in the classic definition of a bureaucracy (pioneered by the German sociologist Max Weber) employees are strongly committed to their specific work role or vocation and to following formal rules. Indeed, it is the specificity of that commitment that creates some of the pathologies of bureaucracy, according to Weber, because it fosters an excessive division of labor whereby bureaucrats can perceive themselves as bearing no responsibility for matters outside their "office." Also, it is important to bear in mind the context here—small high-tech start-ups, dominated in their early stages by scientific and technical personnel. Thus, the "bureaucracy" moniker here should really be thought of in *relative,* rather than absolute, terms. Founders espousing a bureaucratic approach did not envision running their young companies like a huge government agency; rather, they intended to place more early emphasis on things like formal controls and specialization of functions than did other founders.

9. In early work based on the SPEC sample, the researchers employed a four-category typology that did not differentiate between the autocratic and bureaucratic types. However, subsequent investigations highlighted the importance of distinguishing between these two different blueprints.

10. For those compulsive readers obsessed with the statistical significance of these results, simple (Chi square) tests yield the following probabilities for the null hypothesis that the dimensions are independent: selection and control, 0.000003 (i.e., three chances in a million); attachment and control, 0.000063; and selection and attachment, 0.00000028. To give a slightly more complex statistical test (and rejection) of independence: Under the null hypothesis that the founders chose along the three dimensions independently, according to the marginal percentages in the sample, the chance that we would find 2 or fewer organizations in the eight (out of 36) cells corresponding to the "anomalous" blueprints is a mere 0.00225. (Because the null hypothesis is to some extent conditioned by the data, we don't advance this as a serious statistical test. But two chances in a thousand is pretty reassuring.)

11. In lectures given on this topic, we have sometimes begun with the following drill: The three dimensions and the $3 \times 3 \times 4$ set of blueprints are explained to the audience. Then the audience is asked, "Which of the 36 blueprints would you call a star-based (or elite university) organization; which is a bureaucracy; and so on?" In most cases, audience participants report that they get three or four of the five completely correct, and when they miss, it is usually only on one dimension. The point is that these names

seem to mean something to a lay audience, and in particular seem to mean what the SPEC researchers say they mean.

12. Among SPEC firms in the medical technology or research sectors (including biotechnology), 42.3% were founded along the lines of the pure star model, compared to only 1.6% of firms in other industry sectors.

13. See Hannan, Burton, and Baron, *op. cit.*

14. See James Baron, M. Diane Burton and Michael Hannan, "Engineering Bureaucracy: The Genesis of Formal Policies, Positions, and Structures in High-Technology Firms," *Journal of Law, Economics, and Organization,* forthcoming. For other preliminary evidence on founders' choice of HR models, see M. Diane Burton, Michael T. Hannan, and James N. Baron, "Employment Models in Entrepreneurial Companies," unpublished manuscript, Harvard Business School, 1998; M. Diane Burton, *op. cit.*

15. This excerpt from a founder interview, as well as the other quotes cited below to illustrate founders' strategies, are excerpted by permission from Hannan, Burton and Baron, *op. cit.*, pp. 515–7.

16. Excerpted by permission from Hannan, Burton, and Baron, *op. cit.*, p. 518.

17. Yet there are some reasons to believe the effect of any such biases is minimal in this sample. First, bear in mind that the founder reported on initial conditions, so when the current CEO is not a founder (as in 40% of the companies), he or she is not necessarily aware of what the founder reported. In addition, some of the SPEC team's analyses examine quantitative outcomes based on information typically provided by neither the founder nor the CEO (such as managerial intensity—see below), so demonstrated effects of the founding model on those outcomes seem unlikely to be the result of a selective retrospection bias by founders or CEOs. Moreover, in some analyses (such as those examining managerial intensity), the researchers find that the *founder's* model is a better predictor of current arrangements than is the CEO's model, which is consistent with notions of path-dependent organizational evolution but not with the premise that the CEO is concocting his or her reported HR premises to mesh with the present-day reality (see Baron, Hannan, and Burton, *op. cit.*).

18. In addition, one other firm changed from one type of "quasi-commitment" blueprint to another. The remaining 76 all changed "category" as well as blueprint. For more on the pattern of these changes, see below.

19. For readers addicted to statistical tests: Tests against a null hypothesis of independence using the marginals in the data have significance levels of 5% or lower, except for the association between changes in selection and control. Of course, the various tests certainly aren't independent, and because the null hypothesis is generated from the marginals in the data, this isn't very clean as a statistical test. But it does reinforce our priors based on theory.

20. This is net; four firms out of the original seventeen abandoned formal controls, while thirty-eight adopted formal controls.

21. The thirty-eight firms that did not espouse formal controls initially but embraced them later (according to the CEO's model) were 7.25 years old on average, nearly a year and a half older than the rest of the firms in the sample, a statistically significant difference ($p = .0026$, one-tailed). Twenty-two firms instituted formal controls and made no other changes in their HR blueprint: They too were significantly older than the rest of the sample (7.53 years on average; $p = .0060$, one-tailed). Of course, there are a lot of competing explanations for these differences in means, the most straightforward be-

ing that the longer a firm has been around, the more likely it is to change *something*. But these numbers are (at least) broadly consistent with our rationales.

22. Thus, this logistic regression supports the rationale that formal controls arise because of increased opportunity to codify them. But the rationale that formal controls arise because they are desirable as organizations grow in size is not supported. Not surprisingly, in this sample of relatively young technology companies, age is moderately correlated with size and growth.

23. Baron, Burton, and Hannan, "Engineering Bureaucracy," *op. cit.* Interestingly, in that paper, which analyzes what the companies actually *did* by way of formalization over time, replacing the founder with a new CEO had no net effect. Yet as we just noted, replacing the founder–CEO *does* predict the tendency for firms to have changed their HR blueprint toward an emphasis on formal controls. This is another piece of evidence against the claim that the CEO interview responses used to characterize their blueprint were concocted to fit the current (changed) reality in the company. If that were true, we would have expected replacing the founder with a new CEO not simply to predict changes in *assumptions* regarding formal control, but also to predict changes in actual formalization and bureaucratization.

24. For example, see Yehouda Shenhav, "From Chaos to Systems: The Engineering Foundations of Organization Theory, 1879–1932," *Administrative Science Quarterly* 40 (December 1995): 557–85.

25. In the data file from which these results are culled, it is unclear for fifteen of the 154 organizations whether the CEO in 1994–95 was a founder. Hence, these results are based on a subsample of 139 firms.

26. Specifically, suppose we assign the pure and quasi-pure types to autocracy, star, commitment, engineering, and bureaucracy categories, with all other cases grouped into a "hybrid" category, thereby reducing the 36 possible blueprints to six categories. Only 32.1% of companies with a founder–CEO shifted across these six categories, compared to 69.1% of firms in which a founder was no longer CEO. Another indicator of the differential magnitude of change is that among firms in which a founder is still CEO, only 9.5% changed two or more dimensions of the HR blueprint, compared to 40.0% of companies in which the current CEO was not on the founding team.

27. However, there is also an apparent negative interaction between age and size, which we interpret as indicating that either the *need* to bureaucratize (indicated by growth in scale) or the *opportunity* to do so (indicated by organizational longevity) is sufficient to promote this shift.

28. The researchers found similar patterns when studying another manifestation of formalization, namely, the creation of specialized roles within the top management groups of the SPEC companies. Also see the discussion below regarding differences in managerial overhead as a function of founders' HR models.

29. See Paul S. Adler and Bryan Borys, "Two Types of Bureaucracy: Enabling and Coercive," *Administrative Science Quarterly* 41 (March 1996): 61–89.

30. Commitment firms were also fastest to implement employee voice and participation policies (suggestion systems, quality circles and job rotation), however, too few firms had implemented these practices to enable stable and precise estimates of the statistical effects. For additional evidence on differences in the rate of adopting various HR policies as a function of founders' employment models, see Baron, Burton, and Hannan, "The Road Taken," *op. cit.*

31. Autocracies seem harder to characterize (and likely to vary more) along this dimension, because treatment is more likely to depend on the founder's whim. Some autocrats may relate idiosyncratically to each individual employee, seeking a personalized tie, akin to a parent–child relation, whereas others may view all employees as members of the "troop," whom the autocrat commands in a uniform manner.

32. See Baron, Hannan, and Burton, *op. cit.*

33. Consult the SPEC Web site, referenced in note 4 above, if you are interested in updated results.

34. Baron, Burton, and Hannan, "The Road Taken," *op. cit.,* p. 35. Recall that in 40% of the companies (and 60% of the firms that changed their HR blueprint), the CEO interviewed in 1994–95 was someone other than the founder whose interview provided the information used to characterize the founding model. Consequently, those CEOs presumably had no way of knowing that any of the dimensions had "changed" because they did not provide the information used to characterize the founding period.

20

ORGANIZING HR

AES Corporation is a global power company with assets in excess of $10 billion (as of mid-1998), managing about 30,000 people worldwide (as of year-end 1997)—about 10,000 of its own employees and roughly 20,000 people working in its joint ventures.[1] The company's Web site publicizes its distinctive values and management philosophy:

> In order to create a fun working environment for its people and implement its strategy of operational excellence, AES has adopted decentralized organizational principles and practices. For example, AES works to minimize the number of supervisory layers in its organization. Most of the Company's plants operate without shift supervisors. The project subsidiaries are responsible for all major facility-specific business functions, including financing and capital expenditures. . . . The Company has generally organized itself into multi-skilled teams to develop projects, rather than forming "staff" groups (such as a human resources department or an engineering staff) to carry out specialized functions. . . . [T]here is no one person in charge of teams and there is no Human Resources department.[2]

Now, we don't believe everything we read on the Web, but think about what this must mean. No HR department! The firm certainly has human resources: People are paid, they get benefits, they are hired, they change assignments, one assumes they are evaluated. Somebody, somewhere, has to be paying attention to these things. But who?

Contrast this with the following caricature of central HR (and, no less importantly, how it is *perceived* by general managers) in large American corporations. Structurally, the HR function tends to be subdivided into quite distinct areas of specialization. A typical large bureaucratic firm boasts separate units for such functions as central employment (including job posting and recruitment assistance), employee relations, health and welfare programs, training and organizational development, retirement programs, child and family services, total compensation, and systems. In addition, there may be other specialized units devoted to such activities as managing layoffs, legal and regulatory compliance, temporary employees, and the like. In larger companies, one is likely to see an even more detailed division of labor and, depending on the industry, possibly even more specialized subunits, focused on such areas as occupational medicine, human resources information systems, labor relations and collective bargaining, affirmative action and diversity initiatives, HR planning, corporate headquarters (or executive) personnel, and specialized areas of recruitment and benefits (pensions, health plans, etc.). Typically, these specialty areas will all report directly to the corporate head of human resources (or to one of that person's deputies). The chief HR executive, in turn, will typically be a step or two below the top executive ranks, reporting to the CFO or a senior vice president for Administration, or occasionally to a senior manager in another area.

Continuing the caricature, HR professionals are sometimes perceived as enacting their role with regard to the workforce analogously to how the traditional Information Technology (IT) department discharges its duties vis-à-vis computers. Line managers may be responsible for deciding how many computers to buy, but IT will insist on standards that ensure a requisite degree of uniformity in the company's network. The IT folks will bear responsibility for inventorying purchases of new hardware and software, delivering and installing new equipment (and decommissioning equipment once it outlives its usefulness), answering specialized questions and providing forms of internal consulting, maintaining relations with hardware and software vendors, and assisting business units to ensure that employees receive the ongoing training they need to utilize the technology. To a large extent, the traditional HR role consists of doing comparable activities with respect to employees: promulgating HR standards that are uniform throughout the company; "installing" new employees (ensuring that they have been given the necessary orientation and training); helping to "de-install" employees when they leave, voluntarily or otherwise; maintaining an inventory of employees and their skills; providing specialized assistance and internal consulting (including helping to solve the HR equivalent of "bugs" and "crashes"); maintaining relations with sources of labor supply; and providing various forms of training.

Pursuing this analogy a bit further, an accusation sometimes leveled against both HR and IT departments is that they are turf protectors—intent on bolstering their own precarious positions by hoarding knowledge; promoting rules and regulations that maximize their oversight role, overlooking the distinctive needs of various parts of the organization; and sometimes furnishing advice and solutions that seem guided more by their professional allegiances than by informed consideration of business needs. Indeed, the HR area may be susceptible to becoming even more divorced from the business reality than the IT function. Many organizations nowadays have someone who is a chief information officer, whose job consists of thinking strategically about the role that information technology can play and then supporting that vision through the IT organization. Far fewer organizations have a *bona fide* "chief people officer," whose job consists of doing the same thing within the HR organization. And it is easier to find examples of organization charts showing the CIO reporting directly to the president or CEO than it is to find ones that show the head of HR as a direct report to the CEO.

This is not a flattering portrait of the HR function, and it is obviously a somewhat distorted caricature (and one that some observers believe is changing in American businesses). But we believe it nonetheless reflects how a lot of line and staff managers truly feel, deep in their guts, about their HR colleagues, especially the corporate HR department. To put it starkly, notwithstanding all the talk lately about HR as a "strategic business partner," ask any CEO you know who is doing succession planning to identify the internal candidates who are viable contenders for the top job in the company, and then count how many of them work (or have worked) in HR.

By now, you should be able to anticipate things about this caricature that we find disconcerting. First, the highly fragmented and specialized nature of the personnel function—with oversight for different HR practices parceled out into separate domains, coordinated principally by the corporate head of HR (who often lacks a seat at the top management table)—hardly seems conducive to ensuring that specific elements of the HR system are internally consistent and well-aligned with the business context faced by particular line managers.[3] An HR organization preoccupied with managing the minutiae of personnel administration is unlikely to be capable of attracting, developing, or retaining individuals who can understand the strategic business imperatives impinging on HRM. And even if it did, top management would probably be no more likely to listen to those folks than they would be to entrust the company's financial and risk management strategies to the nice folks in Accounting who are responsible for processing travel reimbursements.

We wrote this book because we believe HRM—especially the strategic side—is too important to be left entirely to HR specialists. It should be the province of every general manager. Moreover, we've emphasized throughout this book the virtues of consistency and (somewhat contrarily) of fit with the local environment. We've also noted the substantial psychological benefits that can come from personalizing the delivery of the goods (if not, for consistency's sake, the goods themselves) from the firm to its employees, at least for organizations seeking something more than an arm's-length market relationship with their employees. Thus, our basic view is that the central HR function in most organizations generally ought to do *more* and *less*—*more* in the way of providing strategic guidance, assessing the organization's capabilities, and supporting line managers in developing and managing human assets; and *less* by way of actually creating and overseeing HR policies and practices. The traditional way of organizing and doing HR is simply ill suited to getting this done.[4]

So how does one organize the HR function to get it done? Numerous scholars, HR practitioners, and high-priced management consultants have lately been advocating generic templates for a modern, leaner and sometimes meaner, strategically minded HR function. You probably won't be surprised to hear us express some skepticism about these one-size-fits-all templates, or to hear us assert that the appropriate structure and mission of the central HR function and satellite HR organizations will necessarily vary as a function of an organization's strategy, technology, culture, workforce, and external environment. In this closing chapter, we will sketch some thoughts along these lines to guide general managers in thinking about the role and structure of HR. Those thoughts will ultimately lead us to suggest that, notwithstanding the absence of any single best model for the HR function, the general direction in which AES is headed is promising, relative to our caricature, even if AES may have gone further than some large organizations will want to go.

WHAT ARE THE HR TASKS TO BE DONE?

Our analysis begins with answers to the question, What tasks are involved in doing HRM and, more importantly, what is the nature of those tasks? (Think of this as an exercise in job design in the spirit of Chapter 13. Before you can bundle tasks together into jobs, you have to compile a list of the tasks that are required and think through their attributes.)

At the risk of gross oversimplification, we suggest thinking of the tasks to be done as falling into three categories: formulating HR strategy and general policies; implementing that strategy in individual cases; and record keeping and service delivery to employees.

Formulation of HR Strategy and General Policies

The formulation of the organization's HR strategy begins with basic questions concerning how employment will be structured, what corporate culture will be fostered, how careers will unfold in the organization, what sort of employees will be sought, and so forth. Within this general category of tasks we include both organizationwide HR strategy and the tailoring of that strategy to specific business units, regional units, functions, or divisions. Especially important in terms of organizationwide strategy are answers to the questions: How consistent should HR policies and practices be throughout the enterprise? Where are distinctions in policies and practices (across locales or employee subgroups) desirable? How much latitude should particular organizational units be given in formulating their own HR strategies?

After the broad outlines of strategy have been set, questions about general policies arise, such as: What will be the broad bases of compensation and performance management throughout the organization or in particular units? What tasks will be outsourced, and will the outsourcing be done via labor contractors or independent contractors? What training will be done in-house, and what will be outsourced, and to whom? It is hard to draw a line between strategy and policy, and we will not make any attempt to do so: In this category we will include any HR-related activity that sets rules for the management of human resources that apply broadly to groups of employees.

Formulating strategy and general policies, it seems to us, is a managerial task of the utmost importance. It is fraught with ambiguity; there is no checklist of what to do or what to think about. The outcomes are noisy—how do you know if you've succeeded? Results often take a long time to be realized. Interdependencies with other parts of business strategy are tight. At the same time, dependence on local environmental conditions can be important, so the local environment must be well understood by those who formulate HR strategy and policies. Finally, the tasks here strongly mix guardian and star elements. Poorly aligned or inconsistent HR policies and practices can be devastating for an organization. At the same time, we've seen throughout this book that the ability to see beyond conventional wisdom, to put together an HR system that works especially well, is as potent a competitive weapon as one can imagine.

Implementation of Strategy and Policies

In this category we have in mind tasks that involve nontrivial judgment in fitting general policies and procedures to specific cases. Performance evaluation of individuals and teams, crafting job designs, decisions on whom to hire (and where specifically to look, although this could be construed as part of policy formation), decisions on whom to promote, decisions on training for individuals, specific layoff decisions, and the like all fit here.

Ambiguity in these tasks is not particularly high if a well-formed set of HR policies and practices is in place; however, outcomes are noisy and feedback can be substantially delayed. Interdependencies with other parts of the business can be substantial; decision-makers should have a fairly well-developed "big picture" of the organization or, at least, of the specific function involved. Because of reputation and social comparison effects, these tasks are predominately guardian roles, although especially when it comes to recognition of talent and accurate placement of individuals, some star aspects are involved.

Record Keeping, Compliance, and Personnel Service Delivery

Here we have in mind those tasks that, unfortunately, have come to dominate many line managers' perceptions of what the HR Department does: compliance reports; keeping employee records; filling out forms for benefits and payroll; and so forth, on down to buying the beverages and pizza for the regularly scheduled employee beer blast.

There isn't a lot of ambiguity here and performance is fairly easily monitored. The job is a mix of some guardian and mainly foot-soldier tasks: Screwing up compliance reports can get the firm in trouble with legal authorities, and a bad benefits office can reduce employee morale pretty quickly, but management that isn't completely asleep or complacent can usually avoid the big disasters in this realm.

Of course, the lines dividing these three categories are not sharp. Is the choice about whether a particular provider of mental health services should be part of the organization's medical benefits package an aspect of HR strategy, a specific implementation decision involving judgment, or part of routine service delivery? We'll return to the lack of sharp dividing lines in a bit.

DIAGNOSIS: THE "LOWEST COMMON DENOMINATOR" SYNDROME

This enumeration of the tasks involved in doing HRM helps clarify a root problem with how HR is traditionally organized. In the traditional HR organization, which bundles together all these tasks, a small fraction of the activities account for a huge proportion of the value added by the function, by creating potential upside and/or helping the organization avoid downside disasters. In contrast, most of the activities conducted, measured by time expended or paper consumed, are the custodial, routine foot-soldier tasks, perceived as adding little value (or sometimes worse!) by managers and employees. Complying with rules and filling out forms imposed by central HR regarding job searches, performance appraisal, or compensation and benefits—or being required to have an HR representative present during a sensitive conference with a subordinate—are frequently not viewed as helping matters very much. And employees, once they are hired, often interact with the HR department only when they have a problem or concern, so they may not have an especially positive view of the function either.

In any event, it is not altogether surprising that a function that is perceived as responsible for explaining benefits programs, processing change-of-address forms, complying with governmental regulations, and enforcing policies that limit managers' discretion on how they can treat employees—or that is touted as the "conscience" or "kinder, gentler side" of the corporation—is unlikely to be viewed as a hard-charging, tough-minded, strategic business partner.

So why does the lowest common denominator predominate in the minds of managers? Why isn't HR known for the high-value-added stuff? One reason is salience: If most of the time spent and paper generated by HR is employee service and compliance, that's what will stick in the minds of general managers.

In addition, an issue of performance evaluation kicks in. It's easier to measure how well the HR department is doing in terms of filling out forms and delivering routine services; it's a lot harder to measure how well it does at formulating and implementing an HR strategy. Firms aren't going to ignore the service delivery and paper processing aspects of HR. These tasks may be mundane, but they are important; think how an employee with a sick child feels if his HMO is giving him a runaround and his appeals to the Benefits Office are met with obfuscation, delay, or indifference. Or imagine what the consequences might be to the organization if compliance data required by the government are sloppy and tardy. But in this situation, as we discussed in Chapters 10 and 11, the more easily measured tasks will tend to command a disproportionate share of attention by the HR department—better to devote time and attention to things where a measurable impact can be seen immediately.

Finally, the emphasis—natural as it is—on the mundane side of HR, combined with the salience of these tasks, has an effect on who chooses a career in HR (or even a posting in HR as part of a career-long progression). People with an inclination to provide service, aid, and comfort will be drawn to HR, while those with a skill set appropriate for strategic planning may find the mix of tasks in other specialties more to their liking and comparative advantage. Let us be clear that we have nothing against warm-and-fuzzy types; they are very valuable in HR administration, and we strongly advise as part of a hard-nosed HR strategy that you have some of them around to handle the service aspects of HR administration. But the people drawn to an HR function that is heavily weighted toward (and *perceived* to be heavily weighted toward) the service tasks may be less likely to have some of the attributes needed to command respect from their managerial colleagues when it comes to hard-nosed decisions.

A POSSIBLE CURE, PART I: DELEGATING THE MUNDANE

We've undoubtedly overstated the case. But insofar as there is some truth to this lowest common denominator syndrome, a syndrome that arises because of the organizational structure of the HR function, cures are apt to be found in reconfiguring HR.

We don't have a simple cure for this syndrome. Indeed, if a simple cure existed, it probably would have been implemented already. But we think the lines of a possible cure are suggested if we consider the analogy to the distinctions between marketing and customer service, or between the corporate finance function on the one hand and the accounting/comptroller function on the other. We generally see fairly clear organizational distinctions drawn between those who are responsible for helping an organization formulate its strategies for reaching markets and creating brand equity on the one hand, versus those who manage routine transactions with customers on the other hand. Similarly, most organizations have fairly clear distinctions (in organizational subunits, career paths, etc.) between those who formulate financial strategy and steward the company's fiscal resources versus those who process routine accounting transactions.

We suggest that a similar logic should apply here. To the extent possible, the mundane, foot-soldier, low-judgment, low-ambiguity tasks should be sent elsewhere in the organization. Outsourcing these tasks is well worth considering. Setting up an "Employee Services Department," in analogous fashion to Customer Services, might be considered. Shipping these things off to a joint Payroll/Comptroller Function is yet another option worthy of consideration. The HR departments—at the corporate level, at the division or regional or business unit level, and at the subunit (i.e., plant) level—should be reduced in size, upgraded in status, staffed with people closer to general management, and focused on those HR tasks that require the serious exercise of judgment and knowledge of the business.

Unhappily, it's considerably easier to write the previous paragraph than it is to follow through on this recommendation, because of the murky boundaries between mundane bookkeeping tasks and high-value-added judgment tasks, and because the delivery of employee services will have an impact on how much value does get added by the high-value-added judgment calls. Tasks on the boundary—the selection of health plans, the design of specific training programs—will have to be assigned to one side or the other. It makes some sense for an employee to have a single HR contact to turn to, whether to do career planning (which we certainly lump in with the high-value-added stuff) or to register complaints about mistreatment by the organization's HMO. So *at least* a dotted-line relationship between our hypothetical "Employee Services" department and the HR department will be useful. And a direct reporting relationship is not ridiculous.

Nonetheless, we see some serious advantages in trying as much as possible to push the mundane tasks out of HR. These are service tasks, and the same mindset and incentives that make for good customer services ought to make for good employee services, a conviction shared by Southwest Airlines, the enormously successful short-haul, low-cost air carrier, whose "People Department" reports to the "Executive Vice President–Customers."[5] Indeed, our suspicion is that having the more routine operational aspects of central HR report into the organizations that oversee customer care and/or internal audit and control would promote several useful objectives: (a) help clarify the internal "clients" for those activities; (b) facilitate economies of scale (e.g., in the use of communications media employed by those in customer service or the use of information systems technologies employed by the accounting function); and (c) create back pressure to outsource as much of this activity as possible.

But far and away, the most significant benefit we are after is to break the lowest common denominator syndrome. HR will no longer be known as the folks who handle benefits, fill out forms, and buy the chips and dip for the office parties. Instead, they will be the people who set up employment policies and then make the nontrivial calls about what those policies mean in specific cases. Or, rather, they'll be the people who *help* in these two remaining sets of tasks, which brings us to our second main recommendation.

OUR CURE, PART II: TOP AND LINE MANAGEMENT VERSUS "SERIOUS" HR PROFESSIONALS

You probably won't be surprised to hear us assert that general managers should be involved up to their eyeballs in setting HR strategy and policies, adapting the strategy and policies on a divisional or regional basis (and then on a plant or facility basis), and implementing the policies by adapting them suitably to particular employees and groups. In fact, we believe that general managers should take the lead on these tasks. Why? Given the interdependencies with other aspects of the organization, it takes general management perspective or, if you prefer, general management *gut feel* to integrate HR strategy with other aspects of strategy. And, moving onto the line, because of her day-to-day contact with her subordinates, it is the line manager who is best situated to provide evaluation, meaningful feedback, and useful advice up the line about what a specific employee requires. (But we are quick to note that line managers can be subject to very mixed motives when it comes to the treatment of specific employees. Our assertion for now is that the line manager has the best information, not that she will necessarily employ that information equitably. Read on for an important role for the on-the-spot HR specialist.) Moreover, we are keen in most cases on maintaining a "personal touch" when it comes to HR administration, because employees tend to appreciate it. Who better to give this personal touch than one's immediate supervisor?

It is worth observing here that if general managers are going to be given primary responsibility for *implementing* nontrivial HR policy on the line, then there is another good reason to have general managers be responsible for *formulating* those policies in the first place: When the people who make policy don't have to implement it, the discipline imposed by having to bear the costs of implementation is lost. And, to reverse the argument, when those who must implement a policy did not help formulate it, we can anticipate less commitment to that policy in the first place. Having policy set by top management back at headquarters and then implemented by line managers in the field doesn't conform precisely to the rule that "those who implement should decide," which will lead us later in this chapter to some thoughts about which general managers should set HR policies. But we believe there is likely to be a tighter connection between those who set policy and those who implement when both groups are drawn from the ranks of general management than if HR specialists are primarily responsible for either policy formulation or policy implementation.

Those who are responsible for formulating HR strategy and handling the implementation of HR policies confront a set of tasks that are ambiguous and uncertain, involving outcomes that are noisy and that can take a very long time to be realized. This makes it very difficult to rely on direct, explicit tools to motivate and reward those who are responsible for these HR tasks. When we discussed pay for performance in Chapter 11, we emphasized how hard it is to achieve good extrinsic motivation for mixed star–guardian tasks. Handing these HR tasks over to general managers doesn't solve this problem, by a long shot. Indeed, to the extent that general managers (more than HR specialists) must attend to many different agendas, some of which may be more easily monitored, measured, and motivated, this may lead to the bad outcome whereby HR management is put on a far-toward-the-back burner. But if a culture and performance management system can be put in place for general managers that emphasizes the critical importance of human resources—if there is a sense that this is an important prerequisite for rising within the organization—then the motivational problems may not be insoluble.

Think for a moment of the typical career path of a general manager in an elite Japanese firm (see Chapter 9). Young managers "produce"—they design, manufacture, sell, and so on. Mid-career executives manage the young managers—they spend the bulk of their time developing the human resources in their care and are evaluated in large measure according to how well they do so. And senior managers manage big-picture issues and external affairs. The point is twofold. First, the (historical) lack of labor mobility means that mid-career managers develop a fairly long and detailed track record as managers of human resources. For performance data that are both noisy and delayed in coming, this is a great advantage. (Unhappily, it is not an advantage that can be replicated in all environments.) And second, the culture of management in these firms attaches primacy to HR. This is a lever that many organizations can pull.

Roles for HR Specialists

But if the mundane tasks are shipped out, and the high-value-added, judgment-call tasks are assigned to general managers, what is left for HR specialists sitting in an HR department?

Starting from the "top"—the formulation of HR strategy and policies—HR specialists should act as advisors to and educators of top management. It is important that all of general management, and most especially top management, is HR-literate. That's why we wrote this book. But being a general manager usually means being literate about a lot of stuff and an expert on rather little, and unless the CEO or the division (or business unit or regional) chief has an HR background, she is unlikely to be an HR expert. Some of HRM is pretty straightforward common sense. But we also hope to have convinced you that other parts are fairly subtle. Take, for instance, the design and redesign of performance appraisal systems. Given the number of different goals that performance appraisal serves, it is far from easy or clear or commonsensical how to achieve an appropriate balance. It's even harder to anticipate all the feedback effects that a change in performance appraisal practices will bring. Perhaps most subtle of all is the notion that change in performance appraisal for its own sake may have benefits. (Recall our discussion of these issues in Chapter 10.) Or, to take a somewhat more mundane but still very critical aspect of staffing and recruiting, consider job interviews: Should they be unstructured, so that a skillful interviewer can follow leads that develop in the course of the interview; or should they follow a script, so that there is a firmer basis for the inevitable cross-person comparisons that follow interviews? Should they be conducted one-on-one, which may encourage the candidate to relax; or many-on-one, to reduce interviewer caprice? These questions have been carefully studied; if you don't remember the findings, see Chapter 14. The general point is that a specialist—someone who follows the literature on HRM and is educated to appreciate the nuanced conclusions of HR research—can help find answers to questions that general managers have and, even, to recognize important questions that might not otherwise have occurred to the general manager.

Indeed, even when the CEO or division chief is highly HR-literate, the conflicting demands on that person to pay attention to marketing, finance, operations, and so on are likely to mean that he or she won't have the time to follow the latest thinking on the subject, or even to devote careful thought to HR issues. A staff that concentrates on these matters—not to the exclusion of other matters, but with HR on the front burner all the time—is important, as long as the chief doesn't abdicate her decision-making authority (or the authority of the executive committee) on these issues.

A good example of this role being enacted by HR specialists is provided by the vice president for HR in a prominent, *Fortune 500* high-technology global corporation, who recently gave a presentation to a group of managers participating in an internal management development program. The company, which had grown at an astounding rate, was less than two decades old, founded very much along the "engineering" model described in the previous chapter. The firm had been at the cutting edge of a number of major technological developments in computers and networking, and it had been able to attract extremely talented technical personnel by offering opportunities to work at the technical frontier. The company also offered extremely generous and comprehensive benefits, financial and otherwise. Yet as the company had grown and matured, it had inevitably lost some of its initial "start-up" allure, and its innovations had prompted heightened competition from other leading technology companies. The head of HR had become increasingly concerned about how the firm would continue to attract and retain the technical elite. Accordingly, he commissioned a comprehensive and carefully designed survey of current and former employees, as well as information obtained from prospective employees, designed to answer the question: What differentiates this firm in the labor market and what are the dimensions on which it can be the employer of choice in a world of increasingly fierce competition for technical stars? According to the VP for HR, after they methodically analyzed the data, the answer came back loud and clear about what distinguished his company from competitors in the labor market: *absolutely nothing*. As a result, the head of HR persuaded senior management at this company to launch an initiative aimed at redefining the company's culture and HR practices around the idea of being a "career" employer. He believes this will give the company a competitive edge against other technology firms, which have tended to deemphasize commitments to their employees and play up the notion that individual employees must be responsible for their own careers.

Whether or not this gambit succeeds, it certainly illustrates the sort of enterprise in which we think the head of HR should be engaged. In this firm, as in most, the CEO is far too busy dealing with strategic, technological, legal, and regulatory issues to design and oversee such a thorough study of the company's reputation in the labor market (even if the CEO had the skills to do so, which many do not.) And line managers and their HR partners are too worried about staffing particular positions and fighting local personnel fires to be reflecting on the longer-term issues of HR strategy.

HR professionals also have an important and unique role to play when it comes to the judgment calls that arise when implementing the HR strategy in specific cases. We argued that this should be a line management responsibility because the line manager "on the spot" has the best specific information, and because we believe that the personal touch is usually a good thing when it comes to something as personal and personally important as an employee's career or job. These are solid reasons for leaving judgmental HR administration to line managers. But they aren't entirely conclusive, on at least two grounds: (1) HR specialists can help to preserve the appearance and fact of objectivity; and (2) they can helpfully intervene in cases where the personal touch is not an unalloyed positive.

To take the second point first, human resource management is not always or solely the presentation of gifts. Sometimes bad news has to be delivered. We aren't thinking here of bad news as in, "You're fired," in which the relationship is ended. Think instead of "You didn't get the promotion" or "We won't fund that training in your case." It sometimes helps to be able to lay off at least some of the blame in such instances. Doing so can help preserve cordial relations between a superior and subordinate. In addition, hearing bad news from a third party may help the person getting the bad news to save face, a psychological fact of life that has a lot to do with the persistence of management consulting as an industry.

As for objectivity, it is sadly the case that some general managers are less than paragons of objectivity and virtue. Some are susceptible to corruption, some attend to private agendas, some are prejudiced, and some are simply capricious. (We don't mean you, we emphasize.) To place the administration of HR practices solely in the hands of such a manager is unlikely to produce good outcomes. Moreover, to place the administration of HR practices solely in the hands of a virtuous paragon can lead to (incorrect) feelings of ill use, caprice, corruption, prejudice, and so forth. Not all paragons have had the time and track record needed to develop the untarnished reputation they deserve, and an employee who is denied a promotion or raise by a paragon can be forgiven for sometimes confusing his own unhappy outcome with managerial discretion exercised unfairly. And when an individual manager is given a lot of authority, even if she is incorruptible, the temptation to try to corrupt her might prove too strong for those whose futures she will influence.

Even a line manager who is a veritable paragon of virtue and who is recognized as such has a lot of concerns to balance. When some of those concerns involve measures of performance that can be influenced quickly (such as product shipping date) and others involve noisier, long-delayed outcomes (such as the manager's and firm's reputation with the workforce), line managers might make compromises that are not in the organization's long-term interests.

Finally, individual line managers may not fully understand or appreciate the organization's HR strategy and policies, and the long-term reputation sought with employees. This can be a particular problem in settings characterized by relatively high rates of managerial mobility, which can impede stability, consistency, and "memory" as far as HRM is concerned. We have emphasized that simplicity, consistency, and clarity in HRM are all virtues, in part because they make it easier for individual managers to conform consistently with the strategy and policies of the organization. But simplicity, consistency, and clarity must be traded off against the complexities of real life.

For all these reasons, HR experts in particular specialty areas can play an important role in advising and educating line managers; helping sustain a coherent and consistent HR philosophy throughout the organization; and even, in some cases, acting as independent authorities or appeal officers, in case employees feel aggrieved by line management decisions.

In-the-field HR specialists can also help in evaluating and improving the HRM performance of line managers. We have noted already how challenging it is to evaluate managers' performance in this domain. It is perhaps hardest to evaluate performance in the area of HR strategy and policy formation, but even evaluating how well policies are implemented is difficult. General managers have a lot of things to attend to, and it is therefore expected and natural that HR will be pushed toward the back burner. We advocate dealing with this first of all by promoting a culture that elevates the management of human resources, relying on intrinsic motivation of line managers to some extent. But some accountability—some measurement of performance—will support the desired culture. HR specialists are likely to have the best training and widest range of evidence for conducting comparative evaluations of managerial HR performance. Hence, they are well positioned to provide measures of HR performance on which line manager accountability can be based and to counsel line managers regarding how to improve their effectiveness in formulating and implementing HR policies for their units.

The case of the new 360-degree feedback system implemented at the Morgan Stanley investment bank (now part of Morgan Stanley Dean Witter) is illustrative in this regard.[6] Upon assuming the presidency of the firm in 1993, John Mack implemented a number of organizational changes aimed at creating a unified, continuously innovative "one-firm firm," with greater collaboration and cooperation across units in the service of Morgan's global clients. Mack viewed implementation of the 360° feedback system as an important part of this organizational and cultural change. He hired Tom DeLong, a former professor and university administrator, to serve as his chief development officer (effectively, the senior HR person) and appointed DeLong a managing director of the firm.[7] As a condition of taking the job, DeLong insisted on reporting directly to Mack and having an office located close to Mack's.

Under the new feedback system, input was solicited on a number of dimensions for professional employees from superiors, peers, subordinates, and internal clients, with the list of evaluators selected in consultation between the person being evaluated and that person's "evaluation director" (typically, the manager or supervisor). The evaluation director was responsible for collating and summarizing the input received (into an Evaluation and Development Summary), which was the basis for a regular performance review discussion with the employee. In some divisions, these summaries were also the basis for promotion and compensation decisions.

DeLong and his staff—and John Mack—received a copy of all performance appraisals submitted by Morgan Stanley managers above a certain level, as well as a regular report listing managers who had not submitted the required appraisals on time. (In fact, during the first year of the new system, Mack personally called any senior manager whose appraisals were delinquent or inadequate.) Of course, one objective here was for DeLong to become better informed about the individuals being reviewed, as part of the company's executive development strategy. (And because DeLong and his staff were also responsible for training Morgan Stanley executives in the new procedures, they needed to identify instances where they could help coach managers on how to manage and evaluate performance of their subordinates more effectively.) But another equally important objective was to ensure that the senior managers were implementing the new performance appraisal system effectively, conscientiously, and in a timely manner.[8] Line managers conducting these appraisals were presumably well aware that this was taking place and that the head of HR who was reviewing their "work" had Mack's ear and an office in close proximity to the CEO. You can no doubt anticipate that this would have a salutary effect of the quality of these appraisals. Of course, as you can also anticipate, this caused some skeptical managers to view DeLong as John Mack's "spy."[9]

Having HR specialists in the field help appraise, train, and coach the HR performance of their general management peers has an additional benefit—it adds some clout to the HR department. But it's not without problems. Good and objective measures of performance are hard to come by. We'll address this issue later in this chapter, when we discuss measuring HRM performance. Giving HR specialists a role in evaluating general managers may turn recommendations from the same HR specialists into something closer to "commands," an outcome we would very much like to avoid. And, as we'll discuss later when considering the reporting connections between corporate HR and unit- or subunit-level HR personnel, this will make lines of reporting more tangled. On balance, however, we think this is a role that field HR can often play and a role that ought to be undertaken by someone; so this is a task we urge you to consider assigning to HR specialists. And there is ample precedent for such a role. After all, many companies have used a similar approach in other arenas—for instance, having specialists charged with overseeing corporate quality or ethics initiatives be responsible for training, coaching, and helping to evaluate general managers in contributing to those initiatives.

Finally, we have the record keeping, compliance, and routine delivery of employee services. We advised earlier that you consider outsourcing these tasks, or having the departments that provide them report to Customer Service or Accounting and Payroll. We aren't backing down from that recommendation. But there are some interdependencies between these tasks and the more judgmental, strategic tasks that arise in HRM. (Indeed, employee needs and complaints that surface through delivering seemingly mundane personnel services are often a catalyst for broader changes in HR policy.) So, a dotted-line relationship between service providers and (especially) in-the-field HR specialists is an excellent idea.

STAFFING, TRAINING, AND CAREER PATHS FOR THE HR FUNCTION

Now that we've shrunk and focused the HR department, we have to staff it. Whom should you hire for this newly configured HR function? What sort of training should you give them? What kinds of career paths should they follow?

To our tastes, one should think of these people as "nearly" general managers who specialize in HR issues. They should be well trained in business generally. They should be interested in and knowledgeable about business, particularly *your* business. As part of their on-the-job training, they should get exposure to the other business realities facing your enterprise. The reasons should be obvious: To be successful, HR needs to be integrated with other general business concerns. An HR specialist, in an advisory position or otherwise, who doesn't appreciate the larger general business picture facing the organization is poorly situated to provide sensible guidance. And even if the guidance given is sensible, this person is less likely to be able to get the ear and respect of general managers.

You can think of hiring general management types and then giving them the experience and training needed to become HR experts, or you can think of hiring HR types with basic business training, who are ready and willing to migrate into general management. We have no reason to suspect that either of these is generally superior to the other. But it is worth pointing out that each of them poses a particular problem to be surmounted.

If you decide to hire someone with professional training in HR, it may be hard to find someone with basic training in other crucial aspects of business. At least within the United States, if you peruse the curricula of undergraduate and graduate-level programs that grant specialized degrees in industrial relations, personnel management, human resources, and the like, you will discover that graduates frequently are not required to have taken a course in business strategy, and sometimes not even corporate finance or accounting. Not to put too fine a point on it, we don't think the simple net present value calculations used in a few places in this book should be off-putting to any student in any field of management. But one of the academics who anonymously reviewed this book manuscript for our publisher—a professor whom we expect teaches in a well-regarded department or school of Industrial Relations or Human Resources—suggested that such material would make it impossible to use the book for his or her students. We don't find this encouraging, to say the least. If you hire folks professionally trained in HR, you should be careful to ascertain what they know of a general business nature and how willing and able they are to plug any holes in their knowledge. You should verify that they are ready, willing, and able to spend time learning other aspects of your specific business. And then you should follow through, with tours of duty in other functions or (at least) with some in-house training in what your firm does and how.

Senior HR executives frequently complain that their biggest challenge is finding smart, talented people for their HR organizations who know or can learn *the business*. Give us those people, they say (including to the schools responsible for producing HR professionals), and we can train them in the specialized HR knowledge they need to do their jobs well. So the answer might be, instead, to hire general managers and steer them toward an HR specialty. However, they may resist, at least in the current American business environment, worried that this is a dead-end career path. Managerial recruits and lower-level managers, seeking to rise in the corporation, will have to be disabused of those worries—and the most convincing argument will be the existence of clear career paths leading from or through HR into the highest reaches of top management. Of course, the best way to communicate this is with vivid examples. For instance, Herbert Allison Jr., President and Chief Operating Officer of Merrill Lynch, the global financial management concern, served for some time as that firm's head of human resources as part of his career development en route to the top. As another example, when John Reed of Citicorp (now Citigroup) visited our HR class at Stanford several years ago, he mentioned that he had identified a small number of possible internal candidates to succeed him in the future, one of whom was his head of HR. You could see the immediate impact of this registered on our MBA students' faces. (And of course the message would be even stronger if Reed's successor were indeed to be his head of HR.) If Stanford MBA students divine these cues in speeches from CEOs, you can bet that employees in your organization pick up on them in spades.

But beyond proving the point with a CEO who used to head HR, there are other steps that can be taken to signal that HR is not a dead end. Even if the head of HR—call him or her the chief talent officer (CTO) or chief people officer (CPO)—is not in a particular instance a viable candidate for succeeding the CEO, he or she should have a place on the corporation's Executive Committee. And heads of

HR at the divisional, business unit, or regional levels should have similar positions in the highest councils within their respective units. In organizations that rotate fast-track managers through various functions for purposes of seasoning and broadening, HR should be a stop on the grand tour, and HR specialists should be tourists themselves. Even in organizations that aren't so explicit about crafting such tours of duty for "seasoning" purposes, we should observe transfers from the line into the HR department and out of HR into line positions. The point is to develop HR specialists who are still general managers, to promote the idea that HR is not a dead-end job, but also (and perhaps more importantly) so that the HR specialists can understand and contribute to the integration of HR strategy with other aspects of the overall business strategy.

CORPORATE VERSUS UNIT AND SUBUNIT HR

In the discussion so far, we have taken it as more or less axiomatic that there will be a corporate-level HR department, unit-level HR departments (at the divisional, business unit, or regional level), and then subunit-level departments at specific plants or facilities. We will concentrate here on the relationship between corporate and unit-level HR, but what we will say is easily extended to the relations between unit and subunit HR departments.

There are two important issues to discuss here. First, how should reporting lines be arranged? Second, which issues, questions, and topics "belong" to corporate HR and which to the units?

Needless to say, these two questions are connected. The more that corporate HR strategy dictates unit-level HR policies—that is, the more that unit-level HR simply involves implementing policies and practices set down at the corporate level—the more sense there is in having a direct reporting relationship from unit-level HR to corporate HR. But on balance, we tend to favor having unit-level HR report to unit-level top management, with a dotted-line relationship to corporate HR. The reasons are: to encourage HR customization, to fit the specific environment, strategy, demography, and technological needs of the unit; to work against an HR-is-staff mentality; and to reinforce the idea that it is general management at the appropriate level that should formulate and implement HR strategy. If unit-level HR specialists advise unit-level top management, then they should report to unit-level top management. We can only envision a good case for having unit-level HR report directly to corporate HR when consistency of personnel practices throughout the organization is ultra-important—say, because people and information move across unit boundaries all the time—or when corporate reputation and even survival is at stake in the actions of any unit (for instance, some global financial and transportation companies meet these conditions).

Note that this recommendation concerning reporting relations, if followed, has some natural consequences for one role we've assigned to in-the-field HR specialists—namely, to evaluate the HRM performance of their general management colleagues. It would be tricky, to say the least, to have a division chief's HRM performance evaluated by the division CPO (chief people officer), when that division

CPO in turn reports to the division chief being evaluated. Instead, it would probably be best to have the division CPO report to the division chief about the HRM performance of other, lower-ranking general managers in the division, leaving the evaluation of the division chief's HRM performance to the appropriate official in the central HR department. Yet even so, the division CPO probably will need at least to be consulted, as he or she usually will have the best information on how seriously the division chief takes HRM, what actions were taken and why, and how the division chief might become more effective at HRM. Of course, this issue is not unique to the HR function—it arises whenever one considers systems such as 360° performance feedback. But the fact that this issue arises here should be carefully noted.

As for the allocation of responsibility between corporate- and unit-level HR, we imagine that the forces of centralization will often push toward formulating strategy, policies, and procedures at the corporate level, with unit-level HR left to handle minor adaptations and implementation. But there are some implementation matters that should properly be left with corporate HR. For instance, even in a very decentralized, multinational corporation—a (self-described) multidomestic company such as ABB, for instance—there is usually a core cadre of global managers who move among the different units and then up into the central corporate hierarchy. The nurturing of this cadre of managers, which in our experience tends with surprising regularity to number between 250 and 500 within large corporations, generally should reside with central HR. There are at least three reasons for this prescription. First, it usually will be supremely important to the organization to keep track of these people, to fill holes in the corporation's upper managerial ranks, and to provide these individuals with career paths that make them better candidates for corporate succession. Second, division, business unit, or regional managers may be loathe to surrender such sterling human assets for the greater good of the corporation as a whole—at least, motives may be mixed if these high-potential individuals are "handled" by unit-level HR departments. And finally, forces of social comparison are apt to be particularly high for this mobile cadre of global managers, and consequently consistency of treatment among them is likely to be particularly desirable.

But aside from special cases like this, the corporation should consider the virtues of decentralizing HR policies and procedures, subject to very general HR strategy. The trade-off, of course, is between consistency in HR strategy and practices across units versus fitting those strategies and practices to specific situations. For instance, activities intended to improve diversity of the workforce are, in our experience, typically quite centralized. As we noted in Chapter 14, this is due at least in part to a belief that efforts to improve diversity involve (through externalities) local costs and global benefits, so that decentralizing these efforts might jeopardize getting the job done. Although we realize that some affirmative action imperatives may favor or even require centralization, our general inclination here is to move in the direction of *decentralizing* these activities as much as possible, except for those operational aspects (mostly reporting- and compliance-related) that must be managed centrally. Numerous commentators have noted that the mixed results achieved by many organizations in seeking to promote diversity partly reflect the fact that corporate programs and initiatives in this area are often not well integrated with the strategy and normal operations of the business at the line level and consequently are not "owned" by line managers.

The larger point here is that compelling arguments can usually be made about why the sky will fall if virtually *any* HR activity is decentralized, not to mention self-serving arguments that can be made by an HR organization interested in protecting its turf. Yet the recent success of firms like ABB and AES—which have pursued radical decentralization while also sustaining strong organizational cultures with little or no central HR oversight—suggests that it may be sensible to shift the frame from "What might happen if we didn't do this at headquarters?" to "Is there any compelling argument *against* letting the line managers and their HR partners handle this?"

In every specific case, a five-factor analysis is called for along two lines: What are the costs of potential inconsistencies in policy and practice across parts of the organization; and what are the benefits of customizing HR activities to the particular context? A general analysis of these questions is impossible—it will depend too much on the specifics of the company. But to give a very broadbrush illustration of some of the issues involved, let us consider the more specific analysis of these questions in the context of a global organization.

A Five-Factor Analysis: Companywide versus Unit-Specific HR in Global Corporations

Strategy

The catchphrase "globalization" is invoked often these days, but corporations can follow quite different global strategies that bear on HRM. For instance, one form of globalization involves developing the capability to serve locally differentiated markets, which vary markedly in their particular characteristics and needs, while leveraging corporatewide resources. This strategy would seem to presuppose a considerable amount of hiring of local personnel, well versed in their specific markets, and consequently entail a fair amount of differentiation in HR policies and practices across business units and especially across locales. Hence, one would expect to see a fairly low degree of centralization in HR.

In contrast, some globalization strategies are predicated more on developing global brand equity and facilitating the transfer of knowledge, products, and technologies from one business unit or locale throughout the organization, particularly when the client or customer being served is itself a global enterprise. In this setting, we would expect to observe a higher degree of uniformity and consistency in HR practices sought across business units and locales; this will support coordination and facilitate transfers of personnel, which are likely to be important in implementing this form of global strategy. Consequently, we would expect to observe a somewhat stronger role for the central HR function in firms pursuing this type of strategy, which would include balancing the need for locally competitive HR practices against the need for companywide consistency, assisting with global rotations, and serving as internal consultants to maximize organizational learning and teamwork across intraorganizational boundaries. In addition, this version of globalization is likely to rely more extensively on expatriate hiring, to ensure that new operations established in far-flung locales are appropriately integrated with corporate strategy and culture. This will increase the need for central HR to assist with expatriate issues.

An important issue that melds strategy with culture concerns the *process* by which the corporation is globalizing. Is it creating greenfield sites overseas, or is it purchasing existing firms (as, for example, in the contemporary worlds of book publishing and entertainment)? You can probably anticipate what we will have to say on this point, and you can check your guess in a page or so, when we get to cultural concerns.

Technology

It is also easy to envision ways in which technology and work organization will shape the critical HR tasks and how the HR function should be organized. For instance, as already noted, the degree of interdependence among regional units or locales will influence the desirability of decentralizing versus centralizing various HR functions, with consistency and uniformity being more important where interdependence is high. One characteristic attribute of guardian technologies is high interdependence among business units or locales, if only because of the reputational consequences for the firm of a disaster in any part. (Think of the effect of a large airplane crash on the rest of an airline or the impact of a chemical plant explosion on the rest of the corporation.) When the misdeeds of one business unit or locale can impose large negative externalities on the rest of an organization, we would expect to see more stringent companywide HR policies and practices regarding selection, training, evaluation, pay for performance, and career development, which are at least monitored, if not crafted, centrally. To underscore the point, the collapse not too long ago of Britain's prestigious Barings PLC should persuade you that a single rogue trader—whose country or business unit manager may have implemented an ill-conceived incentive scheme or utilized a flawed process for screening, training, and monitoring hires—is capable of bringing down a huge financial services institution.[10]

Workforce

The important issues here tie back to strategy and technology, and tie forward to organizational culture. Consider firms that globalize by siting different pieces of the overall production process in different countries. For instance, an electronics firm might site R&D and corporate HQ in the United States, manufacturing in Japan, and sales in separate national offices throughout the world. The different national workforces may be quite different in terms of education, career aspirations, age distribution, and the like, making a strong case for distinctive HR practices. Or consider a European car manufacturer that puts a design facility in the United States with a mandate to design specialty cars primarily for the U.S. market. To the extent that the employees of the U.S. facility will not demographically resemble the employees back in Europe and there will not be a huge amount of interdependence between the U.S. designers and employees back in Europe, decentralization of HR is more desirable.

A similar pressure toward home-grown HR policies and practices can arise based on occupational, rather than demographic, distinctions. For instance, scientists and engineers working in a remote research lab within a large corporate bureaucracy are likely to view a system of personnel practices crafted by (or at least specifically *for*) their community of professional colleagues as much more legitimate than a bundle of "not invented here" procedures transplanted from headquarters.

Organizational Culture

Organizational culture is likely to influence the extent of centralization versus decentralization of HR policies. We would expect to find greater centralization: in organizations whose cultures value central control over autonomy, egalitarianism over meritocracy, and tradition over change (an emphasis on change will tend to favor decentralization to facilitate more rapid local adaptations); where there is a presumption of distrust and a belief that workers will shirk unless they are monitored and controlled; where processes and rule compliance are valued over outcomes; and when the organization professes some higher calling (requiring consistency of messages and intense inculturation, which are likely to favor centralization of at least some facets of HRM).

We have stressed repeatedly that culture, and HR practices more generally, display strong inertial tendencies. Implementing major changes can be difficult. So a firm that is globalizing by acquiring ongoing businesses overseas may well be forced into highly decentralized HRM. Consider, for instance, a media or publishing giant that is buying up book publishers, periodicals, and newspapers worldwide. A French corporation, say, that buys a medium-sized American publisher is, to be sure, purchasing a backlist and some brand equity. But perhaps most importantly, this firm is buying (or hopes to be buying) the human resources that are at the center of the publishing firm—contacts between editors and authors, knowledge and contacts among the sales force that help the company compete in securing precious shelf space for its books in the large retail chain stores, and so on. To the extent that the publishing firm being acquired already has in place a culture with accompanying HR policies and practices that differ markedly from those of the French parent, the parent company should proceed with extreme caution in centralizing HR policies and practices. Too rapid a change or too much enforced uniformity risks losing the central asset that was purchased, a lesson that has been learned at great cost by more than one large corporation that has tried to superimpose its corporate HR blueprint on an entrepreneurial acquisition.

Environment

Finally, the economic, social, and legal environments will exert a profound effect on how a global organization should structure its HR activities. To state it succinctly, the environmental variations can range from substantial to enormous, and as a consequence the pressures to decentralize can range from "substantial but not decisive" to overwhelming.

At the "not decisive" end of the spectrum, we have global organizations that primarily hire professionals from a global labor market. Investment banks are a prime example. On the "overwhelming" end of the spectrum are engineering service firms, such as Bechtel or ABB, which frequently must hire a high percentage of local labor, either due to formal domestic content laws, efforts to appease local unions, or attempts to appeal to government agencies that are awarding public works contracts. Laws about labor representation, social norms about work, and differences in local labor markets all need to be "fitted," and a one-size-fits-all HR strategy is clearly going to be inappropriate. Indeed, companies facing such overwhelming diversity may elect to adopt a business strategy that avoids the most dramatic differences by, say, outsourcing extensively. For instance, engineering firms will often subcontract pieces of the overall project; or think of a global package delivery firm—such as Federal Express—which in some countries may choose to ally itself with an existing courier firm for local pick-up and delivery, rather than setting up a pick-up and delivery network of its own. We might expect this to occur especially in countries that must be part of the network so that a truly global service can be offered—perhaps to satisfy a major global corporation that is an important client—but that are not otherwise a major part of the firm's mainline business. And siting decisions can help avoid the worst of conflicts; we've noted several times in this book how the major Japanese car manufacturers, when they set up assembly facilities in the United States, chose locales best suited to the type of HR systems they wished to establish.

An interesting interaction of strategy and environment (along with workforce) that bears on centralization versus decentralization of HRM concerns geographical mobility among personnel. Extensive rotations may be sought because of the business strategy being pursued (recall the extensive movement of *Gentils Organisateurs* among resort properties within Club Med, as described in Chapter 13, to provide a uniform "product" and for language reasons); or because the type of employees the firm requires value mobility as part of their career development; or because long-term postings are not viable due to labor market conditions and the social environment (for instance, expatriate workers may not be able to remain in a given foreign posting for more than a limited period due to visa issues or dual career constraints). For whatever reason, extensive geographical mobility among personnel within an organization will tend to favor centralization of the human resource function, for the same reasons that interdependence across business units does.

Labor unions are another important feature of the environment that will bear on how human resources are structured. Firms facing a single international union will typically migrate toward greater centralization of the HR function. Unions' political agendas often involve the pursuit of equitable and uniform treatment (across regions, firms, industries, etc.) to create a homogeneous and cohesive constituency. (But see Chapter 6 for some exceptions to this.) This pushes unions and management toward more centralized bargaining over the terms of employment and favors the creation of uniform policies that are applied widely, which also favors centralized HRM. In addition, in settings where unionization is industrywide, management may encounter occasions when it seeks to collaborate informally with competitors or through industry associations in formulating stands vis-à-vis the union (steering clear of labor law and antitrust violations, of course), and this will generally be easier when employment relations are centrally controlled. Finally, the more politicized character of employment relations in unionized settings puts a premium on distributive and procedural justice, which will tend to favor centralization of HR policies and practices.

Unions that operate on a truly global scale are rare, however. Large national unions may embrace several closely connected countries (the United States and Canada, say, or the countries within the United Kingdom), and there may be informal relations among unions in different nations (e.g., between some crafts unions in North America and the U.K.), but at present unions remain more national than international in character. (It is interesting to speculate on how creation of the Euro-zone, not quite reality as this book was being written, will affect this in Europe.) Of course, having to deal with multiple powerful unions based in different countries, subject to different labor laws and with different labor–management cultures, pushes in precisely the opposite direction, toward decentralization.

A final interaction of unionization and centralization can arise from the firm's desire to either capitalize on or escape from its prior reputation and traditions in dealing with organized labor. Management that has sought overall cooperative labor–management relations may see some benefit in centralizing labor relations, or at least insisting that national units coordinate with corporate HQ on these matters, as they may be able to leverage a reputation for good relations achieved in one part of the company to achieve similar relations elsewhere (for instance, in a new part of the world the company plans to enter or in a separate enterprise the company plans to acquire). In contrast, when the dominant pattern of union–management relations has been antagonistic, there may be benefits from decentralizing this aspect of HR, to try to build local positive relations, as General Motors has tried to do to some extent with its Saturn venture and its New United Motors joint venture with Toyota.[11]

AES, Redux

To illustrate the analysis just conducted, let us again consider AES, the global power company without an HR department, which we mentioned at the start of this chapter. As we understand it, what this really means is that there is no central or corporate-level HR department at AES. Specific business ventures will, as their general managers see fit, have people who are responsible for handling HR issues at the level of the venture.

Based on the analysis just given, this makes a substantial amount of sense, given AES's business context. As a company building and operating power generation facilities worldwide, AES operates in many diverse markets, with relatively low interdependence among them, and they presumably face strong political and other pressures for hiring local personnel. This is a case of "globalization" achieved through economies of scale being applied to relatively distinct local markets. Linking the specific organizational subunits are three things: (1) a very strong culture, created and espoused by the founders, which values corporate social responsibility and putting people ahead of profits; (2) a cadre of "international managers" who form the core human resources of AES and who manage the far-flung specific ventures in AES's portfolio; and (3) financial ties that link these specific ventures back to the corporate center. Although AES has no central HR department, it does maintain a strong central emphasis on promoting shared values, through mission statements and other cultural documents, extensive corporatewide communications, regular employee surveys, and strategic use of job rotations and expatriate assignments to transplant values. But beyond this, the need to match subunit HR practices to local conditions is paramount.[12]

If AES has gone too far in this decentralization (and we suspect they may find down the road that they've done so), this is likely to surface with HR issues that concern the cadre of high-potential international managers at the core of this corporation. Our understanding is that the "care and feeding" of this group of managers is handled by the top managers of AES, who also act as loose gatekeepers on the financial purse strings of the corporation. At the firm's current size, this may work well—and, of course, we like the notion that top management is intimately involved with this cadre of the firm's human resources. But as AES grows, and as members of this cadre begin to mature, we wonder whether some formalization of the HR function for them—which in turn will necessitate some form of central HR function—won't become unavoidable.

FOUR PROCESS ISSUES

We conclude this discussion by considering four specific issues related to the management of human resources and the HR function:

Measuring HR Effectiveness

As we noted earlier, part of the problem in elevating the importance attached to HRM, as practiced both by line managers and HR organizations, is that the HR function doesn't attract a lot of respect among general managers (in the United States, at least). Until HR gains respect and credibility within the organization, it is unlikely to reach the levels of importance we think it deserves.

We've given our analysis for why this is, but here we want to add a further reason: It is usually hard for the HR function to prove its worth in terms of the bottom line, because HR outcomes are rarely measured very well. In a business culture in which demonstrating your impact on the bottom line or on the market price of equity is the *sine qua non,* this can be crippling.

Think for a moment about the following query: How did organizations in which you have worked evaluate the effectiveness of their HR policies and their HR function? If you were a manager, how was *your* performance in managing human resources specifically evaluated? Prevailing practice at many firms is pretty dismal in this regard. Sometimes there is little or no formal evaluation along these lines at all. With the increasing popularity of benchmarking, companies now increasingly will compare themselves to other firms in terms of their turnover rates, HR head-count and costs per capita, training costs per employee, or employee satisfaction (sometimes by hiring an outside firm to do the survey and provide comparison statistics on comparable firms). But such efforts often provide limited insight for several reasons:

- Efforts to benchmark sometimes do not take adequate account of strategy and technology differences. Consider a firm that has elected to run a high-commitment HR system in an industry dominated by firms that do not. It probably won't learn very much by comparing its HR costs or turnover rates to those of its competitors.

- Turnover and job satisfaction data may be of limited value in gauging the effectiveness of HRM, at least without adjustments for employee perfor-mance and other factors likely to determine turnover and morale in a spe-cific subunit. Presumably an organization would not be deliriously happy to see low turnover and high job satisfaction among its worst performers.

- Conventional hard measures of HR effectiveness (or per capita costs devoted to HR activities) tend to focus on the HR organization, particularly the head-quarters operation. Increasingly, however, the relevant cost and outcome metrics ought to focus on decentralized business units, where activity-based costing and accounting schemes may have an especially difficult time deter-mining which cost pool should be charged for various HR-related activities. For instance, consider training expenses associated with a new capital equip-ment purchase, or travel expenses for a work team to meet with a key cus-tomer and receive feedback that will aid their efforts in the future. Against whose budget should such expenses be charged?

- Relatedly, line managers are seldom held closely accountable for perfor-mance against specific HR-related metrics. This is with good reason: Gener-ally the metrics tend to be much less precise than performance standards in other domains, such as those that concern costs, market share, or opera-tional efficiency. As we discussed in Chapter 10, to motivate explicitly atten-tion to HR concerns based on the noisy metrics available would work poorly with risk-averse managers. But if line managers aren't held account-able, then they don't pay much attention at all.

So what to do? In our view, a two-pronged attack is called for. First, to the extent possible, better measures of HR outcomes should be developed and used. This is really a two-stage process: First, the firm must identify what might be called the "HR drivers" of the business: What are the specific facets of human resource management that translate into tangible business outcomes that the organization cares most about by virtue of its strategy? Then, having identified those HR dri-vers, organizations should develop metrics that permit line managers and the HR function to be assessed in terms of the quality and cost of their efforts to develop and maintain the key HR drivers.

Approaches to this are being attempted, based in general on the increasingly popular "balanced scorecard" approach to managerial accounting.[13] For instance, Skandia AFS (Assurance and Financial Services), a subsidiary of Sweden-based Skandia Insurance Company, has been at the forefront of efforts to revise corporate accounting and measurement activities to capture more thoroughly and accurately the intangible knowledge and competencies that reside in their workforce. The resulting system, called the Skandia Navigator, has received widespread attention from companies and consulting firms around the world, and the company annually produces a supplement to its annual report reporting on its intangible assets.[14]

The specific metrics used in the Skandia Navigator vary across business units and depend on the purpose for which the metrics are being utilized. Metrics are continually revised based on ongoing research concerning the determinants of business unit performance—both Skandia's own internal research and studies by academics and other corporations, which Skandia tracks vigilantly. Examples of metrics used by subunits within Skandia include: personnel turnover; managers as a proportion of the workforce (a measure of ability to reduce overhead through self-management); proportion of female managers (to tap diversity); percentage of employees below age 40; IT competencies, assessed on a 1–5 scale for each employee and then averaged within units; per capita training and education expenditures, including costs of travel and lost time; and an "empowerment index," based on responses to an attitude survey assessing employees' perceptions regarding motivation, organizational support, quality awareness, competence, job satisfaction, and alignment of authority with responsibility.

A key point here is that these metrics—and the HR drivers they are thought to reflect—are neither static nor presumed to be constant across different business units within Skandia. This should be true in general. Within one company or business unit, the key HR drivers may pertain to continuous learning and knowledge transfer, operationalized in terms of training expenditures per capita, patents, employee suggestions submitted and implemented, task forces or team projects successfully completed, or whatever measures are most appropriate for the specific strategy and technology. In another context focused on serving heterogeneous customers, the critical HR drivers may relate to employee diversity, measured in terms of changes in workforce composition, employee multilingualism, and so on. In a manufacturing setting in which flexibility and fast response are paramount, key HR drivers might relate to employee flexibility and autonomy, captured by skills inventories and measures of cross-training, computer literacy among production employees, administrative overhead (to capture the extent of self-management among employees), and the like. Finally, in relationship-based or transactional work (e.g., consulting), the key HR drivers may pertain to developing knowledge and building trust in serving clients, reflected in turnover rates, customer satisfaction ratings and employee morale responses, enrollments in continuing education programs, and the like.

We don't know enough to judge how effective Skandia's system is. To answer this question, whether for Skandia or for any other similar system, one must carefully validate the metrics that are used. This in turn requires research into the HR drivers of key financial and nonfinancial outcomes, incorporating data gathered in-house by the organization itself and from paying attention to (and perhaps encouraging) quantitative studies on comparable organizations that isolate the bottom-line effects of various indicators of intellectual capital and human resource management. But at the same time, one must be careful about how these metrics are used. Academics and practitioners who have been at the forefront of the balanced scorecard movement warn against using their metrics to evaluate and, even worse, to reward or punish individual managers.[15] The various measures in a balanced scorecard are all important, but they vary in their noisiness, in the extent to which an individual manager can affect them, and in the time frame over which improvements can be expected. To combine such disparate measures into a one-dimensional metric of managerial performance is to court the sorts of problems we discussed in Chapters 10 and 11. The value of a balanced scorecard, if we understand the concept, is to communicate to managers the wide range of important outcomes—drivers—that the firm values, but to rely on less formulaic and rigid means for the balancing act that follows.

Setting the Right Tone

If we heed these admonitions not to use HR-relevant metrics as the basis for direct incentives, then the obvious problems arise. We want line managers (and top managers and HR specialists) to pay close attention to the quality and cost effectiveness of their performance on the HR metrics. We want them to achieve a good balance where trade-offs must be made. But how do they know what are the appropriate rates of trade-off? And if there is no direct tangible motivation to pay attention to HR measures, why would they? The answer has to be a mixture of indirect tangible motivation—such as peer pressure and long-term promotion prospects—combined with intrinsic motivation. We've said this already in this chapter, but it bears repeating here: Organizational culture has to be directed at valuing HR-related activities—to activate peer pressure, to clarify criteria for promotion, and to elicit the desired intrinsically motivated responses.

We can't give you a lot of guidance on how to shift organizational culture in the desired direction. Indeed, we've made a big thing in this book about organizational inertia, and culture—norms, implicit understandings, and the like—is one of the most inertial things around. Still, there are some things worth saying. Drama, discretionary resources, and symbolism are all useful in attempts to unfreeze expectations and bring about change. Capitalizing on (or even creating?) crises is often effective, as we observed Burgess Winter doing at Magma Copper in his relations with organized labor in the late 1980s (see Chapter 6). Close attention must be paid to symbolism, which, as we have seen, is often critical in shaping expectations regarding employment relations. Recall Burgess Winter, for instance, standing alongside the union leader in front of the plant to distribute a leaflet announcing a new partnership between management and labor. Or recall John Mack naming Tom DeLong as his chief development officer, locating DeLong's office near his own, and personally calling senior professionals at Morgan Stanley to check on where their delinquent performance appraisal summaries were.

Moreover, leaders must scrutinize their oral and written communications for subtle messages—through what is said and what is *not* said—about the value they place on HRM and on the HR function in the organization. They must be able through vivid examples and stories to articulate their views about HRM concretely and credibly. Virtually every CEO we have heard address students at the Stanford Business School attests to the importance of HR concerns and proclaims that "our people are our most important asset." But students have little difficulty differentiating the rhetoric from the reality. When a CEO is describing a huge acquisition in which her company is engaged, for instance, and she makes no mention of HR issues or the HR function playing a critical role in that process, students hear the subtext. Conversely, when someone like John Reed of Citicorp says publicly that the difference between a good and bad CFO can mean a few basis points better return, but the value of a good head of HR is measured in many billions of dollars annually—and when, as we related earlier, he backs this up by asserting that his head of HR is one of a small number of possible internal candidates to succeed him—the students get that message too. What is true for our students presumably is true for your employees.

Avoiding Dependence on Specialists

A substantial part of managing human resources can be less than exhilarating. In many instances, because it is so complex and fraught with unanticipated feedback effects, HRM is frustrating. And, as we've just finished saying, HRM doesn't always lend itself to sharp measures of performance. For all these reasons—especially when combined with a general culture that devalues HR issues—general managers often prefer to push HRM off onto specialists who, after all, are paid to deal with "that stuff." The longer the specific culture and implicit contracts at the organization have supported this pattern, the likelier it is that what some commentators have described as a "culture of dependency" will arise: general managers become dependent upon the HR specialists, all the while downgrading the services the specialists provide.

The expectations and assumptions that lead to this sort of dependency can be very hard to shift. So anyone who is creating a new enterprise or seeking to change an ongoing one should keep in mind that the HR decisions made today and tomorrow will have powerful long-term consequences.

For example, imagine a newly created organizational unit that the parent wishes to develop into an autonomous enterprise. Struggling to get the new venture off the ground, key personnel are likely to be preoccupied fighting fires and coping with the many vexing challenges they face, which, despite their best intentions, may drive HR concerns off their radar screen. In a benevolent attempt to be helpful, the parent organization may try to enlist the help of the central HR function to deal with the many HR issues being faced by the new venture (staffing, compensation, training, etc.). But this may be misplaced benevolence: Management in the parent organization needs to think hard about whether it truly believes, over the long-term, that effective HRM is a core capability that the new unit must possess. If it answers in the affirmative, then it should do everything it can to resist the temptation to bail the unit out.

Or consider a large organization that has been seeking to create strong line management accountability for HR, and which is unexpectedly faced with the need to implement a large-scale reduction in force. To be sure, there are important legal and HR issues associated with a major downsizing that require attention from headquarters. But even in organizations with strong line HR organizations, there is often a tendency for the line to want to hand off responsibility for such contentious matters back to the headquarters organization, and this inclination is likely to be especially acute when the enterprise has tended historically to manage HR issues centrally. Top management needs to be appropriately concerned about the liabilities (legal and otherwise) of not managing the downsizing coherently and consistently throughout the company. But if decentralization is a high priority, then the organization's leadership ought to be at least as concerned about the detrimental long-term effects of removing or reducing pressure on individual business units to be responsible and accountable for managing their own human resources.

Experimenting with HR Administration

Most large organizations, if they are going to change their HR policies or principles, will choose to experiment with a new way of doing things. We don't necessarily mean a controlled experiment. There may be some of that, but often the new way is rolled out through the enterprise, so that not too much is put at risk all at once. In this way, examples for the rest of the organization can be created, a cadre of "new-way" managers is created who can export their knowledge to other locations, and managers from those other locations can be brought through to see the new way in action and to learn in less controlled fashion what to do and what difficulties are encountered.

Because of the strength of inertial forces, initial attempts to change assumptions about HRM and the role of the HR function in an organization might best be pursued in greenfield sites (or, more broadly, locations where the encumbrances of history are minimized). However, practitioners frequently emphasize how hard it is to transfer learning that occurs in greenfield sites to other units in the same organization and to headquarters, a point that has been made by more than one observer of GM's Saturn venture or its "New United Motors" (NUMMI) joint venture with Toyota. This may simply reflect resistance to change and a "not invented here" mindset. But anticipating that such resistance will be present might shape your thinking in the first place about where and how the experiments should be conducted. Perhaps experiments at (carefully selected) existing sites, although harder and riskier, have greater long-run potential.[16]

To the extent that you really are experimenting with novel HR practices, you should pay some attention, at least informally, to issues of experimental design. A company that elects to experiment with self-managed work teams in six different plants—which vary significantly in their technical interdependence, home country culture, workforce demography, and in numerous other respects—is likely to have a hard time isolating from the results of the experiments any definitive conclusions about the conditions under which self-managed teams are most effective. At a minimum, one would want to identify groups of "matched controls" for each plant, so that each experimental plant can be compared to some roughly comparable plant(s) that continued to run under the old HR model.

Finally, given the well-documented problems organizations face in trying to learn from such experiments, management will also want to have in place *at the outset* a plan that specifies: (a) how, when, and by whom such experiments will formally be evaluated (and there may be informational and symbolic advantages in soliciting independent evaluations from outside the organization); and (b) if the experiment is deemed to be a success, how and by whom "technology transfer" will be effected to other parts of the organization.

IN REVIEW (BUT NOT IN CONCLUSION)

⇒ The HR function has not, traditionally, been thought of as a repository of strategic insight or advantage.
  - Many—perhaps even most—firms pay lip service to the strategic importance of HR, and increasingly many firms regard their human resources as key strategic variables. But this rarely extends to the HR function itself.
  - This reflects a tendency for HR specialists to focus on mundane, day-to-day bookkeeping and service provision; a perception of HR specialists as turf protectors; and an HR subculture that emphasizes (and hence attracts) "warm and fuzzies" rather than strategic hard-edge types.

⇒ To remedy this situation, we propose that you consider the following ideas:
  - Spin off from HR the mundane service and record-keeping tasks, or (at least) separate these "service center" tasks from strategic HR.
  - Have line managers directly involved both in formulating HR strategy and policy and in making nontrivial judgment calls in HR administration.
  - Use HR professionals as advisors to general managers and as evaluators of general management performance in HR.
  - Staff "Strategic HR" with people who are (at least) nearly general managers, with specialized HR training, but also with the training and attitude of general managers.
  - Have unit-level HR report directly to unit-level line management, with (only) an indirect report to corporate HR.

- Push the formulation of HR policy out to units and subunits, unless you have a very substantial reason for centralizing. Decentralization should be the null hypothesis.

⇒ In addition, we recommend that serious attention be given to:
- Creating metrics for measuring HRM performance.
- Designing experiments in HR administration.
- Most importantly, creating a management culture that stresses the importance of HR as a task of general management.
  - Avoid creating a culture of dependency of line management on HR specialists.
  - Because it is generally difficult to find accurate explicit measures of how general managers do in managing their human resources, particularly over shorter time frames, more intrinsic and intangible motivators—in other words, "culture"—must be enlisted.

CONCLUDING REMARKS

Having patiently traveled with us to the end, you are now entitled to reflect back on the terrain we have covered and the road maps we have tried to provide. In so doing, one possible reaction might be that we provided a variety of lenses for looking at a complicated set of issues, but not a comprehensive set of first principles that can be applied to generate precise answers to problems. That's right, and it's the nature of the beast. Human resources respond to economic, social, and psychological factors in ways that generally defy easy categorization, simplistic theory, or straightforward prediction. To be sure, you will get a precise solution from one-size-fits-all nostrums or from theories and analyses that give you one factor or one equation to look at through a single lens. But in our experience, nostrums and one-lens analyses usually address only parts of specific HR problems that a manager faces. They can help illuminate those parts—we've rarely met a nostrum or a tight theory that didn't contain some wisdom—but it's the balancing act missed by such one-lens perspectives that pays the greatest returns. On the other hand, a catalog of the 687 factors you might need to consider in solving problem X and the 432 factors you might need to attend to in addressing problem Y (only some of which overlap with the list for X) isn't of much help either. So we've tried instead to give you a few simplifying frameworks for organizing your thinking about an inherently messy and complicated set of interrelated HR issues pertaining to alignment and internal consistency, as well as to provide you with some theoretical lenses, drawn from several disciplines, to aid your analysis of specific HR topics and practices.

Have we succeeded? In this chapter (and others), we spent some time focusing on metrics and performance appraisal, so it seems appropriate to conclude by suggesting some intermediate-term indicators or proxies that we would use to assess whether HRM in a given organization is moving in the directions we've recommended in this chapter and throughout this book:

- We see increasing diversity over time in the "origin" and "destination" points for individuals posted in the central HR function, with line and general management positions being more and more frequent as routes into and out of postings in HR.

- The organization develops, maintains, and attends to metrics that assess the performance of line managers and individual organizational units in recruiting, managing, and developing employees. These metrics, perhaps experimental at first, are increasingly embedded in the organization's performance management routines and are attended to at all levels of management. These metrics may out of necessity vary from context to context, even within a single organizational unit. In one setting, the appropriate measure might be one of senior management "bench strength": how many talented and qualified candidates exist within the organization to fill vacancies in a set of high-leverage positions. In another setting, it might be a measure of human capital renewal, reflecting the amount of ongoing education employees have obtained through company programs, professional development activities, conferences and workshops, and the like. But what should be common to all such measures is that they are connected tightly to the overall strategy or mission of the corporation and unit.

- The sections devoted to strategic human resource concerns in business plans, annual reports, and SEC filings are more detailed and more informative.

- Beyond formal filings and reports, the company provides informative reports on its human and intellectual capital, so that investors, customers, potential employees, and others can see how the organization defines, measures, and manages its human capabilities. (If your Web site doesn't have a link on its home page leading to Human Resources that provides more information than just job postings and contact information, then you don't pass!)

- Strategic HR is more closely involved in the design of activity-based costing systems, information systems, and quality programs, and is involved sooner and more centrally in long-run strategic decisions, such as mergers and acquisitions, changes in technology, and decisions regarding sourcing and location of facilities.

- Assessments of alignment and internal consistency of HR policies are conducted on a regular and formal basis, not only at headquarters, but also by each line manager. Where the line manager has oversight over a business unit with distinct HR policies and practices, consistency with overall corporate HR strategy should be a focus; where HR is centrally dictated, the focus should be on how well policies and procedures match local conditions. This process would be comparable in regularity and importance to the routine strategy, budget, and planning exercises in that organization (and, ideally, would be closely integrated with them). Among the tools that might assist this effort are: benchmarking studies, enabling a manager to make comparisons against other organizations operating within similar contexts; surveys of current and prospective employees, which allow managers to gauge whether the organization's HR practices have transmitted and reinforced a set of values that are internally coherent and consistent with what management intends; and other research conducted either internally or in conjunction with external partners to evaluate the key HR drivers of profitability.

- *Perhaps most importantly,* all else being equal, we observe a reduction over time in the prevalence of HR staff specialists within organizations, as human resource management comes to be seen as part and parcel of "management pure and simple" and therefore a key determinant of how managers are hired, developed, and rewarded.

If the concepts and frameworks presented in this book help you to move organizations in these directions, then we'll rate our own performance as adequate.

ENDNOTES

1. For descriptions of AES, its distinctive culture, and its radical use of decentralization and autonomous teams, see Jeffrey Pfeffer, "Human Resources at the AES Corporation: The Case of the Missing Department," Stanford Business School case HR3; Alex Markels, "Power to the People," *Fast Company* 13 (February–March 1998): 154–65.

2. See http://www.aesc.com/values/default.html.

3. Our own university is an interesting case in point. Its highly centralized and functionally specialized HR organization was the archetype we had in mind in crafting the caricature provided in the previous paragraphs. Recent changes in central HR at Stanford reflect a recognition that the organization was not being fully responsive to the needs of local subunits within the university. But the nature of those changes is telling: Local HR officers, who previously reported only to their unit managers, now report to an associate vice president within central HR who oversees a new unit called "HR Regional Services." Stanford's CFO, to whom the director of HR reports, described these changes by saying, "[We recognize] the need for local units to be served in their own way. . . . This is what [Stanford's] new [HR] organization is trying to capture: centralization with a local flavor" (see http://www.stanford.edu/dept/news/report/people/february/newhr218.html).

4. For some diagnoses and prescriptions that are broadly similar, see Michael Beer, "The Transformation of the Human Resource Function: Resolving the Tension Between a Traditional Administrative and a New Strategic Role," *Human Resource Management* 36 (Spring 1997): 49–56; Dave Ulrich, "A New Mandate for Human Resources," *Harvard Business Review* 76 (January–February 1998): 124–34; Thomas P. Flannery, David A. Hofrichter, and Paul E. Platten, "Pay and the Changing Role of Human Resources," Chapter 9 in *People, Performance, & Pay: Dynamic Compensation for Changing Organizations* (New York: Free Press, 1996).

5. See Charles A. O'Reilly III and Jeffrey Pfeffer, "Southwest Airlines—Using Human Resources for Competitive Advantage (A)," Stanford Business School case HR1A; James

L. Heskett and Roger Hallowell, "Southwest Airlines—1993 (A)," Harvard Business School case 9-694-023 (revised April 2, 1997).

6. See M. Diane Burton, "The Firmwide 360° Performance Evaluation Process at Morgan Stanley" and "Rob Parson at Morgan Stanley (A)," Harvard Business School cases 9-498-053 and 9-498-054 (respectively).

7. In an investment bank, managing director is equivalent to a senior partner in a partnership, and DeLong was the first nonbanker appointed to that rank in Morgan's history.

8. Source: personal communication with Tom DeLong. DeLong argues that without the sort of political influence and access to Mack that he insisted on having before joining the firm, as well as Mack's personal involvement in persuading managers to embrace the new appraisal system, it would have been particularly difficult to implement the cultural change that Mack desired in a star-oriented, professional services context like Morgan Stanley, where there is an inherent disdain for organizational processes.

9. See Michael Carroll, "Morgan Stanley's Global Gamble," *Institutional Investor* 29 (March 1995): 40–53.

10. Note that considerations of interdependence should also inform how an enterprise handles the HR aspects of integrating acquisitions, whether in a global company or otherwise. When the unit being acquired has HR policies and practices very different from those of the acquirer, it will usually be easier to preserve those distinctive practices when the newly acquired unit is only minimally interdependent with the rest of the organization. For instance, we might expect to see less effort focused on assimilating the employees of the acquired unit into the parent company's culture and HR practices when the acquired unit is expected to contribute at either end of the value chain (e.g., a basic research lab at one end or a call center to handle customer inquiries at the other end). And note that the amount of interdependence is also likely to vary with the stage in the product life cycle. Preserving distinctive HR policies for the employees of a research lab you have acquired may become problematic when it comes time to commercialize some technology developed by the lab's employees, who now must interact extensively with manufacturing, marketing, and finance personnel in the parent organization.

11. As a number of observers have noted, however, a downside of this approach has been limited transfer of the collaborative, team-based approach developed in those ventures back to the rest of GM. According to one commentator, one reason for this is distrust among both GM corporate executives and the union's national leadership of the autonomy inherent in the Saturn experiment. (See Michael Maccoby, "Is There a Best Way to Build a Car?," *Harvard Business Review* 75 [November–December 1997]: 161–72). For another interesting case along these lines, see Charles C. Heckscher, "Lakeville Chemical (A)," Harvard Business School case 9-487-053.

12. See Markels, *op. cit.*

13. See Robert S. Kaplan and David P. Norton, *Balanced Scorecard: Translating Strategy into Action* (Boston: Harvard Business School Press, 1996).

14. See Leif Edvinsson and Michael S. Malone, *Intellectual Capital: Realizing Your Company's True Value by Finding Its Hidden Roots* (New York: HarperBusiness, 1997).

15. Corporate fans of balanced scorecards have not always heeded these warnings. We know of a CEO of a major global corporation who had initiated a balanced scorecard approach as part of a cultural change aimed at increased attention to learning, con-

tinuous improvement, globalization, and HR concerns among his senior management team. At a conference where academics and practitioners (including some from his company) met to discuss research on these issues, he was aghast to learn from one of the presentations that the scorecard was being used at low levels of his organization not only as a basis for evaluating unit performance, but for evaluating particular managers.

16.   Why the parenthetical *carefully selected*? Some of our reasons concerning experimental controls follow in the next paragraph. But you should also mind the aphorism that success breeds success. When an HR experiment succeeds in one facility, it can be held up as something of an example to others, making change easier at other locations. So the sites of such experiments should be selected, at least in part, with the probability of success in mind. Of course—and one of the points of this paragraph—the extent to which a successful innovation at Plant A serves as an example for employees and management at Plant B depends on how closely A resembles B. Trading off these two desiderata (chance of success versus similarity to other facilities) is the crux of the matter.

APPENDIX A

TRANSACTION COST ECONOMICS

This book concerns transactions between employers and employees. Employment is quite different from other economic exchanges, and we focus on the differences. However, labor exchanges do share some characteristics with other types of exchanges. *Transaction cost economics* is an important tool for studying economic exchanges in general, a tool we used in Chapter 4 and will be using intensively, if somewhat informally, to study labor–service exchanges. This appendix provides a somewhat more analytical and complete treatment of the general subject, in case you want one.[1]

BASIC IDEAS

Textbook economics treats transactions as simple this-for-that exchanges; someone gives you twenty-five cents, you give her a donut; you give someone $25,000, he gives you a new car. Both parties to these textbook transactions know what they are giving and getting, and the transaction is completed virtually instantaneously. Because classical microeconomics is built with this sort of transaction in mind, clear and virtually instantaneous transactions are called *classical*.

However, many transactions, perhaps the most important ones, are much more complex than this. The purchase of an education is one such transaction, in which every so often students write out tuition checks, and only much later do they discover what it is that they have bought. Stanford has purchased our labor services as professors and all parties to these transactions are continually learning what the transactions entail as time passes. If you hire a lawyer to represent you in a particular matter, exactly what you have bought is remarkably unclear. If you enter into an agreement with a manufacturer to be a licensed dealer of the manufacturer's products, much of what is material to your eventual profits (e.g., what the wholesale prices will be in the future, what quality the products will be, how often product innovations will be provided, how much national advertising the manufacturer will undertake) is unspecified. Even the simple example above of purchasing an automobile is not so clear and straightforward; you will eventually wish to buy spare parts and servicing for the car, and you don't have an explicit agreement about the price or availability of either when you enter into the contract, nor do you know how well the company will honor its warranties.

Textbook economics implicitly asserts that such transactions as these are simply more complex versions of classical transactions. But the complexities bear closer study. What complicates all these transactions (and others) is the confluence of two distinct sets of factors. One set of factors pertains to the parties involved. People are *boundedly rational*; they can't anticipate everything that might ever happen, and they can't perform complex tasks of optimization except at very high cost (if at all). People also have the potential for acting *opportunistically*; they may try to take advantage of others if the opportunity presents itself and economic or social forces don't prevent this.

These human factors are relatively unimportant when the transaction is clean and straightforward. But they become quite important when a second set of factors come into play—namely, when the transaction is complicated because it involves *time, uncertainty,* and *privately held information.* When a transaction is complicated in this fashion, and when the parties to it are opportunistic, neither party can blithely trust the other's goodwill in meeting contingencies as they arise. To some extent, the parties will try to anticipate what contingencies may arise later and to specify, at the outset, how those contingencies will be met. However, because the parties are boundedly rational, there are *ex ante costs of negotiation.* Moreover, simply making an agreement *ex ante* is not the same as fulfilling it *ex post,* and opportunism by either side may lead to breach of the agreement. Each party will incur *ex post enforcement costs* in trying to ensure that the other side meets its obligations under the agreement. And because of their bounded rationality, the parties will probably be unable or unwilling to anticipate up front all the contingencies that will arise later. As time passes and contingencies unfold, the parties to the agreement will renegotiate their arrangement to meet circumstances; in other words, there will be *ex post (re)negotiation costs.*

Each party to a potential transaction anticipates (at least, in some rough sense) that the transaction will involve these different costs. When deciding whether to enter into the transaction, the parties consider the benefits of the transaction, net of the transaction costs. When the transaction costs are very high, the parties may forgo the transaction altogether. When the costs are low enough so that the transaction can be undertaken, the parties will look for ways to arrange the transaction so that the transaction costs are relatively low.

Transaction cost economics studies these transaction costs and, in particular, how they vary with the form of the transaction, by which we mean the formal and informal institutional arrangements for adapting, adjudicating, and enforcing the transaction as time passes. (We will flesh out this vague definition over the next few pages.) The basic positive premise of transaction cost economics is that transactions will *tend* to take place in a form that minimizes the combined costs of the transaction. To understand all this, a concrete example may help.

An Example of Design and Manufacture

Consider a transaction between two parties, A and B. Party A is a designer who is going to produce the plans for making some item, and party B is a craft worker who will then manufacture the item. Party A's task requires certain pieces of capital equipment—a computer workstation, say—whereas party B's task requires various tools, jigs, and fixtures.

It is easy to think of a number of ways in which this transaction could be arranged. (1) Parties A and B could be distinct economic entities, each owning its own capital equipment, and party A, having completed the design, could hire B as an independent contractor to produce the pieces. (2) A could license the design to B. (3) B could purchase the design from A. (4) A could act as employer, owning all the capital and purchasing B's labor services. (5) B could own all the capital and purchase A's labor services. (6) Some third party C could own all the capital equipment and employ both A and B.

No doubt you can think of specific cases in which each of these transactional forms is employed. The question is: Why one and not another? Does it make a difference? To answer, we first have to be clear on how these different forms really vary.

The main implication of the form of a transaction is in dictating the rights of the parties to make decisions and employ capital (including intellectual capital) as conditions change and contingencies arise. In our example, who owns the right to use in the future the design created by party A, or the right to improve on that design, or to otherwise modify it? Who is able to decide how the jigs and fixtures that are used to make the items will be employed? When it comes to physical capital, the presumptive answer is that the owner of the capital has that right.[2] If A owns all the capital and employs B as a skilled craft worker, then A can presumably fire B for cause and employ some substitute. If B owns all the capital and employs A as a designer, then B presumably has the right to continue production and adapt A's design. When A licenses a design to B, B retains the right to produce whatever quantity he wishes (subject to the original contractual arrangement, and typically with some royalty that is paid), although B will usually not have the right to modify A's design and enter into competition with A. At the same time, A will sometimes be restrained somewhat from making small changes in the design and entering into a licensing arrangement with some competitor of B. This is even more the case when B buys the design from A for a particular good.[3]

These rights are important because the immediate transaction is not the end of the story. The intellectual and physical capital created by this transaction will have value in the future, and the ability to command that value when the present agreement runs out or is voided by circumstances is a crucial part of the overall transaction. Moreover, each party is somewhat at the mercy of the other as the transaction evolves. Imagine, for example, that the two parties retain economic autonomy and each owns its own capital—specifically, B acts as an independent contractor for A. If B must make large investments in jigs and fixtures specific to this particular product, then B will make those investments in anticipation of recovering their cost in the price that A will pay for the work B does. But once B has made those investments, A could engage in a "holdup," demanding that B do the work for a lower amount than was originally anticipated. Insofar as A and B can specify *ex ante* just what B will be paid for the work B does, no problem arises.

But when B's costs or A's quantity demands are uncertain (and especially when they are matters of proprietary information—for instance, when B can misrepresent costs), it becomes considerably more difficult to specify *ex ante* how the transaction will evolve. And what if A comes up with a new and improved model, for which the current jigs and fixtures can be used if modified? The production of this new and improved model is likely to be outside the bounds of the contract A and B originally made, so A is in a good position to proceed with the holdup of B.

The key to this potential holdup is that B's capital is most profitably employed at A's task; B's assets are specific to A. In the jargon of transaction cost economics, we say that this is a problem of *asset specificity*. If B's capital equipment could be employed just as profitably in transactions with various other parties, and if A tried to hold up B, B could just walk away from A with equanimity and employ his capital in some other way. In other words, if there are many As who could equally well use B's capital, then B can rely on competition among them as protection against a holdup.[4] The problem of asset specificity seems to point toward an arrangement in which A pays for and thus owns the capital equipment. Such an arrangement seemingly economizes on the transaction costs incurred if A and B each owned their own capital.

But the story isn't quite so clean as this. If A owns the capital, she may still need to employ someone to use it. One easy-to-see problem with this sort of arrangement is that if B can damage A's capital equipment through negligence or abuse, then in the arrangement where A owns all the capital, A faces a moral hazard problem concerning whether B will take care of her (A's) equipment. In comparing the different ways the transaction could be arranged—(1) where A owns all the capital and employs B; (2) where each party owns some of the capital; and (3) where (say) B owns all the capital and employs A—we have to compare the *relative* transaction costs. Transaction cost economics says that the arrangement that is *relatively* the cheapest is the one that will tend to emerge and persist.[5] If the costs incurred in avoiding a holdup are less than those incurred in dealing with the moral hazard problem, then we would expect to see separate ownership (or B's ownership of the capital) instead of A owning the capital and employing B. If the costs of preventing a holdup exceed those of dealing with the moral hazard problem, then we will tend to see A owning the capital (or, depending on the relative costs, B owning everything).

To see this in an example, consider that when a craft worker's tools are relatively general purpose, such as a carpenter's saw or hammer or drill, then there is a tendency for the tools to be owned by the craft worker. As the tools become more specific to a particular job, however, there is a tendency for them to be owned by the firm that employs the craft worker. Here we see the trade-off between two transaction costs: holdup possibilities if job-specific capital is owned by the craft worker, versus moral hazard costs of maintenance when tools are owned by the firm that employs craft workers to employ those tools. At the extremes, the force of minimizing transaction costs moves us clearly in a particular direction: Journeymen carpenters own their own hammers and saws, whereas Boeing owns the jigs and fixtures for making 777 wings. It is in the middle ground where transaction cost analysis becomes most interesting and muddy.

Asset Specificity and the Push Toward Unified Governance

The story just told picks up one of the dominant themes in transaction cost economics, namely how the holdup problem or, more politely, the problem of asset specificity, pushes transactions toward a form in which some single entity owns all the assets.[6] When physical capital is most economically employed in one and only one exchange, the owner of the capital is at risk relative to partners he or she may have in the exchange. If, for example, A manufactures bottles and B is a soft-drink bottler, it makes some sense for A and B to locate their two plants in close proximity to one another; this way they save on the expense of transporting empty bottles. But if they do this, both are potentially at risk. At any point, either party can try to renegotiate the agreement, seeking to extract a greater portion of the benefits of their physical proximity. If a manufacturer of automobile brakes locates its factory close to the Toyota assembly plant, and if this brake manufacturer engineers its brakes to fit in Toyotas and no other car, then the manufacturer is somewhat at the mercy of Toyota (the more so if Toyota enjoys a similar relationship with one or two other brake manufacturers). The costs of constant renegotiation and adaptation of the transaction to contingencies as they arise can be formidable in such instances, which may make it worthwhile to organize the transaction so that all the assets in question are commanded by some single economic entity.

In the jargon of transaction cost economics, this push toward having all the assets controlled by a single entity is known as the push toward *unified governance,* where unified governance connotes the case of two distinct entities, each initially owning its own assets, which are subsequently unified into a single structure that owns all the capital. The first and most obvious reason for unified governance of assets, then, is that it economizes on the transaction costs of *ex post* renegotiation that would otherwise occur if specific assets were controlled by a number of distinct legal and organizational entities. Moreover, because there is presumably less opportunity for holdups with unified governance, fewer resources must be expended on bargaining and contract writing *ex ante* and on the enforcement of the transaction *ex post.* For all of these reasons, unified governance can save powerfully on some transaction costs.

Pushing in the other direction, however, are a great number of transaction costs that can increase as the ownership of physical assets is unified. Most important are the *agency costs* of labor. Physical assets can all be owned by one firm, but the know-how it takes to work them cannot be; human capital cannot legally be bought and sold. Moreover, the firm, while it owns the assets, employs people to use and care for those assets, and the firm must provide its employees with incentives to use and care for those assets in the firm's own best interests.[7] At the same time, employment creates other specific assets, namely *firm-specific human assets* or *human capital.* The basic idea (developed at length in Chapter 4) is that a worker develops skills and personal connections that are specific to his or her current employer. This leaves both the worker and the firm vulnerable to being held up. The employer may attempt to take advantage of the worker's inability to redeploy his or her skills elsewhere as advantageously as can be done with the current employer. At the same time, if the worker acquires a monopoly of knowledge or skills that are specific to the employer, the worker can hold up the employer by threatening to depart.

Thus, by bringing a set of activities in-house, an organization may alleviate holdup problems with external suppliers, only to exacerbate potential holdup problems vis-à-vis the firm's own employees. To repeat, there are trade-offs to consider in moving to an arrangement in which one party controls all the physical assets, and chief among these trade-offs are the transaction costs associated with employment relationships.

BETWEEN UNIFIED GOVERNANCE AND CLASSICAL TRANSACTIONS: RELATIONAL CONTRACTING

Between the extremes—having all the assets held by a single entity (unified governance) and having them controlled by many individuals who deal with each other in simple, discrete, and isolated classical transactions—are intermediate transactional forms known to economists as *relational contracting*. The idea is to have the assets in the hands of different entities, but to economize on transaction costs of negotiation and renegotiation by enlisting the beneficial effects of long-term relationships and reputation.

A good example arises in the case of automobile parts manufacture. In Japan, many of the parts of a car come from manufacturers that are economically distinct from the assembler. On a Toyota, the brakes, engine cylinders, and even the bumpers are manufactured by firms other than Toyota, firms that own their own manufacturing equipment and sell parts to Toyota.

On the face of it, this would seem to expose the Japanese to large transaction costs of the sort that normally push toward unified governance. At least some of the equipment for making bumpers and brakes for Toyotas is very specific to Toyotas; the bumper manufacturer would have a hard time turning to Nissan or Honda if Toyota tried a holdup, especially because physical proximity is very important in Japanese car assembly. (Toyota, on the other hand, is less liable to a holdup by its bumper supplier, because it typically has two or three suppliers for every major subcomponent that it buys.)

Because of precisely these considerations, auto assembly is organized much differently in the United States. The major U.S. auto assemblers are very highly integrated; they make internally many of the pieces that go into the cars they assemble (though this has been changing in recent years). Thus, they own many diverse assets for auto manufacture; in terms of the last section, they are exemplars of unified governance. Indeed, in the 1920s and 1930s, the degree of vertical integration in automobile assembly was extreme; the major manufacturers (General Motors and Ford) manufactured their own steel, glass, and tires!

How do the Japanese avoid the transaction costs that seemingly pushed the American auto manufacturers into being highly integrated? They do so by relying on long-term relationships between the major auto assemblers and their suppliers and, especially, on the reputation of the major auto assemblers. Toyota has dealt with its suppliers for many years, and each side anticipates that the relationship will continue.[8] As contingencies arise, Toyota and its supplier "work out" how to modify their relationship, trusting that, to safeguard the relationship, neither party will attempt to take advantage of the other. In fact, the working-out in this case takes an extreme form: Toyota makes all the important decisions. As contingencies arise, Toyota pretty much tells its suppliers what they must do. And the suppliers feel protected in this relationship because they trust Toyota not to abuse its authority; Toyota won't abuse its authority because it has an overall reputation for not doing so with all its suppliers. If Toyota treated a brake supplier badly, this would be noticed by the suppliers of its bumpers, lights, cylinders, and so on, and they would begin to demand contractual safeguards. Toyota, to avoid the costs of negotiating and enforcing such contracts, will treat all its suppliers fairly.[9] Thus, by relying on long-term relationships and on reputation, Toyota and its suppliers can avoid the transaction costs normally associated with diffuse governance of specific assets. And Toyota and its suppliers gain by avoiding unified governance and some of the other transaction costs that unified governance would occasion.[10]

Three Pure Forms of Relational Contracting

The foregoing is just an example, but it gives the basic idea of relational contracting. Parties deal repeatedly with one another, relying on the value of their ongoing relationship or the value of their reputation as insurance against opportunistic behavior. Consider the following three general types of relational contracting.

In *balanced bilateral relationships,* two parties to a transaction both retain a fair degree of autonomy, and contingencies are met as they arise through joint consensus. One might imagine that this would greatly increase the transaction costs of *ex post* renegotiation, as the two parties haggle over how to proceed in every instance (given that consensus is required to proceed). However, each party has a powerful incentive to be reasonable in its dealings with the other because it values the ongoing relationship, and any unreasonable behavior might lead to a rupture of the relationship. A good example of this is any ongoing joint venture between two corporations, where each is expected to add resources in the form of knowledge or capital to the joint venture.

In *hierarchical (bilateral) relationships,* there are two parties to a transaction (the bilateral part), and one of the two, called the hierarchical superior, is chiefly responsible for deciding how contingencies will be met as they arise. The other party, called the hierarchical subordinate, retains the right to rupture the relationship but is otherwise largely under the power of the superior. The hierarchical superior can be trusted because the superior has a reputation to protect, either with this single hierarchical subordinate or more generally with a large number of hierarchical subordinates, all of whom monitor how the superior acts in its relations with its many subordinates. An example here is the previously mentioned relationship between Toyota and its suppliers.

In *trilateral relationships,* there are two primary parties to the transaction and a third outside authority is invoked when the two cannot decide how to meet contingencies as they arise. Any time two parties sign an agreement that provides for binding arbitration in the event of a dispute, they are engaging in a trilateral relationship. The arbitrator is normally trusted by each side because she has her reputation as a fair arbitrator to protect; an outside authority that ruled capriciously or in a manner that was generally perceived as unjust would soon lose her customer base. In a sense, in any bilateral exchange taking place within a society with a well-developed system of contract or administrative law, the courts (or quasi-judicial authorities, such as the NLRB in the United States) act as trilateral authority.

Let us return briefly to a couple of examples mentioned earlier. The first involves you (if you are a student), contracting with your university. As noted above, you pay tuition to the university without getting in return a very detailed contract of what you will get as a function of the contingencies that arise. The reason a detailed contract isn't written in this instance is obvious: The contingencies are wide and varied and hard to anticipate. (Will you like Finance? Will you find the need for another course in Accounting? What if you get a failing grade in a required course? What if a professor whose courses you were eager to take becomes ill and cannot teach?) Writing a contract that covered all contingencies, or even just the ones that could be thought of, would be exorbitant. What you buy instead is a loosely defined procedure by which you and your university will collectively decide how those contingencies will be met. This procedure largely consists of: You ask, and the Dean (and administration) decides. Of course, you reserve certain rights of appeal, both to higher university authorities and to the courts. But the presumption is that the school's administration calls the tune, as long as you are treated according to standards of due process as they are employed at your university. You can petition the administration concerning your desires, but the administration decides whether to grant your petitions, and there is very little you can do or say if the answer comes back "No." In other words, what we have here is a very hierarchical relationship, with you as the subordinate.

So why did you enter into such a powerless position? Why did you trust your university not to abuse its power over you? (Consider how much you put at risk by going to school, and you will see just how much you have at jeopardy.) In part, we assume, you chose to come to your university because of its reputation (and its fit with your interests and desires for an educational program). The university's interest in maintaining its reputation both with you as a future alumnus and with other students is the best guarantee you have that you will not be exploited as a student.

This asymmetrical relational form is no accident, according to transaction cost economics; it precisely parallels the balance of reputational stakes in the relationship. A university's reputation is far more at stake than is yours, because you are apt to be a student only once, whereas a university looks forward to many generations of students. So it is efficient to give the university administration the greater share of authority in adapting a specific transaction to circumstances.[11] Note well: We aren't saying that your education isn't as important to you as it is to your university. In fact, your educational experience *per se* probably matters a lot more to you than it does to your dean. But the argument isn't that authority should be given to the party with the most at stake. Rather, authority should be given to the party (or parties) whose *reputation* is most at stake, because it is a reputation stake that can serve to protect the interests of the other party.

To take another example, a textbook author is obliged to guarantee to her publisher that she will not write another book that competes with the one being published. But publishers do not guarantee that they will not publish some other, competitive textbook. Why the asymmetry? Because authors can rely on publishers guarding their reputation. If a publisher were to publish X's book and then that of a competitor (and if the publisher slighted X's book in advertisements, and so on), word would quickly spread among the close-knit community of potential academic authors, and the publisher would have a hard time signing contracts for other books. For a publisher, acquiring a bad reputation would be catastrophic, as publishers rely on an ongoing flow of new books for their profits. Authors can rely on their publisher's desire to maintain a good reputation to safeguard their interests. In contrast, a publisher can't rely as well on an author's desire to maintain a reputation to safeguard the publisher's interests; an author is unlikely to have very many books in her, and so she is much more likely to want to milk any one for everything possible. Thus, authors must give publishers binding and written guarantees of their behavior, whereas authors can rely on implicit guarantees from publishers.

Carrying this example a step further, contracts to publish a book are roughly 95% about the author's responsibilities and only 5% about the publisher's responsibilities. The contract reserves to the publisher unfettered rights to decide on price, advertising, sampling policy, and so on.[12] Indeed, the boilerplate contract that publishers send out gives the publishing company the power to call for revised editions whenever it suits the company (or not at all), regardless of the author's desires. But this clause is rarely if ever invoked (except via jaw-boning), because the culture of academic authors holds that this is unfair, and a publisher invoking this clause would suffer in reputation, even though the publisher has a full legal right to insist on a revised edition.

When authors negotiate with publishers, they typically negotiate on things like the retail price of the book and sampling policy, and they exchange letters recording their informal agreements. But those agreements don't turn up in the contract, and the contract is quite clear that such letters are not made part of the contract. Nonetheless, those letters are of value, given what the publisher has at stake in terms of reputation; although they have no legal force, those letters can be shown to other potential authors. Again, we have a case of a hierarchical relationship that is hierarchical because of the relative reputation stakes that are involved.

Most relational contracting situations do not fit neatly into one of the three pure categories above. Indeed, in the hierarchical form, the hierarchical subordinate generally retains the right to sunder the relationship, which can be a very significant right indeed. Most real-life relational contracts are a mixture in various degrees of the three forms. It is the degree to which the three are mixed, and even more the *ways* in which the mix is concocted (who retains what rights), that determine the transaction costs associated with any specific form.

EMPLOYMENT RELATIONS AND TRANSACTION COST ECONOMICS

Now that we have the general ideas and jargon of transaction cost economics at our disposal, we can quickly reconstruct and review the essential argument of Chapter 4.

- Employment is a complex transaction involving time and uncertainty.
- The bounded rationality of the parties involved implies that the terms of the employment "contract" cannot be spelled out *a priori* in their entirety, but must be formed as time passes and contingencies arise.
- Also because employment is long-term, both employer and employee develop transaction-specific assets, leaving each liable to holdup by the other party as time passes and the relationship develops.
- Unified governance of the human assets involved is not possible, because of laws against indentured servitude.
- Hence, the parties must resort to relational contracting. It may be that one party is given the preponderance of authority to determine how the relationship will proceed; in fact, a caricature image of employment is that it is hierarchical, with the boss deciding and the worker acceding. But other forms, such as balanced bilateral or trilateral governance, can be found, with hybrids also appearing.
- As with any relational contract, either a balance of power between the two parties involved or the stake of one party (or both parties) in a general reputation provides each with assurances against abuse by the other.

ENDNOTES

1. For even more complete and analytical treatments, see Oliver E. Williamson, *The Economic Institutions of Capitalism* (New York: Free Press, 1985); or David M. Kreps, *A Course in Microeconomic Theory* (Princeton, NJ: Princeton University Press, 1990), Chapter 20.
2. This is subject to obvious caveats. It characterizes capitalist societies to greater or lesser extents, and it is subject to the state's rights of eminent domain.
3. An example of this arises in the case of publishing. A textbook author is obligated by her agreement with her publisher not to write a competitive product and sell it to a different publisher. In contrast, the publishing company does not have any formal requirement not to publish some book that competes directly with another book it is publishing. We will get back to this asymmetry in a bit.
4. Even if there are many As, B must still worry if there is the chance that they will form a cartel or otherwise collude against B's interests. He must also worry about develop-

ing a reputation as someone who will walk away from an agreement, thereby reducing the propensity of other potential exchange partners to enter into agreements with him (see Appendix B).

5. This is subject to an important caveat. In comparing the costs of different arrangements, you often must consider more than the individual transaction. Institutional arrangements are rarely fine-tuned for each individual transaction, but will tend to economize on an array of related transactions for the sorts of reasons discussed in Chapter 3. See Appendix B for more on this.

6. Note that this can't work completely in the context of human assets, as it is essentially precluded by laws against slavery and indenture.

7. Note also that to the extent that managers of specific organizational subunits have divergent interests, with decision-making rights delegated from the owner(s) to those subunit managers, there are ample holdup possibilities under unified governance.

8. These long-term economic ties are often supported by personal and social ties—for instance, the management of a Toyota supplier often includes individuals who once worked at Toyota and so have personal relationships with managers of the parent company.

9. You might object that we've slighted the social forces that keep Toyota from abusing its suppliers. This objection is completely correct—we have slighted the important social forces—but then this appendix concerns transaction cost *economics*.

10. It is too far off the point to catalog all those transaction cost savings here, but one is worth mentioning: By not integrating, Toyota can segment its "workforce" in ways that Ford and GM cannot. Because the employees of the bumper manufacturer are not Toyota workers, they needn't be extended all the benefits and safeguards that go to Toyota permanent employees, for example. And this sort of arrangement permits the assembler to impose sharper incentives on the parts manufacturer when necessary; the argument is a bit involved, but it comes down essentially to consistency and distinctions as outlined in Chapter 3. Indeed, American assemblers, noting the power and advantages of relational contracting in Japan, have in the recent past begun to mimic the Japanese, disintegrating vertically in some respects.

11. Compare this to instances in which a school engages in contract executive education for a large corporation. In this case, both the school and the corporation will endure, and each has something at stake in a continued relationship. Hence, in these cases, disputes can be (and often are) settled not by the dictates of one side but instead by negotiation and consensus.

12. Sampling policy means the number of books that will be distributed free of charge to colleagues of the author and potential adopters of the book.

Appendix B

Reciprocity and Reputation in Repeated Interactions

In Chapter 4 and Appendix A, we used some notions from game theory concerning how self-interest can lead to trust and cooperation between employer and employee, based on either balance-of-power or reputation considerations. This appendix reviews the essential game-theoretic ideas and then gives some illustrative applications.

THEORY

Background: Games and Nash Equilibria

By way of background, we begin by discussing the formal techniques of analysis that we will use, the techniques of *noncooperative game theory*.[1]

A *strategic form game* is a formal description of a competitive situation consisting of: a list of participants or *players*; for each player a list of *strategies* that the player can use; and for each *strategy profile* or combination of strategies, one strategy for each player, a *payoff* for each player. The payoffs are abstract (utility) measures of the desirability to each player of the outcomes, where a higher payoff is better, and we assume players choose strategies in order to maximize the expected value or mean of their payoff.

For two participants, we sometimes use pictures like Figure B-1 to describe one of these situations. The two participants are called *player 1* and *player 2*. The rows of the matrix in Figure B-1 correspond to player 1's strategies; there are three rows in the matrix, so player 1 has three strategies, labeled N, M, and S (for North, Middle, and South, respectively). There are four columns, so player 2 has four strategies, labeled W, CW, CE, and E (for West, Center West, Center East, and East, respectively). The participants must simultaneously *and independently* choose strategies. Their choice determines one of the twelve cells in the matrix, and the pair of numbers in the corresponding cell describes the payoffs to the two players. The first number represents the payoff to player 1, and the second number is the payoff to player 2. So, for example, if player 1 chooses M and player 2 chooses CW, player 1's payoff is 4 and player 2's payoff is 2.

PLAYER 2

		W	CW	CE	E
	N	8,0	3,5	0,4	6,6
PLAYER 1	M	5,0	4,2	0,1	5,0
	S	9,9	2,10	0,0	4,10

Figure B-1   An example of a two-player game.

We want to predict how the players might act in situations described in this fashion. Our chief formal tool for doing this is a *Nash equilibrium*. This is a list of strategies, one for each player, such that each player is doing as well for herself as possible, measured by her expected payoff, if she (correctly) anticipates that the other players will follow their parts of the Nash equilibrium. So, for example, M and CW is a Nash equilibrium of the game in Figure B-1: If player 1 anticipates that player 2 will choose CW, then M is better than N or S; while if player 2 anticipates that player 1 will choose M, then CW is better than W, CE, or E. Note that N and E is another Nash equilibrium of the game in Figure B-1.

In what way is a Nash equilibrium helpful in predicting how the game will be played? The idea is that *if* each of the players is able to anticipate how the other(s) will act, then it must be that their joint behavior constitutes a Nash equilibrium. The reason for this is that *if* all the players anticipate what will happen, and if each is trying to maximize his or her payoff, then each must be doing as well as possible against the strategies of the others.

Note well, this isn't saying that in every situation we study each participant will actually be able to anticipate how others will act. We must have some reason to believe that the participants can correctly anticipate the actions of their fellows. It may be that correct anticipations are the product of prior discussion among the participants, or experiences that they share, or sometimes the result of logical reasoning. As we go to *apply* the ideas of game theory to real-world situations, we will need to ask, more or less constantly, whether it is reasonable in the situation being modeled to suppose that each participant can anticipate fairly accurately how the others will act.

This is the sort of formal analysis we will use in the rest of this part of the appendix. We close this background section with two remarks. First, in what follows we will look at situations that are somewhat more complex than the simple sort of game given in Figure B-1. In particular, we will be describing situations in which the list of strategies available to a participant is never made explicit, but instead is implicit in a description of actions the participant can take and information the participant will have when the actions must be taken. Second, because of these complications, we will *not* be mathematically precise in our arguments. You should be prepared for a fair bit of sloppy hand-waving. If you want to see things done absolutely formally, with all the mathematical *i*'s dotted and *t*'s crossed, you will need to look at an advanced textbook.[2]

The Prisoners' Dilemma

We start with the very simple situation described in Figure B-2, which is known as the *prisoners' dilemma*. There are two individuals who take part, called ROW (female) and COL (male). Each has to choose between two possible courses of action, called *cooperate* and *fink*. They must do so without consultation and without the ability to form binding agreements between them, although each is aware of the situation that the other faces.

A story goes with this game. Our two individuals are two prisoners, held by the police as suspects in a crime they did in fact commit. The police lack the evidence needed to get a conviction on the full charge, although they have enough evidence to make a lesser charge stick. So the police put the two prisoners in separate cells and ask each whether he or she wishes to fink on the other. The police offer the following deal: If both fink, both will go to jail for a considerable length of time, but if one finks and the other doesn't, the one who finks will go free and the other will spend an even longer time in jail. If neither finks on the other, then each will spend a short time in jail on the lesser charges. Hence, each prisoner has an ordering over the outcomes as suggested by the numbers in Figure B-2. Best of all is to fink while your colleague refuses to fink. Next best is neither to fink nor to be finked upon. Next is to fink and be finked upon. And worst of all is to refuse to implicate your colleague while that colleague is finking on you.

This game is called the prisoners' dilemma because of what a game-theoretic analysis suggests will happen. Take the perspective of ROW. If her colleague COL is going to fink on her, she is better off finking than not. (That is to say, better to get 2 than 0.) If her colleague is going to cooperate (not fink), it is better for her to fink. (Better to get 8 than 6.) So whatever ROW believes COL will do, as long as ROW believes that her choice of action will not have any influence on COL—and it is hard to see how it could, since they are acting independently—she is better off by finking.[3] COL's situation is entirely symmetric, so he too will fink. They both will fink, and they both will wind up with a payoff of 2, which is a dilemma in the sense that each could wind up with a payoff of 6, if only they could form and keep to a binding agreement not to fink on one another.

In the language of game theory, fink–fink is a Nash equilibrium. Yet it is much more than that. For each player, finking is a *dominant* strategy; it gives the player a higher payoff than cooperating no matter what the other player does, as long as the other player selects his or her strategy independently. Hence, absent other con-

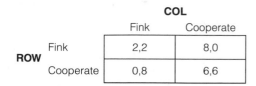

Figure B-2 The prisoners' dilemma.

siderations, and under the maintained hypothesis that players act independently to maximize their payoffs, the conclusion that both will fink is very strong.

Cooperation that Ensues from Repetition and Reciprocity

We could try to attack this dilemma by looking at ways that the two could form a legally enforceable, binding agreement. Instead, we will look at another way they can avoid the dilemma, by modifying the scenario in which they find themselves. Specifically, suppose that the two individuals will play this game not once but a number of times. To be completely concrete, imagine that they will play the game once, with the results revealed at the end of play. Then some random event will be conducted such that with probability .8 the two will play a second time, while with probability .2 the encounter ends. If and when they play the second time, the results are again revealed, and again the random event is conducted (independently), so there is probability .8 of going on to a third round of play, and probability .2 that the second round is the last. And so on. After each round of play, the chance of proceeding to another round is .8 and the chance that the encounter ends is .2, independently of what has happened in the past and how they have played.

Do the two face the same dilemma as before in this changed circumstance, or can they now reach a cooperative outcome? The two face a more difficult situation, to be sure, but one in which cooperation *may* be sustained as a Nash equilibrium. To see this, we first describe a strategy for ROW:

> Begin by cooperating. As long as the game continues and as long as both players have cooperated at every previous stage, cooperate. But if ever either player finks, then in all subsequent stages (as long as the game continues) fink.

Note that this is a strategy on a higher plane than is *fink* or *cooperate*; those are actions that are available in any single round of play, whereas this is a strategy for the repeated interaction between the two players. In particular, what ROW is doing in each round according to this strategy is contingent on what transpired in earlier rounds; ROW is adapting her behavior to COL's (and her own) earlier actions.

What is COL's best response to this strategy by ROW? Suppose COL responds by always cooperating. Then each side will cooperate in each round of play, for as long as the game goes on. COL will get 6 in the first round, 6 in the second (if there is a second), and so on. COL's *expected* payoff will be:

$$6 + (.8)(6) + (.8)^2(6) + \ldots = \frac{6}{.2} = 30.$$

To explain: The first 6 in the sum is COL's payoff in the first round. The second term, $(.8)(6)$, is the payoff in the second round, 6, times the probability .8 that there is a second round. The third term, $(.8)^2(6)$, is the payoff in the third round times the probability $(.8)^2$ that there is a third round, and so on. Then the right-hand side—showing that the infinite sum gives the total [6/.2] = 30—is just a mathematical formula.

Would COL do better to fink in the first round? If he does, he gets a payoff of 8 in the first round, but if ROW follows the strategy above (and if COL correctly anticipates this), then COL can do no better than 2 in any subsequent round, because ROW will be finking forever after. Thus, the best COL can do if he finks in the first round is the expected payoff:

$$8 + (.8)(2) + (.8)^2(2) + \ldots = 8 + \frac{(.8)(2)}{.2} = 16.$$

This is considerably worse than always cooperating. It takes a fair bit of mathematics, but it can be shown that COL's best response to the strategy given above for ROW is any strategy that has him (COL) cooperating as long as ROW does. For example, one best response by COL to ROW's strategy is:

Always cooperate, no matter what.

Another best response is:

Cooperate at the start, and continue to cooperate as long as ROW does. If ever ROW finks, then fink forever after.

Yet another is:

Cooperate at the start. After this, do in round T whatever ROW did in the previous round, $T - 1$.

Let us give these three names: The first is called *nice guy (or gal)*; the second is called *grim cooperation*; and the third is called *tit-for-tat*. Note that the strategy we are supposing for ROW is her version of grim cooperation.[4]

Suppose ROW plays *grim cooperation* and COL plays *nice guy*. Is this a Nash equilibrium? We have already asserted that COL's strategy is a best response to what ROW is doing, but the reverse is not true: If COL is always going to cooperate, ROW does better to fink in every round.

On the other hand, *grim cooperation* against *grim cooperation* is a Nash equilibrium, as is *grim cooperation* against *tit-for-tat*. In the first pair of strategies, each side has the incentive never to fink—each is playing a best response against the other. This is also true in the second pair, although to convince you of this we would have to demonstrate that, against tit-for-tat, it is better not to fink than to fink at every point of play. It turns out that this is so for the numbers we are using—one round of punishment for finking is adequate to keep the other side in line—but it does take a demonstration that is not supplied here.

What is going on here? It is nothing very profound. Because of the repeated nature of the interaction, each side can threaten the other that any breach of cooperation will be met with reciprocal noncooperative behavior. The threat of punishment is adequate to keep each side cooperating. Doubtless in some ongoing interaction in your life, you have participated in this sort of "reciprocally cooperative" scheme, where you didn't take short-term advantage of someone with whom you have ongoing relations because you feared the other would then punish you to the extent he or she could.

There are three things to note about this:

1. In the story told, the (.8) discount factor represents the probability of making it to another round. We could tell a different story in which there is probability one that the interaction will take place over and over again, but the payoffs are accrued with sufficient time delay so that the overall payoff from a stream of rewards is given by their discounted sum. As long as the discount factor is .8, we would get exactly the same analysis.

2. We have described two Nash equilibria, both of which result in perpetual cooperation. Yet there are other Nash equilibria in this situation, which give very different outcomes. For example, if each player chooses to play the strategy *Fink in every round, no matter what your rival has done in the past,* then we have a Nash equilibrium in which perpetual finking is the outcome. Note carefully why this second pair of strategies is a Nash equilibrium: If ROW is always finking, then the best COL can do is to fink. Neither player, changing his or her strategy alone and taking the other player's strategy as given, can do better. You may at this point object that *both* are better off with the grim against grim equilibrium than with the always fink against always fink equilibrium, and you would be correct. However, this doesn't mean that always fink against always fink isn't a Nash equilibrium. We have a Nash equilibrium whenever neither side has an incentive to change what it is doing *unilaterally.*

3. It is important to the cooperative equilibria that there is a significant probability that the two will continue to play and that the stakes are somewhat balanced from one round to the next, because cooperation is based on a calculation that any short-term advantages from finking are outweighed by longer-term advantages of maintaining a cooperative arrangement. If, for example, there was only probability .1 of continuing for another round after each, and if ROW played the grim cooperation strategy, then COL's calculations would be:

    If I cooperate, I net 6 in each round, for an expected payoff of:

    $$6 + (.1)(6) + (.1)^2(6) + \ldots = \frac{6}{.9} = 6.67.$$

    But if I fink, then in the very first round I get 8. Clearly I'm better off finking.

    Or, to put this another way, suppose that the size of the stakes changed from round to round, and in the third round of play the stakes were increased thirtyfold, with little chance that they would ever be that high again. Then in the third round each side would have a very strong incentive to deviate to finking in the short-run, even if that destroyed cooperation in all subsequent periods.

The Folk Theorem of Game Theory

The basic idea in the example above is formalized in what is known as the *folk theorem* of noncooperative game theory.[5] The formal setting is as follows. We have a simple game played by some number N of players. This game is played once, then a second time, a third, and so on. Each player receives as total payoff from the sequence of plays the discounted sum of her payoffs in each round, discounted with some discount factor $a < 1$. (You can think of a as reflecting the time value of money or a probability of continuing. It doesn't matter.)

For each player, we compute the player's *max-min* payoff. This is the worst punishment that all the others can inflict on the player, if the player anticipates what the others will do. For example, in the prisoner's dilemma, each player's max-min payoff is 2, because each player, by finking, can get at least a payoff of 2 no matter what the other player does.

> **The Folk Theorem** (roughly): *Take any outcome of the game that gives to each player a payoff that exceeds the player's max-min payoff. Then if the discount factor a is close enough to one, there is a Nash equilibrium of the repeated-interaction game that gives this outcome round after round.*

This is a rough version of a precise mathematical result—you can see the precise result in textbooks on game theory—but it conveys the basic idea. As long as the future matters enough—which is what it means for the discount factor to be close enough to one—any outcome that gives players more than their max-min payoff can be sustained as an equilibrium. In fact, it is easy enough to describe the Nash equilibrium: All the players play the chosen outcome as long as no one deviates. If ever one person deviates, they all punish the deviator to the fullest extent possible, which puts the deviator at her max-min payoff level. And it is easy enough to see why this is a Nash equilibrium: If the future matters enough, and if the chosen outcome gives each player more than she gets if she is punished by the others, it is better for the player to go along with the deal than to deviate and be held afterward to her max-min payoff.

There are all sorts of mathematical questions that arise about this result. For example, we might wonder for a particular discount factor (such as .8) whether a particular outcome can be sustained. All the theorem says is that if the discount factor is close enough to one, it can be (if it gives each player more than her max-min). But is .8 close enough? Also, we might wonder if players would actually have an incentive to carry out the punishment of a deviator. And what happens if more than one player deviates from the scheme? In formal treatments of the folk theorem, all these questions are addressed.

From our more applied point of view, it is the idea that is important, not the formalities, and the idea is already clear from the example of the prisoners' dilemma.

Also clear is the biggest weakness of the idea, which is that the folk theorem gives us too many Nash equilibria. We began by wondering if there was some way to sustain cooperation in the prisoners' dilemma game; we began by wanting to find a cooperative Nash equilibrium. Repeated play answers this desire; cooperation can be sustained if the discount factor is close enough to one. However, repeated play answers this desire with an embarrassment of riches. Cooperation is an equilibrium. So is continual finking. So is alternating between the two. So is alternating between cooperate–cooperate and fink–cooperate (where we give ROW's action first). So is *anything* that gives (on average) to each player more than they get by continual finking (which gives the max-min payoffs in this case). When we get to applications, sorting through this embarrassment of riches to figure out what will happen will be our first order of business.

Models of Reputation

Before going to applications of this basic idea, however, we need to discuss two further theoretical developments.

In the prisoners' dilemma story, and more generally in the folk theorem, it is assumed that the same N players engage in the game over and over again. Each can be punished by the others if and when the one deviates. Yet in many applications, only one (or a few) of the participants will be enduring. What happens then?

To take an example, imagine the following situation. Two individuals, called *Player A* and *Player B,* play the game shown in Figure B-3. This is a little different from the games in Figures B-1 and B-2, but the idea is simple. Player B starts the game by choosing whether to trust Player A or not. If Player B chooses not to trust A, the game is over, and each gets zero. If Player B chooses to trust A, then A must decide whether to abuse B or treat B fairly. If B is treated fairly, each gets a payoff of 1. If B is abused, A gets 2 and B gets −1.

If we imagine this game played once between A and B, and if we imagine that A is interested only in her expected payoff, then the outcome would seem-

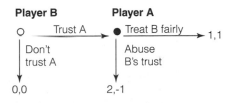

Figure B-3 The trust–abuse game. (In this game, Player B must choose whether to trust A or not. If he trusts A, then A must choose whether to abuse B's trust or treat B fairly. Payoffs to the two are listed at the end of each possible sequence of actions, with A's payoffs given first.)

ingly have to be that B does not trust A. Because if B trusts A, then A has a choice of a payoff of 2 or a payoff of 1. If A only cares about her payoff, she can be expected to abuse B and take the payoff of 2. B, anticipating this at the start, sees his choice as being either to trust A and be abused or to refuse to trust A. Refusing to trust A is better for B under the circumstances.

This is like a one-sided prisoners' dilemma. The dilemma part is that the two wind up with payoffs of zero apiece, while payoffs of 1 apiece are available. If A could make a binding commitment at the outset not to abuse B, both would be better off.

If A and B engaged in this game repeatedly, discounting payoffs in each round with a discount factor, say .8, then we could solve the dilemma. B could play the strategy:

> Trust A in the first round, and continue to trust A as long as A never abuses that trust. But if A ever abuses trust, then refuse to give trust to A forever after.

Faced with this strategy in the repeated interaction, A's best response is always to honor B's trust, because the short-term gain of abusing trust (from 1 to 2) is more than outweighed by the loss thereafter of B's trust. (Note that behind this assertion is a calculation, a calculation that would go the other way if, say, the discount factor were .1 instead of .8.)

Is it important that a single B engages in this relationship with A repeatedly? The point of this section is: No, this is not important, in the following sense. Suppose that A engaged in this game with a given player B today. Tomorrow, A engages in this game with another, completely different B. The day after tomorrow, A engages in this game with a third B, and so on. And suppose that each of the Bs is able to learn how A behaved in the past, with A's previous "partners" B. Then each individual B could adopt the strategy:

> Trust A as long as A has never abused the trust she was given by an earlier B. But if A has ever abused the trust of any previous B, then refuse to give trust to A.

Faced with these strategies by the different Bs, it is in A's best interest always to honor trust. The calculation for A that shows this is A's best response is the same as before.

We can describe what is happening here in the terminology of *reputation*. Essentially, A's past behavior gives her a good or bad reputation as a partner. If A has always behaved honorably with past partners, she has a good reputation. If she ever abuses someone who trusts her, she gets (and keeps) a bad reputation. And the strategy of the players B can then be stated quite simply, as: *Trust A as long as A has a good reputation.*

This reputation construction shares many of the features of the "reciprocal rewards and punishments" constructions of the folk theorem. In particular, many outcomes can be Nash equilibria, corresponding to many different sorts of reputation. For example, there is an equilibrium in which A simply begins with and keeps a bad reputation—no B ever trusts her, and she would abuse any B foolish enough to try her out—and there is an equilibrium in which A's reputation is to behave honorably with every second B (i.e., alternating between abusing one B and honoring the trust of the next B), in which only every second B trusts A.

Notwithstanding the similarities, there are some differences:

- The fact that only one side can be "punished" for bad behavior can sometimes be killing. For example, suppose we had a single A engaged in the prisoners' dilemma game against a sequence of Bs, with A taking the role of ROW and the Bs taking the role of COL. Because each B engages in the game only once, each B's individual interests will lead that B to fink. And as long as each B will fink, the enduring A has no reason to do other than fink. In the prisoners' dilemma game, to escape the fink–fink outcome we need both sides to have something long-run at stake.

- When we pass from bilateral reciprocity to multilateral reputation, a potential free-rider problem intrudes. If B trades repeatedly with A, B will know based on past experience how A has behaved. However, when today's B trades (at most) with A today, he must find out how A has behaved in the past. Will he expend the resources needed to do so? If he does not, he may wind up caught in a relationship with a bad-reputation A. But A is disciplined not by this B, but by future Bs. Whether B checks on A or not, if A anticipates that future Bs will be checking on her, she has just as much incentive to treat this B equitably. Hence, perhaps it is worthwhile for B to trust that others have monitored and will monitor this A, and that this A will therefore obey honorably to preserve her reputation. This sort of consideration leads to three conclusions: (a) If the free-rider problem is severe enough (if the cost of checking A's history is high enough), the reputation construction can fail entirely. To revive it, there must be enough of a chance that A has a bad reputation that it is worth the while of a single B to check. (b) Thus, it can actually be in A's interest to lower the costs to potential trading partners of accessing her (A's) reputation. (Of course, when A is providing the information, Bs have to worry about credibility; see the following section.) (c) Alternatively, the Bs may benefit from forming a collective whose role is to monitor A and coordinate responses to A's behavior (see Chapter 6).

Noise

In both the prisoners' dilemma–folk theorem construction and in the trust–reputation construction, it is important that each side observes what the other does. (More precisely, in the trust–reputation construction, it is important that each B knows what A has done in the past.) The punishments that hold together the cooperative outcomes are based on the idea that if there is a deviation from cooperation, it will be known about and dealt with.

When, in a moment, we turn to application of some of these ideas, this theoretical ideal will no longer hold true. Participants will have a rough idea what others are doing, but only a rough idea. Actions will be observed that could be consistent with either deviation from a cooperative scheme or adherence to the scheme. What will happen then?

To shed light on this question, formal models have been investigated in which individuals obtain noisy indications of what others intended to do.[6] The formal investigation of these ideas quickly becomes very complex, and we will spare you precise formulations or detailed calculations. The basic ideas behind the formal details are relatively easy and intuitive, and they run as follows. There are many ways to formulate this idea, but one way that is typical is to suppose that participants can try to implement certain actions, but sometimes (against their will) what is realized is other than what was intended. For example, we might imagine ROW and COL playing the prisoners' dilemma game repeatedly, with the following change in the rules. In each round, ROW and COL simultaneously and independently choose their *intended* actions, either to fink or to cooperate. Then, with a given probability, what they intend is what transpires. But with complementary probability, what transpires is the reverse of what was intended. And what is observed is not their intentions but what actually transpires. Or, in the case of the trust game, we imagine that every time B trusts A, A chooses between abuse and honorable behavior. Yet these are only A's intentions: Even if A intends honorable behavior, there is a probability that the Bs observe A's actions as abusive.

Think in terms of the prisoners' dilemma formulation, and in particular think of trying to sustain the *always cooperative* outcome. Things proceed smoothly for a while, with cooperate–cooperate the outcome. Then, say on round four, B apparently fails to cooperate. B claims that this is an unintentional mistake; he intended to cooperate, but his intentions were reversed by the forces of nature against his will, and he implores A not to resort to finking, which will hurt both of them. Should A accede to B's arguments? If she does so, then she is open to wholesale finking by B, who can always claim that he intended to cooperate. Should A permit a certain amount of finking by B? If she does, then B will have an incentive to try to fink just that amount. The point is that at some point A will have to meet finking with punishment, or B will fink all the time, and A will have to do this even if she is relatively sure that B's finking was unintentional. To do otherwise is to invite B to fink intentionally.

On the other hand, the inevitable punishment, when it comes, should not be the sort of severe punishment in the grim-cooperation strategy (i.e., finking forever in response to the other person's first incident of finking.) This punishment is more extreme than is needed. The punishment for an apparent act of finking should be just severe enough to keep B honest (and vice versa: B should punish apparent finking by A just enough to keep A honest).

The more noise there is, the harder it will be to sustain cooperation and the more punishment will be required to keep each in line. As the level of noise increases, at some point cooperation becomes impossible to sustain. The effect is just the same as decreasing the discount factor, because when noise rises, the future becomes less a product of the player's intentions and more a product of nature's chance-determined actions. Hence, there is less in the future to trade off against short-term gains. Indeed, stepping outside the model for a moment, it will be in the interests of the participants to find ways to reduce the noise in their observations of what each one does.

Similar things happen when there is noise in the reputation type of construction. If A seemingly abuses a given B, subsequent Bs will have to punish A to some extent, or A will have an incentive to abuse Bs and then blame it on happenstance. But the punishment inflicted on A should not be more severe than necessary to keep A in line. And A and the Bs should look for ways of constructing A's reputation so that it can be monitored relatively noiselessly, to reduce the adverse effects of noise.

The general phenomenon of noise enters into the reputation constructions in a second way. In the theoretical analysis of the trust–abuse game sketched before, it was assumed that each B, when it is his turn to decide whether to trust A or not, is able to learn how A acted in previous encounters with earlier Bs. More generally and more robustly, it is enough that the behavior of A can be credibly communicated from one generation of Bs to the next. Reputation, in other words, passes by word of mouth, modified perhaps by the current actions of A. But suppose B in round N cannot see how A acted previously, and that B in round N either has difficulty in comprehending what B from round $N-1$ is passing along or finds the testimony of B from round $N-1$ to be less than fully credible. Insofar as A can anticipate these difficulties, A has less incentive to treat B fairly in round $N-1$, as it is less likely that abusing this B will hurt A's prospects with the next B in round N. If this is so, and if the Bs anticipate this, then they have less reason to trust A. In other words, in a reputation construction, we must worry about noise in observing in any period what A does; and, especially when reputations are communicated by word of mouth, we must also worry about "noise" in the process of communicating reputation.[7]

APPLICATIONS

Now we turn to the application of these ideas. A number of general economic applications may already be clear to you. For instance, the reputation and reciprocity notions discussed above can help illuminate the origins and maintenance of explicit and implicit collusion among oligopolists; the long-term commitment of a "quality goods" manufacturer to maintaining quality standards; the fervor with which monopolists will deter new entrants and resist price cuts (in order to preserve long-term market power via their reputation); and the efforts of governments to acquire reputations for credible anti-inflation monetary policies.

Here, we wish to focus on applications of these ideas that bear on HRM.

Hierarchical Governance

A lot of time was spent on this in Chapter 4 and Appendix A, so little more needs to be said. Let us insert one remark, however, concerning the impact of noise on the reputation of an employer. If we are relying on a reputation construction, in cases where the employer is enduring but employees come and go, we must worry about the means by which the employer's reputation is transmitted from one generation of workers to the next. When the workforce is drawn from a large area, when the population in the area is in constant flux, and when the workforce is particularly heterogeneous, problems in transmission can be anticipated, at least when compared to situations in which the potential workforce is geographically stable, homogeneous, has abundant social ties (promoting the ability to communicate), and in which the employer looms large in the local labor market.

Balanced-Bilateral Governance

In balanced-bilateral relational governance, both parties to the contract have authority concerning adaptation to contingencies that arise and that are not specifically provided for in the contract. Sometimes the form of governance is that the two must reach consensus before the arrangement is adapted; in other cases, each has specific decision-taking authority over particular items—for instance, in many franchise arrangements, the franchiser sets the wholesale price, and the franchisee determines the quantity he will purchase at that price. In either case, the smooth working of the relationship is meant to arise from displays of reciprocal goodwill by the two parties. Each has more at stake in the continued relationship on good terms than can be obtained by taking momentary advantage of the other side, and so each looks out for the interests of the other side.

Many employment situations resemble this form of contracting—for instance, the relationships between a manufacturer's representative and the manufacturer or between a hospital and its physicians. Note that in both examples, the person performing the labor services may or may not be a legal employee of the organization purchasing those services.

Trilateral Governance

In trilateral governance, a third party is called upon to arbitrate disputes between the two prime parties to the arrangement. Each of the prime parties is thus somewhat at the mercy of the third party, and each must have some guarantee that the third party will not act capriciously or otherwise unfairly. The usual source of such guarantees is the reputation of the trilateral authority. For example, in some labor contracts, an arbitrator (or an arbitration panel) is relied upon. Arbitrators are typically lawyers who specialize in labor law, and in many cases they make their living as arbitrators. To continue making a living in this profession, they must be acceptable to both labor and management, and so they cultivate a reputation for fairness and good judgment. In any single instance, the two prime parties can trust that the arbitrator's interest in maintaining her reputation, and thus her livelihood, will guarantee for them a fair hearing and decision. This is more complex than the simple two-party reputation construction because it involves three parties, but it shouldn't be hard to see the basic form of a reputation construction at work here.

Mandatory Due Process Protections

As a trilateral authority, overseeing and refereeing employment relationships, the courts very often insist that certain actions be taken only after "due process" has been applied. For instance, a worker cannot be dismissed for cause unless there is a well-documented paper trail of evaluations and warnings. Hiring practices that aim at improving diversity must follow procedural guidelines, and so forth. Often these guidelines are set up by the organization negotiating with the courts (e.g., in order to settle an initial finding of discrimination), but once established, the guidelines must be followed to the letter, unless and until an amendment is agreed to by the supervising court and the firm.

The relevant third-party authority that imposes the rules of due process need not be a court or governmental regulator. For instance, professional associations, accreditation bodies, licensing boards, and similar entities sometimes play important gate-keeping roles and can impose high costs on organizations that fail to abide by prescribed practices and codes of conduct, including regarding HRM. A firm being criticized for its labor practices (or those of its suppliers) in developing countries may arrange for audits and public reports from an independent party, as Nike, the sports apparel company, has recently done for its activities in Indonesia, China, and Vietnam. To be sure, compliance in these cases may not be quite as mandatory as in the case of a court of law or government agency, but neither are the due process protections quite as voluntary as in the case where an organization simply seeks to promote trust with its workforce (see next section). In any event, the key point here is that adherence to somewhat formulaic procedures is the *sine qua non* for the courts and other third-party authorities: If agreed-upon procedures are followed, the organization is presumed to be in the right; if the procedures are corrupted, ignored, or bent, the organization is deemed to be in the wrong.

This flies somewhat in the face of efficiency. It is hard to draft *ex ante* a procedure for discharging employees, or improving workforce diversity, or whatever, that accommodates the rich variety of contingencies and conditions that are encountered in the real world. *If we could be sure of the good intentions of management,* we would get better outcomes by permitting the exercise of subjective judgment in what to do and how to do it. Perhaps subjective judgment would be necessary only occasionally, but nonetheless in at least some cases its exercise could presumably improve efficiency.

So why don't we see more subjective judgment applied? The italicized antecedent explains why due process procedures are generally somewhat formulaic, eschewing subjective judgment. The courts and other third parties can't always be sure of the good intentions of management. In fact, the courts are called in precisely because one or more parties alleges that management's intentions were *not* good. And then it becomes important for the courts to be able to inspect the record and decide, based on the evidence, whether management seems to have been acting with good intentions or not.

Judging after the fact whether management exercised wisdom and had good intentions, if management's procedures were subjectively tied to specific contingencies, can be a nightmare. On what basis did management choose to follow this or that procedure? What information did they have? What possibilities were they considering? On the other hand, if the procedure is formulaic—if management is supposed to do A, and then B, and then C—it is relatively easier for the courts to inspect the record and answer, Did management in fact do A, and then B, and then C? Note well, the key here is the *ex post* reconstruction of the process that management followed. It is fine to give managers discretion as to what they may do and how, as long as the courts can reconstruct history after the fact and verify that management exercised its discretion as it is "supposed to."

In terms of the ideas of this chapter, this is a question of noise in observables and the ability of the parties involved to verify *ex post* whether one of the parties kept to the agreement. We may sacrifice subjective discretion, which means that the outcome isn't going to be as efficient as it would be if we didn't need to worry about verification. But worry we must, and therefore the sacrifice in subjective discretion becomes necessary, to avoid other inefficiencies that would arise from attributing bad intentions to management due to an inability to reconstruct managers' decision processes.

Even if this sort of formulaic rigidity or lack of subjective discretion can produce particular outcomes that are suboptimal, it can also lead to a set of outcomes that are on balance more efficient overall. Hence, it may be to the benefit of *management* that such formulaic processes are in place. In fact, given that we've been discussing this issue in the context of court enforcement of due process, some of the benefits for management should be relatively clear: If the courts had to verify good subjective judgment, a firm that had exercised its subjective judgment with good and appropriate intentions would still have to worry that the courts would misread the evidence and find otherwise. When following a formulaic process covers your backside, you needn't worry that, by mistake, you'll find yourself exposed to court-ordered damages.

Please don't read us as arguing that, in the current business and legal environment in the United States (or in any other jurisdiction), the balance between *ex post* verifiability and subjective discretion is perfect. Many commentators argue that damage awards (including punitive damages) in the United States are excessive; if they are correct, it follows that the level of formulaic rigidity is probably too high—at least, limiting damage awards ought to increase levels of subjective discretion applied by firms in these sorts of cases. But the key point is that there is a balance to be achieved here; formulaic rigidity plays an important economic role, and it shouldn't simply be dismissed cavalierly as a useless drag on efficient employment relations.

Voluntary Due Process Protections

Everything we just said about court-mandated due process applies to voluntary due process protections, protections that a firm in its own self-interest gives to employees. You might think that such things—giving employees the right to appeal decisions by their supervisors, requiring documentation by supervisors of performance appraisal procedures, and so on—are a benefit provided to employees, in just the same way that health care or higher salaries are provided. That is, these things are good for the employee and bad for the employer, and so are simply a form of compensation provided the employee, at a cost to the employer.

But this isn't correct. The situation here is far from zero-sum. Of course these things are of value to the employee. But they can also be of value to the firm. By voluntarily providing these protections, the firm helps create and sustain a reputation as a place that treats people well. In addition, the existence of such structures and well-defined procedures (as well as the folklore of most organizations) provides a mechanism for expectations and reputations to be transmitted across generations of the workforce. And, in line with the discussion of the previous subsection, such protections can enhance efficiency by promoting trust: Especially where the procedures are formulaic enough that it can be verified after the fact whether they were followed, employees will be better able to monitor the actions of employers with relatively little noise or error. This, in turn, can help sustain the virtuous cycle of mutual trust that—as we observed in Chapter 4—is crucial to efficient employment relations.

THE LIMITATIONS OF GAME THEORY

The game-theoretic approach to reciprocity and reputation teaches us a number of important lessons—for instance, about the destructive role of noise; about the need to enhance communication from one generation of employees to the next; about conditions under which a hierarchical relationship can be supplanted by one that is more balanced-bilateral. But the game-theoretic approach doesn't answer two crucially important questions: How are expectations formed? And what determines the objectives of the parties involved?

Taking expectations first, the theory we have discussed here is predicated on the notion that the parties involved are in a Nash equilibrium. As we saw at the outset, this means that each has correct expectations about how the other parties involved will act and react. These expectations are key. The difference between positive labor–management relations and relations characterized by grinding confrontation can come down to nothing more than the simple fact that in one case, each side *expects* the other to reciprocate good for good (and bad for bad) and hence each side gives good; whereas in the second case, the expectation is "bad for good and bad for bad," and hence each side metes out bad. We see this vividly in the folk theorem, which attests to the wide variety of equilibrium outcomes, each held together by expectations. But which expectations hold in a particular instance? Here the theory is silent.

As for "objectives," we mean (in game-theoretic terms) the process by which real, tangible outcomes are translated into those ubiquitous payoffs that the theory throws around. Take the prisoners' dilemma. The analysis of this situation is based on an assumption that to fink while your confrere refuses to fink is better for you than the situation in which both of you refuse to fink. Honor among thieves is invalidated *by assumption*. But in real-life applications (including inducing thieves to fink on one another), intangible factors—such as honor, gratitude, kinship, and, on the other side, revenge—all affect what people want. Game theorists by and large consider these things as outside of their domain; "Tell me what people want," a game-theory-plying analyst will say, "and then I'll start my analysis." But in human interactions generally, and in the domain of employment and HRM in particular, figuring out what people want (and sometimes even affecting those desires) is central.

From the perspective of this book, this is where economics—which is largely rooted in the ideas of game theory as described in this appendix—meets the other social sciences. If we believe that expectations are formed out of experience, psychological theories of perception and cognition can help us to understand what sorts of messages are most easily and effectively learned. That is one of the main reasons why (in Chapter 3) we emphasize having simple and consistent messages communicated through the various HR practices within an organization, to enable employees to understand more quickly and effectively what is the implicit contract—what can be expected of others and what is expected of you—in the organization. It is also one of the main reasons why (in Chapter 2) we underscore consistency between HR systems and the external social environment: Employment relations are embedded in a larger context of social exchange, and consonance with that larger social context is generally a plus, because it reinforces the process of expectation formation. Turning to what people value, in Chapter 5 we discuss ideas such as under- and oversufficient justification, escalating commitment, social comparisons, gift exchange, and perceptions of procedural justice. These are all psychological and social mechanisms by which preferences are determined. As such, they help us to fill in the substantial blanks left in the game-theoretic treatment of reciprocity and reputation.

To take an example, the constructions of this chapter lead nearly immediately to a theory of trust: Party B trusts party A because A knows that B, or B's successors, will punish A for a breach of trust. In jargon, trust is *calculative*: B trusts A because B assumes (and calculates) that A can also calculate that acting in trustworthy fashion is in her (A's) own self-interest. Commentators have viewed this as somewhat deficient as a theory of trust, pointing out that another form of trust, which is *noncalculative*—an economist would say, "blind"—works as follows: B trusts A because . . . well, because he does.[8] And A reciprocates by honoring B's trust because . . . well, because she does (although see below). Commentators will sometimes offer the opinion that calculative trust is inferior to noncalculative trust, in the sense of overall efficiency. This opinion surprises and puzzles many economists, who can scarcely imagine a firmer foundation for trust or cooperation than the mutual and conscious self-interest of the parties. But they shouldn't be too surprised or puzzled: If, for example, we believe that noncalculative (or "blind") trust gets party A to internalize party B's welfare (processes like gift exchange or insufficient justification could be at work, along the lines discussed in Chapter 5), then this helps clarify the mechanisms fostering noncalculative trust and reasons why in some cases it might promote greater efficiency.

ENDNOTES

1. This will be a very fast and incomplete summary of these techniques. Most textbooks in microeconomics will give you some exposure to these ideas, if you want more detail and/or a slower pace.

2. For example, see David M. Kreps, *A Course in Microeconomic Theory* (Princeton, NJ: Princeton University Press, 1990), Chapter 14.

3. The usual objection raised at this point is: Will ROW be able to live with the guilt of having finked on her partner COL? Mightn't she choose not to fink on the basis of not wanting a guilty conscience? In reality she might do so, but we want in our model for the payoffs to capture everything that a player wants. If ROW's conscience would bother her, we would change the payoffs in Figure B-2 to reflect this. Thus, by analyzing Figure B-2, we are assuming that any feelings of conscience of this sort are outweighed by monetary or other considerations of the situation and that all this is reflected in the payoffs associated with each strategy.

4. The name *grim cooperation* comes from the fact that if ever the player using it is finked upon, he or she grimly finks forever after. There is never any forgiveness for being crossed, even once.

5. It is called the folk theorem because it seems always to have been known. No one is brash enough to take credit for such a simple and obvious basic idea.

6. The term "noisy" pertains to the presence of statistical noise or uncertainty in the signal that a party receives about another party's actions.

7. For example, it is interesting to speculate on how the burgeoning Internet affects reputation. On the one hand, it is becoming far easier for potential trading partners of A to gather data about how A has acted with respect to other parties; Web sites and newsgroups abound in which individuals recount their experiences in dealing with a particular exchange partner. But the credibility of things posted on the Internet must be taken into account. Of course, there are institutional arrangements—credit rating organizations and the like—whose function is to provide fairly reliable summaries of past behavior by economic actors, and whose own concern for maintaining a favorable reputation exerts discipline on the types of information that are gathered and disseminated.

8. See, for example, Oliver E. Williamson, "Calculativeness, Trust, and Economic Organization," *Journal of Law and Economics* 36 (April 1993): 453–86.

APPENDIX C

AGENCY THEORY

Agency theory, the *economic theory of incentives,* and the *principal–agent problem* are different terms used to describe a collection of models economists have created to study aspects of pay for performance. The purpose of this appendix is to give you a taste of what this literature is like and what it has to say. But you should understand that the literature on this topic is vast and, in places, rather difficult; we have selected the simplest formalizations we can for this appendix. If our overview piques your interest, we suggest reading further on the subject.[1]

The basic model of agency involves two individuals, a principal and an agent. The principal (whom we'll call "her") offers the agent ("him") the opportunity to work for her. If the agent accepts the offer, there is an observable outcome x, measured in terms of profit to the principal (which excludes any compensation paid to the agent). This outcome x is influenced by the amount of effort e exerted by the agent but in general is also random: We will write $F(x;e)$ for the cumulative (probability) distribution function of x given the level of effort e. The principal's offer to the agent is a compensation function y that depends on x. For example, the principal might offer the agent $y(x) = B + bx$, meaning a base salary B and in addition a share b of the gross profits. Note that this contract would leave the principal with a net profit of $x - y(x) = (1 - b)x - B$.

The agent is risk averse; he evaluates risky streams of income according to their expected utility, for a concave (risk-averse) utility function,[2] which we will call U. He also dislikes effort, so if he is offered (and accepts) contract y and he chooses effort level e, he evaluates his situation by computing the expected value of $U(y(x)) - e$, treating x as a random variable with distribution function $F(x;e)$.[3] The agent has a next-best opportunity (taking employment with someone else) that would give him expected utility u, and the agent is in a take-it-or-leave-it position vis-à-vis the principal; that is, the agent considers the offer $y(x)$ made by the principal and asks himself two questions:

> Question 1: "If I accept the contract and go to work for this principal, what level of effort should I choose?" To which he answers: "I should choose that level of e that makes me as well off as possible, which is the level e that maximizes the expected value of $U(y(x)) - e$, where the distribution of x is given by $F(x;e)$."

It is natural to assume that U and y are increasing functions and that an increase in e shifts the distribution of x "rightward," toward higher levels of gross income.

Given these assumptions, notice the trade-off here: Increasing e increases (stochastically) the distribution of x, thus the distribution of $y(x)$, and thus the expectation of $U(y(x))$. In other words, increasing e means more expected utility from the "bonus scheme" offered by the principal. But it also means less utility for the agent in terms of the effort expended; the agent has to balance the positive impact that his effort has on his compensation against his basic distaste for working hard.

Let e^* denote the "answer" to the first question—the optimal level of e for the agent (in terms of the agent's own preferences) if he accepts the contract. Then the second question the agent asks himself is:

> Question 2: "If I take the contract and choose the level e^*, my overall utility will be the expected value of $U(y(x)) - e^*$, where the distribution of x is given by $F(x;e^*)$. I should take the contract if this expected utility exceeds u, the utility of my next-best opportunity, and I should turn it down if this expected utility is less than u. So, how *does* this expected utility compare with u?"

Let us stress here that the model assumes that the agent takes or leaves the principal's offer. If the expected utility exceeds u, he doesn't try to bargain for an even better contract; he simply takes what is offered. If the expected utility falls short of u, he just turns it down.

That is how the agent reasons, if he is offered the contract y. Now, what questions does the principal ask herself? First, the basic model assumes that if she doesn't hire an agent, she nets zero, and that all the available agents are just the same as this one. Hence, if she can't induce this agent to take the contract, no agent will work for her. Second, we assume that she knows enough about this agent to know his utility function and to be able to put herself into his shoes, to figure out the answers he will give to the two questions above. Third, we assume she is neutral to risk; her objective is to maximize the expectation of her net profits. Thus, the (very mathematically complex) questions she asks herself are:

> "Of all the possible contracts y that I could offer the agent, which one nets me the highest expected net profits? Specifically, for each contract y that I could offer, let $e^*(y)$ be the effort this contract induces from the agent, assuming he takes the contract. (That is, $e^*(y)$ answers the agent's first question given the contract y.) Then, among all contracts y that induce the agent to accept my offer—that give the agent expected utility u or more—which contract maximizes the expectation of $x - y(x)$, where the distribution of x is given by $F(x;e^*(y))$? And given the answer to this question, is it worth my while to hire an agent, in the sense that my expected net profit, net of the wages I pay him, will exceed zero?"

This is, we reiterate, a tremendously hard problem. The principal is maximizing not over a variable—the normal stuff of calculus—nor over a variable subject to a constraint—the stuff of harder, constrained-maximization calculus—but over a function subject to constraints. This is the sort of thing that is answered by the *calculus of variations* or *control theory* (if you've ever run across those subjects).

But it turns out that this problem is tougher than the standard sorts of problem one encounters in control theory or the calculus of variations, because of the nature of the constraints that arise from the agent's two questions. Moreover, we have to wonder what we do if the agent gets ties in the answers to either of his questions—for instance, if the utility associated with the contract offered by the principal matches exactly the utility that would be associated with taking his best alternative job. (In general, economists assume that ties in terms of the agent's utility are always resolved to the favor of the principal.)

And, even though the problem formulated in this way is very complex mathematically, the formulation is extraordinarily simplistic in terms of the real-world problem the model is attempting to address. There are any number of grounds for attacking this model as unrealistic, but the three that follow are perhaps the most salient:

1. The model assumes that the agent is effort averse. But real-life workers are not entirely averse to effort (see Chapter 5). In part this problem arises because the model assumes that effort is one-dimensional; in real life, effort is multidimensional, and although the agent may not be averse to effort *per se,* he may not necessarily agree with the principal on how best to direct his efforts.

2. The model assumes that the principal knows everything relevant about the agent and that, given a contract *y,* she can predict perfectly how the agent will respond to her contract offer—whether he will accept the contract and, if so, what level of effort he will select. In the real world, employers don't know the precise tastes of their employees; employers can't figure out precisely how their employees will respond to changes in their compensation contracts but instead must rely somewhat on trial and error.

3. In the real world, there are usually different sorts of prospective employees in the pool from which the employer can choose, and the employer's problem is to design a contract that is acceptable to and attracts the best possible worker, where best possible means *from the employer's point of view.* If we put this sort of consideration into the model, we'd be led to aspects of the economic theory of screening, which we will describe in Appendix D. For now, we only note that our model formulation doesn't take this into account and doing so makes the model even harder to solve.

So we have a model that is simultaneously very complex mathematically and quite deficient as a model of reality. What's the point? The point is, even if we simplify the model further so that we can solve it (and we'll proceed to do this in a moment), and even if the model thus simplified is even more at odds with the richness of reality, nonetheless working with the model can help us understand *some* aspects of real compensation contracts. Economists and other social scientists build models that capture some aspects of reality, not to compute the answer to a real-world problem, but in the hope of gaining some insight into real world problems. We'll only be able to assess whether that happens with this model after we complete the analysis, for which we need to simplify the story still further.

A SIMPLE VERSION

The agency problem described above is too complex to be solved in a fashion that will make sense to most readers of this appendix. So we simplify even more. In particular, we will deal with the following ultra-simple version of the story:

1. We assume that the agent's risk aversion takes the form of so-called mean–variance preferences—the agent likes higher average pay but dislikes greater dispersion (variance) in his compensation, and he trades one against the other in linear fashion. Formally, faced with a random income stream y and effort level e, the agent evaluates his situation according to: $E(y) - k\sigma^2(y) - k'e$, where $E(y)$ is the expected value or mean of y, $\sigma^2(y)$ is the variance of y, and k and k' are two nonnegative constants.

2. We assume that the principal only considers linear compensation contracts, which means contracts that take the form $y(x) = B + bx$, for constants B and b. That is, we rule out nonlinear compensation schemes, schemes with hurdle levels, and everything else, except simple contracts with a base wage B and a bonus that depends linearly on the outcome x, with bonus rate b.

3. We assume that as the agent shifts the level of his effort e, he shifts the mean but not the variance of x. Specifically, the function that gives the mean of x as a function of e is written $m(e)$, which is furthermore assumed to be the function $e^{1/2}$, the square root of e. Thus, increasing effort means a higher mean level of gross profit (because the square root function is strictly increasing), but increasing effort increases gross profits at a decreasing rate (because the square root function is concave). The variance of x is a fixed constant, which we'll denote by v.

Some comments: (a) If you have taken a course in the economics of uncertainty, information economics, or even the modern theory of finance, you probably ran across a discussion of the merits and demerits of using mean–variance style preferences to capture elements of risk aversion. If you haven't ever seen a discussion of this, the executive summary is: This is a model with some substantial problems, but one that works adequately in some contexts. This is one of the contexts where it does reasonably well. (b) The restriction to linear contracts, with a base rate of pay and a constant commission on gross profits, has some theoretical justification.[4] But it is a substantial simplification that will result in some nice results that don't generalize. Note that this makes the principal's optimization problem a lot easier; instead of optimizing over a space of functions, we now have to optimize only two (real) variables, B and b. So standard calculus can be employed. (c) Once we get to the assumptions listed under (3), we have clearly restricted attention to a very particular example. We assume that effort has no impact on the variance of gross profits. (One might imagine, instead, that higher effort means higher mean gross profits, but also higher variance in profits). Furthermore, we rely on a very particular functional relationship between expected gross profits and effort. (If you are mathematically inclined, try as a first step in generalizing our analysis to redo what follows with a general concave and strictly increasing $m(e)$ function. Almost everything of a qualitative nature that follows generalizes to this case, although you won't get solutions in closed form.[5])

With these assumptions in place, we can proceed to the analysis. We will run through the entire analysis before commenting on the "answers" we get.

Step 1. The agent's problem. Suppose the principal offers the agent a contract with base pay B and bonus rate b. The agent, if he accepts this contract, faces the income stream $y(x) = B + bx$. If he takes effort level e (so that x has mean $m(e)$), the mean of $y(x)$ is $B + bm(e)$ and its variance is b^2v. Hence, the agent evaluates his welfare according to $B + bm(e) - kb^2v - k'e$. Simple calculus tells us that the first-order condition for the optimal choice of effort level e is $m'(e) = k'/b$, where m' means the first derivative of the function m. Because $m(e) = e^{1/2}$, its derivative is $e^{-1/2}/2$, and we get, for the optimal level of e (which we denote by e^*):

$$(e^*)^{-1/2}/2 = k'/b \text{ or } e^* = b^2/(2k')^2.$$

Note that this gives $m(e^*) = b/(2k')$. And the agent will take the offer and work this hard if $B + bm(e^*) - kb^2v - k'e^* \geq u$, which, substituting $b/(2k')$ for $m(e^*)$ and $b^2/(2k')^2$ for e^* is

$$B + b^2/(2k') - kb^2v - b^2/4k' = B + b^2/(4k') - kb^2v \geq u.$$

Step 2. The principal's choice of B. What level of B will the principal choose? Adopt the working hypothesis that the principal wants this agent to work for her. (We'll check this working hypothesis in step 4.) Then given the principal's choice of b, she will want to pay the agent just enough of a base salary so that he will choose to work. The agent chooses to work as long as he is better off working than at his next-best opportunity; in fact, given our assumption that ties are resolved in favor of the principal, he chooses to work for this principal as long as he is just as well off as at his next-best opportunity. Thus, the smallest base pay B that the principal can offer, if she offers b, and still get the agent to work for her, is:

$$B = u - b^2/(4k') + kb^2v.$$

Step 3. The principal's choice of b. What level of b is optimal for the principal? Continue to maintain the hypothesis that the principal will choose to employ the agent.

Then if the principal chooses b and thus the B computed just above, and if the agent responds by accepting and choosing effort level $e^* = b^2/(2k')^2$, then the principal will net expected profit equal to:

$$(1 - b)m(e^*) - B = (1 - b)b/(2k') - u + b^2/(4k') - kb^2v =$$
$$b/(2k') - u - b^2[1/(4k') + kv] = b/(2k') - u - b^2[1 + 4k'kv]/(4k').$$

This is maximized in b by taking the derivative in b and setting it equal to zero. If you do the algebra that is entailed, you will find that the optimal level of b to set is

$$b = 1/[1 + 4k'kv].$$

Step 4. Is the agent worth his cost to the principal? Working backward with this value of b gives us the following two expressions:

The base wage is $B = u - [1 - 4k'kv]/[4k'(1 + 4k'kv)^2]$, and
The principal's expected net profits are $1/[4k'(1 + 4k'kv)] - u$.

Hence, the principal will offer this contract to the agent as long as the last expression is positive; otherwise, she will forgo hiring an agent entirely.

Summing Up

That finishes the derivation. Breathe deeply and relax. Before beginning discussion, let us recap what we learned.

For a general compensation scheme $y(x) = B + bx$, if the agent takes the job, he will choose effort level $e^* = b^2/(2k')^2$. And he will take the job (given B and b) as long as $B + b^2/(4k') - kb^2v \geq u$.

If the principal is restricted (as the model assumes) to compensation schemes of the sort $y(x) = B + bx$, she finds it worthwhile to hire the agent if $1/[4k'(1 + 4k'kv)] \geq u$, in which case the optimal scheme for her to offer to the agent is:

$$b = 1/[1 + 4k'kv] \quad \text{and} \quad B = u - [1 - 4k'kv]/[4k'(1 + 4k'kv)^2].$$

At this scheme, the agent chooses effort level:

$$e^* = 1/[2k'(1 + 4k'kv)]^2 \text{ so that } m(e^*) = 1/[2k'(1 + 4k'kv)].$$

The agent nets utility u; the principal's expected net profits are $1/[4k'(1 + 4k'kv)] - u$.

Now to discuss all of this.

If the Principal and Agent Could Contract on Effort

Suppose the principal and agent could in fact write a contract that specified the effort level to be taken by the agent. Assuming a worthwhile deal can be struck at all, the optimal contract would specify the level of effort that makes expected gross profits net of the agent's disutility of effort as large as possible, which is the level e^0 that solves

$$m'(e^0) = k', \text{ or } e^0 = 1/(2k')^2.$$

The agent would be guaranteed a payment of u precisely, and the principal would bear all the risk. And all this would happen as long as $1/(4k') > u$, with the difference between these two representing the principal's net expected profits. Otherwise, even if the two parties could contract on the agent's level of effort, there is no deal available that entices the agent away from his next-best opportunity and simultaneously leaves the principal with positive expected (net) profits.

We are just asserting all these things—they don't follow from the derivation—but they are easy to derive. First, it is clear that if the two parties can contract on the level of effort, then it is best to shield the agent from any risk; the agent discounts risky gambles (as long as $k > 0$) from their expected value and so must be compensated for any risk he takes on, compensation that comes straight out of the pocket of the principal. And then, once we know that the agent will get a certain (nonstochastic) payment, we know that the principal will pay precisely $u + k'e^0$, and we find the optimal level of effort for the two to agree upon by noting that the principal's residual net expected profits are $m(e^0) - [u + k'e^0]$. Maximizing this in e^0 and then computing the principal's expected net profits (and comparing with zero) gives the asserted answers.

The Cost of Being Unable to Contract on Effort

This lets us compute how much it costs the principal and agent to be unable to contract on effort. For the agent in this take-it-or-leave-it model, it doesn't matter. He gets utility u at his next-best opportunity, and he gets u from the principal whatever happens, so by design he is indifferent.

But for the principal, her expected net profits drop from $1/(4k') - u$ to $1/[4k'(1 + 4k'kv)] - u$, with the proviso that her expected net profits drop to zero if the second term is negative. As long as k, k', and v are all strictly positive, this is certainly a drop; the term $1/(1 + 4k'kv)$ is strictly less than one. Moreover, this term is decreasing in each of k', k, and v; the more effort averse the agent, the more risk averse the agent, or the more uncertainty in the connection between effort and profits, the bigger is the cost of being unable to contract on effort.

The Sources of This Cost, and the Impact on Effort
of Being Unable to Contract on Effort

Where does this cost come from? It is important to recognize that there are two sources of cost. The first and more direct source is the need to load risk onto the agent, to get any effort out of him. If the agent were fully shielded from risk, he would be getting a certain (nonstochastic) payment. But because he is effort averse, if his income is guaranteed (and we have no other lever with which to motivate his choice of effort), he will choose as low a level of effort as he can (which is $e = 0$ in the model). This could be acceptable in some contexts, but in this model, $e = 0$ means $m(e) = 0$; the principal isn't going to pay for that! So the principal must motivate the agent with pay for performance. But by construction the agent doesn't completely control the observable output measure (in this model, x), so this means a random income for the agent for which the risk-averse agent must be compensated, giving us the first source of cost to the principal.

The second source of cost is less direct and a bit more subtle. For a general compensation scheme $y(x) = B + bx$, the agent chooses effort level $e^* = b^2/(2k')^2$. Hence, to get the level of effort $e^0 = 1/(2k')^2$, which is what is best when the parties can contract on effort, the principal must set $b = 1$. But this loads a lot of risk on the agent. It is better for the principal to compromise between the effort level induced and the amount of risk loaded onto the agent, by setting $b = 1/(1 + 4k'kv)$. This bonus rate, which is strictly less than one if k, k', and v are all strictly positive, induces $e^* = 1/[2k'(1 + 4k'kv)]^2$, which is less than e^0. That is, the second source of cost comes from a compromise between effort inducement and risk sharing, a compromise that leads to an effort level lower than e^0.

It is probably worth observing at this point that some of what we are seeing here is due to the particular parameterization of the model. In general in agency theory, if the principal is risk neutral and the agent is risk averse and effort averse, we find the first source of cost: To induce the agent to put in anything besides the minimum level of effort, the principal must resort to pay for performance, which means an inefficient loading of risk onto the agent's shoulders.[6] And in general, when the optimum incentive pay scheme is devised, it results in a level of effort different from the level that would have been selected if the two parties could contract directly on effort. Yet one cannot tell in general whether the effort level that is (optimally) induced is more or less than the direct-contracting-on-effort level. To explain why takes us into some fairly technical stuff, so we won't try. However, please note: Not everything we are getting out of the model would obtain in a more general model. In particular, there is probably some intuitive appeal to the idea that the principal will have to settle for lower effort than if she and the agent could contract on effort level. And in this very special model, this is what we see. But in other parameterizations of the principal–agent model, this result does not obtain.

What If the Agent Isn't Averse to Risk?

In this model, the agent's level of risk aversion is captured by the constant k. If $k = 0$, the agent isn't risk averse. From the preceding discussion, we know already that, in this case, the inability to contract directly on effort is immaterial to the principal, but it is worth being careful to note how this comes about: If $k = 0$, then the optimal contract for the principal to offer has $b = 1$ and $B = u - 1/[4k']$. It is worthwhile to write down the corresponding share left to the principal: Since $b = 1$, the principal gets no variable share of the profits, but takes $1/[4k'] - u$ for certain.

To disentangle what just happened, first recall that there is no deal at all if $1/[4k'] < u$; in this case, the principal simply gives up on the project (or job, or whatever). So when we say that, for $k = 0$, the optimal contract has a base wage $B = u - 1/[4k']$, understand that this base wage is *negative*; the agent is *paying* for the right to earn the bonus.[7] The agent gets 100% of the gross profits (that is, $b = 1$). So what we have here is quite simple in fact: If the agent is risk neutral, it is just as efficient on risk-sharing grounds for him to assume all the risk. To deal efficiently with his effort aversion, it is best for him to completely internalize the impact of his choice of effort on the gross profits, which is done, essentially, by having the principal "sell him the business." The agent gets 100% of the profits he creates by dint of his efforts, and he pays the principal up front the expected value (less his opportunity cost) of those profits.

This, it turns out, is quite general. Whenever both principal and agent are risk neutral (or, even more generally, whenever just the agent is risk neutral, as long as the principal isn't risk loving), and as long as the agent is the only party whose actions need to be motivated, it is ideal for the principal to give the agent 100% of the marginal value the agent creates, with the principal taking in return a certain (nonstochastic) payment. Thus, incentive problems must at some level stem from risk aversion on the part of the agent, or from some market imperfection that prevents this simple and elegant solution from transpiring.[8]

What If There Is No Risk?

Consider finally the extreme case of $v = 0$. This is easy. There is no uncertainty, so we are back to the case where, effectively, the parties can contract on the level of effort. But, in fact, this isn't what the math says will happen. Instead, we find $b = 1$ and $B = u - 1/[4k']$, just as in the no-risk-aversion case: The principal sells the business to the agent, although this time there is no uncertainty about either what is paid or what is gained from the sale.

Comparative Statics

We can go on to talk about how the answer changes as the agent becomes more risk averse or more effort averse, or as the level of uncertainty in gross profits increases. These all work in the same way: The principal is made worse off, the bonus rate b declines toward zero, and the level of effort chosen by the agent declines. We won't spend a lot of time on these separate effects—you are free to ponder them if you wish—but we do note that these things depend at least in part on the special parameterization we have chosen.

BEYOND EFFORT AVERSION, A SINGLE PERIOD, AND ONE SIGNAL OF EFFORT

This is a good place to end our excursion into the mathematical world of agency theory. By studying this model and other, more general forms of the same thing, economists come to the conclusions listed on page 249 of the text. But because this model is so simple and stylized, economists have gone on to study more realistic and detailed models of agency, leading to the sorts of conclusions given on pages 250–6. A few examples:

- They consider models in which effort is multidimensional. (Suppose the agent isn't averse to effort at all, but has a constraint on his time. That is, the agent can allocate his forty hours per week among several activities, with e_j representing the amount of time allocated to activity j. He faces the constraint $e_1 + \ldots + e_n = 40$. And the gross profits from activity j, x_j, have mean $m(e_j)$ and constant variance v_j. If you are adept at mathematics, you can try with this start to work your way toward finding the optimal compensation scheme for the principal to offer the agent, assuming a compensation scheme of the form $B + b_1x_1 + \ldots + b_nx_n$. (Assume the variables x_j are independent, for simplicity.)

- They consider models with more than one agent, where the profits earned by different agents are correlated, leading to benchmarking and tournament schemes. (Try a model with two agents, labeled $i = 1, 2$. Agent i chooses effort level e_i for the activity he controls, which gives gross profits x_i to the principal with mean $m(e_i)$ and variance v_i. The key is that x_1 and x_2 are correlated; let r be their coefficient of correlation. Look for optimal schemes where the principal pays agent i according to a function $B + b_ix_i + c_ix_j$ where j is the other agent. If you push through this, you will have to decide how each agent treats the effort choice of the other when choosing his own; the standard beginning assumption in the economics literature is to assume that each optimizes his choice of effort assuming the other's choice of effort is fixed, although collusion between the agents is a next step.)

- They consider models in which agents work in teams. (What happens if two agents *1* and *2* each contribute effort e_i, to give a gross profit x with mean $m(e_1 + e_2)$ for m concave? This leads first to free-rider problems and then to considerations of peer pressure.)

- They consider models in which efforts are made over time, and the agent observes as time passes how he is doing. (We won't suggest a formulation for this model, which is technically fairly difficult. This sort of model can be used to motivate our restriction to linear incentive schemes.[9])

To reiterate from the start of the appendix, we have only barely scratched the surface. Chapter 11 reports some of the conclusions and implications of the technical literature. If you found this brief excursion into agency theory interesting and wish to pursue the theory further, and if you are not too effort averse, you can consult the readings listed at the start of the appendix (note 1).

ENDNOTES

1. For this purpose, we recommend Paul Milgrom and D. John Roberts, *Economics, Organization, and Management* (Englewood Cliffs, NJ: Prentice-Hall, 1992), Chapters 6, 7, 12, and 13; David M. Kreps, *A Course in Microeconomic Theory* (Princeton, NJ: Prince-

ton University Press, 1990), Chapter 16; Andreu Mas Colell, Michael D. Whinston, and Jerry R. Green, *Microeconomic Theory* (New York: Oxford University Press, 1995), Chapter 14. These are all textbook treatments of the subject, which give additional suggestions for further reading.

2. We are assuming that you know about expected utility and related topics such as risk aversion; if not, some of our discussion may not make a lot of sense. But you may still be able to follow the simpler specification begun in the next subsection.

3. Simply subtracting the effort level is typical in this model, but more generally we might suppose that he evaluates contract y and effort level e according to the expectation of $U(y(x),e)$, where U is a function that is increasing in its first argument (he prefers more money to less) and decreasing in its second argument (he prefers less effort to more).

4. See Bengt Holmstrom and Paul Milgrom, "Aggregation and Linearity in the Provision of Intertemporal Incentives," *Econometrica* 55 (March 1987): 303–28. Good luck; this takes a lot of math.

5. A concave $m(e)$ function means diminishing marginal returns to effort, which might reflect physical and mental fatigue or the "low-lying fruit" phenomenon—on a tree it is easiest to pick the fruit located closest to the ground, and thus increasing effort will be required to pick fruit as the tree becomes depleted. This phenomenon applies to a broad range of activities—think of a saturated sales territory, fundraising, scientific discoveries, and process innovations. But this is not a law of nature; for example, there might in some cases be *increasing* returns to effort in pursuing process innovations, at least at the start, as the fixed costs of understanding the process must be paid for during the first few innovations but can be amortized increasingly well as further innovations are made.

6. It is generally true that if risk is being shared between two parties, one of whom is risk-neutral and the other risk-averse, it is efficient on risk-sharing grounds alone for the risk-neutral party to bear all the risk. See Kreps, *op. cit.,* Chapter 3.

7. This may strike you as unrealistic. But, recall the real-world example from Chapter 2 of RE/MAX, a large, international real estate agency, which uses precisely this compensation structure: Realtors get 100% of the commissions they earn, and they pay RE/MAX for the privilege (and for some clerical services). But there is more going on in RE/MAX than risk-neutral realtors; we discuss this example further in Chapter 14.

8. To detail the sorts of market imperfections that give rise to incentive problems is outside the scope of this appendix, but we will mention two. First, there may be an informational imperfection; the principal controls the accounting system and can't credibly provide the agent with an accurate accounting of how much he earned. (This is another form of moral hazard problem, with the hazard on the side of the principal.) Second, the agent may be unable to raise enough funds to buy the business up front, or limited liability considerations may make this impractical.

9. See Holmstrom and Milgrom, *op. cit.*

APPENDIX D

ADVERSE SELECTION AND MARKET SIGNALING

The general theory of adverse selection and market signaling is briefly recounted below, using the used car market as a motivating example.[1]

THE PROBLEM OF LEMONS

There are many cases in which the seller of a good or service knows more about the quality of the item being sold than the buyer does. The standard example is that of used cars; the owner of the used car knows whether the car is a *lemon* (a poorly performing vehicle) or a *cream-puff* (a superior vehicle), whereas buyers cannot tell for sure which it is. Other examples abound. For instance, a manufacturer may be better informed about the quality or reliability of some product being sold than are customers. An individual shopping for insurance may be better informed about his state of health than is the company considering whether to issue health or life insurance to him.[2] More germane to the subject matter of this book, a job applicant may be better informed about her abilities or her likelihood of resigning in the future than is a prospective employer. In all these cases, the uninformed party faces a potential problem of adverse selection: When deciding what price to pay (or charge) for the good or service, the uninformed party offers a price appropriate for the average good offered for sale. If the price appropriate for the average good in the population as a whole is unappealing for those who own higher-quality goods, owners of higher-quality goods will withdraw from the market; the goods or services that are offered for sale (or the people who queue up to buy insurance) are the relatively less reliable, lower-quality ones. But then the buyer must offer a still lower price, because the average good for sale is worse than the average of the entire population. This lower price potentially drives even more high-quality goods out of the market; the feedback loop in this process enhances the adverse selection problem.

To take a very simple illustrative caricature, imagine that every used car is of one of three types: a lemon, okay, or a cream-puff. Of all the used cars in the world, suppose one-third are lemons, one-third are okay, and one-third are cream-puffs. Imagine that there is only one model of car, so that this is the only way in which used cars differ.

Now suppose that there is some fixed number of used cars in the world, say 30,000. Imagine that to their owners, contemplating the sale of their vehicles, a lemon is worth $3,000, an okay used car is worth $4,000, and a cream-puff is worth $5,000. (In other words, owning a vehicle produces utility to the owner equivalent to these respective dollar amounts.) If the market price of a used car is less than $3,000, no car is supplied for sale. If the price is at or above $3,000 but below $4,000, all the lemons are offered for sale. At prices between $4,000 and $5,000, all the lemons and all the okay cars are offered for sale. And at prices at or above $5,000, all the cars are offered for sale. Hence we get a supply curve as in Figure D-1.

As for the demand side of the market, imagine that many people are interested in buying used cars. A car's value to a potential buyer depends on its quality: A lemon is worth $3,300 to potential buyers; if the car is okay, it is worth $4,300 to potential buyers; and a cream-puff is worth $5,300 to potential buyers. We'll suppose that buyers are risk neutral; a car that they assess as being a lemon with probability .4, okay with probability .4, and a cream-puff with probability .2, is worth to them the amount $(.4)(3300) + (.4)(4300) + (.2)(5300) = $4,100. Note that in this example, every used car ought to be exchanged if we are going to have a market that works as well as conceivably possible, because by assumption every car is worth more to a buyer than to its current owner.

In Figure D-1 we have supply. What about demand? The demand at any price depends on expectations concerning the quality of the car being supplied. Suppose that buyers have *naive* expectations, which means that at any price, they believe that a car they buy is chosen at random from the population of all used cars—that is, it is equally likely to be a cream-puff, okay, or a lemon. Thus, the price they would pay for any car is: $(\frac{1}{3} \times \$3,300) + (\frac{1}{3} \times \$4,300) + (\frac{1}{3} \times \$5,300) = \$4,300$.
We get the naive demand curve shown in Figure D-2: no demand at prices above $4,300, and unlimited demand at any price below $4,300. If this is the demand curve, 20,000 cars change hands at a price of $4,300.

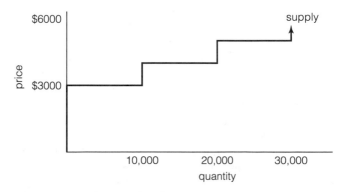

Figure D-1 The supply of cars.

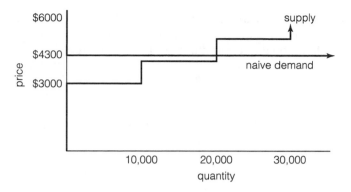

Figure D-2   Naive demand and equilibrium.

But in this equilibrium, the 20,000 cars that are supplied are equal numbers of okay cars and lemons. No cream-puffs are coming on the market, because they are all worth more to their owners than the market price of $4,300. This being so, car buyers will come to learn over time that cream-puffs never come on the market; cars that are sold are equally likely to be okay or lemons. Thus, the most consumers will pay for the cars that are coming to market is: $(\frac{1}{2} \times \$3,300) + (\frac{1}{2} \times \$4,300) = \$3,800$, and demand at $4,300 falls to zero. Moreover, demand at $3,800 falls to zero as soon as buyers begin to understand the new market reality: At a price of $3,800, owners of okay cars will hold on to those cars, and the only used cars supplied will be lemons. A lemon is worth only $3,300. So, taking all this into account, the *sophisticated demand curve* is as shown in Figure D-3: zero demand at prices above $3,300, unlimited demand at prices below $3,300, and an equilibrium in which the lemons change hands at a price of $3,300.

To reiterate: The price that buyers will pay for a used car depends on the *average quality* of the cars that are brought to the market. This discourages owners

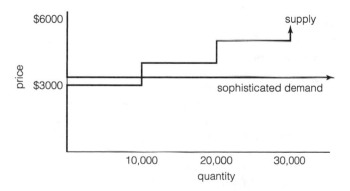

Figure D-3   Sophisticated demand and equilibrium.

of good used cars from selling their cars, and it means that the average of the cars that are brought to the market is lowered. In this case, the presence of lemons drives (ouch!) higher-quality cars entirely out of the market.

MARKET SIGNALS

So if you own a cream-puff, what are you going to do? You know that if you can somehow have your cream-puff certified as being a cream-puff, then you can get $5,300 for it, which is $300 more than it is worth to you. If you can get it certified as a cream-puff for less than $300, you will do so; this might be done by having it inspected in a garage. But suppose that direct certification is not possible. There still might be actions you can take to distinguish your car as a cream-puff. For example, suppose that you offered a limited warranty on your car. You offer to pay for any repairs necessary for the first four months after you sell the car. Of course, this is costly for you, but it may be less costly for you than it would be for someone who owns a car that is just okay or for someone who owns a lemon. Suppose, for example, that the cost to a seller of a warranty depends on the length of the warranty and also the type of car being sold. Specifically, suppose that to a lemon owner, every month of warranty costs an expected $1000. To the owner of an okay car, the first month of warranty costs $100; the second, $300; the third, $600; and all subsequent months cost $1,000 apiece. If you own a cream-puff, the first four months of warranty costs you $100 apiece; the fifth costs you $200; and any additional months cost you $300 each. Suppose as well that a warranty has value to a buyer. Specifically, each month of warranty is worth $75 to the buyer. Now suppose that, somehow, markets reach the following equilibrium:

- If you offer a four-month warranty, you can sell your car for $5,600.
- If you offer a two-month warranty, you can sell your car for $4,450.
- If you offer no warranty, you can sell your car for $3,300.

Suppose you own a lemon. If you offer no warranty on your car, you can sell it outright for $3,300. If you offer a two-month warranty, you can sell it for $4,450, but the warranty will cost you an expected $2,000, so you will realize only $2,450. If you offer a four-month warranty, you can sell the car for $5,600. But the four-month warranty will cost you an expected $4,000, so you will net only $1,600. If you hold on to your car, it is worth $3,000 to you. So it is best to offer no warranty and sell your car for $3,300.

Suppose you own an okay car. If you offer no warranty, you can get $3,300. If you offer a two-month warranty, you get $4,450, from which $400 in expected costs must be subtracted, for a net of $4,050. If you offer a four-month warranty, you get $5,600, less expected costs of $2,000, for a net of $3,600. If you hold on to your car, it is worth $4,000 to you. So you do best by offering a two-month warranty and selling for $4,450.

Suppose you own a cream-puff. If you offer no warranty, you get $3,300. If you offer a two-month warranty, you get $4,450, from which warranty costs of $200 are subtracted, leaving you netting $4,250. If you offer a four-month warranty, you net $5,600, from which warranty costs of $400 must be subtracted, leaving you at a net $5,200. And if you hold on to your car, you have netted the equivalent of $5,000. It is best to sell your car with a four-month warranty, for $5,600.

Do the prices being offered make sense? If a car is being offered for sale without a warranty, it is sure to be a lemon, and so it is worth $3,300 to the buyer. If a car is being offered for sale with a two-month warranty, it is sure to be okay, and so it is worth $4,300 plus $150 or $4,450 to buyers—the $4,300 is the basic value of the car, and the $150 is the value of two months' worth of warranty. If a car is being offered for sale with a four-month warranty, it is sure to be a cream-puff, and so it is worth $5,300 (for the car) plus $300 (for the warranty), or $5,600. All the prices do indeed make sense. This is an example of *market signaling*. Sellers of a good or service who have private information about its quality communicate their private information by "signals" they send. Sellers of higher-quality goods send signals too expensive for sellers of lower-quality goods to send, thereby distinguishing themselves from those selling lower-quality goods. Warranties are an excellent example of market signals, though there are many others; in the labor market context, education is another good example of market signaling, which we discuss in detail in Chapter 14.

This may be a good place to remind you that economists use models as illustrative parables and not as faithful depictions of reality. In the used car market, cars aren't graded so neatly into types along a single-dimensional scale. Moreover, the scale is continuous and not discrete, and not every owner of a cream-puff has the same reservation price as every other owner for his car. In a more realistic model of the used car market (or the labor market), different signals involve partial pooling (see below) of characteristics in which the buyer is interested: That is, a four-month warranty, if that is a market-place standard, will lead to the inference that the car is probably a cream-puff, but may be okay and may even be a lemon, whereas a two-month warranty leads to a different (and more adverse) selection from the population. In a more realistic model, different levels of signals are associated with different distributions or selections from the market, based on experiences and knowledge that market participants have about what the signals mean.

The real world is complex in another way: Not every buyer agrees about what every signal means. In the context of HRM, for example, firms can and do disagree on what the "distribution of talents" is among those students who have signaled with an MBA from, say, Harvard versus the University of Chicago. It isn't simply that different firms have different tastes over these attributes; they disagree over the very meaning of the signal itself.

The complexities of the real world obviously imply that the stark and precise equilibrium of our caricature model will at best be approximated in real life. You should maintain a healthy skepticism about this sort of thing. But notwithstanding healthy skepticism, the economic model of market signaling gives substantial insight into real-world phenomena:

- Signals sent by informed parties can be used by those with less information to infer something about the parties sending the signals.
- Those inferences, though far from precisely correct, are usually relatively valid.
- A key to an effective signal is the relative cost versus quality trade-off: A signal that is *relatively* more costly for the lower-quality types in the market is more apt to be effective, because it is more expensive for the lower-quality types to mimic. Thus, finishing high school may be a good signal of acceptance of authority. But for someone who wishes to send this particular signal, enlisting in the Marine Corps is probably better still.
- A second key to how well a seller's signal works, in terms of indicating the qualities of interest to the buyer, is whether sellers understand that the signals will be "read." For example, if high-school students are incapable of understanding that it may be valuable to get their diploma, then the diploma may be a strong signal of, say, acceptance of authority (i.e., willingness to heed the wishes of authority figures like parents or teachers, even when the student sees no clear value in it). But suppose high-school students understand that this inference will be drawn by employers. If high school diplomas aren't too costly to obtain for some students who reject authority, then some of the more rebellious students will choose to remain in high school, seeking to "fool" employers into thinking that they (the students) aren't rebellious. Having these rebels included in the population of high school graduates weakens the quality of the "authority acceptance" signal provided by a high-school diploma. To signal acceptance of authority, a stronger signal may now be required, such as a diploma from a parochial school or a stint in the military.

OUT-OF-EQUILIBRIUM SIGNALS AND THE PROBLEM OF INFERENCE[3]

The market equilibrium described for our caricature model of used cars is:

- If you offer a four-month warranty on your car, you can sell it for $5,600.
- If you offer a two-month warranty on your car, you can sell it for $4,450.
- If you offer no warranty on your car, you can sell it for $3,300.

This is an equilibrium: Each of the three warranties on offer, coupled with the price that warranty obtains, leads to a particular class of cars being offered with that warranty, which justifies the corresponding price. But the argument that this is an equilibrium is circular: The price at each warranty level leads to the set of cars offered with that warranty, which leads (back) to the price.

A second equilibrium is:

- If you offer no warranty on your car, you can sell it for $3,300.
- If you offer a two-month warranty, you can sell it for $4,450.
- If you offer a five-month warranty, you can sell it for $5,675.

The difference between this equilibrium and the previous one is that, if you have a cream-puff, you have to offer a five-month warranty. To verify that this is an equilibrium, we have to check that cream-puff owners would rather offer a five-month warranty than keep their car, offer no warranty and sell for $3,300, or offer a two-month warranty. But it works out: The five-month warranty costs the previous owner $600, so he gets $5,075 net from selling with a five-month warranty, versus utility equivalent to $5,000 if he keeps the car, and something less than $4,450 if he sells it with a two-month warranty or none at all.

The buyers don't care which of the two equilibria is in force, and the sellers strictly prefer the first equilibrium.[4] So why does the second equilibrium hold together? In particular, why doesn't the buyer of a cream-puff offer his car with a four-month warranty?

This is a specific example of a more general question. What in, say, the first equilibrium is the market supposed to make of someone offering a car with a three-month warranty? Three-month warranties aren't part of the market equilibrium, so it would seem that the person offering a car with a three-month warranty is making a "mistake." Still, it makes sense for buyers to try to figure out how likely this car is to be a lemon, or okay, or a cream-puff, and then to bid on it, based on their beliefs. But, to rephrase the question, what is a buyer supposed to believe, when a car is offered with a three-month warranty?

The basic theory of market signaling is silent on this question. It allows buyers to be so shocked by a mistaken (or so-called *out-of-equilibrium*) offer that they can draw any inferences they wish—for instance, that the car is sure to be a lemon. In fact, the basic theory allows buyers to be so shocked by such a mistaken offer that they refuse to bid on it at all. This means that in the basic theory, there are lots of possible market-signaling equilibria; we have given two above, but there are lots more. For example, another equilibrium is that used cars sell for $3,300, no matter how long a warranty is offered. The trades that take place in this equilibrium are: Only lemons are offered for sale, with no warranty. Owners of cream-puffs and okay cars think to themselves, "I wonder how the market will react if I offer a warranty?" But in the basic theory, they are allowed to conclude, "No one will pay me anything for a warranty and all buyers will therefore conclude that my car must be a lemon, because all used cars that ever go on the market are lemons."

More refined theories of market signaling try to hone in on a particular market-signaling equilibrium (or, at least, to rule some out) by coming to grips with the out-of-equilibrium inferences that a buyer might reasonably make given a "mistaken" offer. For example, in the second equilibrium above, a four-month-warranty offer would cost the owner of an okay car $2000 in expected expenses, so even if the car is perceived to be a cream-puff and can (therefore) be sold for $5,600, the owner of an okay car would net $3,600, versus $4,050 if the owner of this car sticks to the equilibrium offer of a two-month warranty. Hence this four-month warranty offer can only (sensibly) come from a cream-puff owner, and hence it must be met with buyers willing to pay $5,600. If cream-puff owners can figure all this out, this in turn leads owners of cream-puffs to offer four-month instead of five-month warranties, upsetting the second equilibrium.[5]

This is tough and fairly subtle stuff. And it is the subject of a lot of controversy among economists who study market signaling. So don't feel bad if it doesn't quite make sense, and don't take it too seriously if it does. The point we wish to make here, which we will use in the text, is simple: There can be lots of market signaling equilibria in a given context because the question *What inferences are drawn from a signal that isn't part of the equilibrium?* can have many answers, all of them consistent with a signaling equilibrium. When signals are sent outside of an equilibrium, there is no way for the parties receiving them to figure out (statistically) what those signals mean, and if they could mean *virtually anything,* it is easy to see why no one would venture to send them, which is why they could mean virtually anything. Once again, you see the revolution of an economic vicious circle.

INEFFICIENCY

Most models of market signaling tend to conclude that, relative to the case in which there was no private information, market signals are economically wasteful. This isn't to say that people don't send signals, and willingly so. But recall our example of the warranties: Each month of warranty was worth only $75 to the buyer; but each month cost the seller at least $100 and sometimes more. Every four-month warranty by a cream-puff owner is a "waste" of $100, and every two-month warranty by an okay-car owner wastes $250. It is clear that what this market needs is a good garage and an honest, objective mechanic, who can cheaply examine a car and reliably infer its quality.

The economic waste or inefficiency here compounds two effects. First, information has to be produced. Presumably, we'd have to pay the mechanic something, so comparing against a situation in which the buyer can costlessly assess a car's quality is a bit of a red herring. But more than that, what is needed is not simply to produce the information, but to produce so much at the top end of the quality distribution that the next lower level of quality has no incentive to misrepresent. Warranties for cream-puffs have to be long enough so that okay-car owners aren't attracted into offering them. This can be the cause of a lot of inefficiency.

POOLING

For our used-car caricature, we described equilibria in which each quality level sends a different signal. (In the third equilibrium, where only lemons change hands, this isn't quite so; the owners of okay cars and cream-puffs are sending the same signal—namely, no signal at all.) Don't be misled by this. In other examples, we can find equilibria with *pooling,* where more than one type of car is sold for the same price, under the same terms. The example we've created doesn't give simple examples of this. But pooling in real life is a very general and common phenomenon; what is unrealistic is complete signaling separation, where each level of quality is associated with a distinct market signal, so buyers know (from the signals) precisely what they are getting.

SCREENING

In the story of selling used cars, we told the story as if the party with the superior information takes the active role and *signals* to trading partners that he or she has a good car. In other contexts, the uninformed party offers to a population of informed parties a menu of options, from which the informed parties select, and the selection of a particular option from the menu screens the informed parties according to their qualities, or abilities, or whatever.

The story doesn't change much. Instead of having the seller of the used car offer a warranty, we have the buyer saying something like: "If you will give me a four-month warranty, I'll pay you $5,600. For a two-month warranty, I'll pay $4,450. And for a car without a warranty, I'm willing to pay $3,300 only." The seller chooses accordingly: If he owns a cream-puff, he takes the first offer. If he has an okay car, the second. And if he has a lemon, he takes the money and runs.

Actually, there are some differences in what can be an equilibrium, depending on who makes the offer. But you'll have to consult the more advanced literature for that.[6] For our purposes, what is useful is to recognize that signaling means that the informed party takes the lead, and screening means that the uninformed party offers the informed party a menu of choices or contracts. (Or, in some cases, uninformed parties make different offers, so that the informed party faces a menu in the market as a whole.)

Real-life examples of screening abound. When an insurance company offers different premium rates, depending on the size of the deductible chosen, it is screening insurees: More risk-prone insurees are apt to choose the lower deductible, and thus should be charged a higher premium rate. When choosing a mortgage, the prospective homeowner can choose along many different dimensions: different interest rate schemes (fixed versus variable, how much the interest rate can change per year and over the life of the loan, etc.); different times to full liquidation; different (or no) prepayment penalties; and different up-front fees. The lender in such cases understands that the choice of terms by the borrower indicates (statistically) the borrower's likelihood of prepaying or even defaulting on the loan, and interest rates for different packages of features are set accordingly.

Numerous examples of screening exist in the domain of HRM. For instance, several chapters in this book mention RE/MAX, the real estate network that offers a distinctive compensation package, which enables agents to retain 100% of the commissions they earn, in contrast to the standard compensation packages offered by other, more traditional firms in the industry. The effect of this is to screen for more aggressive and talented agents. (This information is then useful to customers seeking such an agent, and thus for those agents who want to be so identified by those customers.) Or recall our discussion in Chapter 11 of how piece-rate pay (e.g., at Safelite Glass) allows workers with different tastes for income versus effort to self-screen; those willing to work harder for more income have that option. Similarly, firms may screen by permitting employees to select from a menu of benefit options (e.g., some of which involve deferred compensation) or a cafeteria plan; or by letting new employees choose between an initial specialized job assignment versus participating in an extended internship or training program that offers the potential for broader job assignments in the future. In each of these cases, workers' selections will reveal private information that potentially is quite useful to the employer (and possibly to clients or customers as well).

ENDNOTES

1. For a more complete and formal version of the theory, see David M. Kreps, *A Course in Microeconomic Theory* (Princeton, NJ: Princeton University Press, 1990), Chapter 17. The seminal references for these ideas are: George Akerlof, "The Market for Lemons: Quality Uncertainty and the Market Mechanism," *Quarterly Journal of Economics* 84 (August 1970): 488–500; A. Michael Spence, *Market Signaling: Informational Transfer in Hiring and Related Screening Processes* (Cambridge, MA: Harvard University Press, 1974); and Michael Rothschild and Joseph E. Stiglitz, "Equilibrium in Competitive Insurance Markets: An Essay in the Economics of Imperfect Information," *Quarterly Journal of Economics* 90 (November 1976): 630–49.

2. Because the good being purchased here is an insurance policy, you can think of this as a case where the buyer is better informed than the seller, and the seller cares about the information possessed by the buyer.

3. This section delves into the finer details of market signaling. Only the brave should venture in alone.

4. Recall that each month of warranty was worth $75 to buyers, who are therefore indifferent between a cream-puff with a four-month warranty costing $5,600 and one with a five-month warranty for $5,675. On the seller side, in the first equilibrium, sellers take in $5,600 for a cream-puff and incur the costs of a four-month warranty (which are $400), netting $5,200. In the second equilibrium, a cream-puff sells for $5,675 but the seller must provide a five-month warranty (which costs $600), for net proceeds of $5,075.

5. If you make your way through Chapter 17 of Kreps' *A Course in Microeconomic Theory* (and live to tell about it), you will recognize this as an example of equilibrium domination.

6. See Kreps, *op. cit.*, Chapter 17.

AUTHOR INDEX

SUBJECT INDEX